Film: Form and Function

Film: Form and Function

George Wead / The University of Texas at Austin

George Lellis / Coker College

Houghton Mifflin Company / Boston

Dallas   Geneva, Illinois   Hopewell, New Jersey   Palo Alto   London

To Adam, Alex, Martine,
and Rufus—and Céline and Julie.

Cover photograph by James Scherer.

Illustration credits begin on p. 501.

Cover: ballet slippers—*The Red Shoes*; chess set in sand—*The Seventh Seal*; umbrella—*Singin' in the Rain*; Rosebud sled—*Citizen Kane*; broken clock—*The Pawnbroker*; Mount Rushmore postcard—*North by Northwest*.

Printed in the U.S.A.
Library of Congress Catalog Card Number: 80-82804
ISBN: 0-395-29740-0

Contents

v

Chapter Three / Space 55

Chapter Four / Continuity 97

Chapter Five / Sound 143

Chapter Six / Color 175

PART TWO / THE HOLLYWOOD NARRATIVE TRADITION 199

Chapter Seven / Hollywood's Social Aspect 203

Preface

Film: Form and Function introduces students to a new approach to films, and enables them to observe, absorb, and understand what is actually taking place during any film experience.

In this text, we consider the motion picture as a highly complex medium of communication. Our aim is to make the student more knowledgeable about this particular communication system by describing it as objectively and factually as possible and avoiding what are only personal opinions and personal values. No doubt your students have, and will continue to have, distinct preferences in movies, but we want their judgments to be well considered and their opinions educated, based upon a fundamental knowledge of movies—the form they take and the functions they serve.

The distinctive approach of *Film: Form and Function* allows us to present an unwieldy, amorphous subject in an orderly, systematic way. To characterize both the form and function of any film, we have divided the subject into three simple but well-defined parts: basic techniques of filmmaking, traditional Hollywood filmmaking, and alternative approaches to Hollywood, usually foreign or innovative films.

We define the four functions that films basically serve as (1) *realist*—to document the world as closely as possible, (2) *persuasive*—to influence the viewer toward a particular point of view, (3) *personal*—to convey the filmmaker's individual vision of the world, and (4) *esthetic*—to serve as a medium for innovative artistic expression. By contrasting Hollywood with non-Hollywood films, we suggest that traditional Hollywood filmmakers tended to maintain an evenhanded balance among the four functions so that no one function was obtrusive. We call this traditional Hollywood approach *balanced* filmmaking. In the case of non-Hollywood films, filmmakers tended to produce movies in which one or several of these functions were predominant. We call this approach *weighted* filmmaking. There is not, however, an exact mathematical formula for our categories: in the world of movies such a degree of precision is not possible and should not be expected.

In the introductory chapter, we emphasize the essential concept that the medium of movie communication is a machine, an instrument whose evolution can be traced to a human fascination with simulating reality and movement that appeared very early in Western culture. In Part 1 (Chapters 2–6), we describe the basic techniques of filmmaking, dealing with the evolution of each filmmaking tool as simply and as clearly as possible. To clarify and diagram the technical information, we have provided sixty drawings of various film mechanisms and processes. In describing the filmmaking process, we detail its evolution from the *camera obscura* to the highly evolved battery of instruments—camera, projector, optical printer, sound systems, and so forth—used in present-day filmmaking. We feel strongly that an understanding of these techniques allows the student to see how the technology profoundly affects the form of the movie that the viewer experiences.

Since their first flickering, halting efforts at imitating smooth motion, filmmakers have developed many techniques to simulate our experiences of movement, space, time, sound, and color. We have included explanations of these techniques—the uses of lighting, framing, film composition, shooting techniques, cutting, and film editing—to show that the modern movie instrument can now imitate very well a wide range of human perceptions, reproducing, if not reality, at least a close imitation of the way we perceive reality.

In Part 2, we focus on the traditional Hollywood cinema and its balanced approach to the four functions of film communication. We study Hollywood's effect on the society at large—how it expresses and clarifies the values of the society, in general, and of each generation, in particular. The symbolism, explicit or implicit, in the Hollywood genres of the Western, the gangster film, or the horror film reveals additional levels of meaning—the conflict between civilization and savagery or the sense of shared community or the irrational versus the rational—to the viewer. Chapter 9 is devoted to characterizing the energy and exuberance of the Hollywood comic spirit from Buster Keaton to Woody Allen.

In Part 3, on alternatives to the Hollywood tradition, we categorize innovative, foreign, and idiosyncratic cinema by the particular function—or combination of functions—that each film serves. The realist film—whether fiction or nonfiction—tries to document the world around us. The persuasive film, in its most obvious manifestations, has been used by governments and propagandists to serve political purposes. The personal film reflects the artistry and subjective sense of the world of certain highly regarded directors who are able to convey an individual style, recognizable in all their films. As examples of esthetic cinema, we point out innovative filmmakers who use the medium of film as an art for art's sake. Finally in Chapter 14, we show how the viewer is asked to adjust to the continuously shifting elements that make up the overall film experience, and we summarize the ongoing process in specific films such as *Citizen Kane, The Rules of the Game,* and *Apocalypse Now.*

Although this text is not an exhaustive study of filmmaking or of film history, it provides students with the essential elements for understanding film—an understanding that they can apply to all their future movie experiences.

This text is intended for an introductory course in film. We have illustrated the text with 250 halftones, which are carefully integrated with the ongoing text. In the notes following each chapter, we suggest sources, particularly the work of film theorists, for additional or advanced study. The text can either be used as a whole course of study or individual chapters can be used independently in any sequence that suits the instructor's particular approach.

Many people have helped with this book, and they deserve special thanks. The staff at Houghton Mifflin gave patient and genial encouragement. Film archivists solved many problems: Sam Gill at the Academy of Motion Picture Arts and Sciences; Mary Corliss and Carlos Clarens at the Museum of Modern Art; Barbara Humphreys of the Motion Picture Section, Library of Congress; and Jane Combs, William Crain, Roy Flukinger, May Ellen MacNamara, Ed Neal, and Decherd Turner at the Humanities Research Center of the University of Texas at Austin. Carol Crowder and Carol Lynn Greene at Audio Brandon Films provided data on as well as prints of *The Love of Jeanne Ney*, *Mother*, *October*, and *Goliath and the Dragon* for our research. Nancy Cushing-Jones at Universal and Ruth Zitter at RKO provided particularly useful assistance with permissions. And many consultants gave valuable information and criticism: Louis Black and Pamela Menteer at CinemaTexas; Muriel Hamilton at Hampton Books; Lydia Blanchard, H. Philip Bolton, Kim Chalmers, Robert E. Davis, Bill Huie, James W. Lemke, Ron Malec, Patrick Ogle, Lauren Rabinovitz, and Monica Weber.

We would like to express our appreciation to those colleagues who reviewed our manuscript: Churchill Roberts of The University of West Florida, Stanley H. Forman of San Diego City College, Garth Jowett of the University of Windsor, and Stuart M. Kaminsky of Northwestern University.

We also thank Diane Swinney and Annette Wint for some very professional typing, Malcolm Doubles for his support and encouragement, and finally our wives who were of much more help than we ever let them know at the time.

George Wead   *George Lellis*

Chapter 1 / Introduction

The Instrument

of Communication

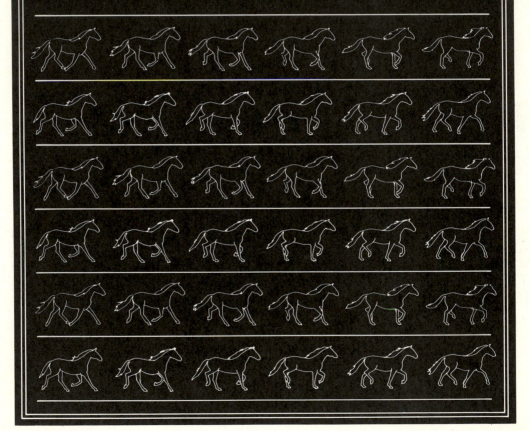

In 1895 the moving picture machine emerged as an instrument of mass communication. No single element of it was wholly unique, nor was it the creation of a single person. It was in many ways the perfectly logical result of psychological, economic, and social forces that had been building since the dawn of human history. And yet, once it was achieved, the motion-picture mechanism became a unique new force in society. It effected illusions in a peculiarly different way, with peculiarly different impact. Nothing it borrowed from had ever worked quite like this before.

In Figure 1.1 we see the mechanism. No particular camera or projector will look exactly like this, but the view illustrates the basic elements that countless years of invention managed to bring together and over eighty years of improvements have not radically altered.

In the movie *camera* (Fig. 1.1a) a strip of light-sensitive *film* passes under a *pressure plate* in which there is an *aperture*, or gate. The film is moved by the workings of *sprocket wheels* and a *claw* that engages the film's *sprocket holes*. The claw is particularly important because, after pulling each new segment of film down behind the aperture, it pauses momentarily, leaving the film stationary behind the aperture. At this moment the *shutter*, which spins at a constant speed, lets light fall on the film through a pie-shaped opening. This light is coming through an optical system—a convex *lens* and *diaphragm*—that has been adjusted to let the proper amount of light fall in sharp focus onto the film. In this manner, at the normal rate today of twenty-four times a second, the motion-picture camera captures a sequence of still pictures, or *frames*, of action.

The movie *projector* (Fig. 1.1b) has the same elements with some rearrangements, since the light comes from a projector *lamp* behind the film. The shutter, with three openings to allow maximum light, is between the lamp and the film, along with some thick pieces of glass, called *condensers*, to diffuse the light and keep the heat from burning the film. And the usual projector lens is optically much simpler than a camera's.

Only a cinematographer or a person who repairs this mechanism needs to know it intimately. But we know it better than we think. We take it for granted. The movies depend on this mechanism. The impact and meaning of their communicative power begin here. The mechanism evolved out of certain urges, drives, conflicts, and assumptions that persist, and ever since its creation, the mechanism's way of operation has imposed certain conditions and limits on those who make movies and those who look at them.

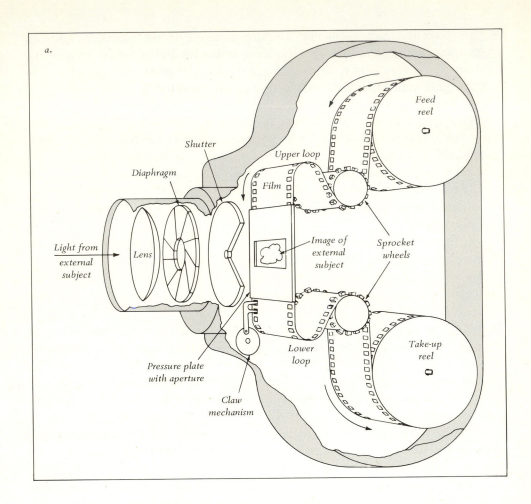

a.

Light from external subject

Lens

Diaphragm

Shutter

Upper loop

Film

Feed reel

Image of external subject

Sprocket wheels

Pressure plate with aperture

Claw mechanism

Lower loop

Take-up reel

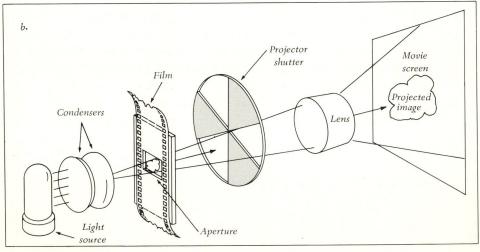

b.

Condensers

Film

Projector shutter

Movie screen

Projected image

Lens

Light source

Aperture

The mechanism involves us in cultural and cinematic *codes*, systems of organization whereby groups and individuals make sense out of the many details of life. The codes are powerful because they are inseparable from what we think of as ordinary life. They *are* the way we live, and it is difficult to stop and study ourselves living. For example, if we try to analyze the structure of our speech while we speak, we soon stop speaking. Though spoken language is actually a complicated code that *can* be studied, it works best when it is taken for granted. In much the same way, we take many things about movies for granted that our culture and the movie mechanism have coded for us.

In Chapter 1, we will examine some of the codes that *fed into* the movie mechanism: some general assumptions about magic and play, illusion and reality, and art and science.

In Chapters 2 through 6, we will examine the more specific coding that *came out* of the mechanism and its subsequent technological development.

A MACHINE OF ILLUSIONS AND LEGENDS

The long evolution toward a movie machine started with a human urge to create lifelike illusions. The urge appears in the first traces of human history and takes forms that foreshadow modern movie instruments. When Stone Age artists painted animals on cave walls some fourteen thousand years ago, they captured stages of movement with an accuracy that, as one art historian puts it, is "hardly surpassed by today's camera."[1] By 2000 B.C. the Egyptians had probably begun to sculpt columns with realistic figures in successive stages of movement so that when riders drove past in chariots, the figures on the columns appeared to move—through a type of illusion similar to that used in the movie projector.

The cave drawings had a practical function: to help early peoples feel that they controlled their lives. Stone Age artisans apparently strove for a lifelike image to capture an animal's spirit. They did not treat the picture as an artful illusion but as magical reality: the animal was present and alive on the wall, for use in hunting and fertility rituals.[2] But the sculpted columns of the Egyptians had another function: they had obviously become playful illusions, designed to fascinate the eye with deliberate trickery. These images gave pleasure, not magical power. Thus these early cultures introduce us to the practical and the playful functions of moving images. Something of both functions persisted as humans pursued their fascination with the illusions of captured movement through the following centuries.

1.1 The movie mechanism. a. The *camera*: light from an external subject leaves an image of the subject on film. b. The *projector*: with certain changes in the same basic mechanism, light projects the subject's image onto an external screen.

In time, scientists replaced magicians, but they continued to study the illusion of movement. In 65 B.C., the Roman philosopher Lucretius noted how the image of a moving object persists briefly in the eye after the object itself has actually moved, a phenomenon that would become known as *persistence of vision*. By A.D. 200 the Roman astronomer and mathematician Ptolemy had carried out various experiments demonstrating how easily the eye could be fooled.

Roman artists skillfully used sculpted figures against painted backdrops to create illusions of captured life; by the seventeenth century, Italian painters had mastered techniques to deceive the eye into taking flat painting for three-dimensional reality. This technique was what the French very appropriately termed *trompe-l'oeil* ("fool-the-eye") painting.

In 1656, Dutch physicist Christian Huygens contributed the "magic lantern" (Fig. 1.2), a picture projector used to display realistic drawings (Fig. 1.3). By the end of the seventeenth century, the German monk Johann Zahn and others were adding movement to magic lantern shows by actually moving the slides or by using masks that created optical illusions (Fig. 1.4). By the 1800s traveling showmen were carrying magic lanterns throughout Europe.

The "peep show" was another popular form of illusionism. A spectator would look into a small box where realistic illustrations were manipulated with strings held by the showman. Battles were fought, London was burned, or highwaymen were hanged in jiggling cardboard. The *panorama*, or *cyclorama*, gave grander effects, encircling a large number of spectators with big battle scenes or landscapes. Sometimes the scenes were moved, carefully lighted, or joined with sound effects for

1.3 Realistic lantern slide, about 1870. This slide is titled, "Be it ever so humble, there's no place like home."

1.2 Magic lantern.

greater realism. *Dioramas* used an opposite technique, moving spectators past the pictures, sometimes in imitation carriages or train coaches.

Any of these inventions could be called a forerunner of the movies, but two in particular mark the beginning of the real push toward a movie machine. Both incorporated basic forms of illusion, and both emerged, by coincidence, in the year 1826. In England, a toy called the *thaumatrope* (Fig. 1.5) appeared, a pasteboard disc with different pictures on either side. When the disc was twirled on strings, the pictures appeared to come together, through the old trickery of persistence of vision. In France, a lithographer named Joseph Nicéphore Niepce exposed a chemically treated pewter plate to sunlight for eight hours and came away with an etching of his back yard made by light. He called the result a *heliograph* (Fig. 1.6). Today we call it the first photograph.

Since this was the nineteenth century, a new sense of industrialization and of corporate endeavor was beginning to make itself felt. With these two inventions, the old traditions of pictorial art and moving entertainments were jolted, almost imperceptibly, and began slowly to converge on a new species of communication.

1.4 Comic lantern slide, about 1850. By moving a mask, the projectionist covered the monkey's arm and the woman's head (left) and then revealed the raised cap and startled face that were hidden (right). The figures thus seemed to move.

1.5 Front and back views of thaumatrope sold
in London, about 1827.

1.6 The first photograph, 1826.

THE ILLUSION OF MOVEMENT: MOVIE TOYS

Like the Egyptian sculpture trickery, the thaumatrope (Greek for "magical turning") created a continuity between separate pictures. According to legend, at least three scientists played a part in its creation. Sir John Herschel reputedly bet Charles Babbage that he could see both sides of a coin at once, then spun a shilling to prove it. Babbage went to William Henry Fitton, who figured out the principle involved and made up other examples. Continuity is pure and primitive in a thaumatrope. The two images are quite different forms that appear together. Neither appears to move, but the toy represents the first modern example of the *pictorial continuity* essential to movies.

Two other essential elements of a motion picture machine had been revealed shortly before—though not in a toy. In a paper delivered in 1824 to the Royal Society, England's official institute of science, Peter Mark Roget, a physician, reported on a phenomenon that intrigued him: when a rolling wagon wheel was watched through the slats of a picket fence, its spokes seemed to *bend* (Fig. 1.7). Roget reproduced the effect in his laboratory and explained it as persistence of vision. Without using the terms, Roget was noting that such an illusion required a *shutter* (the slats repeatedly shutting off the light) and an *aperture* (the narrow openings between the slats). These are the two other basic elements of any movie machine.

1.7 Roget's wagon wheel. Roget used the diagram on the right to explain the phenomenon on the left. A wheel moves (in the direction of the arrow) behind a picket fence (dotted lines), whose apertures (gaps) produce optical illusions. At VO and OW, all of the flashing spokes are seen in a vertical position. But at RO (as one example), with an aperture in Position 1, only the end of a spoke is visible. As it descends to x, the aperture is moving to Position 2, producing curve Ra, since the images of all points of the descending spoke are persisting in the eye—and so on, through curve Rabcd. All the spokes are similarly affected, creating the illusion on the left. Roget published these diagrams in 1825.

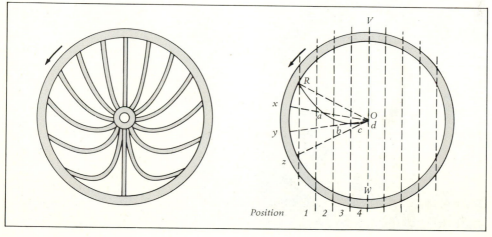

Roget showed no awareness of any potential here for moving pictures, but between his study and the thaumatrope, all the missing links were now available.[3]

In 1832 the links came together. Joseph Antoine Ferdinand Plateau of Belgium and Simon Ritter von Stampfer of Austria, two scientists totally removed from each other, created nearly identical instruments that made still pictures seem to move. In Plateau's *phenakistoscope* ("deceptive view") or Stampfer's *stroboscope* ("spinning view"), we can see all the basic elements working together for the first time. A wheel is designed with pictures of successive stages of an action. In one variety (Fig. 1.8) viewing slots are cut in the same wheel, which is then placed in front of a mirror; in another, there is a separate slotted wheel (Fig. 1.9). The viewer looks through a slot, and when the wheel is spun the figures seem to move. An aperture (the slot) is the only source of light for the eye, and the shutter (the space between the slots) shuts off the view between slots, providing the viewer with flashes of light carrying separate still pictures of a continuous action. The eye can take in several images through one aperture, but all of them appear to move in what we can now call the movie illusion.

For the next sixty years, more or less, Western culture's fascination with motion settled onto a dozen variations of these two simple toys. Mathematician William George Horner conceived of a cylinder design for the *zoetrope* ("turning life"), a revolving, open drum with regular apertures cut in the upper half of the cylinder and sequential pictures placed inside below them (Fig. 1.10). Several viewers could watch the action at one time and none of them needed to get extremely close to see. In effect, the zoetrope was Roget's picket fence running endlessly.

The zoetrope spawned many variations, but the most impressive was the *praxinoscope,* first patented in 1877 by Emile Reynaud (Fig. 1.11). He removed the zoetrope's apertures and placed mirrors in the center of the drum, each mirror facing one of the pictures, which were translucent. By throwing light from a magic lantern

1.8 Phenakistoscope wheel, 1933.

1.9 Double-disc phenakistoscope.

1.10 Zoetrope.

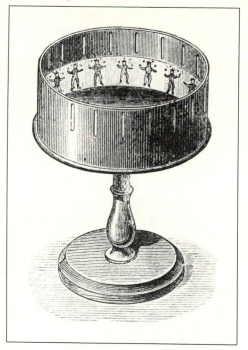

1.11 Reynaud's praxinoscope, 1877.

through the pictures, Reynaud could project them on a screen, where they moved against a background scene projected from the same lantern. By 1889 Reynaud had enlarged this apparatus into the *théâtre optique*, which used a band of pictures that could run indefinitely. The machine told stories projected in six-foot images, and some of the presentations ran for fifteen minutes. The pictures were in full color and are said to have tripped electric circuits as they ran, providing sound effects.

Reynaud had developed the movie toy beyond a point that anyone had reason to expect. To tell a fifteen-minute story, a zoetrope would have to be 900 feet in diameter, a phenakistoscope some 4,500 feet. Reynaud had overcome major technical problems and demonstrated that complex motion-picture shows were possible.

The *théâtre optique* was the high point in the evolution of movie toys, but it could not keep up with the interest it fed. It died out after 1900, apparently because its animated drawings were not realistic enough for people fascinated by the new movies. Movie toys settled back into simpler varieties of the phenakistoscope and zoetrope, still found in toy stores today. The movies needed the greater realism found in another strain of evolution: the development of photography.

THE ILLUSION OF CAPTURED LIFE: PHOTOGRAPHY

The fascination with photographic realism began as a fascination with the sun. Many early cultures worshipped the sun, and some of them came to study it scientifically. One result was the camera. Somehow people discovered that if they poked a small hole in a wall or ceiling of a darkened room, they could watch eclipses without hurting their eyes. The sun's image, upside down and reversed, appeared on the wall or floor opposite the hole.

By the eleventh century, Alhazen, an Arab scholar, assumed that everyone had seen such a room. Scholars later gave it the Latin name *camera obscura* ("dark room"). The development of photography began here.

The Optics of the Camera

From any point on the sun, countless light rays are emitted in all directions. Only a few can strike the tiny hole of a camera obscura. From all the points of the sun, these rays converge on the hole and then pass through it, like the lines of an X (Fig. 1.12a). The rays from any given point of the sun remain clustered together but reverse their relative positions, as in an X, so that rays from the bottom of the sun are

1.12 Evolution of the camera obscura. a. The first *camera obscura* was used to project the sun's image indoors. b. Outside scenes were later dimly captured. c. But the images from the sun's reflected light were very faint until the camera obscura was fitted with a lens and diaphram, allowing a larger aperture and admitting more light. When the camera obscura also became portable, the modern camera was born.

now on top, those from the right are now left, and so on. The image of the sun that all the rays project is therefore a *focused* image (with rays from any point clustered together), an inverted *mirror* image (upside-down and reversed), and a *dimmer* image (employing a small percentage of the total light).

Even when there were no eclipses, people who had made holes in their walls found that the scenery outside would also appear indoors—but only on very bright days (Fig. 1.12b). The light directly from the sun was powerful enough to project a visible image into the camera obscura; however, when the sunlight reflected off of objects before coming inside, the image became much dimmer. Even in darkened rooms and with white paper held near the hole, an outside scene was very faint.[4]

As the Renaissance dawned, focusing greater study on humankind, scholars turned toward improving the camera obscura. By 1550 a physician and mathematician named Girolamo Cardano had suggested using a lens with the camera obscura, and by 1568 Daniel Barbaro, a Venetian nobleman, created the prototype of the camera.

Barbaro enlarged the hole in his wall so that from every point of the scene outside more rays came in, improving illumination. They spread out in a cone, however, overlapping with other rays from other points, blurring the image. So Barbaro took a nearsighted man's eyeglasses and used one of the convex lenses to bend the light rays, bringing them back into focus. Finally he made an adjustable opening, now called a *diaphragm*—a more convenient form of the original hole in the wall (Fig. 1.12c). By adjusting the diaphragm opening and his paper's distance from the lens, Barbaro could obtain an extremely sharp image of anything outside.

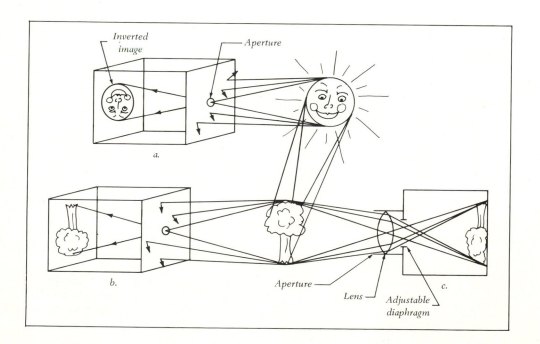

Inverted image — *Aperture*

a.

b.   *Aperture* — *Lens* — *Adjustable diaphragm*   *c.*

"Here," as Barbaro put it, "you will see the images on the paper as they *are*."[5] Nature now came in bright and controllable, and many scientists pointed out that it was ready to be turned into realistic copies by artists. By 1685 Johann Zahn had developed a neat, portable box camera, complete with a mirror inside (today called a reflex system) that reflected the camera's image right-side-up so that it could be copied correctly (Fig. 1.13). As we mentioned, Zahn also improved the magic lantern, which was simply a by-product of the camera's development: the magic lantern was basically a camera with light projected from the inside.

By 1700 the camera obscura was rarely a room and far from obscure. It was a fad. Mobility and the tastes of the Age of Reason had taken it out of the scientists' hands. People were getting images from nature at every opportunity. They crawled into crate-sized cameras; they sat down to table cameras; they rode in carriages that converted into cameras. There were pocket-sized cameras and cameras hidden in books and walking canes. Scenes were copied and colored on paper or canvas like paintings, or on glass slides for magic lantern shows. Camera fans challenged painters to achieve such realism, and inventors improved lenses for greater clarity and different angles of view. During this camera madness, the scientists turned their attention to another peculiarity of the sun: light can paint itself.

The Chemistry of the Photograph

Many chemicals are sensitive to sunlight, but the silver salts (including silver nitrate, chloride, iodide, and bromide) turn black. In 1725 Johann Heinrich Schulze proved

that it was the sun's light, not its heat, that caused the salts to turn black, but he never attempted a practical application of his discovery. Others did. Thomas Wedgwood and Sir Humphry Davy theorized that if one played light and shadow through a camera obscura onto a plate coated with silver salt, one would get a *negative image:* the whites would be blacks and vice versa. Even with the best lens, however, the camera didn't admit enough light to record an image under ordinary conditions. The experimenters had to use direct sunlight to make silhouettes of figures—but the image kept getting blacker unless it was kept out of the light. The two Englishmen never found a way to stop this darkening action—that is, to *fix* the image permanently.

Nicéphore Niepce, a lithographer, found a way to etch an image with light. Having made some copies of drawings with light, he took the next step of letting nature etch itself onto a treated pewter plate that he placed in a camera obscura. For eight hours on a summer day in 1826, light from his back yard played upon bitumen of Judea, a kind of asphalt that hardens when exposed to light. When Niepce washed away the unhardened bitumen—that is, those areas untouched by light—with oil of lavender, he fixed the image. The difference between the hardened bitumen (light) and the bare pewter (shadows) was extremely faint, but it was perceptible.

Niepce did not live to perfect his process, which he called *heliography* ("sun writing"), but he passed on valuable ideas to a young partner, Louis Jacques Mandé Daguerre. Daguerre earned a living by laboriously drawing lifelike diorama scenes with the aid of a camera obscura, and he had tried for years to find a way to get silver salts to do his work for him. He did better than that: he evolved Niepce's etched-plate approach into a new form. And apparently he stumbled onto it. One day in 1835, says a legend, Daguerre gave up trying to etch some silver iodide plates with images, and he laid them in a cupboard in which mercury was stored. When he returned some time later, he found clear images on them. In the cupboard, he learned, mercury fumes had worked on the plates, bringing out the images that had not been visible before. Daguerre had discovered what is now called *developing.* One did not need to wait hours for the sun to etch a faint image unassisted. In a very brief time, light would make an imprint on the silver salt, leaving a *latent image* that other chemicals could develop into a completely visible scene.

Daguerre was also lucky enough to have found a developer that left a white residue on the exposed parts of the plate. In effect, this left a *positive* mirror image of the subject: light areas were whites, shadows were blacks and grays. In 1837 he had found a way to fix this image. He now had a process to obtain a permanent mirror image of any scene in Nature. Daguerre had returned magic to the sun. As one

1.13 Zahn's reflex camera obscura, 1685.

1.14 Daguerreotype, taken in 1851. Caesar, aged 113, the last slave owned in New York State. The photographer is unknown.

1.15 Making photographs using the negative process. In the camera, a subject is rendered as a negative mirror image: blacks are white, whites are black, and the subject is reversed. The negative is then used to make any number of positive copies. These reverse the negative, restoring the original tones and position. ▶

excited viewer put it, all you had to do was say "Show yourself!" to the world.[6] In 1839 Daguerre announced this new process to the public, christening it the *daguerreotype* (Fig. 1.14).

This is where modern photography begins. In fact, the term *photography* ("writing with light") was coined by Sir John Herschel, a British scientist, in 1839 when the daguerreotype was causing a frenzy of excitement—"daguerreotypo-mania," as it was called. Everyone wanted to capture mirror images of life. The daguerreotype required a six-minute exposure (with head clamps for human subjects) and an hour's work over dangerous mercury fumes, but it was a vast improvement over eight-hour exposures or laborious hand copying. Daguerreotypes enjoyed an illustrious career, providing us with impressive portraits of early nineteenth-century life and personalities.

But by the 1850s, Daguerre's direct positive process was losing ground to a better alternative: the *negative* process (Fig. 1.15). In 1841 William Henry Fox Talbot, a British inventor, had patented the *calotype*, which used paper negatives. At first, it offered little competition to the simpler, sharper images of the daguerreotype. But by mid-century, the calotype was much improved. Frederick Scott Archer introduced the wet plate, or *collodion*, process in 1851, reducing calotype exposures to as low as five seconds on glass as well as on paper. This enhanced the calotype's greatest advantage over the daguerreotype: any number of positive copies could be made from one negative. After obtaining the negative (mirror) image, the photographer made a copy by letting light pass through the negative onto a different kind of sensitized paper. This contact printing gave a reverse mirror or double-negative image: a *positive print*. Such copying could be repeated indefinitely.

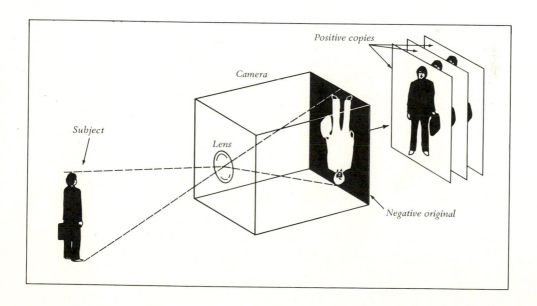

Positive copies

Camera

Subject

Lens

Negative original

Western culture could now mass produce powerfully lifelike illusions: images captured rapidly from the flow of time with what seemed a minimum of human intervention. This new magic, along with the varieties of movie toys, gave the nineteenth century a fresh fascination with realistic illusions. The century was also experiencing revolutions in the traditions of art and science, and these helped push technology toward moving photography.

TWO CULTURAL REVOLUTIONS

The evolution had been more or less leisurely before this time, but now events accelerated in response to massive cultural change.

Eli Whitney, known for the cotton gin he patented in 1793, ushered in a new industrial age in 1798 when he established the basic system of mass production: he made machines that made interchangeable parts for other machines. By the mid-1800s Europe would feel the impact of his system, and after the Civil War the United States would begin to take the shape that mass production implied: a collective society.[7] Photography and the modern movie toy came into existence in 1826, just as this commercial change was beginning to be felt, and they were caught up in the culture's new collective spirit, what we might characterize as a democratic sense of art and science.

Before the nineteenth century, as we have seen, many artists and scientists made discoveries that pushed forward the evolution of realistic illusions. But these earlier inventors were from privileged classes. The scientists were monks, philosophers, astronomers, members of the nobility—people set apart in society, devoted to the detached study of truth. Artists were also set apart, by specialized talents and by a capacity to see and embody the eternal beauty in things. Art was fostered and promoted by classes that had the leisure to devote to the rules of Truth and Beauty.

Since the nineteenth century, such elitism has had to confront, or try to ignore, the democratizing of art and science. The roots go back in history—to forgotten scientists sharing experiments in the seventeenth century, to the camera obscura fad of the eighteenth—but the nineteenth century drove home two cultural revolutions. Principles of *collective* commercial enterprise intruded into the old scientific spirit; and the *masses* entered realms formerly restricted to artists.

Collective Invention

Louis Daguerre introduces us to a new breed of inventor: part artist, part scientist, and large part huckster. He was the first of the inventors we have studied to name his invention after himself. Even before he had perfected the daguerreotype he was advertising its success. He wouldn't reveal the process until at least a hundred subscribers had contributed money to the venture, and when that didn't happen fast enough, he beseeched the French government to buy his process and grant him an annual pension for his discovery. His claim that other countries were making tempting offers was never verified, but he got his pension.

Fox Talbot had a grander plan. Setting out to create a monopoly, he patented every improvement of his calotype process and required users to pay £20 (more than $300 today) for a license that forbade them even to give away photographs without his approval. Talbot's personal claim to improvements that had been freely circulated in the scientific community for years was rejected in 1854 by a court. Talbot, having published his findings first, was acknowledged as the inventor of the calotype, but he was not allowed to patent the unprotected discoveries of others.

Although Talbot's plan failed, he had carried Daguerre's hucksterism to a logical extreme that would become the dominant pattern by the end of the nineteenth century: collective invention.[8] Technology was pushed forward by shrewd individuals who knew how to manipulate the discoveries of others, the complexities of patent law, and—most of all—publicity. Combining the talents of showmen and corporate executives, they became "the great" and got personal credit for achievements that were really collective endeavors. Many uncelebrated inventors made crucial contributions to the development of photography and the motion picture. But they have not become "great," either because they could not compete with the dazzling publicity of those who followed the footsteps of Daguerre and Talbot or because they preferred the more remote pleasures of traditional scientific discovery.

Emile Reynaud, the inventor of the praxinoscope and *théâtre optique,* was a solitary artisan in the Renaissance tradition. He designed and executed everything himself: machinery, optical system, drawings, stories, sound effects, even the exhibition of his shows. But his unique talents and tastes became drawbacks because he could not adapt them to the demands of the masses for realism. Ironically, his genius had fed a technology that ruined him. He becomes the prototype of the individualist who cannot or will not deal with the collective power thrusting the motion picture's evolution forward.

Democratized Art

Photography obviously disturbed the old assumptions about who were artists and who were not. By putting realistic reproduction into the hands of common people, photography vulgarized art—or, at least, art as it had usually been understood.

Photography *was* a threat in that sense. Even Daguerre was thought to be defenseless before the power of his own invention, for "everyone will be able to apply it; the most clumsy operator will be able to take views as perfect as those of an experienced artist."[9] Such cries would echo through the century.

In fact, photography was not at first something that everyone could do easily. Daguerreotypes involved laborious work over dangerous mercury fumes. Calotypes were safer, but wet collodion plates had to be prepared just before use, placed in the camera while still wet, and developed at once. As photography improved, picture taking did become more and more accessible to more and more people. By 1881, a succession of inventors had perfected a dry plate process. Photographic chemicals were held on the plate by a coating, or *emulsion,* of gelatin. They could be prepared ahead of time, would keep indefinitely, and could be exposed at speeds of around 1/25 second. Now *instants* of movement could be captured—so simply, as one fan put it, that "a person of average intelligence could master it in three lessons."[10] But another degree of individuality was sacrificed: photographers could no longer make their own plates. Emulsion making was complicated and the new photography required large companies and a more solidly industrial order.

George Eastman epitomized the new order. Starting out as a dry-plate maker who designed and built his own machinery, he founded the Eastman Company in 1884 around the collective concept of invention: a large number of researchers and inventors would work under the Eastman name to develop new and very competitive products aimed directly at the *amateur* photographer. Eastman's most famous product, the Kodak camera, first released in 1888, incorporated earlier inventions into a fresh form: the emulsion was arranged on a long, movable strip inside a camera with a fixed focus. The photographer simply pointed it at a subject, pushed a button, then rolled the strip to set up another picture. When the roll of pictures was finished, the whole camera was mailed back to Eastman for processing. (Smaller, removable rolls came later.) As the ads proclaimed: "You press the button, we do the rest."

It was the ultimate democratization of art, and now professional photographers joined the artists in lamenting the vulgarization. The number of Kodaks being used jumped from twelve thousand to ninety thousand within the first three years. Eastman noted in the instruction manual that it was now easy for "any person of ordinary intelligence to learn to take good pictures *in ten minutes.*"[11] Even the name *Kodak* was chosen for mass appeal. It was neither a scientific term nor an inventor's name. As Eastman said, it was a pure trademark: "Terse, abrupt to the point of rudeness . . . it snaps like a camera shutter in your face. What more could one ask?"[12]

The first Kodak used a paper strip to carry the emulsion, but by 1889 Eastman was using the substance we today call *film*. The company is often credited with having invented film. It didn't. The history of film is another story of communal invention turned largely to one individual's advantage. In 1856, Alexander Parkes patented celluloid—a material, as legend has it, that he discovered while looking for a synthetic ivory to use in billiard balls. By 1888, John Carbutt introduced the first emulsion-coated films as a substitute for glass plates. In 1887 an Episcopal minister, Hannibal Goodwin, had already applied for a patent on a roll film made from an improved form of celluloid, but then the Eastman Company patented its "invention" and "introduced" film. Neither Carbutt nor Goodwin had the resources to organize or advertise as efficiently as Eastman, whom Goodwin sued. In 1914 the matter was finally settled: Goodwin's estate received $5 million, but Eastman retained a virtual monopoly on roll film.

And so the revolutions of collective invention and democratized art helped push technology to film and the Kodak—and thus to a time ripe for the invention of movies. Film was a flexible substance, tough enough to be driven through the machinery of the movie camera without tearing. The Kodak made the speedy and accurate capture of reality eminently convenient, literally at everyone's fingertips, and therefore prominently on everyone's mind. This was an environment in which inventing movies made much sense. The culture was at a focal point where such a thing almost *had* to happen. And very shortly, it did.

THE MOVIE MACHINE EMERGES

At the beginning of this chapter we pictured two parallel lines of development being jogged by important achievements in 1826 and moving toward an inevitable union. Photography took awhile to evolve several essential elements; the movie toy defined its elements quickly and waited to join photography in a completely realistic illusion. Photography, capturing images through optical and chemical means, had by now expanded to control these means (lens and diaphragm; development, fixing, copying, emulsion, and film). The camera had become a durable, portable, tough, and fast means of freezing movement into a still picture, creating an illusion of captured life. At this point it could be adapted to the peculiar illusion of the movie toy, which simulated motion through a sequence of still pictures viewed by means of an aperture and a shutter.

The idea of wedding the two illusions seemed to come automatically. As soon as cameras could stop rapid motion, inventors wanted to make photographs move. Their exploits continued the spirit of collective invention and gave the masses an even more powerful machine of democratic art.

Stopping Motion

Even before the invention of dry plates, a Californian who called himself Eadweard Muybridge managed to stop fast motion very well. His real name was Edward J. Muggeridge, and he hailed from England. As a pioneering photographer he had hauled a huge camera (it took eighteen-by-twenty-two-inch negatives) into Yosemite Valley to obtain beautifully detailed pictures, and as an aggrieved husband he had killed his wife's lover and been acquitted. So Muybridge was something of a legend even before the famous story of the Horse Bet That Created the Movies.

It may be that there never was a bet after all, but the story nicely illustrates how little anyone knew about movement until high-speed photography came along. No one could prove that a horse did or did not have all four hoofs off the ground while trotting. There were opinions but no proof; the unaided eye was not good enough. Governor Leland Stanford reputedly had a $500 bet (in some versions $25,000) that the horse *did* have all hoofs off the ground at some point, and he suggested to Muybridge that they prove it with a camera. It was still the era of wet-plate photography, and no one had stopped fast movement very well, but Muybridge got to work, funded by Stanford. He ordered special Dallmeyer lenses from London for Scoville cameras from New York, the best available equipment. He set the cameras in a row beside a track and ran wires on the ground from each camera across the track

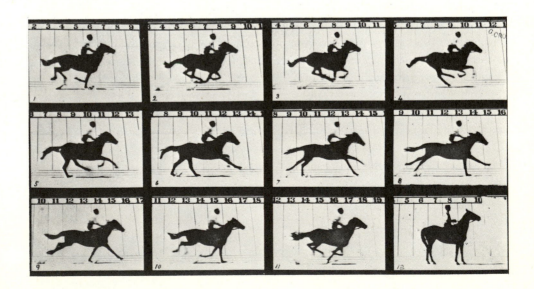

to a shed. As the horse trotted by, it tripped each camera's shutter electrically, taking successive shots of its run (Fig. 1.16). In June 1878, Muybridge made a series of these experiments, obtaining clear proof that Stanford was right. By that time, on the basis of an earlier photo, Stanford had won his bet, at a reputed cost of between $28,000 and $40,000.[13]

Muybridge's achievement was a boon to science. The *Scientific American* published his pictures, and Muybridge went on to more efficient studies of animal and human movement that would benefit not only zoology and medicine but also pictorial art and sculpture. In 1878 he was achieving perhaps 1/2000th-second exposures, a considerable accomplishment, but in later work he achieved speeds of 1/4800th-second—until then thought to be impossible. For the first time, any ordinary movement in real life could be firmly stopped. But that wasn't enough.

Moving the Photos

Muybridge made drawings from his photos and projected them in his invention, the zoopraxiscope, a variation on a projecting phenakistoscope. He used the moving pictures to illustrate the lectures he gave across the world.

In 1888, Muybridge's lecture tour took him to Orange, New Jersey. There he met Thomas A. Edison, who had recently opened a research laboratory in West Orange. Edison was "the Wizard of Menlo Park," celebrated as the inventor of the incandescent light bulb, multiplex telegraphy, the stock ticker, the electric battery, and the phonograph. He would take out more than a thousand patents in his name before he died. His greatest achievement was none of these things, however, but the whole operation embodied in the words "invented by Thomas Edison." More than Eastman, Talbot, or Daguerre, Edison gathered many experimenters to his own name. By 1890 there were more than eighty assistants working at Edison's laboratories, few of them even known today, much less credited for their discoveries. Even the light bulb was not basically Edison's invention. He improved on the technical failures of more creative minds by a method of trial and error that he enlarged into a massive instrument of collective invention. This was certainly a great achievement, though it needs another word than *invention* and it has finally—ironically and probably unfairly—turned against its own maker. Edison's system, through which he allowed himself to be advertised as the inventor of so much that others did, has finally cast a great doubt that we can trust any of his claims.

Edison and Muybridge apparently discussed the possibility of using moving pictures to accompany Edison's favorite creation, the phonograph. By the end of the

1.16 Horse in motion. Muybridge's first successful motion studies, made in 1878.

year Edison began to lodge caveats (descriptions of pending inventions) in the U.S. Patent Office. They reveal a man who knew and learned little about photography or movies, and yet from Edison's shrewd propaganda and the adulation of his admirers two famous legends grew: that all motion-picture machinery descends from him, and that by 1889 his laboratory had actually projected talking pictures.

Neither is true. The meticulous research of historian Gordon Hendricks into the records of the Edison lab found no evidence of a practicable motion-picture camera, much less a projector of talkies, before May 1891.[14] What the lab did achieve depended heavily on other explorers—more than we have noted. The man who gained Edison his reputation as the Father of Movies was William Kennedy Laurie Dickson, a Scot who joined the Edison staff in 1883. An eccentric whom Edison apparently didn't like, Dickson kept tinkering with the problems of motion-picture photography and learned from the other inventors. Edison did not offer much encouragement, apparently because he hadn't been able to adapt his beloved phonograph into a movie camera (to take round pictures in a spiral on a cylinder—a sort of barber-pole approach) and because he thought that Dickson's eventual successes were too silly to create much of a market for moving pictures.

By 1892, Dickson had made a workable camera using film. The reluctant Edison went along with plans for constructing in Feburary of 1893 what has since become known as the first movie studio. It was a practical, ugly building pasted over with tarpaper and arranged to pivot so that an overhead opening could be adjusted to let in maximum sunlight at any time of day. It was called the Black Maria because it looked like the police wagon of the same nickname. Dickson and his associates made test films there, and in March 1893, an Austrian strongman named Eugene Sandow and a Spanish dancer called Carmencita took time off from their vaudeville appearances to flex and twirl for Dickson's camera. On April 14, 1894, their films were among several exhibited by the Holland Brothers in New York City, the first commercial presentation of the new "Edison" machine, the *Kinetoscope.*.

It was a peephole machine: a patron, after dropping a nickel in a slot, looked through a small hole in a cabinet and watched several seconds' worth of moving pictures. The film was joined into a continuous loop that passed over a series of spools (Fig. 1.17). A shutter with one aperture was spun in synchronization with the film so that each frame of film briefly flashed onto the viewer's eye. Despite Edison's initial dream, and his later wild claims, his lab never created a successful synchronization of sound with picture, nor was the lab, by itself, able to project films successfully. It took outside assistance.

The Kinetoscope's first impact was staggering. The vaudeville presentations were so successful that soon the machine had made debuts across the country, and the Black Maria was bringing in Buffalo Bill's Wild West acts, boxing dogs, minstrel shows, dancers, acrobats, and dozens of comedy acts. By July, Carmencita's ankles had been declared indecent at Asbury Park, New Jersey, in the movies' first brush with censorship, and by September the first filmed prize fight was drawing sports fans to Kinetoscope parlors. Apparently impressed, Edison kept tight control of revenues, patents, and publicity.

By September 1895, however, Edison's initially gloomy predictions about the future of movies seemed to be coming true. Exhibitors were having troubles with the quality of Edison's prints and the deterioration of negatives, and, apart from such technical problems, the public seemed to be getting tired of the fad. The greatest flaw in Edison's machinery was its inability to achieve projection. Only one person at a time could watch the Kinetoscope. It would always be a private entertainment—still too close in concept to a toy.

In France, meanwhile, another industrialist was moving ahead. Louis Lumière worked in his family's photographic supply factory in Lyons, together with his brother, Auguste. The two shared credit for a variety of inventions, but the motion picture was Louis's particular specialty. Like Edison, whose Kinetoscope had inspired him, Lumière was competing with a number of other inventors who managed successful projection in early 1895, but by cumbersome and complicated methods.

1.17 Edison's Kinetoscope, first displayed to the public in 1894.

Louis Lumière's method was so simple that his machine, the *Cinématographe* (approximately 12 inches square and 6 inches deep), was less than half the size of its competitors (Fig. 1.18). Most importantly, it managed to record and project clear images by a simple clawlike device that held each frame of film briefly in place, a great improvement over the cams and beater movements of other machines.

In March and June of 1895, Lumière demonstrated his machine to meetings of

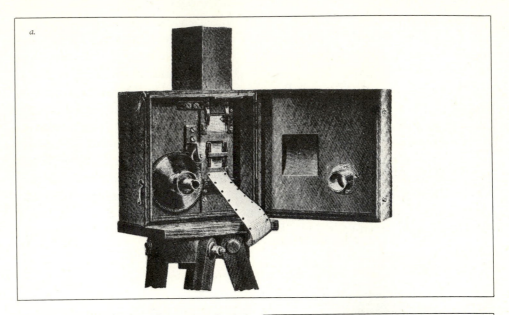

1.18 Cinématographe. a. The camera loaded with film. b. The camera in operation. From the angle shown, the camera's lens is not visible.

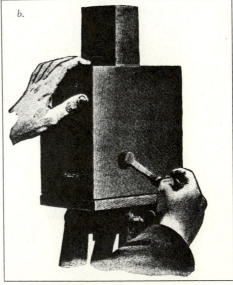

professional societies (Fig. 1.19), and on December 28, 1895, he presented the first screening for a paying public in Paris. Thanks more to Louis Lumière than to anyone else, the year 1895 has come down to us as the beginning of the motion picture. Lumière was not the first—no matter what we finally decide "first" means in such a long, collective process—but, as one historian has put it, "the time of experiment was over and the 'cinema' began to affect the world."[15]

It affected Edison. Before Lumière's success, Edison showed no particular eagerness to continue with the movies. The businessmen who had bought concession rights to the Kinetoscope had been paying him handsome royalties (one group had promised no less than $10,000 a year), which more than overcame Edison's expenses in allowing the machine to be invented. He was more interested in other projects. Then came December 1895. Some Kinetoscope exhibitors, about ready to give up the business, looked at a projector Thomas Armat claimed to have invented. In fact, Armat's collaborator, Charles Francis Jenkins, deserved most of the credit for the projector, the *Phantoscope*. It impressed the exhibitors, who went to Edison with the news not long before word of Lumière's impact also arrived.

Edison was not a man to take second place lightly—certainly not to be "beaten at his own game" as a newspaper had put it, reporting on the Phantoscope's success.[16] The game was now business competition based on entertaining the public. Technology's evolution had come a long way from the disinterested speculations of

1.19 Frame from the first Lumière movie, 1895.
Note the two circular sprocket holes.

elite scientists, yet the business in which Edison would become immersed for a while was a logical continuation of all that had gone before. Edison would now, in fact, move very quickly after the same goal that Talbot had failed to achieve: monopoly on machinery that people liked to believe was wholly his anyway.

By February 1896, Edison had seen the Phantoscope. He made a deal with Armat: the Edison lab would make fifty machines (enough, thought Edison, to cover the country) from Armat's model. They would be leased to exhibitors, never sold, and Armat would get a share of the royalties. On April 23, 1896, the machine made its American debut in New York City. Armat himself was at the controls, projecting Black Maria vaudeville acts and one scene of breaking waves. When the waves appeared, Armat remembered, the audience went wild, shouting "Edison! Edison! Speech!"[17] It was understandable that they didn't shout for Armat or for Jenkins, since the machine that had surprised them was now called the *Edison Vitascope.*

SUMMARY

From the beginning, humans have been fascinated with the illusion of movement and the illusion of captured reality. After 1826 these illusions found expression in a number of movie toys and in the development of photography. At the same time, two cultural revolutions accelerated the evolution of these forms into a movie machine: (1) collective commercial enterprise took over from the old, more individualized scientific spirit, and (2) the new technology, particularly of photography, put realistic reproduction into the hands of the common people. Thus no one person can be credited with being *the* inventor of movies. They arose out of collective invention and the mass popularity of realistic reproduction. In 1893 the Kinetoscope, a peephole device, finally joined the movie toy with photography. In 1895 the Lumières developed the Cinématographe, an efficient and simple machine that projected movies. Their success marks the beginning of movies as a powerful force of mass communication.

NOTES

1 Helen Gardner, *Art Through the Ages,* 7th ed., rev. Horst de la Croix and Richard G. Tansey (New York: Harcourt, Brace & World, 1980), p. 25.

2 For a full explanation, see H. W. Janson's *History of Art* (Englewood Cliffs, N.J.: Prentice-Hall, and New York: Abrams, 1977), pp. 23–27.

3 Roget's paper, printed in 1825, was "Explanation of an Optical Deception in the Appearance of the Spokes of a Wheel Seen Through Vertical Apertures," *Philosophical Transactions of the Royal Society of London,* pt. 1, pp. 131–140.

4 Today we can substitute film for the paper. The *pinhole camera* is a portable camera obscura: a light-proof box with a tiny hole in one end. It gives good pictures but requires lengthy exposures.

5 Quoted in Helmut Gernsheim, *The History of Photography* (New York: Oxford, 1955), p. 5.

6 Quoted in Beaumont Newhall, *Latent Image* (New York: Doubleday, 1967), p. 97.

7 For a complete discussion of this, see Roger Burlingame, *March of the Iron Men: A Social History of Union Through Invention* (New York: Scribner, 1938).

8 The finest single work on collective invention is Roger Burlingame, *Engines of Democracy* (New York: Scribner, 1940).

9 Gernsheim, pp. 50–53.

10 Gernsheim, p. 268.

11 Gernsheim, p. 302.

12 *American Photographer,* 1924. Quoted in Josef Maria Eder, *History of Photography* (New York: Columbia, 1945), p. 489.

13 There are several erroneous versions and pictures of this famous experiment. The most accurate information, and our main source here, is Gordon Hendricks, *Eadweard Muybridge: The Father of the Motion Picture* (New York: Grossman, 1975).

14 *The Edison Motion-Picture Myth* (Berkeley: California, 1961). Hendricks's work remains a model of what film historians ought to do before drawing any conclusions about how the movies came about. It has been a major source of information for the discussion of Edison on these pages.

15 C. W. Ceram (pseudonym of Kurt W. Marek), *Archaeology of the Cinema* (New York: Harcourt, Brace, & World, 1965), p. 157.

16 *Baltimore Sun,* October 2, 1895. Cited by Gordon Hendricks in an unpublished manuscript.

17 "My Part in the Development of the Motion Picture Projector," *Journal of the Society of Motion Picture Engineers,* 24 (March 1935). Reprinted in Raymond Fielding, *A Technological History of Motion Pictures and Television* (Berkeley: California, 1967).

Part 1 / The Techniques

of Communication:

Stylized Perceptions

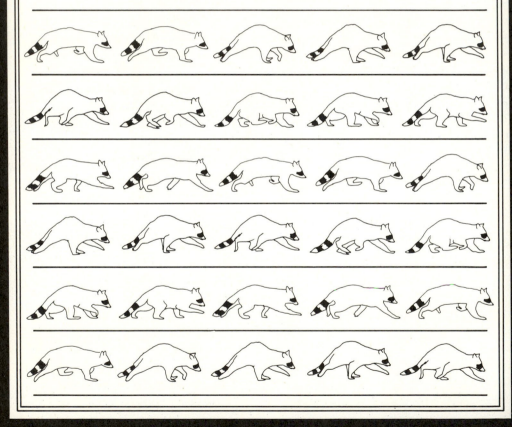

Movies were basically a surprise. There had been no popular demand for movie machines, and many of the inventors thought of their creations as strictly scientific instruments or—as Edison thought—passing commercial gimmicks. But when they were displayed to ordinary people, the machines created an enduring need. People wanted to see more of these moving pictures, and businessmen quickly emerged to supply them. The machines thus roused anew the primal forces of industrial developments: demanding consumers and competing suppliers. From the interplay of these forces there developed a complex system of visual communication. But what lay at the base of this powerful fascination? We will consider that question in Part 1.

The new mechanism, like many other entertainment forms before it, played with the ways humans normally experience the world. The movie camera imitated the human eye's method of recording moving objects as images in space, and later on, color film imitated the eye's mixing of hues. Microphones imitated the eardrum's response to sound waves. The projector was a kind of mechanized brain, throwing up a continuity of images like our imagination and memory. Inspired by the original quest for realistic illusions, the movies thus learned to mechanize our perceptions of reality. But what results is not a copy of reality but a close imitation of the way we perceive reality.

This makes movies fascinating, not simply accurate. They are a mechanical version of our experience—that is, reality done in a mechanical style. The stylization of our perceptions catches us up in a world of play, trickery, and illusion, while the close imitation of our processes makes the movies more realistic compared with other forms of play. Most of the time we ignore a movie's techniques; they are transparent devices we look through to become involved in the movie's action. Sometimes, though, we notice techniques and take pleasure in how they operate. The full experience of movies involves this interplay or counterbalancing between transparent and noticeable as an essential part of our fascination.

In this section we will cover the five principal areas of fascination that movies have evolved: stylized movement, space, continuity, sound, and color. In each chapter we will dwell in some detail on (1) particular techniques and the technology from which they spring; (2) their use in movies; and (3) their influence on audiences and theorists.

By studying filmmaking in this book, we obviously take a much more analytical approach than the ordinary viewer. We will study some basic technological details in order to appreciate these styles more clearly. Movies come from a machine, and filmmakers use that machinery to convey the unique movie experience. It is not magic, but a manipulation of technology, and we need to understand that. Although a complete understanding of technology takes more study than this book can provide, we should become familiar with some essential details and thereby increase our overall sensitivity to the movie experience.

31

Chapter 2 / Movement

There is a legend, passed on by many film histories, that highlights the power of the movies' illusion of movement. It is said that members of the first movie audiences in Europe and America shrank back in shock when trains or waves were shown moving toward them. And yet they were watching silent, black-and-white scenes projected with a perceptible flicker, and often on screens that were little more than bedsheets.

It is possible that the legend derived from a publicity gimmick. It still illustrates the central issue of this chapter: Movement in a movie is obviously fake and yet mightily realistic—to a point where it can be disorienting. Nor is its fascinating impact restricted to the past, when audiences were less familiar with it. We are still capable of ducking while watching wide-screen roller coaster rides, and in 1975 some very sophisticated people stood in line for *Jaws*, to be scared by a shark whose movements they knew were mechanical.

The movie projector plays upon peculiarities of the human eye, tricking us into seeing something that really is not there: a fascinating illusion of movement.

THE MACHINERY OF THE ILLUSION OF MOVEMENT

The perfect illusion of movement demands regular intervals of no movement at all. To enjoy the simple delights of movie toys, viewers can ignore the obvious flutter and flash between the spinning images, but a movie camera cannot get a decent image if the film moves even slightly, and the projector cannot present anything intelligible if the images flow behind the single aperture. The movies require *intermittent motion*: the moving film must keep pausing behind the gate. You have perhaps seen what happens when the film does not pause. A movie's action is suddenly replaced by a wash of blurred forms. The breakdown, called *losing a loop,* occurs when the film pulls loose from the sprockets and moves continuously past the gate. It demonstrates how crucial pauses are to the illusion of movement.

Intermittent motion was the link between movies as private fun and as mass impact. Each image had to be held stationary before the gate long enough to allow sufficient light to throw a bright image onto the screen. At the Edison lab a simple intermittent-motion device allowed the camera to get images, but it was not acceptable for projection, and so the Kinetoscope remained a peephole machine only. The film moved continuously between a lamp and the spinning shutter with its very narrow aperture. The aperture passed over each moving frame of film, allowing

33

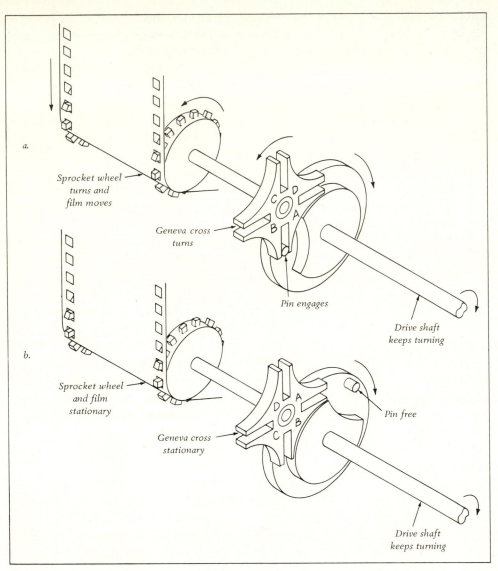

a.

*Sprocket wheel
turns and
film moves*

*Geneva cross
turns*

Pin engages

*Drive shaft
keeps turning*

b.

*Sprocket wheel
and film
stationary*

*Geneva cross
stationary*

Pin free

*Drive shaft
keeps turning*

2.1 The Geneva cross movement. a. The moving pin engages the cross between the leaves marked A and B, spinning it and the film's sprocket wheel a quarter turn before moving free. b. The now stationary film waits for the pin to engage the cross between leaves B and C.

only a very quick flash of light to catch the image. The viewer had to stay glued to the eyepiece to see anything at all. Such a mechanism might have been projected with a very powerful lamp, but that would have burned up the film.

The Phantoscope solved the problem with a device that Armat knew as the star wheel, or *Geneva cross movement* (also called a *Maltese cross movement*), long used in clocks (Fig. 2.1). The star gear is caught and given a quarter turn each time the pin in the continuously turning disk goes by. The disk is attached to the projector's drive shaft, and the star gear drives the film's sprocket wheel. The film remains stationary during most of the disk's journey, then jumps forward one frame, then stops, allowing time for bright projection. Armat referred to this intermittent motion as the heart of all projection machinery. The Geneva cross movement itself is found today only in projectors that need to carry heavier gauges of film (35 mm and 70 mm). It transports them without damaging the sprocket holes, and projection is not greatly affected by the slight differences in turns that tend to develop in the cross movement due to small manufacturing errors.[1] For projectors that carry lighter films (16 mm and smaller) and for cameras that carry a film only once but must do so with absolute accuracy and consistency the cross has been replaced by another device.

The idea for this crucial instrument reputedly came to Louis Lumière one night as he lay sleepless with a migraine headache. His brother Auguste later remembered how Louis explained the mechanism, pictured in Fig. 2.2. "It consisted of a claw with eccentric movement, like the foot of a sewing machine. At the top of its movement, the claw thrusts into the sprocket holes on the edges of each frame, then draws the film down, withdraws and returns back up to repeat the movement, leaving the film momentarily immobile."[2] Lumière's has proved the simplest and most accurate device for achieving intermittent motion. The heart of his machine, and of today's movie camera, consists of two essential organs: the *eccentric cam* and the *claw*.

Left to itself, however, either the Geneva cross or Lumière's claw will eventually break the film. If the camera's take-up reel is pulling away at a regular speed and the intermittent-motion device is holding back the film several times each second, a great tug is going to develop. Inventors discovered the problem very early, and someone suggested an easy solution: loop the film above and below the gate. As the film stops, the upper loop gets larger and the lower loop loses its slack, but then regains it again as the film jumps forward, taking up the extra slack in the upper loop—and so on (Fig. 2.3). An ingenious and absolutely essential idea—but so basic that no one has been able to prove who deserves credit for it.[3]

The loop is associated with another legendary figure in the history of technology. Edison claimed that he held patent rights to the loop. It had been developed, he said, by Woodville Latham, whose inventions had come under Edison's control. When this claim was made (1911), Edison was deep in his attempt to control all American filmmaking through an organization called the Motion Picture Patents Corporation (called "the Trust"). In the tradition of Fox Talbot, Edison wished to lay claim to every basic element of American movie cameras and

2.2 Lumière's claw mechanism. a. At the top of an eccentric cam's movement, the claw engages the film below the camera's or projector's aperture. It then draws the film downward. b. At the bottom of the movement, the claw disengages and then moves back up to re-engage the film. During the pause between the two movements, the film remains stationary—to be exposed or projected through the aperture. Lumière used film with just two round sprocket holes for each frame of film (see Fig. 1.19). Although modern film has more sprocket holes, the modern claw is simply a variation of Lumière's.

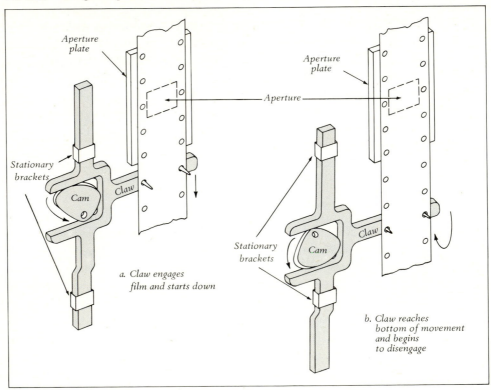

Aperture plate

Aperture plate

Aperture

Stationary brackets

Cam

Claw

a. Claw engages film and starts down

Stationary brackets

Cam

Claw

b. Claw reaches bottom of movement and begins to disengage

demand royalties for their use. Since every movie machine had to have loops, anyone with a movie camera had to pay Edison or fall prey to the Trust's lawyers. To escape the harassment that developed, many filmmakers moved away from the East Coast and looked for happier climes—like California. So the *Latham loop* was one force in creating Hollywood.

There were other forces, to be sure, and the Latham loop wasn't Latham's anyway. Edison lost his try at monopoly, in part because the loop was shown to be in common use prior to Latham's machine. The loop keeps Latham's name more for convenience and irony than for anything else. It reminds us again of how many factors get taken for granted in our assumptions about film history.

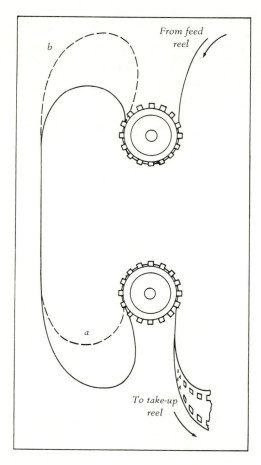

2.3 The loop's function. When the claw or Geneva cross movement stops the film at the gate, the take-up reel continues turning, pulling the film taut at the lower loop (dashed lines a). The feed reel also continues turning, enlarging the upper loop (dashed lines b). When the film is released at the gate, the original loops are regained, and the process repeats.

PERCEIVING THE ILLUSION OF MOVEMENT

The movie projector flashes a succession of still pictures upon the screen, and two things happen: (1) because the pictures are flashing rapidly, the viewer does not notice the moments of blackness between each flash; (2) because the pictures show successive stages of a particular movement, the viewer accepts the flashing frames as a picture that moves. The projector's achievement depends on *two different peculiarities* in human perception.

Persistence of Vision

We have already mentioned the first peculiarity, called persistence of vision. The eye briefly retains the image of an object after the object itself has moved. The phenomenon was widely known before Roget, who is sometimes credited with discovering it.[4] In fact, Roget did not mention the illusion by name in his famous paper, but assumed that everyone knew what he was talking about. Modern science has specified the cause of the illusion. The cells in the retina normally continue to fire—that is, send signals to the brain—for about a tenth of a second after they have been stimulated.

The thaumatrope exploits this phenomenon. One side of the twirling card leaves an image on certain cells of the retina. The cells continue firing while the card turns, leaving the new image, which in turn persists briefly. As long as the twirling movement is completed within a tenth of a second, the eye "sees" a complete figure that is not really there—an optical illusion.[5]

In the same way, the eye will not see the moments of blackness between each still picture of a movie, provided the flashes of light are rapid enough. In the earliest days of motion pictures there was a long period of blackness, so that audiences were aware of a brief gap between pictures. (This registered as a flicker, so that "flickers"—now shortened to "flicks"—became a popular name for movies.) The modern projector overcomes this problem by using a shutter with two or three openings (see Fig. 1.1b), synchronized so that each frame of film is projected twice before it is moved forward by the intermittent-motion device. The shifts from darkness to light now occur about ninety-six times a second, and the eye is fully deceived into accepting the movie's pictures as continuous.

But persistence of vision has been given more credit than it deserves. Since scientists had isolated the phenomenon in ancient times, and early inventors used successive still pictures in their movie experiments, most film historians accepted persistence of vision as the complete explanation of the movie illusion. In fact, it only explains why we don't see blackness between the pictures. The pictures seem to move for another reason.

Acceptance of Phenomenal Identity

A demonstration of this second phenomenon is built into the book. On the corners of certain pages, we have placed drawings of a dog chasing a rabbit. In the first twelve drawings, the rabbit advances 60° from one picture to the next. Flip pages 39 to 63 slowly, and you will perceive the chase moving in slow, choppy movements. In the remaining pictures, pages 99 to 197, the rabbit advances only 7½° from one picture to the next. If you fan through the drawings rapidly, you will improve the smoothness of *apparent* motion until, like the movie's inventors, you achieve a fine quality of apparent movement. But even in the slowest, crudest stage, you will probably perceive the rabbit and dog as *moving*.

    This rules out persistence of vision as the cause of the illusion, for, when flipped slowly, the pictures are not traveling fast enough to allow a new image to arrive while the old one is persisting. If you have doubts about your flipping speed, run a movie through a viewer or special projector that can be set to run precisely at very slow speeds. When film is projected as slowly as three and sometimes two frames per second, the eye will perceive images of very slow *motion*. There is obvious flicker—as though you were watching the movement through the slowly moving blades of a fan—but the illusion of movement remains. Laboratory experiments with perception have revealed the same thing: even with relatively long gaps between one discrete image and another, the eye still perceives apparent movement.

    We can call this second peculiarity the *acceptance of phenomenal identity*, though there is no generally accepted term for it. No one is sure what causes it, though it has been thoroughly recorded. The followers of gestalt psychology maintain that perception depends on the grouping of sensations into identifiable forms, or *gestalts*. In 1912, Max Wertheimer noted that viewers perceived separately flashing points of light as movement of light from one point to another. In 1926, Josef Ternus flashed successive arrangements of lights in a line. In the first arrangement, the lights were positioned ABC. In the second arrangement, DEF, lights D and E replaced B and C in exactly the same positions. Since only one light actually changed position, Ternus theorized, we might expect a viewer to see light A moving to the F position when the arrangements were flashed. In fact, most viewers perceived *all three* lights shifting

On the next twelve right-hand pages, the rabbit in the drawings will advance 60° from one picture to the next. Flip these pages, and you will perceive the chase moving in slow, choppy movements.

back and forth as a unit. This *Ternus effect* suggested that there was an inherent principle of organization at work in human vision, a tendency to see objects moving as units, with each part keeping its same function in the configuration. This is what Ternus called *phenomenal identity.*[6]

Watching a movie, we usually accept such identities without thinking. The projection speed fully exploits persistence of vision, providing apparently constant movement, and the degrees of difference between one frame and the next are more like 6° than 60°. Despite this maximum deception, everyone has probably noticed phenomenal identity in Western movies, where stagecoach wheels seem to go backward. Here, ironically, our wheel experiment has gotten so realistic that it gets tricked by its own trickery. The result is the *wagon-wheel effect* and comes about because one spoke of a wagon wheel looks the same as another. The wheel in Fig. 2.4 has eight identical spokes, with 45° between each one. If the wheel is moving rapidly forward, each spoke moves about 25° per frame of film, as we see Spoke A doing from frame a to frame b. In the second position Spoke B has moved closest to Spoke A's original position but is 20° *behind* it. Since all the spokes look alike, we infer the phenomenal identity of the closest spokes, and the wheel appears to go backward.

This acceptance of phenomenal identity contributes to a variety of illusory movements, known collectively as the *phi phenomena*. Wertheimer's discovery and the Ternus effect demonstrate only one form: *beta movement,* or apparent lateral movement between flashing lights or stationary figures. Outside of movies we commonly experience it in neon signs that use moving letters or figures. In other common illusions, a viewer will tend to perceive an object as getting closer if it grows

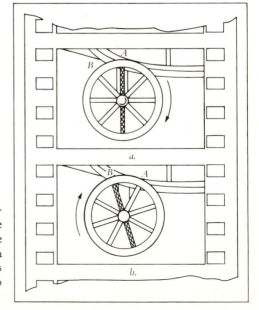

2.4 Wagon-wheel effect. Spoke A actually advances in the direction of the arrow from frame a to frame b. But because we cannot tell one spoke from another, our eyes link Spoke A in frame a with Spoke B in frame b. Since our eyes do this with each spoke, the wheel appears to go backwards.

either larger or brighter; conversely, if it grows smaller or darker it seems to move away. The size illusion is *alpha movement*; the brightness illusion is *gamma movement*. When apparent movement in depth is joined with apparent side-to-side movement, the phenomenon is *delta movement*.[7] Beta movement predominates in movies, but the other varieties may contribute to the total illusion.

Acceptance of phenomenal identity is clearly the true source of illusory movement in movies, whereas persistence of vision contributes to the quality of the illusion. Science has not explained the cause of the illusion. We know that under the right conditions we tend to perceive discrete objects as continuous units, but no one yet knows why this trickery occurs. There are only theories. Here at the most basic level of all, our perception of movement, we encounter a fact that will reappear throughout this book: cinema is not a simple phenomenon but a fascinating complexity.

THEORISTS AND THE ILLUSION OF MOVEMENT

When theorists assumed that the illusion of movement depended only on persistence of vision, matters were relatively clear. There was a measurable physiological cause: movies automatically stimulated the retina. The eye couldn't know it was being tricked, so movie movement was as real to the eye as movement in the real world. This assumption naturally led some theorists to emphasize the realism of movies.

But the acceptance of phenomenal identity opens up contrary possibilities. Either it is just physiological, like persistence of vision, or it involves some kind of positive choice by the brain, a matter of cognition. This second theory is that the mind cooperates in its own deception, that movies are therefore a sort of psychological game.

Though there is not yet proof either way, this second theory has become the more popular one among perceptual scientists, and film theorists, rather belatedly, have picked up on the insights it provides. We will dwell on these more heavily here, saving the discussion of realist theory for a later chapter. But first we must distinguish the contrary possibilities.

Basic Theories of Perception

The various theories of perception can be reduced to two schools. According to the *theories of direct sensory mechanism*, the impression of movement is based on an automatic tendency of the nervous system to react to artificial, flashing stimulations exactly as it would to real, successive stimulations. With either stimulations, perceiving movement would simply be a matter of energy passing between cells. This theory sees perception as *passive,* the mere reception of data.

According to *cognitive theories,* of which gestalt psychology presents the best-known example, when the mind receives from the retina the discrete stimulations of flashing images, it interprets them in the best way it can. Thus, when you flip the pages of an illustrated magazine past your eyes, your mind interprets it as a chaos of forms. At best, now and then in the chaos, it reacts to some fleeting sensation of one form becoming another. When you confront a movie, where the changes in the separate forms of, say, a walking figure (head, body, legs, arms) are consistent, your mind fully exercises its awareness of formal integrity. It identifies the successive images as new positions of the same unit and interprets that the best way it can: as movement. Cognitive theories see perception as a positive *activity,* a grasping by the organism.

We may be tempted to call this a reasoning process, but we must be careful. Some research suggests that even new-born insects and guppies respond to beta movement as though it were real movement.[8] Theorists who hold to direct sensory mechanism could cite such research as evidence in their favor. It may also be, however, that there is a cognitive activity here that is far more immediate than the high-level human problem solving we associate with reasoning. The difference is that humans can know it is trickery. Recall what happened when you flipped through the pictures of the dog-rabbit chase: you *knew* how the effect was occurring, yet you *accepted* the flashes as apparent movement. Cognitive theories suggest that even with the perfected illusion in movies there is always some "double bind" in viewers. They know one thing and accept another. The trickery is thus not physiological, but psychological. This implication has begun to make itself felt in film circles, largely through the delayed impact of one psychologist.

The Pioneering Insight of Hugo Münsterberg

By 1916, when Hugo Münsterberg wrote *The Photoplay: A Psychological Study,* the popularity of photography had created an opinion among many art critics that whatever merely reproduced reality mechanically could not be true art. Movies also fit into that category. The famous legend that begins this chapter suggested to everyone that viewers shrank back because they thought trains and waves were real. This was mere sensationalism, not art. Of course, within three months after the first American movies were projected, at least one writer noted that movies were fascinating because they were *not* real: "The emotion produced upon the spectator is far more vivid than the real scene would be."[9] But this attitude seems generally not to have flourished; at least, no one had made any serious attempt to explain what a "realer-than-real" experience might entail. Münsterberg was the first to try it, and his work had to wait over fifty years to earn the respect it deserved.

Münsterberg believed that the motion picture was a form of art because its technology created "entirely new mental life conditions" whereby the mind collaborated in providing a unique experience that was indeed more vivid, fascinating, and unified than any real scene. As a psychologist, he was aware that research had discounted persistence of vision as an explanation of the movie illusion. In Münsterberg's opinion the illusion was "produced by the spectator's mind and not excited from without," and this "really essential trait" was a key to the distinctive way film art operated. The mind creates the motion; it also accepts the depth of an obviously flat image; it also recognizes in visual devices like close-ups and editing the mental acts of attention, memory, and imagination: at every level of the movie experience, the mind knowingly goes along with a kind of game being played with its powers, so that, like motion, all the effects of the so-called real movies are to a high degree creations of the spectator's own mind. The movies do not reproduce real life. They provide images that come to us "not as hard facts but as a mixture of fact and symbol," and our minds invest them with meaning.[10]

Münsterberg's work created little stir at the time, but after its republication in 1970 it began to strike home. J. Dudley Andrew, in his introduction to major film theories, praises the directness and consistency with which Münsterberg set forth, at virtually the dawn of modern filmmaking, a view of the nature of film that seems remarkably fresh today. As Andrew notes, Münsterberg justifies film as art by claiming that it "exists not on celluloid, nor even on the screen, but only in the mind which actualizes it."[11] This sense of film as a projection of psychological truths and needs is shared by such contemporary theorists as Jean Mitry, who argues that cinema's function is neither to copy nor avoid reality, but to use the human psychological processes to give us unique comments on life. Mitry, who did not discover Münsterberg's work until late in his career, once remarked to Andrew, "How could we have not known him all these years? In 1916 this man understood cinema about as well as anyone ever will."[12]

What Münsterberg most clearly understood were the perceptual processes involved in the movie experience, notably the illusion of movement. By using modern science to explain how technology created unique experiences, Münsterberg became a pioneer film theorist in this new mechanical age which challenged old esthetic traditions.

Foreshadowing Münsterberg's psychological data there was a widely known concept that had been used for years to explain how people are always knowingly deceiving themselves when enjoying art. The concept is worth special mention.

The Willing Suspension of Disbelief

In 1815 the British poet and critic Samuel Taylor Coleridge wrote that his poetry had been an attempt to create unreal characters, but in such a way that they would

transfer from our inward nature a human interest and a semblance of truth sufficient to procure for these shadows of imagination that willing suspension of disbelief *for the moment which constitutes poetic faith.*[13]

Münsterberg's knowledge of psychology provided scientific justification for Coleridge's poetic insight. A human viewer's acceptance of phenomenal identity was a similar kind of willing self-deception. It occurred at a much more basic level, but Münsterberg presented it as an equally cognitive process, and therefore a clue to the many other layers of mental play which esthetic experiences evoke.

Joining Coleridge to Münsterberg, a modern cognitive theorist of perception might say that in the movies there is a suspension of disbelief, but it begins at a level deeper than what we usually call "willing." The mind cannot ignore the persuasive movement of the images, and so it accepts them. There, and through all the stages of perception that follow, the viewer encounters a dynamic tension between the undeniably real and the palpably false—or, as we will put it, between transparent devices and noticeable ones.

The movies presented new levels of perceptual play, going far more deeply into our inward nature to create illusions that did not depend only on poetic faith but on primary self-deceptions of the human organism itself. It was the unprecedented, psychological depth of this tension that transformed the traditions of cultural self-deception in 1895 and gave the world a new esthetic experience. It was a revolution in perception.

THE ILLUSION OF MOVEMENT IN MOVIES

The typical movie assumes the illusion of movement. It does not remind viewers that persistence of vision and acceptance of phenomenal identity are being required of them. Since technology overcame the flicker between images, the wagon-wheel effect is the only inherent flaw left in the illusion, and it is a minor disruption. Nevertheless, some filmmakers have deliberately played with the processes of motion, more or less emphasizing them to the exclusion of other things, and their achievements are worth pointing out.

Playing with Persistence of Vision

With a projector running at today's normal speed of twenty-four frames per second, the eye sees each frame of film for 1/48 second. The frame's passage takes 1/24 second, but during half that period, 1/48 second, the shutter is blocking off the light.[14] Communication in the movies takes place in increments of 1/48 second.

This raises possibilities for experimentation. A normal action—say, the raising of an arm—might take a hundred frames or more, so that the viewer has plenty of time to recognize the arm. But how *little* time is needed? Would a viewer notice one frame of different information in the middle of a normal, continuous action? Could a film communicate with a succession of very different single frames? Would there be true recognition in such cases, or only some kind of suggestion? In other words, if we play with the images' persistence on the eye, what happens to the viewer's awareness?

Subliminal Imagery   We can begin with yet another legend. Once upon a time an advertising firm claimed that it flashed "Buy Coca-Cola" and "Buy Popcorn" very briefly on the screen during a movie in a public theater. The messages appeared every five seconds in flashes of three milliseconds—about 1/7 the length of time that a single frame of movie film appears. The firm claimed that despite this infinitesimal exposure, the audience's demands for Coca-Cola jumped 56 percent, for popcorn 18 percent.

This report raised both interest and alarm that *subliminal* advertising was possible: selling to people without their awareness of the message. However, the firm never made any details of the experiment available, and several attempts to duplicate its reputed effects led nowhere. There have been scientific experiments suggesting that *some* degree of perception without awareness is possible, but just as many proving the opposite. The least successful involve subliminal words—and subliminal advertising does not seem to work at all. There have been some consistent results with subliminal pictures or designs.[15]

At least one major movie has tried subliminal effects. During *The Exorcist* (1973), a story of diabolical possession, the image of a death's head momentarily interrupted an action taking place in one of the character's dreams. Publicity suggested that it had a strange, subliminal effect, and there were reports of people passing out or becoming unaccountably ill after experiencing it. Technically, the effect was not subliminal, since the face could be seen as a brief, scarcely distinguishable image—perhaps one or two frames of film. Moreover, the bizarre context of the whole movie, and the dream in particular, sets up a viewer for the unexpected and terrifying, maybe even the sickening. Subliminal, or even near-subliminal, imagery's effect on a viewer's awareness or emotions has yet to be proved with any scientific accuracy. For publicity purposes, it seems to come in handy.

Minimal Imagery   A filmmaker can reduce a movie's information to drastically few impressions: minimal imagery. Such communication can be nearly subliminal, like the example above, only it carries on the effect much longer.

An extreme example of the technique is *God Is Dog Spelled Backwards* (1967). It is essentially a joke (and the title has nothing to do with the visuals), but it is visually intriguing. Dan McLaughlin took shots of over two thousand paintings, each shot only two frames in length (that is, visible for only 1/24 second), and joined them together. In this way his film presents three thousand years of art in less than 3½ minutes. What you actually *see* depends on your familiarity with art and on the number of times you view the film. You can pick out familiar paintings, though it is doubtful you could train yourself to recognize even half of them. Nevertheless, the film's entertainment value comes from its deliberate manipulation and frustration of persistence of vision.

A master of minimal imagery is Norman McLaren, whose short films for the Canadian Film Board have experimented with every aspect of movie trickery. In *Blinkety Blank* (1955) McLaren uses drawings to tell the story of two birds who meet, fight, finally mate, and have an offspring. Prior to making the five-minute film, McLaren had discovered that, shown three or four frames of a moving image, the eye retained the last image longest, the first image next, and the middle images least. Instead of drawing all the stages of movement on successive frames, McLaren left frames blank between the beginning and end of movements. The images appeared in flashes of one frame or sometimes in clusters of two or three frames. The blank passages between images ranged from one to four frames.[16] Because the images are surrounded by darkness, the viewer has no trouble picking up even the briefest flashes, but the deliberate flicker effect that results breaks down the realistic deception of the eye's persistence of vision. In a sense, the movie analyzes the optical illusion as we watch.

McLaren also forces viewers into a new acquaintance with their own acceptance of phenomenal identity. The mind creates apparent movement from greatly separated phases of action. The result is a more obviously illusory movement. The viewer is able to realize more distinctly that the mind is accepting a trick, and this awareness increases the excitement of the effect. This introduces us to another range of visual play.

Playing with Phenomenal Identity

When filmmakers play with the relationship *between* the still segments of an action, they necessarily engage the viewer's usual acceptance of phenomenal identity in an unusual way. Like McLaren they may leave literal gaps in the action, or they may omit intermediate phases from one position to another. In this way they *animate* the images in different ways. On the other hand, they can keep an image exactly the same from frame to frame, *freezing* apparent movement altogether.

Styles of Animation   *Animation* is (1) the creation of apparent movement with drawings, photos, or inanimate objects, and (2) the manipulation of live-action cinematography so that animate objects move in unusual ways. Animation handles a wide range of *material,* from live figures to very abstract art, and provides various *styles of movement,* from extreme realism to extreme distortion. The latter concern us here.

We accept all animated *cartoons* as moving, but there are great differences in what we are accepting. In traditional cartooning, animators draw each position of a figure's movement on a different celluloid sheet, or *cel,* and they draw background and foreground scenery on separate cels so that they can animate the figures independently of the surroundings. They place the cels on an animation stand (Fig. 2.5) where the movement from frame to frame can be precisely controlled. For very realistic movement, animators change the figure's position every one or two frames. This is *full* animation, duplicating the smoothness of movement in a live-action movie. Other animators prefer less realistic styles, and many producers want to turn out cartoons more rapidly than painstaking full animation allows. For either group, some degree of *limited* animation is practical. It uses fewer cel changes per foot of film and creates more stylized movement.

Animators turned to special machines to achieve their desires. In 1915, Max Fleischer invented the Rotoscope, which projected individual frames of live-action movies into a panel from which very accurate cartoon drawings could be made. In the late 1930s Walt Disney's studio developed a multiplane camera and animation stand to allow greater depth between cels and provide lifelike subtleties in its full animation. By the 1950s, however, television's demand for cartoons had made limited animation a commercial necessity and led to the use of computers to speed up animation even further. Movements were reduced to a set number of positions. The numbers were arranged in the order desired and fed into a computer, which did the actual animating, projecting the figures onto a television tube. A typical television cartoon today reduces action to stock, repetitive movements, changing a figure's position no more than four times in twenty-four frames. This is the most extreme, and most mechanical, form of limited animation.

Not all cartoons move the same way. Disney's work after the mid-thirties shows maximum realism. In the cartoon shorts, animal characters like Mickey Mouse, Donald Duck, or Pluto might get into outlandish situations with extreme bodily contortions, but their actions are smoothly constructed exaggerations of real body movements. The figures are drawn with a natural, rounded look, and the multiplane technique allows near movements to move faster than those farther away, imitating the appearance of movements in real life. Disney's realism is most evident in the animated features, beginning with *Snow White and the Seven Dwarfs* (1937), which join animal characters with human ones. All their actions are so accurate and subtle that much of the visual pleasure comes from the sheer precision in the movements of what are obviously drawn figures.

In contrast, at the Warner Brothers studios in the 1940s, animation directors used a simpler variation of full animation. There was less emphasis on depth, and the

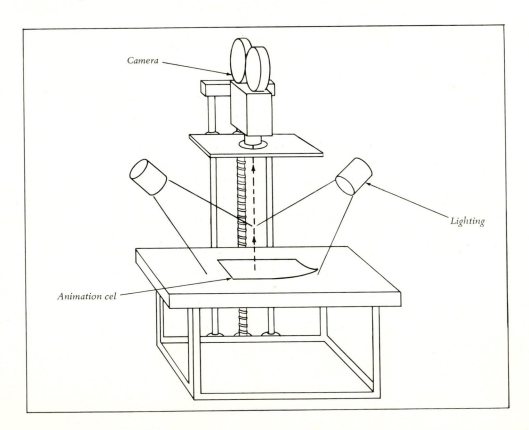

figures of characters like Daffy Duck, Bugs Bunny, and Wile E. Coyote were not as rounded. The mad logic of the stories often involved very rapid movement and bizarre bodily contortions—not realistic at all, but the full animation provided subtle *timing*. When a character like Coyote realizes he is standing in mid-air, his body falls first, stretching down out of the frame, before his head, with some final glance of exasperation on the face, follows. Such split-second touches required the exactitude of full animation.

In the same period, another group of animators broke away from full animation, forming United Productions of America (UPA) specifically to explore less realistic forms of cartooning. Gerald McBoing-Boing and Mr. Magoo are examples of UPA characters. In their cartoons backgrounds appear very flat and deliberately artificial, while body movements are stylized—that is, the animator reduces the many different positions of a realistically flowing action to a few basic positions so that the figure moves in a stiffer, conventionalized way. UPA aimed at this kind of stylized reality.

Computerized animation is typified by the work of William Hanna's and Joseph Barbera's studio, established in 1957 and reputed to employ over half the cartoonists now working in Hollywood.[17] Their work is represented by the Pink Panther, the Flintstones, and Yogi Bear. Action in such cartoons is kept very simple, with few figures in the frame at one time, and movements are extremely stiff and repetitive.

To compete with television the movie industry has specialized in features since 1960, ending the production of cartoon shorts, so your best opportunities to experience animation styles is on the television set. *The Wonderful World of Walt Disney* sometimes runs classic multiplane cartoons, and many of the old Warner Brothers and UPA cartoons have been bought up for children's television shows. The dominant style, though, is the computerized mass product originated by Hanna-Barbera. The advantages are obvious: a Hollywood team that turned out eight to ten 7-minute cartoons a year during the 1940s and 1950s now turns out four half-hours a week for television—a 13,000 percent increase in production.[18] Despite this advantage, some animators pursue the full-animation style, usually for television specials. Chuck Jones, formerly of Warner Brothers, has produced full-animation works like *Yankee Doodle Cricket* (1974) and *Riki-Tiki-Tavy* (1975).

There are still feature-length animated movies, though not so many as in Disney's heyday. *The Yellow Submarine* (1968) capitalized on the popularity of the Beatles, whose songs inspired its innovative techniques of limited animation. With *Fritz the Cat* (1971) Ralph Bakshi introduced a series of animated features that have dealt with harsh issues like urban conflict and world destruction. Bakshi's most recent

2.5 Animation stand.

work, *The Lord of the Rings* (1979), shows a range of animation styles. There are fully animated drawings, some employing the exactitude of Rotoscope copying, as well as special processes that reduce straight cinematography of actors to the appearance of moving etchings.

Elsewhere, animators have followed in Norman McLaren's footsteps to experiment with novel forms of full and limited animation. In Czechoslovakia and Yugoslavia, particularly at the Zagreb studios, cartoons have been turned to purposes of political allegory, with a wide variety of animation styles.

The animation of *three-dimensional* inanimate figures is common to many feature films, particularly science fiction movies, and again we can detect a range of styles. *King Kong* (1933) set a standard of realism, animating an eighteen-inch model frame by frame. Today Kong's movements may seem somewhat stylized—but his successors, particularly since *Godzilla* (1955), use limited animation, which is more noticeably unrealistic. The most realistic modern animation of models is found in space adventures like *2001: A Space Odyssey* (1968), *Star Wars* (1977), and *Alien* (1979). The animation of space ships and monsters is so precise that the trickery is virtually undetectable.

When animators turn to *animate* subjects, they usually wish to create deliberately unreal movement. Norman McLaren provides an example in *Neighbors* (1952), an antiwar fable about two men who kill each other over a flower. McLaren used a method he calls *pixillation*. It involves two basic techniques. In one, a single frame is photographed after each step an actor takes. The stepping action is left out, so that on film there is only a succession of standing figures. When the result is projected, the figure seems to *glide* over the ground, as though on invisible skates. In the second technique, the actor jumps up and down while moving forward, like a dribbled basketball. The filmmaker now removes all the frames except those in which the actor is in mid-air. When the result is projected, the person glides along in mid-air. Other animators have used pixillation in trick films and television advertising.

Filmmakers can give living subjects a mechanical kind of animation in a number of other ways. The simplest method is to change the camera's shutter speed so that figures speed up drastically on the screen. This is *fast-motion cinematography*. We will discuss it in more detail in Chapter 4, where we consider how movies play with time. In addition to speeding an action, the filmmaker can also remove frames at various intervals, adding even more choppiness to the effect. The technique was originally known as Keystone editing, after the Keystone Comedy studios, which used it extensively in the early 1910s.[19] Carrying the principle to an extreme leads to *time-lapse cinematography.* A filmmaker fixes the movie camera in front of, say, a blossoming flower and shoots two or three frames every hour. The resulting film will show a flower opening magically in seconds. If the filmmaker fixes the camera on a building site and shoots five seconds a day, we can watch six months of construction reduced to fifteen minutes. The flower film is likely to show the smoothness we associate with full animation, and the construction film will look like very choppy limited animation.

The making of animated movies includes a good deal more than just movement, but essentially the very term *animation* means a playing with our acceptance of phenomenal identity, and the history of animation provides a wide and subtle variety of such play.

Frozen Motion   A filmmaker can decide to do away entirely with the illusion of movement. There are times in otherwise moving pictures when motion stops on the screen; and there have been movies made entirely or predominantly with still pictures.

The first technique is known as *freeze framing.* Classic examples of it occur in *Jules and Jim* (1961), which tells of two friends' infatuation with a beautiful woman. At one point in the story, by way of accenting the woman's effect on the men, her different expressions within one long movement momentarily freeze, then continue: a succession of stilled images within an otherwise continuous motion. Technically, the effect is achieved by repeating certain frames of a movement after the original film has been shot. It is visually powerful, probably because it plays upon the very thing we take most for granted about a movie: that it moves.

Brief freeze-framing has become a conventional device, particularly to signal the end of a movie or television show. But when it is carried on at great length, freeze-framing creates a peculiar tension in some viewers.

We can see this in *La Jetée* (*The Pier*, 1962), a science-fiction study of people living in a France destroyed after World War III. The filmmaker, Chris Marker, originally intended it as a regular moving picture, but then changed his mind and told the story with still pictures. In effect Marker cancels out the viewer's need to accept phenomenal identity between slightly different pictures. The successive pictures are the same. But, as viewers of *La Jetée* often note, there is a kind of *longing* to accept phenomenal identity—to see a movement that is not possible. Viewers will report that they have seen movement in several parts of the movie, but in fact there is only one point where Marker does have an image move, and the effect can be electrifying, even though the movement is slight.

Marker thus carries the play with phenomenal identity to its furthest extreme: forcing viewers to try to do without it though they are conditioned to accept it. They have seen many movies, for one thing. For another, a stilled movie frame is not the same as a still photograph. The need for phenomenal identity may be canceled, but persistence of vision continues to work. There are twenty-four frames flashing each second, and so a kind of motion is still there. Faced with this predicament, viewers apparently try to feed illusory movement into images that are not even trying to elicit the illusion. And this takes us back to Hugo Münsterberg's observation that it is the mind, after all, that creates the movie's powers.

SUMMARY

Movement in the movies is the product of mechanical devices that play upon peculiarities of the human organism. There are four devices: the Geneva cross movement, the claw, the cam, and the Latham loops. These make intermittent motion possible, and that motion allows the eye and brain to create a realistic illusion. The eye's persistence of vision enables the darkness between images to go unnoticed, and the acceptance of phenomenal identity between the discrete still pictures of a movement enables the viewer to see the process as movement.

The cause of this second phenomenon is not yet known, but the most prevalent theory among psychologists is that the mind is performing an active function, not simply receiving the illusion passively. Psychologist Hugo Münsterberg applied this theory to movie perception, suggesting that the mind helps create the realism of the movie experience knowing full well that it is not real—and in this regard Münsterberg echoes the insight of Samuel Taylor Coleridge that the experience of art involves "the willing suspension of disbelief."

Filmmakers have played specifically with the illusion of movement in a number of ways. They have tried to see how little exposure to an image is needed to leave some impression in the mind, thus creating movies that use subliminal and minimal imagery. In the different forms of animated filmmaking they have played in a variety of ways with the viewer's acceptance of phenomenal identity. At one extreme, animators create very subtle changes from frame to frame, imitating the realistic illusion of the live-action movie camera. At the other extreme, they ignore subtle differences or leave gaps between frames, thus creating extremely stylized and mechanical movements. Such animation includes not only drawings and inanimate models, but live objects that take on peculiar forms of movement depending on how the filmmaker chooses to play with the intermittent images.

The illusion of movement sets up a dynamic tension between the undeniably realistic and the palpably false, and we will see the same pattern of fascination continuing at different levels in the other major elements of motion-picture communication.

NOTES

1 Here and elsewhere the authors have learned a lot from the research of Patrick L. Ogle, whose forthcoming work on motion-picture technology promises to clarify the impact of invention on movie art.

2 Translated from Maurice Bessy and Lo Duca, *Louis Lumière: Inventeur* (Paris: Editions Prisma, 1948), pp. 29–30.

3 Eugene Lauste is a strong contender.

4 It used to be said that Roget was better known for his *Thesaurus of English Words and Phrases*, a book of synonyms, but with all the interest in film study that may not be true anymore.

5 The proper term is *afterimaging*. It varies depending on the intensity and length of the stimulus. A bright light twirled in complete darkness leaves a circular *positive* afterimage that remains for much longer than 1/10 second, seemingly burned on the retina. If you stare at a colored image for a long time then close your eyes, you will see a *negative* afterimage: yellows become blues, reds greens, whites blacks, etc. Flashing movie frames leave less dramatic afterimages.

6 See Irvin Rock, *An Introduction to Perception* (New York: Macmillan, 1975), pp. 193–197. For a translation of Ternus's "The Problem of Phenomenal Identity," see Willis D. Ellis, *A Source Book of Gestalt Psychology* (London: Kegan Paul, 1938), pp. 149–160.

7 The varieties of apparent movement are thoroughly outlined in Gerald M. Murch,

Visual and Auditory Perception (New York: Bobbs-Merrill, 1973), pp. 279–282.

8 Rock, p. 198.

9 Henry Tyrrell, "Some Music-Hall Moralities,"*Illustrated American*, 20 (11 July 1896), 76.

10 *The Photoplay: A Psychological Study* (New York: Appleton, 1916), pp. 39, 57–71.

11 *The Major Film Theories: An Introduction* (New York: Oxford, 1976), p. 24.

12 *Major Film Theories*, p. 26. Mitry's major work is *Esthétique et psychologie du cinéma*, 2 vols. (Paris: Editions Universitaires, 1963 and 1965).

13 In his *Biographia Literaria*, chapter 14, not published until 1817.

14 To be exact: the leaves of the shutter break each frame's projection into two flashes of 1/96 second and two blackouts of 1/96 second; during the second blackout the projector moves the next frame into position.

15 Murch, pp. 320–323.

16 Maynard Collins, *Norman McLaren* (Ottawa: Canadian Film Institute, 1976), pp. 14–15, 46.

17 *Film Dope*, 2 (March 1973), 36.

18 Chuck Jones, "Animation Is a Gift Word," *American Film Institute Report*, 5 (Summer 1974), 27–28.

19 Kalton C. Lahue and Terry Brewer, *Kops and Custards: The Legend of Keystone Films* (Norman: Oklahoma Press, 1968), p. 40.

Chapter 3 / Space

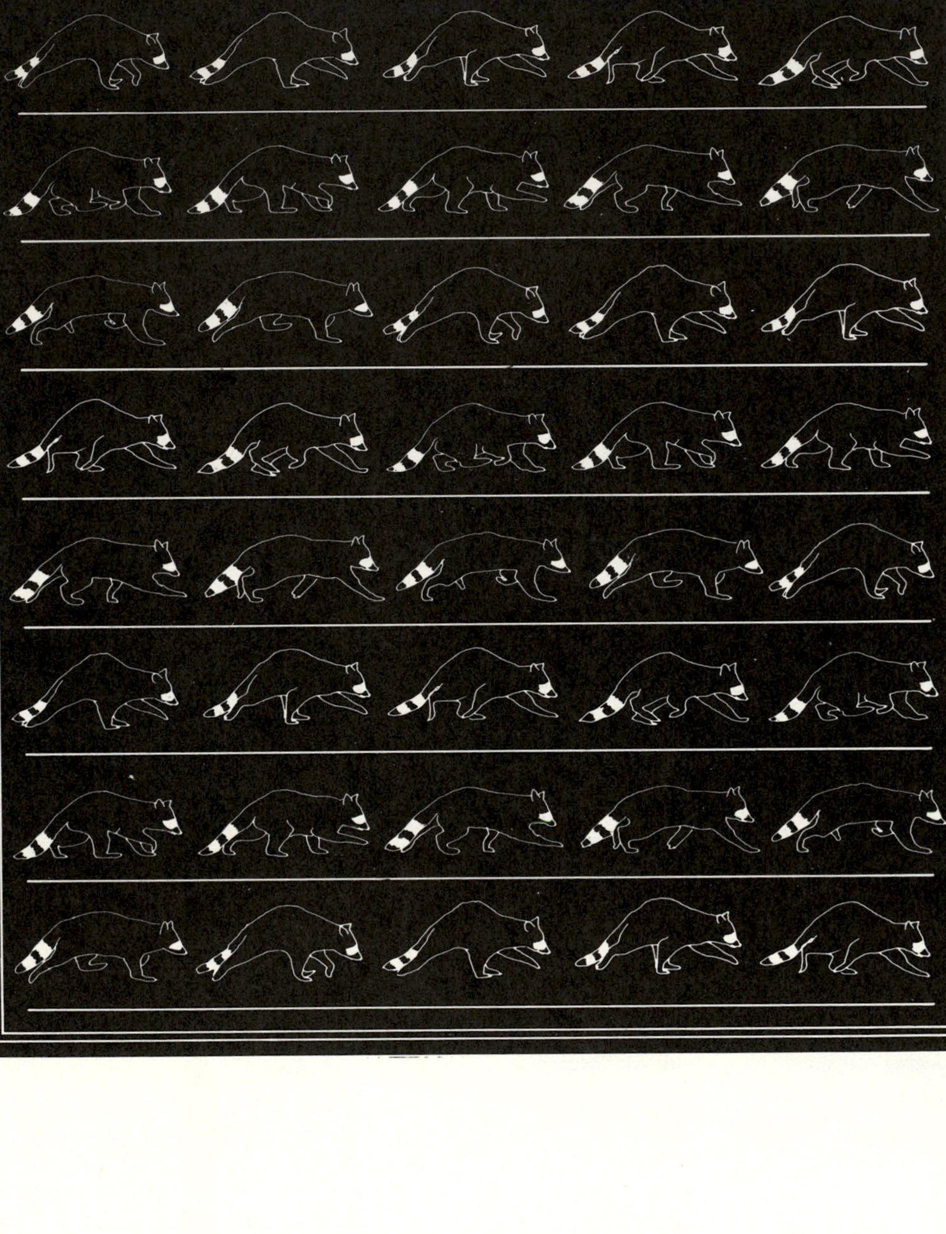

A movie audience sits in relative darkness watching a dominant, framed area on the screen. There is movement there, and it powerfully draws the eye. There are two other attractions as well. There are patterns of light: shifting textures and contrasts. And there are shifting arrangements of figures inside the apparent depth of the picture. In the movie house, then, space is no longer a given factor of ordinary life but something special—a *design* of movement, light, and spatial relationships.

This designed space is a movie's *mise en scène*. Derived from a French term for a stage setting ("that which is placed on stage"), *mise en scène* refers to the whole complex of pictorial elements inside the movie image. It includes the placement and movement of performers, costuming, and set design as well as the use of light. It excludes dialogue or any effects that result from joining shots together in the editing process (which we discuss in Chapter 4). Some writers employ the term as a general synonym for a film's overall visual style. *Mise en scène* is specifically a matter of composition. To discuss it, we look at movies as moving *pictures*. We consider how filmmakers work with light, framing, and depth.

WORKING WITH LIGHT ON FILM

Movies are a variety of photography: what we see as images are literally writings with light. In the movie camera, light makes its marks on chemical emulsion. They are the lines and textures that, in the theater, a projector's lamp will throw onto a screen. To work with light is to apply this photographic technology, much as one applies any writing instrument, to communicate. This has produced various styles with different effects.

The Technology

The filmmaker uses a particular kind of film—properly *film stock*—and finds a particular way to get light to it. The resulting images will have a particular look, then, depending on these two technological factors: the properties of the film stock and the lighting technique.

Properties of Film Stock   The clumps of silver bromide grains in a photographic emulsion may be compared to the receptors in the human retina, but there are significant differences. Emulsions come in varying sizes, and the chemical grains are less adaptable than the cells of the retina to changes in the intensity and color of light. These properties allow movies to "see" differently at different times.

55

The size of the emulsion's grains determines the stock's *texture* and *speed*. A film stock with very large grains of emulsion produces images which present a coarse texture to the eye. The grains are too large to reproduce tiny details and shades of difference in the subject, so the stock is poorer in *definition*. But it is high in *speed*. Its large grains react quickly to light: it is a *fast* film, producing acceptable pictures where there is little light or where you have to take whatever light you can get—in short, for unstaged, on-the-run situations. At the other extreme is the fine-grained, high-definition, slow film stock. It requires far more light but provides richly detailed images (Fig. 3.1).

Slower films are obviously well suited for large-scale commercial movies made in studios where abundant light is available. Japanese movies like *Gate of Hell* (1953) and *Kwaidan* (1965) are particularly noteworthy for using extremely slow color films to achieve rich detail. MGM musicals of the 1950s, using a slow Technicolor process (see Chapter 6), have much the same quality. Fast films are common to newsreels and documentaries, though they also appear in studio films. You can generally tell, for example, when a story film uses newsreel footage. The images are no longer crisp. And since audiences associate increased grain with on-the-spot photography, filmmakers can use fast film stocks throughout fictional stories to achieve a documentary appearance. The grainy images of *The Battle of Algiers* (1965), for example, give a sense of immediacy to the actions. So texture is sometimes imposed on a filmmaker by shooting conditions; and sometimes the filmmaker deliberately chooses a texture for particular effects.

The filmmaker must also deal with the fact that film stock has limited sensitivity to the intensity and color of light. When you look at a person against a window on a

a

b

3.1 Images with different grain. The picture of Bob Dylan (a) from *Don't Look Back* (1966) was taken on fast film. The picture of Pamela Britton (b) from *Anchors Aweigh* (1945) was taken on slow film.

bright day, you distinguish both the outside scenery and the details of the person. Film does not. If you take a picture of the person against the window, you can either record the outside scene and turn the person into a silhouette (Fig. 3.2a) or record details of the person by letting in more light and overexposing the background until perhaps it disappears (Fig. 3.2b). Film has a limited *range of contrast.* You can compensate by introducing another source of light to brighten the person so that the contrast range is not so great, and you get a picture with both distinct background and detailed figure (Fig. 3.2c). But you have had to make choices on the basis of film's limited sensitivity, and each choice gives an image with a different "look" or style. Lighting techniques are therefore important to the filmmaker, and we will turn to them in detail in a moment.

A film emulsion's peculiar sensitivity to colors also affects contrast. An emulsion reduces colors to white, grays, and black, but there are two basic kinds of emulsion whose responses differ. Movies made before the mid-1920s used *orthochromatic* ("correct-colored") film. It distinguished most colors but was insensitive to red and overreacted to blue. This created the generally higher contrasts that give early movies their distinctive look. *Panchromatic* ("all-colored") film, introduced into movies in 1926, rendered virtually all colors as different shades of gray. This gave lower contrasts and a generally "softer" look. Today, panchromatic film stocks are standard in all movies (color film is panchromatic, as we will see in Chapter 6), and orthochromatic stocks are used for special effects and titles.

A filmmaker may also alter an emulsion's color sensitivity or even its texture through the use of *filters.* Since colored filters allow only a certain range of the light spectrum (the range represented by the filter's color) to strike the film, a filter enables the cinematographer to stress or deemphasize elements of a scene. A deep red filter darkens skies; a green filter brings out detail in foliage; and a blue filter darkens some complexions and makes blue eyes paler (Fig. 3.3). There are also filtering devices that affect texture. From the earliest days, gauze and other porous materials have been placed in front of the lens. Being so close, they are too out of focus to be visible, but they diffuse the light, giving a soft "glow" to images. Various kinds of coated glass or tiny screens are also used to diffuse light or to turn the brightest spots of an image into gleaming "stars."

Techniques of Lighting   Cinematographers watch the position and quality of light, measuring it as accurately as possible, for two basic reasons: to get a decent image on the film, and to create a consistent lighting style. A decent image is the primary

a

b

c

d

e

f

3.2 Different effects due to contrast. Because of a film's limited range of contrast, one may choose (a) to create a silhouette, (b) to eliminate background details, or (c) by introducing additional light in the foreground, to register both foreground and background details.

3.3 Different effects due to filters. Image (d) is unfiltered. Image (e) was shot with a red filter, which lightens the lips and complexion and darkens the eyes and foliage. Image (f) was shot with a dark blue filter, which lightens the eyes and foliage and darkens lips and complexion.

consideration. In documentary or newsreel situations, this may be all they worry about. In studio situations, where lighting is a deliberate process, consistency becomes equally important. The director wants to use light to establish moods or direct the viewer's attention, but without shifting arbitrarily from one scene to another. The creative cinematographer will try to adapt a basic style to suit various demands. The development of technology has made a wider and wider range of options available to the cinematographer, and we can break them down into three general areas: flat lighting, three-point lighting, and existing light technique.

Flat lighting dates from the first movie companies. They used sheets of cloth or glass roofs to diffuse the sunlight on film stages. When artificial studio lights appeared in 1906, the same flat-lighting approach was followed. Rows of mercury-vapor lights were set at a high angle overhead, to cast shadows onto the floor and out of the camera's view. The lighting provided even illumination in which there were few dark shadows and few very bright, "hot" spots. By 1910 some filmmakers used light for dramatic contrasts, lighting characters from behind or throwing strong shadows deliberately. This was not easy, because mercury-vapor lamps, like the sun, were floodlights, not spotlights: they threw a wide cover of light, not a narrow, controllable beam. To change the intensity or direction of such light, filmmakers had to employ mirrors or other reflectors (Fig. 3.4).

Technology soon overcame this limitation. By 1920 there were various arc spotlights that threw beams of intense light, giving hard-edged shadows. The middle of the 1930s saw the development of modern tungsten spotlights. Their incandescent lamps gave softer, more attractive shadows. They were built much like projectors, with internal condensors and a front lens. Filmmakers could change not only the direction of the beam but its focus and size. In more recent years, smaller quartz halogen lamps have replaced tungsten lamps in spotlights. They provide more intense, yet essentially soft light and more efficient, lightweight equipment.

This evolution in lighting instruments accompanied the growth of an efficient studio lighting system, generally referred to as *three-point lighting*. It depends on three

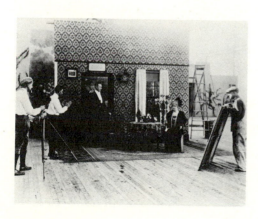

3.4 A typical flat-lighting set-up, about 1910. Daylight is diffused by a glass roof overhead. The man on the right is using a reflector to soften shadows.

basic sources, or points, of illumination. (1) A *key light* is the crucial source that defines the most important details of a scene. Under the plainest conditions there is only a key light. (2) Since strong key lighting throws strong shadows, a *fill light* is usually employed to bring out details in shadow areas or, in general, to soften the contrast between light and shadow. Reflectors may serve this function, particularly outdoors. Indoors it is more common to employ floodlights or soft-focused spots. (3) To give dimension to a subject, a *back light* is used. It sets the subject off from the background.

Since about 1920, all studio cinematography has used this three-point system (Fig. 3.5). That does not mean there must always be three lights, or only three, playing on a scene. The three-point system simply isolates basic areas of lighting for film. It enables cinematographers to play with lights, or eliminate them, as they wish.

Playing with the three-point system is traditionally divided into two broad categories. When one uses predominantly bright key lights and uses the other lights to avoid deep shadows and reduce contrasts, the result is *high-key* lighting, associated with a light mood and an air of sophistication. Most of Hollywood's romantic comedies and musicals of the 1930s display classic high-key technique (Fig. 3.6). When one uses few bright areas and depends on hard contrasts between light and shadow, the result is *low-key* lighting. It suits a more somber mood and what is often called "expressionist" style. The filmmaker uses sharp shadows and pools of light to create a heavily emotional atmosphere—what you are apt to find in the movies of Orson Welles and Ingmar Bergman, or in any number of thrillers and horror movies (Fig. 3.7).

3.5 Three-point lighting. On the set of *Roberta* (1935), various lights are used to provide three-point lighting for actress Irene Dunne. Director William Seiter, in hat and scarf, sits beside the camera, just under two key lights.

3.6 High-key lighting. Shirley Ross and Jack Benny in *The Big Broadcast of 1937* (1936).

Finally, the development of better lenses and faster films has made it possible for cinematographers to operate efficiently using whatever lighting they find on location. This is *existing-light* technique. Outdoors it means using plain daylight with its tendency toward strong shadows and bright highlights—hence, greater contrast (Fig. 3.8). Indoor scenes shot under ordinary house lights may look murky and dim, but the images will be acceptable.

Existing-light cinematography is usually carried on with fast films in documentaries and newsreels, and so it contributes to the look we associate with unrehearsed reality. A filmmaker may use it as a deliberate realistic device, not simply as the fastest or most practical way to get essential information. Thus *The Battle of Algiers* is a fiction film, but the contrasty existing light combines with the grainy texture to give it a documentary look. The technique is not restricted to suggesting documentary. *Barry Lyndon* (1975), a color film whose story is set in eighteenth-century England, uses candlelight as the only illumination for one scene, creating very textured images with an unusual red-yellow glow. In examples like these we see existing light technique becoming another creative option available to the filmmaker.

Applying the Technology

Cinematographers learn to "write" with the technology we have just outlined. Some of them develop characteristic styles, but each style must serve the design of particular films. These designs range from the more transparent, which remain consistently unobtrusive, to the more opaque, where design will stand out strikingly. Let us consider a range of examples.

3.7 Low-key lighting. A scene from *Victory* (1919).

3.8 Existing light technique. Scene from *The Battle of San Pietro* (1944). The use of a fast film makes the image extremely grainy.

The work of cinematographer Joseph Walker is a good example of generally transparent lighting design. In the 1930s Walker shot several movies written by Robert Riskin and directed by Frank Capra, sophisticated comedies in which the values of the small town and the poor triumphed over those of the big city and the rich. Walker, like other cinematographers in American studios at the time, used essentially high-key lighting. But we can see him adapting it to various situations. In *Mr. Deeds Goes to Town* (1936) or *It Happened One Night* (1934) we see high key used on everything from sophisticated interiors to night scenes in parks and woods, most of them actually indoor sets. Overall, Walker's work shows a kind of romanticized realism, without sharp contrasts but also without extravagant sparkle. It is an unobtrusive style appropriate to the down-to-earth optimism of such comedies.

James Wong Howe's work in *Hud* (1963) is another kind of realism, using another variety of consistent lighting. In presenting a harsh West Texas environment dominated by a very cynical main character, Howe selected filters to make the skies appear cloudless, and he carefully filled in shadows with reflectors and additional "booster" lights during daytime shooting so that all details stood out. In nighttime scenes he sought very sharp shadows, even taking glass condensors out of spotlights to increase the sharpness.[1] The result might be called subtle harshness, painstakingly constructed out of high-key, low-key, and existing-light techniques. It is quite different from the look of Walker's movies, yet we can call it essentially realistic. It is consistent and unobtrusively tailored to the harsh story it serves.

During the 1940s and 1950s, extremely low key lighting was popular in many American films, particularly in underworld and horror movies. French critics called the new development *film noir* ("black film"), both for the brooding, cynical quality of its stories and for the visual style which stood out sharply from what had gone before. The lighting design was what we are calling more opaque, using more noticeably calculated effects.

Detour (1946) is a good example of *film noir*. A man now hunted by the police tells us the story of how, through bizarre accidents, he became hopelessly involved in theft and murder. Cinematographer Benjamin H. Kline establishes the story's ominous mood at the outset, using a very striking device. The main character enters a diner and, hearing a piece of familiar music on the juke box, begins to reflect on what has happened. A small spot of light comes up brightly on his eyes as the background scene dims into darkness, and the story flashes back to the beginning. Most of the story takes place at night and in relatively dark interiors where Kline maintains high contrasts and areas of deep shadow. Visually it is a dark, bizarre world, and at the end we are taken back to the diner with the same striking lighting effect that began the story.

During the 1940s cinematographer Nicholas Musuraca worked on a number of horror films produced by Val Lewton at RKO studios. *The Cat People* (1942), in particular, illustrates the effective low-key lighting that marked all the films. The story is about a woman who is afraid that she is capable of turning into a panther and killing people. The story keeps us uncertain whether she really suffers from a supernatural curse or from a psychological phobia triggered by jealousy of another woman. Musuraca's lighting keeps us literally in the dark. For example, in a night scene in Central Park the other woman senses that a cat is stalking her. She finally flees to an indoor swimming pool and stands alone there, knowing that the cat will not enter water. But neither she nor the viewer ever sees a cat. It is something that *may* be in the deep shadows of the low-key lighting. The technique reverses normal expectations and draws our attention to what we cannot see. Musuraca keeps using shadows in this obtrusive way throughout the movie, creating a very appropriate design for this particular story.

In itself light is an obvious necessity for any movie. We need it to obtain an image. But none of the filmmakers we have considered here have used it merely out of necessity. They have provided different *kinds* of light, different styles of experience adapted to the context of particular movies. These range from the transparent to the obtrusive, and they suggest the range of options implied when we speak of working with light.

WORKING WITH FRAMING

The very term *moving pictures* reminds us that the screen is a precisely defined area of *framed* space. Whereas the arc of human vision extends to about 120° with the edges tapering off into indirect (peripheral) vision, the rectangle cut into the aperture plate of the movie machinery takes in no more than 50°, with the edges neatly defined. This means two things. First, the technology of the aperture plate allows the filmmaker to restrict or redefine the framed area in different ways. Second, the presence of limitations on the movie screen involves issues of composition. The screen is a selection and an arrangement of space. These are the factors the filmmaker considers in working with framing.

The Technology

An aperture has relative dimensions, called a *format*, designed to fit inside the width, or *gauge*, of film being used. For example, a 22-mm by 16-mm format is used on 35-mm gauge film. It is common to indicate such a format in *aspect ratios*, the relation of width to height, rather than in actual dimensions. The 22-mm by 16-mm format would thus be 1.375:1. And because an aperture is simply a rectangle cut into metal, its opening may be partially or wholly blocked off with masks, or *mattes*, at any time during shooting. This is the basic technology of framing.

Choosing a Gauge   Inventors have developed some twenty-five different film gauges over the years, ranging from the 75-mm gauge used by the Lumières to a 3-mm gauge invented in 1960. Only a few are practical options for the filmmaker (Fig. 3.9). The standard gauge for professional filmmaking, dating from Dickson's first experiments, is 35 mm, and most entertainment movies use this gauge. Since the 1950s, 65-mm and 70-mm films have been used for super productions. In the 1930s, 16-mm film was introduced, largely for home movies, and in World War II it was widely used by newsreel and combat cinematographers. After the war, 8 mm and later super-8 mm

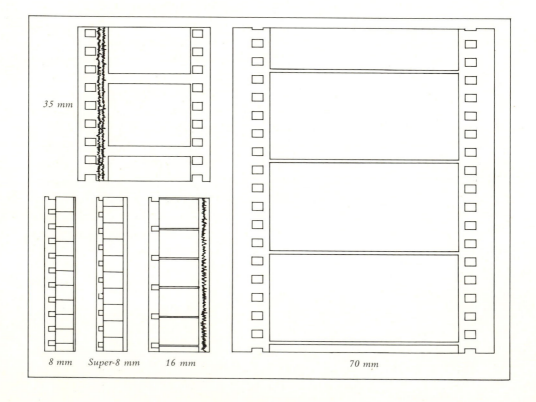

35 mm

8 mm   Super-8 mm   16 mm   70 mm

(a larger format on the same gauge) became the home-movie gauges; 16 mm became a popular vehicle for documentary and experimental filmmakers and is also widely used in film schools.

These gauges offer different advantages. For the documentarist or amateur the smaller gauges offer great portability and less expense. A 16-mm or super-8-mm camera can be handled easily by one person and uses a fourth or a sixteenth of the volume of film stock that a 35-mm camera would use. If projected to fill a commercial theater's screen, however, 16 mm and super-8 mm show increasingly coarser texture: the grains of emulsion are being enlarged tremendously.[2] Professional filmmakers prefer the larger gauges. Their greater expense is offset by their better image quality when projected—and 65 mm and 70 mm give the kind of excellent detail one wants in a top-quality production. But image quality is not the only advantage. Working with a 35-mm or larger gauge puts a variety of formats at the filmmaker's disposal, providing professional filmmakers with a choice of image dimensions.

Choosing a Format   Prior to the 1950s movie formats were standardized. By 1907 the *full screen*, or silent-camera, format was established at 1.33:1. In the early 1930s, when sound tracks had to be fitted onto the film, the Academy of Motion Picture Arts and Sciences established a new standard: the *Academy aperture* of 1.375:1. Then, in the 1950s, came cameras built around a variety of *wide-screen* formats (Fig. 3.10). These arose largely because the movie industry, trying to compete with television, emphasized the film medium's greater potential to play with space.

Wide-screen ratios vary, as do their gauges. Using 65 mm and 70 mm, the Todd-AO process attained 2.2:1, and Ultra-Panavision got 2.75:1. Other processes used 35-mm gauges. VistaVision ran the film horizontally through the camera and projector, getting a 1.85:1 ratio. CinemaScope used an *anamorphic* lens to "squeeze" a wider picture onto 35 mm, then to "unsqueeze" it in the theater. Its aspect ratios changed over the years from 2.66:1 to 2.35:1. Cinerama, which started the wide-screen rage, ran three 35-mm pictures side by side to achieve a ratio of 2.62:1 but finally had to give up the complicated three-projector approach, settling for one projector and a ratio of 1.85:1.

With such a variety available, complicated arguments have risen over which ratio is best. As early as 1930, in answering an inventor's claim that 1.85:1 was a "golden ratio," a scientist studied both outstanding artistic masterpieces and various proportions in nature to arrive at 1.681:1 as a "classical rectangle."[3] In the 1950s some critics and filmmakers argued that wide-screen formats were too clumsy, making

3.9 Common gauges of film in use today.

3.10 Evolution of formats on 35-mm film.

3.11 Typical camera mattes.

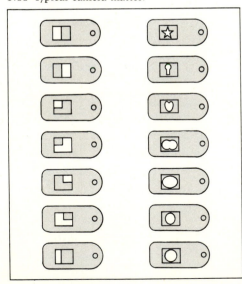

3.12 Optical printer. A projector beams an ▶ image into a camera. With the optical printer the following effects are possible: mattes may be inserted to mask the image; the camera lens may be moved off center, with the movements measured by gauges; the camera lens may be adjusted to achieve the magnification desired; and the printing can be speeded up or slowed down in any pattern.

close shots in particular seem strange and contrived. Others pointed out that wide screens attracted viewers' attention in a new way: they became more involved in the interactions between different areas of the framed space.[4] Since the 1960s, when the passion for extremely wide screens cooled, the typical American 35-mm format is the "golden" 1.85:1, achieved simply by masking off an Academy aperture. European filmmakers prefer to mask their apertures to 1.66:1, as close to a "classical" ratio as the movies have come.

Masking the Frame   A mask, or matte, is a piece of metal slipped into a slot of the camera or projector to block off some part of the aperture (Fig. 3.11). As we just mentioned, American filmmakers today often shoot pictures with an Academy aperture (1.375:1) but compose them with the understanding that a matte will be inserted in the projector, masking to 1.85:1. This is a standard projecting practice.

Mattes are used in the camera for more creative effects. For any shot a filmmaker may block off a portion of the frame. Thus, a matte with a circular opening is commonly used to signal that we are looking through a telescope. Silent movies liked to employ the *vignette,* a fancier form of matte mounted in front of the camera, through which the image was reduced to a small circle while one watched. A filmmaker may also expose the same film more than once, masking different areas each time. In this way the screen is split into two or more areas with different actions in each, or for tricks like creating twins with one performer. Originally filmmakers had to create such effects in the camera without removing the film, but in the late 1920s a technician at one of the American studios found a better method: the *optical printer,* an instrument that faces a camera into a projector (Fig. 3.12). Previously

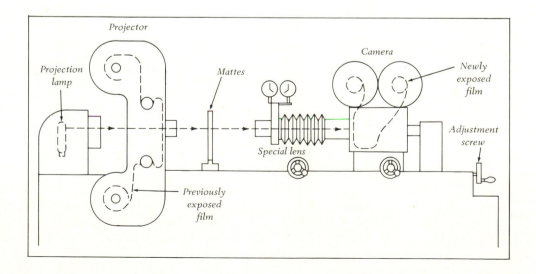

taken scenes are projected into the camera, which copies them with whatever effects the filmmaker wishes, and with frame-by-frame precision if necessary. The optical printer has proved to be one of the filmmaker's most valuable and versatile instruments.

Overall, the technology of framing provides any filmmaker with options ranging from the very tricky to the very subtle. All of them, however, involve the filmmaker in composing subjects within the frame, and that is our next concern.

Techniques of Composition

The screen must provide viewers with the information they need to follow the movie. This is the crucial rule. The filmmaker may also arrange the information to create pleasing and emphatic compositions. These are not crucial, but effective. They are matters of design. The filmmaker decides not just *what* to show but *how* best to arrange it to focus the viewer's attention. The filmmaker must keep four areas of attention in mind: movement, brightness, position, and point of view.

Using Movement   Something that moves gets attention. The more unusual the movement, the quicker one notices it. Some movements are stronger than others, then, because they are more unusual. For example, movements from left to right are considered "normal" to the eye, so that any opposite (right-left) movements on the screen seem more emphatic.[5] If there is a continuous movement in one direction (like that of a waterfall), movement in the opposite direction (rising steam) will draw attention. We are all familiar with the shock of sudden movements coming from unexpected directions on the screen.

Unusual absence of motion also attracts the eye. A character who has been moving about rapidly can get immediate attention by suddenly staying still.

In painting or still photography, strong diagonal lines are said to be more dynamic because they lead the eye around the screen, while strong vertical and horizontal lines tend to create a more static, calming effect. These principles can be applied to movies, also, particularly when the camera is fixed, and movement upon the screen is relatively slight. But when there is a continuous, strong movement it tends to lead the eye so strongly that the viewer will look ahead to where the movement is going. Gregg Toland, one of Hollywood's most respected cinematographers, called this movement a "compositional pointer." He cited the distant shots in *Stagecoach* (1939) as an example. As the tiny coach moves within the vast landscape, it dominates the picture and draws the eye along the trail to finish off the movement, even though the coach is not shown actually traveling across the whole picture.[6]

Using Brightness   After motion, brightness holds the strongest attraction for the eye. If the screen imagery involves no movement, or if a motion is familiar and repetitive (for example, passing scenery behind a character in an automobile) we tend to focus our attention on the brightest area of the screen, wherever it appears. There is a moment in *Apocalypse Now* (1979) which particularly plays on this attraction. The screen is completely dark, forcing us to scan all over the frame looking for some information. Then an ear appears, which rivets our attention.

Cinematographers use brightness much as photographers and painters use it. First, the strongest *light* normally strikes the center of interest. Even when a face is the only subject, filling the screen, small spotlights ("eye lights") are commonly used to draw attention to the performer's eyes. Second, brighter *tones* are used to attract attention. In an evenly lit scene, the character in the lightest-colored clothing tends to get first attention. A blonde tends to get more notice than a brunette, and this is one explanation for Hollywood's emphasis on blonde heroines. Western heroes in the 1930s and 1940s usually had white hats and light clothing. White came to represent the hero's virtue, but the essential idea was to set him off visually.[7]

None of these techniques are rigid rules, however. The central aim is to contrast an area of interest with whatever surrounds it (Fig. 3.13). This can be done by working against the usual emphasis on brightness. If a character's face is the only shadowed area of the frame, we may not be drawn to it immediately, but the contrast becomes noticeable; in the same way (as we noted with *The Cat People*), shadows around a center of interest may gradually attract our attention precisely because they are *not* bright. As Hollywood movies with Katharine Hepburn or Joan Crawford have shown, brunettes provide striking contrasts. Among cowboys the heroic Hopalong Cassidy always wore dark clothes because he had very blond hair and a white horse. Obviously, then, the particular context affects the way a filmmaker plays with our attraction to brightness.

3.13 Use of light and tone for emphasis. Notice how light and tone emphasize the figure at the far left, whereas light on the faces at the right sets up a visual counterpoint. A scene from *Citizen Kane* (1941) with (left to right) Ruth Warrick, Ray Collins, Dorothy Comingore, and Orson Welles.

Using Position   When one arranges sentences, rooms, or static pictures, good composition depends heavily on the position of items. In the movies, however, position has less importance because movement and brightness will draw our attention to anything, no matter where it is. Nevertheless, movement and brightness are most effective when they are arranged in the most emphatic positions. The general practices of cinematographers do reveal some classic principles for balance and emphasis.

Generally speaking, cinematographers avoid a perfectly symmetrical image, where an object of interest is centered and everything else evenly positioned around it. Such compositions lack emphasis. To overcome this, cinematographers tend to displace the center of interest from the mathematical center of the image. They may follow the traditional *rule of thirds,* placing the object of interest along one of the imaginary lines that divide the image into thirds laterally and horizontally (Fig. 3.14). Or they may follow other patterns. Gregg Toland once noted that the point of strongest interest will usually be found to lie roughly along a diagonal line from the lower left to the upper right corner, with the most emphatic positions somewhere in the upper right third of the image. We may call this *Toland's rule* (see Fig. 3.15). There are many exceptions to it, but even when there are, a less prominent line, tone, or mass along the left-right diagonal will usually redirect the viewer's attention to the main point of interest.

We speak of giving greater "weight" to things that impress us, and the expression also applies to positions on the screen. Following Toland's rule, for instance, we would say that the top third and right third of any composition are the "heaviest" segments. We give them more weight, and this determines our sense of "normal" balance in a composition. Our sense of equilibrium is satisfied if a figure on the extreme right is counterpoised with two or three figures on the left. Though the left figures have greater mass, the right figure seems balanced with them; without them, the composition seems too "heavy" on the right. This peculiar sense of balance seems to derive from the eye's tendency to scan from left to right, a tendency related to the brain's construction. Assuming that there are no distractions of strong movement or brightness, a viewer tends to look at the left side first but then is drawn to the right side. This strong attraction makes the right the more emphatic, or heavier, side (Fig. 3.16). One theorist has called this the "curious difference between being important and 'central' at the left, and being heavy and conspicuous at the right."[8] Since the top of the frame is also heavier than the bottom, one figure at the top asks for two or more below it for balance. Thus *pyramid* compositions are common.

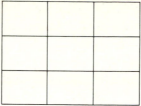

3.14 The rule of thirds. Ernest Borgnine (left) and Jim Brown in *The Split* (1968). Notice the positioning of the faces and the table top along the lines of the imaginary thirds.

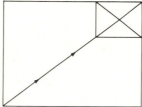

3.15 Toland's rule. A scene from *The Great Ziegfeld* (1936) with (left to right) Virginia Bruce, William Powell, and Luise Rainer. Notice that the composition supports the dramatic tension.

3.16 Left-right balance. In a scene from *Gone with the Wind* (1939), Olivia De Havilland and Vivien Leigh create a balanced composition with Clark Gable.

Since movie images are rectangles that favor the horizontal, there tends to be more interplay between left-right balance than between top-bottom. Wide-screen formats exaggerate the tendency. They increase the eye's scanning distance, so that we become more physically involved in the constantly shifting balance points within the frame. Though today's formats are not extremely wide, they still assert the left-right interplay strongly.

As with traditional rules of movement and brightness, the principles of weight and balance are not meant to be imposed rigidly. The movie frame regularly goes out of balance, for example, on the way to asserting a new balance. And a filmmaker may deliberately unbalance compositions, playing against our sense of equilibrium. The films of Claude Chabrol, the French director who specializes in suspense stories, regularly use unbalanced composition to create a sense of expectation or dread in the viewer. The context calls for such creative imbalance.

Using Point of View   The camera may take different points of view, depending on its level or angle. The most common camera position is at *eye level,* about five feet from the ground or floor, but the cinematographer may change the camera's level or position to get *high-angle* or *low-angle* shots and left or right *oblique-angle* shots. By moving the camera away from the perpendicular, one gets *raked,* or *canted,* shots, commonly called *Dutch angles* (Fig. 3.17).

There are traditional implications to certain angles. A low-angle shot, because it increases the apparent height of figures in the foreground, may imply a character's dignity, dominance, or power. A high-angle shot, decreasing apparent height, may suggest that a character is weaker, defeated, or insignificant. Very high angles may be used for what literature calls an omniscient or godlike view. The raked shot implies anxiety, disorientation, and the bizarre, and so it is often used in science fiction and horror movies.

But there are practical reasons to use angles, so one has to be careful not to turn them into handy symbolic formulas for deciphering a movie's meanings. An oblique angle enables us to see that objects have three dimensions, increasing our sense of

a

3.17 Typical angle shots. a. A low-angle shot from *The Passion of Joan of Arc* (1928). b. A high-angle shot from *The Singing Fool* (1928). c. A raked shot from *Bringing Up Baby* (1938).

depth, and a high angle sometimes reveals objects that would otherwise be blocked from view. Angles may make it clear that the camera is taking a particular person's point of view. If one character is on a ladder and the camera takes a high-angle shot of another character, we assume that the camera has momentarily "become" the other character. This *point of view* shot may say nothing of the dignity or power of the character it shows. Some shots even contradict the traditional implications. *Psycho* (1960) uses an extremely high angle to show a white-haired figure who suddenly appears on a stair landing and kills a man. We may like to feel omniscient about it, but the advantage of the angle is that it *keeps* us from knowing. The figure is not an old woman, as we are supposed to think, and a lower angle would reveal this and ruin the story. In *Citizen Kane* (1941) a very low angle shot shows a friend consoling a losing politician in an empty campaign headquarters. The characters are not dominating heroes. By showing the ceiling of the room, the low angle heightens the sense of emptiness. As with every other technique in filmmaking, the implications of any shot depend primarily on the context in which we see it.

The various potentials in using point of view simply round out the creative options that stem from the fact that filmmakers must work within a frame. They adapt traditional techniques to particular contexts.

Applying the Technology

Unlike the painter or photographer, the filmmaker is working always with *moving* compositions. There are constant shifts in the direction of movement, in areas of brightness, and in balance points within the frame. As a result, the viewer's eye is rarely, if ever, allowed to dwell for long on any arrangement. Still pictures, which we necessarily have to use in a textbook, give no sense of this moving composition, but it is the power that the filmmaker exercises in working with framing. And, again, one may use the power unobtrusively, as a transparent method to involve us in an action, or may shock our awareness more noticeably.

In the typical Hollywood movie of the 1930s and 1940s we find efficient, economical composition, designed to be transparent, to draw no attention to itself.

b

c

The films of director Howard Hawks exemplify this design. Although he dealt with a variety of adventure stories and comedies, Hawks's movies maintain a consistently fluid sense of balance and emphasis. The viewer's attention is not surprised or shocked, not made particularly aware (as in remarks like this) that the movie is quietly keeping one focused on the center of interest. French critics were quicker than Americans to point out this quality. "Obviousness is the mark of Howard Hawks's genius," said Jacques Rivette.[9] And Raymond Bellour did a very careful analysis of twelve shots from *The Big Sleep* (1946), which points out how the movie's repetitive eye-level shots and compositions make us more aware of the subtle changes between characters.[10] Not surprisingly, Hawks was one of the directors who expressed dismay over using wide-angle formats. And yet he used them with the same sense of transparent balance and emphasis. In *Hatari!* (1962), one character enters left, trips, and spills food over two other characters on a bed right. The movement is very simple and unobtrusive; it even follows the eye's natural movement from left to right (Fig. 3.18). This simplicity and "obviousness" help keep the very contrived gag from drawing too much attention to itself.[11]

Horror films, on the other hand, usually try to surprise us with their calculated effects. We need to accept the basic reality of events but also to become sharply aware of a *mise en scène* that might shock us at any moment. In *Curse of the Demon* (1958), for example, a character has just walked down a flight of stairs, moving toward deep shadows below, when, precisely in the top right corner of the screen and in brightness, a gnarled hand appears. The context of the action has led us to expect the worst, and if we have become involved with the action we might jump with fright no matter where the hand appeared. But the framing has also used the pointers of motion, brightness, and position to maximum effect. The hand grabs our attention.

If a horror film puts us on guard against the surprises of its space, then obviously we have moved toward a less transparent *mise en scène*. We can see this shift occurring within the style of one film, *Invasion of the Body Snatchers* (1956). Cinematographer Ellsworth Fredericks handles a story in which people gradually become aware that alien creatures are possessing the bodies of their friends. The

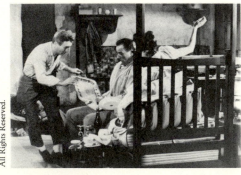

3.18 Composition in *Hatari!* (1962). Red Buttons spills food on John Wayne. The emphasis follows the eyes' natural movement from left to right.

opening scenes are kept "natural" looking, though Fredericks avoids very high-key lighting, keeping a medium contrast ratio. Then, when the aliens' presence becomes clear, Fredericks slips fully into a low-key and, at particularly shocking moments, into dark shadows and extremely distorted angles. Throughout the film the cinematography demonstrates Toland's rule with remarkable consistency, plotting the main line of attention along the lower left to upper right diagonal. Fredericks thus creates a threatening environment that grows out of an ordinary one. The consistent composition gives a sense of controlled space, while other techniques, including severely raked angles at crucial moments, suggest disruption and insecurity. The *mise en scène* is an environment full of spatial tensions that support the main line of action.

The Westerns directed by Sergio Leone use the wide screen in ways that become almost playful at times. In *Once upon a Time in the West* (1969), while three gunfighters wait at a train station to kill a man, one of them begins to play with a fly buzzing around him, and another enjoys a leaky water barrel dripping on his hat. When the intended victim arrives, the composition uses low angles and very deep focus to increase the sense of conflict (Fig. 3.19). In *Duck, You Sucker* (1971), as some wealthy characters are insulting a peasant, there are shots only of their mouths, so that the frame is filled with the movements of lips and teeth, turning the characters into bizarre objects.

Finally, by their very nature, documentary films often make us very aware of changing balance and focus. For example, *Company* (1970) documents the cast and musicians of a Broadway musical, making a record of the show. As the camera observes the performers' changing tensions and interrelations, the framing may be temporarily imbalanced, then regain itself, and focus has to be adjusted sometimes in an ongoing shot. We become aware not only of the performers' craft, but also the cinematographer's discovering and leading us to new points of interest as we watch.

In many ways, then, the cinematographer composes images to make them more interesting and pleasing, not only to give information. Working with framing creates another level of the viewer's involvement with *mise en scène*.

3.19 Composition in *Once upon a Time in the West* (1969). The confrontation at the train station.

WORKING WITH DEPTH

The movie image is really a flat, two-dimensional picture, but the viewer accepts it as having depth. Filmmakers draw the viewer's eye *into* the composition. Any of the movements we have already discussed can operate in depth as well as across the frame. For example, the left-right diagonal line favored by Toland's rule can also carry an object toward or away from the viewer. So can any other movement. In the process of doing this, the filmmaker adapts the optical technology of the camera to exploit the viewer's sense of planes in the image. This is working with depth.

The Technology

It is convenient to consider the movie camera's optical system as a mechanical eye. Like the human eye, it has a *lens* that bends rays of light into a sharp *focal point* on sensitive material. But, unlike the eye, a camera's lens provides different *kinds* of depth perception. Filmmakers can exploit its technological properties for very varied effects.

Properties of the Optical System To appreciate a lens's stylization of depth perception, we need to center on two of its optical properties. A lens has a particular angle of view. The limits and distortions of that view depend on the *focal length* of the lens. The lens also has a limited range of clear focus within its angle of view, and that range is called its *depth of field.*

Lenses are designated in general categories according to focal length. There are *wide-angle* (from 15 to 35 mm), *normal* (50 or 55 mm) and *telephoto* or "long" (from 85 to 300 mm) lenses. There are also *zoom* lenses with variable focal lengths (for example, 43–86 mm, 50–300 mm, 80–200 mm).[12] Focal length determines the angle of view. Wide-angle lenses take in a large field. The different figures in Fig. 3.20 take up a relatively small part of the frame when seen through a 28-mm lens. At the other extreme, a 105-mm telephoto lens takes in a small field, and so the figures take up more of the frame. In between is the 50-mm lens, which gives a normal angle of view—that is, approximately the same as the human eye.

The peculiarities of focal length provide the cinematographer with three methods for bringing objects nearer or moving them farther off. Each method has a distinctive look. First, as the illustrations we just cited demonstrate, the cinematographer may simply change the lens's focal length without moving the camera at all. This changes the *apparent* distance of objects. Notice that the depth relationship, or *perspective,* of the different figures remains the same through the three shots because

a

b

c

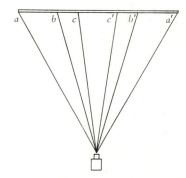

3.20 The effect of changing focal length. The camera remains fixed, but the focal length of the lens is changed from (a) 28 mm to (b) 55 mm to (c) 105 mm. When focal length is changed during a continuous shot, a zoom effect is produced. The line drawing illustrates the camera's different angles of view.

a

b

c

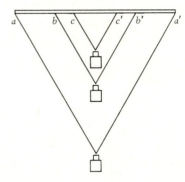

3.21 The effect of changing camera distance. The focal length of the lens remains fixed at 28 mm, but the distance of the camera is changed from (a) ten feet to (b) five feet to (c) three feet. When the camera is moved during a continuous shot, the dolly effect is produced. The line drawing illustrates the camera's different positions.

the camera, despite appearances, does not move. If the cinematographer used a zoom lens, changing focal length while shooting continuously, we would get the *zoom effect* of movement in depth. There is the appearance of actual movement, but a consistent perspective, for the picture is simply being enlarged or diminished as we watch.

Second, the cinematographer may prefer to keep the same lens but move the camera. This changes the *actual* distance. Notice in Fig. 3.21 how the foreground figure seems to "grow" twice as fast as background figures as the camera gets closer. This striking change comes about because a lens renders perspective with objective mathematical accuracy whereas a human viewer always makes mental adjustments. To us, an object ten feet away seems twice as large as it does when twenty feet away; but to the camera lens the object becomes *four* times larger. If the cinematographer moves the camera while continuing to shoot, we get the *dolly shot*, with far more dynamic perspective changes than the zoom shot allows.

Notice, too, that distortion appears in the close shot of our second example. The foreground face in Fig. 3.21c is framed as in Fig. 3.20c but does not look the same. In the 28-mm shot (Fig. 3.21c) the subject is actually close to the camera, where differences in perspective are exaggerated, so that the distance between nose and eyes seems greater, elongating the face. In the 105-mm shot (Fig. 3.20c) the subject is much farther from the camera, where the difference between nose and eyes is not so crucial, and the face seems flatter.

As a third option, the cinematographer may combine both previous methods, changing *both* focal length and distance (Fig. 3.22). This distorts perspective to a maximum degree. If done in a continuous shot, these changes create the *zoom-dolly* effect.

These three methods allow cinematographers to play with perspective in many ways. In *A Clockwork Orange* (1971) and *Touch of Evil* (1957) characters move in close to the camera, and the wide-angle lens grossly distorts their features. In *Seconds* (1966) an extremely wide angle lens warps all the perspectives of the nightmarish closing scene. In *The Graduate* (1967), the hero, rushing to stop his girl from marrying someone else, seems to be getting nowhere because an extremely long lens has made the distance he is moving seem much shorter. The battle scenes of *Throne of Blood* (1957), a tale of medieval Japan, are shot with long lenses, giving them the flat appearance of a tapestry. At the end of *La femme infidèle* (1968) a husband looks back at his wife as he is led away by police for murdering the wife's lover, and the camera takes his point of view in a zoom-dolly shot with its sense of conflicting movement in opposite directions. These are creative exploitations of focal length.

a

b

c

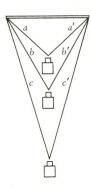

3.22 The effect of changing both focal length and camera distance. The focal length of the lens is changed in each shot from (a) 28 mm to (b) 55 mm to (c) 105 mm. The camera, however, has been moved to keep the foreground figure always the same size in the frame. When both focal length and camera are moved during a continuous shot, the filmmaker produces the zoom-dolly effect. The line drawing illustrates the camera's different positions and angles of view.

By exploiting depth of field, the cinematographer involves us in another aspect of depth perception. On the film—and ultimately on the movie screen—a lens can bring only one *plane*, or layer, of a scene into absolutely sharp focus. But there is a range of planes on either side of this focused one that our eyes will accept as relatively in focus. This range of acceptable focus is that scene's depth of field. [13]

The cinematographer may increase or diminish depth of field in various ways. Reducing the camera's diaphragm opening will increase depth of field. Also wide-angle lenses have greater depths of field than long lenses. Notice that everything seems relatively sharp in Fig. 3.20a, but in Fig. 3.20c only one figure is sharp and everything else is fuzzy. These examples illustrate another range of options whereby the filmmaker creates particular kinds of images in depth.

Techniques of Depth Arrangement   The technical variables discussed in the previous section finally boil down to one important fact: movies present us with specialized illusions of depth. Within the frame the angles of view change, perspectives vary and the range of sharpness may widen or narrow. Any combination among the variables is possible, but we can break them into four typical styles of depth arrangement that have evolved in film history: pan focus, shallow focus, deep focus, and three-dimensional cinematography.

Movies made before 1915 operated under what would be considered primitive conditions today. The very slow orthochromatic film, being insensitive to red, gave very contrasty images, and the camera lenses lacked the complex elements that in today's lenses let in a lot of light. Because of the slow film and simple lenses, movies had to be shot under very bright sunlight or very strong indoor lights. But there were advantages. The small apertures gave great depth of field; the simple lenses did not reflect away much light, and so gave sharper images; and the film's high contrast gave a very precise delineation of details.

Some filmmakers exploited these limitations, arranging images in depth so that the distinct planes led the eye into the picture and gave scenes layers of crisp detail. This is now sometimes referred to as *pan-focus* ("all focus") style (Fig. 3.23). [14] Much of it has been lost to modern viewers because, in reducing films to 16-mm copies many generations removed from the originals, we have dulled the image quality. Now and then, however, film students can still experience some of the power of pan-focus style in films directed by D. W. Griffith, Maurice Tourneur, or Henry King. Tourneur, in particular, liked to provide some framing material, such as an arch or trees, in the foreground so that the eye is drawn from it toward the center of interest.

From 1915 onward another style became increasingly popular in American films. It was borrowed from still photography. Going against the natural sharpness of orthochromatic film, portrait photographers used the shallowest possible depth of field so that all planes on either side of the center of interest were out of focus. This usually meant that only the subject's eyes were sharp, with the rest of the face in "soft" focus. Gauze or special filters could heighten the effect. The movies began to copy this technique for close-ups, and by 1925 *shallow focus* was common to most American movies (Fig. 3.24).[15] Filmmakers kept lenses at maximum aperture, so that even in longer shots the planes around the center of interest were softened.

This softer imagery better suited the new panchromatic film, which arrived in the mid-twenties. Because it was sensitive to red rays, which have a slightly different focus point than blues and greens, panchromatic had an intrinsically softer focus than orthochromatic, at least at first. It was several years before specialists in optics

3.23 Pan-focus style. A scene from *Intolerance* (1916).

corrected the problem. But even after sharp focus became possible with panchromatic, American film studios continued to exploit shallow-focus depth. It was the characteristic style throughout the thirties.

Shallow focus is least evident in outdoor adventure scenes, where distance and bright light automatically provide great depth of field. In the typical indoor melodramas and comedies, which have less light and tend to keep action closer, we get the full shallow-focus effect. There is a layer of sharpness at the center of an otherwise soft-edged picture. The sense of being led into a shot is usually less strong, for the camera gives us the one plane we can focus on.

This single plane of focus can be shifted during a shot. Most of the time this is for corrective purposes: if a character moves outside the shallow depth of field, the focus changes accordingly. This is called *pulling* or *racking* focus. Since the 1960s it has become fashionable to rack focus extremely during a shot, so that a very unfocused (and therefore virtually invisible) plane suddenly pops into focus as we watch. In *Jaws* (1975), a character is scanning a crowded beach, fearing that a killer shark may attack at any moment. The focus suddenly racks from a group of swimmers to a shark's fin in the distance.

Also related to depth arrangement are the various techniques of *process work* that developed especially in the 1930s. These are various special effects used to add realistic depth to shots where otherwise it might be difficult or impossible to render. The most common was *rear projection:* still or moving images are projected behind performers in the foreground (Fig. 3.25). This was a typical method used to show people sitting in an automobile with a moving street scene behind them; it gave a sense of depth and made lighting easier to control. In some cases, *front projection* was preferred for the same effects. In *glass shots* scenery is painted in miniature on glass then placed near the camera so that it becomes a kind of frame around the live action at a distance (Fig. 3.26). To the viewer, the painted and live scenes are indistinguishable. Many of the exotic scenes in *King Kong* (1933) were achieved in

3.24 Shallow-focus style. Al Jolson in a scene from *The Jazz Singer* (1927).

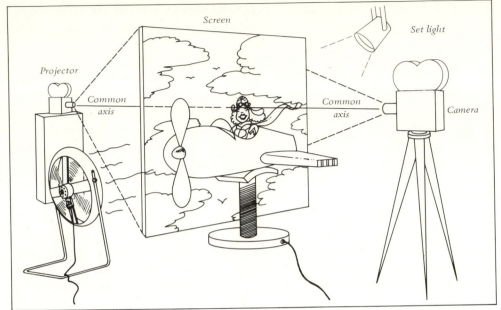

3.25 Rear projection. Facing the camera on a common axis, the projector provides back- ground scenery for an action staged on the set.

3.26 Glass shot. The second story and roof of the house are painted in miniature on glass, which is positioned close to the camera and photographed with the first story of the house, actually constructed on the set. This shot creates the illusion of a complete house in the final movie.

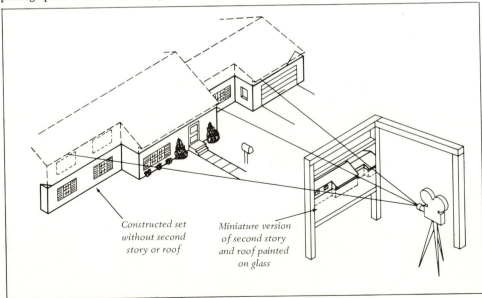

Constructed set without second story or roof

Miniature version of second story and roof painted on glass

this way. Finally, special techniques using *traveling mattes* allow two separate scenes to be brought together (Fig. 3.27). Handled in the laboratory with the optical printer after shooting, they are the most common such special effects used today. In movies like *Star Wars* (1976) and *Alien* (1979), for example, images of planets and the like are shot with miniature models, then matted into windows of space-ship scenes shot in the studio. This gives the illusion that the characters are traveling in outer space.

By the end of the 1930s many filmmakers, influenced by a widespread trend toward realism in photography,[16] were moving away from the shallow-focus style. Gregg Toland's work for Orson Welles on *Citizen Kane* (1941) is an outstanding example of this technological change. Toland set about achieving the greatest possible depth of field. He did it by combining several separate technical improvements. By 1940 lenses could be coated so that fewer rays of light bounced off the glass of the lens; new twin-arc lamps, developed for color films, threw much brighter light; and the speed of black-and-white film had increased considerably. By using fast film, the new lamps, and a coated 18.5-mm (extremely wide angle) lens, Toland pushed all the factors affecting depth of field (light, film speed, focal length) to a point not considered possible at the time. He increased depth of field from two to four times what it had been.[17]

3.27 Traveling matte technique.

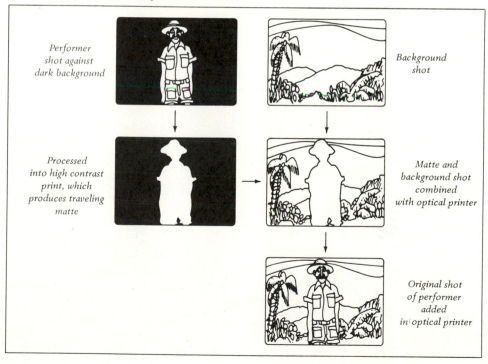

Performer shot against dark background

Background shot

Processed into high contrast print, which produces traveling matte

Matte and background shot combined with optical printer

Original shot of performer added in optical printer

This is *deep-focus* style (Fig. 3.28). It usually employs long-running camera shots which allow the eye time to move about the screen. The shallow-focus approach suits rapid shots where the eye needs to assimilate information quickly. But we should not draw too neat a distinction between the two styles. *Citizen Kane* has some shallow-focus scenes, and some 1930s films will draw the eye into compositions, even if some planes are not quite as sharp as they might be.

The ultimate deep-focus effect would seem to be the "true" depth provided by *three-dimensional cinematography*. In fact, 3-D movie depth has proved neither true nor, finally, very effective.

The 3-D technique antedates movies by many years. In 1832, Sir Charles Wheatstone invented what he called the *stereoscope* or "watcher of something solid" (Fig. 3.29). It took advantage of *binocular disparity* in human vision. When we look at a scene, the image strikes the retina of either eye in a slightly different position. This

3.28 Deep-focus style. A scene from *The Magnificent Ambersons* (1942) with (left to right) Tim Holt, Anne Baxter, Joseph Cotten, and Dolores Costello.

is a major cue to the brain that objects in a scene are at different distances. Wheatstone arranged it so that two pictures of a scene viewed at slightly different angles (from about 2½ to 3 inches apart, like the eyes) would be seen by each of the viewer's eyes separately. The viewer's brain put the two views together as one three-dimensional image.

Binocular cameras were built, and stereoscopic photography was all the rage for awhile. By 1891, Louis Ducos du Hauron had found a way to make a single picture take on three dimensions.

Movie inventors dabbled in 3-D from the beginning, but in the 1950s Hollywood took it up seriously, along with wide screens, to combat the threat of television. The success of *Bwana Devil* (1952) led to the release of thirty-eight 3-D features between 1953 and 1954.[18] To view such movies, audiences used glasses that adapted an invention of Edwin H. Land, inventor also of the Polaroid camera. Each lens of the glasses was a *polarizing filter*. It allowed only one plane of light rays to strike the eye. One lens was set to pass only vertical rays, the other horizontal. The same kinds of filters were used on the projectors. Each eye saw a separate image without any appreciable distortion of color, and the viewer's brain combined them into full-color 3-D.

The craze for 3-D lasted not quite two years. Some argue that the glasses caused its early death; they were a nuisance and gave some viewers headaches. Others blame the unimaginative movies that were simply excuses for tricks. By the time more sophisticated productions were ready, 3-D had lost its charm. *Kiss Me Kate* (1953), released in two versions, did better business in 2-D, and *Dial M for Murder* (1954),

3.29 Stereoscope from about 1850.

shot in 3-D, was released in the traditional form. Since the 1950s occasional features have used 3-D, either to sell an otherwise mediocre product or, like Andy Warhol's gory production of *Frankenstein* (1974), for blatantly bizarre effects.

Contrary to any assertion that it shows "true" depth, 3-D has an extremely unreal, "layered" look. It exaggerates the overall depth of the picture—we are very aware that some planes are closer or farther away than others—but it does not give much solidity to individual figures. They seem rather to be painted flat on separate sheets of celluloid and arranged in depth. This is nothing like the solidity we perceive in real objects, for our eyes depend on more than binocular disparity to see three dimensions. In particular, the almost constant, involuntary movements of the eyes seem to cue the brain that objects are solid. Such subtle cues are not possible in the 3-D situation. It exaggerates overall, or gross, depth while leaving individual planes relatively flat. This situation helps explain why 3-D movies have so strongly exploited gross depth effects, and it may explain 3-D's failure to become an integral part of the movie illusion.

Applying the Technology

Most filmmakers do not follow one style of depth exclusively, any more than they compose their frames according to one formula. As we have said, part of the movies' attraction lies in the constantly shifting balance points, weights, and lines as well as in varying textures and contrasts. The same applies here. We can think of shifts from soft to deep focus and the movements at different planes of a deep-focus shot as changing points of attraction *in depth*. In other words, movies attract us with a constant "juggling" of spatial weights and balances not only side to side, but front to back also. A movie asks your eye to do, in effect, what your hand does when it tries to keep a stick perfectly vertical on a fingertip: to adjust itself to constantly shifting pulls. In this section we will first consider some transparent and less transparent uses of depth, but then finish with examples of how composition in depth unites with lighting and framing techniques to create a unified *mise en scène*.

Melodramas of the thirties do not draw great attention to the depth of their compositions, for their soft-focus technique generally requires them to select the single plane we can focus on. Figures are arranged in depth, and often quite effectively, but the soft focus of those planes around the center of interest keeps the effect more transparent. The films starring Greta Garbo are good examples. In *Camille* (1936) and *Anna Karenina* (1935) Garbo plays a sensuous woman who dies of love. The films depend heavily on close shots of the woman and the men in her life.

Here the soft-focus technique is used to maximum advantage. Not only is the plane of attention precisely controlled, but the focus is often kept as narrow as possible, so that softness predominates in the frame. This provides a fitting environment for the sensuous romanticism of the story. A later, and very different, example of transparent technique is *Key Largo* (1948), which involves gangsters terrorizing a remote hotel during a hurricane. The *mise en scène* relies heavily on pyramid compositions in depth to emphasize the psychological tensions between the characters, and yet this is carried on unobtrusively within a soft-focus style.

During almost any movie, however, we may become sharply aware of depth. In *Winchester '73* (1950) an outlaw tells a woman he is going to betray his companions, and just at that moment, between them, forming a pyramid construction, the companions appear in the far distance on horseback, pulling our attention toward them. The silent comedies directed by Buster Keaton often emphasize depth to bring off a gag. In *Our Hospitality* (1923) the hero, to escape men who are trying to kill him, has put on a woman's dress and raced off on horseback. The men, in the foreground of the frame, spy the horse standing in the distance with its back to them, the rider apparently still on its back. They take aim. Then the horse turns, and we see that the hero has simply draped the dress over the horse to fool his pursuers. The gag uses depth to fool the audience as well (Fig. 3.30). In *The General* (1926), set during the Civil War, the hero is in a locomotive chasing spies in another locomotive. He has attached a mortar behind his engine to fire shells at the spies. He lights the fuse, but then the mortar comes uncoupled and bounces on the track, and its barrel lowers until it aims right at the hero. We watch what happens next in a continuous shot composed in depth: the hero's engine swerves as it rounds a bend, and the mortar fires, missing the hero but dropping its shell near the spies in the distance. This kind of in-depth action is frequent in Keaton's movies, which take great advantage of the pan-focus possible with orthochromatic film.

As we have already noted, *Citizen Kane* (1941) is an outstanding example of deep-focus style. Indeed, the movie emphasizes *mise en scène* so strongly that one may

Audio Brandon/ © Raymond Rohauer, 1980

3.30 Depth in a Buster Keaton movie. A frame enlargement from *Our Hospitality* (1923).

not be able to look *through* its spatial design at all (Fig. 3.31). Its very contrived space takes full advantage of all the design factors we have outlined in this chapter. Its lack of transparency is one reason why it remains fascinating, attracting viewers back to see it long after the ending of its story has lost its surprise value.

The story is simple: a famous man, Charles Foster Kane, speaks a word as he dies, and a reporter spends the rest of the movie interviewing the man's acquaintances to discover what the word meant. The *mise en scène* is far from simple: it regularly displays layers of detail that attract the viewer's eye into and around the frame. Early in the movie, for example, the reporter interviews Kane's ex-wife, now an alcoholic nightclub singer, and after failing to find any clue he makes a telephone call. The action during and after his call takes place within a continuous, deep-focused scene. In the center sits the singer, accented by light; on the right, framed within the frame by a telephone booth, is the reporter, who remains in shadow; two waiters counterbalance the composition; and on the back wall, in the top left where the viewer may not notice it until the eye has roamed the whole frame, is the drawing of a castle much like the one where the singer once lived with Kane. Thus, the composition allows the viewer to interrelate distinct elements of the scene. One discovers implications in an unbroken space.

This happens throughout the movie. In other scenes involving the wife we see Kane forcing a voice teacher to train the untalented woman, and we see her finally attempting suicide in desperation. Each scene is shown in a continuous shot. In the first, Kane enters from the background, forming the apex of a triangular composition with the singer and the teacher, and as he advances he comes into increasing domination. In the second, a glass and a bottle of medicine dominate the foreground in extreme closeup as Kane and others break down the bedroom door and come forward to minister to the wife. The incredibly deep focus had, in fact, to be tricked through process work, but this emphasis on depth is more captivating as a result.

Even when filmmakers do not put so much emphasis on deep focus, they may stress *mise en scène* heavily to achieve a richly artificial environment. A good example is *Dracula* (1979), the remake of Bram Stoker's classic vampire story, directed by John Badham. It creates a world of striking design. Unlike the 1931 *Dracula* with its typically high-key studio lighting, the new version uses very low key lights, to a point where the viewer may have to strain to catch details and so, in a reverse of the usual effect of brightness, become more aware of the threatening dark. Even in daylight, cinematographer Gilbert Taylor maintains a dim, overcast look to everything. Regularly the composition draws the eye diagonally across the 1.85:1 frame toward the upper right corner—for instance, along a dimly lit road toward Dracula's castle silhouetted against the setting sun. The framing does not follow a mechanically consistent pattern, but we can notice its effect at important moments. Thus, Dracula is frequently shown on the right side of the frame, but his adversary, Van Helsing, occupies the left side for his first appearances in the story. When Dracula talks of his eternal life, the composition provides an ironic contrast: he stands to the left, while in the stronger right position, more brightly lighted but in soft focus, there is a skull. Depth is used for startling effect. In one shot, the camera pulls focus suddenly from a vial of blood to the face of a young woman receiving a transfusion. In another scene, as a woman enters Dracula's banquet hall, we are given an overhead point of view through a spider web. As Dracula moves toward the woman in the distance, the spider makes the same movement across the web in the foreground. In other blatant intrusions, a woman's eyes shine in blood-red eye lights after she has become a vampire. Albert Whitlock provided the special process work for the scene in which Dracula attains the woman of his desire, a scene that explodes into black and red optical distortions.

The overall spatial design of *Citizen Kane* or *Dracula* illustrates the constantly shifting attractions that the movies' technology makes possible. It is a *heightened*

3.31 Depth in *Citizen Kane* (1941). This still shows the typical deep-focus style used throughout the movie. Orson Welles is on the left.

experience of space. It is only one aspect of the total cinematic experience, but a very perceptible one. And it has made its impression on critical theory, too.

MISE EN SCÈNE AND CRITICISM

The movie screen's framed space presents such a powerful sense of captured reality that some theorists see it as the core of the cinema's power. They constitute the *realist* school of film theory, and their ideas build on the realism of the photographic image. We can find a foreshadow of realist theory in the title that Fox Talbot gave to his first collection of photographs, *The Pencil of Nature* (1844). It reflects an awareness that for the first time an image of the world was formed, as it were, by invoking nature to draw itself, not through the creative human intervention. Realists see cinema carrying this illusion of captured reality to a culmination, and they believe that, by studying the implications of this, we better understand what makes the cinema unique.

The fundamentals of realist theory stem from two works: Siegfried Kracauer's *Theory of Film: The Redemption of Physical Reality* (1960) and André Bazin's *What Is Cinema?* (four volumes, 1959–1962).[19] We discuss Kracauer's ideas in Chapter 10, because they are particularly appropriate to movies that stress the relation of a message to real life. Here let us focus only on Bazin, for he provides helpful insight particularly for the point we are making in this chapter: a movie's *mise en scène* is a record that *heightens* our experience of space. It is thus a form of illusion, too.

For Bazin a movie's *mise en scène* is a record that, like photography, provides a realism of *space*. It is a mechanical, objective record of spatial relationships. It may reflect the camera operator's personality and selection, but it possesses a credibility that is absent from the other arts where the human maker must directly intervene. In spite of the differences we detect, said Bazin, "we are forced to accept as real the existence of the object reproduced, actually re-presented, set before us."[20] This was the unique reality of cinema, what Bazin termed its "ontology." For him, cinema fulfilled the dream of inventors to create total "myth," a complete world of the imagination that reconstructed "a perfect illusion of the outside world in sound, color and relief."[21] This was not reality itself, but what Bazin compared to a tracing: something more directly linked to real objects than any other art form.

Bazin argued that deep-focus cinematography was the most proper form of cinematic expression, but he did not use it as a yardstick to measure what was "true" cinema. He insisted that the critic's role was to *describe* what happens, not *prescribe* what should be done. He extoled deep focus because it fully demonstrated a principle that all movies followed: "What is imaginary on the screen must have the spatial density of something real."[22] Filmmakers who manipulate the space with editing (to be discussed in Chapter 4) or other techniques (for example, racking focus or using extreme angles) do make films with some degree of spatial density, but they *use* space for their reasons and so impose meanings on the viewer. For Bazin the more appropriate path is to *reveal* space as something valuable in its own right. He preferred the "neutral" style that deep focus provides, where the director selects from reality, avoids explicit symbols, and lets the camera observe and follow action for long periods of time without interruptions. This approach does not impose a viewpoint on viewers, but rather gives them time to experience a new sense of the real world through a free interplay between themselves and the movie's framed space.[23] He considered *Citizen Kane* a superb example of this.

Bazin believed in the transcendent value of the physical world. For him cinema provides an unparalleled opportunity for the artist to reveal nature's rich ambiguity—what Bazin called its mystery. To him life defied clear or simple explanations. It was layered with a variety of meanings, confusions and contradictions that could not be simply resolved. By capturing this ambiguity so well, cinema's *mise en scène* fulfilled the revolution in art begun by photography. Movies *freed* the other arts from an obsession with copying reality. Painting, for example, could now "be swallowed up in color" without worrying about representing real things.[24]

But Bazin freely acknowledged that the illusion of captured reality *is* an illusion—something that, to some degree, is always manipulated. He had little trouble reconciling this apparent contradiction, because he revered captured reality *as* an illusion. Faced with a movie's *mise en scène*, he notes, we simply "need to believe in the reality of what is happening while knowing it to be tricked."[25] He preferred this realistic illusion and felt it is the noblest trick that movies bring off, but he was too open-minded to ignore the power in other tricks or seek to define cinema permanently. He believed that "cinema has not yet been invented!"[26] It is not a fixed form, but a creature still discovering what it is.

André Bazin's work represents a clear and sensitive presentation of realist film theory. In the next chapter we will look at its opposite, *formative* theory, which places heavy emphasis upon the manipulations made possible by editing and montage. Bazin never denied the power of such manipulations, but for him the primacy belongs to the power of cinematic space.

SUMMARY

The movie machine's film emulsion, aperture plate, and optical system provide a mechanized version of human space perception. What results is stylized space, referred to as a movie's *mise en scène*. It has distinctive qualities, elaborated by filmmakers through particular techniques. Working with the film emulsion's reaction to light, filmmakers create different kinds of texture and contrast. Working with framing, they change the shape of the screen image and arrange motion, brightness, position, and point of view to vary emphasis within the frame. Working with the optical system's focal length and depth of field, they create various sensations of depth. The apparently captured reality inside the frame is, as a rule, very carefully manipulated. Realist theorists like André Bazin who believe that the movies' central power lies in its imitation of reality have had to deal with the fact that its realism is an illusion.

We can see that *mise en scène* involves us in a number of tensions and counterbalances within the screen image. The eye must adjust to shifts in texture, contrast, compositional balance, and range of depth. The frame also displays different degrees of transparency, so that the eye sometimes looks *through* design to the action it displays, and sometimes *at* the design for its own sake. Taken together, all the tensions wrought by the various techniques help explain the fascination that movie space holds for viewers.

NOTES

1 Charles Higham, *Hollywood Cameramen* (Bloomington: Indiana University, 1970), pp. 94–96.

2 Since the common projectors in U.S. schools are 16 mm (with some Super-8 mm as well), students usually see grainier versions of movies shot originally on 35 mm or larger formats, with a necessary loss of quality. In addition, prints of old movies may be many copies, or generations, away from the original; this can severely increase their contrast, damaging detail even further.

3 Richard Patterson, "Highlights from the History of Motion Picture Formats," *American Cinematographer*, 54 (January 1973), 42.

4 For a full discussion, see Charles Barr, "CinemaScope: Before and After," *Film Quarterly*, 16 (Summer 1963), 4–24. An abridged version is in *Film: A Montage of Theories*, ed. Richard Dyer MacCann (New York: Dutton 1966), pp. 318–328.

5 Some argue that this is because we read from left to right. However, Japanese movies, made by people who read downwards, do not empha-

size vertical more than lateral movement. It seems more likely that the left-right tendency is conditioned by differences between the halves of the brain. See Rudolf Arnheim's *Art and Visual Perception* (Berkeley: University of California, 1969), pp. 18–19.

6 Gregg Toland, "Composition of the Moving Image," in *The Movies as Medium,* ed. Lewis Jacobs (New York: Farrar, Straus and Giroux, 1970), p. 73.

7 Toland, p. 69.

8 Arnheim, p. 19.

9 "Génie de Howard Hawks," *Cahiers du cinéma,* 23 (May 1953), 16.

10 "The Obvious and the Code," *Screen,* 15 (Winter 1974/1975), 7–17.

11 See Barr, pp. 17–18.

12 These are the ranges for the 35-mm gauge. They vary with other gauges. For 16 mm, "normal" starts at the 25-mm lens; for Super-8 mm, at 12.5 mm. Beyond the typical ranges indicated, there are also special telephoto lenses reaching out to 2,000 mm.

13 Do not confuse this with depth of *focus,* which is inside the camera. The precise focal point for a plane within a scene can land far or short of the film's surface and still be within the depth, or range, of acceptable focus. This information is more important to optical technicians than to cinematographers.

14 For example, by Richard Koszarski in "Maurice Tourneur: The First of the Visual Stylists," *Film Comment,* 9 (March–April 1973), 27.

15 Barry Salt, "Film Style and Technology in the Thirties," *Film Quarterly,* 31 (Fall 1976), 24–25.

16 Barry Salt, "Film Style and Technology in the Forties," *Film Quarterly,* 31 (Fall 1977), 49; Patrick Ogle, "Deep Focus Cinematography: A Technological/Aesthetic History," *Filmmaker's Newsletter,* 4 (May 1971), 24–26.

17 Gregg Toland, "How I Broke the Rules in *Citizen Kane,*" in *Focus on "Citizen Kane,*" ed. Ronald Gottesman (Englewood Cliffs, N.J.: Prentice-Hall, 1971), pp. 73–77.

18 Kenneth MacGowan, *Behind the Screen* (New York: Dell, 1965), p. 454.

19 Kracauer's work was published in English by Oxford University Press (New York, 1960). Bazin's was published in French by Les Editions du Cerf (Paris, 1959–1962). Hugh Gray translated selections from Bazin into English in two volumes (Berkeley: University of California, 1967 and 1971). Quotes here are from the English volumes.

20 Bazin, I, 13–14.

21 Bazin, I, 20.

22 Bazin, I, 48.

23 For a fuller discussion, see J. Dudley Andrew, *The Major Film Theories* (New York: Oxford, 1976), pp. 153–155, 162–163, 169.

24 Bazin, I, 16.

25 Bazin, I, 48.

26 Bazin, I, 21.

Chapter 4 / Continuity

In Chapter 3 we discussed the space in which movement occurs on the movie screen. This movement also takes *time*. It *goes* somewhere. A movie's design involves a temporal as well as a spatial aspect. The camera converts every second of time into twenty-four frames of film, and the projector communicates this material as a continuous movement in time. This means that, on the one hand, movies record time; and, on the other, they change time into material that can be manipulated.

These patterns of movement in time are referred to as a movie's *continuity*. The word carries the idea of a constant flow of events, one thing leading to another. Filmmakers refer to the detailed shooting script from which they work as a *continuity*, a word generally used as the more exact film term for what one would call plot in literature. It is time as we experience it in the movies: as a *sequence* of events. Our sense of sequence is largely psychological: we apprehend that a certain movement begins, goes somewhere, and ends. It may link to a new action that also begins, develops, and ends—and so on, until the whole continuity is completed. A movie's continuity is thus a series of psychological closures. They take two basic forms:

(1) Sequencing may occur *within* a single, continuous camera shot. An action begins, develops, and closes in exactly the amount of time it did in reality, its space shown without break. This is *recorded continuity*, what some distinguish as the *sequence shot*. The first movies of Edison and Lumière were simple examples of it: one-minute transcriptions of real events, taken in single, continuous operations of the camera. Movies that exploit deep-focus *mise en scène* (like *Citizen Kane*) usually exploit the power of recorded continuity at the same time, developing action within long-running shots. They involve us in rhythms of movement within such shots.

(2) Sequencing may occur *between* shots. The filmmaker builds a complete action with separate shots, each contributing only one link in the chain of development. This is *constructed continuity*. It creates what is generally referred to as a *sequence*, a group of interrelated shots unified by psychological closure. It involves us in rhythms and tempos between shots.

The great majority of movies use *both* recorded and constructed continuity. At one moment a movie will emphasize the passage of real time; at another, it may alter time, make the impossible happen, or it may break space into visual beats of time. This chapter discusses these techniques and the stylized sense of time they create.

WORKING WITH RECORDED CONTINUITY

Recorded continuity involves the power of the *shot*. When the cinematographer turns on the camera, records an action, then turns the camera off, the strip of film that results is a single shot. When projected on the screen it presents something happening uninterrupted while we watch. The longer the shot, the greater this emphasis on unified space and time. A recorded continuity exploits this power by presenting a complete sequence of events with a continuous run of the camera—known as a sequence shot. It allows the filmmaker to emphasize the presence of time and the rhythms of movement within the shot. In this section we will look at the technology involved in recorded continuity and the ways it allows filmmakers to vary our experience of recorded continuity.

The Technology

Two technological factors affect recorded continuity. First, there is the movement of the shutter. It creates a film time out of real time by a dual process of selection and re-presentation. The camera's shutter selects moments from a real movement and flashes them on the film; the projector's shutter re-presents them in flashes on the movie screen. Second, there is camera movement. During a shot, the camera may remain fixed in one position, or it may be moved in a number of ways. Because of shutter and camera movement the filmmaker can stylize recorded continuity in different ways.

Shutter Movement   A movie camera may run at various speeds; these are called *shutter speeds*, not camera speeds, and are designated in *frames per second* (fps). They range typically from 1 to 128 fps; "normal" camera speed is 24 fps. This matches the modern projector's fixed speed of 24 fps and provides accurate, or "normal," time reproductions. With the camera and projector shutters both operating at the same speed, there is no difference between the time of the original event and the time of the movie's re-presentation. The process duplicates real time—so that, for example, a one-minute horse race takes one minute of film time.

Since the camera can run at different speeds, however, the cinematographer can play with time. Consider what happens when one increases the shooting rate to 60 fps. The horse race still takes one minute in reality, but at 24 fps in the projector the film that recorded the race runs for two and a half minutes. This creates *slow motion*. The horse seems to float along with unusual grace. The effect has become common on television, where instant slow-motion replays allow us to analyze an athlete's moves. The degree of slow motion varies with the shooting speed: the faster the shooting speed, the slower the apparent movement.[1]

On the other hand, if one shoots the race with a slower shutter speed than normal, the horse's apparent speed is proportionately increased on the screen. This is *fast motion,* or *accelerated motion.* Shot at 12 fps, for example, the horse's speed is doubled on the screen at 24 fps. Its movements will appear choppy and mechanical— and today's viewers almost invariably find this funny. The ultimate is shooting at 1 fps, making the race twenty-four times faster and absurdly choppy, with about 96 percent of the horse's real movements omitted. (The ultimate in fast motion is *single-framing*—shooting only one frame at a time, with great gaps of real time omitted between each frame. It is generally restricted to effects like showing flowers coming into bloom, as in time-lapse photography. See Chapter 2.)

Shutter speed clearly provides a number of ways to play with the viewer's experience of time's passage.

Camera Movement A shot taken with a fixed camera simply records the rhythms of movement and composition within its alloted time. When the camera itself moves, however, it adds an additional element of sequencing, going from one position to another and thus affecting the action in a number of ways.

In certain movements the camera turns on its mount during the shot (Fig. 4.1). In a *pan* (its name derived from *panorama*) the camera moves sideways; in a *tilt,* it moves vertically. We have seen the movements exploited in many Westerns. A slow pan emphasizes the desert's endless horizon, or a quick tilt connects settlers in a valley with a band of outlaws or Indians about to pounce on them from a hilltop. *Stagecoach* provides classic examples of both techniques. The camera provides a smooth, stylized imitation of the human head's movements, making a complete sequential "statement" within a single shot.

A more acutely stylized technique is the *roll,* a panning movement that rakes over from the perpendicular. It is rarely used, for unless done in mid-air or under water, it becomes an obvious intrusion by the filmmaker. *Women in Love* (1969) uses an ironic roll in which the camera slowly turns on its side so that, as two standing lovers kiss, they become horizontal to the viewer.

Another very stylized panning movement is the *swish pan,* or *flash pan,* a very rapid sideways movement. Though used in point-of-view shots to imitate the quick turn of a character's head, the swish pan has also become a convention for representing the passage of time. In *Citizen Kane,* for example, we see a husband and wife at a breakfast table in a series of brief shots that show their love decaying over several years. Between each shot a swish pan signals that time is passing.

For *traveling shots* the camera moves together *with* its mount. Imitating a walking human viewer, it creates a smooth, "floating" stylization that enhances shifting perspectives within a scene. The movement is so attractive that some directors—

On every right-hand page from here through page 197, the rabbit will advance 7½° from one drawing to the next. Flip these pages, and you will perceive a smooth movement.

notably Max Ophuls in Germany and Miklós Jancsó in Hungary—have created movies in which the camera is constantly traveling.

The technique takes different forms and names. The smooth lateral movement we have just described is called *trucking* (after the original method of mounting a camera on a truck or railroad car), *dollying* (from the small mount, or dolly, developed to carry the camera as shown in Fig. 4.2), or *tracking* (referring to the light rails, or tracks, laid down to carry the dolly as smoothly as possible). The *hand-held*

4.1 Basic camera movements: pan, tilt, and roll.

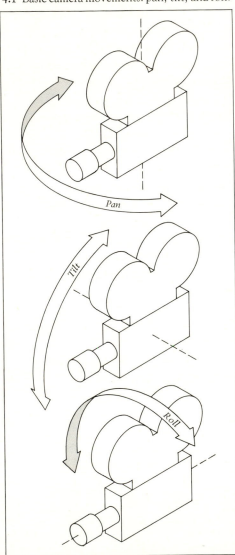

4.2 Dolly in use. On location for *Portrait in Black* (1960).

4.3 Crane in use.

traveling shot became popular in the 1960s to simulate a walking or running character's point of view. Since it exaggerates the sensation of sideways or vertical movement, an opposite effect from the dolly shot's fluid movement, a hand-held shot may also suggest confusion or panic. In very recent years, however, the development of special camera mounts, or *steady cams,* has made it possible to hand-hold a shot as smoothly as a dolly shot. Thus, in *A Clockwork Orange* the camera follows characters for several minutes, floating through a wooded area that a normal tracking technique could not easily handle.

For smooth vertical traveling shots, filmmakers used balloons or elevators until the late 1920s, when the first camera cranes were brought into studios. The *crane shot* may move in any direction, though it usually exploits the striking effect of rising above or dropping onto a scene (Fig. 4.3). Outside the studio, the camera operator may achieve the same rock-steady smoothness with a gyroscopic mount in an airplane or helicopter. In *Funny Girl* (1968), for example, the camera circles down from high above New York harbor, swings completely around a moving tugboat and moves in onto the singing heroine until her figure fills the screen.

In different ways, then, the camera's movement may contribute sequentiality to a scene, going from one position through space to another position.

Applying the Technology

Technology thus provides methods for playing with time inside a sequence shot. At normal shutter speed, the camera simply records time; but by changing shutter movement, one can elongate or shorten apparent time within the shot. From a fixed position, the camera simply records the sequence of events; but by moving the camera, one can give a scene beginning, development, and closure in a striking way. And, as with other techniques, a filmmaker may use these in subtle, transparent ways or in obvious, noticeable ways.

Obvious changes of shutter speed are exceptional in today's movies. Most variations in speed are introduced subtly. They heighten the effect of travel in outer space, for example, and for years adventure stories have been shot in "Western 18," a shutter speed that makes action move faster than in reality, but not obviously so. It does not disturb our sense of "normal" movement. In the silent era (before 1928), however, there was a different sense of "normal." Most films were shot at about 16 fps and projected at about 24 fps—but both cameras *and* projectors were run at varying speeds. This meant, first, that audiences were used to seeing most movies at somewhat accelerated speed; and, second, projectionists could slow or speed movement as they wished.[2] Many films came with precise suggestions for showing different scenes at different speeds. It might be better to call the silent era the Era of Elastic Time. With the arrival of sound, projectors were fixed at 24 fps, and the play with time became much more conservative. Obvious slow motion is still used occasionally for "poetic" effect; director Sam Peckinpah has used it in *The Wild Bunch* (1969) and *Straw Dogs* (1971) to dramatize moments of death. Accelerated motion is a more or less guaranteed comic device, as director Stanley Kubrick uses it in *A Clockwork Orange* (1971) to turn acts of violence into bizarre, black comedy.

Using normal shutter speed, a filmmaker may emphasize the presence of time with long takes. In adventure stories this is often done to increase the viewer's sense of anticipation or dread. In *The General* a locomotive moves onto a burning trestle, and in a single long take we watch the span buckle, then break and drop the locomotive into a river. The one shot encloses a complete sequence of events. When soldiers move into battle in *The Big Parade* (1925) the continuity uses more than one shot to sequence events, but there are longer takes with a trucking camera, emphasizing the gradually increasing danger of the slow advance as men begin dropping under enemy fire. In both examples the emphasis on recorded time brings a different quality of excitement, and yet these are passing shifts of emphasis inside a generally transparent approach.

Other films may carry long takes to an extreme, drawing far greater and more noticeable emphasis to ongoing time. We can see this in *The Best Years of Our Lives* (1946), a melodrama about the anxieties of three servicemen returning to civilian life after World War II. Shot by Gregg Toland, the movie exemplifies the power of deep-focus composition, its long takes drawing the eye to shifting rhythms of emphasis within the frame (Fig. 4.4). This also involves us in a build of events within long passages of real time. In one scene, a veteran awakes after his first night home, during which he went on a drinking spree to cover his insecurity and finally passed out. His wife brings him breakfast, and in one very long take we watch him move nervously about, an unspoken tension growing between them, until finally he takes her into his arms. In another scene, a veteran asks a bank official for a loan to buy his own farm. The only thing he can pledge as security for the loan is his war record, and the official, himself a veteran, must decide if that is enough. We watch the discussion in a continuous shot, composed so that we look into the petitioner's face but are able to see the official at the edge of the frame. The shot thus counterpoints the two men but allows us to watch as the veteran gradually reveals his character, moving the official to okay the loan. In these examples the recorded continuity involves us in

4.4 A typical shot from *The Best Years of Our Lives* (1946). A long take of this shot emphasizes, at various times, the wedding couple at the right (Harold Russell, Cathy O'Donnell), the older couple in the center background (Myrna Loy, Fredric March), and the couple at the left (Dana Andrews, Teresa Wright). Movement of the figures in the shot draws the viewer's attention and shifts emphasis from one group to another.

tensions, rhythms, and character insights that grow to a climax and close within a lengthy, unbroken passage of time. As a result, we may become very much aware of the presence of time.

The most extreme examples of this are two of pop artist Andy Warhol's experimental films in the 1960s. For *Sleep* (1963) Warhol spliced together ten-minute shots of a sleeping man to make a six-hour movie. *Empire* (1964), which is eight hours long, joins ten-minute shots of the Empire State Building. Whether or not we sit through either movie in its entirety, we soon become aware that *any* movement within the fixed frame—a twitch of the sleeper's shoulder, fog passing over the building—becomes very important. And this appreciation of movement seems to stem largely from our acute awareness of time.[3]

By moving the camera, the filmmaker can lead us through a sequence of events in time. This can be relatively unobtrusive, as in *The Big Parade*. But camera movement is innately powerful. The more there is, the more striking its effect. The work of Max Ophuls illustrates this. In his best-known films, which he made in the 1940s and 1950s with cinematographer Christian Matras, the camera constantly moves through elegant scenes of European life at the turn of the century. Some viewers criticize the style as mere decoration, a sophisticated exterior without much substance. Others find it an effective way to picture elegant people attempting to lead poised lives while caught in the rush of events beyond their control. We can see the

epitome of Ophuls's style in *The Earrings of Madame De . . .* (1953), which tells how earrings, passed as gifts between several people, bring tragedy. The film opens with the camera on Madame De . . . as she goes through her possessions, deciding which she will pawn to pay a gambling debt. Only when she comes before an oval mirror do we finally see her face, framed as though it were a cameo (Fig. 4.5). Later, when she has fallen passionately in love, Ophuls shows her in a swirl of constant motion at a formal dance. Even when we see figures seated at tables, a large mirror reflects the dancers, extending the swirling movement deep into the background. Later still, we watch the woman's husband trying to come to grips with her affair. He moves through rooms, and the camera stays with him as he closes all the windows. Thus Ophuls shows characters caught in their own vanity, passion, and frustration; but all are surrounded by the elegance of their own living space, with the camera imposing movement and keeping everything in flux.

The moving camera has such power that, as French filmmaker François Truffaut has put it, "A director is tempted by the dream of linking all of a film's components into a single, continuous action."[4] Technically, a one-shot feature-length film is impossible, for a studio camera's film magazine holds only ten minutes of film. Filmmakers tempted by the dream of total linkage can put only a relative emphasis on recorded continuity, using longer shots and fewer changes of shot. But in 1948 Alfred

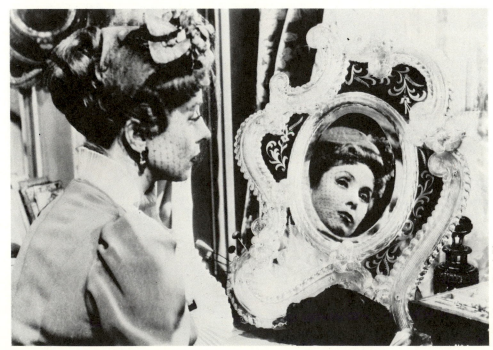

MOMA/ Courtesy Corinth Films

Hitchcock went as far as possible. He made *Rope,* an eighty-minute movie, in one *apparently* continuous shot. He arranged the action so that, as the camera reached the end of each magazine, a performer or piece of furniture would be in front of the lens, blocking the light momentarily and allowing a change of film at that point. Later, all the shots were joined, but the connections are invisible to the ordinary viewer.

The result is an illusion of a single, continuous record. What takes eighty minutes on the screen takes exactly eighty minutes in an apartment: a murder, the hiding of the body, a party during which one man becomes suspicious, and finally the discovery of the body. There are no sudden changes of viewpoint or distance. This creates a unique suspense. Time moves steadily forward as the camera records space constantly yet controls what the viewer can see by its framing and rate of movement.

Rope comes closer than any other movie to fulfilling the dream of a single, unbroken action; but it is not a practical option. Hitchcock himself, apparently not too pleased with his experiment, withdrew *Rope* from circulation some years ago. In commenting upon his movie, he enunciated a rule that applies to the vast majority of all movies: "No doubt about it; films must be cut."[5] This brings us to the subject of constructed continuity.

WORKING WITH CONSTRUCTED CONTINUITY

Constructed continuity involves the power of the *sequence.* An editor builds a complete action out of clearly distinct shots. Each shot becomes a link in a unified chain of events, a brief moment in a larger action rather than a complete action in itself. This linkage of shots is a sequence. When presented on screen, the images of a sequence break up the normal unity of space and time. For example, distance and viewpoint can shift abruptly and rapidly as we watch, or totally separate locales can be linked in time. Constructing continuity allows filmmakers to create tempos and rhythms between shots, adding these to the rhythms within shots. In this section we will consider the technology that filmmakers use to construct sequences, the basic traditions of constructed continuity that have developed, and the varied experiences they provide.

The Technology

Two technological factors affect constructed continuity. First, film can be cut into pieces and reassembled in any desired order. Second, there are a number of conventional visual signals for different experiences of time. Through cutting and

4.5 A shot from *The Earrings of Madame De . . .* (1953). Danielle Darrieux framed within a mirror at the end of the long tracking shot that opens the film.

optical conventions, then, filmmakers construct continuities to suit particular purposes.

Cutting   We do not know who invented film cement, but it allows filmmakers to arrange any pieces of time in any way they choose. Film cement softens celluloid so that the base of one piece of film can be dissolved into the base of the other, making a permanent weld, called a *splice*. Viewers do not see a splice, but a sudden change in scene or point of view. The change is called a *cut,* the same term used for various aspects of creative splicing. An editor *cuts* the pieces of film together, and the pieces themselves may be called *cuts*. In the 1920s film was joined by hand, one piece pressed onto the other and the results checked by being held up against the light. Today, editors use footage counters and magnifying editing machines to decide where to cut the film, and the pieces are joined with precision splicers. The assemblage of machines is called a *cutting bench*.

Originally, filmmakers cut shots together simply to lengthen movies, but soon they developed a whole system of new conventions and techniques—everything we are discussing as constructed continuity. For example, in a certain context a cut is not simply a join but a conventional signal that a character is remembering something. And cuts are combined with optical effects to create other conventional time signals.

Optical Conventions   By manipulating the camera mechanism, filmmakers found visual ways to signal time relationships. These have become the movie's common optical conventions. Originally created in the camera itself, they are more often handled today in the optical printer. But the basic methods remain the same.

Rather than start and stop each scene abruptly, filmmakers may create a *fade*. They sometimes did this in the earliest days by reducing the lens's diaphragm opening while shooting. A fade works best, however, in cameras or printers that have variable shutters, where the pie-wedge opening can be closed completely and reopened as the shutter turns. The mechanism is started with the shutter closed down, allowing no light to enter. Gradually the shutter is opened, *fading in* the scene to full brightness. At the end of the scene the process can be reversed, *fading out* to black. Fades mark the beginning and end of most movies, and they may occur inside a movie to mark a passage of time: one scene fades to black before the next fades in.

One scene can blend gradually into another, a process called the *lap dissolve*, or simply *dissolve*. This is one fade on top of another—that is, as one scene fades out, its successor fades in. One seems to dissolve into the other. Before there were optical printers, dissolves took careful planning. The camera operator, after fading out the first scene, had to crank the camera backward to the correct spot (using either "feel" or a footage counter), then set up to fade in the next scene. The same basic method is used in the optical printer today, but it is exact down to the precise number of frames desired, and filmmakers need not decide where to use dissolves until all shooting is completed. Unlike the fade, the dissolve has no easily specified meaning. In the twenties it simply emphasized the importance of some character or action within a scene. Today it more often suggests that two separated actions are happening simultaneously or are connected in some way. It also may suggest internal processes of memory and reflection.

Another effect with various implications is the superimposition—*super,* for short—in which the filmmaker literally lays one image (or several) on top of another. Supers may suggest a chaos of activity or a character's multiple impressions. Some filmmakers like to use very slow dissolves, so that for perhaps several seconds the viewer experiences a supering effect. Among recent films, *Apocalypse Now* (1979) stands out in its use of slow dissolves and supers to suggest the imagination linking images together.

Effects that were conventional in earlier times have become today's specialized devices. In the twenties and before, it was common to *iris in* and *iris out* between scenes—that is, close in a circle of blackness on one image, then open it out on the next. In the thirties the *wipe* was popular: a vertical or horizontal line moving across or down the frame to bring on a new picture. Neither device is common today, though both are still found, usually as deliberate imitations of old styles.

Experimentation goes on, and specialists working with optical printers and computers can provide modern audiences with flipping and spinning images, intricate split-screen effects, and images that freeze and fly off into darkness, as well as any of the manipulations once handled only in the camera. Technology thus provides audiences with an ever-widening range of conventional time signals.

Basic Traditions of Constructed Continuity

The possibilities inherent in cutting and optical conventions have led to three basic traditions of technique that evolved in film history. First came trickery, the construction of bizarre and fantastic stories. Then filmmakers modified this approach to create the more realistic effects of what is now considered standard editing procedure. Others elaborated this into complex systems of montage. The three traditions have tended to blend together so that all of them may be found today within the same movie.

Trickery   Filmmakers realized very early that the movie mechanism allowed them to play tricks with time. It is said that Louis Lumière liked to run one of his movies, *The Demolition of a Wall* (1895) frontward, then backward, so that the wall would seem to fall and rebuild itself.[6] While making *The Execution of Mary, Queen of Scots* (1895) for the Kinetoscope, Alfred Clark briefly stopped the camera to substitute a dummy for the actress, so that in the final film the queen's head seemed to be cut off while the viewer watched.[7] Clark's trick, termed *stop-motion cinematography* today, became a standard device in hundreds of movies during the first decade of film history.

The classic examples of trickery are the movies of Georges Méliès, a Parisian magician turned filmmaker, who made over five hundred trick films from 1897 to 1913. Some were what he called "transformation scenes," single shots about three minutes in length, within which devils, clowns, monsters, or gods would appear and disappear under the command of some wizard or magician. For more adventurous subjects Méliès linked shots together into genuine stories, using not only stop motion but supers, dissolves, and matte shots as well to create bizarre and magical effects. *A Trip to the Moon* (1902), probably his most popular work, ran about ten minutes. Like all his films, it looks very theatrical. Each segment is like the rounded scene of a play: the actors come in, perform in very theatrical gestures, and exit. But within the theatrical style, Méliès carries on his stop-motion magic. For example, the moon's face gradually floats toward us, then gets a rocket in its eye. The space travelers encounter "Selenites," monkeylike creatures that burst into smoke when struck with an umbrella, and at one point the expedition's leader lifts the Selenite king into the air and throws him on the ground, where he explodes.

The pure trick film, of the sort Méliès made, has virtually disappeared, but stop motion is an integral part of the process work and special effects that contribute spectacular illusions in adventure stories down to the present day. In *Star Wars* (1977), for example, stop motion allows swords to be turned on like flashlights.

Unlike other continuity techniques, stop motion is a *hidden* play with time. It constructs a continuity that only pretends to be happening in unbroken space. The era of this trick's great popularity has long passed, but stop motion is important in film history. It marks the discovery that film continuity has no obligation to follow real continuity. One may interrupt an action many times within a passage of film that, when projected on screen, will seem to go on as a continuous experience. By making it clear that film allows one to manipulate the normal unity of space and time, stop-motion trickery became a foundation for experimentation in constructing continuity.

Standard Editing   Filmmakers like Méliès were *editing* their movies—that is, they were linking together what we described earlier as sequence shots, each of them representing a scene of a story. But gradually filmmakers moved away from Méliès's kind of theatrical fantasy and toward stories with obvious, not hidden, breaks and a more open flow of action. In the process, they evolved a system of editing that is standard filmmaking practice today. Two early short films show this transition from trickery to standard editing.

In 1903, Edwin S. Porter, a director at the Edison Company, made *The Great Train Robbery*, a twelve-minute story in which outlaws waylay a train, dynamiting the safe and robbing the passengers, and then are hunted down by a posse. It is violent American realism, yet it shows the influence of Méliès's kind of trickery. When the robbers slug a man and throw his body off the train, Porter uses stop motion to substitute a dummy. (A sudden change in scenery gives away the trick, because Porter didn't stop the train.) Like Méliès, too, Porter uses each shot to develop a complete scene, with a unity of space and time, as in the theater (Fig. 4.6). In fact, Edison's catalog listed titles like "The Fight on the Tender," "The Train Uncoupled," "Battle to the Death," and so on. But Porter is also getting away from the theatrical look, where each scene comes to a neat conclusion. Instead, some of the movie's scenes are linked by a flowing continuity of action—as when the robbers leave the telegraph office in one shot and move toward an outside water tower in the next.

In *Rescued by Rover* (1905) British filmmaker Cecil Hepworth went further with this interrelation of shots. The eight-minute movie tells of a collie dog that finds a kidnapped baby and leads the child's father to the rescue. Hepworth breaks each of the collie's trips into a series of shots. On the first trip the dog moves down a road, up a street, and across a stream. After finding the baby it reverses its route (stream, street, road), then brings the father back (road, street, stream). Hepworth thus ignores the old theatrical unity of scenes, building their action through patterns of distinctly different shots (Fig. 4.7).

Today, filmmakers still organize movie continuity along the lines we see

4.6 A single shot used for one scene. A frame enlargement from *The Great Train Robbery* (1903). When the telegraph operator's daughter brings his dinner, she discovers her father has been tied up by robbers.

emerging here. A continuity links units of closure, commonly called *scenes* ("Finding the Baby," "Going for Father," "Bringing Father to the Rescue"). A filmmaker may record scenes in single shots, keeping space and time unified. This is Porter's method. It constructs an overall continuity by linking sequence shots, but it keeps emphasis on recorded continuity within each scene. Filmmakers usually prefer to construct the development and closure of action within each scene out of a series, or *sequence*, of separate shots. This is Hepworth's method. "Finding the Baby," for example, develops through shots of road, stream, and street; the next scene, "Going for Father," develops through shots of street, stream, and road. This emphasizes the power of constructed continuity, for now there is linkage within scenes as well as between them, and the filmmaker more freely breaks up the normal unity between space and time. The great value of this structure, however, is that no filmmaker need follow either Porter's or Hepworth's method exclusively. Through editing, a film can exploit action in ongoing time or emphasize any portion of a scene at any moment.

Between 1908 and 1915 filmmakers developed these structural principles into an efficient system. Narrative movies grew from one reel in length (about fifteen minutes running time) into fully-developed *features*, defined as five reels (approximately fifty-five minutes) or longer. Historians refer to these years as the time when

a

b

c

d

film found its language, and they cite particularly the work of director D. W. Griffith. Beginning with one-reelers in 1908 Griffith used an innovative sense of editing to develop movies with remarkable emotional power. His success was capped with *The Birth of a Nation* (1915) and *Intolerance* (1916), twelve and thirteen reels long respectively, impressive monuments to the power of the new systematic editing.

The system divided all shots into three general categories, according to the viewer's apparent distance from the subject: long, medium, or close. Each category provides a different emphasis. The *long shot* lets us know where we are, and so is also called an *establishing* or *cover shot*. It emphasizes the whole environment of an action, whether it is a room, building, city street, or broad landscape. People in it are always full figure, and when they are distant—in *extreme long shot*—they are simply part of the environment. The *medium shot* moves in to frame about half or three-quarters of human figures, so that it necesarily puts more emphasis on actions between characters or between a character and some important part of the environment—such as a man's struggles to climb a cliff. Medium shots are commonly described by the number of characters in them: a *one-shot, two-shot,* and so on. A variety of the two-shot, the *over-the-shoulder shot,* keeps two characters interrelated, but emphasizes only one.

Close shots provide maximum emphasis. The *close-up,* a shot that frames a person's face or only part of it, brings us into very powerful intimacy with a character. A tear sliding down a person's cheek takes up as much space on the screen as the fall of a burning building in a long shot. And an extreme close-up, pushing past ordinary intimacy, may turn a person into a strange object—a disembodied mouth or eye. A close shot used to emphasize an ordinary object—a gun in a drawer, the face of a clock—is properly called an *insert.*

The usual *film script* breaks each scene into these traditional shots, thus showing what emphasis is wanted at particular moments. Suppose, for example, that in one scene of a mystery story a woman, suspicious of her husband's behavior, enters his bedroom and finds an incriminating letter in his bureau (Fig. 4.8). The following gives some idea of what a typical script might indicate, with parentheses added by us to point out what is being done with each shot:

a. Long Shot—Bedroom Door opens. Woman looks in cautiously, then enters and moves to bureau. (This establishes the scene's locale, and lets us see the relationship of things in the room.)

b. Medium Shot—Woman at Bureau Woman reaches bureau. She begins looking through papers on its top. Something suddenly distracts her attention. She looks

4.7 Several shots used for one scene. Frame enlargements from *Rescued by Rover* (1905). Rover discovers where the baby has been taken.

4.8 A dramatic scene broken into traditional camera shots.

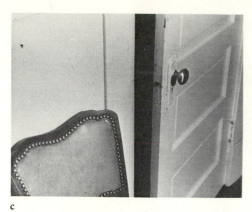

c

d

g

h

k

back toward door. (Our attention is narrowed to one area of the scene, and we can clearly see what the woman is doing.)

c. *Medium Shot—Door*   The door is slightly ajar, and now it begins to open. (Another area of scene is now important.)

d. *Medium Shot—Woman*   She quickly tries to arrange papers as they were, fearing she is about to be discovered. (Emphasis on her activity.)

e. *Medium Shot—Door*   Door opens only slightly. A cat comes in. (Emphasis on activity at the door.)

f. *Close-up—Woman*   Relieved, woman laughs nervously, then turns back to bureau. (Emphasis on character's emotional response, personality.)

g. *Medium Shot—Woman at Bureau*   She looks through some more papers, then begins checking drawers more and more rapidly, finding nothing important. She hesitates at last drawer, afraid of what she may find. (Our attention is again narrowed to the search at the bureau. We follow her movements and the growing suspense they involve.)

h. *Close-up—Woman's Hand at Drawer*   The hand is still at first, then pulls the drawer open. A single, open letter lies in the drawer. (Our attention is narrowed to precisely what she sees.)

i. *Close-Up—Woman's Face*   She is now clearly afraid. She has found what she didn't want to find. (Emphasis on a new emotional response.)

j. *Insert—Letter*   We see the words "You must kill your wife." (Emphasis on a small detail of major importance.)

k. *Medium-Long Shot, Different Angle—Woman at Bureau*   We see the woman through the partially open door. She turns slowly toward the door and stares ahead, not knowing what to do. (Emphasis returns to woman's relation to environment.)

In filming such a scene, the movie's director sets up each shot with a crew and may record several *takes* of it before getting an acceptable one. When shooting is finished, the film is cut together, or edited. From among the takes, the director selects the shots that make up the final movie. (Properly speaking, *take* refers to the process of shooting, and *shot* to the result on screen; the terms are often used interchangeably.) To mark the closure of the scene, the director may want to use a fade or dissolve rather than a cut, depending on the kind of linkage desired with the next scene. Fades or dissolves would be handled in a laboratory after shooting, using an optical printer.

Our example comes from the type of studio film production that we associate with Hollywood, a type we will outline in greater detail in Chapter 7. Keep in mind that this is only one way to make a film. Independent and experimental filmmakers may work from very sketchy scripts, very small crews, and few, if any, special optical effects. Some films, like documentaries and newsreels, are not scripted at all. What our example illustrates is the most formal codification of a system for organizing space in time. Even a newsreel cinematographer works within this system's principles: establishing locales with long shots, moving into medium distance for interactions, getting close for crucial details, and then editing together these separate pieces of space into a meaningful continuity. It is the standard method for constructing continuity.

In themselves, shots are different areas of space, but when they are edited together we experience them also as events in *time*. A cut from one shot to another is a beat in time; fades, dissolves, and other conventional devices are different shifts and blendings in time. The filmmaker thus adds external tempos and rhythms to the rhythms of movement and the shifting compositional balances within the shots. Look again at our scene with the woman at the bureau. The opening two shots will run longer, centering on the rhythms of the woman's movements to and at the bureau. Then will come much shorter takes: cut to door, cut to reaction, cut back to door and cat, cut to reaction. The next shot, a long take, records the tempos of the woman's movement and pause. This leads to a cut to drawer, cut to face, cut to words, followed by a longer take of slow movement that finally stops. Much as in a passage of music (but without the regularly recurring pulses we have in musical beats), this scene has two peaks of tempo. The filmmaker has constructed them out of longer and shorter lengths of film to accentuate certain moments and to reinforce the rhythms within the shots.

At first, filmmakers worried that this external manipulation would disorient, even scare, an audience. After all, using a sudden close-up is cutting to a bodyless head. In practice, though, filmmakers found that if there was some *logic* in the editing, audiences had no difficulty. A number of logical methods have become commonplace techniques. In joining separate shots of the same action, standard editing uses *match-action cutting*: what begins in one shot continues into the next. In our example, the woman moves toward the bureau in long shot and arrives there in medium shot; she hesitates at the last drawer in medium shot, then pulls it open in close-up. When used between shots in separate locales, matching cuts can help establish that they are *parallel actions*, separate events happening simultaneously. The continuity may continue *cross cutting* between the two, developing the separate lines of parallel action together. Another editing tactic, *cause-and-effect cutting*, assumes that one action following another must result from the first. That would be a fallacy in an argument, but in filmmaking it is commonplace logic. If a hand pushes a button in one shot, and a man drops through a trap door in the next, we assume that one caused the other. If a rider gallops through a valley in one shot, and six riders gallop through in a later shot, the six are pursuing the one. Or, with the woman at the bureau, when she turns her head in one shot and we see the door in the next, the logic of match-action and cause-and-effect cutting tells us that she is looking *at* the door. A variation of cause-and-effect logic is the *flashback:* the continuity cuts or dissolves to some causal action, reminding us of something we have seen earlier or suggesting that a character has remembered something.

Editing logics are conventional arrangements that audiences come to take for granted. The examples above are very standard editing techniques that generally try to draw the viewer's attention to the action, not to the editing process itself. This is *soft cutting*, or *invisible editing*. The changing emphases and tempos have their effect, but the conventionality of the techniques keep the impact unobtrusive.

This tradition is most clearly represented in the American Hollywood cinema from about 1915 through the 1940s. Since the 1950s, however, the soft-cut approach has shown the influence of another tradition, one that stresses more obtrusive, hard cutting and operates from assumptions that date from the 1920s. This brings us to montage.

Montage　After World War I, European filmmakers developed systems of editing that reflected political and social situations different from those in the United States. These systems have been distinguished by the word *montage*. Technically, it means exactly the same thing as "editing," being derived from the French *monter* ("to mount, build") used to describe the cutting together of any film. The separate term hangs on, however, because it accurately marks a distinction between American and European cutting. The difference is not in the *act* of editing, but in the motives behind it.

After the ancient czarist government collapsed and the Communists took control of Russia in 1917, Lenin, the chief architect of the revolution, set out to establish a new cultural unity. He chose the motion picture as a major instrument of communication, for it was a visual medium that could directly instruct people in the ways of the new Soviet government and in the techniques of industrial development.

Americans are not accustomed to think of movies as flagrant propaganda, but the new Soviet filmmakers were inspired, in fact, by the persuasive power of American films, particularly those of Griffith. They were fascinated by his editing. From this came pioneering work in Soviet montage.

Lev Kuleshov, in charge of a workshop for young filmmakers at the Soviet film school, made some editing experiments. One sequence showed a man and woman walking along, hailing each other, then coming together, both apparently on the same street. The sequence in fact used widely separated parts of Moscow and ended with a shot of the American White House. Another sequence cut together close-ups of different women to create the illusion that only one woman was putting on make-up. These experiments demonstrated that editing can create "synthetic" or "artificial" spaces that do not really exist.[8]

The workshop's most famous experiment went further. It suggested that editing can condition an audience to see events that do not actually occur. Kuleshov took identical shots of an actor's emotionless face and intercut them with different scenes: a bowl of soup, a woman in a coffin, and a child with a toy bear, among others. Viewers of the resulting sequence swore that the actor's expression changed in each context—from hunger, to sorrow, to sweetness, and so on, though in fact his face remained the same throughout. Accounts do not clarify how Kuleshov constructed the strange continuity without either confusing his audience or tipping them off to what was happening. But this *Kuleshov effect* is now considered a basic premise in the psychology of editing.

Kuleshov insisted that the cinema's power lay in the act of cutting. In the present context it is more accurate to refer to that act as *montage*, not editing in the American sense. For Kuleshov and his followers cutting carried the idea of *analysis*. The filmmaker carefully, even scientifically, breaks down action into individual pieces. Each shot becomes more emphatically important: it becomes more obviously symbolic, and it conditions ideas and attitudes through its relation with other shots. The acts of cutting remain the same, but they are designed to engage the viewer in a more deliberate way. "The spectator himself," said Kuleshov, "completes the connected shots and sees in it what has been suggested to him by the montage."[9] Such editing does not simply pull viewers into an involvement that ignores the junctures between shots. It also engages our awareness that space is being analyzed for us, broken down into its important components. This is *hard cutting*.

Soviet filmmakers used montage within a strongly political context. *Storm over Asia* (1928), directed by Vsevolod Pudovkin, intercuts scenes of Buddhist priests and British soldiers preparing for an official ceremony of state. The sequence does not advance the story's action so much as make ironic commentary on the similarity between the trappings of state religion and the trappings of capitalist government. Director Sergei Eisenstein spoke of "intellectual montage," in which the filmmaker used editing to open up ideas, much like a visual essay. In *October* (1927), which recounts the Communists' rise to power, Eisenstein cuts from shots of Kerenski, president of a provisional government hated by the Communists, to shots of a gilded mechanical peacock (Fig. 4.9). The sequence is an intellectual analysis that breaks in on any emotional involvement we might have with the story. The montage suggests that Kerenski is like an artificial peacock. Eisenstein's work demonstrates the most analytical forms of Soviet montage, pushing it toward metaphor and the expression of abstract ideas. Of all the Soviet filmmakers he has had the most enduring effect on film history and theory.

In Germany, filmmakers used montage within a different context. From the start, German movies had emphasized the complexity of the human mind. They told stories in which men had diabolical split personalities or created vengeful monsters. They used distorted sets and acting to create landscapes befitting the tortured mind. These early movies show the heavy influence of theater and painting, but as the 1920s progressed, German filmmakers developed different styles under the influence of American production techniques and of Soviet montage. Unlike the Russians, German filmmakers did not see montage as the essence of cinema. They were too interested in the lighting and composition of individual shots to go that far. But they used montage to dwell on psychological details, linking continuities by the inner associations of characters.

Variety (1925), directed by E. A. Dupont, displays this psychological montage in telling the story of a husband who learns that his wife is cheating on him with a man who is their partner in a trapeze act. The continuity often cuts between different characters' viewpoints—so that, for example, we see the wife from the husband's, then the lover's viewpoint—so that we are constantly taken into the characters' attitudes and feelings. But the continuity goes further. In one sequence we see the husband, aware of his wife's affair, sitting miserable at his dressing table. The continuity cuts to shots of the trapeze act, and we see the partner miss the husband's grasp and fall to his death. Then the film cuts back to the husband at the dressing table. We have been shown his imaginings. The movie's montage presents and even analyzes the workings of the mind. It creates a psychological space and time.

German movies like *Variety* had an influence on American editing practices in the 1920s, but Hollywood movies in general maintained the tradition of a softer-cut, more invisible style. American studios did use the term *montage*, however, to

4.9 Eisenstein's intellectual montage. Frame enlargements from *October* (1927), in which Kerenski is compared to a gilded peacock.

distinguish a technique especially popular in the 1930s and 1940s. This was the *montage sequence*. It compresses time. If a movie wants to say that a man has been out for days looking for a job, the continuity shows a rapid montage of feet walking the pavement, men shaking their heads, and doors slamming. If a character is undergoing a long court trial, it is summarized in a rapid series of newspaper headlines (some of them spinning, perhaps) with shots of printing presses, newsboys, and crowds on the street. *The Roaring Twenties* (1939) has classic examples. To summarize the history of gang wars, there are sequences of skidding cars, flying bodies, explosions, and gunfire. To signal the stock market crash of 1929, there is a montage

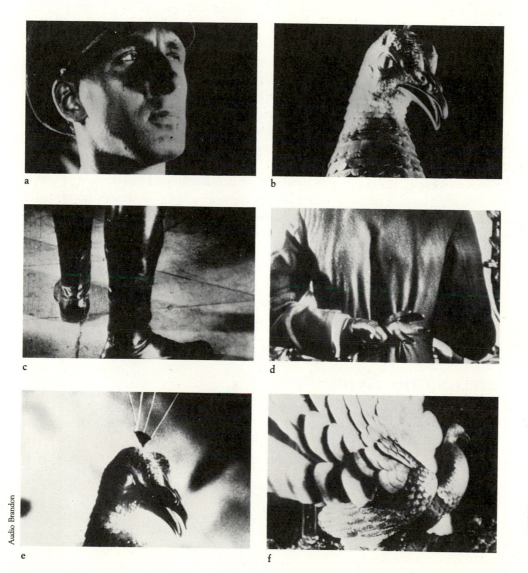

Audio Brandon

a

b

c

d

e

f

with a swelling ticker-tape machine, a mound of money, and then a Wall Street that melts. To create such effects, studios had montage departments with their own directors and editors. In this way, Hollywood adapted the hard-cutting, analytical concept of editing to the conventional American system.

American filmmaking has continued to evolve and adapt, and it is no longer accurate to describe American editing as typically soft-cut and invisible. Filmmakers have done new variations on old techniques, and European editing practices have had further influence. Since the 1950s, for example, American audiences have become very familiar with *jump cuts*, cuts that ignore any matching between shots. A jump-cut version of our scene with the woman discovering the letter might show shots of her at the door, at a window, at the bureau, with the cat, at the drawer, then with the letter—but without any matching actions joining the continuity. Traditionalist filmmakers once considered jump cutting merely bad editing, but it is now a common device for eclipsing time or bringing sharp tempos of emphasis. It derives from European montage techniques. By playing against standard editing conventions, a filmmaker tends to create a more obtrusive, hard-cut kind of continuity. It may begin a scene with extreme close-ups, deliberately leaving us unsure where we are, or it may surprise us with an apparently match-action cut that is, in fact, a jump-cut. In *The Graduate* (1967), for example, a character leaps toward a rubber raft in one shot and lands in bed in the next: a kind of visual joke. *Easy Rider* (1969) and *Don't Look Now* (1974) turn the flashback convention around and do *flash-forwards*: cuts to what has not yet happened. Disorienting at first, the cuts are used consistently within the story contexts, and the viewer can grasp this peculiar editing logic—though it is not likely to become a standard editing device.

Working with constructed continuity, filmmakers have evolved fantastic tricks, unobtrusive editing devices that pull viewers into the action, as well as analytical montage that plays more obtrusively with space in time. These traditions are not totally distinct "schools," with precise rules, but patterns of operation that may intermix within the same film. Through these patterns filmmakers apply the basic technology of cutting and optical effects to create complex manipulations of space in time.

APPLYING THE TECHNOLOGY

All movies create heightened experiences of time and rhythm, but each draws from traditional methods to suit its particular purposes. It may place great emphasis on one method. More typically, a movie builds various techniques into a visual design where time and tempo interplay with movement and *mise en scène* in different ways at different moments, and with different effects. And, as we have already pointed out, some movies are relatively transparent or soft-cut in their approach; others are more obtrusively hard-cutting. Let us consider a range of examples.

For a good example of conventional Hollywood continuity, we can turn to a movie directed by Frank Capra for RKO in 1946. *It's a Wonderful Life* uses a number of strong characters and a variety of situations to create a sentimental fantasy. George Bailey, who has always dreamed of becoming a famous architect and traveling the world, is forced by economic circumstances to stay in his small home town and run his family's savings and loan company. The struggling company helps the poor people of the town and protects them from the vengeful power of Henry F. Potter, a millionaire who wants to take over control of the town for himself. At Christmas time one year, however, the company's manager misplaces $8,000, and George is finally at the mercy of Potter, who threatens to jail him and take over the company. Frustrated by what he feels is a useless life and convinced that his insurance policy makes him worth more dead than alive, George decides to commit suicide. But his guardian angel, taking human form, shows George what it would be like if he had never lived: the townspeople would have been miserably unhappy and degraded. Aware now of his own value and buoyed by the many friends who come to his support, George finally realizes that his is a wonderful life after all.

The movie's continuity, handled by William Hornbeck, follows very consistent patterns. It uses standard shot arrangements and editing logic. Long shots establish and reestablish the overall *mise en scène;* medium shots isolate interactions within scenes, and closeups isolate an individual character's reactions. The generally soft cuts between shots keep action flowing within scenes; dissolves and wipes between scenes keep transitions smooth.

These familiar patterns set up a context of conventional Hollywood realism in which there is a great flexibility. For example, when the story involves a character insight or an action that is meant to grow on the viewer's awareness, the camera may simply linger for a long time on the shot, subtly emphasizing the presence of ongoing time. This happens in a scene where George tells his mother that he has decided to remain at home and allow his brother, who had been groomed to take over the company, to follow a career elsewhere. It is a delicate moment that depends on the gradual understanding between mother and son, and the camera simply holds on a medium shot of the two while George unfolds his decision. The continuity certainly might have cut away to the mother's reactions, but the particular choice allows us to feel the moment as a development *in* time, without any counterpointing tempo.

On the other hand, when the story involves rapid changes, the continuity may shift to quick shots, emphasizing tempos. This happens when the movie shows the changes that come to the town with the outbreak of World War II: some citizens go off to war; George is rejected as 4-F but takes over the town's civil defense; Potter controls the draft; and George's brother becomes a war hero. The quick shots provide a rapid synopsis, much like a montage sequence, forwarding the story smoothly.

The continuity changes for different actions, setting up effective contrasts. One instance is the scene in which George comes home after he has discovered that the money is missing (see Fig. 4.10). The continuity begins by emphasizing the new locale, the Baileys's living room being decorated for Christmas. Rhythms of movement and speech develop within a fairly long take. As the scene proceeds, George sits with one child while his wife and another child decorate the tree. The continuity separates the two groups into medium shots, and as George momentarily breaks down while the wife works at the tree, the continuity intercuts between the two areas. When the wife notices that something is wrong, the continuity cuts to a closeup of her face, emphasizing her awareness. Then, as the moment passes and

4.10 Classic Hollywood editing. A sequence from *It's a Wonderful Life* (1946) with James Stewart and Donna Reed.

a

b

e

f

George regains some control, the wife pretends not to notice, and the continuity goes back to the intercut medium shots. In this fashion the continuity organizes one brief sequence into a design that first establishes an area and emphasizes internal shot rhythms, then builds to a climax of tempos, then settles back again into regular rhythms and tempos.

This one sequence can be said to epitomize the flexible, unobtrusive design we associate with classic Hollywood cinema. When desired, it may place emphasis on internal rhythms, using lengthy takes; or it may use shorter takes to punctuate action with rapid, external tempos. Melodramas, which rely strongly on character development rather than exciting adventure, are likely to place heavier emphasis on internal rhythms, using longer takes. *Dark Victory* (1939), for example, is the story of a doctor who marries a woman he knows is dying. In its climax the continuity joins a series of lengthy takes that show the woman going to her room to face death alone. It builds from long shots into a final closeup, but without emphatic editing tempos. However, adventure stories are more likely to use such tempos to set chases, battle scenes, or moments of high suspense apart from the rest of the action. In D. W. Griffith's *The Birth of a Nation* a terrified woman flees a man threatening her with rape. Her brother, sensing her danger, follows their trail. Shots of woman, rapist, and brother become shorter and shorter, the increasing tempo enhancing the

c

d

g

h

growing suspense. It reaches a culmination as the woman throws herself from a cliff, then the continuity returns to a slower pace. In *Stagecoach* (1939) the editing tempo increases as Indians launch an attack, relaxes after the cavalry comes to the rescue, then begins to build again when the hero goes into town to face gunfighters. *Bullitt* (1968), a modern detective story, punctuates its story with exciting chases. In one the hero outwits killers in an auto race through the streets of San Francisco, and in the story's climax he pursues another killer through a crowded airline terminal. In each scene the continuity heightens an exciting moment with sharply increased editing tempos.

As we would expect from classical Hollywood cinema, the predominance of match-action cutting and the familiarity of the editing logic help create the "invisible" effect. The filmmaker may push beyond that, though, shading into more obvious calculation. We can see this in Vsevolod Pudovkin's *Mother* (1926). Much like a Hollywood storyteller, Pudovkin motivates his performers to create precise character types, and he arranges his shots in generally smooth continuities of rapid cutting with clear editing logic. But Pudovkin analyzes the action into precise symbols of strife, courage, and oppression. They stand out from the story itself. At the beginning, for example, a wife tries to prevent her husband from selling their clock for more drink. The montage breaks the struggle into groping hands and determined faces, culminating in a rapid sequence of shots where the clock slips from the man's hand and smashes on the floor, the final movement only the rolling of a solitary clock gear (Fig. 4.11). At the end of the film, when the wife joins the Communist revolution, Pudovkin rounds out the symbolism begun in the early sequence and continued through the film. The woman's hands hold her murdered son's body and then pick up the fallen Red flag, and she is cut down. Pudovkin affirms the ultimate triumph of the revolution by intercutting between the striking workers and a swollen river that has begun to break up its frozen surface in the first signs of spring.

Pudovkin called this approach *linkage*. It converts actions into a chain of isolated symbols that carry strong emotional overtones. He tells intense, often gripping stories, but he strips them down to crucial details, which he imposes on the viewer. He moves away from a simply invisible continuity.

Sergei Eisenstein's work went further. Eisenstein described montage as a collision of one image against another, forcing the viewer to a new realization. This was a *dialectical* concept, based on the philosopher Hegel's view of reality as a constantly dynamic clash of one entity (*thesis*) with another (*antithesis*), leading to a new unity (*synthesis*). Eisenstein's montage was designed to involve the viewer, but

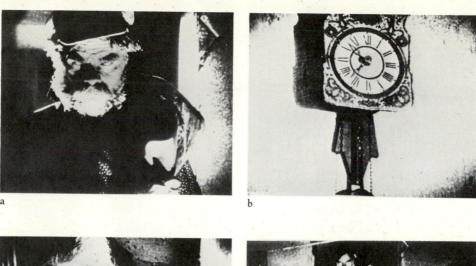

a

b

c

d

e

f

4.11 Soviet montage. Frame enlargements from
Mother (1926), with A. Khristiakov and Vera
Baranovskaya (continued, pp. 126–127).

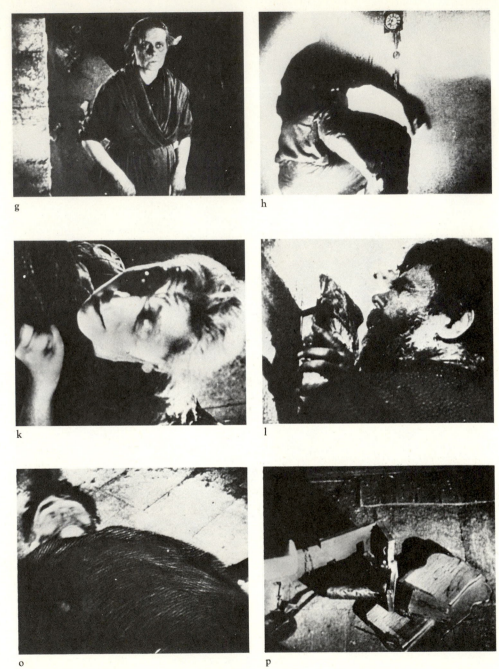

g

h

k

l

o

p

i

j

m

n

q

r

intellectually. He considered perception as an active participation, not passive experience, and so he developed a very analytical form of montage. *Potemkin* (1925), probably his best known work, typifies his striking manipulation of editing. The story recalls a 1905 incident in which the citizens of Odessa, because they befriended mutinying sailors, were attacked by czarist troops who marched down a long row of steps firing into the helpless crowd. In rendering this scene, Eisenstein uses jarring and forceful cuts. We have little time to develop any emotional identity with the people, who are types rather than individuals: a student, a cripple, a mother and her son. Instead, we watch an analytical demonstration of oppression, as Eisenstein elongates the actual time of the massacre, clashing together images of the confused people with those of the relentless soldiers, whose orderly boots, rifles, and uniforms we see. The sequence builds to a kind of Kuleshov effect. A baby carriage rolls to the bottom of the steps, a Cossack slashes downward with his sword, and the student screams out. We do not actually see what happens: we are invited to complete a horror that is only suggested. The jolting clashes between shots ignore the idea of "invisibility," and we more easily become aware of what is being done with the action.

Pudovkin and Eisenstein made maximum use of montage, and in their movies rapid tempos and hard cuts predominate. Few filmmakers have followed their lead. One exception is Richard Lester, whose British movies in the 1960s were exercises in montage. In *A Hard Day's Night* (1964) and *Help!* (1965), two madcap movies featuring the Beatles, and in *Petulia* (1968), a serious study of human loneliness, Lester fully exploits the frenetic, disruptive effect of montage. In the 1970s, however, Lester settled into a much more traditional editing style for comedies like *The Three Musketeers* (1973) and for more serious work like *Robin and Marian* (1976). His later movies fall into the pattern common to most filmmakers who exploit montage: they use montage sequences as counterpoints to more traditional continuity.

During the silent period German filmmaker Georg Wilhelm Pabst transformed melodramas with passages of psychological montage. One such sequence occurs in *The Love of Jeanne Ney* (1927), when a blind young woman enters a darkened room in which her father has just been strangled (Fig. 4.12). She has heard something and is frightened. She calls her father's name as she gropes into the room, her sightless eyes staring ahead. The murderer shrinks back before her. She stumbles over her father. Her hands move slowly up the body, until they reach the face. With a shriek of horror she throws her head up, then falls onto the body, her blond hair covering the dead man's face. Pabst's technique blends the smooth continuity of American editing with the analytical approach of Soviet montage to emphasize symbols of compulsion, vulnerability, death, and terror.

Alfred Hitchcock became the most famous manipulator of psychological montage. As early as *The Lodger* (1926), a silent movie, Hitchcock used rapid, hard cuts to jolt our awareness and to keep us off balance. By the time of *Psycho* (1960) and *The Birds* (1963), he had perfected an editing style that forced us to look at frightening things, sometimes directly but more often by playing upon our own mental associations. The celebrated sequence in *Psycho* in which a woman is stabbed to death in a shower illustrates the Kuleshov effect. The horror is not so much in what Hitchcock shows, but in the connections we make between the images he carefully arranges to exploit our imagination. In such passages Hitchcock was a master of montage, but as his experiment with *Rope* indicates, he did not limit himself to one continuity technique.

Classic Hollywood continuity has given way to more elastic styles. Striking montage sequences appear in otherwise traditionally edited stories. At the end of *The Godfather* (1971) the continuity rapidly crosscuts shots of an infant's baptism with those of bloody Mafia assassinations. The technique as such is conventional, but the content of the two lines of action is so different that we can become aware of the editing as commentary. It ironically contrasts religion, innocence, and cleansing with Mafia, death, and revenge—and so resembles the sort of hard cutting that we find in Pudovkin. Its connections are meant to be noticed.

The Wild Bunch (1969), directed by Sam Peckinpah, uses passages of unconventional editing to bring a sharp emphasis to important moments in its story of hounded outlaws trying to pull off one last big robbery. Early in the story, a posse ambushes the outlaws in the middle of a town. The continuity builds suspense with conventional editing, intercutting shots of the hidden posse with shots of the unsuspecting outlaws and townspeople. Then, when the posse opens fire, the continuity explodes into a montage of very rapid, hard cuts. It also cuts slow-motion shots into the action. One person's fall, for example, is in a long, slow movement interrupted by rapid cuts to other actions in normal time. Later on in the story, the continuity intrudes slow-motion shots at key moments: when the outlaws shoot a wounded comrade and when they blow up a bridge as the posse crosses it. Then at the end of the story, when the outlaws choose to die in a massive shoot-out with an entire Mexican army, the continuity explodes again into a violent montage with slow motion underlining the death of each outlaw. Here again we see Hollywood conventions repeatedly giving way to analyses of action that are comparable to Soviet montage but used for very different purposes.[10]

a

b

e

f

i

j

m

n

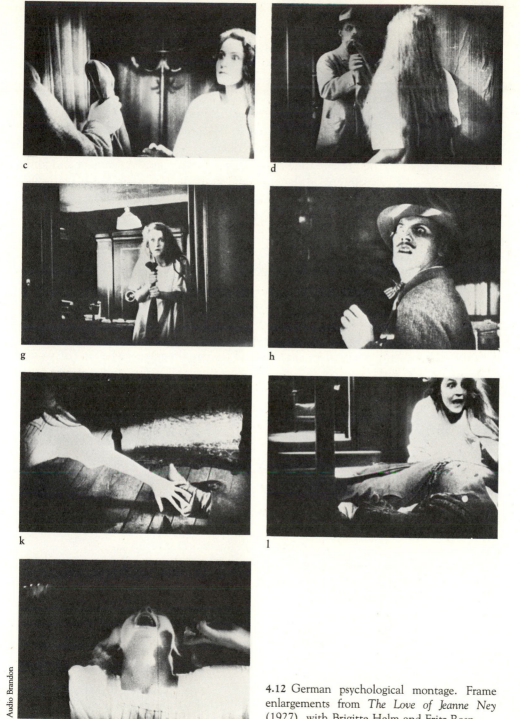

c

d

g

h

k

l

Audio Brandon

o

4.12 German psychological montage. Frame enlargements from *The Love of Jeanne Ney* (1927), with Brigitte Helm and Fritz Rasp.

Some of Hollywood's changing sense of continuity can be attributed to the influence of much more self-conscious forms of montage in Europe, particularly in the 1950s. Alain Resnais's work is an example. Resnais came into fiction filmmaking out of documentary, where he developed an extremely proficient editing style. In documentary, jump cutting is common, since it is difficult to match action between shots of unstaged events. Resnais capitalized on the jump cut, for his work often dwells on the relationship between present and past time. *Night and Fog* (1955), his study of German concentration camps, intercuts color sequences of the camps as they look now with black-and-white sequences (all documentary footage) of what went on there in the past. In the present-time shots, Resnais uses a moving camera and long passages of recorded continuity; in the past-time shots, he jump-cuts among terrible, seering images that illustrate the narrator's descriptions of camp life. The film is not just a picture of the camps, but a contrast of two times; it ends by wondering if the future will not have to face such terrible things again. In his features, Resnais went on to interrelate present and past in creative, disjunctive montage. *Hiroshima mon amour* (1959) and *La guerre est finie* (1966) involve characters who dwell on memories of the past. Resnais's most extreme experiment is *Last Year at Marienbad* (1961), which involves the viewer in perplexing time relationships that are never clarified. Again, Resnais blends long moving-camera shots with disjunctive jump cutting to present a world in which the power of time dominates.

Resnais was only one of many French and Italian filmmakers who, in the words of Jean-Luc Godard, wanted "to take a conventional story and remake, but differently, everything the cinema had done."[11] This included more than just continuity, but the interrelation of constructed and recorded experiences of time drew much of their attention. In his *Pierrot le fou* (1965), for example, Godard edits a sequence in a kind of reverse, casual time pattern: shots of two characters escaping from killers alternate with their plan of the escape. In *Masculin féminin* (1966) he jump-cuts between apparently unrelated daytime and nighttime shots to accompany characters philosophically discussing freedom and love. One writer has suggested that such tactics reflect Godard's desire to get away from traditional methods and to create a dialectical tension between reality and abstract ideas.[12] Godard thus carries Eisenstein's principles into new realms of intellectual montage.

American studio films, with their strong ties to conventional storytelling, play with the technology of continuity in a less self-conscious fashion. Nevertheless, the techniques of classic Hollywood editing and European montage have intertwined in the last thirty years, so that today viewers encounter both transparent and obvious plays with time, interrelating the rhythms of recorded continuity with the tempos and trickery of constructed continuity. As we have noted about movement and space, our experience of time in movies is always heightened, and the evolution of techniques has made it more and more diversified and complex.

CONTINUITY AND CRITICISM

No comprehensive film theory ignores continuity, but different theorists value different aspects of it. Hugo Münsterberg speaks of editing as an imitation of human memory and imagination, and realist theorists are taken with the presence of actual time in recorded continuity, which completes the viewer's sense of captured reality. There are two other schools of theory, however, whose ideas about continuity seem particularly important, and we will center on them here.

The *formative* school argues that editing and montage are ultimately the major source of cinema's power because they make movies totally unique from all other forms of art. The *semiotic* school deals particularly with one aspect of the formative school's view: that editing and montage also help make cinema a language system.

The Formative School

We can credit formative theory, which began to emerge in the 1920s, with stirring the first widespread interest in cinema as an art form. There are three central spokesmen of the theory. In Hungary, Béla Balázs wrote various essays, eventually published together in English as *Theory of the Film* (1952). Rudolf Arnheim's work was translated from the German in 1933, then expanded into *Film as Art* in 1957. And Sergei Eisenstein's many writings first appeared in English in *The Film Sense* (1942) and *Film Form* (1949).[13] There are differences among the writers, but in all three we find the same hallmarks of the formative approach.

First, formative theory stresses that cinema's true value is in its *difference from reality*. To Arnheim, filmmakers who seek naturalness in movies are engineers, not artists. An artist diverts the viewer's eyes from mere subject matter to a movie's form: the unusual ways it arranges things. And so he concluded that mechanical devices like editing, fades, supers, or backward motion, which some consider drawbacks to a perfect illusion, "actually form the tools of the creative artist."[14] In his turn, Balázs denied that movies give us pictures of reality. The film artist seeks those qualities that a movie "does not reproduce but produce and through which it becomes an independent, basically new art."[15] Eisenstein said the filmmaker should "sever the passive everyday connection" and establish a new one.[16]

Eisenstein used montage as one method for creating a formative film experience.

He distinguished five types of montage. Only the first two deal with our sense of time: *metric* montage, defined by the length of each shot, determines tempos; it should be synchronized with *rhythmic* montage, which involves the movement within each shot. Eisenstein's other categories are more abstract. *Tonal* montage organizes shots according to the "dominant emotional sound" of each piece: a "gloomy" or "bright" shot depends on degrees of illumination, and a "shrill" or "quiet" shot depends on the angles or straight lines in the frame. Eisenstein noted that *overtonal* montage could occur when the previous types of montage interrelated with one another. He compared this effect to musical overtones, vibrations that cannot be written into a score but can be heard or felt when the notes are played. Finally, a sequence could achieve *intellectual* montage, which would agitate the mind as other kinds of montage agitated the senses. Using outlines and complicated charts to organize his montage system, Eisenstein presented the most elaborate method for stressing film's difference from reality.[17]

Second, these theorists stress that movie art should have *no uncertainty or ambiguity*. This explains the theorists' strong attachment to montage. By a careful construction of images, the filmmaker *leads* the viewer to see exactly what is desired. Eisenstein spoke against long takes, for example, because they led to uncertain meanings and showed a lack of artistic intelligence, for the filmmaker was asking the viewer to look at something long after its significance should have been clear.[18] Arnheim believed that film art must manipulate images as purely as possible. No realism for its own sake, not even color, should intrude. Montage was "a first-class formative instrument . . . the royal road to film art." Adding sound, he felt, interfered with the pure expression of images, which he found only in the silent, black-and-white cinema prior to the 1930s.[19]

From this stress on purity emerges the third hallmark. Formative theory stresses clarity of technique so strongly that it treats cinema as *language*. Arnheim catalogues techniques as if he were writing a grammar, explaining the meaning of each and how it should or should not be used. Supers, for example, are "likely to give the feeling that the artist has achieved his effect too cheaply"; dissolves are "impossible within a scene in which the unities of space and time are unbroken."[20] Eisenstein thought that movie imagery indicated a more basic kind of language than verbal speech. Ultimately he searched for what he called *synesthesia*, a synchronization of all the senses, which film artists would bring about by manipulating the forms at their disposal. It would be a kind of consummate montage, providing a multisensory experience.[21]

Following Arnheim more closely than Eisenstein, writers in the formative school have produced many books that treat cinema as though it were literary composition. Shots are like words, they suggest, and filmmaking can be learned like grammar. Many have also picked up Arnheim's definition of the artistic film as "film which is produced without regard for the general public."[22] These approaches tend to turn cinema into a closed system, where certain techniques always mean certain things, where one learns to make "correct" artistic choices, and where only a select group knows the rules. Carried to extremes, then, the formative approach becomes a new version of the artistic elitism that the realistic qualities of photography and movies threatened in the nineteenth century.

Despite their assertions, the fathers of formative theory reveal a struggle with the pull of realism. Arnheim modifies his extreme position by speaking of film art in terms of a balance between contrary tendencies. The filmmaker should not avoid nature but find an equilibrium between merely sensational reproductions of reality, which show *no* human artistry, and ambiguity, which shows no *precise* organization.[23] Balázs, for all his avowed disinterest in reproduction, spoke eloquently of the immediate, realistic power of the close-up.[24] Eisenstein's concept of montage may suggest an assembly-line process with everything neatly patterned ahead of time, but he also spoke of film art as an organic process that grows through insights discovered as one works. He refused finally to accept formative filmmaking as strictly a matter of applying abstract principles.[25]

Eisenstein's tendency to explore contrary, even contradictory possibilities makes his theory the most difficult to read, but he is probably the most stimulating, certainly the most open of formative writers. Much like Bazin, he acknowledges that cinema is an on-going process that will not hold still for any closed-minded extremes.

Semiotics

The formative school simply assumes that cinema is like language, but there is a science that seeks to define the nature of that similarity. This science studies all systems by which humans pattern what they employ as *signs* to mean something to someone else. The basic principles of the science derive from two thinkers: Ferdinand de Saussure, a Swiss linguist who called it *semiology*, and Charles S. Peirce, an American who called it *semiotics*—the term now preferred in the United States.[26] The foundations were laid by the early 1930s, and by the 1960s semiotics had evolved into a network of studies aimed "to take in any system of signs, whatever their substance and limits; images, gestures, musical sounds, objects and the complex associations of all these, which form the content of ritual, convention or public entertainment."[27]

To study verbal signs, linguistics developed a very precise framework, or *model*, to describe the "building blocks" of sound and meaning (phones, phonemes, morphs, morphemes) that structure human speech. Though technically only one branch of sign study, linguistics has come to hold such a dominant place that semiotics today usually refers only to the study of nonverbal sign systems, and the linguistic approach has heavily influenced all sign study. Film theorists have become interested in building a comprehensive model that will describe how a movie signifies all its meanings to an audience. They have grappled with the issue of film as language, and, in the process, they have sparked wide discussion and controversy.

Semiotics distinguishes two aspects of language. The system of rules and conventions established by society is *langue;* the individual act of communication is *parole*. Because two speakers share the same knowledge of grammatical rules, for example, they can communicate through a virtually unlimited range of individual utterance. They take the rules for granted. If they do not—if they try to think about the rules while using them—their speech becomes difficult or impossible. All communication depends on some complex system that remains *assumed* between people. The movies are no exception. They have evolved compositional practices, photographic techniques, and editing logics as means of communicating. They use familiar story forms, characters, and actions drawn from other media within the culture (novels, theater, comics) or from other forms of cultural expression (such as fashion, slang, or myth). Like language products, any movie is a *text*, a collection of signs organized into various patterns, or *codes*, that make sense to us. Through the shared codes we understand a movie's messages.

In discussing language, semioticians consider two axes of meaning: a *syntagmatic axis* and a *paradigmatic* (or *systemic*) *axis*. The syntagmatic axis refers to the way in which words, or other verbal or nonverbal units called *signifiers*, must be linked to be conventionally meaningful. The paradigmatic axis refers to the choice of words available to the speaker or writer given the context that has been set up. If we take the words "John hit the . . . ," we know by the syntagmatic organization of the language that the next word will most likely be either a noun like *ball* or an adjective preceding a noun, like *furry*. To say "John hit the abruptly ball" is to break a rule of the language, although the listener may still guess what you're talking about. The syntagmatic level of language involves the rules whereby words are joined together.

When we talk about the paradigmatic aspects of communication, we mean the number of possible words or signifiers that could be used in a given situation. That is, if I were to say "John hit the sphere," my choice of word *sphere* is meaningful because in English I could have used *ball*, which would indeed be the more common word.

My choice of *sphere* is not just meaningful in itself, but in implicit comparison with all the words that could be used following "John hit the . . ."—such as *ball, policeman,* or *punching bag.* The paradigmatic level of language systems refers to the choices available to a communicator within the system of signifiers the medium uses.

An example based on the language system of a restaurant menu may clarify the two components. On the syntagmatic level, one eats an appetizer followed by a soup, an entree, and a dessert. On the paradigmatic level, one can choose between clam chowder and onion soup, between roast chicken and steak, between apple pie and chocolate pudding. One *can* break the rules of dining and eat one's chocolate pudding before clam chowder, or a restaurant could list steak under desserts, but these actions would respectively break the syntagmatic and paradigmatic grammar of our culture's system of eating. Yet only by studying the menu as a whole could a foreigner get some sense of what the eating "codes" of our country are.[28]

Different forms of literary expression favor an emphasis on one axis or another. Conventional storytelling novels, for example, emphasize the syntagmatic qualities of language, the linking together of described events, words or ideas. Poetry, on the other hand, emphasizes the individual word chosen for what may be a multitude of ambiguous meanings. In early film history, the narratives of Griffith would emphasize the syntagmatic, the use of editing to tell a story. The silent comedies of Charlie Chaplin, on the other hand, are filled with poetic digressions and amusing sight gags that can be seen as directly meaningful on several different levels.[29] This is paradigmatic emphasis.

In much of the pioneering work in film semiotics there has been an emphasis on the syntagmatic aspects of the medium. Christian Metz, the major figure of the movement, has postulated that there are eight different kinds of shots in movies, in relation to what their meanings may be for the film's narrative continuity. The language system of film is constructed out of these syntagmatic categories.[30] Umberto Eco, an Italian theorist, sees all human perception, even perception of still images, as a process involving syntagmatic connections.[31] Metz and Eco give a privileged place to continuity, especially montage, in film communication.

Recently the work of theorists like Metz and Eco has been attacked for its emphasis on the syntagmatic. Bill Nichols, a Canadian film theorist, argues that in no way do we get meanings strictly through connections between shots. Even montage like Kuleshov's experiments joins units whose meanings are affected by the *way* they are shown—by changes in lighting or camera angle, for example. In movies a particular *style* of presentation always carries and affects ("mediates") messages.[32] In addition, critics have objected that Metz's concentration on narrative carries with it the implicit assumption that narrative is somehow the "natural" form of film expression, an attitude disputed by critics who favor poetic or noncommercial forms of film expression.

Whatever their point of view, semioticians struggle toward some model that will detail the whole *context* of film communication, for it is only within the context of both moviemaking in general and the culture in general that we understand the particular meanings of any given film. Semioticians strongly emphasize that codes are taught by one's culture. We learn what to look for, how to act, what is important, and how to arrange ideas. There may be universal traits among peoples, but each culture organizes a distinct world view (what semiotics terms "ideology"). This colors our perceptions and thought processes. In Spanish or French, two languages that reflect strong class-oriented cultures, one must decide whether to use the familiar pronoun (*tu* in both languages) or formal pronoun (*usted* in Spanish, *vous* in French) when addressing someone. English speakers long ago dropped the distinction, which survives as the familiar *thou* in prayers. In one scene of Claude Chabrol's film *Les bonnes femmes* (1961), a pair of lovers who have used *vous* up to a certain point in the story begin to use the familiar *tu*. The distinction is lost to American viewers reading subtitles. They understand through other signifiers that the couple is becoming more intimate, but may miss the particular nuance of the scene. French filmmakers have often used the switching from formal to familiar forms as a convention to indicate that a couple has begun to have sexual relations.

Film, with its techniques of editing, *mise en scène,* and sound, is what is known as a polysemous communication: it uses more than one coding system to express ideas. Within these various systems, there are also cultural codes operating, on the level of subject matter and attitudes expressed in the film. Film is an example of what literary critic Roland Barthes calls a *plural text* in which there is not one simple meaning but a range of interrelated implications. A movie does not have a single meaning; it has any number of meanings, and they differ from one viewer to the next.[33] These meanings may at times conflict or contradict one another, in which case the film communicates *dialectically,* through a tension or opposition between different codes rather than through simple agreement.

To study polysemous media, semioticists believe, one should begin with manageable subdivisions of general codes. Within a culture whose members use the same basic language there are groups with their own variations in speech and behavior (college students, politicians, cowboys, filmmakers, New Yorkers), and there are social trends and attitudes that come and go, influencing the speech and behavior of a certain period (the flappers, the 1930s Hollywood studio system,

McCarthyism, rock 'n roll). These subcultures and historical influences provide *subcodes,* variations on the culture's general rules, which are easier to define and study. One approach is to study the changes in a single subcode or cluster of subcodes from one period to another. Works on the evolution of montage or close-up techniques or on the changing treatment of women and men in movies fall into this category. Another approach is to study the subcodes that affect a movie at one particular time. In an essay on the Warner Brothers movie *Marked Woman* (1937), for example, Charles W. Eckert points out that—although the movie follows typical codes of melodrama, with a clear-cut hero who stops the outrages of a stereotyped villain—there are other codes at work (in the lyrics of songs, in the different ethical and social backgrounds of the hero and heroine, in the unromantic ending) that contradict the audience's usual expectations, underlining class differences and the hopeless state of the poor in the Depression.[34] *Marked Woman* is a film in which a French viewer might miss the overtones of American class conflicts.

Semiotic study has also become the basis for attacks on Western cultures. French semioticists in particular, under the influence of Sigmund Freud's psychology and the economic theory of Karl Marx, stress that cultures use traditional movie codes to exploit and control their members. The codes repress unruly drives for sex and power by filtering them through hypnotic illusions, and they support the capitalist ideology of the ruling class.[35] For such theorists semiotics is not a neutral ("pure") science but a political instrument. They want viewers to notice how codes operate so that they can resist, even act against, cultural exploitation.

It remains to be seen whether semiotics can construct its comprehensive film model or use it to change behavior. The theorists themselves are not naive about the massive task facing them. They take their cue from Christian Metz, who may revise or even reject his own previously expressed ideas from essay to essay, for "it is the nature of intellectual investigation to be progressive and, of semiotics, to be a work of patience."[36] Working initially from a concern for the languagelike structure of movie continuity, Metz has spearheaded the most rigorous approach so far to the nature and impact of movie communication.

SUMMARY

The movement of the shutter and of the camera, as well as the film's capacity to be edited, allow the filmmaker to sequence events in a stylized experience of time called continuity. Working with shutter and camera movement, the filmmaker alters the apparent time of recorded events, uses different angles of view, or lets the camera run in long takes, during which it may move about. These techniques emphasize the recorded aspect of continuity, using rhythms within shots. By cutting the film, the filmmaker controls the relations between shots, creating trick effects or building long, medium, and close shots into edited sequences. These techniques emphasize the constructed aspects of continuity, using the rhythms and tempos between shots.

Film history shows us three major traditions of constructed techniques. Trickery creates apparently recorded continuities that are really constructs. The standardized editing approach, most clearly represented by the Hollywood studio system of the thirties and forties, uses soft, "invisible" cuts that pull the viewer into the action. It more evenly balances the powers of recorded and constructed techniques. Montage, rising from European political and psychological contexts, more noticeably analyzes the action; it may even comment on the action in passages with hard cuts between rapid shots. Montage places more obvious weight on the impact of constructed continuity. These three traditions have intertwined so that, particularly since 1950, all three may be found in a single movie.

Constructed continuity has had a strong influence on critical theory. The formative school of theorists stresses that editing and montage are crucial in making movies an art: they divert us from mere records of events to unique forms of experience. The semiotic school stresses that editing and montage are crucial in making movies a true languagelike system, building a grammar of signs in ways similar to verbal language's structure of words. Semiotics has used constructed continuity as the first step toward building a comprehensive model that will describe how a movie signifies all its meanings to an audience. Within both schools, however, thinkers have had to deal with the strong impact of recorded continuity. They suggest that a movie's meanings come just as much from what the filmmaker does within shots as between them.

Continuity's play with space in time, varying from the transparent to the obvious, involves us in a variety of changing rhythms and tempos. This complex experience of movie time is another major contribution to the fascination of movies.

NOTES

1 There are special cameras that record images at 18,000 fps or more. They use a rotating prism to "spray" images onto the film, for a conventional claw mechanism would melt at such speed. They provide an extremely slow motion, useful for analyzing high-speed objects like bullets or atomic particles. At 18,000 fps a one-minute horse race would take twelve and a half hours to run through a standard projector.

2 For an old projectionist's information on this, see Walter Kerr's *The Silent Clowns* (New York: Knopf, 1975), p. 36.

3 For a full discussion of this, see Gregory Battcock's "Four Films by Andy Warhol," in *The New American Cinema*, ed. Battcock (New York: Dutton, 1967), pp. 233–252.

4 François Truffaut, *Hitchcock* (New York: Simon and Schuster, 1966), p. 134.

5 *Hitchcock*, p. 134.

6 C. W. Ceram, *Archaeology of the Cinema* (New York: Harcourt, Brace & World, 1965), p. 151.

7 Gordon Hendricks illustrates Clark's trick in *The Kinetoscope* (New York: Beginnings of the American Film, 1966), pp. 137–140, illus. 31.

8 Jay Leyda, *Kino: A History of the Russian and Soviet Film* (New York: Collier, 1960), p. 164.

9 Leyda, p. 165.

10 Andrew Tudor uses the climax of *The Wild Bunch* to illustrate Eisensteinian montage in *Theories of Film* (New York: Viking, 1973), pp. 49–58.

11 *Godard on Godard*, trans. Tom Milne (New York: Viking, 1968), p. 173.

12 Richard Roud, *Godard* (Garden City, N.Y.: Doubleday, 1968), pp. 97–98.

13 *Theory of the Film*, trans. Edith Bone (London: Dobson, 1952); *Film as Art* (London: Faber, 1958); *The Film Sense* and *Film Form*, ed. and trans. Jay Leyda (New York: Harcourt-Brace, 1942 and 1949). Meridian Books, New York, published a combined edition of the Eisenstein works in 1957.

14 Arnheim, p. 109.

15 Balázs, p. 46.

16 "Colour Film," in *Movies and Methods*, ed. Bill Nichols (Berkeley: University of California, 1976), p. 386. Originally published in *Notes of a Film Director* (New York: Dover, 1970).

17 *Film Form*, pp. 69–83.

18 J. Dudley Andrew, *The Major Film Theories*, pp. 48 and 158.

19 Arnheim, pp. 79, 80, and 183–189.

20 Arnheim, pp. 103 and 104.

21 For condensed discussions of synesthesia, see Andrew, p. 49; and Peter Wollen, *Signs and Meaning in the Cinema* (Bloomington: Indiana University, 1969), pp. 50–59.

22 Arnheim, p. 98.

23 *Art and Visual Perception* (Berkeley: University of California, 1967), p. 31; also see Andrew, pp. 39–40.

24 Balázs, pp. 60–66.

25 Andrew, pp. 61–67.

26 Saussure, *Cours de linguistique générale* (Paris: Payot, 1916); English ed. *Course in General Linguistics*, trans. Wade Baskin (New York: Philosophical Library, 1959). Peirce, *Collected Papers of Charles Sanders Peirce*, ed. Charles Hartshorne, Paul Weiss, and Arthur W. Burks, 8 vols. (Cambridge: Harvard, 1931–1958).

27 Roland Barthes, *Elements of Semiology*, trans. Annette Lavers and Colin Smith (New York: Hill and Wang, 1967). Also quoted in *Cinema*, 31 (Spring 1972), p. 41.

28 Barthes, p. 63.

29 Barthes, p. 60.

30 Christian Metz, *Film Language: A Semiotics of the Cinema*, trans. Michael Taylor (New York: Oxford, 1974), pp. 119–146.

31 "Articulations of the Cinematic Code," in *Movies and Methods*, pp. 590–607.

32 "Style, Grammar and the Movies," in *Movies and Methods*, pp. 607–628.

33 *S/Z*, trans. Richard Miller (London: Cape, 1975), pp. 4–10.

34 "The Anatomy of a Proletarian Film: Warner's *Marked Woman*," *Film Quarterly*, 27 (Winter 1973–1974), 10–24.

35 Andrew, pp. 237–241.

36 Metz, p. 133.

Chapter 5 / Sound

So far, we have been discussing movies in terms of visual experience. They involve aural experience as well. Movement, spatial design, and continuity operate in relation to sound in the form of dialogue, music, and sound effects.

It was a while before sound could be precisely synchronized with the movie mechanism, but sound was involved with movies from the start. Emile Reynaud created sound effects inside his apparatus. Thomas Edison wanted movies to accompany his phonograph. During the so-called Silent Period, theaters provided live music and sometimes sound effects for the movies (Fig. 5.1), and various inventors kept experimenting with different systems for synchronizing speech. The most dramatic change came in 1928. Great numbers of the public wanted movies to talk. The sound that swayed opinion was poor and clumsy, but people desired it—and once again, as with the movie craze of the 1890s, showmen and technicians clamored to answer the new expectations and keep them alive.

Since then, sound has become fully integrated into the movie experience. It is an added device of technology that the filmmaker applies to create another range of effects. This chapter deals with this movie sound.

THE TECHNOLOGY OF SOUND

Sound occurs when a vibrating body (a string, reed, or vocal chord) sets up oscillations of energy in the molecules of a medium of communication (air, water, or a solid). The molecules form a series of waves. These *sound waves* have *amplitude* (the height of their peaks) and *length* (the distance between peaks) while moving in a given direction at speeds of around 1,125 feet per second (Fig. 5.2).[1] Technology has developed mechanical systems for recording these waves, and so the filmmaker has been enabled to manipulate sound through various techniques. Let's consider the structure of sound waves, to clarify some familiar qualities of sound, before moving on to technology's systems and filmmakers' techniques.

The Structure of Sound

Amplitude determines the *loudness* of a sound, measured in decibels (dB). The sound's amplitude will gradually decrease, or attenuate, as the wave continues, so that in everyday experience we tend to associate amplitude with a sound's distance: the louder the sound, the closer it seems to be.

A sound's wavelength determines the number, or frequency, of waves moving per second at the set speed, and this establishes the *pitch*, or tone, of the sound. A

143

low note, for example, has a longer wavelength and so a lower frequency of waves—described as *cycles per second* (cps) or *Hertz* (Hz), after the famous radio physicist, Heinrich Rudolph Hertz. Middle C is about 262 Hz; the A below it is 220 Hz. A loud note has a higher wave crest (amplitude) than a soft one, but the same frequency of waves (Fig. 5.3). If you double (or halve) the number of waves per second, you raise (or lower) a pitch by what is known in music as an octave.[2]

Only laboratory tuning forks produce such pure tones, however. Everyday sounds are complex tones. They have a fundamental pitch, the basic tone, whose vibrations give rise to several *harmonics*, or *overtones* that are multiples of the basic

5.1 Music for a silent movie. A page from a piano score for *The Hunchback of Notre Dame* (1923). The movie is divided into numbered segments, each with a musical theme. D indicates a dramatic cue signaling a new theme; T indicates an onscreen title signaling a new theme.

5.2 Basic wave pattern.

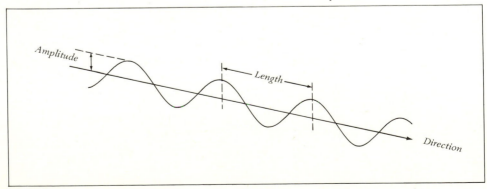

wavelength. For example, an A of 220 Hz has harmonics of 440 Hz, 660 Hz, 880 Hz, 1100 Hz, 1320 Hz, and so forth. The particular overtones that are most noticeable in a particular A depend on the sound's source. A contralto's A is fundamentally the same note as a baritone's, a tuba's or a violin's—but the metal horn,' the wooden sound board, and the resonating chambers of the woman's and the man's skulls reinforce different overtones and therefore produce different sound qualities. A sound's distinctive quality is its *timbre*.

Pitch and timbre have much to do with the mood or character conveyed by music or voices. A high-pitched violin can be said to "shriek," and a low-pitched, deeply resonant cello is "sad." Peculiar timbres—with squeaks, rasps, or gravelly qualities, for example—can make people sound comical; an overly precise enunciation or exaggerated resonance in an ordinary situation may suggest' a phony or pompous person.

Disorganized sound, or *noise*, lacks clear harmonic relations between tones. A breaking plate and the roar of a subway train are common examples. Some sounds that we consider noise—such as horns, sirens, and airplane motors—may by themselves exhibit some harmonic structure. The line between noise and harmony is not always neat.

Sounds come to us, then, in a complex *system* of waves, or oscillations, that provide volume, pitch, harmonic timbre, and noise. A sound wave strikes an

5.3 Amplitude and wavelength. The amplitude, or height, of a sound wave determines loudness; wavelength (Hz) determines pitch. A doubled wavelength is an octave higher in pitch.

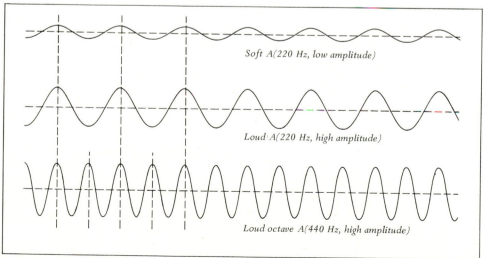

Soft A(220 Hz, low amplitude)

Loud A(220 Hz, high amplitude)

Loud octave A(440 Hz, high amplitude)

eardrum, causing it to vibrate in the same pattern, and the movements are transmitted through the fluid-filled canals of the cochlea, an organ that translates the vibrations into impulses picked up by the auditory nerve and conducted to the brain. This system is versatile, and humans can hear tones from about 20 to 20,000 Hz within a 120-dB range of amplitudes. Our hearing system is also selective, for we can direct it to sounds that draw our attention. We can ignore outside sounds when talking with friends or studying. If you stop and listen now, for example, you will probably pick up sounds that you did not notice before reading this sentence.

Technology found ways to *mechanize* this human system, converting its wave motions into modulations of electricity and light. These mechanical systems are less versatile than the human system. They handle at best about a 50-dB range of amplitude, and record sounds with absolute objectivity. In using them, a filmmaker must limit the range of tone and amplitude to avoid distortion and must find various means to select and emphasize important sounds. The filmmaker can create a precise, consistent, and stylized experience—a heightened sound to accompany a stylized visual experience.

Recording Systems

The evolution of sound recording systems shows the same corporate invention and squabbles over patent rights that marked the evolution of the movie mechanism. We find the essential concept of all the systems in various nineteenth-century instruments for transmitting sound. These instruments translated, or encoded, sound waves into some channel of communication through which they could be transmitted and then decoded. For example, in the telephone, invented about 1876, sound waves strike a diaphragm in a mouthpiece, causing a magnet to fluctuate and send alternating electric current through a wire. Radio, whose fundamental principles were known by 1888, converts sound waves into electromagnetic energy and transmits them through space.

Sound recording systems encode sound into some kind of relatively permanent form from which one may decode the sound at any time. The phonograph introduced the masses to recorded sound in 1877. Edison derived his phonograph ("sound writing") from scientific instruments that measured sound waves. When he directed sound into a large speaker horn, the sound waves would set in motion a diaphragm to which a stylus was attached, and the stylus left a graph of the sound on a moving cylinder. Edison discovered that when one placed the stylus (or needle, as it soon became known) in the grooves of a graph made on tinfoil, the stylus vibrated,

5.4 The sound system of an early phonograph.

activating the diaphragm and playing the sound back out the speaker (Fig. 5.4). Later, others replaced the tinfoil with wax, from which durable copies could be made; eventually discs replaced the original cylinders.

Well before the movies arrived, then, listening to records was a popular pastime, and it is not surprising that Edison first thought of motion pictures as something to synchronize with sound, not the other way around. But the phonograph's huge "morning glory" speaker did not provide enough volume. A performer would have to speak directly into it, so that it would appear in the camera's shot; when the sound was played back it was too feeble even for a small movie house. The dream of sound movies had to wait for inventors to solve the problem of *amplification*, and very soon they did.

Prior to 1912, neither telephones nor radio communicated for very long distances, because the transmissions soon lost the little amplitude they had to begin with. But experimenters discovered a peculiar power in the *Audion tube*, or triode, a device Lee De Forest had invented earlier to strengthen radio signals. When he fed part of the triode's current back into the tube, the Audion amplified the signals a thousand times; after further adjustments to the feedback, the Audion transmitted

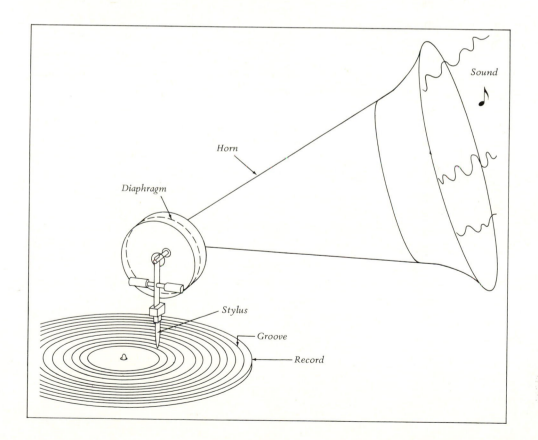

the strengthened waves. It was another corporate achievement. De Forest claimed to have invented the feedback circuit, but many feel that Edwin Howard Armstrong, who discovered feedback in 1912, probably understood its principle better than De Forest did.[3]

The Audion tube and feedback circuitry marked the beginning of long-distance telephoning and of modern broadcasting, and they opened the way to practical systems for synchronizing sound with movies. One system in particular, built from Edison's original dream of sound on disc, had much to do with rousing public desire for sound movies. Western Electric created what was considered a practical sound-on-disc system for motion pictures and in 1926 formed the Vitaphone Corporation with Warner Brothers to make movies employing the process. Vitaphone was to contribute another legendary event in film history.

At first, Warner Brothers used Vitaphone only for music. A New York audience heard it for the first time on August 6, 1926, in eight short subjects and in *Don Juan,* a feature. Elsewhere Vitaphone was not very successful—probably because few theaters risked buying the expensive sound equipment (estimated to cost between ten and twenty thousand dollars), so that most people saw *Don Juan* in the usual silent version with live music. Warner Brothers continued the experiment, releasing *The Better 'Ole* late in 1926, then *The Jazz Singer* on October 6, 1927. It featured Al Jolson, one of vaudeville's most popular stars, in what was essentially a silent movie with a recorded score and a few recorded songs. Just before the first song, Jolson blurted out, "Wait a minute! Wait a minute! You ain't heard nothin' yet!" It was his trademark line from vaudeville, and this spoken line excited the audience as no previous sound experiments had done. By this time, too, Warners had installed many more sound systems in theaters, so that *The Jazz Singer* reached great numbers of people as a "talkie." Its success convinced more theaters to convert, and Warners cast Jolson in a truly *all*-talking picture, *The Singing Fool,* released in September 1928. At the close of the next fiscal year Warner Brothers, until then a minor studio, showed the film industry's greatest net gain: a profit of $17 million, an incredible increase of 745 percent over the previous year. The Sound Era of the movies had arrived.

Ironically, the instrument of the revolution was soon discarded. The sound-on-disc system was entirely too clumsy. Projectionists had to synchronize a sixteen-inch record with each reel of film, but they might either miss the mark on the record or synchronize reels with the wrong records. Any reel of film that broke and was respliced was missing a few frames and would lose sync at the splice. The projectionist had to change projector speed to correct synchronization problems. It is hard to imagine the system working well for long—but it *did* work long enough to have great historical impact. By 1931, the movie industry discarded sound on disc as too unwieldy. Movies today use two other systems that are far more practical: optical and magnetic recording.

The Optical System: Sound on Film   Light affects certain metals in peculiar ways. It turns silver salts black, making photography possible. It also causes certain alkali metals to emit a flow of electrons—that is, electricity. Inventors exploited both reactions to record sound with light. If a sound wave can create fluctuations in a beam of light, (1) it can leave a record, or *optical sound track*, on a photographic emulsion; and (2) when light is played back through that track onto a sensitive metal in a *photoelectric cell*, the metal's reaction converts the light into sound by the speaker's diaphragm. This is the optical system for recording and playing back sound.

As early as the 1870s, Alexander Graham Bell and others had experimented with transmitting telephone messages by light, and by 1906, Eugene A. Lauste had patented an efficient apparatus for recording sound on film. Like other unheralded inventors, Lauste could not get the capital he needed to continue experimenting. Lee De Forest incorporated the work of other inventors into an optical system he patented in 1921. Theodore W. Case collaborated for a while with De Forest and, with Earl I. Sponable, built an improved system. And in Germany, inventors Josef Engl, Joseph Massolle, and Hans Vogt developed an improved photoelectric cell for their Tri-Ergon system. Some movie studios experimented with sound-on-film movies, and in 1926, William Fox, owner of Fox Pictures, decided to give major attention to them, gambling that they had more future than sound-on-disc movies. Fox set up the Fox-Case Corporation with Case and bought up the Tri-Ergon patents. All this led finally to ten years of wrangling over patents; but Fox's hunch was right, for optical sound became the movie industry's standard system. Today it creates the sound you usually experience in movie theaters.

In Figs. 5.5 through 5.7 you can follow the details of the optical system developed from Lauste, De Forest, Case, the Tri-Ergon inventors, and many others. In the *optical recorder*, sound waves leave a track of light on moving film by one of two basic methods. In one (Fig. 5.5), the microphone's vibrating diaphragm creates fluctuating electricity, much as in a telephone. These fluctuations affect a "light valve" that opens and closes, leaving what is called a *variable density track* on the film. In another method (Fig. 5.6) the microphone's diaphragm affects a mirror that rotates with the variations of sound, leaving a *variable area track*.

An *optical sound projector* re-creates the original sounds from any optical track by the method pictured in Figure 5.7. After the film has passed through the projector gate, it passes over a *sound drum*. The drum ensures that the film moves smoothly, without the variations in speed that cause distortions ("wows"). The film moves past a small *exciter lamp*, which beams light through the sound track. The variations of density or area in the track cause modulations, or fluctuations, in the waves of light—re-creations of the light movements that made the track. This *modulated* light then falls on a *photoelectric cell*, which converts the modulations of light into fluctuations of electricity. These then pass through an *amplifier*, cause the diaphragm of a *speaker* to vibrate, and thereby re-create the original sound.

The optical system has great efficiency because it uses *film*. The track is joined with the pictures, and the playback mechanism is joined to the projector. Synchronization is precise and invariable, because on the film a particular sound is permanently related to the frame of action where the sound is made. If we lose portions of the visual continuity through breaks and resplicing, we lose portions of the sound track, too; but what is left of the whole movie remains synchronized.[4]

Professional filmmakers usually record and edit images and sounds separately from each other, bringing them together onto the same piece of film only when the movie is ready for release. During the 1930s and 1940s sound editors worked with strips of film, just as continuity editors did, because all sound recording was optical. In the 1950s this procedure changed, because a more manageable material appeared: magnetic tape.

The Magnetic System: Sound on Tape   The principle of modern tape recording dates from a discovery by Danish inventor Valdemar Poulsen in 1898. When passed into an

5.5 Variable density soundtrack.

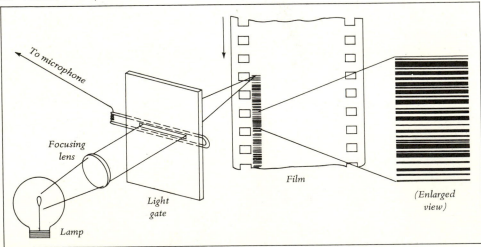

To microphone

Focusing
lens

Light
gate

Lamp

Film

*(Enlarged
view)*

electromagnet, a modulated electric current will give off modulations of magnetic force, which can be picked up and stored by a strip of metal passed over the magnet. Some of the inventors working on movie sound tried to develop magnetic systems using wire, but with little success. It was not until after 1945, when American sound engineers became aware of the significant improvements made by German technicians during World War II, that magnetic recording became a practical option for the film industry.[5]

5.6 Variable area soundtrack.

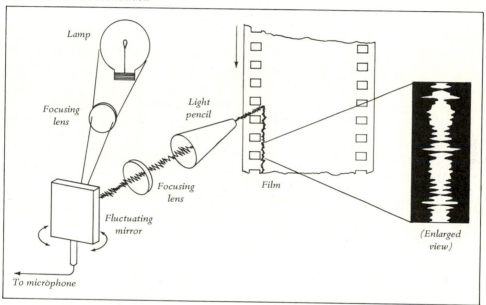

5.7 Optical sound projector system.

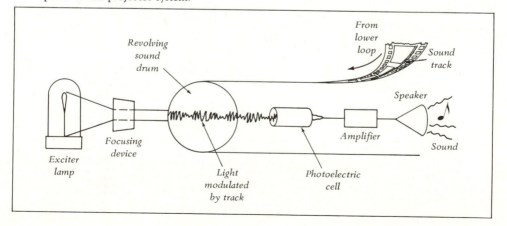

The material used in such recording is plastic tape thinly coated on one side with iron oxide (Fig. 5.8). The same tape (in varying widths) is used in all audio and video tape recorders. For recording, the tape passes over the *recording head,* an electromagnet wired to a microphone. The microphone changes the sound waves to electrical variations, as usual; the recording head gives these off as magnetic modulations; and the iron oxide stores them in a *magnetic sound track.* An additional electromagnet, the *erase head,* carries an inaudible signal and is placed before the recording head to remove any previously stored signal from the tape. For replay, the tape passes over the *playback head,* an electromagnet wired to a speaker. The recording process is now reversed, with the stored modulations going from a magnetic to an electrical to a sound signal. The tape will retain the signal for years unless it is erased.[6]

The development of magnetic tape came just a little ahead of what can be called the solid-state revolution in electronics. For years, the Audion amplifier and its descendants operated by vacuum tubes that were roughly the size of light bulbs. But by 1948, three engineers at the Bell Laboratories—John Bardeen, W. H. Brattain, and William Shockley—had developed the *transistor,* which transmits electrons in solid materials through chemical interactions. Tougher and more efficient than the Audion, the transistor was roughly the size of a very thinly sliced pencil. And it was only the beginning. By 1959 several dozen electronic components were being fitted into a single *integrated circuit* no larger than a pinhead. This revolution has ushered in a new era of portable electronic devices—everything from space satellites to pocket calculators.

Tape and solid-state technology have given filmmakers easily portable equipment that produces high quality sound and can be handled efficiently. Lightweight tape recorders have replaced cumbersome equipment for recording and editing sound, and sometimes magnetic tape replaces the optical track on the film itself. Let's outline the options that sound on tape provides the modern filmmaker.

The most popular sound technique is to record and edit picture and sound separately. This is *double system* filmmaking (Fig. 5.9). It is the same procedure followed in the thirties and forties, except that magnetic tape is now used to record and edit all the sound. When final editing is completed, the separate magnetic track is usually converted into an optical track and joined with the edited pictures.

It is also possible to put a magnetic track directly onto the film. A strip of iron oxide, called a *mag stripe,* replaces the optical track, and the film runs through a

5.9 Double-system filmmaking. Sound and picture are recorded separately but off the same electrical source to maintain camera and recorder at exactly the same speed.

magnetic sound projector. The film industry has used mag-striped prints for super productions in 70 mm with stereophonic sound. As many as six separate magnetic tracks may be laid on a 70-mm format. The tracks run to different speakers in the theater, so that, for example, when an auto moves from left to right in the background of a shot, the audience first hears it on the far left before it appears, then on across the auditorium and off right, each speaker in turn picking up the sound (Fig. 5.10). This is the film industry's most elaborate sound technique.

Mag-striped film has also made good *single system* filmmaking possible. In single system, the camera records both picture and sound onto the film at the same time (Fig. 5.11). The filmmaker uses film with a single mag stripe, running it in a camera equipped with a magnetic recording head connected to a microphone. The head lays a magnetic track onto the tape as the film is being exposed. After processing, the film is ready for projection with sound.

5.8 Magnetic sound system. a. For recording. b. For playback.

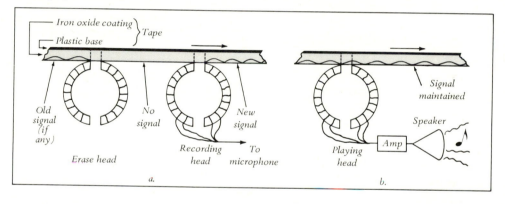

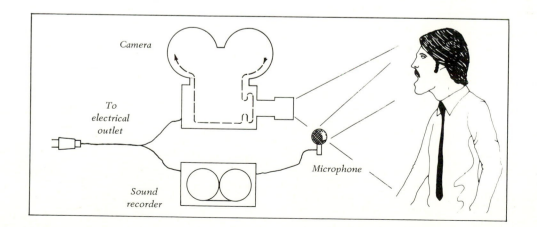

There are great advantages to single system, but one built-in drawback. The necessary separation between the aperture and the sound recorder places any cut into a shot one or two seconds away from the corresponding sound, depending on the film format. This tends to eliminate tight or intricate editing of images. It is possible to transfer the original sound onto a separate tape, edit it, then transfer it back onto the mag stripe—but this reduces quality. Filmmakers drawn to single system, however—

5.10 70-mm film with six magnetic sound-tracks. One of the six tracks is used to cue the other five to different speakers.

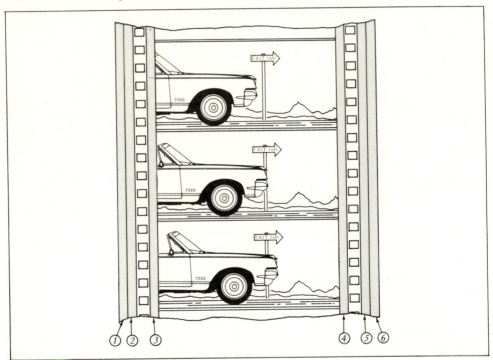

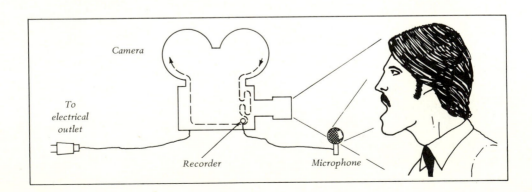

like documentarists or newspersons—are less concerned with editing effects than with recording important information. Portable single-system gear has pushed filmmaking into corners never imagined at the beginning of the sound revolution.

Most professional filmmaking is still double system—in fact, single systems are not available in formats larger than 16 mm. And most entertainment movies are still shown with optical, not magnetic sound. Since the sixties, the use of magnetic stereo has declined because of the expense required to produce it. The future of stereo seems to lie in the *Dolby stereophonic system,* introduced in 1977, which uses multiple optical tracks in much the same way that magnetic stereo does.

In the realm of sound, as in the visual areas of the film experience, advances in technology have given filmmakers a versatile medium and a wide range of options. From the range available at a given time, the filmmaker makes particular choices, applying the technology to create a particular kind of stylized sound. Let's now consider what that entails.

APPLYING THE TECHNOLOGY

Our experiences of sound fall into three general categories: speech, music, and everything else. In ordinary situations our ears take in a wide range of all these sounds, but the brain is always selecting what is important among them. For example, when we talk with a friend we ignore music playing on the radio, but the ringing of a telephone will get our immediate attention. In movies the filmmaker is dealing with a purely mechanical, nonselective system. The recorder's microphone will give equal attention to friend, music, and telephone, so that on the sound track we may not be able to tell which is more important. The filmmaker must do the selecting for us, applying the technology to create an environment of sound and to emphasize the most important sounds at given moments.

To understand this creative process better, let's break it up into some basic categories. Speech, music, and other sounds in the movies will appear to have a source that is visible or implied in the action we see on screen or a source outside that action. The one form of sound is *actual* or synchronous, since it occurs in exactly the same time frame as the visible action. The other is *commentative,* or nonsynchronous sound.[7]

Actual speech is *dialogue:* the speech or other meaningful vocal sounds (grunts, chuckles) of on-screen characters. Commentative speech is *narration* or *commentary:* off-screen speech, or voice-over, as it is popularly termed. *Actual music* has a source

◄ 5.11 Single-system filmmaking. Sound and picture are recorded together onto the same piece of film.

in the frame of action—for example, a visible orchestra or the radio a character turns on. *Background music,* that conventional device borrowed from nineteenth-century theater, provides moods or extra emphasis with no source in the movie action itself. *Sound effects* are all other sounds that go to round out an environment. They are usually actual sounds (animals, machines, thunder, crickets, crowds), but there are also commentative effects: artificially produced sounds (electronic modulations, unidentifiable squeaks) that operate like background music, coming from nowhere to provide moods or emphasis.

These are the elements from which filmmakers construct movie sound. One filmmaker may choose to keep a movie as realistic as possible, blending and emphasizing different actual sounds in close imitation of the human ear. This approach is what we have been calling transparent, or unobtrusive, technique. Another filmmaker, wanting a very stylized environment, may emphasize nonsynchronous sounds, in effect separating visual and aural impact in the viewer's awareness. This is opaque, or obtrusive, technique. Most movies land between the extremes: they have certain stylizations (background music being the common example) but an overall sense of actuality.

Whatever a particular movie's style of sound, the filmmaker has had to manipulate an available technology to achieve it. The movie's sound, like its visual technique, will show the marks of its period, whether the filmmaker has opted to be transparent or obvious in manipulating the sound. It is useful, then, to break this discussion of applied technology into three basic periods, during which sound technology presented problems, then efficiency, then fluidity.

Early Sound, 1927–1932

Sound recording brought chaos to movie crews and casts primarily because it required silence, whereas silent moviemaking had allowed for a lot of sound on the set. Directors instructed performers *as* they acted, and there was live music on most sets to provide the proper mood while the cameras whirred and the arc lights hummed (Fig. 5.12). With sound came a large, cumbersome microphone that picked up sounds from all directions. Technicians placed them as close to performers as possible and shielded them from other sounds on the set. That ended vocal direction and mood music. Cameras and cameramen resorted to large soundproof boxes called blimps, where no camera movement was possible and temperatures rose to 120°. Desperate technicians hid the microphones in potted plants or telephones to get as good a sound as possible, and sound effects personnel hovered just out of camera range to provide environment.

5.12 A silent movie set with accompanying music.

You can get a good idea of the chaos by looking at *Singin' in the Rain* (1952), a musical comedy about the early days of sound. Though obviously spoofing its troubles, the movie is quite accurate about a period of filmmaking that its critics described as "canned theater." As on the stage, sounds had to be put together during the live performance. They were fed into a single optical sound recorder. Just when the camera had developed into a highly mobile instrument, sound anchored it in place as though time had jumped back to 1895.

Sunny Side Up (1929), a musical comedy from that day, shows us canned theater's technical and stylistic problems. Performers project their voices loudly, playing to the insensitive microphone. The microphone gives their voices a light, airy quality, a distinctive timbre that changed as microphones improved. Shots have been taken simultaneously by several blimped cameras with different lenses, making three-shot editing possible, and background music and dialogue have been recorded at the same time. It looks at times as though the camera is simply recording a stage performance. But the moviemakers are also trying to overcome some of the limitations imposed on them. The opening scene uses a surprising crane shot that moves through a crowded tenement street and then along upstairs windows, recording several different bits of dialogue. To achieve this, director David Butler had to "conduct" the entire set like an orchestra. As the camera moved from one scene to

another, the performers would "fade out" and "fade in" their voices, so that the dialogue of the on-screen action at that moment was always the loudest sound recorded by the single microphone. Butler's technique does not overcome the movie's generally stagey look, but it shows us one attempt to break away from the restrictions imposed by sound equipment.

In other films of this period we can note a range of techniques running from the conservative to the innovative. *Grand Hotel* (1932), a very successful movie made by MGM, shows a conservative approach. It is rich in stars—John and Lionel Barrymore, Greta Garbo, and Joan Crawford—who handle the melodramatic material with rather exaggerated diction and gestures. The movie sticks to the basic power of canned theater: presenting strong personalities in very theatrical performances. For *Love Parade* (1929), on the other hand, director Ernst Lubitsch wanted to make the continuity more fluid than the conservative theatrical approach allowed. In one scene, for example, he cross-cuts between two different couples singing the same duet—and to do this he had to shoot both couples simultaneously from two blimped cameras on two separate sets in the sound stage as a live orchestra played off camera. For *Blackmail* (1929) director Alfred Hitchcock tried another method. He had an actress mouth her dialogue on camera while another actress spoke the lines into an off-camera microphone. This provided better sound and somewhat freer, more realistic action.

Other filmmakers simply ignored the illusion of captured reality. For example, French director René Clair argued for what he called "asynchronous sound." He deliberately destroyed the realistic connection between sound and picture. In his *À nous la liberté* (1932) a flower sings, and the sound of a woman's voice suddenly runs down because, as the movie then reveals, it comes from a nearby record player. In Clair's *Le million* (1931) a bass drum booms when one character hits another, and the sounds of a football game accompany a big brawl in a theater. Such obvious playfulness was not so evident in American filmmakers of this period, though director Rouben Mamoulian was one exception. For *Dr. Jekyll and Mr. Hyde* (1932) he created a mixture of unrelated sounds, including his own heartbeat, to accompany Jekyll's transformation into the monstrous Hyde. It was called "Mamoulian's stew" at the time, and it opened the way to the use of artificial effects on sound tracks.

Because of the clumsy technology, the sound in any film from this period may seem peculiar or stilted to us today, and so become obtrusive whether the filmmaker intended it that way or not. The films still show a range of creative variation, and the major problems were soon to be overcome.

5.13 A barney in use, around 1934. Note that the microphone is still large and cumbersome and that the performers are playing to it.

Sound from 1933 to 1949

In this period emerged the clear, complex sound tracks that one considers typical of the modern sound movie. Several technological refinements made this possible. The large, omnidirectional microphones gradually gave way to smaller ones able to pick up sounds within a narrower, more manageable range. The huge blimps were replaced with "barneys," soundproof coverings of metal and later padded cloth that fit over the camera housing, allowing the camera to move as freely as it had before sound (Fig. 5.13). And, probably the most important single achievement, the development of noise suppressers made it possible to blend several separate sound tracks together onto one track: a crucial technique known as *mixing*.

Mixing sound tracks separate from the pictures had been tried from the start of the sound revolution, but the first optical recording systems gave off so much background noise that when one added tracks together (say, background music or sound effects to dialogue) the accumulated noise became too loud and hurt sound quality. You can hear the results in Laurel and Hardy's *Helpmates* (1931) or *The Music Box* (1932). Sound tracks were generally kept simple, with any blending done on the set—as in *Sunny Side Up* and *Love Parade*.

Technicians soon developed noise suppressers, and by 1933 filmmakers were creating mixed tracks according to a system that is standard filmmaking procedure

today (Fig. 5.14).[8] The various sound components are recorded onto a *dialogue track*, a *music track*, and an *effects track*. Each track may itself be constructed of several separate recordings. There may also be a *presence track*, a recording of sounds that a particular environment gives off by itself (the rustlings of people in an auditorium, the hush of a still night, the "presence" you can hear now if you stop reading and listen). The filmmaker mixes these tracks together to create an appropriate sound environment that is recorded onto one track and joined to the pictures.

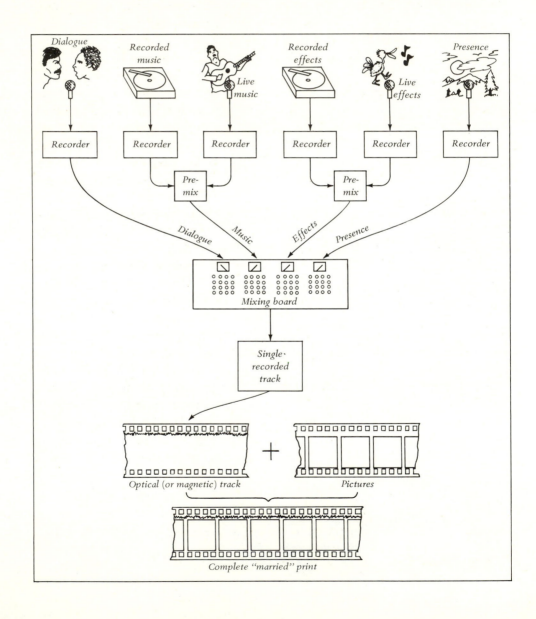

Mixing gives the filmmaker total control. We referred earlier to the selective quality of human hearing. The effect can be imitated on a mixed track through electronic selection. If two characters in a movie say important things beside a street, we hear traffic noises *under* their speech (on the dialogue track); and if at some moment the traffic (on the effects track) becomes important—say, a truck threatens to run down one character—then that sound will suddenly come *over* everything else.

Mixing provides very "clean" sound: each element of the track is recorded under flawless conditions. Even before noise suppressers, filmmakers had tried whenever possible to record dialogue completely separate from action, so that performers would be close to the microphone and perhaps in a sound booth for the finest quality. We noted Hitchcock's experiment in *Blackmail*. One reason for the popularity of musicals was that a musical number could be prerecorded, then played on the set when the number was shot. This practice, called *prescoring*, freed the camera nicely but did not work well with nonmusical scenes. With the advent of mixing, it became easier to *dub* or *postsynchronize*—to record dialogue *after* the pictures were shot and edited. The performers return for "looping" sessions in a sound booth. The film is broken into segments, each of which is joined in a loop so that it runs continuously in the projector. The performers repeat the scripted dialogue, cuing their voices to the silent images until the synchronization and inflections suit the director. This dubbed sound then constitutes the dialogue track. Studios try to record as much good dialogue as possible directly on the set, since dubbing is expensive and time consuming, but dubbing allows the cleanest possible dialogue.

During the thirties American studios perfected techniques that are now typical devices of classic filmmaking. To appreciate them, it may be helpful to think of them as *aural equivalents of visual devices*. We have noted, for example, how one sound can suddenly come over another on the track. This is a kind of *sound cut*, a change of emphasis. Such cuts are generally unobtrusive. We watch characters in an extreme long shot, for example, without noticing that their voices sound as though they are right next to us in the theater. A more obtrusive sound cut is represented by background, or mood, music. It can intrude at a big moment—though it may have been introduced so subtly that we did not notice its presence until that moment. There are sound "dissolves," too, referred to more properly as bridges. A significant sound will carry over from one scene to another, making an implicit connection between what would appear to be different actions without the bridge. Or at any

5.14 Mixing. Until 1949 optical recorders performed all steps of mixing. Today magnetic tape recorders do all the recording, including the mixing of the single, complete track, which usually is then converted to an optical track. But the track may be transferred directly onto a magnetic stripe on the film.

moment a familiar sound can be introduced to remind us of something we have seen and heard earlier: an aural flashback.

Thus, filmmakers in this period perfected what we can speak of as sound editing and sound montage: arrangements of sounds, like images, for either transparent or obtrusive effect. Specifically, this tends to come down to an interplay between actual and commentative sound. The typical American narrative movie blends the two. Dialogue and sound effects, though selectively mixed into a cleaner-than-real world, stem from the scene being shown. On the other hand, background music and voice-over narration are unrealistic devices obtruding into the action, though in practice such devices have become so conventional that we usually don't notice them. During the forties, for example, it was fashionable in underworld movies to have the major character remember the story and comment about it in a voice-over as we watch. *Murder, My Sweet* (1944) and *Double Indemnity* (1944) are good examples of the convention.

The filmmaker's use of conventional devices may surprise us, though. In *The Best Years of Our Lives* (see Chapter 4), for example, a veteran who has become discouraged by his inability to get a good job goes to an airfield lined with wrecked bombers about to be scrapped. He sits in the nose of one, where he used to sit as a bombardier—and we hear the sound of bomber engines gradually building in volume on the track. He is reliving the past. Suddenly someone shouts at him from below, and we come back to the realistic sound we had before. Here the sound track has functioned like the psychological montage we discussed in Chapter 4. It stems from the on-screen action, yet it takes us inside the character's feelings, as a commentary might. A similar surprise occurs in *You Only Live Once* (1937). Eddie Taylor, a young man found guilty of a crime he didn't commit, breaks out of a prison and, in a confused moment, kills a priest who is trying to help him. Eddie is hunted down and finally killed as he is trying to cross into Canada and freedom. At that moment, the voice of the priest is heard on the track, calling "Eddie! You're free! The gates are open!" This voice-over is not simply commentative; it brings the story into a different level of meaning.

French director Jean Renoir is notable for his unconventional use of sound in this period. For one thing, he did not concern himself too much with "clean" sound, preferring to free his actors as much as possible and settle for whatever sound he could get. The quality is rougher, but this provides a documentary quality to the action. Renoir also liked to use music as an integral part of the action, not just for outside moods. *Boudu Saved from Drowning* (1932), the story of a tramp who disrupts the household of a man who saves his life, nicely illustrates Renoir's style. The sound is rather murky by American standards, and the tramp's dialogue is often unintelligible even to those who understand French. Especially in one scene, Renoir plays with the convention of background music. A woman is resisting the tramp's amorous advances, and as she gives in, the camera dollies in on a picture of a trumpet player. The trumpet sounds triumphantly, and we believe that this is a humorous bit of commentative music. But it isn't only that, for as the movie cuts to an outside scene, we discover that the trumpeter is in a marching band—part of a crowd coming to present a reward to the woman's husband for saving the tramp's life.

Orson Welles, who came to movies from radio, had his own ways of playing with sound conventions in this period. In *Citizen Kane* the collapse of one character is signaled noticeably on the sound track by mood music that dies, as though the plug of the recorder had been pulled out. In Welles's *Magnificent Ambersons* (1942) a voice-over narrator who is not part of the action sometimes almost gets into a dialogue with the characters, suggesting what they are going to say—much as a director might do. And Welles is the narrator.

It is also worth pointing out—as many writers have—that filmmakers discovered the value of *silence* once the initial excitement over sound had passed. The swimming pool scene of *The Cat People* (see Chapter 3) gains from the relative absence of sound: we cannot hear or see anything, and this increases the terror. In *Fury* (1936), an embittered man who believes he can live without people is walking in the street when he hears music and voices in a bar. He goes in to join the throng, but the bar is empty and silent. The sound track has again provided psychological montage, but this time with silence.

The distinctiveness and peculiarity of certain sounds—what we discussed above as timbre—came to be fully exploited in this period. The distinctive vocal quality of certain stars marked them: the calm self-reliance of Gary Cooper, the brassiness of Jean Harlow, the Eastern sophistication of Katharine Hepburn, the gutsy arrogance of Jimmy Cagney, the emotional tremolo of Jimmy Stewart, the cool sensuality of Lauren Bacall. Such stars were popular in radio programs like the Lux Radio Theater (which retold movie stories) precisely because their stardom involved timbre, not just looks. And cleanly mixed sound allowed full exploitation of peculiar sounds. It is interesting, for example, to compare *Frankenstein* (1931), the classic monster tale made during the days of clumsy sound, with *The Bride of Frankenstein* (1935). Sound in the first film has little to do with heightening the horror; the film simply records the dialogue of characters involved in pre-eminently visual horror. The second film exploits the bizarre sounds of Dr. Frankenstein's laboratory, the horrendous storm that rages outside when he creates the bride, and the huge explosion that ends the story. The sound has become a real helpmate of the images.

The appeal of filmed theater hung on, most noticeably in the musical, which was frankly theatrical in style. It often dealt with backstage life, and it was full of songs and dances that took place onstage or in stagelike settings. Mixing freed the musical from the limitations of the earlier technology, allowing audiences a visual experience that would never have been possible at an actual Broadway musical; but the film musical kept its allegiance to the stage, as it has down to the present day. The popularity of filmed stage plays continued. Among Hollywood directors, George Cukor stands out as a filmmaker who had great success with theatrical cinema. In films like *Dinner at Eight* (1933), *Holiday* (1938), *The Philadelphia Story* (1940), and *Gaslight* (1944), Cukor transferred popular Broadway plays to the mass film audience. The emphasis was on great performances and dialogue. Near the end of the period Sir Laurence Olivier, an outstanding theatrical figure in his own right, directed and starred in *Henry V* (1946) and *Hamlet* (1948), which attracted a great deal of American attention to Shakespeare. Especially in *Henry V*, Olivier sought to combine the visual display and poetic diction of theater with the exciting potentials of cinema. The movie begins with a documentarylike re-enactment of a performance at Shakespeare's Globe theater, progressing through various rich theatrical settings— some like medieval paintings—arriving at a realistic battle scene in straight cinematic style, and then returning through theatrical settings again to the Globe. Olivier used different styles of sound, too. In some scenes he uses the exaggerated diction we associate with "canned theater." He shifts into quieter delivery for more intimate scenes, and during Henry's soliloquy before the big battle Olivier employs voice-over, so that we hear Henry's musings while watching a silent actor.

Between 1933 and 1949, the movies defined and systematized all the essential techniques available to the sound film. Sound became something to be broken down and reassembled in various ways, like film. Sound became an integral part of the movie experience, providing new levels of shift and balance to attract the audience's attention. Since this period, the sound film has not changed essentially, but it has benefited from improved quality and portability of the equipment.

Sound Since 1950

Just as in the thirties and forties, studios since 1950 have depended on sound stages for many movie scenes, but getting good sound on location by direct recording is easier than it was. Cameras with lightweight barneys move almost anywhere without disturbing sound reception. "Shotgun" microphones with very narrow cones of sensitivity pick up clear dialogue at some distance with little surrounding noise, and wireless microphones can be hidden on performers and picked up by remote control. With the adoption of magnetic tape recording in 1949, sound personnel now hand-carry the equivalents of equipment that used to be pushed around on large dollies.

With such improvements dubbing has become less common. Besides, the independent status of performers, who now sign specific agreements for each film and are not under long-term studio contract, has made it even more expensive to bring performers back after shooting to record dialogue. But dubbing has become crucial to the success of many imported movies. When a foreign movie aims for the largest possible audience, its producers dub all dialogue into English. In Italian productions, in fact, it has long been a policy to dub almost every major film—especially those in which the performers speak several different languages. Aficionados of the foreign film complain about what dubbing does to the tempo and pace of a movie. Voices may sound distant and stilted, and the chances of achieving an accurate translation are very slim, since words are usually matched to vowel and consonant sounds more than to meaning. Unless synchronization is extremely good, dubbing can leave characters looking as though they are talking to each other while strenuously chewing gum. But producers feel that dubbing pays off at the box office.

The new technology has had subtle effects. In narrative movies, the pure sounds provided by the dubbing booth have given way to a more ordinary realism, less technically clean but more suggestive of "caught" reality, with more random background noise. Background music, while still a popular convention, is not taken for granted. Some movies avoid it altogether, using actual music where necessary to support action; others use background music sparingly.

Stereophonic sound has been touted as a new dimension in realism, though in fact it sometimes provides a very obtrusive emphasis. When sound comes from different parts of the theater rather than from behind the screen, as in monophonic sound, it takes sound *away* from the visible action. This is another variation on the possibilities for manipulating sound and space, and many viewers find it very attractive.

Portable movie equipment has greatly benefited newsreel and documentary filmmakers, so that today audiences have been widely exposed to what can be called *direct sound*. It usually goes with existing-light cinematography. The filmmakers must adapt to whatever conditions they find, and they are usually armed with a minimum of equipment. They must select all the important sounds on the spot, often with only one microphone; thus the final sound track may depend almost entirely on one recording. This does not leave out the possibility of music and effects tracks, but most news crews have no time for such nuances, and many documentarists prefer to keep their work as straightforward as possible. There will probably be little or no mixing of tracks and very simple editing—particularly if the original was shot single system.

The result is that direct sound combines with existing-light shooting to create a rough-textured, fuzzy-sounding movie world that audiences associate with untouched reality. To some extent, filmmakers who deal with fictional narrative exploit this illusion of immediacy in image and sound—but almost invariably they create their effects through very sophisticated recording and mixing.

Among American filmmakers, director Robert Altman has a reputation for keeping his sound tracks full of diverse and random sounds, such as one might expect to hear in an on-the-spot recording of a real event. *Nashville* (1975) and *A Wedding* (1978) illustrate the technique. Careful listeners will find that the apparently random background sounds are often neatly related to particular actions. A character offscreen, for example, may say something barely audible that supports or ironically counterpoints the visible action.

Among European filmmakers, French director Jacques Tati stands out for his creation of comical sound environments involving barely audible and apparently random sounds that are in fact carefully constructed. In *Mr. Hulot's Holiday* (1953), about one man's disruption of a summer resort, Tati makes obvious use of a squeaking door, a sputtering auto and a bouncing ping-pong ball to counterpoint the comedy. Less obvious are the fainter background sounds. A woman offscreen says "What's going on here?" in the middle of a comic scene, and Tati uses the quiet wash of waves on the beach to begin and conclude sequences in a subtle aural "dissolve." In *Playtime* (1967), a parody of technologically oriented society, much of the humor is strictly aural: the peculiar buzz of a malfunctioning neon light, the squeak of a man's shoes as he walks down a polished corridor, or the whoosh of a man's nasal spray. Like Renoir, Tati uses actual, not background, music to develop certain scenes—as when he resolves a scene of comic chaos at a restaurant by having one character sit at a piano and play, prompting others to sing together, bringing in a sense of harmony.

Since 1950, new technology has opened up a greater range of options: filmmakers have a far more portable system at their disposal and may readily depart from the cleanliness and conventions of studio sound. But the essential techniques remain the same. In movies our experience of sound, like our experience of continuity, comes about through careful construction as well as through recording. The filmmaker selects and builds a track that, subtly or blatantly, enhances our sense of the power of sound.

SOUND AND CRITICISM

Considering that sound created a revolution in the movie industry, we might expect it to have had great impact on film theory. In fact, theorists today still give far more attention to movies as visual experience, treating sound as an assistant to the visual but not an equal partner. Their assumption is that movies are designed primarily to *move*. Sound should enhance that fact, not compete with it. Otherwise, we get canned theater or, worse, photographed radio. One theorist sums it up: "Film sound has no distinctive qualities in itself, and can be meaningfully discussed only as an adjunct to the visual."[9] Music presents a challenge to that assumption, as we shall see, but, in general, theories of film sound are essentially variations on theories of film imagery, and fall into the two basic schools we discussed in earlier chapters.

Insofar as there was any conscious theorizing behind the invention of the sound movie, it was *realist* in nature. In the terms that André Bazin would use years later, the sound revolution in 1928 was a big, new step toward "that complete illusion of life" desired by the realist theorist.[10] It was precisely this realism that disturbed many filmmakers and performers about the arrival of sound. Mary Pickford, one of America's foremost silent film actresses, gave a nice summary of this antipathy to sound: "It would have been more logical if silent pictures had grown out of the talkie instead of the other way round."[11] Pickford was not a theorist, but she expressed a basic tenet of the *formative school:* cinema is supposed to be different from reality, not a copy of it. From a formative point of view, movies should logically develop by moving away from mere copying, by evolving more and more techniques for stylizing real-life experience—not by reverting to copies again.

After their initial chagrin, however, many filmmakers and theorists began to see that sound need not just duplicate reality. It, too, was a formative instrument. It could be stylized, or—to maintain the emphasis that Bazin himself puts on his theory—it was part of an *illusion of reality*. For example, René Clair, whose silent films had exhibited a strong sense of stylized visual comedy, expressed dismay initially that spectators leaving a talkie "were not plunged into that comfortable numbness which a trip to the land of pure images used to bestow on us. . . . They had not lost the sense of reality."[12] But then he found a way around the problem. He suggested a new "law" of technique: one should not use a sound *simultaneously* with an image of what produces it, but rather *alternate* one with the other. You do not need to see a door slam if you hear it. Image and sound had separate powers, and the filmmaker should organize them into a different experience, not one that maintained strictly natural connections. He acknowledged that one usually had to keep a natural connection between a speaker and the speaker's voice, but even here one should orchestrate voices, much like the conductor of a symphony, in relation to alternated images and sound effects.[13] Clair demonstrated his law in the asynchronous sound of his own movies. It was an extreme technique, and it worked best in comedies; but the theory behind it is the foundation for what still goes on today in any mixed track. The filmmaker selects from among natural sounds, using them in actual and commentative fashion, sometimes maintaining the natural connection, sometimes alternating between strictly visual and strictly auditory impressions.

Sergei Eisenstein had no trouble fitting sound into his concept of dialectical montage. For him sound completed the montage form, which he saw as a means of reconstructing the laws of human thought processes. Thus, the proper material of the sound film was not dialogue between characters, but one person's internal monologue. Sound added one more conflict within the montage sequence, between optical and acoustical experience, leading to what he called audio-visual counterpoint.[14] In practice, Eisenstein did depend on some dialogue in his movies—but it was more typical of him to isolate a character's manner of speech, giving it a uniqueness, so that "dialogue" between characters in an Eisenstein movie is more like interrelated monologues. And this corresponds to his visual design, where continuity is an interrelation of particularized images.

The most precise example of his formative approach to sound is in Eisenstein's writings on movie music. For *Alexander Nevsky* Eisenstein worked with composer Sergei Prokofiev to achieve the audio-visual synchronization he desired. Eisenstein used graphs to show how each shot was arranged to correspond to the musical score. In one shot, for example, (Fig. 5.15) there is a helmeted female soldier prominent in the left third of the frame, a narrow space to her left, and a row of highlighted distant helmets (the X's in the graph) balancing the composition to the right. As the graph shows, Prokofiev's score at that moment used a single eighth note, a chord, then three more eighth notes to create the musical equivalent of the visual design. Eisenstein realized that some might find this formative technique far-fetched. But he argued that just as musical composition involves a movement in time from one note to another, pictorial composition consists of leading the spectator's attention in a movement in time across the screen—and the two movements can be made to coincide in form and emphasis. "We must know," he wrote, "how to grasp the

5.15 Eisenstein's analysis of visual and musical composition.

movement of a given piece of music, locating its path (its line or form) as our foundation for the plastic composition that is to correspond to the music."[15]

Eisenstein made it clear that a theory of the sound film ought to incorporate a theory of film music. Some musicians took up this issue, too. Notable among them was Hanns Eisler, a German composer and theorist who scored a number of American and European movies, including Fritz Lang's *Hangmen Also Die!* (1943), Jean Renoir's *The Woman on the Beach* (1947) and, perhaps his finest work, Alain Resnais's *Night and Fog* (1955). Eisler agreed with Eisenstein that movie music had to be planned objectively and carefully in relation to the images. But he did not agree that music had to be in empathy or correspondence with the imagery. This only contributed to what Eisler felt was the worst tendency of music in movies: its style is neutralized. It has no independence, nor does it express the composer's attitude. It only introduces sounds into a machine that "spits them out again in a digested, blunted, and conventionalized form."[16]

Eisler argued that music should be a genuine element of contrast. He evoked Eisenstein's concept of collision montage and, much like Clair, stressed that there should be a disparity between image and music. In one of his most striking passages, Eisler points out that the talking picture is really not very different from the old silent picture. Speech in movies, he argues, is as artificial and impersonal as the old printed captions, and it is just as separated from the characters' gestures. The two are not

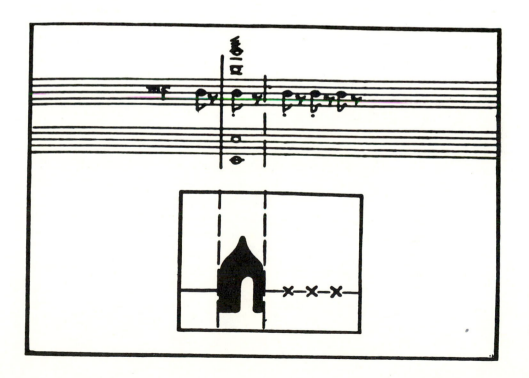

identical at all, and music should not try to express or to duplicate the characters' movements. Like good ballet music, it should supply momentum but remain separate, not expressing the dancers' feelings or aiming at identity with them, but simply summoning the dancers to dance. For Eisler the models for good movie music were the production numbers of musical comedies. "These may be of little musical merit," he admitted, "but they have never served to create the illusion of a unity of the two media or to camouflage the illusionary character of the whole, but functioned as stimulants because they were foreign elements."[17]

Eisler conceded that there were times in a movie when music ought to remain unobtrusive—but it should do so as part of the filmmaker's and the composer's plan. At times it could break in or break off abruptly, not fade out discreetly, and it could rise to completely "outshout" the action, as Eisler put it. To translate Eisler's theory into terms we use throughout this book, he argues for music that shifts in emphasis (balance) with word and picture, creating a sometimes transparent, sometimes intrusive effect.[18] Even more than Eisenstein, he argues for a use of sound that departs from any illusion of reality. In *Night and Fog* we find a model of Eisler's theory at work. The documentary images include no synchronized speech, only a voice-over narrator and Eisler's music. The elements have separate powers, which the movie sometimes fuses or sometimes sets apart, so that our experience of the movie involves an awareness of the independent contribution of each.[19]

Kurt Weill, another German composer, took more of a middle position between the demands of the filmmaker and the muscian. Weill, famous for his collaboration in 1928 with playwright Bertolt Brecht on *The Threepenny Opera,* a revolutionary musical drama (filmed in 1931), also scored a number of American movies, including Lang's *You and Me* (1938), Mitchell Leisen's *Lady in the Dark* (1944), and William Seiter's *One Touch of Venus* (1948). Weill compared the film industry to the medieval Church: it was a powerful institution that sponsored musical creation. There was little difference, he suggested, between what the Protestant church did for Bach and what Hollywood did for someone like Weill. But he also felt that music's potential in movies had hardly been tapped. He felt that someday the movies would replace the musical theater as an outlet for the composer's imagination, but "only when a formula for a truly musical picture is found and developed." Weill posed the basic problem more simply than Eisler: should music follow the dramatic action or emphasize the emotional development? He accepted the practical problems of mass film production—the need to score a movie within four weeks, and the need to mix it with dialogue and sound—and he accepted the concept of transparency in movie music: namely, that a good score is "one which you don't hear but which you would miss if it were not there." But he pointed out weaknesses. American movies often overorchestrate scores, overwhelming dialogue and action with sixty-piece orchestras. And, in general, the movie industry works backward: composers are presented with completely finished works before they start writing. Weill praised the movie work of composers like Aaron Copland, who scored *Of Mice and Men* (1940) and *Our Town* (1940), and Bernard Herrman, who scored *Citizen Kane* and many of Hitchcock's movies. But he felt such creativity was wasted if a composer was not allowed to collaborate on a movie from the beginning.

Weill was writing from his experience with classic studio filmmaking. Today, the production system is more elastic, and there is more chance that a composer might collaborate from the start, not be called in just to add the musical element. The old weaknesses are still around, however, pointing out the general failure of music theory to affect the production of typical feature films.

Finally, though, Weill gives us a chance to appreciate other movies from the standpoint of musical structure. He divides movies into three categories according to how much active, creative participation they offer a composer. The first category is the documentary, in which the composer often works with the filmmaker during the editing process to provide emotion and tempo to the images. In the second category, the animated cartoon, the composer usually writes the music first, and the characters are then animated to its rhythms and accents. In the third, the film musical, music and action are interwoven from the outset. As a composer, Weill had high praise especially for the latter two forms. For him, the cartoon is the ballet of movie entertainment, and some of Disney's scores fine examples of popular ballet music. And the musical was film opera. If there was ever to be an "American opera," Weill felt, it would come out of the movies.[20]

Some music theorists, then, have challenged the film theorists' general assumption that sound is only an adjunct to the visual in movies. Despite the exceptions we have cited, however—and even though albums of movie music sell well—sound still holds a subordinate position in film theory and criticism. The revolutionary suggestions of Hanns Eisler have yet to be fully explored.

SUMMARY

Though sound was associated with movies from the start, it was some time before recording systems with efficient amplification developed to provide precise synchronization of sound with imagery. By 1928 the Warner Brothers' Vitaphone sound-on-disc system and the Fox-Case sound-on-film system had impressed American audiences so strongly that sound came to be expected in films. After an early period (1927–1932) of clumsy experimentation in which "canned theater" predominated, the sound-on-film system became the industry standard, and technology provided noise suppressors and other improvements. Filmmakers could systematically mix words, music, and sound effects into clean, precise sound tracks, creating a range of techniques and styles that we can compare with the range we find in the editing and montage of images. This classic approach to sound developed from 1933 to 1949. After 1950, the use of magnetic tape provided even greater freedom, widening the range of effects further from stereophonic sound to single-system recording and the flexibility of direct-sound technique.

Sound is considered in all the major film theories, which treat music and dialogue as important supports to a movie's visual style. Realist theorists praise sound's contribution to the complete illusion of life, and formative theorists point out how mixing and sound montage can create a nonrealistic experience. Although realists may stress sound's transparent effect of unobtrusively assisting the imagery's impact, formative theorists remark on sound's ability to counterpoint and contrast with the imagery, even—particularly with music—accruing a clearly separate power of its own.

Like movement, *mise en scène*, and continuity, movie sound sometimes blends into a transparent design or sometimes draws our attention to its own operation. It is one more element of changing emphasis, shifting in its relationship with the other elements, adding an aural dimension to the fascinating play occurring on the screen.

NOTES

1 This is the typical speed of sound in air. In denser media like water or wood, sound travels faster.

2 Musical notation is not based on wave cycles, but on seven basic tones (A to G). An octave is an interval of eight tones, hence a skip to the next tone of the same letter.

3 Sidney Head, *Broadcasting in America* (Boston: Houghton Mifflin, 1972), pp. 126–127.

4 We should explain that a particular sound is not stored directly beside the frame of film whose sound it represents. The exciter lamp is situated a few inches below the projection lamp, so that when we watch lovers kiss, for example, the image of the lips meeting is several frames away from the area in which the sound of the kiss is stored. Since movies require intermittent motion at the aperture and smooth motion at the sound drum, this gap between picture and sound is necessary. The gap may

cause a momentary loss of sync if a movie has been spliced after a break.

5 Head, pp. 93–94.

6 On video-tape recorders there are one or more additional heads for recording and playing the images.

7 These terms are commonly used by film-makers. See Karel Reisz, *The Technique of Film Editing* (New York: Focal Press, 1963). Some semioticians call actual sound *diegetic* and commentative sound *nondiegetic*.

8 Barry Salt, "Film Style and Technology in the Thirties," *Film Quarterly*, 30 (Fall 1976), 30.

9 F. E. Sparshott, "Basic Film Aesthetics," *Journal of Aesthetic Education*, 5 (Apr. 1971). Reprinted in *Film Theory and Criticism*, ed. Mast and Cohen (New York: Oxford, 1974), p. 224.

10 *What Is Cinema?* I, 20.

11 Quoted in Kevin Brownlow, *The Parade's Gone By* (New York: Knopf, 1968), p. 577.

12 Clair, *Cinema Yesterday and Today* (New York: Dover, 1972), p. 141.

13 Clair, pp. 133–141.

14 Eisenstein, *Film Form*, pp. 54–55, 105–106.

15 Eisenstein, *The Film Sense*, pp. 168, 188–190.

16 Eisler, in collaboration with Theodor W. Adorno, *Composing for the Films* (Freeport, N.Y.: Books for Libraries, 1971), p. 87.

17 Eisler, pp. 73–74.

18 For the full discussion of his esthetic principles, see Eisler, pp. 62–88.

19 Unfortunately, American prints of *Night and Fog* use subtitles, so that the impact of the French narration is blunted.

20 Kurt Weill, "Music in the Movies," *Harper's Bazaar* (Sept. 1946). Reprinted in *The Movies as Medium*, ed. Lewis Jacobs (New York: Farrar, Straus and Giroux, 1970), pp. 289–296.

Chapter 6 / Color

L ike sound, color was involved in the movie experience from the beginning. Edison's first Vitascope presentation in 1896 included a color movie, *The Dance of Annabelle*. By today's standards, it was unusual color, painted on the print by hand, but it contributed to the impact of that big event. And throughout the silent period various paint and dye processes continued to enhance movies, combining with the live musical accompaniment and the projectionists' manipulations of shutter speed to create far more stylized experiences than those we encounter today.

Unlike the history of sound, there was no sudden revolution that ushered in the modern color film. There were many experiments with processes for recording natural colors directly onto the film. By 1935, Technicolor had solved the big technical problems, and audiences responded strongly. But black-and-white movies continued to prevail for many years. The balance shifted only gradually until, since the 1960s, few major American film productions have been in black and white.

Color has been fully integrated *into* the machinery of movies until it shares the illusory realism of all the other components and has become a subtle, complex, and versatile instrument at the filmmaker's disposal. This chapter deals with this movie color.

THE TECHNOLOGY OF COLOR

The electromagnetic spectrum is a band of energy that supplies us with radio and television waves, x rays, sunburn (from ultraviolet rays), and light (Fig. 6.1). Modern physics considers this energy to be matter, particles moving at 186,000 miles a second and oscillating as they go. Their movement is sometimes described as straight "rays" or "beams," but they are more easily discussed in terms of vibrating *waves* that have the configuration of sound waves, with amplitude, length, and direction (Fig. 5.2). What we call light is the visible portion of the electromagnetic spectrum.[1] We see the movement of this visible spectrum as brightness and color. Let us consider the structure of light before moving on to technology's systems and filmmakers' techniques.

The Structure of Light

The amplitude of a light wave determines its *brightness*. Sunlight is the brightest light possible—all wavelengths at maximum amplitude. When sunlight comes through clear glass or water, the amplitude of all its waves will be reduced a little. They will

175

also lose some of their speed, which causes the light to refract, or bend—a tendency that makes it possible for camera lenses to focus an image.

Every individual wavelength of light is a different *color*. When sunlight is refracted by water or glass, each of its wavelengths actually bends to a different degree. The shorter the wavelength, the greater the bending. Normally, we don't notice this, but if light passes through rain mist under the right conditions, or through a prism, the spectrum fans out into its component waves and we see bands of color—a rainbow (Fig. 6.2).

There are nearly four hundred different colors, or *hues*, in a rainbow—one for every wavelength in sunlight. This spectrum is usually divided into three general categories: (1) the *shorter* wavelengths (violets and blues); (2) the *middle* wavelengths (greens and yellows); and (3) the *longer* wavelengths (oranges and reds).

No one is sure exactly how our eyes perceive colors. The most popular theory—based on the work of Thomas Young and Hermann von Helmholtz in the nineteenth century—states that the human eye has three different kinds of color receptors, primarily sensitive to red, green, and blue. When light from an object

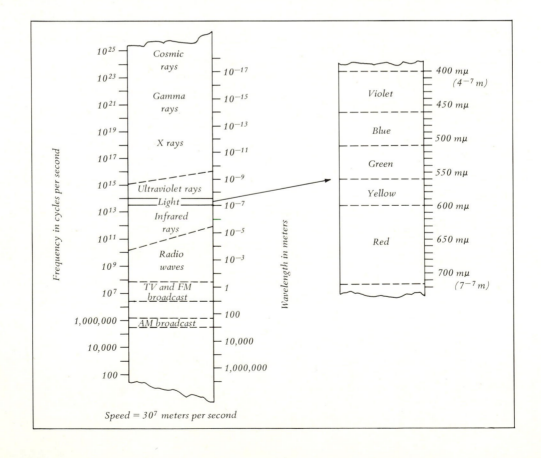

stimulates these receptors, each responds in proportion to the number of wavelengths in its area of sensitivity.[2] All the colors that we distinguish are therefore being mixed by the eye from the primary colors red, green, and blue.[3]

Direct sunlight is the purest *white* light because it includes all possible colors, and all the eye's color receptors respond equally. When objects pass on all the sun's visible wavelengths, we see white; as objects absorb the rays in increasing amounts we see shades of gray or black. These are the *achromatic* colors. This page appears white because it passes on red, green, and blue, evoking an equal response from all the receptors in your eyes. The type appears black because, absorbing all the colors, it evokes no response from the color receptors. The grays in our photos evoke a weak response from all the receptors, for all the colors are partially absorbed, the degree of absorption determining the darkness of the gray.

The *chromatic* colors (all the colors in a rainbow) occur when objects disturb, absorb, or hold back, some wavelengths of light but do not affect others. Skies are blue because the earth's atmosphere scatters about only the short, blue wavelengths as light passes through. Apples reflect reds predominantly, absorbing most greens and blues. A green eyeshade holds back most reds and blues, passing on only its own color.

All human color making is based on what we find in nature. The essentials are detailed in the color wheel (Fig. 6.3). Red, blue, and green are the *primary colors*. We can mix any hue by *adding* primaries together. As we move around the wheel from red to blue, for example, the red is being mixed with greater amounts of blue. At the midpoint between the two primaries is magenta, which represents equal proportions of red and blue. In a similar way, we can create any color we want by mixing any primaries.

The three mid-points between the primaries are magenta, cyan, and yellow. These are the complementaries, or *secondary colors*. They are also called the *minus colors* because we can use them to create any hue by *subtracting* colors. Each secondary color subtracts the primary color opposite it on the wheel—that is, if we hold a magenta filter against a white light, it will hold back the wavelengths represented by the green opposite and pass on red and blue. Thus magenta is called *minus green*. Cyan is *minus red*, passing on blue and green; yellow is *minus blue*, passing on red and green.

This manipulation of color follows one basic principle: a filter will pass on its own color but hold back all others. This *minusing effect* works between all opposite

6.1 The electromagnetic spectrum. The higher the frequency of energy, the shorter the wavelengths. Thus a television station broadcasts on waves of about one meter in length, at frequencies of 100 million (10^7) cycles, or 100 megacycles, a second. X-rays, however, may have wavelengths of .00000000001 (10^{-12}) meter traveling at about 10 quintillion (10^{18}) cycles a second.

6.2 Prism effect. As white light passes through a prism, the different wavelengths, or colors, are bent to different degrees.

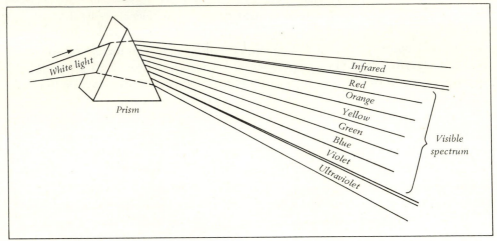

6.3 Color wheel. Solid lines link the primary colors; dotted lines link the secondary, or minus, colors.

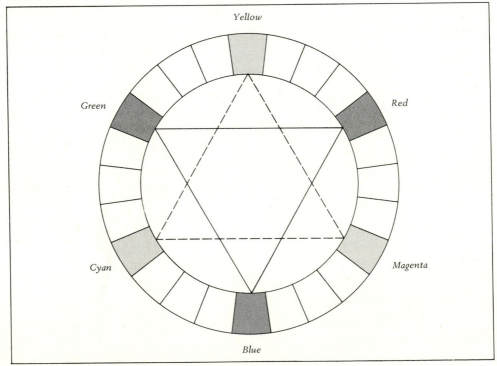

colors on the wheel, and in both directions. Thus, a green filter will hold back magenta, and sunglasses are blue-green to hold back red-yellows. But magenta, cyan, and yellow are considered *the* minus colors because they affect the primaries. We can create all hues by adding primaries, and we can do the same thing by subtracting the secondaries (Fig. 6.4). Thus there are two processes for creating color: the *additive* and the *subtractive*.

To prevent any confusion about our terms, we should point out that we are discussing color processes strictly in terms of manipulating *light*, not pigments. When painters talk of color, they may say that they create any hue of paint or dye by mixing the three "primary colors" of "red, blue, and yellow" in various proportions—and that seems to be an "additive" process that fits nowhere in what we are discussing here. This problem comes from a lack of precision. Paints and dyes are mixed together, but they actually operate on light *subtractively*, like filters: they hold back certain wavelengths of the white light being passed through or reflected off of them. They reproduce any hue with one of three basic colors, generally called "red, blue, and yellow," but more properly defined as magenta (red-blue), cyan (blue-green), and yellow. Our usual sense of color is not too picky, and we know that we can mix almost any "blue" with any "yellow" and get some kind of "green." To be exact, though, we should say that the so-called primary colors of paints and dyes are really the *secondary* colors of light: magenta, cyan, and yellow.

Color film, like paint or dye, creates color by imitating the eye's method of distinguishing the three primary colors. Color film is a more complex form of panchromatic film. It uses emulsion that renders different colors as different degrees

6.4 Additive and subtractive color processes. a. The additive method overlaps beams of light that are colored red, green, and blue. b. The subtractive method overlaps magenta, cyan, and yellow filters on a single source of white light.

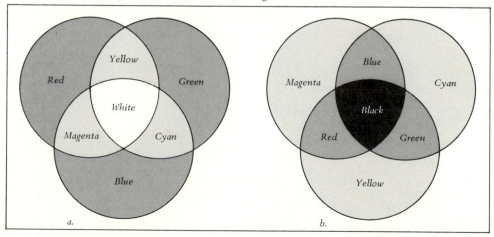

of brightness: white, black, and the shades of gray between. Panchromatic ("all-color") film is so called because it gives a different shade of gray to almost all major colors. As a result, it opens color to the possibility of manipulation. A dark red filter over a camera lens will reduce blue skies to almost black, and a dark blue filter will whiten eyeballs and blacken lips. (We discussed this in Chapter 3; see Fig. 3.3.)

Color filmmaking, then, depends on two capacities of panchromatic film: to distinguish all the major colors and, through filtering, to let only certain ones register. This is far from the elasticity of the human eye, but it allows movies to imitate natural colors.

Color Systems Used in Movies

Since film emulsion records nothing but black, grays, and white, one must use paint or dye to achieve color. One may apply color as painters do, or one can use it to convert the shades of brightness in the black-and-white picture back into the colors they represent. The first method we will call *applied color*. The second is the basic method of color photography: what is considered natural or *recorded color*.

Applied Color   The earliest color movies, like *The Dance of Annabelle*, were *hand*-painted. The color was applied directly onto the image with tiny brushes. This was the same technique that had been used on magic-lantern slides throughout the nineteenth century. By 1905 this method had been streamlined: a *stencil* was cut for each color, and the film was run through dyes with the stencil attached. Eisenstein had a flag dyed red in *Potemkin* (1925), and Erich von Stroheim demanded that symbolic objects in *Greed* (1923), a study of money's power over people, be hand-colored in gold. But direct coloring of figures in the frame was rare after 1920. Today some cartoonists employ it deliberately for an effect that was once considered a major flaw: since the edges and density of the coloring are not perfectly consistent from frame to frame, the colors become animated and "jiggle" separately from the movement of the figures. Depending on what you are after, then, hand- or stencil-coloring is either a clumsy imitation of real color or a unique kind of animated color.

Throughout the silent period, the most common color technique was *tinting*: coloring the film stock on which the image was printed. In effect, this created a black-and-colored picture, though there was only one color. Tinting was organized into a code. Exteriors were often bright yellow, battles or fires red, and seascapes green; and different colors might be used to set off different sequences and even different sides of the same frame. The most consistent policy was to render night scenes in blue. Since these scenes usually had to be shot in daylight (because of the slow film speeds at that time), blue tinting gave a clear indication of nighttime. Today we usually see only black-and-white copies of the old tinted movies, so we not only lose their sense of style but we may mistakenly assume that those filmmakers were too naive to make any distinction between day and night scenes.

Color *toning* was also popular. Toning introduced dyes into the emulsion, so that the lines and tones of the image itself were colored, not just the stock on which it was printed.[4] When filmmakers used toning with tinting, they provided two different colors in a movie. It became a common practice to sepia-tone images on yellow-tinted stock, for example. Possibly over 80 percent of Hollywood features were being tinted or toned by 1920, and the practice continued into the sound period.[5]

But all during the silent period there were also experiments with "natural color" processes to provide copies of colors as they appeared in the original subject. These processes were perfected in the 1930s.

Recorded Color   The development of modern color films began in 1855, when scientist James Clerk Maxwell demonstrated how to capture natural colors from black-and-white film. He used a strictly additive method.

Figure 6.5 illustrates Maxwell's method. Red, blue, and green filters are used in turn to get three separate pictures of a subject. Each filter lets through only its own color, registering it only in black, white, or shades of gray. Thus, if the subject includes a shade of red that is the same hue as the red filter, that shade will appear in the red-filtered shot as white; if some portions have no red, the picture will register them as black; and if there are some red wavelengths reflected by different parts of the subject, those will register as brighter or darker shades of gray—and so on, for each filtered image. We now mount these images as positive slides in separate projectors, each fitted with the same color filter used to take that image. In doing so, we convert the whites, grays, and blacks into different intensities of the color they recorded. To go back to the red example: now the white areas let through pure red; the blacks absorb all the red; and the shades of gray give proportionate shades of red. The same process would occur for each projected image. When we project the images on top of one another—that is, in *register*—we have a reproduction of the subject's original colors. We have imitated the additive process of the human eye: recording natural colors by blending together the data of receptors sensitive to the three primary colors.

Maxwell's demonstration triggered a great deal of experimentation, and today's color television is simply a more sophisticated version of his work. A television set broadcasts images by firing a row of electrons from a "gun" onto a sensitized plate in the television tube. In color sets there are three tubes, each filtered to receive and transmit only one of the three primary colors. The guns transmit a picture as particles of red, blue, and green blended in various proportions to reproduce the hues of the original subject.

Unlike television or Maxwell's apparatus, however, movies require a single source of light for their pictures. And so they depend on a method that goes beyond the additive process, combining it with the subtractive process. The fundamentals of this method date from 1869, when two French inventors, Louis Ducos du Hauron

6.5 Maxwell's additive experiment. Maxwell used filters in taking black-and-white pictures and in projecting them in registration, thus reproducing the original colors.

Black-and-white picture taken and projected with red filter

Black-and-white picture taken and projected with blue filter

Black-and-white picture taken and projected with green filter

Composite picture reproducing original colors

and Charles Cros, independently discovered them. One may reproduce the original colors of a photographed subject by dyeing separate negatives with the secondary colors (cyan, magenta, and yellow) which, when placed in register, operate by *holding back* portions of light.

Figure 6.6 illustrates the steps of this method, the basic procedure in all modern color photography. The first step duplicates Maxwell's approach, except that it sensitizes the emulsions without the use of outside filters. The subject is exposed on

6.6 Steps in modern color photography.

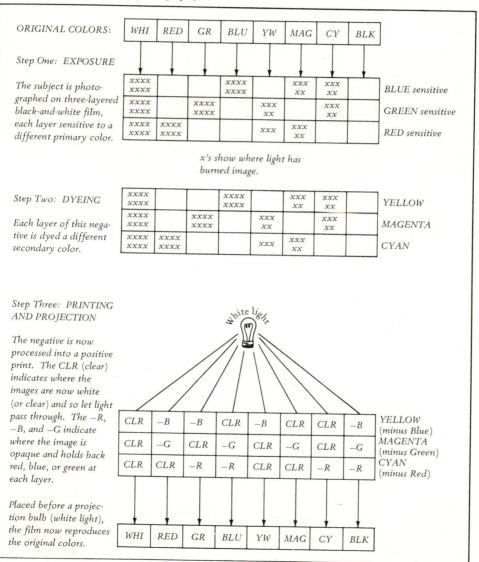

the three separate emulsions, each sensitive only to one of the primaries. This step yields three different negative images of the subject. Any reds, greens, or blues in the subject will leave marks (the x's in the drawing) only on the appropriate negative. White affects all of them; black affects none.

In the second step, these negatives are dyed with the secondary colors. The blue-sensitive negative is dyed yellow (minus blue). The green-sensitive is dyed magenta (minus green), and the red-sensitive is dyed cyan (minus red).

In the third step, the negatives are processed into positive prints. They are ready for projection in register. All the marks left by the exposure step (the x's) become whites and grays—that is, they are clear or translucent on the positive print (the CLR's in the drawing) and transmit the color they have been dyed. Those areas where there were no marks remain opaque—that is, they hold back their opposite (or minus) primary color. We have marked those areas "−R" (minus red), "−G" (minus green) and "−B" (minus blue) to clarify this.

When placed before a projector bulb (a lamp designed to give off as white a light as possible mechanically), this frame of film renders the subject's original colors through the "minusing effect" of the secondary colors. For example, red has left no marks on the blue-sensitive or green-sensitive layers so that the opaque yellow and opaque magenta hold back the blue and green, allowing only red to come through the clear portion. The same process is repeated for all the colors illustrated.

Keep in mind that Figure 6.6 illustrates only a *model* of all modern color films. Particular film systems are variations on this model. Some have kept the three negatives totally separate through the steps of processing, bringing them in register only at the projection stage; others keep them joined through all the steps. Some systems yield color negatives in register, from which any number of positives can then be printed; others must do all the processing at one time, and so yield only color positives. The differences here have a bearing on the filmmaker's work, discussed in the next section.

The point here is that by using dyes and chemical filtering in conjunction with black-and-white film, technology developed a method for recording natural colors. Like the movies' other illusions of recorded reality, this one opened up a range of possibilities with which the filmmaker could play.

APPLYING THE TECHNOLOGY

The history of color as a creative tool is as rich as the history of any other visual element in the movies, but there was little to say about it before the development of

6.7 The Technicolor camera's optical system.

color photography in the 1930s. Earlier filmmakers used it very creatively, but few good examples survive. There are copies of *The Great Train Robbery* (1903) that retain the original hand-coloring of costumes, explosions, and gunfire; and there are copies of films like *Intolerance* (1916) or *Tol'able David* (1921) that retain sequences tinted in orange, green, or blue. But only random stills remain of tinted-and-toned movies, and we simply have to imagine what other effects looked like—Eisenstein's red flag, or Stroheim's touches of gold. Such movies have come down to us only in black-and-white copies, and this loss reminds us of a fact that often gets overlooked: technology is fragile. We can fool ourselves into believing that because they are machine-made, movies are permanent records. They are not. A discussion of color, as it turns out, is a convenient place to bring up that fact, and we will return to it again in a moment.

The movies that employ color photography fall into two fairly distinct eras, each with a predominant color system, and particular qualities and problems: the Era of Three-Strip Technicolor and the Era of Eastman Color.

The Era of Three-Strip Technicolor, 1932–1949

Starting in 1914, filmmakers had experimented with various color photography systems. In the twenties there were several features photographed entirely in color, but there were too many problems to suit the movie industry. Then, in 1932, Herbert T. Kalmus perfected the Technicolor system he had initiated in 1917 with another inventor, Daniel F. Comstock. From then on, color became a force to be dealt with.

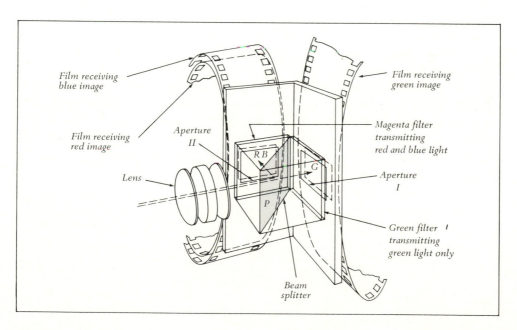

Film receiving
blue image

Film receiving
green image

Film receiving
red image

Aperture
II

Magenta filter
transmitting
red and blue light

Lens

R B

G

Aperture
I

P

Green filter
transmitting
green light only

Beam
splitter

Technicolor had evolved from a clumsy two-color system into an efficient, but costly and complex, three-color one. It required a special camera, three times wider than the typical Mitchell cameras in the studios, to run three entirely separate strips of film through its mechanism, splitting the incoming light with a mirror-prism device so that the three strips were exposed simultaneously (Fig. 6.7). The film used was initially very slow, demanding some 80 percent more light than black and white, and it required special processing and dyes that the Technicolor Corporation kept a well-guarded secret. To use Technicolor, a studio had to lease the corporation's cameras, film, and services, which included special operators and consultants. Technicolor was three to four times costlier than black and white.

Studios were, of course, none too eager to jump into such production, and they risked their resources at first only on cartoons and short subjects. Walt Disney tried Technicolor for *Flowers and Trees* (1932), a "Silly Symphony" cartoon, which won the first Academy Award for animation. Pioneer Pictures released *La Cucaracha* (1934), a two-reel musical, which became the first theatrical movie in three-color Technicolor. After that short's enthusiastic reception, Pioneer produced the first three-color Technicolor feature, *Becky Sharp* (1935), an adaptation of William M. Thackeray's novel *Vanity Fair* (Fig. 6.8). From that point on, the orders for the Technicolor Corporation's services increased sharply. The era of three-strip Technicolor was fully under way.

The good points of Technicolor were, in effect, its drawbacks looked at from another angle. The slow film gave a sharp delineation to figures. The three-strip mechanism tended to heighten contrasts. And the Technicolor dyes, together with the bright lighting, created *saturated colors*—that is, colors that are very pure, with little or no gray mixed with them. Although Technicolor's consultants insisted on rendering colors as realistically as possible and were anxious to display the subtlety of the system,[6] Technicolor's images were far more brilliant and clear than anything in real life, and its "subtlety" often consisted of very striking hues.

During most of this era, Technicolor maintained its standards of quality, mainly through Natalie Kalmus, Herbert's former wife, who was the corporation's chief color consultant until 1948. She resisted the arguments of cinematographers like Stanley Cortez, who felt that Technicolor created only "Christmas package colors" that needed to be toned down. "Even though a thing might be technically wrong, to me that wrong thing can be *dramatically* right. . . . You must *distort* color, play around with it, make it work for *you*, intentionally throw it off balance."[7]

6.8 The first three-strip Technicolor feature. Rouben Mamoulian, seated by the lights, directs Miriam Hopkins in *Becky Sharp* (1935). Notice the large Technicolor camera.

The most familiar examples of classic Technicolor quality are *Gone with the Wind* (1939) and *The Wizard of Oz* (1939), movies where the brilliant colors are well suited to the heroic and fantastic themes of the stories. Though the colors follow the dictates of Technicolor "realism," they enrich everything and sometimes set apart certain sequences in contrast with others. The burning of Atlanta in *Gone with the Wind*, for example, is particularly memorable for its reds and oranges. *The Wizard of Oz* carries the contrast to its logical extreme, opening and closing with black-and-white scenes for Dorothy's "real" world, and setting her adventures in Oz apart with Technicolor green woods, the purples and blues of the wizard's lair, and the famous yellow brick road.

Jesse James, also made in 1939, is perhaps a more striking example of Technicolor because its story is a more ordinary adventure, and yet its colors are equally unordinary. Jesse has leaped on top of a train he is about to rob, where he is silhouetted against the deep blue sky while the car windows below glow in orange. Everything else in the frame is blackness, setting up an implicit contrast between the "cold" world of the outlaw and the "warm" world of the law-abiding passengers.[8]

Elsewhere in the movie, the rich greens and blues of the outdoors set up a similar contrast with the warm browns and golds of interiors, creating an appropriately heightened world for the romantic story.

Among Westerns made under Technicolor's auspices, we should also single out *Duel in the Sun* (1946). One sequence, in which a range lord gathers his men to attack a railroad gang, combines classic Hollywood editing with the power of Technicolor. The cowboys gather under rich blue and purple skies and ride down on the gang, only to confront a phalanx of blue-clad Union soldiers. The range lord, facing the army and the flag he had served in the Civil War, backs down. The sequence is already rich in drama, continuity, and spatial design—but the color adds effectively to a sense of larger-than-real conflict.

The musical benefited greatly from Technicolor because it was a larger-than-real genre to begin with. Even after the autonomy of the Technicolor Corporation had ended (we'll turn to that shortly), the MGM musicals in particular exploited the system's classic saturated colors to great effect. In *It's Always Fair Weather* (1955) dancer Cyd Charisse does a number in a replica of Stillman's Gym, the famous training ground of prize fighters. She wears an electric green dress, setting up a level of contrast with the environment that would be impossible in black-and-white. In the "Broadway Melody" dance number of *Singin' in the Rain* (1951) the colors maintain their saturation, but become more pastel—that is, less bright—as the scene develops. The number involves a young dancer who comes to New York, gets a job in burlesque, then moves up to the big time. At the beginning the colors are deliberately garish, with intense greens and reds contrasted in particular for one long dance passage. At the end, the dancer does a ballet, and the colors subdue into pastel purple and white—a change in color scheme that matches the change in style and sophistication.

This range of examples gives us some idea of what the Technicolor Corporation meant by realism and subtlety. Some filmmakers chafed against it for various reasons. Director Henry Hathaway refused to use Technicolor consultants on *The Trail of the Lonesome Pine* (1936), which was praised in the press as better than any previous attempt in color.[9] Cinematographer Leon Shamroy angered Natalie Kalmus when he insisted on using yellow light instead of white light for a sunset in *The Black Swan* (1942). He wanted to ignore realism, like Rembrandt and Van Dyck, and "make a deliberate mistake." Though told that was no way to photograph color, he won an Oscar for his work.[10] And in *Moulin Rouge* (1953), director John Huston and cinematographer Oswald Morris broke Technicolor's ban on using colored filters.[11]

6.9 Eastman Color's monopack construction. The three emulsions are joined together through all the steps of processing.

By that time, however, Technicolor's autonomy was coming rapidly to an end. A new film system had evolved and was beginning to affect the look of color movies and the old ideas of realism.

The Era of Eastman Color, 1950 to the Present

During the thirties and forties, inventors labored to overcome the most clumsy and expensive aspect of the Technicolor system: that it required a special camera to run three separate film strips. In 1935, Eastman Kodak introduced Kodachrome for home movies (in 16 mm)—a film that kept the three strips of emulsion permanently bonded in what is called a *monopack* (Fig. 6.9). The images, which cannot be separated, are colored by introducing, or "coupling," dyes to the emulsions during processing. But Kodachrome was not acceptable for professional movies. Working with Kodak, the Technicolor Corporation had developed a professional monopack by 1941—and it was used in some movies—but it was still inferior to the old separation system. Finally, in 1949, Kodak introduced Eastman Color, a monopack negative film for professionals. This ended most of the previous difficulties and launched a new era in filmmaking.

Eastman Color was a cheaper, simpler system with obvious advantages. It was a much faster film and by 1976 it could be used under the same light conditions as most black-and-white films. Though still more expensive than black and white, Eastman Color freed the studios from Technicolor's leasing policy. They regained full control of their productions, and ultimately this meant a greater range of visual styles.

There is one overriding problem with Eastman Color, however: very poor stability. So far, no way has been found to fix the dyes used in any color system. After

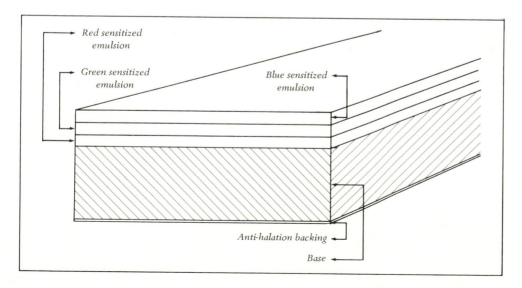

Red sensitized emulsion

Green sensitized emulsion

Blue sensitized emulsion

Anti-halation backing

Base

a while, they will begin to fade. Color movies lack the stability of black-and-white ones, which may last over two hundred years with proper fixing and care. Three-strip Technicolor has the best record among color systems: its dyes had relatively high stability, and its system allowed the studio to keep three separate black-and-white negatives from which freshly dyed prints could be struck at any time. This explains why *Gone with the Wind,* now over forty years old, looks brand-new when re-released. Fresh dyes can be used in new prints off the original negatives.

The Eastman Color system allows no such luxury. The dyes coupled to the emulsions have poor stability to begin with, and the emulsions themselves are inseparable. There is no easy way to remedy fading—which may occur, depending on how carefully the film is processed and stored, anywhere from six months to twenty years after a movie's release. The cyan dye, which has a lot of control over yellows and greens, is usually the first to go. Prints of *Cleopatra* (1963) and *Lawrence of Arabia* (1962) are beginning to take on a rosy or purplish look, much like a silent movie tinted red. *Man of the West* (1958) is largely pale reds and thin yellows—and without knowing about the stability problem, one might think the color was designed that way to give a dry, harsh look to the story.

Because of technology's fragility, gains often involve such losses. In forty more years *Gone with the Wind* can still be made fresh, but a film like *Elvira Madigan* (1967), shot in Eastman Color and touted for its exquisite color, may fade away or else be converted into less exquisite copies, prints made from prints, several generations away from the original. Some archives have resorted to cold storage to at least slow down the deterioration, and some studios employ a separation process, similar but less reliable than the old Technicolor method, to strike three black-and-white negatives off the movie itself—but this costs around $30,000 a movie and doesn't always work. The stability problem has, of course, spurred new explorations: into special optical printers, colored lasers, computers, video disks, holograms—and, of course, stabilized dyes.[12] So far, nothing has solved the problem, but the Era of Eastman Color has gone on unabated. The convenience and adaptability of the new process have turned studios almost completely away from black and white, so that color is the standard in commercial entertainment films. Eastman Color is the universal tool. Terms like "WarnerColor," "Deluxe Color," "MetroColor," or (since about the mid-fifties) even "Technicolor" indicate only the studio or plant that did the processing of what is basically the Eastman Color monopack system.[13] Ironically, the movies they produce represent the most advanced forms of cinematography as well as the most fragile.

The great gains have been in those areas of "playing around," as Stanley Cortez had put it. Eastman Color freed filmmakers from an enforced "realism," allowing them to explore the variables latent in the technology of the color system. Here we will outline some key ones. The filmmaker can play with saturation and brightness, adjust the sensitivity of the film stock, and change the color of light.

We said before that Technicolor's system yielded highly saturated, brilliant colors: that is, colors that are pure (involving few wavelengths in a particular hue) and give off a lot of light. Eastman Color can do the same (though it never quite approaches the look of three-strip Technicolor) or not, depending on how it is shot. For Ingmar Bergman's *The Passion of Anna* (1969) cinematographer Sven Nykvist carefully reduces the amount of light striking the film. This lowers brilliance and, within a certain range, increases apparent saturation: because less random light strikes the film, the range of wavelengths involved in any hue is reduced. This gives a rich, but subdued range of hues—nothing is brilliant, but the hues are fully saturated and intense. For Michelangelo Antonioni's *The Red Desert* (1964) cinematographer Carlo di Palma uses the same technique but carries it further. He reduces exposure in some scenes so much that the hues begin to *desaturate*—to become grayer and duller. This desaturated color is particularly appropriate to that film, which deals with the dehumanizing influence of modern society upon a sensitive woman. Di Palma can still contrast colors effectively; in particular, reds stand out in many scenes as symbols of the woman's frustrated passion. And in one sequence di Palma suddenly uses fully saturated color to make a striking contrast. The woman is telling her son a story about a little girl on a desert island—a story that reflects the woman's own fantasies—and the movie shows her story in rich sea greens, blue sky, and golden sand and rocks. The color shifts themselves tell us how much richer her fantasies are than her real life. These are changes in saturation and brightness, brought about by manipulating the *volume* of light striking the film.

The filmmaker may also manipulate the *color* of light striking the film. Any color film designed for outdoor shooting will give orange tones under tungsten (ordinary incandescent) light; and indoor film used outdoors will give blue tones. This is an intrinsic chemical factor, having to do with the temperature of light, and filters are normally used to compensate in such situations. But filmmakers can exploit the factor. In *2001* (1968) director Stanley Kubrick depends on the blue tones of fluorescent lights to give a cold, antiseptic mood to many scenes, whereas for some interior scenes of *Barry Lyndon* (1976) he depends on the extremely warm tones of candlelight. In these instances the source of light has been selected with a certain mood in mind. Another way to achieve such effects is by using colored filters. For his *Romeo and Juliet* (1954), director Renato Castellani had pale red and yellow filters placed before the lens to imitate the tonalities of Renaissance paintings. Director Federico Fellini used similar filtering for scenes in *Fellini Satyricon* (1969). Certain filters help dull the brightness of colors. Cinematographer Stanley Cortez chose them for this purpose in *The Bridge of Remagen* (1969) to give director John Guillermin the overall drabness, the look of grim war, he wanted.[14]

The technology of color processing also allows any filmmaker to play with the relationship of dyes to create various effects. John Huston had almost all color bleached out of initial prints of *Reflections in a Golden Eye* (1967) allowing only some pale red-yellows to come through (but the bleached prints were later withdrawn). In one scene of *Deliverance* (1972), directed by John Boorman, the dawn's light suddenly grows strangely dark as one character waits for a killer. The effect was achieved by introducing black into one of the color dyes.

By playing with the volume or color of light and by manipulating the color process itself, filmmakers make movie color accurate to their purposes, not just to reality. The color is manipulated without disturbing our basic sense of "realism." Thus, in *Ulzana's Raid* (1972), the story of a cavalry-Apache war, Joseph Biroc's cinematography accentuates reds and yellows, creating a kind of sepia-and-gold world reminiscent of Frederic Remington's and Charles Russell's paintings of the Old West. But any filmmaker may bias color toward an explicit and noticeable symbolism. We have noted the use of red for passion in *Red Desert*. Antonioni also had vegetables painted in one set of that movie to increase the pallidness of the world through which his heroine wanders. According to director Ingmar Bergman, the deep red sets he used in *Cries and Whispers* (1973) reflect his vision of the soul as a red membrane. In *The Umbrellas of Cherbourg* (1964) director Jacques Demy opts for extremely rich colors in what one writer calls a kaleidoscopic effect. The bright, artificial colors set off the otherwise banal lives of the characters: reds and oranges to set off big moments, or strong, solid colors to distinguish certain characters.[15]

In the Era of Eastman Color, then, color has become as diversified a tool as any other at the filmmaker's disposal. No color is precisely accurate or "real" to true life in the abstract, because its technology is less elastic and adaptable than the human system it imitates. The filmmaker uses it to create different worlds of color. It works inside an overall context, determined by the purpose behind the movie. Whether used transparently or with very noticeable symbolism, it is always a peculiar kind of *movie* color.

Movie color had to wait a while to gain respectability. Formative theorists quarreled with the garishness of Technicolor, and realists with its obtrusive prettiness. But as time went on, and particularly within the freer era of Eastman Color, critics and theorists began to wrestle with the predicament color posed to both formative and realist schools of thought. On the one hand, the filmmaker cannot usually ignore the physical links of colors and objects in real life; a purple apple suddenly appearing in the typical movie would throw the viewer off, destroy the illusion game, force us to ask why the apple is purple. On the other hand, the filmmaker has a great deal of control over color and creates an experience quite different from that in real life.[16] In trying to resolve this dilemma, theorists followed their own biases, of course, but in the process they converted color into a movie instrument.

Sergei Eisenstein, for example, treated color as another montage element. Like the individual shot in a sequence, every color was active in its own right, but it was also subordinated to and orchestrated within the whole ensemble. Just as sound montage severs the everyday connection between an object and the sound it makes, so color montage separates an object from the impact of the color it generates. Eisenstein called it "color sound" and thought it was crucial to any artistic use of color. "Before we can learn to distinguish three oranges on a patch of lawn both as three objects in the grass *and* as three orange patches against a green background, we dare not think of color composition." By making viewers see this distinction, the filmmaker separates color from its mere senuous connection with real objects and creates dramatic, expressive patterns. "The *color* of red becomes *thematic* red," as he put it. The viewer is moved from the sensuous to the intellectual and esthetic levels of awareness. Eisenstein saw colors working in crescendos like music—or indeed, to go back to his terms, like montage sequences: for instance, "the orange color, going through reddish orange, finds its consummation in red, and azure is born from bluish green engendered by pure green with a spark of blue in it."[17]

Eisenstein left only one work that uses color: *Ivan the Terrible, Part II* (1946), his last film. It has one color sequence that uses stark red and green lights to support a bizarre dance episode leading up to an assassination. Though strange and powerful, it is not a clear example of the color orchestration his writings describe. On the other hand, as Paul J. Sharits has pointed out, Jean-Luc Godard's *A Woman Is a Woman* (1961) uses colors in an intellectual, functional way to form a theme, just as Eisenstein's theory suggested. Godard emphasizes primary blue and red, tying them to characters and to continuity. Red is associated with the story's effervescent woman; blue with her cool, reserved lover. Their apartment contains a balance of red and blue objects. When they argue, blue and red neon lights outside reflect the mood. She becomes attracted to another man who, feeling no real affection for her, wears gray. When the lovers reconcile at the end, it is in a blaze of red neon light.[18] This seems to have come closer to Eisenstein's color orchestration than Eisenstein himself managed to do.

If Eisenstein's theory stressed color as a unit of montage, Rudolf Arnheim's theory treated it as an element of balance and imbalance within the *mise en scène*. Arnheim theorized that unmixed, or saturated, hues or equal mixtures of two hues tended to provide stability within the frame, whereas hues with slight mixtures, what he called "afflictions," of other colors introduced a strong dynamic quality. A saturated red has dignity and seriousness; a saturated yellow is serene. But a yellow red is shocking, and a red yellow takes on energy and becomes more powerful. Pure red and pure blue are not particularly warm or cold, but add red to another color and you warm that color; add blue and you make it cooler.[19]

As Arnheim himself admits, his theory has not been tested. But, like Eisenstein, Arnheim converts color into film terms. It is no longer something reputedly "realistic," nor is it something arty borrowed from painting: it is another aspect of daily experience that filmmakers transform. When color comes into movies, it becomes involved in the power of *mise en scène* and of continuity. It is no longer the same color we experience in nature or in other art forms. First, within the framed screen space, color strikes the viewer more sharply than natural color does, but without losing its connection with reality. Second, movie color works in time, too, and becomes increasingly powerful; painting has no such continuity. The filmmaker who fully exploits the medium puts color into a unique spatiotemporal context, organizing striking patterns of hues to develop in time.

In "Coming to Terms with Color," a concise essay on the esthetics of color in movies, William Johnson outlines four basic approaches used by filmmakers.[20] The first is to let a single hue dominate the entire movie. Director David Lean's spectaculars seem generally to follow this pattern: blue-white snow in *Dr. Zhivago* (1964), orange-yellow deserts in *Lawrence of Arabia* (1962), yellow-green forests in *The Bridge on the River Kwai* (1957). Second, what Johnson considers the most common pattern, is to keep color looking natural but organized to contrast sequences with one another. In *Red Desert* the woman's story is set apart by its saturation, and in the "Broadway Melody" passage of *Singin' in the Rain* the raucous and genteel dance numbers are in contrasting styles. Third, a filmmaker may display a great variety of colors for their own sake. This can be in fun, as in Richard Lester's *Help!* (1965), or it can be used in more serious fantasies, like Fellini's *Juliet of the Spirits* (1965). It runs the risk of looking messy or superficial, but it can be a very rich, invigorating experience. Finally, the filmmaker may create a naturalistic world of color that counterpoints, even comments upon, the movie's action. In Alain Resnais's *Muriel* (1963), the clutter of gritty and sometimes jarring colors reflects upon characters whose lives are shattered by guilt and emptiness. In *Le bonheur* (1965), Agnès Varda creates a world of very sensuous colors to tell the story of a cabinet maker who is perfectly happy having both a wife and a mistress and goes right on being happy after the wife kills herself. The color is the reflection of a man's selfish immersion in his own happiness—though Varda's irony was lost on many viewers, who saw the movie as supporting the man's attitude.

Color is still a largely uncharted wilderness for the film theorist. Physiologically and psychologically, we can compare color perception to the illusion of movement: no one is sure yet how it occurs. As one book on the subject puts it, "it is still only possible to speculate about how color responses are produced."[21] Esthetically, we can compare color to music in movies: too few theorists have yet explored it as a separate factor, preferring for the most part to subordinate it to their general concepts of realist or formative theory. Ironically, color remains one of the most powerful appeals within the film experience, and one of the least discussed.

SUMMARY

Color was involved in moviemaking from the beginning, applied directly to the film image through hand painting, stencil painting, tinting, and toning. Throughout the silent period, however, inventors experimented with systems that would capture natural colors directly on film in the camera, using a combination of the additive and subtractive methods known to photographers since the mid-nineteenth century. By 1932, Herbert T. Kalmus had perfected the three-strip Technicolor process, which required a special camera and a careful dyeing process. By 1935, *Becky Sharp,* the first feature to use the new system, had appeared, and the Era of Technicolor was on its way. That era was to end effectively in 1949, when Eastman Color arrived. It was a professional color movie film with the three emulsions joined in a monopack that could be run through an ordinary camera and processed by the studios. Eastman Color brought new freedom at less expense—though its monopack construction and unstable dyes have meant that most color movies made since 1950 are extremely perishable and will probably fade within twenty years. Despite this problem, the Era of Eastman Color continues unabated to the present day.

Color styles within the Technicolor era were marked with high saturation and brilliance and sometimes a reputation for mere prettiness. Since 1950, filmmakers have been able to play with the volume and color of light and the sensitivities of film stock to create a wide range of styles. Critics and theorists have come to view color as one more enhancement of reality that the filmmaker exploits as a unique contribution to *mise en scène* and continuity. The full implications of color within the movie experience, however, have yet to be explored.

NOTES

1 The visible spectrum includes all the particles, called photons, whose vibrations range in wavelength from about 400 to 700 millimicrons (millionths of a millimeter). They move at frequencies of about 700 to 400 trillion waves, or cycles, per second. Film can record ultraviolet and infrared, the bands at either end of the visible spectrum, but the eye cannot perceive them.

2 Organic differences in any eye can affect the color receptors, however, leading to partial or total color blindness.

3 For a more complete summary of the three-color theory of color vision, see Gerald M. Murch, *Visual and Auditory Perception* (Indianapolis: Bobbs-Merrill, 1973), pp. 56–61.

4 Writers sometimes describe both tinting and toning simply as toning, but they are distinct processes.

5 James L. Limbacher, *Four Aspects of the Film* (New York: Brussel and Brussel, 1968), p. 5.

6 William Johnson, "Coming to Terms with Color," *Film Quarterly*, 20 (Fall 1966), 4.

7 Quoted in Charles Higham, *Hollywood Cameramen* (Bloomington: Indiana University, 1970), p. 98.

8 Johnson, p. 11.

9 *New York Times*, Mar. 15, 1936, sec. 10, p. 3.

10 Higham, pp. 33–34.

11 Johnson, p. 4.

12 For illustrations and fuller discussions of

the stability problem, see Bill O'Connell, "Fade Out," *Film Comment,* 15 (Sept.–Oct., 1979), 11–18; and Paul C. Spehr, "Fading, Fading, Faded: The Color Film Crisis," *American Film,* 5 (Nov. 1979), 56–61.

13 Rudy Behlmer, "Technicolor," *Films in Review,* 15 (June–July 1964), 351.

14 Higham, pp. 99, 118–119.

15 Johnson, pp. 20–21.

16 Johnson, pp. 6–7.

17 Eisenstein, "Colour Film" in *Movies and Methods,* ed. Bill Nichols (Berkeley: University of California, 1976), pp. 381–388. See also "Color and Meaning" in *The Film Sense,* pp. 113–156.

18 Paul J. Sharits, "Red, Blue, Godard," *Film Quarterly,* 19 (Summer 1966), 24–29.

19 Arnheim, *Art and Visual Perception* (Berkeley: University of California, 1965), pp. 276–282.

20 Johnson, pp. 17–22; see Note 6 for full citation.

21 *Color: A Guide to Basic Facts and Concepts* (New York: Wiley, 1963), p. 179.

Part 2 / The Hollywood

Narrative Tradition

*I*n the previous section (Chapters 2 through 6), we discussed the means by which filmmakers build fascinating creations. They stylize our perceptions. The illusion of movement tricks the eye; points of attention constantly shift within the frame; continuity alternates real time with spatial tempos; movie sound intermixes volume levels; and color, although bound to reality, is artificial in many ways. Sometimes we notice these interplays, more often we do not; the whole system of stylization is alternately transparent and noticeable. At the level of perception, then, we find a system of counterpoints and balances that help explain the overall fascination of the movie experience.

This experience is also a system of communication—one of many that we use to get messages across to one another. It is not just sensory stimulation, but works at a cognitive level, too. We understand things through the movie experience.

We need now to consider the implications of this last fact. Stylized perceptions are the means . . . but what are the ends? What functions do movies serve at the cognitive level?

We can distinguish the factors at work in any communication by plotting them into a basic pattern, or model (see figure on p. 200). A movie is a communication that, like any other, involves a communicator (sender) who encodes a message within a medium for an audience (receiver). This sentence, for example, encodes its message in a sign system that uses written words and punctuation. Movies encode messages in a system that stylizes perceptions.

Any message that results serves four linked but distinct functions:

1. *The message has some reference to objects in the real world.* This realistic function is the basis of all communication, in that a message must refer to something we know about in order to make sense. "Zipper the hashed rocks" uses English words in an idiomatic sequence, but it does not refer to anything we know about zippers, hash, or rocks. We may associate this kind of message with poetry, which often creates deliberate nonsense, ambiguity, or confusion. Textbooks, on the other hand, try to avoid confusion. Both forms must refer to what we know. This realistic function defines the relations between the message and the real world. Some movies emphasize this function heavily. They represent a strongly realist cinema.

2. *The message stirs the receiver to some kind of reaction.* This is its persuasive function. It differs in kind and intensity, depending on the message. "Look out for that truck!" enjoins you to action. "I love you" asks for emotional response. Both have a persuasive function, which defines the relationship between the message and the receiver. Movies made for advertising purposes strongly emphasize this function. Among traditional features there are those we can classify as propagandistic cinema. They emphasize persuasion.

3. *The message says something about the sender. This is the* personal function. *It reveals the communicator's attitude or feelings. From the way someone says, "I love you," you may infer that the person is kidding, trying to con you into sympathy, or sharing a deep revelation. To some degree the message is stamped with the person's character. In movies this personal function is complicated by the fact that so many individuals are involved in the message system. It is hard to decide who is "talking" to you. And yet, most of us treat a movie as the statement of "someone" to us. The personal function defines this relationship between the message and its sender. Movies that strongly emphasize this function are often described as* personalist cinema.

4. *The message is some kind of construction, which may be pleasing or beautiful, clumsy or ugly in itself. This is the* esthetic function *of the message: how it strikes us simply as a construction. "I . . . um . . . could be . . . that is, uhr, might be . . . no am, that's it, am in love with you." This is not a well-made message in its own right—no matter how true it may be, how strongly it moves us, or how revealing it is of the speaker. The esthetic function defines the interrelation between elements of the message itself. In some communications—what elitists like to call the "purer" forms of poetry, painting, or music—the message itself is its main reason for existence. In movies we find the esthetic function heavily emphasized in what are sometimes called* art films *and* spectacle films.[1]

By isolating these four functions we can see that there are both external and internal forces at work on a movie. The realist and persuasive functions involve external forces: the outside world, the codes of society, its history and beliefs. Every movie represents the world in some way and calls us to some kind of response. On the other hand, every movie to some extent stands on its own terms, separate from any factors except the internal ones that created it. The personal and esthetic functions involve the "voice" that a movie conveys in itself and the particular construction that this movie displays.

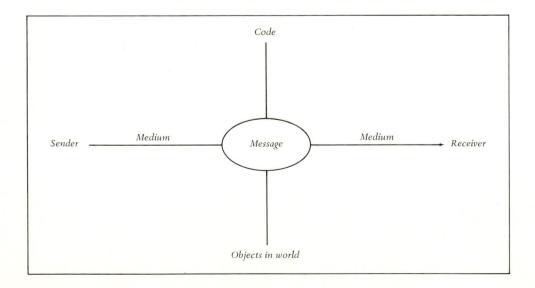

What have we now got? Well, counterpoints and balances at another level. The functions are all present in any movie, and yet the relative emphasis of one over another can vary. A particular movie may be strongly realist, or political, or personalist overall. One political movie may maintain an objective, realist form, but another may show the director's personal biases and passions. And a great number of movies maintain a more or less even balance among all the functions. These we can say are the most transparent in their approach: they exploit all the functions without drawing great attention to any one of them.

No one approach is necessarily any better than another. When you come out of a theater and say "That was a good movie," you might mean one or all of several things: it really showed me something about life; it taught me something important; I particularly liked its attitude; it was beautifully put together. As we have already seen in our discussions of criticism, a person's idea of good filmmaking depends a lot on that individual's particular sensitivity to the functions. One person may overlook clumsy structure in responding to a movie's sense of honest reality. Another may feel that the personality of a movie director or star is the major criterion. Another may respond mainly to splendid storytelling and craftsmanship. Yet another may feel that a good movie is one that clearly tries to change the viewer's attitude.

Our aim in this book is to lay out a system that deals with filmmaking both as unique experience and as communication. That, we feel, will provide at least a sensible base from which you will make your personal judgments.

In this section (Chapters 7 through 9) we turn to the most familiar movies: those made in the Hollywood narrative tradition. We will look at the way Hollywood forms interrelate the four functions in a generally balanced, or transparent way, but with subtle shifts of emphasis at different times.

In the next section (Chapters 10 through 13) we will turn to the basic alternatives to the Hollywood approach. There we will deal with filmmakers who more specifically commit their work to one function or another.

1. Varieties of this same model can be found in Pierre Guiraud, Semiology (London: Routledge and Kegan Paul, 1975), p. 5; in Laurence Behrens, "The Argument in Film: Applying Rhetorical Theory to Film Criticism," Journal of the University Film Association, 31 (Summer 1979), 3–11; and in Don Fredericksen, "Modes of Reflexive Film," Quarterly Review of Film Studies, 4 (Summer 1979), 299–319. The major source for the model is Roman Jakobson, "Closing Statement: Linguistics and Poetics," in Thomas A. Sebeok, ed., Style in Language (Cambridge, Mass.: M.I.T., 1960), 350–377.

Chapter 7 / Hollywood's

Social Aspect

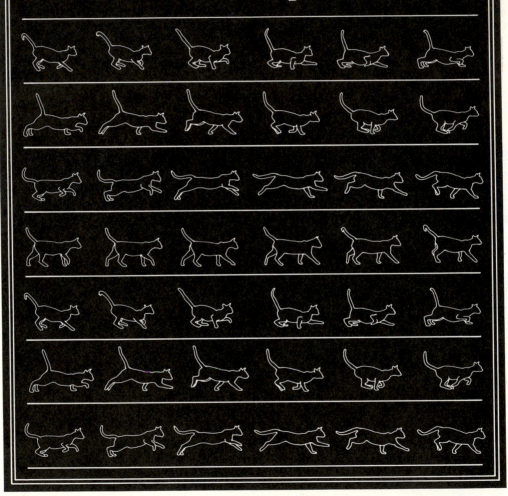

The Hollywood tradition of filmmaking is both the product of American society and an influence upon that society. Hollywood came into prominence through a number of external forces. Some of these were specifically technological and economic: they led to a strongly organized system of movie production, much akin to the factory systems that have become typical in all walks of American life. Other forces involved more generalized cultural attitudes: Hollywood gave body to fundamental needs and ideals of the American people. In its turn, Hollywood has had impact on that culture. By focusing social forces into very popular forms, Hollywood movies have affected styles, attitudes, and the social order in general.

Hollywood represents a particular *narrative* tradition. Most of its movies tell stories, and in formulaic ways that have become synonymous with the word *Hollywood.*

A narrative has several characteristic elements. It implies a storyteller who involves the audience in a rising complexity of imaginary events. There is a progression of events in time and an intensification of experience as the story progresses. A narrative typically begins with a situation in which various conflicts develop around some central figure, or *protagonist,* who faces one or more opposing forces or characters, the *antagonists.* The conflicts give rise to a new situation that in a brief story may end the action, or else the second situation may then develop new conflicts, continuing on to new situations and conflicts until there is some major clash, or *climax,* bringing things to a stable condition that ends the rising action. We can speak of a story as a work of the imagination that moves through imbalance from one kind of tentative equilibrium to another.[1]

There were many traditions of American narrative before the movies arrived, but what Hollywood did was to turn earlier traditions into new formulas that proved highly successful with the public—successful on a mammoth scale. These formulas were organized to manufacture effective stories as efficiently as possible.

The functions that Hollywood stories serve can be divided into two groups. One, which includes the personal and esthetic functions, represents the internal forces at work in the movies, or what we will call the artistic impact to be discussed in Chapter 8. There we will look at the individuals who tell or present the stories and at structural principles they demonstrate. Here we are concerned with external functions, the realist and persuasive, that form the social aspect. First we will ask, What is a Hollywood movie's relation to the real world? Second, What kinds of reaction does the Hollywood movie elicit?

HOLLYWOOD NARRATIVE AND THE REAL WORLD

Hollywood developed formulas that operated at every level of storytelling. Most stories fell into certain overriding popular types, or what today would be called *genres*, with characteristic conflicts and settings. Situations and characters fell into typical categories, long familiar from the stage and popular fiction. Popular characters reappeared in series of stories, just as in the old dime novels. Screen acting was organized into a movie *star system* that used particular performers for particular kinds of roles. The construction of movies also became tightly systematized, organized by scripts into numbered shots, so that stories could be broken down by location or type of shot to facilitate shooting and editing. Popular devices like poignant close-ups or last-minute rescues were structured in precisely, and production was broken down into specialized jobs.[2]

Hollywood's genre system was not entirely a deliberate construction, like a bridge or house. It was also a cultural inheritance that was transformed as time went on by the communication between society and filmmakers—an unsure and chancy kind of communication that has been immortalized in the word *box office*. Filmmakers sought new ways to exploit the public's interests while remaining at the mercy of public whims. There was no logical consistency in what resulted. It was an evolutionary process that might best be compared with a river system, whose tributaries (theatrical and literary traditions) feed into new mainstreams (movie genres) that may divide into branches (subgenres) or mix with other streams. Plotting the whole river system is the task of a genre encyclopedist. Here we can bring up some major issues, though, beginning with the realist issue: what has this peculiar river system of storytelling got to do with ordinary life?

Narrative: The Function of Myth and Folklore

People use stories to deal with the world. The modern forms of popular narrative in literature, drama, and cinema are extensions of a much more ancient system of storytelling. It originates in the stories every culture tells of its origins, recounting the deeds usually of gods or supernatural beings to explain the relations of mankind to the universe. These are *myths*: large, controlling images that give meaning to the details of that culture's everyday life.[3] As philosopher Susanne Langer has explained, myth making stems from the human need to symbolize, a process more fundamental than the desire to organize or classify material. We transform our everyday experience through "the sheer expression of ideas," creating dynamic and dramatic conceptions of the world.[4] Each culture has its own conceptions, collected into a mythology. We are familiar with the Judeo-Christian images of a single, personal God creating humans in a Garden of Eden that they lose through disobedience, afterwards suffering a flood, captivity, wandering, and tribal conflicts. These stories are collected in the biblical Book of Genesis ("book of origin"), which provides a code of belief that is simple and clearly defined—compared with the wide variety of myths found in other cultures. The ancient Germanic tribes told many versions of stories about fallible, gaming gods who created people from trees. The Aztecs pictured humankind created by gods who sacrificed themselves to feed the sun. In some Eskimo belief, humans are created accidentally by a Crow Father who quarrels with them and takes away the sun.

The value of such stories is predominantly religious. They closely relate to a culture's rituals and theology. Thus Jews and Christians emphasize repentance and personal prayer; ancient Germans venerated trees and lived in dread that stronger demons would destroy the world in a "twilight of the gods"; Aztecs sacrificed humans in a spirit of renewal; and Eskimos once told an anthropologist, "We do not believe; we fear."[5]

But people do not generate stories only to explain the cosmic forces that trouble them. They also symbolize dreams, social relationships, and historical events. Out of this come legends, ballads, and various kinds of tales—or *folklore,* whose characters are often more specific and personal than those of myth. Folklore deals with more *secular* problems than myth, and often asks for simple enjoyment more than for strict belief. It gives us culture-heroes like King Arthur, the Cid, or Beowulf, whose powers border on the supernatural though the heroes stem from historical figures. Folklore also gives us commoner heroes like Davy Crockett, Wild Bill Hickok, or Molly Pitcher, historical persons whose exploits tend to be exaggerated beyond normal bounds.

Folklore may remain an *oral narrative* tradition, passed on and embellished by singers and tellers, or it may be recorded in one way or another, and it may become commercial. Then it moves into the arenas of popular fiction (from the nineteenth-century dime novel to the modern paperback), theatrical melodrama (on stage or on television soap operas), and the movies.

These entertainment media refer to the culture's assumptions and codes of value—its *ideology* or way of thinking. Popular stories exhibit the tendencies of their ancient predecessors. They repeat familiar character types in familiar situations, but with many variations on the basic story formulas, and while providing an "escape" from ordinary reality, they also present cultural beliefs and doubts. It is not their function to pass on accurate history. They usually take liberties with facts, passing on what history *means* to the storytelling community. In a way, then, the "escape" we speak of in movies is not escape at all. We confront ourselves in a different mode that allows a focus, emphasis, and release not attainable outside the movie theater. However entertained, we confront what Langer has called "moral orientation, not escape."[6]

Hollywood Genres as Mythic Forms

At the mass popular level, Hollywood movies function in the manner of myth and folklore. They repeat formulas, and yet with virtually infinite variations; and they provide American society a way to reinforce its beliefs about reality while also expressing the doubts that always arise around our beliefs. Thus movies help give us a national identity.

There cannot be a one-movie genre. A genre *repeats* its particular kinds of characters, settings, situations, and themes. It repeats a basic pattern of relationships, but with elements that are all variables. In oral folklore there are traditionally repeated phrases, names, situations, and choruses. They help tellers and singers anchor down the type of story while leaving them free to introduce variables as they wish. In this way, epics developed hundreds of varying verses, and a rich variety of shorter ballads and legends evolved from a single topic. In the movies, basic story patterns are anchored down by tradition and box-office success. After that, the filmmakers, somewhat like old bards and balladeers, play upon the variables.

We might expect that Hollywood movies would reinforce cultural beliefs: tell people what they want to hear, assure them that their code of values is secure. Most of them do end with the norms of society triumphant: love conquers all, the protagonist protects defenseless people, and the villains are defeated. In fact, though, the mere setting up of social values in terms of a conflict raises questions about the security of those values. Many stories raise a kind of mature doubt, even when they end to society's advantage. Anthropologist Claude Lévi-Strauss thinks that myth operates in a dialectical way: the many characters and situations in traditional stories create sets of relationships that keep opposing each other, so that "mythical thought always moves from the awareness of oppositions towards their progressive mediation."[7] The very terminology we use when speaking of stories reinforces this insight. Conflicts in stories are not *solved:* they are *re-solved* (resolved), brought back into mediation once more, until another variation on the same story forces us to take up the struggle again, and resolve it again.

These patterns of repetition with variation and belief with doubt are as strong in movies as in myth and folklore. We can see them in familiar Hollywood genres: the

7.1 The stereotypical Western setting.

Western, the underworld film, the horror movie, the science-fiction film, the war film, and the love story or romantic melodrama. These genres present conflicts that mirror major beliefs and doubts in American culture. These ideological issues can all be summarized simply: society's values sometimes come into conflict with an individual's values. But there are various aspects of this conflict. Let us consider only four of them and the ways that genre films present them.[8]

The Meaning of Civilization   Civilized society depends on codes of belief and conduct that individuals agree to in order to make sense of the world. Without such codes—legal, philosophical, ethical, economic—there would be chaos. What this means, in effect, is that a civilization draws a boundary between itself and chaos and is therefore always threatened by that chaos. This fact is so basic that it may be found in some form in almost any story, but two genres make particular use of boundaries: the Western and the horror movie. Let's consider each in turn.

    We identify a Western immediately by its setting: a frontier, a border of society's progress (Fig. 7.1). This determines the nature of its crucial conflicts. On the one hand is civilization with its towns, laws, and family life; on the other is a rugged wilderness peopled by savages and outlaws. The protagonist, usually a man,

confronts the inevitable threats to civilization and takes violent action to overcome them. He may be a lawman or some other emissary of the frontier community—or his own character may itself be somewhere between wild and civilized, so that he must choose where his ultimate allegiance lies.[9]

In the simplest Western stories we may find a virtuous man in a white hat outshooting a black-hatted villain and saving an innocent, helpless town. They present a hero who follows a clear, absolute code—without any doubts (Fig. 7.2). His clear-cut victories are particularly appealing to youngsters, who find in him someone they can identify with in dealing with their typical feelings of inferiority and insecurity.[10] But there are many Westerns with more ambiguous situations that appeal to more mature viewers. In these the villains may not be simply evil, the town simply innocent, or the hero simply virtuous.

In *Stagecoach*, a cowboy named Ringo, who has killed one man to avenge his brother's death and is on his way to kill two others, joins a band of travelers and helps lead them through hostile Indian territory. The band includes a prostitute, a pregnant woman, a gambler, a drunken doctor, a traveling salesman, a crooked banker and a sheriff—a sampling of civilization's strengths and weaknesses (Fig. 7.3). Under Ringo's leadership they band together, survive a ferocious Indian attack, and reach safety. In gratitude, the sheriff lets Ringo confront the last of his brother's killers, then sends the cowboy and the prostitute off to find a happier life together in the wilderness . . . away from civilization.

The story shows the values of human community and a personal moral code, with full awareness of civilization's corruptions and the limitations of revenge. The movie works out all the story's conflicts in strong action, using its different settings—the open wilderness, the closed coach, the dark town where Ringo finally faces down the killers—to enhance the different kinds of conflict. The strong central hero is both savage and civilized, and the story's action interweaves close personal conflicts with sweeping engagements that reach epic proportions.

7.2 Simple Western confrontation. The hero (Rod Cameron) deals with a villain (George Douglas) in *Riders of the Santa Fe* (1944).

This is the Western's way of depicting the boundaries of civilization. The horror movie involves a more fundamental frontier—one that is meaningful to more than Americans. We identify horror movies by situations where what we confront *cannot* be possible yet *is* happening. Sometimes the events are shown to have a rational explanation (for example, unimagined powers of science); sometimes they demonstrate absolutely supernatural powers (devils or demons); and sometimes we are left unsure if they are one or the other.[11]

The horror in *Frankenstein* (1931) is rationally explained, though fantastic in form. A scientist, Victor Frankenstein, creates a living human from parts of corpses, only to have the creature break away from his control and become a threat to society. Boris Karloff's acting and Jack Pierce's creative make-up combined to give Americans a classic monster: a huge brute shambling in leaden shoes, eyelids drooping, with electrodes jutting from its scarred flesh. The creature has a pathetic, sensitive side, as though good instincts were struggling with the malevolent ones. Audiences may

7.3 Complex Western situation: the strong and weak characters in *Stagecoach* (1939). Standing (left to right) are Donald Meek, Andy Devine, George Bancroft, Tim Holt, and John Carradine. Seated (left to right) are John Wayne, Claire Trevor, Louise Platt, Francis Ford, Barton Churchill, and Thomas Mitchell.

sympathize more with the monster than with the hero or heroine he threatens (Fig. 7.4). In *The Bride of Frankenstein* (1935), the monster becomes positively heroic. An evil scientist forces Frankenstein to create a mate for the monster—but when the mate rejects him, the forlorn monster orders Frankenstein and his wife to leave, then blows up the lab, sacrificing himself but destroying all the evil in it. The very name *Frankenstein* has come to mean the monster, not its creator. The monster has become the protagonist.

Like other traditional monster movies, *Frankenstein* crosses the boundary between the known and the unknown—between what civilization agrees is good knowledge and what is, if not outright evil, at least terribly threatening. As an evil doctor in *The Vampire Bat* (1931) puts it, "There are many mysteries beyond the ability of the human mind to comprehend." And these are not necessarily happy mysteries. America admires scientific advance, but we know it creates threats of social destruction and chaos. The horror movie puts this into some kind of ultimate, fantastic confrontation. And our tendency to sympathize with the hideous creature that results suggests, if nothing else, that we appreciate what it is like to be at the mercy of forces we cannot know or control. This echoes in modern terms what the Eskimos meant when they said, "We fear."

The Value of Civilization   The Western and horror movie focus on external threats to civilization, but there are internal threats, too. We have already alluded to them in relation to the Western town, and they certainly appear in many other stories. But two genres give classic expression to our concern about the dubious values within civilization, its seemingly inherent corruptions. These are the underworld film and the war film. Let's consider each in turn.

7.4 Frankenstein's monster. Boris Karloff and Mae Clarke in *Frankenstein* (1931).

Savages within the confines of civilization dwell in a place that our stories call "the underworld," a kind of hell. They are relatives of Western outlaws, but the underworld is no open frontier. It is a dark, claustrophobic hiding place associated with the city, where deeds are done secretly or with mechanized efficiency: the world of snub-nosed pistols in hidden holsters, Thompson submachine guns, bombs, and black limousines spewing death (Fig. 7.5). We classify the people by different names: gangsters, hoods, private eyes, molls, mobsters, hit men, the Syndicate, the Mafia. Their conflicts are with each other as well as with the representatives of the law—who may be equally corrupt. We cannot speak simply of these stories' central figures as heroes. Some are offenders against society; some are victims of society's corruption; and some stand cynically apart from society.

The *gangster* protagonist sprang up in movies about the time that the bloodiest era of real gangland slayings came to an end in Chicago. Some famous gangster actors were Edward G. Robinson in *Little Caesar* (1930), James Cagney in *Public Enemy* (1931), and Paul Muni in *Scarface* (1932). Physically small men, they personified lower-class figures who rose to immense power in the age of Prohibition, when traffic in liquor and prostitution meant quick wealth. There was something of the "mad dog" in such figures. They were simply society's bad seed. Later, after religious and

7.5 The underworld setting. A scene from *Scarface* (1932).

educational leaders spoke out against the dangerous influence of such characters on impressionable young viewers, some gangsters were shown as basically good men turned wrong by their environment. In *Roaring Twenties* (1939), for example, Cagney plays a war veteran who turns to crime because his country cannot provide him with honest work.

The *bandit-gangster*, another underworld protagonist,[12] was a hybrid character, in part a modern, mechanized figure of the underworld, but in part also a rural figure roaming the countryside in the tradition of Jesse James, Belle Starr, or, for that matter, Robin Hood. Romantic love is an issue in many bandit-gangster stories, far more than in classic gangster tales, where women are flashy molls treated merely as pieces of property. The central bandit-gangster characters are often doomed lovers. In *You Only Live Once* (1937) they are innocents wrongly accused of crime. In *High Sierra* (1941) the man is an ex-convict who falls in love while leading a gang on one last, doomed robbery. And in *They Live by Night* (1948) the woman is an innocent who falls in love with a bandit. In all, the lovers are hounded by an essentially cold-blooded society.

A third variety of underworld protagonist is the *detective* or "private eye." He existed through the thirties, but he became particularly popular in the forties and early fifties. The private eye stood between evil gangsters and hoods, on one hand, and, on the other, law officers who were equally antagonistic and often corrupt. The private eye followed his personal moral code in a dark, chaotic world. We find his most familiar characterization in Humphrey Bogart's portrayal of Sam Spade in *The Maltese Falcon* (1941). Spade puts up with danger and mayhem, and finally turns in a woman who promises him wealth and love, all because he feels that a man ought to solve his partner's murder—even if he didn't like the partner very much.

In the underworld genre, then, it is often the socially unacceptable or questionable figures who stand at the center of the conflict and draw our attention and perhaps our allegiance. The gangster and the bandit-gangster are bound to die, and so they draw sympathy; the private eye is anti-heroic, yet a wise cynic. The attraction of dubious, even evil characters is one element of this genre's fascination. As Marxist critics have been quick to note, the genre is implicitly involved with American class struggle. Its reference point is the tension between those with money and power and those without it—and the viewer's focus often is on the latter. The gangster, often of immigrant stock, takes the American success ethic to a troubling extreme: if money measures success, then the means justify the end. After all, the quest for success in materialist terms often corrupts the figures of law and order themselves. Caught in between are the simpler-minded, even innocent, figures whose failure to fit into society is a troubling challenge to the American work ethic, which says that everyone who wants to work can succeed in the Land of the Free.

Depending on when it is made, a war film may ignore such class issues or strongly challenge them. In a war film the "hero" is almost a corporate entity: the whole squad, platoon, or company who depend on each other and share rivalries and affections as equals. When a war movie is made during an actual war, a time of external threat to the nation, it pushes *morale* issues, assuring the audience that its side is right, strong, and going to win. After the war, the genre is much more emphatic on *moral* issues, questioning the values and motives of society.

After World War I, for example, Lewis Milestone directed *All Quiet on the Western Front* (1930), considered a supreme achievement of the genre. It looked at the war from a German's point of view. Its sensitive central character struggles to maintain some sense of human decency amid the horror and uselessness of the fighting (Fig. 7.6). In a final symbol of frustration, he is killed by an enemy sniper as he reaches for a butterfly beside the trenches. During World War II, Milestone directed *The Purple Heart* (1944), a story of American airmen captured by the Japanese. There is little moral dimension in these enemies, though. They are depicted essentially as depraved monsters insane with blood lust. In one scene they leap about bizarrely, brandishing samurai swords in celebration of a battle victory. After that war, as we shall note shortly, there was another swing back to moral doubt.

The war film's swings toward moral doubt don't, however, change its intriguing ambiguity about the value of war to American civilization. The war film depends on the fact that war is exciting, a natural excuse for dynamic action; and even when a film questions or denounces war, the excitement remains. The audience may

7.6 War film dealing with moral issues. A German soldier (Lew Ayres) helps a dying French soldier (Raymond Griffith) in *All Quiet on the Western Front* (1930).

sympathize when, as in *What Price Glory?* (1926), weary soldiers cry out, "Stop the blood!" But the fascination of epic movie bloodshed has brought the audience to the theater. Within this counterattraction, the moral-oriented war film tends to raise the same questions about class structure as do many underworld films. The lower classes (soldiers) are sacrificed to the power plays of distant upper classes (politicians and generals). Like the gangster, war is a social factor we both loathe and find fascinating, and movies play upon our sense of values.

The Pastoral Myth   Another thread of ideology that runs through American genres is the belief that nature is ultimately better than technology, that "getting back to the country" is a sure way to peace and contentment. This pastoral myth was a popular literary theme long before America was discovered, but it finds strong expression here. It is basically another aspect of the civilization and savagery motif in Westerns, or the bandit-gangster's predicament in underworld films. It predominated in silent-film genres known as "country boy" and "country girl" movies (Fig. 7.7) represented by *Tol'able David* (1921) and *True Heart Susie* (1919). Since the twenties, though, the pastoral myth feeds more quietly into all genres. It is a distinctively nostalgic value that we hold onto and yet challenge all the time. In *The Asphalt Jungle* (1950), for example, a bandit-gangster wants money to return to the country, and he finally races there, after being mortally wounded in the city, to die in an open field. Such imagery means a lot to Americans, even though in films from *Miss Lulu Bett* (1921) to *Peyton Place* (1957) and beyond, we have enjoyed seeing that life can be as traumatic in a small town as anywhere else.

Love, Eroticism, and Marriage   Freudian psychology has made us aware that society seeks to channel the sexual drive into acceptable, useful forms—marriage being the obvious example. But we also know that this channeling process can create frustrated and psychotic individuals who are misfits and threats to society. The conflict

7.7 Scene evoking the pastoral myth. Richard Barthelmess in *Tol'able David* (1921).

between accepted and forbidden love feeds all genres, but two make particularly emphatic use of it: the romantic melodrama and the horror film.

The romantic melodrama is sometimes called the "woman's film." Though it used to carry a kind of derogatory implication, the term makes sense when you consider that women in America have long borne the brunt of having to keep society stable regarding love and marriage. Women's eroticism attracts men, whom they settle into stable marriages. So the woman has typically had to face the trauma of finding "true" love and of maintaining her "proper" role, problems at the heart of romantic melodrama. In *Dark Victory* (1939), for example, Bette Davis plays a headstrong woman whose life seems to have no center until she marries a good doctor, whereupon she gains the strength to face death bravely alone. In *Now Voyager* (1942) she plays a lonely spinster who falls in love with a married man. He offers her everything she has never had, but she finally refuses to marry him, because doing so would wreck his home; instead she devotes herself to his troubled daughter, fulfilling her social function that way. *Mildred Pierce* (1945), on the other hand, shows a woman, played by Joan Crawford, who deserts her husband, becomes an aggressive business woman and showers unhealthy affection on her daughter. The woman comes to grief, though she returns to her husband at last and faces a happier, more socially integrated future.

These films handle romance with what today seems a very repressive attitude toward woman's role in society. She is expected to know her place and keep it, or know the consequences. This is a male-oriented point of view, and it reflects cautiousness about—if not an outright fear of—the woman's power in society, which is ultimately related to sexual power. This changed in the sixties and seventies, as we will see, but in the meantime the horror film was expressing the conflict between sexual power and social order in different terms.

Eroticism is a persistent factor in the horror genre. Consider Dracula, the most famous of those demons beyond the limits of natural science. He is sexually attractive to women, who join him in living death, preying on others, and he and his followers can only be overcome through religious and occult practices. Bela Lugosi's performance in the *Dracula* of 1931 combined a suave and chilling manner in a style that now is outdated and has been parodied a lot. But in the forties and fifties, handsome Christopher Lee updated the sexual attraction of the vampire in a number of British movies built off the traditional formula, and in a new *Dracula* in 1979 American actor Frank Langella created a sensual figure who was touted as a romantic idol (Fig. 7.8). We may no longer believe that a Dracula is literally possible—as more ancient civilizations did—but he is still an image of eroticism's threat to society. And the horror genre treats him with a traditional ambivalence. On one hand, his perversity is part of a living death; on the other, he is a fascinating force who is extremely difficult to overcome. The vampire film can be particularly appealing to adolescents, who have natural fears about controlling sexual urges.

Eroticism is often a factor, too, in those rarer horror movies that leave us wondering if what happens is rationally explained or supernatural, or perhaps both. *The Cat People* (1942), mentioned in Chapter 4, is a variation on the werewolf formula: a woman is afraid that her sexual fear and jealousy will turn her into a panther that kills anyone who threatens her. Is this a supernatural curse or a psychological phobia? The movie never answers this simply—though RKO studios insisted that producer Val Lewton insert one quick shot of a panther to assure the viewer. The ambiguous feeling remains. Lewton's *I Walked with a Zombie* (1943) and *Isle of the Dead* (1945) deal with ghost stories in similar ways. They play upon the viewer's dread of forces that cannot easily be explained, one way or another, and the forces are strongly linked to women's sexual power (Fig. 7.9).

In this section we have only touched on a few of the many cultural issues that Hollywood genre films make reference to. These issues are not restricted to genre

7.8 Male sexuality in the horror film. Frank Langella and Kate Nelligan in *Dracula* (1979).

7.9 Female sexuality in the horror film. Marguerite Churchill (left) and Gloria Holden in *Dracula's Daughter* (1936).

films. Nontraditional stories make reference to the same concerns, for they mark off the world of American identity and belief: our ideology, to which all communication refers. Hollywood genres are simply·conventional, formulaic expressions of it.

We have omitted some familiar genres: the science-fiction film, the suspense movie, the police adventure. Like the others, these have distinctive settings, character, and themes; they may also share some characteristics with other genres. The horror film blends into the science-fiction film and the suspense film; the underworld film shades into the police adventure. Again, Hollywood genres are not neatly isolated from one another: they are like a river system which flows, blends, changes—and has an effect on us. Movies stir *reactions* with their references to American realities. This is their persuasive function, and we need to look at it now.

HOLLYWOOD NARRATIVE AND SOCIETY'S RESPONSES

Like any other message, a movie aims primarily at our intelligence or at our emotions. These are the two basic kinds of persuasive function. An educational film strives to make us understand something, to clarify ideas, to present facts in an objective way. Hollywood narratives, on the other hand, do not seek to educate. They invite our emotional participation. If they raise cultural issues, it is not to discuss them as ideas but as emotion-laden values. Hollywood movies play upon our subjective, subconscious reactions, moving us to fear, sympathy, laughter, and tears.

And because Hollywood has communicated to such a large mass of Americans, it has triggered two kinds of reaction. On one hand, it has had a tremendous effect on national attitudes, mores, codes of behavior, and even styles of dress. The power of the star system is an obvious example of this. Audiences identify with stars and emulate them. Publicity and fan magazines maintain the emotional contact even when stars are not making movies. And this affects more than just individuals. According to one legendary account, when Clark Gable took off his shirt in *It Happened One Night* (1934) and revealed a bare chest, the sale of undershirts in the nation dropped virtually overnight, and the garment industry complained bitterly.[13] Obviously, movies trigger powerful effects. On the other hand, these very effects rouse concern, particularly among parents, educators, psychologists, and those who enforce the law. All feel that Hollywood should not become an irresponsible medium of entertainment. They worry that Hollywood's myths are not historically accurate, that children are led to emulate the wrong kinds of people, and that such communication may threaten the legal and moral fabric of American society. It may be that some critics expect Hollywood to provide a form of cultural leadership that is beyond its nature or function; Hollywood, as we have suggested, does indeed spin myths and folklore; this makes it a channel for our culture's discussions with itself, not simply a medium of accuracy and rational truth. But the quarrels are not baseless. Because Hollywood is so powerful, we cannot expect society to ignore its potential dangers. Society must maintain some kind of control over its elements if it is indeed to be a society.

The issue of social control almost immediately raises the specter of *censorship,* the prohibition of materials deemed unfit for public consumption. It is a particularly troublesome idea to Americans, who pride themselves on living in a free society. The very idea of censorship raises the ire of many, while others insist with equal vehemence that some censorship is essential. The history of social control in American movies shows an interweaving of three factors trying to achieve some kind of sensible control over movies' social effects without violating the American tradition of free speech. The three factors are legal and governmental restraint, economic pressure by particular groups, and regulation by the industry itself. Let us outline each.

Legal and Governmental Restraint

The good of society may require that a certain kind of communication be curtailed or its use punished. In time of war, for example, the government may feel that the publishing of information would be detrimental to the nation; and at any time it is illegal to use communication to incite the public to rebellion against the lawful government, to violence, or to obscenity. There has been considerable governmental restraint imposed at different times on movies, but the thorniest issues have risen over the legal restraint of violence and obscenity.

The movies were a troubling new challenge to the principles by which the law judged entertainment. Movies invited vicarious participation by a large public seated in darkness; there was nothing in previous folk experience quite like them. By 1907 some cities had set up censorship boards to review movies and charge license fees because movies were "liable to degenerate and menace the good order and morals of the people," as one group put it. Such censors believed that "the average person of healthy and wholesome mind" knew what "immoral" and "obscene" meant.[14]

This assumption set up the procedure of *prior restraint.* Any movie could be viewed by city or state censors before it was exhibited to the public, and if the censors decided against it, it could not be legally shown—at least not in that particular city or state. In 1915, the United States Supreme Court supported prior restraint in a judgment against the Mutual Film Corporation, which had challenged Ohio's right to such censorship. The court's opinion clarified that legal restraint was justified because movies were "a business pure and simple" and therefore did not come under the First Amendment rights of free speech.[15]

The decision may seem shocking today, but it codified an attitude toward the movie industry that would not be changed for thirty-seven years and is still invoked by a number of city censorship boards. But in 1952 the Supreme Court handed down a new opinion. It decided in favor of Joseph Burstyn, a film distributor who had been enjoined by the city of New York's censor board from showing *The Miracle,* an Italian film involving a retarded woman who believes she is pregnant by the Holy Ghost. The censors found the movie "officially and personally blasphemous," but the court decreed that "it cannot be doubted that motion pictures are a significant medium for the communication of ideas" and hence come under the protection of the First Amendment. To be declared obscene (or blasphemous, in a religious definition of obscenity) a film must (1) appeal to prurient interest—that is, seek merely to arouse lewd desires; (2) be offensive to community standards; and (3) have no redeeming social or artistic value. The second and third criteria in particular suggested that restraint could not be imposed on a movie before the public had seen it. A movie should not be declared illegal by prior restraint, then, but through the normal *criminal process,* whereby a charge of illegality can be raised by some member of the viewing community, who takes the offending party to court.[16]

The *Miracle* decision brought greater complexity into matters of legal restraint. The "offending party" might be the producer, distributor or—most often—the exhibitor, who had fewest legal resources to fall back on, and thus prior restraint continued to be practiced unchallenged in many places. But the triple criteria codified the awareness that movies were a mature form of expression, and that no one "average person" or small group could assume to know what "immoral" or "obscene" meant.

These attitudes have gone through one more modification, no doubt influenced by a new freedom of expression in movies that, in turn, raised new, conservative worries about their social effects. In 1973 the Supreme Court declared that, while the old criteria of prurience, offense, and redeeming values still applied, they were determined by the *local* community, not by national standards. This has made issues even more complex and thorny. In Austin, Texas, for example, the city attorney brought obscenity charges against *Deep Throat,* a sexually very explicit movie; but after three juries were deadlocked, the charges were dropped. In San Antonio, ninety miles from Austin, *Deep Throat* was also taken to court and found obscene in the first trial. It is therefore illegal to show the movie in one city, legal in the other. In

Memphis, charges were brought against one of the actors in *Deep Throat*—though they were later dismissed.

The system of legal restraint thus reflects the complex responses that movies have triggered in the public. The movies are no longer judicable as simply good or bad for social order, and the public's standards are no longer simply defined.

Economic Pressure

For some groups, movies pose serious problems, even when they stay within the limits of the law. They can undermine morals, thwart the development of equality among peoples, and confuse particularly parents who are concerned about the development of their children. These groups have made their concerns felt by bringing various kinds of economic pressure to bear on the movie industry.

The most effective pressure has been the threat of massive boycott. Among religious groups, for example, the Protestant National Council of Churches has sometimes launched attacks on the morality of movies and threatened to seek federal censorship, but the Catholic bishops got more effective results with the Legion of Decency, established in 1934. The legion previewed and rated movies on the basis of moral content, charging Catholics to stay away from those rated "B" (objectionable in part for all) and "C" (condemned). This was particularly effective because, coming from the edict of the American bishops themselves, the legion's rulings held sway over all Catholics, who represented a sizable percentage of the box office. The legion therefore exerted considerable pressure on the industry. As time went on, the legion became less negative in its attitude, praising good movies rather than condemning bad ones and providing an educational newsletter to teach Catholics more about the art of filmmaking. Reflecting this shift, it changed its name to the National Catholic Office of Motion Pictures in the sixties, and in the seventies became the Office of Film and Broadcasting of the U.S. Catholic Conference. It still brings pressure to bear on film companies to respect its moral sensitivities.

In 1915 the National Association for the Advancement of Colored People spoke out vehemently against the depiction of blacks in *The Birth of a Nation*. But the NAACP was a small group then, with little influence on black filmgoers, and so its pressure was ineffectual. By 1963, however, the NAACP spoke for some twenty million black viewers, and when it denounced the "artistic and moral dishonesty" of black caricatures in Hollywood movies, the industry listened. There was an increase in black players, black stars began to appear prominently, and racial issues were more openly presented on screen (Fig. 7.10).[17]

7.10 Changing image of blacks. a. Willie Best, shown in *Murder on a Bridle Path* (1936), represents the kind of stereotyping that the NAACP resented. b. Sidney Poitier, shown with Elizabeth Hartman in *A Patch of Blue* (1965), represents the new black image that emerged in the 1960s.

Industry Self-Regulation

Hollywood has not ignored the issue of social control. Whenever widespread censorship or pressure has threatened, it has responded with some form of self-regulation. Its motives have been almost entirely economic. If Hollywood rouses too much legal censure or moral indignation, the box office can suffer, and mass filmmaking requires a great deal of money. Thus, through film history there has been a kind of see-sawing activity: demands for control on one hand, and Hollywood's response on the other.

In 1909, in direct response to threats by New York censors to close down movie houses, the film industry gave financial and moral support to the National Board of Censorship—later the National Board of Review—which reviewed and evaluated movies, particularly as an aid to parents. Despite this, thirty-six states were considering film censorship by 1921, and Hollywood hired Will H. Hays, an ex–postmaster general with an impeccable moral reputation, to head the Motion Picture Producers and Distributors Association of America (MPPDA)—thereafter known as "the Hays Office." It was essentially a public relations office, designed to assure the American public that the movie industry was upstanding. Hays made a list of "Don'ts and Be Carefuls" for the guidance of producers. They forbade the use of such things as profanity, nudity, illegal drug traffic, prostitution, sexual relations between people of different races, or ridicule of the clergy; and they urged special care in showing firearms, crime techniques, violence, sympathy for criminals, rape, or lustful scenes.[18] The list gives some insight into the mores of the time, but producers gradually ignored it, finding that the public was more interested in stories with a degree of sensationalism.

In 1930 Martin Quigley, a trade publisher, and Daniel A. Lord, a Jesuit priest, drafted the Motion Picture Production Code, which producers were to promise to follow. It was a more explicit updating of the Don'ts and Be Carefuls, breaking forbidden or cautioned material into areas including crime, brutality, sex, vulgarity, obscenity, blasphemy and profanity, costumes, religion, national feelings, and

a

b

cruelty to animals.[19] The attempt to legislate the code led nowhere until 1934, when federal censorship was again threatened and the Legion of Decency was formed. Then the industry set up its own censor, Joseph I. Breen (succeeded later by Geoffrey M. Shurlock), who was empowered to withhold a Production Code Seal of Approval from any movie that violated the code.

For twenty years the industry's filmmakers worked within the code system, bargaining with the censor over disputed scripts or scenes and appealing if necessary to a review board made up of the heads of major companies. But by the late fifties, the code had begun to relax its hold. Some filmmakers had refused to acquiesce in the censor's demands, even releasing movies without a seal of approval—and the code authorities in turn discovered that American moral attitudes had changed, so that audiences were not necessarily shocked by subjects like drug addiction, as in *The Man with the Golden Arm* (1956), or blatant adultery, as in *The Moon Is Blue* (1953), *Double Indemnity* (1944), or *From Here to Eternity* (1953).

However, this more relaxed attitude, combined with the more liberal legal interpretations of the Miracle Period, led again to cries of moral laxity and the need for federal censorship. So in 1968, Jack Valenti, head of the Motion Picture Association of America (the MPPDA's new title), announced a new ratings system that would, in effect, replace the old code system. Movies would now be rated under four classifications: G, for general admission; PG, where parental guidance is suggested; R, where children under sixteen must be accompanied by parents; and X, where no one under eighteen is admitted. The new classification system was designed to satisfy parents and educators who wanted guidelines to follow in selecting films for children, and it was also intended to help filmmakers avoid lawsuits. Moreover, some filmmakers felt that their freedom of expression was thwarted by a code system that judged all movies by the same criteria. In fact, the classification system has alleviated few pressures. Parents and educators find some listings entirely too lenient—as when *Jaws* (1975), a film with horrific scenes of a shark attacking people, received a PG. Exhibitors discovered that an R or X roused the ire of moralists, and producers still had to bargain with the MPAA administration to get ratings that would not hurt them at the box office.[20] By the late seventies many producers were avoiding G ratings, which signified bland, uninteresting movies to viewers, as well as X ratings, which signified "dirty" movies.[21]

Like the other aspects of social control, the outline of the industry's self-regulation shows us a changing Hollywood having to deal with a changing American society. Some patterns remain consistent. American society is peculiarly sensitive about certain subject matter, notably sex and violence, and about the impact of movies on the young. But society is ambivalent in its responses. Filmmakers have long been aware that sensational subjects often do very well at the box office, even while drawing criticism and outrage. Society's frame of reference has changed, too, so that the thirties' sense of what was acceptable relaxed considerably in the fifties and sixties, only to become more conservative again in the seventies. The industry has not disguised its business nature. It needs to arouse generally positive responses in audiences to survive. But the mass audience does not always respond predictably or as a unit.

HOLLYWOOD'S SOCIAL IMPACT THROUGH HISTORY

The persuasive function of movie communication ties closely to the realistic. Filmmakers ask for responses to the worlds they reflect in their movies. And these worlds are in turn reflections of the immediate period and frame of thought that bred them. We can best see this in the total social context: history. We can break Hollywood's history into four periods, pointing out how the industry and its products reflected and appealed to the society of that time.

The Classic Period, 1915–1946

As the word *classic* suggests, Hollywood established basic principles of operation in this period, producing the most balanced and traditional forms of its communication. Between 1908 and 1915, production companies moved from the East to the West Coast, and they began to develop the systematic scripting, shooting, and editing described in Chapter 4. Classic Hollywood can be said to have declared itself in 1915 with the release of *The Birth of a Nation*, directed by D. W. Griffith. Twelve reels long and shot at a cost of $110,000, it was considered a frightful waste of time and money by other American producers. Telling a very romantic and biased story of the Civil War and the rise of the Ku Klux Klan, it was considered a travesty of history by many viewers. Yet in New York City alone, some estimators say, over 825,000 people saw it in its first run; and it went on to gross at least $5,000,000 (some estimates say $50 million).[22] Thus, *The Birth of a Nation* marks the mass impact of Hollywood mythic narrative as an economic and cultural force.

During the next fourteen years Hollywood's evolution reflected an era of great national prosperity and expansion. Relatively untouched by World War I and annoyed by the Prohibition amendment (1919), which outlawed liquor, Americans turned the twenties into the "Jazz Age," which challenged conservative standards of living. For many, Hollywood became a symbol of decadence. A series of scandals brought public outrage and cries for censorship. The most celebrated involved two very popular actors, Roscoe Arbuckle and Wallace Reid. Arbuckle was accused in 1921 of raping and causing the death of a young actress; though Arbuckle was exonerated in court, the Hays Office saw to it that he was virtually banned from further filmmaking.[23] Reid died as a result of heroin addiction in 1923.

Despite these setbacks, American movies continued strong in overall popularity. They became more sophisticated in subject matter, and they often reflected the clash between older, rural-based ways of life and new city-based attitudes. Movies like *The Thief of Bagdad* (1924) or *Flesh and the Devil* (1926) reflected the exotic and worldly figures of the new generation's taste, while *The Crowd* (1928) reflected cultural uncertainties with what proved prophetic accuracy. This finely crafted movie tells of an overconfident man who comes to the city to make his fortune, only to face bitter defeats that almost destroy him. One year after the movie's release, the stock market crash ended Jazz Age prosperity and ushered in the Depression.

The Depression and the expensive transition to sound cemented Hollywood's studio system in place. Prior to the twenties, filmmaking had been carried on largely by independent producers who found separate distributors for their movies. But Adolph Zukor at Paramount began a move toward what became known as "vertical integration," the implementation under one roof of all phases of movie communication: production, distribution, and exhibition. This led to unified film factories that produced their own movies, distributed them worldwide, and owned chains of theaters that showed only those pictures. Only such strong fortresses survived into the thirties. The most prolific were the "Big Five" (MGM, Paramount, RKO, Twentieth Century–Fox, Warner Brothers) and the "Little Three" (Columbia, United Artists, Universal), studios accounting for 70 percent or more of annual box-office receipts during the rest of the Classic Period.[24]

The studio system was the utmost in efficient storytelling for the masses. Each major studio developed a fairly distinctive way to tell the kind of story it preferred. In this process Hollywood gave America images of itself that were particularly suited to the Depression. This communication is often called *escapist*—and it was, in the sense that, to a large extent, viewers wanted to forget day-to-day economic problems and confront epic, romantic, or fantastic images of life that assured them that American values were strong and good. But the escapist label tends to ignore the social awareness that intruded into many movies, which asked audiences to laugh at their Depression predicaments and sometimes to take a hard, critical look at them. Such movies remained largely affirmative about society, and they were larger and more dramatic than life—but "escapist" does not do justice to their quality.

The studios reflected the times in different ways. At one extreme was Metro-Goldwyn-Mayer, which advertised "more stars than there are in Heaven" and stressed high quality in productions that can be described as having a "well-scrubbed" American look.[25] MGM was the most escapist of studios, being very conservative in method (it was the last studio to adopt sound, for example) and in political philosophy. Its production head, Louis B. Mayer, was a staunch Republican who strongly supported President Herbert Hoover and believed that America's economic system would heal itself if left alone. MGM movies gave little indication that a Depression was going on. More than other studios, MGM stressed literary adaptations and high-class canned theater. In movies like *Mutiny on the Bounty* (1935), *The Great Ziegfeld* (1936), *The Wizard of Oz* (1939), *The Philadelphia Story* (1940), and the Andy Hardy series about adolescents in a small town, MGM stressed individual pluck and the American dream. Its greatest achievement, *Gone with the Wind* (1939), was an adaptation of a novel about an epic American struggle in the romantic past; in it the Hollywood factory system was working at its best.

At the opposite extreme from MGM was Warner Brothers. It devoted itself heavily to classic genres, particularly the underworld film, the musical, and the romantic melodrama, most of them leanly edited seven-reelers made on very tight budgets. At this time production chief Jack Warner was a staunch Democrat, devoted to the New Deal policies of Franklin D. Roosevelt. When Roosevelt became president, in fact, he offered Warner a diplomatic post, but Warner turned it down because "I can do more . . . with a good picture about America now and then."[26] In Warner Brothers pictures the Depression is often evident. They deal frequently with the harsher aspects of lower-class American life. *Marked Woman* (1937) and *I Am a Fugitive from a Chain Gang* (1932) show the hopeless lot of those trapped by prostitution and a vicious penal system. Its underworld films showed corrupted politics and broken-down economic policy breeding evil. Its musicals were essentially about poor people trying to get ahead.

Between the extremes of MGM and Warner Brothers, the other studios created a variety of distinctive worlds. Paramount stressed high quality and European sophistication in literary adaptations like *A Farewell to Arms* (1933), a melodramatic attack on war, or in escapist musicals like *Love Me Tonight* (1932) and *Mississippi* (1935), but the studio also produced a series of low-budget Westerns adapted from Zane Grey's novels. Twentieth Century–Fox specialized in Westerns, musical revues, and religious melodramas, while RKO (Radio-Keith-Orpheum) leaned toward low-budget literary adaptations, though it dealt with various genres. They ranged from the escapism of Fred Astaire–Ginger Rogers musicals, to the hard-edged realism of *Dance, Girl, Dance* (1940). Among the Little Three, Universal specialized in low-budget horror (like *Frankenstein* and *Dracula*), and Columbia leaned to comedies that showed the triumph of small-town American values over those of the corrupt city. United Artists, alone of the Hollywood leaders, was solely a distribution company for independent producers, and so had a wide diversity of product.

A good example of the studios' relationship to audiences in this period is the *A movie–B movie* system of distribution that prevailed. If Hollywood genres can be compared to a river system, then their audience is like a huge school of fish whose members generally rove where they will but can suddenly turn all together to follow some collective urge. In the Classic Period the audience moved pretty much en masse all the time—or at least the movie industry could profitably assume so. Audiences came to expect a three-hour film program during the Depression, and in most towns theaters had three changes of feature, or bill, each week. The studios needed products to fill these bills but didn't want to waste money on weeknights when audiences were thinner. They therefore developed units to make only B movies: those budgeted between $100,000 and $150,000, and seldom more than seventy-five minutes long. Theaters had to take these on weekday nights to get top-dollar "A" movies for weekends. An A movie was at least 90 minutes long and had a budget of at least $500,000. This method of distribution was called *block booking,* and the method of exhibition involved the *double feature,* or *double bill,* in which the theater paired either an A and B or else two B's to make a three-hour package that was less expensive. By 1936, 85 percent of all U.S. theaters played double bills.[27] The B movie was a piece of precisely tailored merchandise, making direct, simple, and concise use of the formulaic elements of genres. The restrictions could be remarkably tight. At Columbia in the forties, for example, B producers kept the budgets of Boris Karloff horror movies between $90,000 and $105,000; if the budget went to $130,000, the movie would lose money.[28] Audiences were consistent in their preferences, and B movies satisfied them.

World War II brought the Depression to an end in 1941 and ushered in the last phase of the Classic Period. Movies were the readiest entertainment available at a time when morale needed boosting, and Hollywood affirmed the American way of life more brightly and positively than before. By 1946 weekly movie attendance had risen to 90 million, the highest since 1930. Whereas the eight major studios took in $193 million in 1939 from U.S. film rentals, they took in $332 million in 1946—an increase of 72 percent, which made 1946 the highest income year in Hollywood history and the climax of the Classic Period. And then things went to pieces.

The Dark Age, 1947–1960

Not as many people went to movies in this period. War veterans had come back, some of them maimed and psychologically disturbed, to look for jobs and take up delayed educations while raising children of the wartime "baby boom." Television emerged in 1948 as a competitive medium of entertainment. In the same year the Supreme Court found movie studios guilty of monopolistic practices. The ruling forced studios to give up some of their old ironclad security and to deal with independent producers and stars. In both 1947 and 1951, the House Committee on Un-American Activities launched investigations into the so-called Communist infiltration of Hollywood. This led to secret industry blacklisting of any writers or filmmakers suspected of being "Red" or "pinko".

By 1950 the United States was involved in a "cold war" against communism in Europe and a "police action" in Korea that would last until 1953 and cost fifty thousand American lives but lead to no clear victory. Overall, there was national insecurity about former values, and it was reflected in Hollywood's structure and products.

The mass audience changed its habits. If we keep the fish school metaphor, we can say that from the fifties onward, audiences have broken into smaller groups attracted to particular genres and subjects and only occasionally converging en masse onto single movies. To deal with this new pattern, the industry in this period began to revamp its distribution system. As movies competed with television, double bills, cartoons, and short subjects disappeared from traditional theaters, which emphasized the single feature at least ninety minutes long. Meanwhile, drive-ins became popular. In 1948 there were 820 of them, or 4 percent of U.S. theaters—but by 1958 there were 4,063 drive-ins, or 25 percent, and they maintained that approximate percentage through the seventies. To handle the traditional and drive-in (and later inner-city) marketplaces, the industry broke into two separate circuits: *mainstream* and *exploitation*.

Mainstream theaters handled a wide diversity of products: children's films, foreign "art" films, and traditional genre movies of all sorts, including multimillion-dollar blockbusters. They bore some resemblance to theaters in the Classic Period, but the audience had changed. One critic has tried to explain the difference by saying that where previously movies talked *down* to the audience, taking its presence for granted, movies now spoke *to* a number of particular groups and interests.[29] The exploitation circuit was able to speak to a very specific and consistent audience. Drive-ins attracted rural and teenage audiences; later, inner-city theaters attracted minorities. Movies could exploit the current interests of such groups—hence the term *exploitation*—and use simple formulas designed particularly for them.

Specific exploitation companies arose. The most prolific and successful was American International Pictures, headed by Samuel Z. Arkoff. Founded in 1955, AIP began the new trend of selling low-budget features in double-bill combinations that appealed to youth. The company started with Westerns, the underworld, science-fiction, and horror, but moved on to include beach party romances, motorcycle films, as well as car chase and truckdriver adventures, striving always as Arkoff put it, "to fathom how far and how fast the youth changes were occurring."[30] Exploitation films were (and are) attacked for their cheapness, their emphasis on sex and violence, and their "disreputable" attitude, reflected in such titles as *Attack of the Crab Monsters* (1957), *How to Make a Monster* (1958), or *I Was a Teenage Werewolf* (1957). But they maintained the powerful appeal of genre formulas while also reflecting the change in audience structure and values.

The period's insecurity was reflected in various trends in movie subject-matter. It was a period in which the last extravagant, escapist musicals flourished, particularly at MGM. But narrative genres went a different route. To describe American narratives after the war, French critics coined the term *film noir*: the dark movie. This was not a new genre, but a mood of cynicism and despair that was most noticeable in love stories and underworld movies (Fig. 7.11). The obvious stylistic mark was their dark settings: city worlds of deep shadows and unseen threats. The movies combined harshly realistic subject matter with precisely controlled craftsmanship. But the darkness went beyond decor or particular genres. All story formulas reflected national cynicism, a concern with psychosis, and a sense of impending doom.

Cynicism was reflected in a number of darkened heroes. The attitude we noted in the private eye earlier now flourished in many underworld characters, not all of them literally private detectives. They were far from self-confident, and often not even very smart. Sometimes they found faith in the future, as does the vengeance-seeking cop in *The Big Heat* (1953). More often they were wry cynics just doing a job,

7.11 The *film noir* setting. Virginia Huston and Robert Mitchum in *Out of the Past* (1947).

as in *Murder, My Sweet* (1944) or *The Big Sleep* (1946). There was usually nothing cheering in the victory of law and order. The Western hero often became remarkably ambivalent toward civilization and savagery. The hero of *Comanche Station* (1960) declares, "I'm not talking about what's good, but surviving." In *Forty Guns* (1957), when a marshal confronts the killer of his brother, the killer uses the marshal's sweetheart as a shield. The Classic Period found noble means to conquer such obstacles; here the marshal simply shoots the sweetheart, then kills his opponent. As one writer has noted, the villain and the hero shared a very similar integrity, the moral being "Everyone finally loses."[31]

The *Searchers* (1956) contains an excellent example of the darkened heroic values. The hero, a wilderness man and ex–Confederate soldier still loyal to the lost cause, spends years tracking down his niece, the last living member of his family, who has been stolen by Indians. In the process he becomes as savage as the Indian chief he pursues and kills—and when he brings his niece back to civilization, he remains outside the settlement. This character, alien both to full savagery and to his own kind, is one of the most powerful images of the period.

Genre films also reflected a concern with psychosis. War movies like *The Men* (1950) and *Bright Victory* (1951) presented the emotional traumas of returning servicemen. The gangster was not just a social misfit, but often insane. The protagonists of *Baby Face Nelson* (1957) and *Al Capone* (1959) are men who love to kill, and a hoodlum in *Kiss of Death* (1947) is a sadist who shoves an old woman in a wheelchair down a flight of stairs. In Westerns like *Winchester '73* (1950) and *The Naked Spur* (1952) the hero is on the edge of hysterical obsession with revenge, solitude, or pride. *The Left-Handed Gun* (1958), touted as the first "psychological Western," shows Billy the Kid as a man driven to revenge by the death of a father figure.

White Heat (1949) is a fine example of the fascination with psychosis. This Warner Brothers film stars James Cagney as Cody Jarrett, a bandit-gangster with an oedipal obsession for his mother. As a child he feigned headaches to get her attention, and now they have become psychosomatic: physical spasms triggered by his disordered mind. While he is in prison his mother dies, and the news triggers a memorable scene in which Jarrett goes beserk in the prison dining hall. Jarrett escapes and goes on a crime rampage. He cannot trust his two-timing wife and finally confides in a man who is in fact an FBI agent sent to infiltrate the gang. Betrayed by wife and friend, he is pursued by lawmen using sophisticated radar and long-range telescopic rifles. Brought to bay at last and mortally wounded atop a gas refinery tank, Jarrett laughs insanely at his enemies and blows himself up in a huge cataclysm, screaming "Top of the world, Ma!" It is one of the period's most troubling and ambiguous movies. Society defeats a "mad dog" criminal, but only by playing upon his pathetic sexual frustrations, betraying his honest trust, and bringing him down with cold, technological efficiency.

White Heat's final cataclysm also suggests another problem on society's mind in this period: nuclear destruction. This was the first era of an Atomic Age in which Americans worried that nuclear annihilation might come unexpectedly either from the Russians or from outer space. The first reports of unidentified flying objects occurred in 1947, and the Soviets successfully launched Sputnik, the first manned space satellite, in 1957. The old monsters of the horror genre gave way in this period to the new monsters of science fiction, with its stress on the mysteries faced by advancing science. *The Thing* (1951) typified the transition. Its story involves an eight-foot creature that looks like Frankenstein and lives off human blood like Dracula, but is a vegetable of superior intelligence with no moral or emotional sense—and it comes from outer space. It was the antithesis of the American way of life. Atomic radiation began to affect the balance of nature in countless movie stories (Fig. 7.12), with fearsome results like *The Beast from 20,000 Fathoms* (1953), *The Creature from the Black Lagoon* (1954), *The Incredible Shrinking Man* (1957), *The Blob* (1958), and *The Attack of the Fifty Foot Woman* (1958).

However fantastic or preposterous, these films dealt with fundamental concerns about scientific and erotic power. *Forbidden Planet* (1956) combined both powers explicitly. The invisible antagonist that American spacemen encounter in the story turns out to be the projection of a scientist's id, trying to keep his virginal daughter free from contact with other men.

The Invasion of the Body Snatchers (1956), directed by Don Siegel, blends science fiction and traditional horror in a noteworthy reflection of 1950s paranoia. A small-town doctor and his sweetheart gradually discover that vegetable creatures

7.12 Science fiction in the atomic age. Richard Carlson and Julia Adams confront the creature in *The Creature from the Black Lagoon* (1954).

from outer space, called "pods," are taking over the bodies of their friends and reducing them to emotionless automatons. Siegel develops an increasingly hopeless situation that he intended to end with the doctor, trying to get the attention of heedless motorists on an expressway, screaming "You're next!" Allied Artists, unable to accept so negative an ending, added a sequence in which officials, realizing that the doctor might be telling the truth, set out to stop the pods.

Even with the happier ending, Siegel's movie reflects the period that created it, picturing a breakdown of mutual trust, a fear of destruction from outsiders, and ending with only a vague hope that anything can be done to preserve life and love as we know them.

The Period of Individuality, 1960–1970

The sixties rang with rallying cries for personal independence and initiative. It was simultaneously a period of great freedom and painful frustration. When John F. Kennedy took office as president in 1960, he spoke of a New Frontier and in 1961 established a Peace Corps that drew young people into work to improve the world. Astronaut John Glenn orbited the earth in 1962, and in 1969 Neil Armstrong walked on the moon. In 1964 the most comprehensive civil rights bill in American history was signed into law. Yet in 1961 the first American military forces arrived in Vietnam to assist allies, and by 1965 had engaged in the first combat offensive of an unofficial and ill-defined war that would cost this country over 56,000 lives, over 300,000 wounded, and over $141 billion before the United States withdrew in 1973. Civil rights marches and antiwar rallies divided the country into bitter camps. John Kennedy was assassinated in 1963; then Robert Kennedy, his brother, and Martin Luther King, Jr., the most prominent leader of the civil rights movement, were assassinated in 1968. Personal independence tended to express itself in "anti-Establishment" attitudes epitomized in a youthful "drug culture" that challenged all the dictates of parental and educational authority.

In the midst of all this, Hollywood learned to take its problems in hand. Rather than fighting television programs, studios produced them and began selling off old movies to TV for prices that, by 1965, rose to approximately $400,000 a feature. In individual deals, the amounts would rise to between $800,000 and $5 million (the latter Twentieth Century–Fox's price for *Cleopatra*) by the end of the decade.[32] Studios used overseas, or "runaway," productions to take advantage of lower foreign taxes and labor. Industrial and religious codes relaxed in the liberal spirit of the times, enabling the movies to appeal to a more educated and selective movie audience. Talent agencies began to take over some of the old producer's functions, putting together "packages" of talent designed for particular movies. And by the end of the decade large conglomerates had taken control of most major studios.[33]

It was a period rife with self-criticism and talk of revolutionary change, and this was reflected in movies in many ways. The old studio concept of transparent storytelling yielded ground to the appeal of the storyteller. It became more common to consider an American movie as the statement of its director. People became more attuned to movies as personal and political messages. The world revealed in such movies was more anti-heroic than ever, with violence developed into a new intensity and with some classic figures and situations changing their functions.

The old heroes lost their glamor. They became insecure, aging, disturbed, sometimes inept and crass, and their stories often forced them and the viewer to confront the end of old dreams and illusions. This anti-heroism was not new, only more noticeable in the sixties. Its impact was strong in Westerns, which depend so much on the romantic past. In *Ride the High Country* (1962) two old-timers, transporting gold ore from a corrupt mining settlement, take on and defeat a band of lunatic thieves and help some young lovers (Fig. 7.13). One of the old-timers lies mortally wounded at the end; with him, the movie suggests, passes a code of personal integrity that modern times have relinquished. In *Hud* (1963) the Western hero has become a crass cowboy who cares nothing for his father's notion of honor and simply waits around, doing as he pleases, until the old man dies and leaves him the ranch. *Hud*'s director, Martin Ritt, was surprised to find that young people admired the cowboy's attitude, which Ritt treated as disreputable.[34]

The horror genre found new monsters in contemporary life inside the mind and the social structure. *Psycho* (1960), *What Ever Happened to Baby Jane?* (1962), and *Hush, Hush, Sweet Charlotte* (1964) depicted horrors inside frustrated and obsessed people. In *The Manchurian Candidate* (1962) Communists hypnotize an American soldier so that when he returns home he can be triggered to kill, and *Seconds* (1966) was a modern Frankenstein story about a middle-aged man given a new body his mind cannot accept (Fig. 7.14).

7.13 The aging Western hero. Randolph Scott (left) and Joel McCrea in *Ride the High Country* (1962).

The stringent dictates of the Production Code against violence and sex melted away under the need to attract a more sophisticated audience. Open discussions of sexual freedom had become commonplace in this period's society, and nightly television coverage of the Vietnam War and of interracial wars in the cities made violence a familiar reality. The movies reflected this. *The Pawnbroker* (1965), a serious study of a Jewish man's attempt to block out his terrible memories of a Nazi concentration camp, included one scene with frontal female nudity. Its reception as a mature piece of work (actor Rod Steiger was nominated for an Academy Award) opened the way to even more explicit presentations of sexual material in mass-audience movies. *The Dirty Dozen* (1967), about misfit and psychopathic soldiers sent on a suicide mission to murder Germans in World War II, exemplified the new violence (and was nominated for four Academy Awards). But many patrons became alarmed at the new trends, and their cries for greater social control helped trigger the MPAA's rating system in 1968.

The dominating stories of the period combined the poignant anti-heroic sense with the shocking new violence. *Bonnie and Clyde* (1967), a bandit-gangster movie initially dismissed by many critics as exploitive, went on to extraordinary popularity. It pictured the bandits as a frustrated couple naively seeking love and fame, then

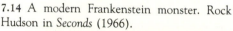

7.14 A modern Frankenstein monster. Rock Hudson in *Seconds* (1966).

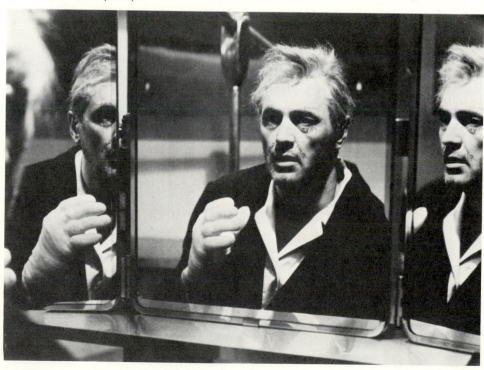

paying the debt of violent retribution it had won them. And Sam Peckinpah's *The Wild Bunch* (1969) pictured a band of old-time desperadoes trying to pull off one last big job, and then finally dying in their own violent style.

In many movies of this period we can see revisions in the traditional roles of narrative figures, reflecting the period's concern with individual rights. Indians had been traditional images of savagery in the classic Western, for example, but that changed. *Apache* (1954) had showed an Indian unfairly treated, and this sympathetic view enlarged in this period. In *Cheyenne Autumn* (1964) the Indians are the protagonists, trying to survive the white man's chicanery. *Soldier Blue* (1970) reeks with outrage at what whites have done to Indians, and *Little Big Man* (1970), taking a more powerfully ambiguous stance, is the story of a white man who adopts the Indian culture and watches whites destroy all he loves.

Young people were no longer those who, like Andy Hardy in the thirties, learned wisdom from their elders. They were rebels against the stodgy *establishment*. The trend had been foreshadowed in films like *Rebel Without a Cause* (1955) but it flowered in this period. *Easy Rider* (1969), directed by the young Dennis Hopper, pictured youth's rebellion in a manner as ambivalent as the old image of sympathetic yet self-destructive gangsters. It was also a reverse Western, in which two renegades head east on motorcycles to settle down in Florida on the money they have made selling heroin, only to meet death at the hands of redneck Southerners. *The Graduate*

(1967) became a rallying film for the young generation. A new variation on romantic melodrama, it featured a confused college graduate who stumbles through an affair with a married woman but falls in true love with her daughter, whom he finally kidnaps from church as she is about to marry someone else (Fig. 7.15). The movie used old establishment clichés to strike out against them.

Directed by Stanley Kubrick, a fastidious technician, *2001: A Space Odyssey* (1968) is a striking exemplar of the whole period. It developed spectacular special effects in showing a sterile world where humans are almost overwhelmed by machinery until one man breaks through into another dimension to become a new creature. Its intellectual subject matter, which left some critics baffled but still admiring, represented Hollywood's new maturity. And its new variations on traditional elements of the horror and science-fiction genres reflected this period's popular concern over personal freedom in the modern age.

The Period of Reorganization, 1971 to the Present

Before the seventies were half over, the nation had withdrawn from a war and survived a massive spasm of internal corruption. Then, freed of many delusions about its purity and invincibility, it settled back to lick its wounds and face an uncertain future. Appropriately, the motion picture industry built its stories to a climax of the iconoclastic independence begun in the sixties, then settled into a new equilibrium that strongly resembled its Classic Period.

The period begins in 1971, the year Richard Nixon, then president, authorized a clandestine espionage group to burglarize data from reputed enemies of the state. In 1973, slightly more than a month after bombing civilian areas of North Vietnam to placate its South Vietnamese allies, the United States withdrew from the Vietnam War. In 1974 Nixon became the first United States president to resign from office. Some of Nixon's top aides were found guilty of conspiracy and sentenced to prison in 1975—the same year that an efficient North Vietnamese army totally routed the corrupt and demoralized former allies of the United States.

By the end of the seventies, the United States was facing more threats to its old confidence. Inflation soared into two digits, its highest since the fifties. The word *ecology* became widely familiar as Americans began to realize that technology was posing ruinous threats to the environment. As petroleum resources dwindled, a society that had prided itself on the mobility and freedom of the automobile had to face serious gasoline shortages and high prices determined by foreign oil exporters.

7.15 Romantic rebels against the establishment. The hero (Dustin Hoffman) disrupts the wedding of his true love (Katharine Ross) in *The Graduate* (1967).

And international terrorism, spawned by worldwide economic and political unrest, began to touch us personally—notably in 1979 when Iranians took American consulate employees hostage as political pawns.

The movie industry reflected the nation's internal dismay and fury in contradictory, overlapping ways. Particularly at the beginning of the seventies, disenchantment and paranoia continued from the previous period and even intensified. But as the political cataclysms of 1974 and 1975 were working themselves out, many movie stories began to reflect a new variety of optimistic heroism. It was in many ways a return to classicism. Blatant sex and violence were declining by 1974. Gross box-office receipts were up that year to over $1.6 billion, the highest since 1946. Even with inflation and the devaluation of the dollar, there was cause for optimism. While many commentators continued to speak of the death or ruin of Hollywood, the industry in fact reverted to the structure it had known before World War I: exhibition, distribution, and production were all separated from one another.[35] This provided far less security than in the Classic Period, when all three were under total studio control, and the new studio heads were not the moguls of the past but rather multicorporate executives with less feel for audiences and a desire for simple package deals. All the same, there was something more individualized about storytelling in seventies movies than even in the sixties. The previous mainstream and exploitation markets were no longer as distinct, with new multiscreen theaters in many cities showing both kinds of movies. And the exploitation circuit had proved a training ground for new directors and performers, some from film schools, who entered mainstream production with a studied awareness of the story traditions they were working with. In the seventies, we find many movies that play upon old formulas deliberately, adapting or subverting them to new uses and exploiting the social affirmations and doubts that genre films employ. At the same time, they operate with all the old efficacy of good stories. They catch us up in traditional conflicts and appeal to our sense of what is culturally satisfying.

We can see two overlapping influences in movies of this period, then: one continues the disenchantment and paranoia from the sixties; the other represents a new classicism, a deliberate evocation of old formulas.

In many movies there was a sense of outright paranoia, a suggestion that one was inevitably doomed by forces one could not isolate, much less overcome. The protagonists of *The Parallax View* (1974), *The Conversation* (1974), *Chinatown* (1974), and *The Omen* (1976) are either physically or psychologically destroyed at the end. There is no conventional sense of relief, or catharsis, at all.

Other movies were more ironic than depressing. Some outstanding examples were Westerns that undercut the old mythic values of the genre. *Bad Company* (1972) and *The Culpepper Cattle Company* (1972) showed young people being drawn into the corruption and glory of violence. *The Great Northfield Minnesota Raid* (1971) was an ironic commentary on the way myths and real life differ. *McCabe and Mrs. Miller* (1972) painted a touching image of a sad and frustrated West—and made an appropriate counterpoint with *Jeremiah Johnson* (1972), a portrait of a man who forsakes civilization for the absolute solitude of the wilderness. *The Missouri Breaks* (1976) totally undercut the traditional Western's values, destroying all sense of heroic integrity or honest violence. But *Ulzana's Raid* (1972) took virtually all the elements of the classic Western and spun them into a superbly counter-balanced conflict. An idealistic young cavalry officer leads a veteran troop out to capture an Apache war band. His scouts are a loyal Apache and a squaw man, a white man who is married to an Apache (Fig. 7.16). During the pursuit they gradually bring the officer to see his own cultural blindness, prejudice, and naiveté. The movie shows both the white mens' and the Indians' brutality and heroism. It exploits all the rich action, space, and color we associate with Westerns, and yet at the end no one has won or lost. It is a reflection of many issues, including the futility of the Vietnam War, the wisdom that lies in understanding nature, and the inability of one people to prove its code superior to that of another people. By bringing a traditional Western conflict to bear on the new cultural disenchantment, *Ulzana's Raid* proved the enduring power of the genre.

Even while disenchantment was expressing itself, a more aggressive and optimistic heroism also began to emerge. One example was the variety of new black heroes, played by actors like Sidney Poitier, James Brown, and Richard Roundtree. The trend had begun in the sixties, in movies like *In the Heat of the Night* (1967), where Poitier plays a tough city detective who changes a Southern sheriff's attitude toward blacks. By the seventies the black superhero had arrived—typified in the

7.16 The Western hero and the Indian as compatriots. Jorge Luke (left) and Burt Lancaster in *Ulzana's Raid* (1972).

series begun by *Shaft* (1971), where the hero triumphed over any number of international and national villains (Fig. 7.17).

An even more successful variety of new heroism asserted itself in *Airport* (1970), the first of many *catastrophe films* that are good examples of what we are calling new classicism. They were expensive superproductions that featured, besides special effects and all-star casts, old-time heroes: one or more individuals who risked and sometimes gave their lives for the group (Fig. 7.18). In these spectacles human courage won out over natural disaster and human shortcomings. *Airport* was about people trapped in a jetliner; *The Poseidon Adventure* (1973) had them trapped in an overturned ocean liner; *The Towering Inferno* (1974) had them in a burning high-rise.

Following catastrophe films came a general return to the formulas of classic storytelling. *Rocky* (1976) was the love story of a washed-up boxer who, against impossible odds, fights the world's champion to a draw, proving to himself and his sweetheart that he is somebody. In *Close Encounters of the Third Kind* (1977), earth scientists make contact with aliens from outer space, and in an almost religious ending the hero goes off with them to learn the mysteries of the universe. *Jaws* (1975) drew from the monster horror tradition to show heroic men saving a whole community from disaster. *The Godfather*, in two parts (1971 and 1975), reaffirmed the drawing power of the classic gangster film. *Star Wars* (1977) was traditional science fiction. *The Exorcist* (1973) and *Carrie* (1977), among many, gave supernatural horror a new life.

If this was nostalgia—"thumb-sucking optimism," as one critic called it—it was obviously popular.[36] *Airport*, *Poseidon Adventure*, and *Towering Inferno* had domestic grosses of $45 million, $42 million, and $50 million respectively. *Godfather I* grossed $86 million, *The Exorcist* $82 million, and *Jaws* $121 million. *Star Wars* became history's most lucrative movie, grossing $127 million. (These figures date from 1978; all are higher by now.)[37] Even with production costs greatly increased and with

7.17 The black superhero. Richard Roundtree in *Shaft* (1971).

inflationary devaluation of the dollar, these statistics suggest that the movie industry in this period was again feeling something akin to the old power of Hollywood storytelling.

The outcome of all this storytelling is yet to be seen. You are already aware of changes that had not occurred when we wrote these words. Whatever has happened, however, it seems fair to say that with the word *Hollywood* we still invoke certain kinds of stories, whose history we have outlined here. That Hollywood still lives, through all the changes in its internal structure.

HOLLYWOOD'S SOCIAL ASPECT AND CRITICISM

In this chapter we have approached the Hollywood narrative cinema from several points of view derived from disciplines outside film theory itself: psychology, philosophy, sociology, anthropology, and literature. We sometimes group these contributions to film study into a single category called *structuralism*. Like semiotics, which it complements and shades into, structuralism seeks to define the forces at work in communication with as much scientific accuracy as possible. Structuralists tend, however, to look at more generalized forces than the semioticians, who get down to very discrete units of messages. Structuralists are interested in the large cultural beliefs mirrored in many kinds of messages, and in their method of conveying shared codes to members of a society—that is, of *enculturating* them.

Like semiotics, structuralism is just beginning to scrape the tip of an iceberg that offers great challenges. And in only a few years structuralism has generated a large volume of literature.[38] We have already outlined some typical structural concerns involved in Hollywood narratives. Here we will touch on basic tendencies of the movement, dividing it into two general groups: structuralists dealing with the nature of communication and those dealing with the social impact of communication.

In the first group Susanne Langer and Claude Lévi-Strauss stand out as important figures. Langer's *Philosophy in a New Key* (1942) made a concise presentation of humankind's manner of imaging belief in other than strictly rational ways. Lévi-Strauss, writing in the 1950s, provided an influential model of mythic communication, picturing it as a series of "bundles" of relations that work in immediate, nonrational ways that he compares to the power of music.[39]

Following Langer and Lévi-Strauss, writers began to take new looks at the structures of folklore and written literature, suggesting insights of obvious value to film scholars.[40] Structuralist writings gave new life to the study of Hollywood genres. One influence was John Cawelti's *The Six-Gun Mystique*, which examined the

7.18 Self-sacrificing hero. George C. Scott in *The Hindenburg* (1975).

formulaic structure of the literary and the film Western and argued for the need to treat any popular genres as stories that serve many valuable social and psychological functions. In *Horizons West,* Jim Kitses used Lévi-Strauss's model to block out the "philosophical dialectic" between the values of wilderness and civilization in the Western. Structuralist genre study has since become widespread.[41]

Among those dealing with the social impact of communication, George Huaco took a structuralist approach in *The Sociology of Film Art.*[42] He divided structural factors of movies into four categories: current events, filmmakers' creativity, technological factors, and audience factors. Other writers, like Garth Jowett and Robert Sklar, have taken a sociological approach that might not be considered structural in the usual sense of the term, but they do provide thorough studies of the cultural factors at work in the Hollywood cinema.

Among film journals, *The Journal of Popular Film and Television* deals almost exclusively with cultural issues in movies. The British journal *Screen* is devoted to very thorough analyses of semiotic and structural patterns. *Film Quarterly* and *Film Comment* regularly feature essays on structuralist topics.

Serious study of the social aspect of movies has developed rapidly in the last fifteen years. Although this scholarship has provided an introduction to the complex nature and impact of Hollywood cinema in particular, many challenging issues are yet to be resolved.

SUMMARY

Like other communications, Hollywood movies refer to the real world and aim at some kind of response from their viewers. These realist and persuasive functions make up the social aspect of Hollywood: the way its movies reflect and appeal to the external American society.

Storytelling is an imaginative form of communication that gives body to traditional codes of belief in society. It collects them into formulas, or genres, that encode the crucial tensions of social life. These formulas and genres change as the culture moves through history, keeping the essential patterns but shifting the elements within them. Hollywood's genres—the Western, the underworld film, the horror movie, the war film, and others—encode fundamental tensions in such themes as the meaning and value of civilization, the pastoral myth, and the problem of eroticism.

This storytelling does not exist in a vacuum. It strikes responses from its audience. On one hand, it focuses cultural values in ways that affect conduct, mores, and styles of living. On the other, it changes according to the responses it gets and the control exerted over it in turn by society. Thus, Hollywood is always evolving in response patterns of audience reaction that are most clearly seen in legal and governmental restraints, economic pressures, and the movie industry's own self-regulation. From the social aspect, Hollywood's history is a give-and-take between mythic views of life and American society's reaction to these views. Hollywood has moved from a precisely organized presentation of cultural values, its Classic Period, to a confused period, its Dark Age. The period of Individuality, in which traditional values came under attack, preceded the Period of Reorganization, which returned the industry to an emphasis on traditional values—though within a different production system.

Throughout this evolution, the basic formulas of traditional Hollywood filmmaking maintain themselves as basic patterns of cultural communication. Whether the filmmaker assumes them transparently, as in the Classic Period, or subverts and undercuts them, as in later periods, the traditional Hollywood narrative genres have a strong influence on what we talk about and how we respond in movie communication.

NOTES

1 Tzvetan Todorov, "Structural Analysis of Narrative," *Novel,* 3 (Fall 1969), 75.

2 We discuss the breakdown of production jobs in Chapter 8.

3 This definition of myth derives from the work of Branislaw Malinowski, particularly *Myth in Primitive Psychology* (New York: Norton, 1926).

4 See "Symbolic Transformation," chap. 2 of *Philosophy in a New Key* (Cambridge: Harvard University Press, 1957), pp. 26–52.

5 Clyde Kluckhohn and Dorothea Leighton, *The Navaho* (New York: Doubleday, 1962), p. 200.

6 *Philosophy in a New Key,* p. 176.

7 "The Structural Study of Myth," *Journal of American Folklore,* 78 (Oct.–Dec. 1955), 432–444 passim. Reprinted in *The Structuralists: From Marx to Lévi-Strauss,* ed. Richard and Fernande De George (New York: Doubleday, 1972), pp. 175–194.

8 The discussion in this section owes much to Robin Wood's "Ideology, Genre, Auteur," *Film Comment,* 13 (Jan.–Feb. 1977), 46–51.

9 John G. Cawelti, *The Six-Gun Mystique,* (Bowling Green University, Ohio: Popular Press, 1971), pp. 52–66.

10 See Frederick Elkin, "The Psychological Appeal for Children of the Hollywood B Western," *Journal of Educational Sociology,* 24 (Oct. 1950), 79–84. Reprinted in *Focus on the Western,* ed. Jack Nachbar (Englewood Cliffs, N.J.: Prentice-Hall, 1974), pp. 73–77.

11 Tzvetan Todorov has identified three varieties of such experience in horror movies: *the uncanny* (apparently impossible events finally

receive a rational explanation); *the marvelous* (events prove that the supernatural clearly does exist and cannot be rationally explained); and *the fantastic* (the audience is left hesitant before either a natural or supernatural explanation). See Todorov's *The Fantastic: A Structural Approach to a Literary Genre,* trans. Richard Howard (Cleveland: Case Western Reserve University Press, 1973), pp. 24–57.

12 Stuart Kaminsky first used the term in *American Film Genres* (Dayton, Ohio: Pflaum, 1974), p. 31 note.

13 Frank Capra, *The Name Above the Title* (New York: Macmillan Company, 1971), p. 177.

14 Richard S. Randall, *Censorship of the Movies* (Madison: University of Wisconsin Press, 1968), pp. 11–12.

15 Randall, pp. 18–21.

16 Randall, pp. 25–32.

17 Murray Schumach, *The Face on the Cutting Room Floor* (New York: Morrow, 1964), pp. 100–102.

18 The complete list is in Raymond Moley, *The Hays Office* (New York: Bobbs-Merrill, 1945), pp. 240–241.

19 The complete code is in Schumach, pp. 279–292.

20 Garth Jowett, *Film: The Democratic Art* (Boston: Little, Brown, 1976), pp. 4, 8.

21 Producer Joe Camp, in an interview with George Wead, June 1968.

22 The exact gross will never be known. Exhibition rights were sold in return for a percentage of box-office receipts, but since there was no accurate accounting system, many exhibitors held back their true earnings. This led to what *Weekly Variety* called a "whopper myth" about the film's being the greatest moneymaker of all time. *Variety's* diligent research has established that *Birth of a Nation* grossed some $5 million domestically and perhaps another $5 million abroad. See *Variety,* Jan. 4, 1978, p. 25.

23 For a fully documented account of the Arbuckle case, see David Yallop, *The Day the Laughter Stopped* (New York: St. Martin's, 1976).

24 For a synopsis of the Hollywood studio structure at this time, see *The American Film Industry,* ed. Tino Balio (Madison: University of Wisconsin Press, 1976), pp. 213–227.

25 W. Dixon Powell, "MGM: The Studio at Its Zenith," *The Velvet Light Trap,* 18 (Spring 1978), 4.

26 Jack Warner, *My First Hundred Years in Hollywood* (New York: Random House, 1964), p. 224.

27 For a thorough discussion of this economic context, see Charles Flynn and Todd McCarthy, "The Economic Imperative: Why Was the B Movie Necessary?" in *Kings of the Bs: Working Within the Hollywood System* (New York: Dutton, 1975), pp. 13–43.

28 From an interview with director Edward Dmytryk, who then worked at the Columbia studio.

29 Charles Champlin, "Who's Watching," *AFI Report* 4 (May 1973), 28.

30 Interview with Linda May Strawn in *Kings of the Bs,* p. 265.

31 Jim Kitses, *Horizons West,* Cinema One Series No. 12 (Bloomington: Indiana University, 1969), pp. 103–109.

32 Balio, pp. 322–324.

33 In 1955 Howard Hughes sold RKO to a subsidiary of General Tire and Rubber Company, which sold it to Desilu Productions in 1957.

Music Corporation of America, a talent agency, took over Universal in 1962. Paramount became part of Gulf and Western Industries (a steel, plastics, and mining conglomerate) in 1966. United Artists went to TransAmerica Corporation, an insurance conglomerate, in 1967. And in 1969 Warner merged with Kinney Services, a building maintenance conglomerate, the same year that Kirk Kerkorian, a builder of multimillion-dollar resort hotels, bought control of MGM. Only Twentieth Century–Fox remained primarily a motion-picture production company. See Balio, pp. 329–331.

34 Ritt, in an interview with George Wead, March 1978.

35 Robert Sklar, *Movie-Made America: A Cultural History of American Movies* (New York: Random House, 1976), p. 290.

36 Andrew Sarris, "After *The Graduate*," *American Film*, 3 (July–Aug. 1978), 35.

37 Box-office figures quoted are from the May 17, 1978, issue of *Weekly Variety*.

38 For a comprehensive bibliography of important works on structuralism, consult Terence Hawkes's *Structuralism and Semiotics* (Berkeley: University of California, 1977).

39 Basic works by Langer and Lévi-Strauss have already been cited. You may also wish to consult Langer's *Feeling and Form: A Theory of Art* (New York: Scribner's Sons, 1953). The best overall study of Lévi-Strauss's thought is Edmund Leach's *Claude Lévi-Strauss* (London: Fontana, 1970).

40 For an application of structural principles to folklore, see V.I. Propp's *Morphology of the Folktale* (Austin: University of Texas, 1958). For a general introduction to structure in narrative, see Robert Scholes's and Robert Kellogg's *The Nature of Narrative* (New York: Oxford, 1966).

41 In *Adventure, Mystery and Romance* (University of Chicago, 1976) Cawelti continues to develop his structural approach to detective stories and romantic melodrama, but only in literature—not in film. Tzvetan Todorov's *The Fantastic*, cited above, is a structural approach to the horror genre in literature. Colin McArthur's *Underworld USA* (New York: Viking, 1972) outlines some structural factors in the underworld film genre. Essays on structuralist issues can be found in *Focus on the Western*, edited by Jack Nachbar (Englewood Cliffs, N.J.: Prentice-Hall, 1974) and in *Focus on the Horror Film*, edited by Roy Huss and T. J. Ross (Prentice-Hall, 1972). Other ongoing structuralist discussions will be found in the journals cited later in this text.

42 New York: Basic Books, 1965.

Chapter 8 / Hollywood's

Artistic Aspect

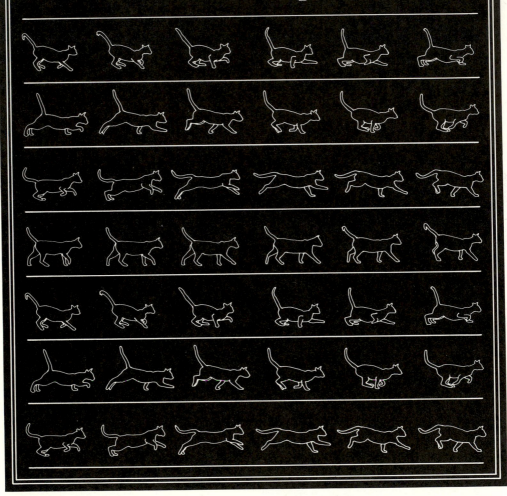

In Chapter 1, we talked about how movies evolved out of a general democratization of art that shocked and dismayed painters and art critics of the nineteenth century. It is time now to look at that democratization of art in relation to the Hollywood movie.

The word *art* usually suggests several interlinked factors: the personal expression of an individual who uses particular talents in a powerful and significant way to create a beautiful form that stands out as an individual expression of the human spirit. But what can such factors mean in a medium that requires factorylike production? Wasn't this precisely the cry of artists in the last century, and doesn't it still echo in the present century?

To answer this we must look at the esthetic and personal functions of the Hollywood cinema: those related to the inner ordering of any message and to the personal voice within any communication. We look at the Hollywood movie in itself, separate from the social pressures outside the act of creating the movie. We can ask by what formal, structural principles we can evaluate the order or beauty of a Hollywood movie, and how a personal voice can arise from the factory. This takes us into the formal and personal factors in the Hollywood system.

THE FORMAL QUALITIES OF THE STUDIO SYSTEM

The idea behind the studio system is to put a story on its feet before movie cameras in the most efficient and powerful manner possible. The complicated task is broken down into specific areas to be handled by specialists. The degree of this breakdown varies with the kind of production involved and with the period in which it was made. But the essentials remain the same.

The construction of a narrative film begins with a concept in someone's mind: an abstract *story idea*. It may or may not originate in a writer's mind, and it may or may not be developed first into a story, play, or novel—but ultimately (and, in the modern movie industry, usually through an agent) a writer approaches a film producer with the story idea developed into a completed *script*, or *screenplay*, or at least into a preliminary *treatment*, a thorough outline of the story.

If the *producer* buys the story, or *property*, the producer arranges for financing and for a *production crew* to turn the property into a motion picture. The producer organizes and supervises the production. In the Classic Period, when production was centered in vast studios, the crew members were all employees of the same company, and the producer was often just the administrator of company policy. Today, the producer is usually an independent businessman. He or she may rent studio production facilities or release the film through a studio outlet, but the producer is in charge of the film—and may write and direct it, as well.

A large-scale production still requires a great number of specialized skills. The leading member of the production crew is the *director,* who is primarily responsible for bringing all the writer's characters and scenes to life before the camera, and who usually oversees all creative aspects of the production from beginning to end. The *director of photography* sees that images are successfully captured on film, arranging the lighting and camera setups that the director wants. Camera operators run the cameras, and *gaffers* arrange the lights. The *art director* concentrates on the space in which the lights and camera play, designing and dressing interior sets and outside locations to create the visual environment of the story. *Grips* arrange the art director's scenery and props. The *costume designer* clothes the cast of performers, which is selected with as much care as the crew. Any number of *sound technicians* handle microphones and recording equipment on the set. *Special effects* and *stunt personnel* may also be required.

On the credits of large-scale productions you may see a number of associate producers, technical advisers, choreographers, swordfight coaches, stunt directors, second-unit directors to handle separate location shooting, many technicians for process work, animators, and perhaps a handful of writers, some of them hired simply to dress up dialogue or "punch up" big scenes. At the other extreme, in very low budget productions, crews may be cut to a bare minimum. A director of photography may hang lights and operate the single camera, or an art director may also design the costumes.

It is all the same method. Filmmaking is characteristically a *corporate* endeavor, especially in the production of feature-length Hollywood narratives. All elements of production are geared to embody the director's vision of the story, but the director relies on many other talents and the way they see the story. This introduces many variables, all the way from differences in shades of color or camera settings down to major revisions of characters or of the story itself because actors are changed or money runs out. Instead of the embodiment of an original vision, the director is more apt to settle for an acceptable consistency between performances, settings, lighting, and camera work.

The story is no longer what it was in the writer's head or on the pages of the original script. A *shooting script,* or *continuity,* has broken the story into specific shots. This is, effectively, the director's version of the writer's script. Some directors construct the shooting script with the help of a *story board,* where each shot is pictured much like a cartoon. On the set the director works off the shooting script with the aid of a *continuity person*, who keeps detailed notes on every shot to maintain a consistency from one shot to another and to keep a record of the many changes made in the script as production goes along.

Further changes may come in *postproduction*, which includes editing and laying the complete sound track. Several *cutters* may do the actual splicing for the *editor*, who usually works with the director to enhance the action and to overcome any continuity problem. The producer may require drastic revisions in the story, usually for the sake of time. In the thirties, studios kept most features to a maximum of ninety minutes. Films made for television have even more precise time limits. Producers have generally maintained their right to the "final cut" on movies—though a few directors demand the right as part of their contracts. In the process of all this editing and re-editing, whole scenes and characters may wind up "on the cutting-room floor." *Sound effects* technicians or *music composers* and *music directors*, who write and play the musical background, do not alter continuity, but they may change moods or emphases. And when different voices are *dubbed* over the original performers (more common in imported foreign movies than in American products), characters' personalities may undergo significant changes.

The original story idea does not come to full life on the screen until all these people have had their hands in it. In the typical movie story there is little sense of one teller spinning the tale. Its creators are many and anonymous. And this mode of creation derives from economic necessity. The Hollywood studio system rested on the assumption that many experienced personnel would achieve maximum quality and create a highly competitive product at a lower financial risk to the investors.

The classic reasoning continues to govern narrative filmmaking, though the style has changed. Since the old studios have been bought up by conglomerates that do more things than make movies, executives at some distance from the storytelling itself are responsible for financing and staffing productions. They are dealing, too, with much more independent workers. Labor unions have placed strict limitations on what crew members may do and what they must be paid, raising production costs and complicating schedules. Virtually all creative personnel—directors, writers, editors, directors of photography, art directors, music directors, and the like—are independents whose specific conditions must be met. And agents often put together "packages" of talent, complete with script, which they sell to studios.

All this, then, is what we refer to when we speak of the *studio system*. Obviously it challenged traditional codes of artistic creation when it came into existence. Arts like painting, sculpture, and literature assumed individual creators who fashioned the forms of their works by themselves. In dramatic and musical composition, individual creators gave their work over to performing artists—actors, dancers, singers, musicians—who then fashioned them into individual presentations. Movies combined both approaches, but broke creativity down into separate functions that seemed very disjointed to traditional artists. Art directors, cinematographers, and special effects personnel sometimes worked on visual forms that the performers and many of the crew never saw until the final movie was screened. Performers were seldom allowed to build their characterizations from beginning to end through a story. The roles were broken down into fragments arranged for the convenience of the shooting schedule—so that, for example, all scenes in one locale were shot together regardless of where they appeared in the story, and the performer might have to be old in one scene, young in another, middle-aged in a third, and so on. This disjunctive approach to art, where bits and pieces were often arranged in totally separate environments, was a thorough "democratization," all right, and in the abstract seemed to elitists to offer little more than the vulgar delights of a circus. There was lots to look at, many "acts" to draw one's attention, but little formal integrity or unity of purpose.

In fact, movies simply have a *different* integrity, not necessarily a weaker one. They interrelate many forms of the esthetic function. Though the system is factorylike, it offers the chance to exploit the qualities of visual, literary, and performing art to the fullest. Looked at from that angle, its nontraditional approach to esthetic creation is an advantage, not a drawback. It creates a form that appeals simultaneously to many senses.

In Chapters 2 through 6 we discussed the particulars of this multisensory appeal. Here we look at it as embodied in the Hollywood narrative. Narrative depends on the structuring of imaginary events in time, and so Hollywood's storytelling, being very conventional, tends to drive the narrative forward as clearly and as emphatically as possible. What results is a distinctive kind of simplicity. For, by trying to do everything in the most polished way, Hollywood filmmaking becomes the epitome of formal qualities that all filmmaking seeks to exploit to one degree or another. We will discuss them under three headings: clarity and coherence, emphasis, and simplicity.

Clarity and Coherence

The esthetic qualities of narrative movies begin with the fact that forms are presented as what they are. The spectator sees images of clearly actual persons and things. A tree is this particular tree, a performer is this blonde woman or this short, swarthy man. They make sense to us—that is, they are coherent—as what they clearly *are*. Their clarity is larger than life, though, because they are on screen. They are not *ordinary* actualities, but symbolic ones. The filmmaking process imposes lighting, color, positioning, and speech upon them in ways that make them particularly meaningful. A film may push this imposed symbolism to extremes—for example, in *Red Desert* (1964) a bedpost turns red to reflect the heroine's fear of passion, and in *Wild Strawberries* (1957) a man drives his hand against a nail to symbolize his Christlike anguish. But even these images are of actual persons and objects, not abstract symbols. As critic V. F. Perkins has put it, "The primary appeal of the movies depends on what we see rather than on the way we see it."[1]

The transparent style that predominates in Hollywood movies is simply a practical, efficient way to display the inherent clarity and coherence of subjects and events. The *clarity* lies in presenting images we immediately recognize. We look through the filmmaking devices to the actualities they present; the transparent style does not ask for any abstract intellectualizing about symbolic meanings. The style's *coherence* lies in making motives and actions credible. If the images presented are first of all recognizable people and objects, then they should look and behave in ways that are recognizable, granted whatever circumstances they find themselves in. For example, in *All That Heaven Allows* (1955), a romantic melodrama, a daughter lashes out at her widowed mother for daring to fall in love with a younger man. As the women argue, their faces and the backgrounds take on different colors—and we can find in this, if we wish, a striking symbol of the upheaval the argument represents in the mother's life. But the color shifts come from a credible source: the women are moving about behind a multicolored window in the room. In *The Poseidon Adventure* (1973), a priest leads a band of survivors through an overturned ocean liner. They arrive at last at an exit port, only to find that it is closed and that the valve controlling it is high up above a flaming room. Knowing he is sacrificing himself, the priest leaps up and grabs the valve. Hanging by his arms over his followers, he twists the valve, opening the exit for them, then falls to his death. For those who care to notice, the scene is rich in symbolic allusions: like a crucified Christ, the priest brings salvation, willfully descending into hell to save others from death in a ship named after the pagan god of the sea. But, first of all, the scene is a credible act of a believably heroic person, and an exciting way out of an unusual situation.

These scenes have no symbols imposed strictly from outside, forcing our minds to register the meaning of the actions. They use *functional* symbols—that is, symbols that, first and foremost, keep us involved in an emotionally charged action, driving it forward in credible ways with recognizable causes. The filmmaker may or may not have intended such symbolism—may or may not even be aware of it. The fact remains that the viewer can find such implications without altering the basic coherence of the story. The window lets in light, the valve opens the exit: that is their basic meaning. We can enrich their meaning, but we need not do so to understand them. They remain basically what they are.

Such functional symbolism is not necessarily random or occasional. It often runs like a thread of coherence through a whole movie, working at a secondary level of meaning like the examples above and tying together different characters or scenes. This encourages the viewer to consider *motifs*, visual or aural patterns that occur repeatedly in a movie, providing a system of organization and giving coherent form to the whole movie.

For example, in *White Heat* (1949), a troubling underworld film we discussed in Chapter 7, there is an aural motif that ties Cody, the psychotic bandit-gangster, to wild forces of nature. Early in the movie Cody's mother first uses the expression "Top of the world" as she is comforting him after one of his psychosomatic headaches; and from outside we hear the sound of a gathering storm. After his mother's death, Cody catches his wife trying to run away; in terror she betrays another man whom Cody then kills—all on a very windy night. On yet another windy night, Cody admits maybe he is "nuts" to miss his mother so much. And then, at the very end, Cody cries out "Top of the world, Ma!" in a huge burst of flame (Fig. 8.1). Without laboring any point or intruding into the credible action, the sounds of natural violence on the sound track create a symbolic motif.

Even when situations are fantastic or bizarre, the symbolism operates credibly within the context that has been set up. *Singin' in the Rain* (1952) is a musical about Hollywood, a place where images are created. Being a musical, it creates a fantasy context in which characters sing and dance to full orchestral accompaniment, even on streets or in ordinary living rooms. This context pushes narrative strongly toward the esthetic function (we discuss the musical more specifically in Chapter 13), where the structure of the message draws great attention. Nevertheless, within this context, *Singin' in the Rain* creates a pattern of "image *versus* reality" that functions credibly yet also serves as a symbolic motif. A silent star, Lena Lamont, has the image of sophisticated beauty, whereas in reality she is ignorant and has a shrill, grating voice. Her costar, Don Meredith, tries to impress a pretty young woman, Cathy Selden, with his star image; but she rejects him, laughing at him as a mere "shadow" image, a cliché, not a true artist as in the theater. But Don really falls in love with her, and she really proves to be a dancer who wants to get into the movies. He helps her by getting her to dub her voice for Lena's in one of the new sound movies, so that Lena

8.1 Functional symbolism: *White Heat* (1949). Cody Jarrett (James Cagney) prepares to blow himself up, capping the motif of natural violence seen throughout the movie.

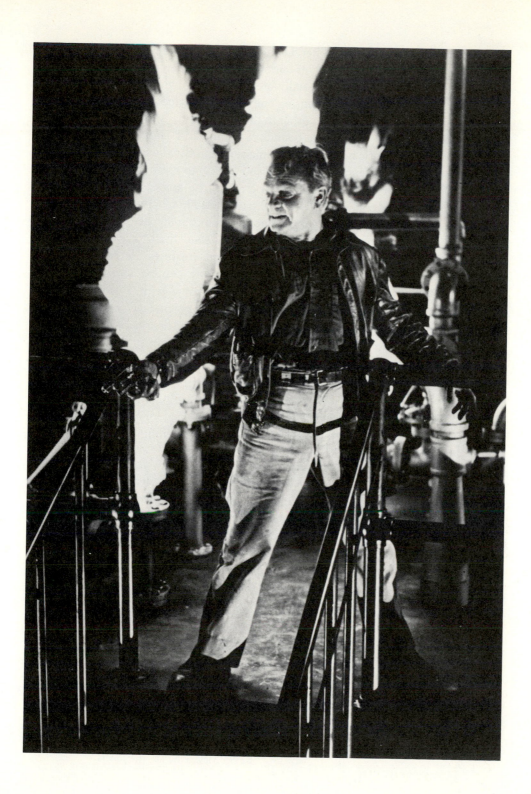

can keep her star image intact. When Lena hears of it, she threatens to ruin Cathy in the industry, so Don and his cohorts arrange at a preview screening to have the audience see how Lena's voice is really created. The movie ends with Don's and Cathy's images on a billboard advertising one of their new movies, with the real Don and Cathy looking lovingly at each other in the foreground. Without any intellectual ostentation and within the credible bounds of the musical's story, *Singin' in the Rain* develops a subtle thematic motif in which image is contrasted with reality: either one overcomes the problem, learning (like Don and Cathy) to speak true feelings through images, or one centers selfishly (like Lena) only on the image, and loses out.

Invasion of the Body Snatchers (1956), also discussed in Chapter 7, is a horror film that sets up a bizarre context. Seeds, apparently from outer space, grow into plants with giant pods that generate humanoid forms that then take over humans, apparently by consuming them. The resulting pod creatures are coldly rational, without any emotions. The movie sets up this bizarre context and then operates credibly within it—that is, confronting ordinary people with a situation where everyone else is becoming a threatening pod, and a few people must try to escape the town to get help. The movie exploits many traditional elements of horror. One of them involves the fear of darkness, which *Invasion* threads into a particular motif. The central protagonists, Miles and Becky, are old acquaintances who find themselves drawn to each other by a new, more erotic attraction. Early in the movie, before they learn of the pods, Miles brings Becky home and, turning out the light, starts to kiss her. Becky nervously turns the light back on. "That way lies madness," she says. At other moments in the ensuing action, Miles approaches Becky warmly again, but something related to their growing awareness of the pods always intervenes. The pods, they learn, attack only when a person sleeps. The dark, then, is a particularly fearful time, and fire is the only weapon that seems to stop the pods. Finally, leaving Becky alone for a moment in a cave, Miles goes to find help. Unsuccessful, he returns and encourages Becky to keep awake. He kisses her—and realizes she is now an emotionless pod (Fig. 8.2). Here the traditional conflict between darkness and light or fire in horror stories has been woven into a motif that includes the element of sexual fear. Darkness becomes an ambiguous value. It harbors the "madness" of being human, which Miles asserts and Becky seems to fear. It also brings relief from being human, which Miles resists and Becky succumbs to. The story is obviously about the struggle of humans to survive, but this "darkness as madness" motif brings in a subtle complexity.

8.2 Functional symbolism: *The Invasion of the Body Snatchers* (1956). The kiss that reinforces the darkness-eroticism motif. Dana Wynter and Kevin McCarthy are the lovers.

Clarity and coherence are not opposed to the kind of calculated ambiguity we find above or in a movie like *The Cat People* (1943), where we are not supposed to be sure whether the woman's urge to kill was psychological or supernatural in origin. The characters face the dilemma in recognizable, credible ways—and we accept it as credible that we cannot finally be sure what caused the horror. There are other calculated ambiguities that might better be called "trick" clarities. The most common are stories that require the viewer to discover at the very end that an image of reality was, in fact, a dream. *The Wizard of Oz* (1939) and *Cabin in the Sky* (1943) use this approach. Because they are musicals, the audience accepts the dream passages as the typically fantastic context of such stories. Then they find out they have been tricked. No one is likely to complain about such deception in musicals, which always play with fantasy. However, some viewers are offended when this is done in a realistic context, as in *The Woman in the Window* (1944), where what we accept as a respectable man's descent into crime turns out to be a dream. The movie presents a compelling story, and with intriguing motifs of eroticism and guilt, but under false pretenses.

We should note, too, that credibility is not the same thing as accuracy or "believability," as that term is often used. *The Big Sleep* (1946), for example, is a credible underworld movie, even though its plot is so technically confusing that neither director Howard Hawks nor Raymond Chandler, writer of the original novel, could ever figure out who murdered one of the characters.[2] Anyone familiar with prize fighting knows that it would be virtually impossible for a worn-out individual to get himself into championship shape in a few weeks, as the hero of *Rocky* (1976)

does—yet it is credible within the romantic realism that movie sets up as its context. Hollywood's worlds are never "real" in that sense. They create illusions with the clarity and coherence of actuality.

Many filmmakers like to move away from this classic Hollywood approach and *impose* a coherence upon the recorded actuality. The most obvious examples are European directors, who like to emphasize the personal function. We have noted Antonioni and Bergman already. They make us aware that they are entering, and to some extent disrupting, the illusion. In *La dolce vita* (1959), to give another example, director Federico Fellini introduces a strange sea creature into his story (Fig. 8.3). Some decadent Roman aristocrats gather around it and wonder at it. It has been introduced in a relatively credible way—the aristocrats are on a beach, watching fishermen—but it doesn't emerge from anything they have been doing, and so its sudden intrusion marks it immediately as an *intellectual symbol*. What *is* it, the viewer is asked to wonder: nature's denunciation of the aristocrats, a symbol of their ugly life, of the meaninglessness of life, of the hopeless lot of nonaristocratic fishermen? Because it is imposed, the creature *requires* our interpretation if we are to appreciate the movie.

MOMA/Audio Brandon/National Telefilm Associates, Inc.

We shall take up this kind of coherence in Chapter 12, where we deal explicitly with personal cinema. Here we need only point out that intellectual symbolism is not the characteristic way of Hollywood, which uses a functional symbolism that may be explored beyond its basic clarity and coherence as a familiar, actual person or thing—but need not be.

Emphasis

Any message that gives us what we need to see or hear when we need to see or hear it has proper emphasis. The communication sciences have pointed out that most messages have a great deal of *redundancy:* repeated and therefore less noticed forms that provide a familiar framework inside of which crucial forms can be emphasized. In newspaper headlines, for example, we find a sentence reduced to achieve maximum emphasis—all or most of the redundant words are removed.

The system exemplified by Hollywood codifies this redundancy and emphasis in a number of efficient ways. Shallow focus technique guides the eye to the most emphatic plane, the unfocused areas being redundant. Movement and compositional patterns, particularly within extended takes of the camera in deep focus, establish emphatic lines of attention. Even by lingering on a subject beyond the time it takes to identify the information, a shot asks the viewer to understand that the subject is important, even if one doesn't yet know why.

Three-shot editing is the most obvious example of a redundant system in which emphasis can be very precise. The continuity gives the story emphasis on environment (long shots), interaction (medium shots), and intimate details or insights (close shots). Scripts are blocked out this way, and so is the story the viewer confronts. This allows a precise emphasis within each shot, and then an emphatic arrangement of sequences.

Let's use *King Kong* (1933) as a typical example. Near the end of the story the giant ape Kong is chained on a theater stage for display to a high-society audience. The shots precisely interrelate (1) the ape as a display (long shots); (2) the interactions between the ape and the audience, the photographers, and his captors (medium and medium-long shots); and (3) details of the ape's growing vexation and attempts to get loose (medium-close shots). This neat isolation of space directs the audience's attention to the aspects of the story that are most important at each moment. The general environment appears in the backgrounds or surroundings of

8.3 Intellectual symbolism: *La dolce vita* (1959). Actor Marcello Mastroianni (left) and director Federico Fellini squat beside the symbolic sea creature.

each shot; this is redundant. But each shot forces us to look at one emphasized portion of that environment.

As we mentioned in Chapter 4, this continuity of shots develops a closed form—that is, each sequence tends to begin, build, climax, and end in a neat closure. And one sequence leads directly to another in an emphatic arrangement of sequences. The theater sequence in *King Kong* establishes the ape's inside confinement in which several forces—the chains that bind him, the crowd, the photographers' flashbulbs—increase the ape's anxiety. The suspense grows until the ape breaks loose, neatly ending that rising conflict by opening out action from the closed theater to the outside streets. The "panic in the streets" sequence then immediately begins with people fleeing from the ape as he wanders about looking for the woman he is trying to protect. The ape's interactions with elevated trains, skyscrapers, and the like then build to a new climax, and so on.

The most traditional Hollywood editing keeps shifting emphasis very transparent. Editing is cut on movement like the theater sequence of *King Kong,* which depends on eye-line movement—that is, as the ape looks at the crowd, the continuity cuts to the crowd looking back at the ape, then the ape looking at the photographers and them looking back, and so on. Such movement is a redundant pattern helping to carry us to the next point of emphasis. In this way we are given what we need to see as we need to see it.

Transparency in itself is not a virtue. A filmmaker may wish to move in the direction of least redundancy—toward what communication science would call *maximum entropy.* In written communication a telegram represents high entropy. "Arrive 8:10 A.M. Wednesday" is the essential information, and if you don't already know the context you might be confused as to whether you are being told *to* arrive or that someone *will* arrive. Similarly, without traditional visual redundancy, an edited continuity may deliberately create confusion or force the viewer to pay close attention, since only crucial data appear with no familiar system to carry them along. A Hollywood montage sequence is more entropic than ordinary three-shot technique, though it is a familiar device and not usually confusing. A sequence may start with abrupt close-ups rather than establishing shots, leaving us unsure where the action is occurring. Or editing may move fully into a rapid, disjunctive technique, as in jump cutting, where entropy is consistently very high—and this forces us into greater intellectual concentration. The obvious examples, again, are European: Eisenstein's intellectual montage or Godard's deliberate disruption of traditional cinematic logic.

As we noted in Chapter 4, Hollywood has been influenced by all these approaches. Particularly since the fifties we can say that its continuities are more often entropic than they were in the earlier days, when there was a classic balance between entropy and redundancy. But by codifying such balance so efficiently, Hollywood exemplifies how emphasis normally works. Entropic editing techniques elaborate upon the system exemplified by Hollywood, just as our telegram plays off of an assumed language system. But again, Hollywood exploits the esthetic value of emphasis without requiring that we rivet our attention to it.

Simplicity of Action

Hollywood's clarity, coherence, and emphasis combine to provide the esthetic quality of simplicity. Abstract and complex issues are usually transformed into simple action. A story often flows in distinct cause-and-effect relationships, for example. When Kong is in the theater, the photographers' flashbulbs provoke the ape's anger, which causes him to strain at his chains until they break. Movie characters are defined by what they *do*, and they directly *perform* solutions to problems that might never be handled so simply in real life. We are familiar with Western and underworld film codes, whereby complicated personal and political issues are resolved in simple contests of arms. There are also many varieties of instant psychological illumination, such as we find in *Marnie* (1964) or *Mirage* (1965), where a character's deep disturbance is quickly clarified and cured.

In a system of traditional storytelling like Hollywood's, the power of simple action is a prime requisite. This does not mean, though, that Hollywood movies must therefore be intellectually simplistic, failing to deal with complex problems in a mature way. Simplicity of form is not the same as naiveté of attitude. As we noted in Chapter 7, the white-hat and black-hat kind of simple Western action seems naive to adults, but only because they are no longer so involved with the issues it embodies. A Western like *The Searchers* puts virtually unanswerable cultural problems into simple forms of action, and an adult can either enjoy the action or be moved by the puzzles it raises—or both. This is not naive or simplistic. The simple forms give rise to complex overtones.

What this finally means is that Hollywood's simplicity of action is, paradoxically, a complex simplicity. Its movies present emphatic actions with a simple clarity and coherence that can surprise us with their implicit power and suggestiveness. All movies have such potential, and most movies partake of narrative form to some degree or another. But Hollywood represents a narrative moviemaking that stresses mass-popular traditions and maximum efficiency, whereby the tasks of cinematic storytelling are broken down into specific areas to be handled by specialists. This has led to movies displaying formal qualities in what we have usually described as a transparent manner.

Let us summarize the implications involved here, because they are crucial to the structure of this text. What distinguishes a non-Hollywood (or simply nontraditional) movie is its extreme emphasis on one particular film function, which results in an upsetting of the balance of the four functions. Such a movie may stress the disorganized open-endedness of real life (the realist function), the viewer's need to recognize particular political issues (the persuasive function), the personal concerns of the filmmaker (the personal function), or the fascinations of the filmmaking process itself (the esthetic function). Or a movie may jar our intellects into noticing all these functions. The Hollywood system resists extremes, working on our emotions with balanced functions. To be sure, this test should not be applied too rigidly. At times in its history Hollywood has come more strongly under the sway of one function or another: the persuasive in its Dark Age; the personal in its Period of Individuality. Hollywood has also become more self-consciously intellectual in the new classicism of its Period of Reorganization. (We will take up these shifts in the chapters devoted particularly to those functions.) But Hollywood's devotion to traditional narrative forms and to factorylike efficiency has imposed restraints. It blends functions, and so its esthetic qualities reflect the transparent approach of the whole system.

PERSONAL VOICE IN THE STUDIO SYSTEM

We take it for granted that a movie says something to us. But who says it? In the factorylike system we outlined in the beginning of the last section, who can be credited with delivering the final filmed message?

There has been a fair deal of controversy over this question. Many viewers credit a movie's big stars, who have the names that draw the mass audience to the movie in the first place. Others, arguing that stars merely act out someone else's message, would credit the writer, who creates the story's basic design, or the director, who integrates the film factors that put the story on its feet. Still others credit the producer, who oversees all the creative forces and usually has the final say about what goes into or stays out of a movie's message. These choices indicate that no one has come up with an answer that suits all movies.

Whose voice speaks in a Hollywood movie? Perhaps the question is out of date. It reflects one of the traditional assumptions about art that the mass-audience movie helped disrupt in the nineteenth century. There is no single, clear voice emitting the Hollywood message. The voice we hear is a "mythic voice," a kind of illusion. It does not really exist, for the corporate technology forbids a simple personal function. "Voice" is something the viewer *ascribes* to a movie—and its source changes to some extent with each viewer and with each movie. *Dark Victory* is "a Bette Davis film"; *Casablanca* "a Humphrey Bogart film." *Rope* and *Psycho* are "Alfred Hitchcock (the director's) films." To some, *Meet John Doe* and *It Happened One Night* are simply Frank Capra (the director's) films; others think the first reveals the influence of writer Robert Riskin on Capra, whereas the second (written by Capra and two other writers) does not. Fans of *Gone with the Wind,* which had three directors and several writers and stars, are apt to see its "voice" as producer David O. Selznick's. But these assessments vary from viewer to viewer. Some call *Meet John Doe* a Capra film, others a Riskin film, still others a Gary Cooper film.[3]

We can reduce all this down to two kinds of voice that viewers give attention to. One is the *dramatic voice,* the voice from the central figure—in Hollywood, the star. Like the theater, movies present people enacting an action; we watch them live it, and we may listen to the main enactor as though he or she were talking directly to us. Another is the *narrative voice:* the voice from the storyteller. Like literature, the movie's story is under the constant manipulation of the narrator, who may also be a character in the story but more commonly is not. We may notice this voice far more than the dramatic voice—and, as we have just discussed, in Hollywood movies the narrator's manipulation is a corporate operation. Nevertheless, when we assent to this mythic voice we are responding to the storyteller behind the action, not simply the voices of those enacting it. We may, of course, assent to both kinds of voice; certainly both kinds are at work in any story movie, which combines the arts of drama and literature. But each voice involves different factors, which we will now take up.

The Dramatic Voice: The Star

In its Classic Period, Hollywood depended heavily on what it called the star system. Vaudeville and the theater had invented the system, building shows around big names; but whereas stage stars were usually restricted to larger cities, the movies went everywhere, and in the movie house's greater darkness each viewer apparently participated more personally in the experience of "identifying" with stars. The movie's system dated from 1910, when Carl Laemmle, head of the Independent Motion Picture Company (later Universal), had it reported that Florence Lawrence, "The IMP Girl," had been killed. The public response to her "miraculous" reappearance convinced Laemmle, and of course his competitors, to sell stories through popular performers. Writers and directors tailored their work to fit a given star's image, and publicity departments kept the image alive off screen, especially through fan magazines. People were drawn to many movies strictly by a star's name.

The thirties and forties saw the heyday of the star system, in which studios like MGM could advertise "more stars than there are in Heaven" while reaping considerable profits off talents they virtually owned. Some stars were held to twenty-year contracts. By the fifties, though, when the Supreme Court called for decentralization of the studios and many performers' contracts began to expire, the star system died, but the star's power continued. Stars became free-lance operators, bargaining for each movie. By the seventies new superstars had emerged—people like Paul Newman, Marlon Brando, Barbra Streisand, or Steve McQueen, who could demand (and get) from $2 to $5 million per movie. With that kind of money at stake today, filmmakers gear movies to the star's taste and image, and financiers are often more concerned with which star is used than with any other creative factor. Stars also develop their own movie projects, which they control from the start.

With many Hollywood movies, then (and there are exceptions to be mentioned in a moment), the message conveys the "voice" of the star: a certain attitude or tone implicit in the star's image. This image is a variety of the mythic Hollywood voice we have already discussed, for the star's image is something larger than life (Fig. 8.4). It is a special emblem, memorialized with terms like "sex appeal" and "the star look." It holds a special, privileged place within any story, representing an attitude toward life

a

b

that is particularly meaningful to the audience. This emblematic voice remains essentially the same, no matter what particular roles it takes. In certain periods, for example, the voices of particular stars rise to prominence over others because they suit the times. James Cagney and Bette Davis in the thirties, Humphrey Bogart and Rita Hayworth in the forties, or James Dean and Marilyn Monroe in the fifties stand out as particularly striking emblems of major social attitudes. Some movies in the sixties and seventies even draw attention to the separation between the star and the role. Joan Crawford in *What Ever Happened to Baby Jane?* (1962) and John Wayne in *The Shootist* (1976) are themselves as well as their roles, and the particular power of their performances comes largely from our awareness that the roles play upon the stars' images: Crawford is a crippled ex-movie star, and Wayne a dying gunfighter looking back over his past, which is pictured at the movie's beginning with clips from old John Wayne movies.

Though an emblem, a star does not necessarily have an unchanging attitude. More often, a star represents a particular set of tendencies or compulsions that set up internal conflicts and change. The star's emblem incorporates the tendency toward change. And so, from movie to movie, the star goes through the same kind of changes in different characterizations. In *Jezebel* (1938) and in *Dark Victory* (1939) Bette Davis plays a willful woman who finds love and peace by heroically accepting what she cannot change: a predicament very much in keeping with Davis's characteristic image of the proud but essentially tender woman (Fig. 8.5). Even in *What Ever Happened to Baby Jane?* Davis plays an insane harridan torturing her crippled sister, and we get another variation on the same emblem. That movie's surprise ending depends to an extent on our identifying the fact that, deep down, the Bette Davis voice has its pathetic, tender side. James Stewart has made a career playing a likable but very intense individual whose strong emotions bubble very near his manly exterior. This voice comes through almost all his pictures, regardless of very different roles (Fig. 8.6). The same, familiar voice speaks, though in very different contexts.

Stars cannot be simply interchanged without affecting the story they function in. Katharine Hepburn and Joan Crawford, for example, were both romantic leads in the thirties, yet "Hepburn love stories" and "Crawford love stories" are quite different from each other because each star represents very different kinds of emotive appeal. Studios in the Classic Period learned that to cast "against type" was to court financial disaster.

The star's dramatic voice, then, may almost entirely take over a movie's personal function in which case every other performer and all the movie's esthetic

8.4 The star's image: Greta Garbo before and after the Hollywood treatment. a. Garbo in 1925 at the time of her arrival in Hollywood from Sweden. b. Garbo as an established MGM star in the 1930s.

a

b

c

a

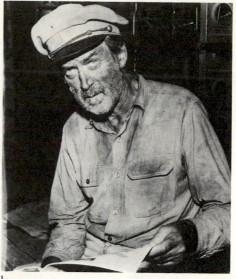

b

c

◆ **8.5** The proud but tender woman: Bette Davis. Shown in (a) *Of Human Bondage* (1934), (b) *The Private Lives of Elizabeth and Essex* (1939), and (c) *Dark Victory* (1939).

8.6 The manly but emotional man: James Stewart. Shown in (a) *Carbine Williams* (1952), (b) *The Flight of the Phoenix* (1966), and (c) *Winchester '73* (1950).

qualities provide the context for this voice to speak to us. But we cannot carry that concept too far, or make it a rule for all movies. Nothing is that simple in movies. There are obviously movies that ignore or disturb the idea of a single dramatic voice. *What Ever Happened to Baby Jane?* has two stars, Crawford and Davis; neither can be said to be *the* voice behind the movie. Even during the classic period of the star system some studios, notably MGM, began the practice of putting two or more big stars in one movie. *Grand Hotel* (1932) and *Dinner at Eight* (1933) were "star-studded" vehicles. And studios regularly released "showcase" movies, designed to give the audience brief glimpses of many stars. Warner's *Thank Your Lucky Stars* (1943) and MGM's *Ziegfeld Follies* (1946) were vaudeville-like musicals that count more as sheer esthetic spectacle (see Chapter 13) than narrative; but the catastrophe movies spun off of *Airport* (1970) use a "showcase" approach to storytelling. It has also happened that, particularly as the classic studio system decayed, some stars and filmmakers have deliberately worked against type. Near the end of their careers, stars like Humphrey Bogart in *The African Queen* (1951) or Clark Gable in *The Misfits* (1961) broke somewhat with their established images, and people like Laurence Olivier and Marlon Brando have made names for themselves as movie stars while remaining essentially talents who change their image considerably from one movie to the next. Director Alfred Hitchcock played with Cary Grant's lady-killer image in *Suspicion* (1941), leading the audience to believe that the Grant character was really going to kill his wife; and Hitchcock shocked many viewers in *Psycho* (1960) by killing off its star, Janet Leigh, halfway through the story.

We obviously cannot ignore the emotive function of the star's voice, but we cannot overlook the presence of the storyteller, whose voice may rise very noticeably over all others.

The Narrative Voice: The Storyteller

The storyteller's function, particularly in Hollywood movies, is necessarily divided among producer, writer, and director. They contribute the mythic single narrative voice we hear. History has made it convenient to talk about this voice in relation to the director. What other people contribute to the narrative voice is usually discussed as an influence on the director, not the other way around. And this traditional assumption (which, of course, is challenged in particular movies by partisans of the other creators) has been fed by history.

Prior to the 1920s directors had pretty direct control over their movies. They coordinated a loosely knit silent film production whose story lines were often sketchy and therefore open to great manipulation, and whose directors often had personally picked their production companies. Directors like D. W. Griffith, Cecil B. De Mille, and Erich von Stroheim developed well-known, distinctive styles, and their names drew audiences as strongly as the stars that appeared in their movies. The rise of vertically integrated studios and the arrival of sound altered the director's power, however. Producers took more control over personnel and administration, and writers' scripts more strongly determined the shape of the complicated sound film. There were some, like De Mille, who maintained more control by becoming independent producer-directors, and there were some, like Capra, whose names were popularly attached to certain kinds of story; but generally the director was a relatively obscure employee of the studio as far as the public was concerned.

After the 1950s, however, directors once more moved into prominence. In France a group of young critic-filmmakers, led by Francois Truffaut and Jean-Luc Godard, attacked the emphasis on mere studio "quality" in French productions and argued that good films were made only by "men of the cinema" who, ideally, wrote and directed their own work and in any case managed to project their own view of life through the cinematic means at their disposal. These French critic-filmmakers praised directors like Alfred Hitchcock, John Ford, and Howard Hawks as such "men of the cinema"—or *auteurs*, as they called them.[4]

In America this became the *auteur theory*, which reached its simplest definition in a remark by Frank Capra that the film message should be "one man, one film."[5] It jibed very much with the sixties' stress on individuality and the growing study of film as an art form in American schools. *Auteur* implied "artist," and people began to study the great *auteurs* and to discover new ones. Obscure and previously unnoticed American veterans were rediscovered as *auteurs*, and young directors with only three or four movies to their credit were praised as new *auteurs*. Auteurism became the most widely known and discussed approach to movies. It focused attention sharply on the emotive function of the director's voice, making that the primary gauge of a movie's value.

The *auteur* theory has spawned attacks from critics outside the camp.[6] Many filmmakers, including directors honored as *auteurs*, have also scoffed at the theory, claiming it vastly oversimplifies a complex process in which directors simply do the best job possible and don't bother about imposing a philosophy of life. Some noted that the French operated within a looser studio system—much like what we pointed out in pre-1920 American movies—where directors have greater control from the outset. Nevertheless, the *auteur* theory has hung on, and with good reason. It points out the undeniable presence of a consistent narrative voice in the movies of certain directors. This voice prevails and matures through such directors' movies—and although we cannot be sure that this "mythic" voice can be ascribed totally to the director, the *auteur* theory certainly gives us a useful framework for analyzing narrative voice.

Using the French insights, we can distinguish two kinds of direction in Hollywood movies. One involves competence and efficiency, the hallmarks of a good studio director. Such a director is called a *metteur en scène* ("placer on stage"). The other kind of direction involves the integration of a personal voice into the studio system. Despite the collaborative nature of the filmmaking process, some directors' work reveals a consistent point of view and attitude. These are the *auteurs*—the authors—who make movies that are distinctly their own. The French terms distinguish what we normally lump together under the single term *director*—and, indeed, some directors are both *metteurs en scène* and *auteurs*. But we need to consider each kind of direction in turn.

The Metteur en Scène   We have said that some directors, especially those in Hollywood's Classic Period, remained relatively obscure employees so far as the public was concerned. Many still are, because their work does not ring with any personal narrative voice—even though some of them were regarded as efficient artisans within the industry. These are the *metteurs en scène.*

They were prolific filmmakers, and they generated impressive and successful movies. W. S. Van Dyke directed over sixty-nine movies in twenty-five years, among them popular films in the Thin Man and Dr. Kildare series. Sam Wood directed fifty-eight movies in thirty years, including the Marx Brothers' *A Night at the Opera* (1935) and *A Day at the Races* (1937) as well as *Goodbye, Mr. Chips* (1939) and *For Whom the Bell Tolls* (1943), popular literary adaptations. Mervyn Le Roy directed over seventy-six movies in forty-three years. He directed *Little Caesar*, an important contribution to the underworld genre, in 1930—the same year he did six other movies. And he directed *I Am a Fugitive from a Chain Gang,* a fine exposé of social problems, along with five other movies in 1932. Among Henry King's sixty-six movies in forty-five years, *Tol'able David* (1921) is a fine example of rural melodrama, the romantic Western *Jesse James* (1939) is striking in its use of color, and *The Gunfighter* (1950) is considered a splendid example of the Western genre.[7]

Because these directors cannot be said to impose any consistent narrative voice onto their material, they have been virtually ignored by film scholars who measure film art in terms of personal expression. Michael Curtiz can be said to epitomize all *metteurs en scène.* His fifty-year career as a director included an incredible 169 movies—some in Hungary and Austria, most in Hollywood at Warner Brothers.

Curtiz handled every genre of American movie, and some of his pictures are considered major works: *The Mystery of the Wax Museum* (1933), *Yankee Doodle Dandy* (1942), *Casablanca* (1942), *Mildred Pierce* (1945), and *The Breaking Point* (1950). He directed a highly successful series of films starring Errol Flynn, among them *Captain Blood* (1935) and *The Charge of the Light Brigade* (1936). All these movies show the high quality and transparent style we associate with the best of Hollywood productions. But his films resist attempts to find any comprehensive vision that threads them together. He is a professional. Film scholars treat him as a "hard, efficient and fast worker" who handled Hollywood's various styles with admirable competence.[8] He was "the best of the Warner action-men," with "no prolonged good or bad periods."[9]

This is hardly faint praise when you consider the number of movies that Curtiz directed. He can hardly be considered inartistic or unsuccessful overall with the film medium. He has no discernible voice in his movies precisely because he is submerged in a storytelling process that creates the mythic voice. His works are Bogart films or Flynn films or just simply underworld or horror films, not Curtiz films.

The attitude of a good *metteur en scène* is reflected in a remark once made by director Victor Fleming. His thirty-year career included more than forty-five movies, and in 1939 he directed two monumental Hollywood works: *Gone with the Wind* and *The Wizard of Oz*. Producer David O. Selznick once stated that "in my opinion he was doing one of the greatest directorial jobs the industry has ever seen." But Fleming is another submerged figure because, as he said to Selznick when he went to work on *Gone with the Wind,* "This is your picture. I am doing exactly what you tell me to do, and I hope it turns out all right."[10]

This is the attitude of the professional. We can certainly see that craft and credit it as such—and in that sense speak of Curtiz movies or Fleming movies. But there is no consistent narrative voice discernible from movie to movie. We can, however, find such a voice in some directors' work.

The Auteur Beyond giving an artisan's coherence and style to the meanings presented to them in scripts, *auteurs* imbue their work with their own particular views of the world. When we look over such a director's films we can find the same recurring motifs. They are adapted to serve the varying requirements of different genres, and their implications change perhaps as the director's career develops; but they mark that director's body of work with a familiar narrative voice.

John Ford is a strong example. Ford was one of Hollywood's enduring professionals. His career spanned sixty years and included over 130 films. And yet what distinguishes him from the prolific directors we have just discussed are the strikingly consistent motifs throughout his work. He directed many action genres, comedies, and literary adaptions, but he preferred Westerns, and it is in them particularly that we see the clearest expression and evolution of his world view. In Chapter 7 we outlined some of the characteristic marks of the Western genre, and these were well suited for Ford's values, but he marked them with his particular motifs; as one saying goes, a viewer can recognize a John Ford Western in five minutes.

Within the Western's context of conflict between civilization and savagery, Ford's movies stress the values of a community spirit that goes deeper than the mere trappings of civilization (Fig. 8.7). The truly worthwhile social values are expressed in the rituals of religion, meals, dancing, and music—rituals that appear repeatedly in the films. The good society joins with the fertility we associate with wilderness and turns it into something enduring and beautiful—and thus images of planting and gardens recur in the movies. Community spirit among men expresses itself in convivial drinking and brawling among cowboys and cavalry troopers. The women may understand and sometimes share this wild camaraderie, but their role is to bring the wild males into the fuller, more enduring community of marriage and family. The evil side of this world is represented by communities with no true community spirit and by those individuals who cannot or will not join in true community. Of all the periods of American history Ford's films allude to, the Civil War probably recurs most often. It is represented by veterans of both sides who either heal or maintain that great division in the nation's community spirit.

Ford's *Stagecoach* (1939), already cited for its classic expression of the Western genre's elements, reveals almost all the Ford motifs. The diverse group of people in the coach, some of them outcasts from a town pictured as essentially cold and unfeeling, learn the values of true community as they proceed across the savage

a

b

landscape. At their first meal together, an ex-Confederate officer insists that the outlaw cowboy and the prostitute sit apart from an upper-class lady who is present. At another stop, the lady gives birth, assisted by an alcoholic doctor who sobers himself up to do his duty. The Indians who attack the coach are representatives of sheer savage force, with no tribal unity that we see; and when the coach reaches its destination, the sheriff allows the cowboy to face and kill savage white men who have murdered his brother in cold blood. At the end, the sheriff sets the cowboy free to go out beyond the town where he and the prostitute will marry and settle into family life. The upper-class lady expresses her indebtedness to the prostitute and the doctor. The only passengers who never come to share the coach's true community are the ex-Confederate, who dies gallant but aloof, and a banker who has joined the group only to escape town with money he has stolen.

Ford's movies can be seen as a continuing exploration of the values implicit in these personal motifs. *Wagonmaster* (1950), by Ford's own admission, "came closest to being what I wanted to achieve."[11] It tells of two cowboys who help a Mormon wagon train cross the prairie. The Mormons introduce the cowboys to true community, and the nomads find hardy women (one a medicine-show performer) and settle into marriage. The wagon train's antagonists are not Indians, but a band of cretinous brothers led by their wily father, Shiloh, whose name recalls the Civil War. What they want is to take gold from the earth, not to plant it with grain as the Mormons do; Shiloh's band finally dies trying to destroy the community.

In *Wagonmaster* the Indians are no longer simply savage forces but other representatives of true community. One of Ford's most evocative passages occurs in this movie. Mormons and Indians have come together around a campfire, and as they dance together, the unifying forces of music and dance, so strong in all Ford's movies, bring them together as one people. Suddenly, breaking up the dance, Shiloh and his sons appear. In the simplest narrative terms, the sequence presents the heart of Western conflict in Ford's films: true community opposed by selfish individuality.

Analyzing personal motifs opens up a new level of movie appreciation. We use them to appreciate each individual Ford movie, but also to study the changes and variations between movies. Presumably they reflect not only the changes in American society but Ford's changing moods about that society. He never left any doubt that he loved America and was apolitical.[12] But not all his movies are as optimistic as *Wagonmaster* or as simple as *Stagecoach*. He never gave up the beliefs implicit in the motifs of his movies, but his vision became more ironic—even sadder—as he proceeded.

8.7 The world of John Ford. Scenes from (a) *She Wore a Yellow Ribbon* (1949) with John Wayne, and (b) *Wagonmaster* (1950) with Joanne Dru and Harry Carey, Jr.

In *She Wore a Yellow Ribbon* (1949), a colorful cavalry story, Ford treats Indians both as antagonists and as another true community. The movie's protagonist is an old man, a retiring colonel, who looks with wisdom on his lieutenants' fights to win a pretty woman and to establish American community life as well as on the cavalry war against the Indians. He finally meets with a chief, his old friend and antagonist, who wants the colonel to come with him to "hunt buffalo, smoke pipe, get drunk together." The Indian agrees that "old men should stop wars," but he knows that it is hard to stop the young, idealistic warriors. Ford was fifty-four when he made the movie, approximately the same age as the colonel, played by John Wayne, who once noted that in his movies for Ford he was basically playing Ford himself.[13] In *The Horse Soldiers* (1959) and in *Sergeant Rutledge* (1960), Ford, with his typical compassion, treats the Southern cause in the Civil War and the troubled place of black men in American society. In *Cheyenne Autumn* (1964) the Indians have become the protagonists, betrayed and oppressed by white men who are finally brought up short by one man who invokes the spirit of Lincoln to heal the breach in community spirit. "Let's face it," Ford said in reflecting on the movie, "we've treated them very badly."[14]

But the most eloquent testimonies to Ford's ironic wisdom are *The Searchers* (1956) and *The Man Who Shot Liberty Valance* (1961). In the first the hero, again played by Wayne, is an ex-Confederate who cannot give up his dedication to that lost cause. In seeking to find the last living member of his family, he becomes as savage as the Indians he hates, and finally he is left outside the settlement. It is probably the most remembered image in Ford's movies: the hero standing in the wilderness as the door of the white man's community is closed to him. Within the world of Ford's motifs, such a hero is neither good nor bad, but both; and the narrative image suggests that he will never resolve his position. *The Man Who Shot Liberty Valance* tells of a man who is acclaimed as a hero for a deed he never did: killing a vicious outlaw. The false hero becomes a renowned statesman, while the real hero lives out his life alone and forgotten. The false hero has won the real hero's woman; by killing Liberty Valance (a name suggesting the value of savage freedom), the real hero has destroyed the last remnant of his way of life, ushering in a new kind of society in which he has no place. In itself, this movie is a splendid example of Western storytelling; but seen in the context of Ford's whole career it is particularly sad and ironic. As the story is structured, the statesman has come back West for the funeral of the hero, who is again played by Wayne, and the statesman tells the true story to a newspaper man who believes it but refuses to print it, saying "When the legend

8.8 The sad irony of John Ford. The closing shots of *The Man Who Shot Liberty Valance* (1961) with James Stewart and Vera Miles.

becomes a fact, print the legend." The last sequence is another of Ford's masterful narrative touches. The statesman is riding back East, but decides he will retire soon and return West. He has tried to square his debt to his friend and failed. A conductor respectfully punches his ticket, asking if everything is all right, for "Nothing's too good for the man who shot Liberty Valance," and the last image is of the train speeding through the tamed wilderness (Fig. 8.8).

But any auteuristic analysis of Ford may raise reasonable questions. First, can't these motifs be ascribed to the screenwriters as much as to Ford? Perhaps, but the movies we mentioned involved several writers—among them Dudley Nichols, Frank S. Nugent, and Willis Goldbeck. No one of them had a hand in all the films. If the motifs originated entirely in the scripts, it is reasonable to assume that the writers tailored the material to Ford's taste. This jibes with the original concept of an *auteur* as a director who either writes or greatly influences the writing of films he makes.

Second, aren't these motifs pretty typical of *all* Westerns? Aren't Ford's heroes, women, and towns pretty much the same as all others in the genre? And the answer is yes and no. The fundamental issues of savagery *versus* civilization remain the same, but the overtones are different. We need to compare Ford to other *auteurs* to see this. Sam Peckinpah is sometimes cited as Ford's heir because he looks upon the West with a fond romanticism that resembles the sad irony of Ford's later movies. But there are considerable differences. In Peckinpah's *The Wild Bunch* (1969) or *Pat Garrett and Billy the Kid* (1973), for example, children are not the happy fruit of a worthy community; they are pure savages who torture dumb creatures and therefore epitomize Peckinpah's ironic view of civilization as innately corrupt, unable to recognize or control the violence it unleashes upon nature. Peckinpah's heroes are always outside the mainstream of society and stay there, living out codes of friendship that bind them to their word and to a controlled use of the violence society has taught them. Men need women in Peckinpah's movies not because women bring order, but because men are incomplete without them. Only the independent woman

who herself stands above the corruption of society can bring Peckinpah's men any value.[15] He goes far beyond the doubts we find in Ford's movies. Peckinpah's bring almost no sense that the heroic individual can find any place in so corrupt a society. The mood varies, but the motifs and consequences remain virtually the same. *Ride the High Country* (1962) is gently bitter, the story of two old-timers who know their code of honor is outdated but who prove its value anyway. *The Wild Bunch* (1969) is a violent epic in which a doomed band of outlaws prove ironically more honorable than the corrupt forces of law and order that hunt them down. *The Ballad of Cable Hogue* (1969), Peckinpah's personal favorite, encapsulates the director's world view in a comically cynical tale. A man who has been left in the desert to die by companions he trusted finds water miraculously and survives. He sets up his own outpost, completely removed from civilization. He outwits thieves and manipulators, gathers a handful of friends who share his code, gets his revenge on the companions who betrayed him, and then dies, run over by a motor car, the product of a modern age he happily leaves. Whereas many of Peckinpah's other films have raised outcries against his emphasis on violence, this film gently and comically reveals a sense of anguish that remains consistent throughout his work. Hogue, its hero, may be said to summarize Peckinpah's attitude about what individuals should do when they need help from society: "Git in, git it, and git out."

Other *auteurs* stress the Western's elements in distinctive ways. Howard Hawks shows a world—as in *Red River* (1948) and *Rio Bravo* (1959)—where men set up their own exclusive society marked with a kind of playfulness toward death and danger. Women are treated as outsiders, even threats—though they are finally accepted. Hawks suggests, in a way that appears more clearly in comedies like *Bringing up Baby* (1938) and *Monkey Business* (1952), that the women have the ultimate power. Budd Boetticher directed a number of Westerns—among them *The Tall T* (1957) and *Comanche Station* (1960)—in which the hero's closest spiritual kinship is with the villain he finally must pursue and kill. The world of Anthony Mann is rife with psychosis (Fig. 8.9). Movies like *Winchester '73* (1950), *The Naked Spur* (1952), and *The Far Country* (1954), feature a near-psychotic hero driven by compulsions that he can never clearly explain to himself. James Stewart's image brought a strong dramatic voice to such films, but Mann's attitude is strong here and in movies where Stewart did not appear.

We have limited our discussion to celebrated *auteurs* of the Western genre, but it illustrates the basic factors involved in any analysis of narrative voice. First, some

8.9 The world of Anthony Mann. The hero (James Stewart) savaged by three psychotics, played by (left to right) Cliff Lyon, Harry Morgan, and Royal Dano, in *Bend of the River* (1952).

films seem to ask for such analysis more strongly than others. The personal storyteller we hear in them may, in fact, be just as much of a mythic assumption on our part as the submerged artisan in ordinary genre movies or the single dramatic voice in star vehicles. But a personal narrator's voice seems an undeniable factor at times.

Second, this approach asks us to look for personal narrative motifs within the pattern of traditional techniques and familiar genre motifs. The *auteur* concept puts particular emphasis on just the emotive function: the personal attitude that the message displays along with its references to typical social values and its esthetic structure.

Third, an analysis of the storyteller's personal motifs is a useful approach to any individual movie that seems to ask for it—but the auteuristic approach ultimately assumes that we see many of the teller's works. It isn't necessary to know who directed a film to enjoy it, but once we become aware of the recurring motifs in an *auteur*'s films, we approach that director's next one with the same sort of informed anticipation that we bring to a favorite novelist's new book. In that sense, the term *auteur*, despite the quarrels it raises, is perfectly appropriate.

Finally, our sense of a particular narrative voice probably has a lot to do with why certain movies within a genre seem more interesting or less clichéd than others. As we noted above, the basic elements of a genre such as the Western are always clichés, repetitions of the same formula. What differs is the kind of voice we hear

speaking through these clichés—and some voices mean more to us than others. John Ford's movies were popular long before the *auteur* theory appeared, and American audiences knew that Alfred Hitchcock's thrillers were peculiarly fascinating long before various critics pointed out the playful perversity he shows toward his stories and his viewers. Despite the corporate process that creates it, a Hollywood movie does convey the sense of an individual voice, which can seem just as personal to some viewers as an intimate conversation.

HOLLYWOOD'S ARTISTIC ASPECT AND CRITICISM

In this chapter we have dealt more directly with common factors of esthetic structure and personal voice that ordinary viewers largely take for granted when approaching a movie. They make immediate judgments on the basis of these factors. They find some movies have silly motivations, don't make a lot of sense, are not fresh—are simply not as "real" to them as other movies. Individuals do not agree among themselves on particular movies, and they may argue over them. But they may not be able to justify their choices to others, and often they do not even try. Their judgment is finally a personal one—but it is, we argue, based on factors of clarity, coherence, emphasis, and personal voice that affect different viewers in different ways.

We can call this kind of response *folk criticism*. It comes from ordinary people, and it is very powerful. Whatever their particular differences, ordinary people can sometimes reach very effective agreement on what they like or don't like. Their taste established such filmmakers as Ford, Hawks, and Hitchcock long before the auteurists arrived, and no amount of intellectual discussion has been able to revive the public's lost interest in filmmakers like D. W. Griffith, Budd Boetticher, or Peter Bogdanovich. This illustrates the democratization of art unleashed over a century ago with the emergence of photography.

Distinct from it is the work of *professional criticism*, the more deliberately intellectual activity of journalists and scholars. Elitists see this camp as opposed to the folk camp. They argue that the common people are intrinsically naive, too easily exploited into accepting what they don't want, too ignorant of the artistic values they would understand if they only listened to the elitists tell them what was good and bad. What this overlooks, we argue, is that professional critics *are* part of the common people. Their responses are triggered by the same factors as anyone else's. Their function is not to dictate what should be—but to explain more clearly what everybody already knows and takes for granted. This task is not as easy as it may sound.

This book barely scratches the surface of what the motion-picture experience involves. That experience itself is continually evolving. Under the influence of television, filmmaking has acquired a different status whose dimensions are still not perceived, and television is itself another type of the motion-picture experience, raising new issues this book cannot begin to introduce.

In dealing with the artistic aspects of the Hollywood movie, however, we arrive at some critical principles that would seem to apply to one's approach to any movie. First, there seems to be little point in trying to remove the element of imprecision and contradiction. It is built into the system. Factory-made movies should have no voice, but they do; movies are blatant clichés, but they're not; they show us an absolutely false world, but they don't. And so on. The elitist professionals' quest for clear rules and correct taste seems to deny the nature of the material they study.

Second, the sensible quest of the critic, whether folk or professional, should therefore be to *describe*, not *prescribe*. We spoke of this in discussing Andre Bazin's sensible attitude toward film esthetics. It makes even more sense in light of the artistic aspects outlined in this chapter. If the esthetic function involves an implicit interplay between intellectual and functional symbols, and if the personal function tends to be a mythic assumption on our part, how can one demand that any film *must* use one kind of symbol or another, *must* speak with a personal narrative voice?[16]

Third, the folk critic and the professional critic are united in the same quest. The elitist presumption that the latter is more important than the former is at best wishful thinking. History suggests that they are constantly teaching each other. The introduction of film study into American universities over the past twenty-five years has led to audiences who are more intellectually aware of techniques and traditions, and this has influenced the style and attitude of Hollywood storytellers, who can, for example, play more self-consciously with genre conventions. But within the same period professionals turned increasingly to semiotics, structuralism, and rhetoric to find the tools to deal with the fact that there was more happening out there among the folk than they could handle with the old tools. The professionals influence the folk, but the folk always challenge the professionals. And in that process we all learn something worthwhile about the motion-picture experience.

SUMMARY

A discussion of the artistic aspects of Hollywood movies involves both its esthetic and personal functions: on one hand, the formal qualities that determine its structure; on the other, the "speaker's" voice that emerges from its message.

The formal qualities include clarity, coherence, and emphasis, which unite to create an overall simplicity of action. The Hollywood narrative depends strongly on the actuality and credibility of objects and actions. It creates functional symbols, which primarily keep credible action moving, rather than intellectual symbols, which would obtrude upon the transparent narrative. Its *mise en scène* and continuity also impose equally transparent techniques, balancing emphatic (or entropic) elements against redundant (or familiar) patterns. And what results is a simplicity of action that nevertheless carries complex stimulations and associations.

The "speaker" in a Hollywood movie is a mythic voice that different viewers ascribe to different sources. One person may hear the narrative voice of the star; another may respond to what is essentially a submerged narrative voice—that of the *metteur en scène* who crafts elements into a unity. Yet another hears an individualized narrative voice, that of the *auteur*, whose films reiterate a more or less consistent attitude.

The *auteur* theory of criticism has had great influence on viewers' attention to the personal narrative voice. But cinema's artistic aspect, as exemplified in Hollywood's corporate system of production, eludes critics who would prescribe one approach as clearly superior to another. We learn more about movies' artistic aspect from critics who describe the complex interlacing of various factors, through which different films call for responses to different esthetic and personal elements.

NOTES

1 *Film as Film* (Baltimore: Penguin, 1972), p. 74. Chaps. 4–6 are an excellent presentation of the esthetic issues outlined here.

2 Michael Goodwin and Naomi Wise, "An Interview with Howard Hawks," *Take One*, 3 (Nov.–Dec. 1971), 22.

3 For a more thorough discussion of what we have simplified into the "mythic" voice, see Michel Foucault's essay "What Is an Author?" *Partisan Review*, 42 (1975), 603–614. Foucault discusses what he calls the "transcendental anonymity" of literary works, but he raises issues that are very important to movies. Foucault qualifies some of the methods he used in his earlier, complex structuralist work, *The Order of Things* (New York: Pantheon, 1970).

4 For the fundamentals of this movement, see Truffaut's "A Certain Tendency of the French Cinema," included with some excellent examples of *auteur* criticism in Bill Nichol's *Movies and Methods* (Berkeley: University of California, 1976); and the writings of Godard, collected and translated by Tom Milne in *Godard on Godard* (New York: Viking, 1968). Peter Wollen's *Signs and Meaning in the Cinema* (Bloomington: Indiana University, 1969) outlines the *auteur* approach and applies it to some American directors.

5 " 'One Man, One Film'—the Capra Contention," *Los Angeles Times Calendar*, June 26, 1977, p. 12. Andrew Sarris, one of the first American critics to espouse the *auteur* theory, presents a defense of its principles in the introduction to *The American Cinema: Directors and Directions, 1929–1968* (New York: Dutton, 1968), which provides filmographies and brief auteuristic analyses of a number of directors. Among film journals *Film Comment, Film Quarterly, American Film,* and the now defunct *Take One* have presented auteurist interviews and analyses.

6 The most vociferous critic is Pauline Kael. See her "Circles and Squares," one of the essays collected in *I Lost It at the Movies* (Boston: Little, Brown, 1965); and "Raising Kane," included in *The Citizen Kane Book* (Boston: Little, Brown, 1971). You may wish to pursue the auteurists' responses in Andrew Sarris's "Notes on the *Auteur* Theory in 1970," *Film Comment,* 6 (Fall 1970), 7–9; and in Peter Bogdanovich's "The *Kane* Mutiny," *Esquire,* Oct., 1972, pp. 99–105, 180–190.

7 *What Is Cinema?* II, 153.

8 Kingsley Canham, *The Hollywood Professionals, Volume One: Michael Curtiz, Raoul Walsh, Henry Hathaway* (New York: Barnes, 1973), p. 10.

9 Markku Salmi, "Michael Curtiz," *Film Dope,* 9 (Apr. 1976), 24.

10 *Memo from David O. Selznick,* ed. Rudy Behlmer (New York: Viking, 1972), pp. 237–238.

11 Peter Bogdanovich, *John Ford* (Berkeley: University of California, 1968), p. 88.

12 George J. Mitchell, "Ford on Ford," *Films in Review,* 15 (June–July 1964), 323.

13 In Peter Bogdanovich's documentary film, *Directed by John Ford* (1973).

14 Bogdanovich, *John Ford,* p. 104.

15 These insights into Peckinpah owe much to Louis Garner Simmons's "The Cinema of Sam Peckinpah and the American Western" (Ph.D. dissertation, Northwestern University, 1975).

16 One of the best sources for descriptive criticism is Perkins's *Film as Film.* Perkins outlines the issues with great clarity and perception.

Chapter 9 / The Distinctive

Mode of Comedy

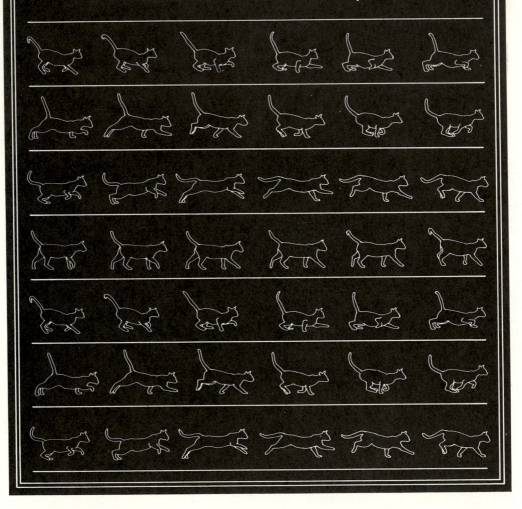

Humor entered movies at the start. Emile Reynaud's projected drawings involved clowns; William K. L. Dickson's experiments were comic scenes; and Louis Lumière's first bit of storytelling was a farce.[1] Since then, most narrative movies, even those whose stories end tragically, have funny moments that vary the mood and provide what is usually called *comic relief.*

This chapter centers on those movies whose more or less continuous aim is to make us laugh—*comedies.* They employ the same visual and aural means, and they reveal the same four basic functions of any communication. But we feel they deserve some special consideration because comedy has a distinctive *mode* of communication: it disrupts the customary system. Comedy cannot simply be called another narrative genre, for it may take over other genres, turning them into comic Westerns, underworld films, horror movies, or whatever. The experience of the comic, whether in moments or throughout entire movies, is one of the most elusive and complex events we take for granted. We have no delusions that we will overcome all the challenges it raises. But they deserve particular attention because they are so common and so distinctive.

We will deal here only with American comedies, which relate to our common experience and which have evolved out of the Hollywood production systems we have already discussed. During the Classic Period there were many companies of personnel who specialized in comedies and produced them in two basic forms: the *comedy short,* which developed essentially one comic episode; and the *comedy feature,* which developed a complex narrative plot with changes of tempo, pace, and mood. Since the breakup of the old studio system, comedy shorts have moved over to television—the situation comedy (or sitcom) being essentially what filmmakers used to call a two-reeler. Comedy features, like other narrative movies, are separate business deals between investors, stars, and filmmakers.

We will discuss Hollywood comedies under the four different functions they serve. We will look first at a comedy's relationship to the real world (the realistic function), then at its structure (the esthetic function), its voice (the personal function), and its social function (the persuasive function).

COMEDY'S RELATIONSHIP TO THE REAL WORLD

Comedy makes us aware that there are all sorts of patterns we normally assume in making sense of the world. For example, we identify objects verbally by particular words or visually by certain shapes and functions; we expect actions to follow certain physical laws, like that of gravity; we dress and behave according to certain codes;

279

and so forth. In noncomic communication we assume such patterns in order to convey meaning. They make meaning possible. They are the "realities" we take for granted in phrasing ideas or stirring emotions about the real world.

Then something comic occurs. It violates the patterns, bungles them, gets us confused about them—in general, disrupts the assumptions on which all proper communication rests. Someone uses the wrong word or gets two meanings of one word tied together; the friend you rush up to embrace turns out to be a stranger who looks like your friend; the heavy rock you went to lift flies up because it's really a sponge; the down elevator goes up; you notice that a man has on two different colored socks; and so forth. When the comic experience happens to you, you may not laugh; but when it happens to someone else you are likely to find it funny or ridiculous. Each is essentially a comic predicament, but one must see it as a disruption of pattern—and not be emotionally involved with what it means or implies—in order to laugh.

This is what comedy exploits deliberately. It emphasizes the patterns that we normally assume. It creates stories whose characters are outcasts from normal behavior (extreme versions of the man with mismatched socks), in which nature does not follow normal laws (an extreme version of the down elevator going up), in which words, people, and objects get confused and scrambled—and it asks us to see it primarily as *pattern play,* not as something to get us emotionally involved. We can create a working definition, adapted from a saying of Horace Walpole, the eighteenth-century British writer: "tragedy is for those who feel, comedy for those who think."[2] Comedy is at its heart an intellectual game. This is what distinguishes it, for example, from noncomic narrative genres like horror movies or underworld films that also involve bizarre circumstances and social outcasts. We experience shock or worry in such movies because we worry *with* characters; we get caught up in the dreadful implications of what they confront or represent. The comic experience is more complicated. It doesn't remove all involvement with characters, but it keeps making us see them as patterned figures as well as people. In many horror stories or mysteries there are moments when, after the audience knows the hero's fearful predicament, something threatening intrudes—a shadow appears at a window or a doorknob begins slowly to turn—and then the intruder turns out to be a friend, even sometimes a friend playing a joke. Usually we laugh. The story's pattern has set us up to expect one thing and then fooled us. This is comic relief: the thinking side, which sees the trick, takes pressure off the feeling side. This helps explain, too, why many old horror movies bring more laughs today than chills: we see their outdated styles merely as patterns, not as communicators of fearful meanings.

All this illustrates the complexity of the comic experience. The meaning of comedy lies in the disruptive way it reveals the patterning we normally assume in finding meaning. We usually respond with laughter. But we use laughter to signal other reactions, too: animal pleasure, hysteria, embarrassment, or fear. (Notice some time how much laughter you hear at horror movies.) Comedy is one thing; laughter something else. Some people like comedy but don't laugh much. And laughter doesn't necessarily signal simple enjoyment of the comic. Some comedies are "dark" or "black," to use common terms: cruel or bitter stories that make jokes of terrible and touching predicaments—and they can rouse bitter and nervous laughter. Our responses to comedy also depend on our ability to understand what patterns are being disrupted. We can miss the point or catch points others overlook. Some people have no "sense" of humor—which perhaps means they can't easily separate pattern from meaning. It is also interesting to watch young children's reactions to comedies. Children are necessarily those people in society who are still in the process of learning the proper patterns. They are very attentive, then, to disruptions that no longer interest adults. And so children may have a keener sense of some comic predicaments, notably those disrupting fundamental natural laws or codes of social behavior. A cartoon tree falling the wrong way or the Three Stooges demolishing a room disrupts the real world at a level the child knows very well.

Movie comedies refer to the world by disrupting it in many ways. We cannot hope to cover all of them here, but we can note some basic forms of comic disruption that are particularly noteworthy at different moments of film history. Since they are basic comic forms they are not unique to their periods; each represents a tradition that has ancient roots and continues to the present day. But within a given period each was particularly popular, which suggests that it had special relevance to that time. We can distinguish the forms under the general terms of physical, social, and critical comedy. We will pinpoint them in three particular traditions of movie history: slapstick, screwball, and satire.

The Slapstick Tradition

The motion picture was initially a silent visual medium. Among the many theatrical talents it attracted were vaudeville comedians who performed routines that emphasized physical action, not words. These performers were *clowns* in the truest sense, part of a tradition generally classified as *slapstick comedy*.

Both terms were, and are, sometimes used disparagingly as synonyms for "low" humor—but they represent the purest and most ancient strain of the comic impulse in human history. Its roots are in tribal fertility rituals, which were transformed into *farces*, plays that emphasized physical pranks. By the sixteenth century the farce tradition was embodied in its most famous form: the *commedia dell' arte* ("comedy of the guild"). Companies of Italian players travelled throughout Europe performing farces improvised on several standard plots using stock figures. At the center of each plot was a pair of troubled lovers. Opposing them were some "old men" characters: Pantalone, a possessive fool; the Doctor, an inept man of learning; and the Captain, a bragging coward. On the other side, usually supporting the lovers, was a group of servants, including Harlequin, a fellow of many moods; Pierrot, a tender simpleton; Brighella and Pulcinella (later Punch), pugnacious fellows; and Columbine, a shrewd woman. Except for the lovers, each *commedia* character wore a distinctive mask and clothing, and each performer developed personal mannerisms and tricks, called *lazzi*, that individualized him or her. The stories emphasized tricks, acrobatics, and beatings. Harlequin carried a kind of paddle made of two slats attached to a handle, and when he hit someone the paddle gave off a loud smack. This was the slapstick, which gave the tradition its name.

The *commedia* fed into the American circus and vaudeville, and then into movies. The clown was a distinctive figure with a bizarre face, absurd clothes, and peculiar mannerisms. A slapstick situation involved clowns in very physical disruptions. They ran into and beat upon each other; they got into peculiar conflicts with ordinary things; they didn't even move in typical ways. By 1914 the Keystone Film Company, supervised by producer Mack Sennett, was generating extremely popular comedy shorts that were basically American *commedia* (Fig. 9.1). They featured human caricatures that moved about like ludicrous machines, bizarre and repetitive in looks and gestures. Mack Swain was "Ambrose," a huge fellow usually trying to elude a dominating wife; Chester Conklin was "Walrus," a creature behind a huge moustache; and Roscoe Arbuckle was "Fatty," a jolly man who often got into or out of trouble by donning female disguises. The Keystone Kops were maladroit policemen in mortal struggles with trains, telephone poles, or their own paddy wagon. Speed was essential at Keystone. A typical situation was begun and

9.1 Keystone: American *commedia*. Phyllis Haver, Jimmy Finlayson, and Ben Turpin (left to right) in an unidentified Keystone comedy.

completed within twenty seconds, and action was not only undercranked but treated to "Keystone editing," in which every third or fourth frame of film was removed to make the movement even faster and jerkier.[3] *The Bangville Police* (1913), *Muddled in Mud* (1913), and *Ambrose's First Falsehood* (1914) are examples of Keystone farce in its early, one-reel forms, where action was very simple and repetitive. Later on, stories were developed somewhat more fully in two-reelers, but still with lots of mayhem—as in *A Desperate Scoundrel* (1914), or *Love, Speed and Thrills* (1915).

The slapstick tradition embodied a lot of violence and physical destruction, and this maintained a strong appeal through the twenties, a time very taken with material prosperity. The crudities of Keystone were tempered somewhat, but the interest in mayhem remained. At the Hal Roach Studios, comedians Stan Laurel and Oliver Hardy appeared in a series of comedy shorts whose standard pattern can be described as escalating chaos. In *From Soup to Nuts* (1928) they destroy a banquet; in *Two Tars* (1928) they set off a chain of destruction along a line of automobiles; and in *Big Business* (1929) they get into a sort of duel with a homeowner, trading acts of violence until most of his house and their auto are demolished.

At the same time, the production of comedy features brought a need for greater sentimentality and realism to serve the demands of more complicated plots. Charles Chaplin, who started at Keystone but soon moved into producing his own comedy shorts, developed a clown character who gradually moved away from the emphasis on violent mayhem. In his features, Chaplin's "Little Tramp" character became a combination of Harlequin and a troubled lover, sometimes moving his audiences to tears—though always within the essentially farcical framework (Fig. 9.2). *The Gold Rush* (1925) included, on one hand, a scene where Chaplin, starving in the Yukon, cooks and eats a shoe as though it were a delicacy, and, on the other, a scene where he dreams of entertaining his true love, only to awake and find she has forgotten her promise to visit him. In both *The Circus* (1928) and *City Lights* (1931) Chaplin plays the same kind of gentle clown, helping women who don't realize how much he loves them.

9.2 Charles Chaplin's gentle clown. With Georgia Hale in *The Gold Rush* (1925).

Buster Keaton took an entirely different approach. In his short comedies Keaton had developed a kind of Pierrot, a solemn-faced clown who performed adroit acrobatic maneuvers. He often created peculiar comic machines for his stories: mechanized households in *The Scarecrow* (1920) and *The Electric House* (1922) and bizarre structures or vehicles in *One Week* (1920), *The Boat* (1921), *Cops* (1922), and *The Balloonatic* (1923). Keaton maintained this interest in machinery in his features, but he put a greater stress on realistic credibility. His unsmiling clown wore ordinary clothes in stories that were comic versions of adventure narratives. In *The General* (1926) Keaton spent $42,000 on one shot, wrecking a real locomotive to tell a comic version of the Civil War's Great Locomotive Chase. *Go West* (1925) is a comic Western, with Keaton putting on a red devil's costume to attract a herd of cattle's attention and lead them through a town. In *The Navigator* (1924) he plays a spoiled rich boy who finds himself adrift in an empty ocean liner and ends up saving his sweetheart from a horde of attacking cannibals. *Steamboat Bill, Jr.* (1928), about a sissy who wins his tough father's respect, contains a scene in which Keaton lets the two-ton façade of a building fall on him, an open window barely clearing his body (Fig. 9.3). Keaton's dedication to film machinery shows in an extraordinary sequence from *Sherlock Jr.* (1924), where, playing a dreaming projectionist, he gets caught in the editing process of a movie and can't get out.

The slapstick tradition's clowns found many other faces and *lazzi* in the twenties. Harold Lloyd probably departed furthest from the idea of a clown, developing what he called the "glasses character," who looked like an optimistic college student in horn-rimmed glasses. His stories had him getting into innocent trouble while trying to hold a job or win a girl. They often shaded toward sentimental melodrama, like Chaplin's, but his features in particular built into exciting displays of physical comedy. In *The Freshman* (1925) the glasses character wins a football game against seemingly insuperable odds, and in *The Kid Brother* (1927) he proves his manhood in a vicious fight with a huge bully. The most famous image of Lloyd, from

Audio Brandon/© Raymond Rohauer, 1980

9.3 Buster Keaton's realism. A frame enlargement from *Steamboat Bill, Jr.* (1928).

9.4 A Marx Brothers' disruption. With Margaret Dumont in *Animal Crackers* (1930). ◗

Safety Last (1923), shows one of his typical physical predicaments: he hangs from the face of a huge clock several stories above the street.

Slapstick comedy has never entirely disappeared from movies, but the *commedia* tradition inherited from vaudeville began to trickle away almost immediately with the arrival of sound. No one has found a simple explanation for its decline in popularity. It may be that physical comedy was too tied down by sound technology, that comedians' material had begun to lose its freshness anyway, or that the Depression era, which happened to arrive along with sound, did not respond as strongly to the old comic attitudes. The new ones had a more specific social reference, as we shall see.

In fact, though, the Depression era's most famous comedy team can be described as the last great flowering of the *commedia* tradition in American movies. The Marx Brothers' movies were as close to the old *commedia* structure as any we will find (Fig. 9.4). Most of them center on two troubled lovers. An aunt or mother forbids their marriage, or an older man wants to marry the young woman. To their rescue come the Marx Brothers, who are lower-class, just like the *commedia* servants, and just as distinctive. Each has his particular attire and *lazzi*: Groucho's moustache and stooped

walk; Chico's cap and accent; Harpo's wig and horn. None of them fit the classic *commedia* characters precisely, though Harpo and Chico share some of Harlequin's and Pierrot's qualities, and Groucho is much like aggressive Brighella, who has been described as "opportunistic . . . egoistic . . . moving always with a prowl-like gait."[4]

The Marx Brothers carried the old tradition over into the sound period. Meanwhile a new movie tradition had developed that was particularly appropriate to the thirties.

The Screwball Tradition

We can think of the slapstick tradition as making fun of life in general; its materials were basic physical and social codes that apply to almost any period. Screwball comedy, on the other hand, is more clearly marked with its time, the Depression.

The term *screwball* refers to movies derived for the most part from a certain variety of Broadway play. Hence, it was a strongly *verbal* tradition of comedy. The plays built stories around irresponsible and often wealthy people confronting the social upheaval represented by the Depression. Screwball comedies varied a lot in style; some employed slapstick elements, others remained sophisticated. They were not established by comedians, but by writers and directors who gave a contemporary twist to age-old comic conflicts between rich and poor, men and women, rural life and urban life.

In screwball comedies the poor tend to represent great simplicity and down-to-earth honesty because, being poor, they are in touch with reality. The rich people live behind masks of wealth and pretension, and many plots arrange for the rich to remove, lose, or at least have trouble with their masks (Fig. 9.5). The worthwhile rich prove they are poor at heart, and the poor hero or heroine finally gets rich. Screwball comedy, after all, had an escapist function: to let people forget, even laugh at, their troubles before returning to very real breadlines and joblessness.

9.5 Social upheaval among the rich. A scene from *Nothing Sacred* (1937).

9.6 The poor versus the rich. William Powell and Carole Lombard in *My Man Godfrey* (1936).

Many comedies showed a poor person becoming involved with a wealthy family. The classic example was Frank Capra's *It Happened One Night* (1934), where a hard-boiled newsman travels across country with a spoiled heiress who has run away from home. He introduces her to the life of ordinary people and finally marries her—to the delight of her down-to-earth father. *My Man Godfrey* (1936), directed by Gregory La Cava, and *Easy Living* (1937), directed by Mitchell Leisen, both follow similar lines. In the first film, a spoiled rich girl brings home a poor man, like a pet, to be the family butler (Fig. 9.6). In the latter, a business tycoon, fed up with his wife's spending, gives her mink coat to a poor girl. In both cases, the poor person winds up saving the rich family's fortune and marrying into it.

Finding true love was always part of such stories, for the screwball was a form of *romantic* comedy. Yet it was apt to surprise assumptions about the roles of men and women. In *My Man Godfrey*, for example, the woman initiates all the romance, not Godfrey. In George Cukor's *Holiday* (1938), the down-to-earth hero finally sees his rich fiancée's true selfishness and calls it quits—but this moves her free-spirited sister, who has loved him all along, to leave the family and go after him.

Other screwball comedies went further than role reversal into something approaching toe-to-toe battles between the sexes. Victor Fleming's *Bombshell* (1933) tells about a studio press agent who battles, tricks, and deludes a Hollywood star until both realize they need each other (Fig. 9.7). In Leo McCarey's *The Awful Truth* (1937) an ex-husband keeps harassing his ex-wife and meddling in her romantic life until she outwits him at his own game, and they return to each other. Cukor's *The Philadelphia Story* (1940) was a variation on the same situation.

In this section we are focusing on the realist function of screwball comedy, to the particularized real world of the Depression it uses as a reference point. Later on, in the section on comic voice, we will focus on screwball as an instrument of personal attitudes, particularly those of directors Howard Hawks and Ernst Lubitsch and of writers Robert Riskin and Ben Hecht.

World War II broke up the Depression and, to some extent, the screwball tradition. Like slapstick, its principles and themes have never entirely disappeared, but it gave way in the forties and fifties to a more biting kind of comedy.

The Satiric Tradition

In the forties and fifties we find the slapstick tradition carried on in a very modified form by verbal comedians, many of them with experience in vaudeville and burlesque, who made a number of popular movies. Bob Hope and Bing Crosby, who were established radio performers, made a series of "road" pictures, beginning with *The Road to Singapore* (1940). "Red" Skelton, another radio veteran, starred as a genial buffoon in features like *Whistling in Dixie* (1942) and *Merton of the Movies* (1947). Danny Kaye, primarily a stage entertainer, developed a subtle clown in movies like *The Secret Life of Walter Mitty* (1947), *The Inspector General* (1949), and *The Court Jester* (1956). And in features like *Dubarry Was a Lady* (1943), *Miss Grant Takes Richmond* (1949), and *The Fuller Brush Girl* (1950), Lucille Ball established a clowning style that carried her to enormous success in television. Perhaps the

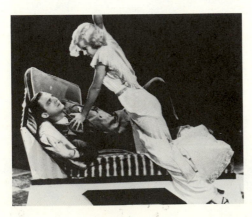

9.7 The battle of the sexes. Lee Tracy and Jean Harlow in *Bombshell* (1933).

epitome of forties clowning was the team of Bud Abbott and Lou Costello, who did a long series of feature comedies using ancient jokes and crude slapstick to kid the armed services, as in *Buck Privates* (1941), or other genres, as in *Abbott and Costello Meet Frankenstein* (1948). Dean Martin and Jerry Lewis provided similar buffoonery for a popular series of features in the fifties, including *At War with the Army* (1950), *Money from Home* (1953), and *The Stooge* (1953).

None of these comedians was particularly controversial. Like the old clowns of visual slapstick, they used contemporary situations to make pretty generalized fun. But the forties and fifties, as we noted in Chapter 7, was a period of great social controversy. Charles Chaplin, by far the most popular comedian of the twenties, ran afoul of this new period's growing fears and paranoia. He had made few features since the twenties, and these had successfully kidded their times. *Modern Times* (1936) showed the Little Tramp running amuck in a modern factory, finally leaving the technological world behind, and walking off to a more hopeful world at the end. *The Great Dictator* (1940) was a comic denunciation of fascism, with Chaplin playing both a Jewish barber and the dictator, a parody of Hitler, whom the barber is mistaken for. But after the war Chaplin's comedies outraged audiences. In *Monsieur Verdoux* (1947) he abandoned the tramp character and played a Bluebeard who murdered wealthy women to provide his family with security, noting ironically that "one murder makes a villain; millions a hero!" (Fig. 9.8). In the paranoia of the McCarthy era, Chaplin came under dark suspicion. It culminated in 1952 when the attorney general effectively banned Chaplin from reentering the United States, and the American Legion boycotted his *Limelight,* a sentimental re-creation of Chaplin's music-hall days. Chaplin settled in Switzerland and made *A King in New York* (1957), where he plays a monarch who visits the United States and comes under government suspicion. In the film's climax the king turns a firehose on a congressional committee investigating him. Before his death in 1977, Hollywood invited Chaplin back for a special Academy Award, a gesture of reconciliation after all the old bitterness. But the bitterness tells us something about the period.

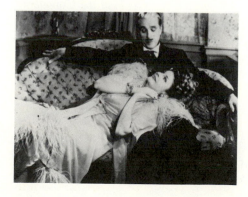

9.8 The comedian turned murderer. Charles Chaplin and Martha Raye in *Monsieur Verdoux* (1947).

The forties and fifties were a time in which a strong sense of *satire* developed in various comic features. Certainly, satiric elements can be found in American comedies of any period, but in this period we find a comedy that does not simply reflect basic physical incongruities as plain slapstick does, nor does it simply make fun of class codes in the screwball manner. Although it borrows from both traditions, satire also *attacks* social patterns.

Chaplin's Verdoux and his king hosing down a congressional committee were examples of satire, and their reception proved in a way how successful his communication was. Generally, though, the satiric tradition in this period was represented by directors and writers, and directors who were also writers, who managed to prick the public's moral assumptions without killing their movies' popularity. For that reason, satire is almost impossible to discuss without reference to the personal function, the narrative voice behind the movie, whose tone tends to drip with *irony*. Though it may employ slapstick elements, satire is generally considered a far more intellectual, or "high," comic experience than either slapstick or screwball comedy. Satire relies heavily on the viewer's ability to detect subtle irony—in particular, to detect that what one means is quite different from what one says. This is why viewers can miss satire's point altogether. It is ironic that Chaplin's Verdoux, a murderer, is a gentle, comic fellow, and his line quoted above is not a defense of murder but a condemnation of war. Still, many of the movie's viewers condemned it for joking about murder and making light of justice. Too few saw Verdoux as a man simply using the techniques that he had learned from a society that increasingly ignored individual rights. (We might also assume that many missed the point but caught the satiric tone and condemned the movie anyway.) Satire is typically a comic form that gets misunderstood; since it is attacking social conventions, that is perhaps understandable.

Preston Sturges fared better than Chaplin. Sturges wrote and directed eleven comedies that spanned the forties and confirmed him as a biting satirist of the war years. The public could never quite decide if he was serious or merely irreverent. He parodied political life in *The Great McGinty* (1940), romantic love in *The Lady Eve* (1941), and artistic ideals in *Sullivan's Travels* (1941). And in a time of war he dared to make fun of small towns, motherhood, and servicemen. In *Hail the Conquering Hero* (1944) Woodrow Lafayette Pershing Truesmith, the son of a dead Marine hero, cannot bear to tell his mother he has been rejected from service as 4-F. Some sympathetic Marines force him to put on a uniform and pretend to be a hero. Anything for a mother. He is nominated for mayor and is about to win when the

9.9 The satire of sexual phobias. Jayne Mansfield, Edmund O'Brien, and Tom Ewell (left to right) in *The Girl Can't Help It* (1956).

incumbent, a crook, exposes him. Woodrow confesses the fraud, but one of the Marines praises his honesty, and so the town elects him anyway. He is a hero to them because he has admitted being a fraud.

Sturges's comedies were popular, but some worried about what one critic called his "snobbery, cynicism, cowardice and a radical lack of love."[5] It has remained for later generations to consider that, in parodying every value held sacred to American life in the forties, Sturges was sincerely critical of society. "He was listening and looking for the reasons for tomorrow's insanity," filmmaker Robert Downey wrote in 1970. "Look at one of his films and then look around you: the man was serious."[6]

Sturges's popularity faded after 1949, but other satirists replaced him. Frank Tashlin was an obscure craftsman in Hollywood until he turned out *Hollywood or Bust* (1956), *The Girl Can't Help It* (1956), and *Will Success Spoil Rock Hunter?* (1957). With these movies he became a director of distinction. His detractors claimed that his garish, comic-strip approach merely exploited the public's inane fascination with rock 'n roll, quick success, and stardom, and particularly with the large breasts of stars like Anita Ekberg and Jayne Mansfield. Tashlin's fans saw him satirizing these American phobias (Fig. 9.9).

Two sharper and more clearly defined satirists appeared at the end of the fifties: writer Isadore A. L. Diamond and director Billy Wilder. They brought an often nasty

wit to bear on contemporary affairs. Their first big success together was *Some Like It Hot* (1959). In it two musicians have witnessed a gangland execution and need to hide from the killers. They disguise themselves as women and join an all-girl band on tour, which eventually brings the musicians back in touch with the gangsters they are hiding from. Meanwhile, one musician falls in love with a singer but can't tell her he is a man, and the other musician is wooed by a rich man. While generally parodying the gangster genre and romantic melodrama, the movie is also a bizarre satire on sexual roles and personal identity (Fig. 9.10). Wilder and Diamond continued their harsh wit into the sixties and seventies with movies like *The Apartment* (1960), a jab at the world of big-business hanky-panky, and *Kiss Me, Stupid* (1964), which slashed so energetically at American sexual mores that many viewers denounced it as an exercise in poor taste.

Since the fifties, American film comedy depends largely on satire and some vestiges of the slapstick tradition. In the sixties, Jerry Lewis broke his partnership with Dean Martin and developed an independent clown character who appeared in a number of features, including *The Bellboy* (1960), *The Nutty Professor* (1963), *The Patsy* (1964), and *The Family Jewels* (1965). His nearest successor in this slapstick approach is Woody Allen, who created a distinctive clownlike figure for the seventies, a bumbling misfit whose adventures in movies like *Bananas* (1971) and *Everything You Always Wanted to Know About Sex, But Were Afraid to Ask* (1972) involved a great deal of social satire.

There is some degree of what can be called comic nostalgia also, a re-creation of older film forms in comic style. Allen plays with Bogart and Casablanca in *Play It Again, Sam* (1972). Producer-director Blake Edwards falls heavily upon Laurel and

9.10 The satire of sexual roles. Jack Lemmon plays a woman in *Some Like It Hot* (1959).

Hardy, as well as other old clowns, for the inspiration of movies like *The Great Race* (1965), *The Party* (1968), *10* (1979), and the series of "Pink Panther" comedies begun in 1964. Writer-director Mel Brooks, a wild satirist whose movies bring back the earthy vulgarity of old burlesque, broke into prominence with *The Producers* (1967), a satire on theatrical life, then moved into lampooning traditional movie genres in *Blazing Saddles* (1974), *Young Frankenstein* (1975), *Silent Movie* (1976), and *High Anxiety* (1977), a takeoff on Hitchcock.

The harshest satires have come from filmmakers not otherwise known as specialists in comedy. One is Stanley Kubrick, whose *Dr. Strangelove, or How I Learned to Stop Worrying and Love the Bomb* (1963) dared to caricature militarists, atomic scientists, and world annihilation itself at a time when paranoid Americans and Russians were building bomb shelters. Another satirist is Robert Altman, who attracted popular attention with *M*A*S*H* (1969) a "black" satire that counterpoints the horrors of the Korean War with the lunacies of the staff running a Mobile Army Surgical Hospital. The Korean conflict was long over, and the target of Altman's irony was the Vietnam War and the moral upheaval it was creating. Altman has not confined himself to satire: his *Nashville* (1975) and *A Wedding* (1978) both stirred very mixed feelings in audiences, turning human relationships into absurd patterns of behavior that are funny but also pathetic and disturbing—a mixture of comic and noncomic.

One frequently hears the lament that American comedy, like Hollywood, is dead. Certainly the classic forms of slapstick and screwball are gone, but the visions of the world they represent live on within a different system, blended often with deliberate satire to provide a continuing outlet for the comic spirit.

COMIC STRUCTURE

A movie creates a comic world by taking the structural elements at its disposal and doing something with them that tends to evoke laughter. We have already noted that such manipulations tend to force a more intellectual awareness of disrupted pattern on our part. This structural disruption fulfills a comedy's esthetic function: it is funny, regardless of whatever social references it may also be making.

To understand a comedy's esthetic function let's refer again to structural qualities we introduced in Chapter 8—clarity, coherence, and emphasis—and see what a comedy does with them.

Comic Clarity and Coherence

A comedy disrupts our sense of what objects are and how they are normally used. It disjoints our ordinary understanding of credible behavior—not destroying it and thus making the behavior wholly unbelieveable, but rearranging customary patterns. It does this visually and aurally. At the simplest level comedy makes an object or a word absurd by itself. It is recognizable, even credible in some logical way, yet ridiculous. At the next level, comedy goes on to create what is generally called the *gag*, a sequence of events or words that operate logically but crazily.

Buster Keaton's comedies are particularly rich in absurd objects. In *One Week* (1920), for example, the hero puts together a prefabricated house, but a rival has misnumbered all the parts so that the result is an absurd construction. Later on, after a rainstorm, the house warps, so that it looks even more comic (Fig. 9.11). The hero finds out he has built it on the wrong lot, so he moves the house, using barrels for "wheels" under it. The weird structure is credible, in that everything in it is logically explained, yet ridiculous. It tends to evoke laughter by itself.

In this example we can see that the object is independently absurd. We can also see that movies tend to build upon a basic absurdity—creating an increasing sense of the ridiculous. This shows us the absurd creation being used in a gag, a logical but absurd sequence of events.

The visual gag is obviously prevalent in silent comedy. Chaplin cooks a shoe in *The Gold Rush* and then eats it as though it were a delicacy; the clash between what it is and how it is used sets up a comic incongruity: it is a shoe, but it is also food. In *The Pawnshop* (1916) Chaplin takes a clock apart as though he were a surgeon operating on a patient. In *One A.M.* (1916) he gets into a mortal struggle with a folding bed. In Keaton's *Cops* (1922) the hero, riding in a wagon, constructs a turn indicator with a boxing glove on a flexible tie rack. It works fine, until he gets to a busy corner and manages to punch a traffic cop twice with the device while making a turn. Structurally, silent comedies were strings of such gags, sometimes linked very tightly. *Big Business* (1929) is essentially one long gag, in which a house and a car become

Audio Brandon/© Raymond Rohauer, 1980

9.11 A comic object. The warped house in *One Week* (1920).

duelling weapons between Laurel and Hardy and their antagonist. Keaton's *The Balloonatic* (1923) is an ingeniously interlinked series of gags. The hero finds himself trapped on a runaway balloon, which finally comes down in a deserted area. We see the hero light a fire to refill the balloon with gas. Then he gets into various conflicts with an Amazonian young lady who is fishing in the area. The hero adapts various things in unusual ways. While trying to grill fish on a tennis racquet, for example, he burns a hole in a canoe. Later we see him paddling the canoe on a stream, and when he spies a rabbit he wants to shoot for supper he simply walks out of the water: he has been using his legs to plug up the burned hole, and this enables him to use the canoe on land or water. The movie ends with the hero and the lady floating romantically down the stream—right toward a waterfall. The hero ignores this peril—and then we see why. The canoe is attached to the repaired balloon we had forgotten about, and the lovers continue forward over the waterfall in mid-air.

In these examples we see ordinary objects turned to comical use in a sequence of events that is both logical and absurd. Various assumptions or "laws" of credibility are disrupted. Though prevalent in silent comedy, this gag technique is fundamental to any physical humor. In M*A*S*H a medical corpsman gets entangled with a wounded man whose neck is spewing blood like a geyser. It is horrible, but funny. Much like Chaplin's gag with the clock, the wounded man is treated as both thing and human. Such disruption of patterns can turn anything comic.

The verbal gag uses words in peculiar ways to create absurd sequences of dialogue. English often becomes funny when spoken by a foreigner who mispronounces, misuses, or misunderstands words, and so dialect humor is common in American comedies. Chico Marx is a classic dialect comedian. In one gag of *The Cocoanuts* (1929), for example, Groucho keeps trying to explain that they will travel by viaduct, and Chico keeps asking, "Vhy a duck?" Dialogue usually becomes funny when it is speeded up, too. Director Howard Hawks had performers speak as rapidly as possible in *His Girl Friday* (1939) to add to the screwball comedy. And in some of his movies comedian Danny Kaye created his own rapid-fire language, speaking and singing gobbledygook. Whether delivered rapid-fire or in a dialect, most verbal gags involve wordplay or some surprising turn of phrase.

Wordplay amounts to *punning*, playing upon two meanings of the same word or upon the similar meaning or sound of different words. Rather than avoiding confusion of meanings, as noncomic speech does, the verbal gag may deliberately smash meanings into one another. One of Groucho Marx's disruptions of logic in *At* the Circus (1939) is a good example. When a wealthy woman announces, "You will sit on my left hand at the banquet and he will sit on my right," Groucho replies, "How do you eat, through a tube?" Some forgotten elitist in the last century labeled such obvious collisions of meaning as "the lowest form of humor," but the principle of punning lies at the heart of many witty remarks, not all as blatant as Groucho's. In Preston Sturges's *The Miracle of Morgan's Creek* (1944) a father complains that his daughters "hang around the house like Spanish moss." And when the audience knows more about a situation than a character involved in it, dialogue acquires many double meanings. In Sturges's *The Lady Eve* (1941), for example, a rich man discovers that the woman he has fallen in love with is a con artist. He breaks off their relationship, and she gets revenge by posing as someone else and getting him to fall in love with her again. He falls madly for her and proposes marriage, wondering how he came to deserve her. She replies, "If anyone ever deserved me, you do. And so richly!" Inside the story's context, her remark is loaded with double meaning. It is an ironic situation, which depends mainly on comic voice, but its verbal wit works on the same basic principle as punning.

A verbal gag may depend simply on some surprising turn of phrase that disrupts the basic flow of information. In Sturges's *The Sin of Harold Diddlebock* (1947) a bartender becomes poetic about a drink he is mixing: "The cocktail should approach us on tiptoe like a young girl whose first appeal is innocence." The disproportion between the language and the thing described is absurd. Sturges characters are also apt to end a remark with a phrase that surprises us with an unexpected connection. The con artist in *Lady Eve* notes, "I need him like the ax needs the turkey," and a man in *Morgan's Creek* philosophizes, "Women are always taking the rap for men; it's called the mother instinct." In *The Cocoanuts* Groucho flirts with a buxom matron, saying "I'll meet you tonight under the moon. . . . You wear a necktie so I'll know you." Carried to a logical extreme, surprising verbal plays like this lead to the *non sequitur* ("it doesn't follow"), a series of connections that lead to nonsense. In *A Day at the Races* (1937) Groucho again takes on a rich matron who becomes outraged at the way he talks to her. His lengthy response is a catalog of all the verbal gag techniques we've mentioned here, and its connections of ideas lead to nonsense:

Oh, I see. We're not good enough for you! Don't forget, you blueblooded Amazon, all men are created free and easy. Have you forgotton Jefferson's immortal words? I have. Say, I've even forgotton the music. Your grandfather wouldn't have been ashamed to mop up gravy with these peasants—of course, he'd have been glad to get any kind of meal. We've come a long way since the Pilgrims landed on the rocks. We've come through muck and mire, rain and sleet, fire and theft, shot and shell, and we won't come back, I said we won't come back, till "Johnny Comes Marching Home Again, Hurrah, Hurrah . . . !"

We have emphasized the Marx Brothers and Preston Sturges in this section because they provide fairly simple examples of some basic structures. Verbal gags provide infinite variations on these forms. The point is not to classify them, anyway, but to point out the structural play going on. The remarkable thing about comedy is that viewers pick up visual and verbal complexities instantly, without any need for rational analysis. This recalls our earlier distinction that comedy is for thinkers—but it is an instant illumination of patterns we take very much for granted.

Comic Emphasis

The illumination we just mentioned requires us to notice distinctive modes of visual and verbal communication. If the comedian does not emphasize this distinctive mode in some way, we can miss the humor. A sense of humor depends on comic emphasis, and a movie comedy develops a continuity that shows us both comic timing and comic construction.

It is common to describe a funny individual as offbeat: with actions and speech patterned strangely. Visual comedians like Chaplin or Keaton and verbal comedians like Bob Hope or Woody Allen have peculiar ways of moving and speaking. It isn't just *what* they do or say, but *how*. You may repeat their actions or dialogue, but unless you have their gift for *timing*, you're not likely to be as funny. There is no way to write such timing down. It is a matter of "feel," which varies with the comedian and with the situation. But it emphasizes the offbeat.

Visual comedy uses beats in "takes," or looks. A double take is a classic form of delayed reaction: the comedian looks at something twice before noticing it is there. Each beat can be prolonged and elaborated in many ways. Harry Langdon, a silent comedian, was noted for triple takes. He could also do a very "slow take," staring at something for a long time, as though hypnotized by it. Harpo Marx used a wild-eyed variety of the same business. Some comedians developed a "hesitation beat," in which every reaction to another person's moves is one beat off. In *Battling Butler* (1926), Buster Keaton follows instructions from a boxing coach while defending himself from a sparring partner—but he is always one beat off, with disastrous consequences. Edgar Kennedy, a regular opponent of Laurel and Hardy, developed the "slow burn," a fury that grew until he slapped his forehead and wiped his hand down his face.

Verbal comedians use speech rhythms in similar ways. An old gauge for joke telling is the so-called rule of threes (not to be confused with composition's rule of thirds), which suggests that the customary time to hit a punch line is on the third beat: "I just flew in from Chicago . . . [one] . . . [two] . . . Boy, are my arms tired!" But such a "rule" is made to be played with. A comedian may "milk" a line for many beats, keeping the listener in suspense; or jump immediately onto the punch line, surprising us. Jack Benny's performance in *To Be or Not to Be* (1942) exemplifies the one approach; the Marx Brothers preferred the other.

Movies exploit comic timing through *recorded continuity*, capturing passages of continuous time where we can watch the rhythm of the beats working. Chaplin's and Keaton's silent movies depend heavily on long takes to capture the intricacies of their movements, and there are similarly long takes in Marx Brothers and Preston Sturges movies. Recorded continuity gives us a chance to understand what the *commedia dell' arte* called *lazzi*—and what today's comedians call *shtiks* (Yiddish for "pieces") or "business"—that is, the peculiar gimmicks and emphases that mark a distinctive comic performer.

Movies also use editing to *construct* stories with comic emphases. Earlier we mentioned "Keystone editing," where frames were removed to create an extremely mechanical action. Keystone also became famous for building almost every comedy into a final chase. It was reputedly a takeoff on the last-minute rescues in D. W. Griffith's melodramas, but it was generally a wildly mechanical device, sometimes involving hordes of people, whether they had much connection with the story or not. Many movie comedies use the same idea, building continuities toward some fast-moving action that tops off the whole story. Almost none, though, have been quite so bizarre as Keystone's.

Within stories, gags are built in a succession of turn-arounds or surprises, each building off the previous one until they reach a peak, or "topper," that ends that particular sequence. Then the next crescendo begins. Short comedies are often simply one long crescendo, whereas features involve a succession of them, sometimes intermixed with romantic or melodramatic scenes. A grand reversal—*the* topper—finishes off the continuity. This is essentially the same technique we find in any classic Hollywood continuity, but the emphases involve constant disjunctions between logic and absurdity that make them comic. We referred earlier to Keaton's short movie, *The Balloonatic.* It has a linked series of gags (getting trapped on the balloon, the balloon's fall, burning a hole in the canoe, hunting in the canoe, and so on), each with its own topper, but building toward a single big topper at the end that completes the crazy logic of the whole movie.

In *The General* (1926) Keaton constructs a more complex continuity. It is the story of a Confederate engineer whose train and sweetheart are kidnapped by Union spies. The story involves three linked problems: the hero has been refused admission into the army, has been spurned by his girl, and has lost his train. The continuity divides into two halves. In the first, the hero chases the spies into Union territory and has to hide; in the second, they chase him after he recaptures his train and sweetheart and is racing back to warn the Southern army of the Union attack. The second half comically reverses the path and logic of the first, for each situation is not only a gag, but a variation of one we saw in the first, except that now the engineer is fully successful. Each of his problems has its final topper. The Union spies, thinking a burning bridge will hold their train, fall into a river; the hero gets his commission, almost shooting an officer in the process; and he wins the girl, though he has to kiss her while returning the salutes of all the enlisted men.

As in these classic examples, all comedies tend to operate with a kind of mechanical efficiency that, in noncomic stories, would detract from the credibility. The comic continuity sets up obstacles and then proceeds to follow a distinctive, consistent logic to knock them down. There is a great diversity in technique, to be sure, all the way from the crude mechanisms of Keystone to the sophisticated wit of screwball comedy and satire, but a distinctive efficiency marks them all. In *His Girl Friday* (1939), for example, a veteran newspaperwoman wants to quit her job and get married, but her editor, who is also her ex-husband, knows she can't resist a scoop. He gets her more and more entangled in a big news story, craftily manipulating events until she finally gives up and comes back to him. *Dr. Strangelove* (1963) has U.S. officials trying to recall a bomber attack on the Soviet Union that will set off a doomsday device of total annihilation. Through a series of insane reversals, the officials find themselves attacking their own forces to get the recall code, offering to help the Russians knock down the planes, and then failing to get through to the last bomber anyway. The doomsday device finally goes off—a black but comic conclusion, being logically the most insane reversal of all.

In this section, then, we have considered film comedy's esthetic functioning, the ways it handles basic structures to make movies that are intrinsically funny. It disrupts our normal sense of clarity and coherence, making ordinary objects, actions, and dialogue credible but absurd. It records the distinctive timing of the comedian, and it constructs distinctly efficient continuities. In these ways it creates a communication that is comic in its very structure.

COMIC VOICE

The personal function in American film comedy involves both dramatic and narrative voices that "speak" its messages. The voice we ascribe to a particular comedy depends a good deal on the tradition from which it comes. Screwball and satiric comedies reflect traditions where the comedian enacts someone else's attitude; the comedian's dramatic voice is separate from the writer's or director's narrative voice. Such a comedy involves us in the same questions of mythic voice that we discussed in Chapter 8. Many comedies, however, carry on a more ancient embodiment of voice, the one represented by the slapstick tradition. As in the circus or in vaudeville, the performer in these comedies is also writer and director. The clown *is* a particular attitude. Dramatic and narrative voice unite. This only rarely occurs outside comic performance, and so a discussion of comic voice needs to specify three sources: the narrator, the performer, and the narrator-performer.

The Narrator

According to ancient medical theory, a "humour" was the dominant fluid in your body which gave you a distinctive personality and viewpoint. Sometimes the narrative voice in movies is "humorous" in a similar way: it *looks* at things in a distinctive way. The comedy factories of Mack Sennett and Hal Roach are good examples. Sennett wanted all stories given "the Keystone slant," which treated people like crazy machines.[7] Roach believed that people became funny when they behaved like children, and so he instilled that sense of humor in his writers and directors.[8] There is not a singular narrative voice, but an overriding comic attitude. The director is a *metteur en scène*, submerged in corporate humor, not an *auteur*.

Sometimes the narrative voice stands out. We are aware of some narrators as *witty*—that is, sharp, intellectual, and incisive. We associate them more immediately with screwball and satiric traditions—though, in fact, slapstick can be witty, too. They are *auteurs*. Whether they use familiar comedians or more generally dramatic performers, the dominant voice tends to be theirs.

Howard Hawks is one example. As we noted in Chapter 8, Hawks's narrative movies emphasized male groups whose codes exclude women, but in his screwball

9.12 Comic reversal in Howard Hawks. A scene from *Bringing Up Baby* (1938) with Cary Grant and Katharine Hepburn.

comedies the women are often more than the men's equals. In *Bringing Up Baby* (1938) the woman dominates the man, a fumbling scientist looking for a lost dinosaur bone, and leads him to realize that she is the only woman for him. At one point the man has to wear the woman's robe while his own clothes dry, thus pushing the role reversal to a comic humiliation of the male (Fig. 9.12). It is all the more noticeable since the scientist is played by Cary Grant, the image of sophisticated love in many romantic melodramas. Hawks used Grant in two other comedies, *Monkey Business* (1952) and *I Was a Male War Bride* (1949), and in the latter Grant spends more than half the time disguised as a woman. This is typical of Hawks's distinctive screwball wit.

Ernst Lubitsch has a reputation for great sophistication, embodied in "the Lubitsch touch," whereby he can suggest sexual intrigues without showing them. *Trouble in Paradise* (1932) has characters who are witty blends of the crass and the elegant. A jewel thief loves his accomplice but wants to seduce their rich target. In *Design for Living* (1933), a woman arranges a "disarmament conference" with two men who are good friends but keep fighting over her. She demands to be accepted on

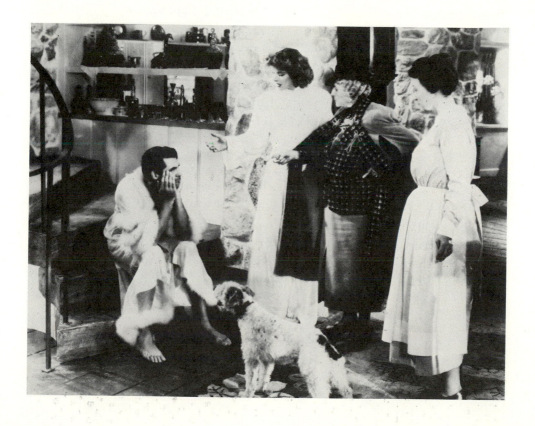

equal terms with both of them, and they all decide that society's idea of marriage simply isn't adequate to their kind of three-way relationship. And *Ninotchka* (1939) stars Greta Garbo as a Russian officer who finally lets out her repressed passion in Paris. Lubitsch has his characters move and speak with such extreme sophistication that they become witty parodies of elegance, very much in the screwball vein.

Though directors continue to be singled out as the *auteurs*, the screwball and satiric traditions have been heavily influenced by writers. Ben Hecht and Robert Riskin stand out particularly. Hecht brought a sharp, cynical wit to various screwball comedies. He adapted *Design for Living* from a Broadway play and wrote *Twentieth Century* (1934) and *Monkey Business* (1952) for Hawks. His lesser-known comedy, *Nothing Sacred* (1937), reflects the essence of Hecht's wit. In it a small-town girl cons some big-city newsmen into believing that she is dying from radium poisoning. They bring her to New York, where "Truth, crushed to earth, rises again more phony than a glass eye," and exploit her situation to sell papers—only to find that she is as big a fraud as they are.

Riskin shared some of Hecht's cynicism, but his most successful work was done for director Frank Capra, an optimist who saw small-town folk as the moral heart of America, which, when called upon, could bring new life to the deadened sensibilities of the big city. Riskin collaborated with Capra on thirteen movies, including *It Happened One Night* (1934), *Mr. Deeds Goes to Town* (1936), and *Meet John Doe* (1941). Each exhibits optimism mixed with cynicism in what another writer has called a perfect blend of schmaltz and acid, which the two managed only when they worked together.[9] The narrative voice we hear belongs arguably to both men.

Mr. Deeds is characteristic of Capra-Riskin screwball comedy. The hero, Longfellow Deeds, resident of a small town, inherits $20 million. He comes to New York, where he falls prey to sharpers and con men, and he falls in love with "Mary," who is really Babe, a news reporter using her contact to sell juicy stories about him. Deeds finally learns the truth about her and, fully disillusioned, decides to use his money to give away land to the needy, then return home. He is hauled into court on charges of insanity. After Babe convinces him she has really fallen in love with him, he refutes the charges and is declared "the sanest man who ever walked into this courtroom."

Summarized like this, the story sounds like straight melodrama, complete with last-minute rescue. Indeed, the movie even gives Deeds the overtones of a Christ figure. A man of simplicity from a small town, he has come to help the poor and confront pharisees, only to be betrayed. One of Deeds's friends compares Babe to a

9.13 Dark overtones in Capra-Riskin comedy. The attempted suicide in *Meet John Doe* (1941) with Gary Cooper and Edward Arnold.

Judas who "crucified Deeds for a coupla stinkin' headlines!" And, like Christ before Herod, Deeds refuses to speak in the court. Deeds is a very sentimentalized clown. He has funny quirks, but we easily become involved emotionally with his despair. What makes things comic are, first of all, the villains. They are caricatures: wicked lawyers, a pompous psychiatrist, a snobbish rich woman, and a spineless relative. Second, there is a drunken poet who befriends Deeds. He is a cynical version of what Deeds almost becomes—a disillusioned man. Third, there are characters who become reformed cynics but who teach Deeds something. One is Babe; the other is Cornelius, a public-relations man, who contributes some very cynical wisdom about the artificial world where Deeds feels lost. Deeds finally teaches Babe and Cornelius to have confidence and to feel love for people, but they teach him to be tough and not give up at the first disappointment. Together they combine the strengths of cynicism and naiveté. They win out in the end through comic reversal, but the narrative voice telling this story has a tone that is both tough and sentimental.

In *Meet John Doe* the narrative tone is harsher yet. The story ends with the simple hero's attempted suicide (Fig. 9.13). It leaves such dark overtones that one may rightly wonder if it really is comedy any longer. The narrative voice is again colored by cynicism we can ascribe to Riskin more than Capra. Together the two create a particularly striking voice that rings with both optimism and pessimism. The

same can be said of Billy Wilder and I. A. L. Diamond. Without the harsh edge that Wilder seems to bring, Diamond's other scripts have not been nearly as successful. Together they create a more complex and striking satiric voice.

Preston Sturges can be called the perfect example of a satiric *auteur*, because he wrote and directed all his major successes. The narrative voice was distinctly his own, imposed on dramatic performers like Henry Fonda and Barbara Stanwyck as well as comedians like Eddie Bracken and Betty Hutton. And, as the *auteur* theory promised, we can find a remarkable consistency in Sturges's comic vision.

The Miracle of Morgan's Creek (1944) exemplifies that vision. It is, at almost every level, an outrageous comedy. It takes courageous and sentimental characters and turns them (in a time of war, no less) into buffoons with ridiculous names and attitudes. An outline of the story catches the essential tone. Trudy Kockenlocker discovers she is pregnant by a serviceman she married one night while dizzy from too much drinking and dancing. Now he has gone overseas and she cannot remember his name—"Ratskywatsky, or something." She talks her friend Norval Jones, who has always loved her but has been rejected for military service and so isn't much of a hero, into impersonating Ratskywatsky and going through another marriage ceremony, so she will have a license as proof. But Norval gets caught and is sent to jail. Trudy has sextuplets, all boys, a big boost to the war effort, and everyone assumes that Norval is the father. He finds himself a hero, a colonel in the National Guard, and Trudy's legalized husband. Then he finds out why. With Norval's screams of protest, Sturges ends his most daring comedy: a satire on motherhood, war morale, and small-town morality in the midst of World War II.

Sturges presents us with a variety of character types, all designed to make us laugh at cherished American values. The central characters are buffoons (Fig. 9.16). Norval is a parody of heroism. He stutters, see spots, and is inept. He knows how to cook and sew, while Trudy is the aggressive one, a parody of traditional romance, given on one hand to melancholy poses but, on the other, using them to con Norval. And there is Trudy's grouchy father, a policeman who usually has no idea what is going on and is given to taking wild, frustrated swipes at people. These three characters are innocent fools. They have no malice and don't realize they are being funny.

At the other extreme are witty characters who comment in ironic ways on the foolishness around them. Trudy's sister knows what is going on and puts things in perspective. Of what use, she wonders, is "a town that could produce shnooks like

9.14 The parody of American values by Preston Sturges. Father (William Demarest), daughter (Betty Hutton), and boy friend (Eddie Bracken) in *The Miracle of Morgan's Creek* (1944).

Papa?" The town lawyer, used to turning human foibles to his advantage, is "anxious and willing to sue anyone, anywhere and at any time." Like the sister, he has a cynical honesty. Other town characters are scalawags who prate about "state honor" and "public weal" while looking to their own advantage; but each is also a buffoon who makes us laugh. Only the town banker is a totally dishonest fool who has no saving buffoonery or wit.

Sturges might seem simply to attack all American values. Nothing is sacred. He even has Trudy's babies arrive on Christmas Day in a fairly obvious parody of Christ's birth. But Sturges also uses two wise characters to contrast with the fools, cynics, and frauds of Morgan's Creek. One is a gentle doctor who cares for Trudy; another is a merchant who brings her a comforting gift at Christmas. Each is quaintly funny, but not foolish, cynical, or dishonest. Sturges can be said to use them as images of a spirit he values enough not to satirize. At the same time, he makes the gentle doctor a German, native of a country that was America's enemy at the time; and he makes the merchant of Christmas spirit a Jew. Even as he provides the audience with positive values, Sturges's voice rises in derisive laughter at American presumptions.

Many viewers—then and now—have found Sturges's movies contemptuous. This speaks for the derisive power of his voice. Yet in each of his movies he uses simple characters or moments of honesty to reveal solid values that place the rest of his satire in perspective. This helps make his movies some of the most intriguing examples of narrative voice in American comedy.

The Performer

Comic performers are very distinctive. They have distinctive faces, mannerisms, or ways of speaking that set them off entirely. More strongly than any other kind of performer, they maintain the ancient concept of the *mask*: the stylized covering which sets dramatic actors aside from reality. The Keystone comics, the Marx Brothers, and the Three Stooges have masks only slightly less exaggerated than those of the *commedia dell' arte*. Chaplin and Keaton kept clownlike masks even in realistic feature films. Later comedians from Eddie Bracken to Jerry Lewis to Woody Allen lost the clown look but exploited funny faces and mannerisms (Fig. 9.15). The same is true of minor comedians, some of whom appear as comic relief in melodramas: they stand apart, thanks to this power of the comic mask.

It is not surprising, then, that the comedian's voice may take charge even over material that is not his or hers. The comedian easily becomes the speaker for the

a

b

9.15 Comic masks. a. Buster Keaton in *The Navigator* (1924). b. Danny Kaye in *The Court Jester* (1956). c. Jerry Lewis in *The Nutty Professor* (1963). d. Woody Allen in *Play It Again, Sam* (1972).

writer and director. We seldom stop to consider that the material for comedians like Bob Hope, Danny Kaye, Lucille Ball or the Marx Brothers is, in fact, written largely by other people. And, conversely, the director's or writer's voice is more likely to come through when the performers are not comedians but dramatic actors in comic roles. This helps explain why Hawks, Lubitsch, and Sturges stand out as *auteurs*, while the directors of Hope, Kaye, Ball, and the Marxes are, for the most part, submerged *metteurs en scène*. The comedian tends to be so distinctive that either the director finds the right clown for his particular vision—as in the case of Sturges with Bracken—or else the director gives place to the comedian's dramatic voice.

The ultimate achievement, of course, is when the director *is* the comedian, and this is our next concern.

The Narrator-Performer

In the circus and vaudeville every clown was his own *auteur*, developing very distinctive ways of handling a traditional stock of comic situations. Many comedians maintained a total control over their work when they moved into silent movies, and some of their distant successors did the same. What they represent are the truest *auteurs* of American film comedy. We have already mentioned some of them— Charles Chaplin, Buster Keaton, Jerry Lewis, Woody Allen—and here we ought to

c

d

consider the expression and growth of personal attitudes within the body of their work.

Charles Chaplin learned the essentials of filmmaking at Keystone, where he attained such success that he was soon able to set up his own company. He took a one-man approach to every phase of filmmaking, from scripting to composing music or arranging an actress's hair. He had little patience with the intricacies of visual technique, preferring to use the camera primarily to record his ballet-like grace and timing. His adroit sense of comedy involved delicate personal touches and amazing feats of agility, so that he transformed the Keystone style of farce into something quite distinctive. As he went on, however, Chaplin became more and more fascinated with what he later called "the combination of the tragic and the comic,"[10] and he finally decided that feature-length comedies were the only outlet for this expression.

What we can see in Chaplin's work is the maturing of his world view. The Charlie of *The Floorwalker* (1916) or *The Cure* (1917) is as mischievous as a child—inquisitive, roguish, vengeful, flirtatious, mocking by turn: a fascinating instrument of comic chaos. As early as *The Tramp* (1915), though, we see a pathetic side to the fellow: after falling in love, only to find that the woman loves someone else, the Little Tramp just walks down the road, alone but chipper. Chaplin's first feature, *The Kid* (1921), carried pathos much farther: the tramp takes custody of an abandoned boy, only to have him taken away by insensitive authorities. Everything turns out happily, but there are some heavily melodramatic moments.

Throughout the rest of his career, Chaplin explored the blend of pathos and comedy. Indeed, the most popular image of Chaplin is probably of his walking down a lonely road—the image from *The Tramp*—repeated at the end of *The Circus* (1928) and *Modern Times* (1936). *City Lights* (1931) ends with another powerful image: Charlie facing a woman who has just realized that the man responsible for curing her blindness is not a wealthy benefactor as she supposed, but a tramp (Fig. 9.16). The movie ends with her reaction still unknown. In fact, though, more often than not, the Little Tramp happily won the girl and triumphed at the end; but the pathetic image remains strong, probably because it so deeply impressed audiences. Even when the tramp triumphs in the features, it is only after he has been hurt by sad ironies and by the insensitivity of those he cares about. The mocking, disruptive rogue of the short comedies has become a sensitive, wronged clown. The early mockery simply made light of what the later pathos made serious: that society crushes individuals. From this point of view, Chaplin's career can be seen building to *Monsieur Verdoux*

9.16 Chaplin's blend of comedy and pathos. The last scene of *City Lights* (1931).

(1947), the point where he discards the tramp disguise altogether and speaks out vehemently against society's crass attitudes. André Bazin has pointed out that Verdoux is the ultimate Charlie the Tramp—except that this time society finally guillotines him. Bazin sees the American audiences' fury over the film as one indication of their guilty, if subconscious, realization of what Charles Chaplin was really saying to them.[11] Whatever one thinks of his message, Chaplin never failed to insist that it was entirely his; and his world view still raises spirited controversies among his viewers.

Buster Keaton worked in a very different way. An acrobat, Keaton loved to set up complex gags that would fully exploit the camera's capabilities. His solemn-faced clown did not appeal to sentiment; in fact, if anything bordering pathos began to develop, Keaton was likely to undercut it immediately with a gag. Unlike Chaplin, Keaton left no philosophical remarks about the nature of his world view. The only testament is the movies themselves. During the silent period, Keaton worked closely with a corps of regular personnel who shared his interests and methods. Though he sometimes assigned directing and writing credit to others, he oversaw the whole operation, stamping it very clearly with a style and an attitude that remain substantially the same through his silent movies.

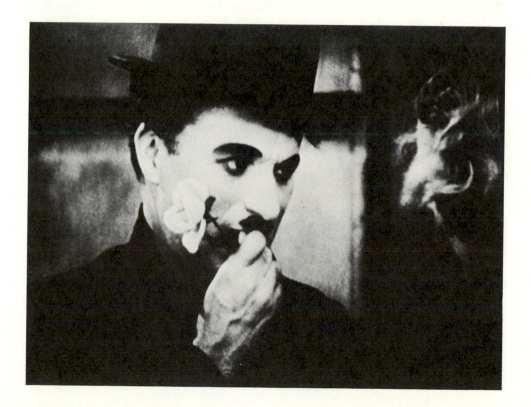

Elsewhere we have noted Keaton's preference for realism and his emphasis on machinery. His hero was almost invariably a man trying to prove to a woman that he could be successful. Sometimes he failed, or Keaton ended things sardonically. *Cops* (1922) ends with Keaton's porkpie hat perched on a tombstone, and after the hero wins his girl in *College* (1927), a rapid montage shows them growing old and cranky and then buried side by side. And we can read into Keaton's unsmiling character a kind of hopeless resignation. On the whole, though, Keaton does not insist on such an interpretation: he simply shows a man coping as best he can, learning to be efficient with things and people, but vulnerable all the time. In this way, man transforms the world into something helpful, but never fully under his control.

Our Hospitality (1923) typifies this comic transformation we find throughout Keaton's work. The hero, Willy McKay, has come South to claim an inheritance. He falls in love with Virginia Canfield, then finds that the Canfield men have vowed to kill all McKays. Willy finally outwits the Canfield men and wins Virginia. His method of survival and triumph is best illustrated by his involvement with a rope. A Canfield finds Willy stranded on a cliff's ledge and throws him a rope so he can swing Willy out to shoot him. Realizing this, Willy yanks on the rope, pulling Canfield off the cliff—but himself, too (Fig. 9.17). They land, tied together, in a stream. Willy runs across a railroad track as a train passes, cutting the rope. He jumps into the train's wood tender, but it comes loose, lands him back in the stream, then capsizes, sending him rushing toward a waterfall. Coming to his rescue, Virginia also falls into the stream. Just as Willy is about to go over the brink, the piece of rope, which is still attached to him, catches on a log. Getting out, he tries to untie the rope, but seeing Virginia coming, he swings out on the rope instead, grabs her, and pulls her to safety. This is comic transformation. Hindrances become advantages, and forces introduced earlier in the story (for example, the train) finally figure in the hero's triumph.

In Keaton's world people try to be compatible with things. The successful hero learns to use things, always in some comical way, to his advantage. Keaton's few unsuccessful heroes fail at it—making clearer what is implied in all the stories, that

Audio Brandon/© Raymond Rohauer, 1980

9.17 Keaton's comic transformation. The hero's use of the rope in *Our Hospitality* (1923).

people are always vulnerable, no matter how efficient. Unlike Chaplin, Keaton does not seem ever to have formulated a particular philosophy of life. He devoted himself simply to making funny movies, leaving it to viewers to notice the remarkably consistent attitude they reveal. Many have pointed out how appropriate the Keaton hero's predicaments are to mankind's dilemmas in the present age of technology.

Jerry Lewis gradually moved into full control of his movies in the sixties, and he worked consciously to satirize American society and to blend comedy carefully with pathos, in the Chaplin manner. He sees himself playing two intermingled characters: a buffoon he calls "the Idiot" and a more needy figure, "the Kid."[12] This split personality can be seen particularly in those features that Lewis also wrote and directed, beginning with *The Bellboy* (1960). The French have been quick to accept Lewis as an *auteur*, pointing out that his work consistently satirizes such elements in American life as hysteria, homosexuality, eroticism, and sadism. American critics seem only to notice Lewis's style, which they tend to dismiss as excessive and childish. Whatever its reception, Lewis's work does show a consistent image of the modern world as schizoid: split between extremes of absurdity and sentiment.

Comedian Woody Allen has emerged through a long apprenticeship in filmmaking to take firm control of the movies he stars in. Beginning with *Take the Money and Run* (1969) Allen directed his own material in a self-conscious visual style that made allusions to a wide variety of literary, film, and political topics, but which even Allen's admirers found clumsily put together. After *Bananas* (1971), *Everything You Always Wanted to Know About Sex, But Were Afraid to Ask* (1972), *Sleeper* (1973), and *Love and Death* (1976) audiences came to assume that poor structure was simply one mark of Allen's style. With *Annie Hall* (1976) and *Manhattan* (1979), however, Allen suddenly achieved a new delicacy of direction and a greater concern with human insights than with broad satire. The change is roughly similar to what we find in Chaplin, though Allen has not claimed to imitate that silent clown. After a period of wild mockery, Allen emerges as the spokesman for simplicity and sentiment. In *Manhattan* Allen plays his usual comic hero, an insecure intellectual, this time involved in what would normally be considered a ludicrous love affair with a high-school girl. But ultimately the affair is not ludicrous. The intellectual discovers the girl has a mature sensibility he doesn't find anywhere else. By the time he discovers this, the affair is over. She is leaving for Europe, and may return to him or may not. The ending is rife with sentiment—and it recalls (perhaps consciously) the ending of Chaplin's *City Lights* (1931), where the Little Tramp waits fearfully to see whether the woman will love him or not.

More than any other comedian of the present day, Woody Allen has reaffirmed comedy's power to be both eloquent and funny. His work shows the emergence of a clear narrative voice, always comic, but expressing the pain and bitterness that is so often the underside of laughter.

And this, logically, brings us to comedy's relationship to society.

COMEDY'S SOCIAL ASPECT

What does comedy ask of a viewer? Laughter, obviously. But that is not yet an answer. What does laughter mean? or, putting it another way: when an audience laughs at a comedy, what is the comedy doing to them?

There is no decisive answer to this question. In fact, to deal with it at all we need to enter the area of critical speculation. There are theories about what laughter means, no concrete facts. And so, in dealing with comedy's persuasive function—its relation to the viewer—we will deal at the same time with the topic of criticism and comedy.

Comedy evokes different kinds of laughter: hearty and vulgar for slapstick, ironic and genial for screwball, sharp or even bitter for satire. Comedies end happily, as a rule—usually with a marriage or some other form of reconciliation and union. They reaffirm social order, but only after they have opened up culture's ways of working to our awareness. This gives comedy a more radically critical role than straight narrative performs. In making us laugh, comedy reminds us that society's beliefs and patterns of order are arbitrary rules that, at best, observe a kind of cautious truce with the impetuous human spirit—or, at worst, are in combat with it. After opening up this situation, comedy heals the wound and leaves society intact.

What this operation finally means to the viewer is open to question. We can divide the wide variety of opinions into two very general camps.

Some would argue that comedy is a cultural safety valve: it allows people to escape from authority's pressures for a while without really threatening authority's control. This idea owes much to Sigmund Freud, whose psychology pictures humans as constantly seeking socially acceptable means of channeling their aggressions. Departing somewhat from Freud, Hugh Dalziel Duncan argues that comedy upholds as well as resists authority, making unsociable forces laughable and thereby reasserting the power of reason.[13] Others put less stress on reason but agree that comedy provides both release and a new kind of social union. Northrop Frye traces the Greek roots of the comic spirit to explain that it leads essentially to a renewed sense of social integration, for in comedy the hero frees himself from social types who are in some kind of bondage to their own compulsions or to the rituals of society.[14]

Theorists of another camp look upon comedy as a constant challenge to society's complacency. Walter Kerr has noted that a comedy's happy ending is simply arbitrary, the only way out of a hopeless situation. Rather than release its characters from their cultural alienation and clumsiness, a comedy points "to the thousand ways in which the admittedly free man is not free."[15] In *Feeling and Form*, Susanne Langer notes that the comic buffoon is the purest expression of the comic rhythm, an amoral creature expressing the sheer sense of life which achieves a temporary triumph over society.[16] And Wylie Sypher points out that modern comedy no longer simply affirms social order but only temporarily relieves the stress between competing ideals. "The modern hero," he suggests, "lives amid irreconcilables which . . . can be encompassed only by religious faith—or comedy."[17]

This simply reaffirms the elusive power of the comic impulse. It is something laughable and relieving, yet it can be paradoxically touching and disturbing. Unlike ordinary narrative, comedy depends primarily on a shock of intellectual recognition from the viewer. Emotional appeal is certainly present in the great comedians, but it is something counterpointed to the comic insight itself. In whatever form and with whatever success, the comic impulse continues to intrude into movies as a disruptive spirit, emphasizing disrespect, doubt, and limitation to counterbalance the culture's dreams of complete social order.

SUMMARY

Comedies involve the basic communication functions, but in a different mode. They provide shocks of recognition by disrupting the patterns we normally take for granted in communicating. This draws us to see the world in terms of patterns, not just meanings.

American movies embody three major comic traditions. The slapstick tradition, which reached its peak of popularity in the twenties, descends from the Italian *commedia dell' arte*, with its emphasis on physical farce and clownish characters. In the thirties the screwball tradition emerged. Based heavily on Broadway theater, its stories gave a contemporary twist to conflicts between rich and poor, men and women, rural and urban life, emphasizing the Depression context and the reversal of social roles. The forties and fifties spawned comedies that were strongly in the satiric tradition, attacking social attitudes with sometimes bitter vehemence.

Structurally, all movie comedy depends on the gag, which disrupts the normal coherence of objects and words, or on different kinds of comic emphasis. Through long takes of recorded continuity, movies may emphasize comic timing; through editing they construct sequences of gags according to various kinds of comic logic.

Comedy's personal function involves both dramatic and narrative voices that "speak" its messages. We find particularly strong narrative voices in the work of Howard Hawks, Ernst Lubitsch, Preston Sturges, and Robert Riskin and Frank Capra. Performers frequently assume the personal function from less dominant directors or writers, simply because the comedian is so strongly set apart. Ultimately, the strongest sense of personal function comes from those performers who direct their own work—for example, Charles Chaplin, Buster Keaton, Jerry Lewis, and Woody Allen.

Considering comedy's persuasive function immediately involves us in critical theories. Some would argue that comedy functions as a safety valve, releasing pressures and reasserting social order; others argue that comedy continues to insist that we live amid irreconcilable forces. Comedy remains a distinctive and very complex mode of communication.

NOTES

1 *Le arroseur arrosé* (*The Squirter Squirted*, 1895) was a one-minute shot in which a boy stepped on a hose and then released it, squirting a gardener in the face. It can be called the first story told with moving images recorded from actual life. Reynaud's little comedies were the first stories using animated drawings.

2 Walpole said, "This world is a comedy to those that think, a tragedy to those that feel" See *The Collected Works of Horace Walpole* (London: Robinson and Edwards, 1798), IV, p. 369. We are giving his insight wider implications than he intended.

3 The best single source on the filmmaking at Keystone is Kalton C. Lahue and Terry Brewer, *Kops and Custards: The Legend of Keystone Films* (Norman: University of Oklahoma, 1968).

4 David Madden, "Harlequin's Stick, Charlie's Cane," *Film Quarterly*, 22 (Fall 1968), 12. This article is a valuable summary of the *commedia*'s influence on American silent comedy.

5 James Agee, *Agee on Film* (New York: Grosset and Dunlap, 1969), I, 410.

6 "Past Master," *New York Magazine*, Aug. 17, 1970, p. 17.

7 Clarence G. Badger, "Reminiscences of the Early Days of Movie Comedies," *Image*, 6 (May 1957), 108.

8 Anthony Slide, "Hal Roach on Film Comedy," *The Silent Picture*, 6 (Spring 1970), 3.

9 Philip Dunne, quoted by David W. Rintels in " 'Someone Else's Guts'—The Rintels Rebuttal," *Los Angeles Times Calendar*, June 26, 1977, pp. 12–13.

10 Chaplin, *My Autobiography* (New York: Simon and Schuster, 1964), p. 33.

11 "The Myth of Monsieur Verdoux," in *What Is Cinema?*, Vol. II (Berkeley: University of California, 1971), p. 102–123.

12 Lewis, *The Total Film-Maker* (New York: Random House, 1971), especially Chaps. 5, 16, and 17.

13 *Communication and Social Order* (New York: Oxford, 1962), pp. 373–428.

14 "The Argument of Comedy," reprinted in *Theories of Comedy*, ed. Paul Lauter (New York: Doubleday, 1964), pp. 450–460.

15 *Tragedy and Comedy* (New York: Simon and Schuster, 1967), p. 146 and Chap. 4.

16 *Feeling and Form* (New York: Scribner, 1953).

17 "The Meanings of Comedy," in *Comedy* (New York: Doubleday, 1956), p. 196.

Part 3 / Alternatives

to the Hollywood Tradition

*I*n the preceding three chapters we have been dealing with the classic Hollywood cinema, a form of filmmaking in which none of the four major functions we have described—the realist, the persuasive, the personal, and the esthetic—stands out over the others. No single purpose dominates the film, to destroy thereby the illusion of the story as a complete mythic world unto itself. We noted in the preceding chapters that the Classic Period of the Hollywood film, the thirties and forties, gave way to more mannerist kinds of filmmaking in the fifties and sixties, as Hollywood filmmakers would become preoccupied with one or another function. More recent Hollywood films have emphasized documentary styles of location shooting (realist), controversial stands on public issues (persuasive), the development of personal styles and attitudes on the part of Hollywood directors (personal), and various forms of formal and technical experimentation (esthetic). Most of these developments have been in the context of the standard narrative film. Hollywood's is never a cinema of great extremes, which is why we have termed it balanced filmmaking.

In the next four chapters we plan to discuss what we call weighted message functions in film. In such alternative film forms, we find one or, at times, two message functions dominant. Some of them will represent these newer directions in the Hollywood cinema; others will involve radical departures from Hollywood classicism that sometimes present the outer limits of the medium's potential in performing one function or another.

In Chapter 10, we will talk about realist cinema. At its most extreme, this is cinema as a mere recording device, as in certain types of documentaries. We also see various types of realism in the storytelling film, some of which come closer to traditional Hollywood forms. Documentary filmmakers emphasize the use of the film medium to observe the world, often from a detached point of view. They may try to tell true factual stories, raise political questions, or explore the medium of film, but in all cases there is a fundamental acknowledgment of the apparent factuality of the filmmaker's material. Some realistic fiction filmmakers follow standards for realism established in nineteenth-century theater and literature; others seek to merge fictional stories with a documentary format or documentary shooting techniques.

In Chapter 11 we will discuss persuasive cinema, filmmaking as a political tool designed to move viewers to action. Included will be both extreme forms of propaganda and the more conventional socially conscious fiction film. In considering persuasive cinema, we will examine how the ways in which films are financed may affect their political message. Fictional Hollywood narratives about social problems are often very different from government-funded propaganda. In other cases, filmmakers may seek to subvert the very economic system that allows them to work. In all cases, the desired result is some sort of awakening of political consciousness in the audience—and perhaps also an awakening toward political action.

In Chapter 12 we will discuss personal cinema. Here we will go beyond the mere identification with characters—that occurs in the standard story film—to discuss film as a more personalized medium that allows directors to express their feelings about the world and their own existence, as well as show their dreams, fantasies, and subconscious lives. Some personal filmmakers work with autobiographical forms; others try to use the medium to duplicate the subjectivity of human experience; still others find inspiration in the philosophical tenets of existentialism to present their views of the individual's place in the world. Personal cinema emphasizes the film artist's vision.

Chapter 13 explores the issues involved in an esthetic cinema. Within the Hollywood genre film, we see forms such as the musical and the science fiction film as suggesting a preoccupation with form for form's sake. Other more experimental filmmakers make animated or trick films or push the medium toward abstract styles unfamiliar to the usual moviegoer. These innovative filmmakers may look to the Dada movement in art to make films that undermine conventional notions of art and good taste. They may make use of various techniques to emphasize the abstract forms rather than the content of their images. Or they may pare their cinema down to the most basic, minimal film elements. Aesthetic moviemaking explores the problem of organizing moving pictures to emphasize their physical, plastic beauty.

All of these kinds of filmmaking have one thing in common: they emphasize the filmmaker as a kind of mediator between the viewer and the world. As films begin to break off from the classic mainstream of narrative, the world they present is no longer the unquestioned mythical reality of the Hollywood film, one organized to conform to the attitudes and expectations of a mass audience. Rather, it is acknowledged as a human artifact, a discourse, so to speak, about reality. Filmmakers who deliberately put the communicative functions of film out of balance call attention to the functions they favor—and hence to themselves as interpreters of reality.

When message functions are balanced, they are invisible. We may be too caught up in the emotional identification with a character to see that the filmmaker is subtly preaching an ideological message through that character. Or we may so accept a photographic image as real that we don't notice the filmmakers' calculated manipulation of it. By making their influence on the material more pronounced or obvious, filmmakers throw off the classic balance.

If the balance of the Hollywood cinema is largely what makes it appealing to a mass audience, a lack of such balance often disturbs many viewers. In general, films with weighted functions are less likely to be mass-media films; they serve more sophisticated, educated, or sympathetic audiences. They are seen in art houses, museums, schools, or cine-clubs. The movie is no longer broadly popular myth, but often something for analysis and discussion. And depending on one's point of view, the self-consciousness that results from weighted message functions is either a gain or a loss for the medium. For some critics, this self-consciousness makes film an art form, a subject for serious study, or a tool for subtle political observation. For others, the result is elitism, a rejection of the illusory qualities that best hold and entertain a mass audience. For these latter critics the unobtrusiveness of a Hollywood film's component parts is the source of its subtlety.

As we consider the four weighted forms in the following chapters, let us remember that our goal here is not rigid categorization of movies. Some works we will discuss will strongly emphasize more than one function. As we have mentioned earlier, every work partakes of all four functions; a work that effaces its political intent or esthetic manipulations does not necessarily lack political or esthetic qualities. The four functions—realist, persuasive, personal, and esthetic—are always present. What we will study is the way in which filmmakers indicate to an audience that it should attend more closely to a particular function—to see in that aspect of the movie its primary meaning.

Chapter 10 / Realist Cinema

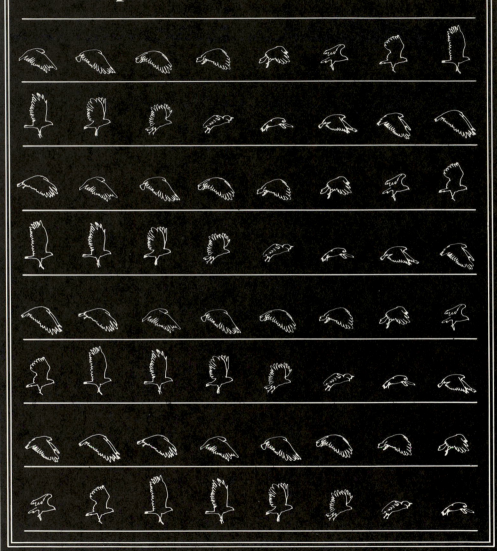

The realist function of communication involves the relationship between the message itself and the people, places, and things in the world that the message describes. Any act of communication refers to the world around us, directly or indirectly. This referential relation between a message and reality is never completely precise, since it is always subject to human error and subjectivity as well as to the limitations that any communication medium has in attempting to duplicate or capture all of reality.

As a medium, film has always seemed to give a good, comprehensive duplication of reality. Yet we are also aware that filmmakers perform countless manipulations to make the "objective" reality in front of the camera conform to a preconceived notion of it. In discussing the Hollywood film, we noted how the classic Hollywood motion picture makes reality mythic. It uses the illusion of reality to create an environment for characters to play out roles dictated largely by the community's accepted value system. The shared values of filmmaker and viewer create a mythic universe in which good and evil battle in largely predetermined conflict. As these value systems change over time, so do the myths; therefore, it is much easier for us to see biases and stereotypes in the movies of forty years ago than in their more "realistic" counterparts today.

Almost from the beginning of cinema, some filmmakers have sought an alternative to the mythicized reality of commercial moviemaking by trying to develop a cinema of unadulterated, unbiased, "raw" reality. The whole notion of the *documentary* film, the film shot directly from life without script, actors, sets, or other artifice, is an attempt to underscore the realist function of film. Because the medium unavoidably stylizes what it records, the goal of total realism is an impossible one. As numerous critics have pointed out, the very acts of deciding where and when to point the camera and shoot film, how to frame and compose a shot, what kind of lens, film stock, or exposure to use all influence the resultant image and create a layer of interpretation over the reality that the filmmaker has photographed. Filmmakers have long been conscious of the tension that exists between the camera as an unbiased recording device and the natural human tendency to shape photographed material to make it meaningful—and thus not truly objective. Objectivity in film is always tantalizingly close but may well be impossible to obtain. The medium can never be exclusively realist.[1]

We will treat in this chapter not just the documentary film but all forms of cinema in which a major goal of the filmmaker is to reproduce reality. Critics have long debated where to draw the line between documentary and realist-oriented fiction films. Although we do not wish to deny the distinction, the difference between these two types is not always clear. Some fiction filmmakers include much factual material in their films; some documentarists make use of such techniques as historical reconstruction or even dramatization with actors. Both documentary and realist-oriented fiction films can use certain techniques that emphasize the realist nature of their medium. Both are designed to keep viewers conscious of the relation between what they are watching and the world outside the theater.

THE CONVENTIONS OF REALIST FILMMAKING

The question of how to emphasize realism in visual and theatrical media is certainly not new, and it is certainly not confined to the medium of film. Since at least the nineteenth century, theorists in literature and theater as well as in painting and sculpture have tried to formulate what is meant by *realism.* They have asked how one produces a work of art whose main justification is its ability to capture the surface qualities of the real world accurately.

Interest in realist forms became particularly keen in the nineteenth century. Artists up to this time had been interested primarily in religious, historical, or mythical subjects, and realism for its own sake was largely absent from art. Rather, the subject matter of a work was used to exemplify some standard of beauty or morality. Although many of Shakespeare's plays are drawn from historical material, our usual interest in them is not in whether they are accurate historically. We are concerned with the ethical and moral problems they contain.

The movement toward realism in art quite tantalizingly accompanied the invention of photography, which allowed the first photographers to copy images from the world with seeming objectivity—without the obvious intervention of preconceived values. Realism put the emphasis more on the world outside the artist and less on the artist's subjectivity. Almost anything from the real world—however mundane, sordid, ugly, or banal—could become a subject for an artist to present as objectively as possible.

Realist communicators traditionally make three major assumptions:

1   They see themselves as rather like scientists, producing works that aim to be accurate, objective documentations of typical human actions and events.

2   They treat subjects of social concern in an attempt to improve society.

3 If working in a narrative form, they deemphasize tightly constructed plots and favor simple representations of passing time or "slices of life."

These assumptions constitute the conventions of realism.

Scientific Detachment

The attitude of realist or documentary artists usually is clinical and detached: they see themselves as something like scientists. The notion of "experimental art" began with Emile Zola, the nineteenth-century novelist and theorist, who wished to use a scientific metaphor for what he saw as the writer's task of "putting men under a microscope." Zola saw himself in part as a collector of data about people and society. Like the scientist who studies repeated, verifiable events in the natural world, Zola advocated that the writer observe ordinary, everyday events for subject matter, noting that "the more banal and generalized it is, the more typical it will become."[2] Zola's novels, filled with lengthy descriptions of people, places and things were as much the work of a journalist as a poet; he paid scrupulous attention to detail in setting, costume, and everyday action.

Documentary or realist filmmakers have easier access to this everyday reality. They have only to point their cameras and shoot. As quasi scientists, realist-oriented filmmakers consider all facts about a subject potentially important and may refuse to be as selective in presenting them as other filmmakers. Since obtrusive details may be as significant as more obvious central points of interest, these filmmakers may let the viewer select what details should be considered meaningful from a mass of visual and aural information.

Small points of setting, costuming, or dialogue may assume major importance. Luchino Visconti's *La terra trema* (1947), a film about the lives of Sicilian fishermen, is considered a classic of realism. Director Visconti took care to have the dialogue in the authentic Sicilian dialect, even though this required a narrator to explain the action even to Italian audiences. Visconti preferred to use this awkward device rather than be untrue to reality as he heard and saw it—an attitude typical of the realist mentality.

Just as the presence of a scientist on the scene of an experiment may distort its results, the presence of the filmmaker may significantly affect a documentary film.[3] In the documentary, a belief in the importance of detail often leads to a bias against editing or other manipulation by the filmmaker. The viewer should be free, the argument goes, to decide what is important. Carried to its extreme, this attitude leads to a documentary like *Portrait of Jason* (1967), a ninety-minute interview with a black homosexual nightclub entertainer (Fig. 10.1). Director Shirley Clarke is careful to indicate the beginning and end of each of her takes by leaving in footage in which she focuses the camera or in which she reaches the end of a roll of film. Each segment of conversation is uncut, in real time, and produces an impression of untouched, unedited reality. The effect is as much that of viewing a case study as a work of art.

Social Concern

Whether making fiction films or documentaries, realist filmmakers frequently treat subjects of social concern. Since the nineteenth century, realist artists and writers have concentrated on the lower classes, perhaps because the lives and preoccupations of the lower classes are more obviously linked to material reality and the struggle for food and shelter.

Critics rarely use the term *realistic* to describe a play or film about the rich. Upper- and middle-class life, with its etiquette, protocol, and concentration on appearances and social roles, is inherently theatrical, even stylized. A realist treatment of the rich would be likely to demonstrate the relation of the upper classes to the "real" world of poverty, social injustice, and oppression. Since there are more poor than rich people in the world, average people usually seem more real to us, and they easily represent the social reality the film portrays. Just as Gustave Courbet's *Stone Cutters* or Edgar Degas's *The Laundresses* glorified the common worker rather

10.1 The uncut interview. In *Portrait of Jason* (1967) Shirley Clarke carries her approach to objectivity in the documentary to a single-minded extreme. A candid, feature-length interview, it is edited only at the obvious moments when the rolls of film are changed.

than saints or mythological figures, movies in realist film movements deal almost exclusively with "little people," representatives of the working class often in angry rebellion against a restrictive society (Fig. 10.2).

Such films border on what we have been calling the film of persuasion or propaganda. Nonetheless, the notion of the writer or filmmaker as a quasi scientist separates, however finely, the realist filmmaker from the propagandist. The line is not always clear, since realist styles are often associated with propaganda; however, realist artists, like scientists, presumably believe they should not convey preconceived notions in their films. The propagandists are more like engineers, applying the knowledge of society to achieve specific, concrete ends. Realists typically show sympathy for the plight of the poor even while offering no concrete solutions.

Episodic Construction

The structure of the realist film, one that attempts to look at the world objectively, differs from that of the usual narrative film in being either very simple or episodic. By *episodic* we mean that the events in the film do not necessarily build directly on one another to tell a story in which every event is interrelated. Each episode or sequence of the film suggests random occurrences that are typical and representative of the people or environment portrayed.

The realist, episodic narrative suggests a span of life that began before the start of the book or film and will continue after it ends. We learn about characters simply by what we see and hear, and we may know nothing of their fate after they have disappeared. The realist, episodic narrative may be filled with incidents only tangential to the story and may leave certain conflicts unresolved. Some critics have argued that this type of narrative structure perfectly suits the film medium; they praise "stories whose common property it is to emerge from, and again disappear in, the flow of life, as suggested by the camera."[4]

10.2 Realist subject matter in the fine arts. *The Laundresses* of Edgar Degas (about 1884) illustrates a nineteenth-century approach to realist subject matter in painting. It shows workers performing everyday actions without reference to myth, religion, or history.

Advocates of realist cinema argue that its quasi-scientific approach, concern for humans in society, and use of episodic narrative structure make a more truthful, authentic type of movie. In some cases they may, but it is well to remember that these are conventions and that their use does not guarantee authenticity or truthfulness. Skilled filmmakers may borrow the devices of realism to lend authenticity to fictional stories that otherwise resemble standard Hollywood material. The conventions are significant because they are designed to call attention to the movie's realist nature. Filmmakers may lie about their material, or accidentally distort it, but their use of realist conventions still asks us to compare the motion picture with the world it represents. Discouraging the response of "It's only a movie," these conventions indicate not a closed, mythic universe in the film, but rather one in which the filmed image represents a part of the universe in which we live.

THREE MODES OF REALIST FILMMAKING

Three major categories of realist filmmaking have emerged in the history of the medium. One category consists of films (largely from the silent and early sound eras) heavily influenced by the traditions of realism and naturalism in the theater and literature. Second is the documentary film in its varied forms. Then there are hybrid forms, fiction films more or less influenced by the documentary, especially following World War II. A short examination of key movements and representative films will show some of the ways in which filmmakers have weighted their work in the direction of realism.

Theatrical and Literary Realism

The high point of naturalism in the French theater, as represented by the works of Emile Zola and his followers, occurred in the late 1800s, just before the invention and popularization of the projected motion picture by the Lumière brothers. Just as the nineteenth-century theater of melodrama influenced D. W. Griffith and set the stage for the development of American narrative, this realist tradition also influenced a significant stream of European filmmaking. Noted for its attempts to reproduce in full richness all the details of real life—and for its comprehensive descriptions of the effects of poverty, disease, alcoholism, and insanity—the theater of Zola and his followers influenced the cinema of the early twentieth century. The pioneer filmmaker Ferdinand Zecca, creator of some of the first major narrative films made by the French, was aware of these trends on the stage, and he even adapted Zola's novel *L'assommoir* into the film *Les Victimes de l'alcoolisme* as early as 1902.

10.3 Germany in the 1920s. G. W. Pabst described the grim economic conditions of Germany in the 1920s in *The Joyless Street* (1925), which showed how middle-class lives were disrupted by inflation and unemployment. For all of Pabst's touted realism, note the strong evocation of mood. The actress on the right is Greta Garbo.

André Antoine, perhaps the most noted stage director of the French realist theater, directed several films at the end of the second decade of the twentieth century and in the 1920s, including two adaptations of works by Zola. He made noteworthy use of natural locations so that the theatrical traditions he brought to the screen were at once linked to the outdoor shooting techniques of Lumière. "The most valuable improvement [in the cinema] that could be made would be to avoid using studios, *even, and especially for interiors,*" Antoine wrote. "Then we would be able to note the difference possible between the cinema, which is living, outdoor *creation,* and the theater, whose principle, on the other hand, is the imitation of nature." Many subsequent French realist fiction films show the combined influence of Zola and Lumière.[5]

In contrast to the French silent film tradition of realism, which emphasized outdoor shooting, German films of about the same period were usually made in the studio. Preoccupation with current social problems characterized the German "Street" film of the twenties, the most famous of which, G. W. Pabst's *Joyless Street* (1925), uncompromisingly portrayed the inflation and unemployment that followed World War I (Fig. 10.3). Greta Garbo, in one of her first major roles, plays the part of

an unemployed government worker's daughter, who almost resorts to prostitution out of economic necessity—a not uncommon occurrence in a society in which formerly middle-class parents could no longer afford dowries for marriageable daughters untrained for any trade or profession.[6]

Pabst was a leading figure in a movement known as the *Neue Sachlichkeit* ("new realism" or "new objectivity"). This movement, in painting as well as film, concentrated on the austere portrayal of external surfaces rather than the exploration of internal worlds and was partly a reaction to German expressionism. Although Pabst worked in a fairly wide range of styles, some of his early sound films like *Westfront 1918* (1930), about World War I, and *Kameradschaft* (1931), recounting a French mining disaster, are admired for their ascetic portrayal of grim subjects. Film historians consider the early sound period to represent a flowering of realism in the German cinema, not only in the works of Pabst but in films like Fritz Lang's M (1931) about the tracking down of a sex criminal, or Slatan Dudow's militantly leftist *Kuhle Wampe* (1931), made from a script by Bertolt Brecht.[7] Even when shot in the studio, these films tried to reconstruct the rich detail of life without necessarily attempting to record life directly.

To this line of theatrical realism one must add the films of Erich von Stroheim, the most famous of which is *Greed* (1924). Based on the novel *McTeague* by Frank Norris, the film originally ran almost nine hours before being cut by three-fourths to the version that remains today. Stroheim sought to record Norris's details with pedantic and comprehensive thoroughness, cinematically capturing the sheer description of realist literature. Although all of his films feature symbolism and stylized passion, Stroheim emphasizes the physical details of reality and such aspects of human behavior as alcoholism, insanity, and sexual perversion, and this links his films to the tradition of literary and theatrical realism.

In the silent era, the films that emerged from the tradition of theatrical or literary realism were something of an alternative to filmed classical theater (static and uncinematic) and to the rich tradition of melodrama (exploited by Griffith and others). Realist filmmakers attempted to carry into the film medium realist dramatists' efforts to show life as it was. The results are often fascinating to us today, for despite the filmmakers' persistent attempts to avoid artifice, we are aware of contradictory and contrived plots, blatant symbolism, and stylized acting. These films may have been more convincingly realistic in their time, for the filmmakers were working without a substantial tradition of the documentary film against which audiences could measure their efforts. Realism as a style was still being invented for the cinema.

The culmination of this line of literary realism may be found in the movement known as *poetic realism,* which flourished in France in the thirties. Directors like Marcel Carné, Julien Duvivier, Jean Vigo, and Jean Renoir were the leaders of this movement. Two films by Carné, with scripts by the poet Jacques Prévert, are archetypes of the movement: *Quai des brumes* (1938) and *Le jour se lève* (1939). In both, Jean Gabin plays a moody anti-hero who becomes a murderer out of love. His life and death are acted out in working-class neighborhoods, cafés, and dirty hotel rooms. Carné builds the atmosphere of these proletarian milieux by the careful use of studio sets and of studied lighting effects. Although highly praised in their time, the films of Carné have disappointed some recent critics. But they were also highly influential, and some commentators see in them, and their downbeat fatalism, a source of the American *film noir.* Somewhat more delicate and more consistently admired today is Jean Vigo's *L'Atalante* (1934), the story of the separation and reunion of a young married couple. The film presents environments—like the barge on which the couple lives or the chaotic streets of Paris—that it skillfully compares to the psychological states of its characters.

Jean Renoir, eccentric and difficult to classify, may ultimately be seen as a bridge between the theatrical and literary tradition of naturalism and the realistic cinema. Some aspects of his work hark back to conventions in literature, theater, or especially painting (he is the son of the impressionist painter Pierre Auguste Renoir); others look ahead to what is now considered "contemporary" film technique.

As a practicer of poetic realism, Jean Renoir synthesized many contrasting approaches to filmmaking, and a good half dozen aspects of his work invite detailed consideration:

1. Renoir was drawn consistently to works of realist and naturalist literature for inspiration. His first major film, *Nana* (1926), was based on a novel by Zola. Although it was shot on rather stylized, decorative studio sets, Renoir claims to have been inspired by a 1921 Stroheim film, *Foolish Wives.* Other adaptions by Renoir are Flaubert's *Madame Bovary* (1933), Gorki's *The Lower Depths* (1936), and Zola's *La bête humaine* (1938).[8]

2. Renoir was a man of substantial political conviction, particularly in the thirties, although he was never a dogmatic propagandist. In *Le crime de Monsieur Lange* (1935) Renoir collaborated with other committed leftists to make a comic parable in which working-class people band together to form a collective publishing house. Lange's crime is that he murders a capitalist to save the collective. Renoir's next film, *La vie est à nous* (1936), was financed by the French Communist party to

gain support for an election. A series of sketches about French politics, the work never forces its attitudes on the audience, but chooses a subtle, satiric approach.

3. Renoir pioneered in the practice of location shooting, and *Toni* (1934), a drama about a crime of passion set in the south of France, is considered a milestone in that technique (Fig. 10.4). *La Marseillaise* (1937), a costume film about the French Revolution, was shot largely outdoors—a novel contrast to the conventions of studio shooting used in its day.[9]

4. Linked to this location shooting was Renoir's insistence on the use of direct sound for many of his films. As early as 1931, he shot *La chienne* without any dubbed sound, although much of the film was shot on location and directional microphones had not yet come into use.[10] Renoir's interest in direct sound was also linked to his love of regional accents and dialects. Many of the actors for *Toni* were natives of Provence, and the use of direct sound allowed Renoir to capture their manner of speaking.

5. Renoir's shooting methods relied heavily on improvisation. He was known to give actors freedom to develop characterizations, and he encouraged spontaneity.

6. Out of this improvisatory method of shooting, Renoir constructed stories that had a free-flowing, relaxed manner—quite in contrast, say, to those of Carné. "I

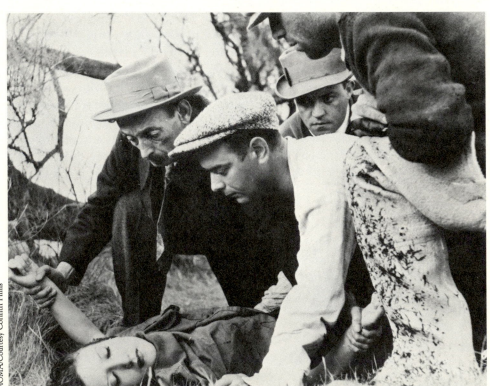

MOMA/Courtesy Corinth Films

hate the sanctity of suspense," Renoir once said. "It's left over from nineteenth-century romanticism."[11] His films are often built around a large number of characters who enter, intermingle, and depart, suggesting a flow of life quite beyond the edges of the motion-picture frame.

Yet Renoir was never simply a realist, striving merely to reproduce the real world. Rather, a constant theme in his work has been the tension between theater and life, and he is clearly aware of the way the film medium combines both. Renoir contrasts the apparent realism of the film medium with deliberately theatrical elements. One of his favorite devices is to frame characters in such a way that the architecture or settings around them suggest a stage or proscenium arch. As he grew older, Renoir made works that were meditations on the nature of theater in their treatment of show-business people. Films like *The Golden Coach* (1953) and *French Can Can* (1954) are works that emphasize the artificiality of film through controlled studio shooting in color. From the watershed realism of *Toni*, Renoir was to come full circle, but his goal remained the same: to explore the various ways in which the film medium can refer to the world.

Renoir was an innovator, introducing much of what we now consider modern in motion pictures. For his sense of the dual nature of film—that it is a realistic medium but one that is always manipulated by its makers—and for such classic works as *Grand Illusion* (1937) and *The Rules of the Game* (1939), some critics consider him the finest filmmaker ever to have lived.

The Documentary Film

We associate the term *documentary* with films shot directly from real-life occurrences, in the style of newsreels, done without the use of the studio, without prepared dialogue, and without professional actors. Theorists of the documentary often argue about where to draw the line between the documentary and realist fiction film, perhaps because there are various hybrid forms between the two. Generally speaking, the components of the documentary are real-life events and actions, performed by people who would be doing them ordinarily, photographed where they really happen.

Documentary is a method of shooting film that emphasizes the medium's references to the real world—its effect of spontaneously captured life—and that deemphasizes film as a form of calculated, planned theater. Because the notion of the documentary suggests an approach to the *process* of filmmaking rather than any particular subject matter, documentary films take various forms. All emphasize the

10.4 The realism of Jean Renoir. In *Toni* (1934), a story filled with passion and jealousy, Jean Renoir pioneered in the use of natural locations, the casting of local people in numerous roles, and the direct recording of authentic regional accents.

film's relation to reality—but also often incorporate one of the other functions of film: some documentaries produce great audience involvement and suggest the filmmaker's own feelings about the subject. These might be termed *personal* documentaries, and some of the first examples were made by Robert Flaherty. Other documentaries are politically militant, or *persuasive;* they seem part of a tradition started by John Grierson. Others, emphasizing formal arrangement of materials, may be called *esthetic* documentaries, and their roots may be found in Dziga Vertov and the "city symphony" tradition. All fuse the realist function with one or another of film's purposes—personal expression, political persuasion, or esthetic experimentation. Still other films, especially some in the *cinéma vérité* movement, develop a shifting of emphases among several of these functions.

Flaherty and the Personal Tradition   Even from the earliest days of Lumière, filmmakers have made travelogues. The travelogue form is arguably the most purely realist form of filmmaking possible, for it presents simply places, objects, and customs for their own sakes, for their intrinsic interest. Yet even in the simplest of the Lumière single-shot pictures, we can see the first signs of narrative structure. In a study of the early Lumière films, Marshall Deutelbaum has demonstrated how Lumière's short reportings of places and events often have a deliberate sense of beginning, middle, and end, the first stirrings of narrative.[12] When we are faced with unstructured life before the camera, our natural human impulse may be to give it emotive—and hence narrative—significance.[13]

If travelogues have always existed in film, however, the term *documentary* begins with Robert Flaherty, when John Grierson, writing as a critic, applied the term to Flaherty's *Moana* (1926). Earlier, Flaherty had explored the northern part of Canada for several years, documenting it on film, before persuading the fur company Revillon Frères to put up the money for him to make *Nanook of the North* (1922), about Eskimos (Fig. 10.5). What made Flaherty's method different from the early travelogues was that he lived among the Eskimos for some time and concentrated on a single subject, Nanook and his family, developing our sympathies for them in much the way a fiction film develops them for imagined characters. With a fine sense of drama, Flaherty recorded not only daily life, but also several dangerous hunting expeditions in an attempt to show the natives' difficult search for food and their struggle for survival. Some critics consider *Nanook* to be the first documentary to make full use of the editing techniques of the fiction film as a means of producing identification and audience involvement.

10.5 Nanook hunting. Many critics accused Robert Flaherty of romanticizing Eskimo life in *Nanook of the North* (1922) and of ignoring the realities whereby the natives were exploited by colonialist practices. Note how the low camera angle makes Nanook appear imposing and heroic.

Some commentators have also criticized Flaherty for dishonesty: in his eagerness to show native Eskimo culture, he provided his subjects with traditional Eskimo clothing, despite the fact that they had been wearing "civilized" dress for some time. To allow for filming, the igloo that was built for the film was twice the size of a usual one. Many events in the film were staged for the camera. Flaherty's defenders argue that it was his intention to show the nobility of a native culture that was fast approaching extinction, and that the film's fabrications are fully justified by Flaherty's desire to show traditional, rather than modern Eskimo life. Seen in terms of the emotive function of film, Flaherty was mythicizing Nanook and primitive culture to make them look heroic. If, in a later film, *Man of Aran* (1934), about poor fishermen off the coast of Ireland, Flaherty had these peasants perform an outdated (and highly dangerous) shark hunt for the sake of the movie, he did so both to generate suspense and to create (or exploit) a mythology. Flaherty's critics faulted *Nanook* and *Man of Aran* for not showing the cruel forms of social injustice experienced by the "noble savages"—but to have done so would have given each film a persuasive tone antithetical to Flaherty's aim. Flaherty's approach emphasizes his films' apparent realism even while he manipulates his subjects; he sacrifices scrupulous honesty to the need to create an exciting story.

Documentarists working in a personal mode must select their subjects with this end in mind. In shooting *Moana*, Flaherty made the mistake of choosing South Sea Islanders, whose heritage included nothing so exciting as seal fishing or shark hunting. Unlike *Nanook*, the film generally failed at the box office. Some of the most successful documentaries of Richard Leacock (a former assistant of Flaherty who was also a pioneer in the use of synchronized sound in the documentary) are built around naturally dramatic events. *Primary* (1960) followed the Wisconsin presidential primary battle of Hubert Humphrey and John F. Kennedy. *The Chair* (1963) dealt with a life-and-death subject, showing the attempts of a man sentenced to die in the electric chair to appeal his sentence. In *Don't Look Back* (1966), Leacock, working with D. A. Pennebaker, built the film around a performance tour by popular singer Bob Dylan, thereby putting a superstar at the film's emotional center.

In other instances filmmakers have exploited accidental occurrences for dramatic effect. We see the drama through their eyes. In *Warrendale* (1967), a film by Alan King about a home for emotionally disturbed children, the unexpected death of a cook who was beloved by the children brought the feature to a climax. In *Gimme Shelter* (1970), Albert and David Maysles photographed the famed Rolling Stones Altamont concert and could therefore record a murder that occurred, involving the Hell's Angels motorcycle gang. The drama was real, but the filmmakers also carefully constructed their film around it, playing on our expectations (derived from the publicity surrounding both the event and the film) of violence. Given the mythic presence of both the Stones and the Angels, the movie has a larger than life effect.

Such relatively personal documentaries borrow techniques from the Hollywood fiction film. They usually concentrate on single characters or small groups of people in order to develop our identification with them. They often emphasize the close-up, that most emotionally charged of shots, and cut materials for coherent dramatic thrust (even at the occasional risk of distorting them).

John Grierson and the Persuasive Tradition John Grierson was a Scottish social scientist who in the twenties became acutely aware of the importance of the film medium in shaping the attitudes of the masses. In 1929, he made *Drifters*, a silent film about herring fishing in Britain. Its success brought about his appointment to form and head the British Empire Marketing Board Film Unit, whose purpose was to promote trade and understanding within the British Empire. When the Empire Marketing Board closed in 1934, Grierson's activities were assumed by the General Post Office, and with the coming of the 1940s he moved on to organize the National Film Board of Canada as well as similar agencies in Australia and New Zealand.

Grierson saw great potential in the cinema as a public service medium rather than as mere entertainment; in the documentary in particular he saw a chance to educate the public in social awareness. He made no further films himself, but the works made under him reflected these preoccupations. Alberto Cavalcanti's *Coal Face* (1936) was about conditions in the mining industry; *Housing Problems* (1935), made by Sir Arthur Elton and Edgar Anstey, focused on slum dwellers as subjects. The latter is considered the first documentary to use direct interviewing techniques. Some works made under Grierson combined formal innovation with utilitarian goals. *Night Mail* (1936), which Harry Watt directed, creatively used a verse commentary by W. H. Auden and music by Benjamin Britten to describe the operations of the post office. Implicit in the work is an admiration for the nobility of the working man and for public service.

With the coming of World War II, the GPO Unit became the Crown Film Unit and began to make films about the war. Humphrey Jennings's *Listen to Britain* (1941) was a poetic portrait of Britain at war, organized around the various sounds of the times. British documentaries about the fighting itself, like Harry Watt's *Target for Tonight* (1941) or Roy Boulting's report on the North African campaign, *Desert Victory* (1943), showed both technical mastery and a decided restraint of tone. Such films had the dual purpose of informing the public about the war (a realistic function) and bolstering morale (a persuasive function). Thus the British wartime cinema moved toward an increased blending of documentary and fiction forms. *Target for Tonight* and Humphrey Jennings's *Fires Were Started* (1943) used RAF men and firefighters playing themselves, with scripted dialogue. At the same time, such realist-fictional war films as *In Which We Serve* (1942), by Noel Coward and David Lean, imitated the look and low-key directness of the documentaries. Given the needs of a country at war, Britain at least partially achieved Grierson's goal of a popular cinema with a sense of commitment to society.

In the United States, the figure most like Grierson was Pare Lorentz, who in 1934 persuaded President Roosevelt's New Deal government to fund a film about the

10.6 *The Plough That Broke the Plains* (1936). Like John Grierson, Pare Lorentz saw film as a tool for educating the public to the social issues of the day. In this film he documented the results of backward agricultural practices and the human misery that followed.

Dust Bowl, *The Plow That Broke the Plains* (1936, Fig. 10.6). The work proved controversial. Its admirers saw it as an artistic and moving portrayal of the problems of conservation; its detractors accused it of being propaganda for the government's proposed farm program as well as a dangerous threat to the free enterprise system (because of its manner of financing). The government then backed Lorentz's *The River* (1937), which also posed questions of conservation in its treatment of the Mississippi River.

With the coming of World War II, many American Hollywood filmmakers were called upon to make documentaries of the fighting effort. John Ford's *The Battle of Midway* (1942) and William Wyler's *Memphis Belle* (1944), which is about aerial combat, are among the best remembered. We may surely examine these movies as much for their political, propagandist intent as for their objective recording of warfare; but while they were intended to maintain home-front morale, they also established certain standards about what the war looked like. These standards carried over into the fiction film. Near the end of the war some Hollywood pictures like *The Story of G. I. Joe* (1945) made a conscious effort to downplay heroics and deal instead with the experiences of ordinary men in wartime. Such films were done in a style that, in the words of Arthur Knight, "seemed to match frame for frame the footage sent back by the Signal Corps."[14]

In the postwar era the domain of the persuasive documentary has become largely the public affairs television program. Despite frequent low ratings, these programs are produced in part to fulfill Federal Communications Commission public service requirements or are produced for public television. One of the most important figures in the contemporary persuasive documentary has been Frederick Wiseman, a former lawyer who turned to film in the interest of publicizing some of the ills of public institutions. The titles of Wiseman's films, most of which are shown on public television, reveal their subjects with direct simplicity: *High School* (1968), *Hospital* (1970), *Basic Training* (1971), *Juvenile Court* (1973), and *Canal Zone* (1977). Wiseman's usual tactic is to take single, simple cases, recording the daily routines of an institution without commentary. In most instances none is needed, for the filmmaker allows the moral ambiguities and social contradictions to emerge on their own.

Wiseman's work represents a dominant philosophy of the political documentary: let the social problem speak for itself. To ignore a problem is, in effect, to advocate the status quo, while the mere fact of presenting it on film can be an implicit call for reform. The political engagement that so often accompanies realist filmmaking is often just a natural outgrowth of attending carefully to the world around us.

The City Symphony and the Esthetic Tradition   Other filmmakers in the twenties were less concerned with the personal or persuasive potential of the documentary but rather wished to experiment with the film medium for its own sake. They sought to use the documentary to explore the medium's capacity for expressive movement, trick photography, lighting, and composition.

Some of the first significant works using this approach became known as *city symphonies.* Alberto Cavalcanti's *Rien que les heures* (1926) and Walter Ruttman's *Berlin: Symphony of a City* (1927) documented single days in Paris and Berlin respectively, looking for poetry in the forms, movements, and rhythms of urban life. Ruttman's work, along with Pabst's, is considered a leading example of the *Neue Sachlichkeit* movement. It was an engaging device. Following the dawn-to-dusk activities in a generalized urban area provided these filmmakers with a sense of sequential organization, a progression of beginning-middle-end. Yet within this structure they were almost totally free to photograph whatever they wished and to structure it for maximum visual and thematic impact.

The most extravagant of the city symphonies was undoubtedly Dziga Vertov's *The Man with a Movie Camera* (1928), a film most likely influenced by Ruttman and Cavalcanti. Some of Vertov's roots were in the persuasive documentary. With the arrival of the Bolshevik revolution, the twenty-two-year-old Vertov began to edit the Soviet government newsreels that were shown on the trains traveling about the country and stopping in towns along the way. In 1922 came his famous *Kino Pravda* ("Film Truth") series, which consisted of twenty-three newsreellike films that appeared monthly and spontaneously recorded various aspects of Soviet life. Their goal was in part to unify a country of disparate cultures. Vertov and his assistants often roamed the streets looking for subjects of interest.

The Man with a Movie Camera is Vertov's most famous feature. He constructed it around three major points of interest:

1. It is about Moscow, showing the city and its way of life—quite possibly with the aim of giving rural peasants a sense of unity with urban dwellers.

2. It is about work. We see in the course of the movie factory work, housework, saleswork, and the work of making the film. And this is contrasted with play, as Dziga Vertov concludes the film with an extended section showing athletic competition, a kind of "work" in itself. In a country trying desperately to increase productivity, the goal of such a film might be much the same as that of a propaganda poster exhorting the laborers to increase production: but by editing these fragments of Soviet life together, Vertov creates a buoyant feeling of exultation, not preachment.

3. It is about the processes of filmmaking itself. Vertov shows us, throughout the movie, a film being shot, edited, and projected. He constantly reminds the audience that it is watching a movie, in a manner completely the opposite of Hollywood illusionism.

An overriding technique of the esthetic documentary is editing. The filmmaker gives order and shape to materials shot directly from life. The editing of *The Man with a Movie Camera* is some of the most flamboyant ever attempted in the history of the medium (Fig. 10.7). Shots are joined to one another not to allow for spatial or temporal unity but to compare similarities of shape, movement, or subject matter. The goal is not a unified whole but rather a mosaic in which each shot of the film is a discrete unit.

Yet even more conventional documentaries often use continuity and editing to unique esthetic effect. For an example, let us consider at length Basil Wright's *Song of Ceylon* (1934), a film produced, ironically, under John Grierson, who was noted for his sponsorship of more overtly propagandistic works. It had the nominal intent of fostering tea trade, but today it seems far more poetic than didactic in tone. Influenced by Soviet montage theory, Wright divided his study of Ceylonese culture into four parts, each introduced by a title card. "The Buddha" begins with the

camera tracking through a forest in which dancers perform a native ritual—a recurring point of reference for the film. Wright next shows us a pilgrimage of Buddhists to a holy mountain. The director does little to personalize these people. He gives us fleeting portraits of individual pilgrims, but also concentrates on close-ups of marching feet or other impersonal details. His point of view is detached—a narrator simply describes the customs or recites a Buddhist prayer—but at the same time the sequence's unique continuity reflects in its way the mysticism of the subject at hand.

This continuity links many shots in this section with dissolves rather than cuts to create a smooth, flowing effect in which time and space relationships become indefinite. Occasionally Wright will pan his camera away from a point of human interest, in much the same way that a person might look away in a state of distraction or meditation. In a shot of two native women, the camera moves down from their heads to show only their torsos. Another shot begins with a group of people, but the camera soon pans right to include only the landscape behind them. The sequence ends with a series of lyrical right-to-left pans following birds flying across the water. In effect, the section depicts how the natural beauty of the island may be the source of its culture's religious beliefs: at the same time, it implies that the Buddhist view of the world may affect one's perception of those same surroundings.

Song of Ceylon's second part, "The Virgin Island," concentrates on the daily lives of the people. Its first images of water—the ocean surrounding the island, women washing clothing or bathing children, a fisherman casting his nets—suggest how the fact of living on an island dictates one's way of life. The narrator then explains a key point of the native Ceylonese economic system: individuals consider no task beneath their dignity if they are doing it for themselves, but to work for another is a humiliation. Wright illustrates this with a series of shots of people at work—a potter, a workman constructing a house, a fisherman fixing his nets. Wright describes and shows the process of gathering and hulling rice. This second part ends with a dancing master instructing a group of children—a foreshadowing of the film's final sequence. Throughout this section, simple cuts replace the dissolves of the earlier one. The subject matter has become earthly, even mundane, in its discussion of work and everyday life.

"The Voices of Commerce" begins with the sounds and sights of a railroad, followed quickly by a shot of an elephant helping fell a tree in the name of progress. Here Wright uses sound inventively, complementing his images of industrial and

10.7 Geometry in *The Man with a Movie Camera* (1928). Many of Dziga Vertov's images were apparently selected to emphasize graphic shapes and formal properties. Subject matter and thematic interests appear of secondary interest.

commercial development with a montage of voices reading from a selection of business correspondence. As the narrator later describes the importance of copra to the economy, we see coconuts being picked, cut open, dried, and shipped. We follow the same process with the production of tea; it is harvested, processed, loaded onto ships. Again, Wright mainly uses simple cuts to link shots about the material world.

"The Apparel of a God" returns us to the native dancing with which the film began (Fig. 10.8). We watch the native men put on elaborate, radiant costumes. As the dancing develops, Wright sets up a pattern of editing whereby shots of dancers—sometimes framed so as to show only their torsos—dissolve into shots of Buddhist shrines and statues. Again the dissolve creates a different space-time system: Wright links the eternity and stillness of the statues to the immediate energy of the dancers, until a final dissolve returns us to the same forest seen in the film's opening. The film has a circular structure.

The art of *Song of Ceylon* is in its editing. Rather than seek a continuity of story or location, Wright edits instead for conceptual meaning. The different shots of pilgrims, workers, or dancers compare varied examples of a kind of activity, forming a composite. Editing shows, briefly and effectively, the processes whereby rice, copra, and tea are harvested and made ready for the marketplace. Editing allows *Song of*

Ceylon to be more than a random collection of footage about the country, making it an analysis of the different elements of Ceylonese culture. Although it was shot in sound, *Song of Ceylon* is similar in its esthetic to the silent film. The natives speak with synchronized dialogue, but their words remain untranslated by subtitles. The verbal commentary explains much of what the film shows, but its force comes mainly from its visual images and the way they are organized.

The documentary thus comes down to us as a form of filmmaking in which, given the right subject matter, movie makers can experiment with varying forms of continuity and structure. In a film like *Song of Ceylon* this experimentation may be serious, even mythical. In a Vertov film it may be playful. In short, documentaries are seldom purely realistic: they rarely say "Look at this!" without having some other interest in mind. Rather, we see either real-life dramas, socially committed film journalism, or displays of technical prowess (or playfulness) using newsreel footage as a basis. The flexibility of this form of filmmaking is one reason it has so many adherents and admirers.

Jean Rouch and Cinéma Vérité   In the late fifties the question of the extent to which filmmakers should call attention to themselves became one of the key issues in documentary filmmaking. A movement developed known as *cinéma vérité*, a term now commonly applied to almost any documentary that uses lightweight hand-held cameras, portable sound equipment, fast film stock, and available light. Richard Leacock and Frederick Wiseman are often referred to as *cinéma vérité* filmmakers, but there has been some controversy over grouping them with European filmmakers in the movement.[15]

Cinéma vérité (French for "film truth," a reference to Vertov's *Kino Pravda*) started with Jean Rouch, a French anthropologist. Rouch originally began using the camera in connection with his work in black Africa; he soon developed working methods in which the film became something of a collaboration between him and the subjects he was photographing. *Moi, un noir* (1958) was constructed, in part, by having a poor dock worker play out his fantasy life on screen and then comment on the soundtrack about the footage Rouch had taken of him. *The Human Pyramid* (1961) went further. Rouch brought together a group of black and white students in Abidjan to perform an experiment in integration and record it with the camera. Rouch even allowed his group to improvise scenes of fantasized events, incorporating a collective fiction into the film. Such techniques, Rouch's defenders would argue, might reveal more of his subjects than conventional ones.[16]

10.8 The dancers in *Song of Ceylon* (1934). Originally produced to foster tea trade, Basil Wright's *Song of Ceylon* emphasized how Ceylonese religious beliefs infuse the whole culture with a certain world view.

What is important about the cinema of Rouch is that he admits that the camera intervenes and affects the events in front of it. The truth of *cinéma vérité* lies in the recognition that any film is something between the mere recording of reality and creative invention. The *cinéma vérité* of Rouch does not pretend to record events that would have happened anyway. Rather, it accepts the fact that the presence of a camera not only affects what happens in front of it but may even cause things to happen.

Chronicle of a Summer—Paris, 1960 (1961), made with Edgar Morin, is Rouch's most famous film. It takes as its subject some people living in Paris in the summer of 1960 as the material for a sociological-anthropological inquest. Rouch and Morin state their intentions at the start of the film: they intend to ask people, "What do you do with your life?" and attempt to record the answers authentically. A series of conversations and interviews follow. Some are brief responses by ordinary people to the question "Are you happy?" Others are lengthy personal revelations.

When Rouch and Morin first ask one of their interviewers, Marceline, what she does with her life, she responds, "Work, mostly." The answer forms the key to what most of the interviews have in common, and they form a kind of reverse negative version of *The Man with a Movie Camera.* Most of the people in the film appear unhappy: they dislike their jobs and would rather be doing something else with their lives. Some auto mechanics indiscreetly reveal having to cheat on their repair records to get by. An artist couple discuss candidly their activities of falsifying antique furniture and the pleasures of a Bohemian life without work. Factory workers talk of the drudgery of their jobs, and a white-collar couple describe their former economic difficulties and current dissatisfactions. The film also follows the exodus of Parisians to the provinces for August vacation—their attempt to escape from the world of work.

The structure of the movie follows two parallel lines. One is chronological and develops an emotive interest in some of the inverviewees. Rouch and Morin talk to some subjects only once but follow others through several scenes, giving brief indications of the passage of time (shots of a Bastille Day dance, or of people leaving on vacation August 1). The film authors talk to Angelo, a Renault worker, both before and after he loses his job. We witness two conversations with Marilou, an emotionally unstable Italian girl, and note changes in her personal life and attitudes. We follow an African student, Landry, in his attempts to understand the French and their culture.

While all this is taking place, the film takes its shape from certain thematic elements. Having established that people are alienated from their jobs, the filmmakers announce midway through the work their intention to expand the film's interests to include not only people's personal lives but their reactions to political events as well. Discussions follow about the confusion and impotence the French have felt about the Algerian war and about racism, but this attempt at political generalization is only partly successful. The conversations invariably return to the subjects' personal feelings.

Scenes follow one another in a kind of free association. A discussion of racism with some African students ends with their being embarrassed about having not understood that a tattoo on Marceline's arm has to do with her having been deported to a concentration camp during the Nazi occupation. Rouch then cuts to Marceline walking through the streets, remembering events of her deportation and articulating her memories of it. Personal lives and political events are, the film implies, in the end inseparable.

Often footage in the film illustrates or amplifies the conversation that comes before or after it. In the scenes with Jean-Pierre, the student, we see first his book-filled apartment and next learn from him of the pressures he is under at school; then he and Marceline talk about the unsuccessful affairs they have had. Immediately afterward, he joins the group in discussing the Algerian crisis, and we see demonstrated the disillusion and cynicism he had previously said he was feeling. Together the scenes form a composite, interrelating his professional, personal, and political problems.

Angelo's discussion with other workers about the oppressiveness of their jobs is followed by a sequence in which we see him get up in the morning, go to work, come home, practice karate alone, and go to bed. Sandwiched in are shots of the factory routine in which we see not Angelo but an assortment of anonymous workers. The effect is significant, for it suggests that at work Angelo becomes a face in the crowd, simply another worker.

What makes *Chronicle of a Summer* different from the traditional documentary is the filmmakers' acknowledgment of their effect on the events they are recording. Much of what the film shows—such as all of its interviews—would never have existed had the movie not been made. Following the sequence about Angelo's working day, there is a scene in which Rouch and Morin introduce Angelo to Landry, the African student, to see how the two will respond to one another (Fig.

10.9). The encounter is artificial (they would never have met under ordinary circumstances), but it is also authentic, since one presumes that the conversation and rapport that develop between them are genuine. Similarly, Marceline's monologue about the Nazi deportations occurred only because the camera and microphone were there to record it, so that it is simultaneously both real (her genuine reactions and remembrances) and staged.

Technique in *Chronicle of a Summer* is at once sophisticated and primitive. Clearly the film was an advance on the traditional documentary of its day in its use of lightweight cameras and sound equipment to go into natural, often unfavorable shooting conditions and record something usable. Yet the film rejects polished technique. Rouch and Morin ignore traditional continuity, so that often jump cuts serve to compress a succession of actions (in Angelo's day, for example). At times the directors will cut from one part of a conversation to another, using what is clearly a later segment of the same interview; only context indicates a temporal shift. Rouch

10.9 *Chronicle of a Summer* (1961). Social scientists Jean Rouch and Edgar Morin experimented with recording events that would not have happened had they not made this particular film. When a factory worker and a student meet here for the first time, we witness their awkward attempts to get to know each other.

MOMA/Courtesy Corinth Films

and Morin rely on simple setups and long, largely uncut takes. Close-ups dominate the interviews, and at times they are painfully close, as in the scene of Marilou's revelation of her drinking, her promiscuity, and her despair.

Only in the quick opening interviews, in which Marceline asks people off the street whether they are happy, is editing used to obvious effect. The brief clips are a perfect example of a filmmaker cutting to show an array of typical, varied responses. Most of the film's important editing is in the juxtaposition of whole lengthy scenes for contrast, with very little emphasis or editorialization within them. At times, however, the content of scenes has an apt poetic justice. The shots of vacationers climbing rocks and falling back down again are a depiction of their activities as well as a metaphor (thoroughly integrated into the context of the film) for the sense of futility that so many of the interviewed people have expressed.

At the end of the film, Rouch and Morin record the contradictory reactions of the people in it to seeing themselves in a preview screening. The reactions are, as the filmmakers themselves summarize, either that they are uncomfortably true to life or falsely dramatic. The subjects of the film discuss and argue the merits of what they have seen. The film seeks to put itself in perspective, acknowledging both the truth it has captured and the false impressions it may have produced in the process.

The final conversation of the filmmakers, as they talk in the lobby of the museum in which the screening has been held, underlines this perfectly (Fig. 10.10). It is a long, elaborate take in which the camera follows the subjects as they walk, turn around, and pace the length of the lobby back and forth. The conversation is both spontaneous (they give reactions to the screening and discussion) and staged (the detailed coordination of camera and walking *had* to have been planned).

A landmark in documentary film, *Chronicle of a Summer* is thus not only about its subjects but also about the ambiguity of making a documentary film. It extends certain traditions of the nonnarrative documentary, like the city symphony or the

10.10 Filmmakers reflect on their documentary. At the conclusion of *Chronicle of a Summer*, Rouch (left) and Morin evaluate their project. The film ends with their handshake and departure.

work of Dziga Vertov. But at times it also plays up personal or even persuasive functions. It marks the beginning of a new era in documentary awareness, one in which filmmakers see themselves not only as recorders of reality but as people who can make events happen and who can try to capture these events on film.

HYBRID FORMS

We have seen in almost every documentary film movement at least some tendency for documentary filmmaking to pick up certain elements of the fiction film. The coming of World War II changed the faces of both types of filmmaking. Audiences, caught up in wartime fervor, appreciated documentaries that kept them informed about the war, and producers found they could make them acceptable and palatable to the masses. At the same time, such documentaries proved how flexible and effective location shooting could be, and we have seen in the postwar period an increasing movement toward the application of documentary shooting techniques to the fiction film. In the Hollywood film, the rise of location shooting paralleled the development of postwar disillusionment and the *film noir,* as discussed in earlier chapters.

It was in the European film, however, that some of the most striking use of natural urban settings was to occur in fiction films, especially in postwar Italy.

Italian Neorealism

At the end of World War II, in Rome, even before the German troops had been completely withdrawn, Roberto Rossellini began shooting *Open City* (1945), a film about the ruthless German occupation and the unification against it of both Catholic clergy and Communist resistance. Based in part upon true events from the war, the film startled audiences with the sense of immediacy it gained from its use of location shooting and performers who were both unfamiliar and unglamorized. Rossellini followed it with *Paisan* (1946), a feature composed of six loosely constructed episodes about wartime Italy. Its emphasis was not so much on any particular message as on how the war looked and how it affected the lives of the people caught in it.

Shortly afterward Vittorio De Sica and Cesare Zavattini collaborated on *Shoeshine* (1946) and *The Bicycle Thief* (1949), movies that dramatized the poverty and economic uncertainty of postwar Italy through the portrayal of children. And Luchino Visconti made *La terra trema* (Fig. 10.11). De Sica, Visconti, and Rossellini

10.11 Visconti's esthetic realism. In one of the classics of neorealism, *La terra trema* (1947), Marxist director Luchino Visconti creates a tension between the subject of abject poverty and an esthetic style of filmmaking. Note here the carefully planned effect of the light shining from the mirror in contrast to the grim surroundings.

all frequently used nonprofessional actors, showed concern for the poor, and rejected the usual glamor of commercial moviemaking. They form the triumvirate of directors who began the movement known as *Italian neorealism,* which achieved both critical success and popular acclaim all over the world.

Of all the films in the Italian neorealist movement, *The Bicycle Thief* represents the archetypal realist film drama. Its working-class milieu, its simple story of everyday life, its nonprofessional actors, location shooting, and functional, unobtrusive style are all trademarks of what is commonly considered cinematic realism.

The story is noted for its simplicity. An unemployed worker, Ricci, finally lands a job for which he must have a bicycle. Someone steals his bicycle on his first day of work, and the movie traces his unsuccessful attempts to retrieve it. A story like this emphasizes poverty and issues of class and society, but it does so on the level of the routine, everyday problems of a common man. The events portrayed are hardly unusual or extraordinary.

De Sica's film works as a document and a drama. Although *The Bicycle Thief* is fiction, it records in its location shooting the streets and physical appearance of postwar Italy. In addition, De Sica incorporates into the story observations about Italian society at the time. The crowd of people at the employment agency where

Ricci gets his job demonstrates the problem of unemployment. When Ricci buys his bicycle, we see a worker put the bedsheets Ricci's wife has just sold to pay for the bicycle on a huge stack of others. Goods are plentiful, the shot implies, but unavailable to the people. When Ricci goes to work, he drops his son off at a gas station where the boy works. Child labor is apparently common. At the police station, the officers are more interested in putting down a demonstration than they are in finding the poor man's bicycle. When he returns to his neighborhood after the theft, the first place he goes to is what appears to be a socialist meeting hall to talk to friends there. *The Bicycle Thief* provides a portrait of a country in the midst of economic struggle and political unrest. Yet it offers neither reasons for nor solutions to these problems. The film merely describes them.

Ricci's search for the bicycle takes us through a cross section of disparate elements in Italian society. At a mission, rich people seem patronizing and condescending: De Sica here subtly suggests a tie between the moneyed classes and the religious establishment. We view the middle classes eating well at a restaurant; when the worker and his son have wine, bread, and cheese, they devour them and consider the food an extravagance. At one point Ricci pursues the supposed thief through an elaborately decorated brothel. Workers and the poor are visible everywhere—sweeping sidewalks, picking up garbage, crowding buses. In its settings, *The Bicycle Thief* could almost be a comprehensive documentary of Italian life.

At the same time, however, De Sica's movie is a carefully structured melodrama that abounds in trumped-up coincidences and chance occurrences. That Ricci should spot the bicycle thief just as he leaves the house of a religious seer who has told him "You will find the bicycle now or not at all" simply strains credibility. De Sica enjoys playing with our expectations of how the narrative will go. Early in the film, when Ricci leaves his bicycle outside the seer's home, one fully expects it to be gone when he returns—if only because the film is titled *The Bicycle Thief.* At another point, he tells his son to wait on a bridge. As the father goes by, he hears cries that a boy has drowned. It is not his son, but for a moment we believe with him that it could be.

What is most manipulative about *The Bicycle Thief* is the way in which it moves audiences to tears. At the end of the film, when the child takes his father's hand, knowing that he is a thief, the surging, romantic music serves as a Pavlovian cue for the audience to start crying. At the same time, however, De Sica has carefully built up this climax. In the preceding two episodes, he adds to Ricci's problem of getting a

10.12 Location shooting and neorealism. The use of spontaneous street photography is perhaps the most striking quality of neorealist films, in general, and of *The Bicycle Thief* (1949), in particular.

bicycle the pressures of humiliation as he first accuses a young man of the theft and later unsuccessfully tries to steal a bicycle himself. Not only is the young man defended by his neighbors and relations, but he turns out to be epileptic. In both instances, Ricci must face an angry crowd that makes him out to be something he is not—a heartless accuser or a common thief. Both episodes magnify the character's sense of frustration and helplessness. His final tears easily become ours.

The Bicycle Thief is thus built up very successfully around a tension between its qualities as a deliberately developed narrative and an objective observation of Italian society. Technically the film is simple so that one hardly notices the use of the camera or cutting. Much of it is done in medium shot, and if De Sica uses some camera movement, it is almost always to follow a subject directly and unobtrusively. André Bazin has commented that the work always implies a broader world outside the frame that De Sica imposes on it, giving as an example the scene in which Ricci is surrounded by German seminarians as he takes shelter from rain. These figures add nothing to the story. They serve no other purpose than to suggest the whole loaf from which the story of Ricci is but a slice.[17] *The Bicycle Thief* becomes a structured drama to which unstructured elements have been added to create a sense of real life (Fig. 10.12).

The balance found in *The Bicycle Thief* between the carefully plotted and the arbitrary is one of the qualities of neorealism. De Sica presents a world that is ruled not so much by fate (as in the classic, mythic story) as by chance. His reluctance to propose political solutions suggests that De Sica finds the problems of the poor too important to ignore but too complex or even too ambiguous to solve. If later films of the Italian cinema have moved in the direction of myth (the Hercules films of the fifties) or political statement (the leftist Italian cinema of recent years), *The Bicycle Thief* represents a blend of the two. It shows the world as an uncertain place that is easier to observe than to interpret.

In the fifties neorealism gave way in Italy both to more personal and more commercial forms of filmmaking, but neorealism affected moviemaking worldwide. Even works from the early postwar period made by directors later noted for very different styles, such as Ingmar Bergman (in *Port of Call*, 1948), Akira Kurosawa (*Drunken Angel*, 1948), or Luis Buñuel (*Los Olvidados*, 1950), show a preoccupation with location shooting and lower-class settings (Fig. 10.13). In France, several works, such as René Clément's *The Walls of Malapaga* (1948), tried to combine the neorealist style of shooting with a revival of the fatalism of the poetic realist movement of the thirties.

The device of showing the horrors of war or poverty through the eyes of a child—used by De Sica in *Shoeshine* and by Rossellini in *Germany Year Zero* (1948)—inspired imitation by filmmakers outside Italy. In France, Clément used it

MOMA/Audio Brandon

in *Forbidden Games* (1952); in Switzerland, Hollywood director Fred Zinnemann made *The Search* (1948); and in America, Sidney Meyers made a documentary about a Harlem youth, *The Quiet One* (1949). Indian filmmaker Satyajit Ray, strongly influenced by Jean Renoir and De Sica, began his career with *Pather Panchali* (1956), carefully observing Indian culture and society in a manner that is in direct contrast to the usual stylization of Indian cinema—with its songs, dances, and discreet romance.

Finally, François Truffaut's autobiographical *The 400 Blows* (1959) pays direct tribute to De Sica. Truffaut uses a child's point of view in portraying dreary urban surroundings. But this brings us to the French New Wave, a subsequent landmark intersection between documentary and fiction forms that redefined cinematic realism.

The French New Wave

Film historians customarily mark the start of the French New Wave as 1959, when three French films—*The 400 Blows* by François Truffaut, *Black Orpheus* by Marcel Camus, and *Hiroshima, mon amour* by Alain Resnais—all won major prizes at the Cannes Film Festival. The New Wave was less a school of filmmaking than a convenient journalistic catchall term for a new generation of filmmakers who had started to make relatively independent films, usually from their own scripts. Some, like Truffaut, Jacques Rivette, and Jean-Luc Godard, had started as film critics for the magazine *Cahiers du cinéma*, which, throughout the fifties, had championed the notion of personal authorship in film. Others, like Resnais, were influenced by the other arts or had had traditional experience in the short film. All felt a commitment to the notion of film as a director's medium.

The first New Wave films were characteristically low-budget affairs made without stars. Directed mainly by young men of about thirty, the films often dealt with aimless, rebellious youth. *The 400 Blows* was an autobiographical movie recounting Truffaut's own childhood.

The New Wave films combined aspects of both realist and personal cinema, and we will deal at greater length with Truffaut and Resnais in a later chapter. Because so many of the filmmakers began as critics and theorists, it is easy to trace certain direct influences on their work. Members of the *Cahiers du cinéma* group championed much of Hollywood cinema, but they also showed the influence of Renoir, neorealism, and Jean Rouch.

From Renoir and Rossellini they took an improvisatory style of filmmaking, working often from notes rather than completed scripts, or writing the dialogue for

10.13 Neorealism as an international trend. After World War II, realist styles of filmmaking became popular worldwide. In a story of a dedicated doctor who fights poverty, pollution, and gangsters in a Japanese slum, Akira Kurosawa combines qualities very similar to neorealism with traces of the American *film noir* in *Drunken Angel* (1948).

each day's work on the morning of filming. From Rouch they borrowed a sense of casual technique—to such a degree that New Wave films were often accused of technical incompetence. These filmmakers shared Rouch's fondness for working in real time, often with long, uncut takes, and shared his attitude that, even in improvised fiction, there is a sense of personal—and hence real—revelation on the part of actors and actresses. The success of the early New Wave films was due, to a great extent, to the skillful work of directors of photography such as Henri Decaë and especially Raoul Coutard, who began as a newsreel photographer before photographing all of Godard's early films and several of Truffaut's. Trained to work fast and economically, Coutard gave a crisp, unadorned, even harsh look to these films, a look that was quite startling when compared with the meticulous lighting and exposure of traditional films at the time. In a scene in Jean-Luc Godard's *Breathless* (1960), shot at an airport on a sunny day, the camera follows a character in and out of a shaded area without cutting, so that the figure becomes very dark, or, alternately, the background becomes overexposed. The style is raw—and, if a bit obtrusive, also exciting.

At their most theoretical extreme, the New Wave directors saw their movies as dialectics between the spontaneous captured reality of photography and the more formalized arts of theater and literature. This quality is most evident in the films of Godard and Rivette. Critic Bernard Dort has written provocatively on the way in which Godard's films always contrast a documentary-style recording of cold, impersonal, contemporary city life with characters who constantly reflect (or long for) an idealized, poetic world of the past.[18] The plots of Godard's movies may be nominally Hollywood genre—the gangster film is represented by *Breathless, Band of Outsiders* (1964), and *Pierrot le fou* (1965), the musical comedy by *A Woman Is a Woman* (1961), the science fiction film by *Alphaville* (1965). Yet these romanticized stories, which invariably deal with melancholy misfits of one sort or another, are only an external layer of conventional narrative supporting through dialogue and action visually pessimistic studies of urban alienation. The two purposely don't gel: plot confronts setting, theater confronts life.

This Renoir-like construction of cinema out of a tension between the artifice of theater and the direct realism of cinema is taken to a radical extreme by Jacques Rivette, especially in his marathon four-hour work, *L'amour fou* (1968), which tells the story of a group of actors rehearsing Racine's *Andromaque*. In the course of rehearsals the director and his wife become estranged. (Some commentators have suggested that Rivette may have taken as his subject Godard's own separation from

10.14 The birth of *le nouveau naturel*. The French have been fond of making low-budget films shot in semidocumentary style about aimless adolescents. Jacques Rozier's *Adieu Philippine* (1962) was a cult film among critics and filmmakers of the French New Wave and foreshadowed a movement in the 1970s known as *le nouveau naturel*.

his wife of several years, Anna Karina.[19]) In addition, Rivette shows a documentary film crew also making a film of the rehearsals, making *L'amour fou* a multilayered study of illusion and reality. Thus we see the play being rehearsed, the play as photographed by the film crew (when the grain of the image changes, we know we are seeing the play as photographed within the film), the "real-life" drama of marital discord (clearly improvised by actors who are *known* to be actors so that we cannot tell how much of their real experience is going into it). Rivette's work is about realism, about the nature of film and theater. Stylistically, the long takes and marathon talk sessions in *L'amour fou* recall Rouch, whom Rivette in 1968 called "the force behind all French cinema of the past ten years, although few people realize it."[20]

The first New Wave was followed by the debuts of several other "waves" of new directors in France, although few have achieved quite the prominence of the first group. One of the relatively unsuccessful films of the first wave—although one quite admired by the *Cahiers* critics—was Jacques Rozier's *Adieu Philippine* (1962, Fig. 10.14). It proved to be surprisingly prophetic when, in the seventies, there came a whole cycle of similar comedies and dramas about restless, aimless youth, done in similar semidocumentary styles. Critics dubbed this movement, represented most

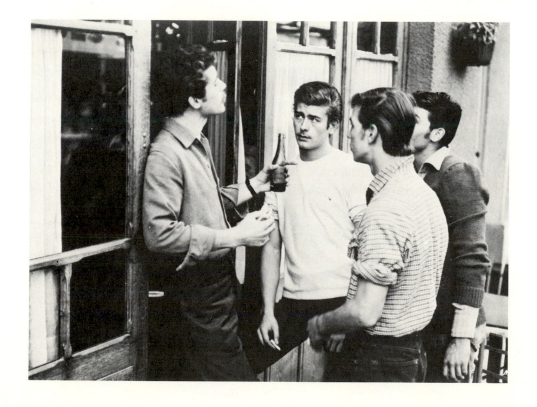

strongly by Pascal Thomas's *Les zozos* (1972) and Jacques Doillon's *Touched in the Head* (1974), *"le nouveau naturel."*

The legacy of the New Wave has been to change the standards of what feature films look like in the sixties and seventies. Jerky hand-held camera work and natural lighting, frequent zooms, and fast, grainy film, which heretofore would have been considered unprofessional in Hollywood, are now standard. Some of these changes may be due to the adoption of techniques derived from television production, but the embracing of them by the New Wave filmmakers has helped in their widespread acceptance.

New Hollywood Realism

These once-innovative techniques have long since become a part of standard commercial filmmaking, in part because younger Hollywood filmmakers favor the freedom of expression they provide. Sometimes the result is something like a new realism in the American film. The films of Michael Ritchie, although they often use highly paid stars and involve relatively commercial story lines, are often structured and shot in a documentary manner. One is hardly surprised to learn that early in his career Ritchie worked with the Maysles brothers, famous for their *cinéma vérité* style documentary work in America.

In Ritchie's *The Candidate* (1972), for example, Robert Redford plays a young liberal senatorial candidate who upsets, at the film's end, an older, conservative incumbent in California. What strikes one about the film, however, is a sense that it looks like a documentary dissection of American politics. We see Redford, as a candidate, the way a television news camera would. Even for shots that could easily have been set up with a tripod, there are slight tremors of the camera, and the style of photography emphasizes natural and bounced light. The documentary look of the film, with its prominent crowd scenes on the campaign trail and ambiguous contrast between the candidate's public image and his "off-camera" reality, helps convince us of its authenticity, even though it is obviously a scripted, acted film.

Ritchie has taken this approach even further in *Smile* (1975), a comic study of a small town's "Young American Miss" pageant. Again, the emphasis is on a portrait of a segment of American life made convincing by emphasis on little-known teenage performers and a realist sense of episode and loose story construction. Ritchie held a real beauty pageant during the shooting of the film, thus intermingling fiction with fact. Perhaps because *Smile* was not a box-office success, Ritchie has moved on to safer commercial projects like *The Bad News Bears* (1976) and *Semi-Tough* (1977), but even these incorporate techniques from modern documentary shooting.

Far more self-conscious and theoretical are the films of Robert Altman, one of the more iconoclastic Hollywood directors of the seventies. Altman's films are examples of New Wave methods of shooting applied to the structure of the Hollywood genre film. Altman has developed an improvisatory, Renoir-like style of shooting, constructing his films around fairly large groups of characters. As mentioned earlier, *M*A*S*H* (1970), Altman's most successful work at the box office, was a satiric comedy about an emergency medical corps in the Korean war. He has since worked in the Western (*McCabe and Mrs. Miller*, 1971; *Buffalo Bill and the Indians*, 1976), the *film noir* (*The Long Good-bye*, 1973; *Thieves Like Us*, 1974), and the science-fiction film (*Quintet*, 1979), but in each case he questions the myth, demythicizes the genre. His Westerns constantly force us to question how much of the film is historically accurate, how much is legend. *Thieves Like Us* plays a rather harsh picture of poverty in the Depression era against our expectations of the bandit-gangster genre. *The Long Good-bye* sets the mythical character of Philip Marlowe down in the contemporary world, where both he and the environment have changed. Altman is in this respect a kind of Hollywood Godard.

Altman's most advanced work may be seen in *Nashville* (1975), a portrait of the country music scene that juggles the stories of some twenty-four characters in a casual, fragmentary style, a technique he repeated with less success in a satire on American nuptial customs, *A Wedding* (1978).

The introduction of techniques emphasing film's realist nature may often invigorate the standard story film. But we hit here a central paradox. Realistic techniques can make a story more credible, but the more obvious such techniques are, the more they call attention to themselves. And the more they call attention to themselves, the more they destroy the illusion that is the film's reason for being. Directors like Godard, Rivette, and Altman seem aware of this paradox; in fact, it seems to be part of the fascination the medium holds for them. And such techniques also provide the basis for some of the major critical controversies about the nature of film.

Realist Cinema and the Critics

We have already discussed how there are, in effect, two kinds of theorists about film: those whose main concern is with the reality the film represents and those who are preoccupied with how filmmakers manipulate their materials. The latter critics we have called *formative*: their interests would be largely in the esthetic and personal dimensions of filmmaking. The former critics, of the *realist* school, would be interested in film as a medium that refers to reality or records it.

We have already discussed André Bazin as a theorist of editing and deep focus. Bazin usually favored uncut takes and deep focus because he found such techniques to be more honest (less manipulative) than elaborate montage. Bazin championed *Nanook of the North* and the films of Renoir and neorealism because he felt they let the photographed reality speak for itself. In other words, the filmmaker does not interpret reality, he simply shows it. For Bazin, the art of filmmaking is to choose the technique that best allows the reality of the subject to show through.[21]

A theorist similar to Bazin but in some ways more extreme and rigid in his advocacy of realism is Siegfried Kracauer. Kracauer works from the premise that the fundamental quality of film is that it is a photographic medium and that photography has certain "affinities" for subject matter. It is most suited to the capturing of unstaged reality, chance occurrences, or what Kracauer calls "the flow of life." The argument is that in effect, the realist presentation of untouched (or minimally manipulated) reality is what the film medium does best and most convincingly. Therefore the realist drama, drawn from real-life incidents and using natural settings as well as unobtrusive acting styles, should be the ultimate ideal of the film medium. Anything that calls attention to artifice—a contrived plot, studio sets, stylized acting, poetic dialogue, flashy editing, or fancy camera angles and photographic effects—is better left to some other medium more suited to it, like theater, painting, or literature.

By this token, Kracauer disapproved of German expressionism, most musicals and historical films, blatant propaganda, and classical tragedy as anticinematic. He would prefer neorealism, the photographic look of the Soviet silents (if not always their editing style), or a well-constructed documentary. Film is at its best when it duplicates the external qualities of reality, formed into simple stories that help us to understand that reality. For Kracauer, movies are an inherently realist medium.[22]

Kracauer, who sees the destiny of film as being in that line of filmmaking begun by Lumière, draws the criticism of those who appreciate the side of film that comes out of Méliès—a side of magic, fantasy, and deliberate illusionism.[23] Yet critics with a strong interest in the realistic nature of the film medium also find fault with Kracauer (and Bazin) on yet other grounds. Opponents of conventional realist theory say that Kracauer and Bazin do not distinguish between the illusion (by which they mean appearance) of reality and reality itself. They argue that certain techniques—grainy film, hand-held camera, or natural light—are simply devices the filmmaker uses to telegraph to an audience: "This is reality."[24] Thus filmmakers can use these techniques to deceive us, or—equally bad—they may be deceiving themselves: they may honestly think they are presenting untouched reality when in fact they are simply duplicating their own perceptual biases of the world on film. In the final analysis, the apparent realism of De Sica, Renoir, or even the greater number of documentaries may be as deceiving as Hollywood fare, for it leaves us with no way to distinguish between real and fake, objectivity and bias.

Critics like Louis Marcorelles or Jean-Louis Commoli have seen one way out of this problem in the *cinéma vérité* movement in film and in works influenced by that movement. That is, by including in the film the presence of the filmmaker making it, one has acknowledged some of the artifice used in the presentation. The honest movie becomes not a representation of reality, but a new reality created for the camera that would not have existed without the camera's presence. The realism of film must refer to a *filmed* world. The filmmakers do not duplicate reality, they intervene in reality.[25]

The question of realism ultimately leads into questions linked to the other functions of film. To ask how the social concern of the filmmaker may be shared by the audience is to consider the persuasive function of film. To ask how the processes of photographing reality may reflect the attitudes of the filmmaker is to consider the personal function of the film. To discuss the alternatives to a realist style of filmmaking is to consider the esthetic function of the medium. But all films beg the question of realism, of their relation to the real world.

SUMMARY

Realist filmmaking is that form of cinema that emphasizes the relation between the movie and the objects, places, and people photographed in it. Realism includes documentary film and certain fictional forms.

The notion of realism comes down to us from the nineteenth century as a set of conventions. We tend to associate with realism the idea of the author or artist as objective observer of the world, a kind of scientist. Realist artists deal most often with subjects of social concern, and their narratives should not be complicated, pat stories filled with coincidence, but simple descriptions of people and events, emphasizing setting, detail, and everyday incident.

We may consider three major modes of realist filmmaking: (1) theatrical and literary realism, (2) the documentary film; and (3) hybrid forms that merge the documentary with the fiction film.

Theatrical and literary realism come directly from the nineteenth-century traditions we have just discussed. The films of G. W. Pabst, Erich von Stroheim, and the French poetic realists of the thirties exemplify this kind of realism, carried from theater and literature into film.

In the documentary form we may examine (1) personal forms of documentary, like the films of Robert Flaherty, which emphasize emotional involvement in the subject; (2) persuasive documentary, represented most markedly by the tradition established by John Grierson; and (3) the esthetic documentary, as found in the city symphony film. The *cinéma vérité* movement has, in films like *Chronicle of a Summer*, challenged previously established notions of photographic truth or honesty in filmmaking; it sees filmmakers as people who shape and influence, rather than simply record, the reality they photograph.

Following World War II, hybrid forms of filmmaking blended documentary and storytelling modes. Such Italian neorealist films as Vittorio De Sica's *The Bicycle Thief* used nonprofessional actors and spontaneous location shooting to tell episodic narratives about the poor or about wartime conditions. Italian neorealism was a significant influence on the French New Wave, which used new technical means like lightweight cameras and fast film to tell fictional stories in an often semidocumentary style. Some Hollywood filmmakers have continued in this vein.

André Bazin, Siegfried Kracauer, and other theorists of realism in film have argued that film is a fundamentally realist medium and that it is in the nature of the medium to capture reality, to refer directly to the real world.

NOTES

1 See in particular Amédée Ayfre, "Néoréalisme et phénomenologie," *Cahiers du cinéma*, No. 17 (Nov. 1952), 6–18.

2 Emile Zola, quoted in Damian Grant, *Realism* (London: Methuen, 1971), p. 28.

3 Fereydoun Hoyveda makes this observation in "Cinéma vérité ou réalisme fantastique," *Cahiers du cinéma*, No. 25 (Nov. 1961), 33–41.

4 Siegfried Kracauer, *Theory of Film: The Redemption of Physical Reality* (London: Oxford, 1960), p. 251.

5 André Antoine, quoted in Georges Sadoul, *Dictionary of Film Makers*, trans. Peter Morris (Berkeley: University of California, 1972), p. 8.

6 Otto Friedrich, *Before the Deluge: A Portrait of Berlin in the 1920's* (New York: Harper & Row, 1972), p. 127.

7 See in particular Raymond Borde, Freddy Buache, and Francis Courtade, *Le cinéma réaliste allemande* (Lyons: Serdoc, 1965).

8 See François Poulle, *Renoir 1938—ou Jean Renoir pour rien?* (Paris: Editions du Cerf, 1969); Peter John Dyer, "Renoir and Realism," *Sight and Sound*, No. 29 (Summer 1960), 130–135.

9 Raymond Durgnat sees *La Marseillaise* as a precursor of modern documentaries or semidocumentaries like *Target for Tonight* or the *cinéma vérité* films of Chris Marker; see *Jean Renoir* (Berkeley: University of California, 1974), p. 169.

10 Jean Renoir, *My Life and My Films*, trans. Norman Denney, (New York: Atheneum, 1974), p. 106.

11 Jean Renoir, quoted in Penelope Gilliat, *Jean Renoir: Essays, Conversations, Reviews* (New York: McGraw-Hill, 1975), p. 27.

12 Marshall Deutelbaum "Structural Patterning in the Lumière Films," *Wide Angle*, 3, No. 1 (1979), 28–37.

13 It also may not be. The authors are aware of the intelligent critique made by some Marxist critics that the seeming affinity of the film medium for narrative may be simply a result of the capitalist marketplace and the ideology it produces.

14 *The Liveliest Art: A Panoramic History of the Movies* (New York: New American Library, 1957), p. 245.

15 The difference would be the way in which the American *cinéma vérité* filmmakers seem to wish to efface themselves in their movies rather than acknowledge their intervention.

16 James Blue, "The Films of Jean Rouch," *Film Comment*, (Fall–Winter 1967), 82–83; Hamid Nacify, "Jean Rouch: A Personal Perspective," *Quarterly Review of Film Studies*, 4 (Summer 1979), 339–362; Mick Eaton, ed., *Anthropology—Reality—Cinema: The Films of Jean Rouch* (London: British Film Institute, 1979).

17 André Bazin, *What Is Cinema?*, trans. Hugh Gray (Berkeley: University of California, 1971), II, 52.

18 Bernard Dort, "Godard ou le romantique abusif," *Les temps modernes*, No. 235 (Dec. 1965), 1118–28.

19 Jonathan Rosenbaum, ed., *Rivette: Texts and Interviews*, trans. Amy Gateff and Tom Milne (London: British Film Institute, 1977), p. 94.

20 Ibid., p. 34.

21 Bazin, *What Is Cinema?*, I and II, 1967, 1971.

22 Kracauer, *Theory of Film.*

23 See in particular Pauline Kael, "Is There a Cure for Film Criticism?" in *I Lost It at the Movies* (Boston: Little, Brown, 1965), pp. 269–292.

24 See in particular Pascal Bonitzer, "Réalité de la dénotation," *Cahiers du cinéma*, No. 299 (May 1971), 39–41; Pascal Bonitzer, "Horschamp (un espace en défaut)," *Cahiers du cinéma*, No. 234–235 (Dec. 1971—Jan. 1972), 15–26.

25 Louis Marcorelles, with the collaboration of Nicole Rouzet-Albagli, *Living Cinema*, trans. Isabel Quigly, (London: Allen and Unwin, 1971; Jean-Louis Comolli, "Le détour par le direct," *Cahiers du cinéma*, No. 209 (Feb. 1969), 48–53, and No. 211 (Apr. 1969), 40–45. Some of Comolli's more recent writings suggest that he may have refined or revised these views.

Chapter 11 / Persuasive Cinema

All film is political has become a slogan for certain movie critics practicing today. By this they mean that all films either directly or indirectly affect their viewers, shaping or changing their beliefs and attitudes—and sometimes even arousing them to take action. This political nature of film is what we mean by its persuasive function. It refers to the relationship between the message and the audience to whom it is directed. The persuasive function of film involves the use of the medium as rhetoric or propaganda.

In discussing the Hollywood cinema, we saw how the quasi-mythological forms of the Hollywood movie tend to support a popular ideology, a kind of collective consciousness of the mass audience. At the same time, commercial movies can clearly be an important influence on the attitudes, morals, and culture of a people, and particularly a young audience. But usually when we speak of Hollywood as an agent of social control, we see the movies as not fully intentional agents in the process. Propaganda is implicit rather than explicit in the classic Hollywood film. From the moral point of view, even the most fervent puritans rarely argue that producers of Hollywood films deliberately set out to corrupt youth. Rather, the influencing of minds or the altering of behavior is always a secondary or corollary function of the classic Hollywood movie. Its first and avowed function is simply to entertain.

Propaganda is always more visible to people uninfluenced by it. That is, the audience that takes the myths of the Hollywood cinema for granted does not notice them as myths. It does not see the message of a Hollywood film as reflecting a specific value system that may indeed be arbitrary. It is easier for us today to see certain old Hollywood movies as carrying direct messages that women should be housewives and mothers, that blacks are racially inferior, that policemen can do no wrong, or that casual sex is always immoral. Since many people today do not share these beliefs, the ideology in these films is no longer taken for granted. Marxist critics have no trouble labeling many Hollywood films as propaganda for an economic system constructed around conspicuous consumption. A capitalist audience may consider it unremarkable that the hero drives a beautiful car and lives in a luxury apartment, or that the heroine wears designer gowns and elaborate make-up, but an anticapitalist critic may not share these assumptions. Similarly, the American viewer who chortles over an obvious bit of Soviet propaganda glorifying the workers and the Communist state may miss the point that a worker in Russia, surrounded by such messages all the time, may take them as much for granted as the American takes Cadillacs and Revlon for granted in a Hollywood film.[1]

361

In other words, a message becomes propaganda (in the pejorative sense) to someone who doesn't agree with it. When propaganda is implicit, the audience simply accepts what it sees, just as filmmakers themselves may never have questioned the validity of the values they present. That is in the nature of myth, of collectively assumed ideology. It is transparent, as we say. But when propaganda is explicit and calculated, we are more likely to be aware of it because the balance of the standard Hollywood film is thrown off. Such "unbalanced" films, which have deliberate and manifest persuasive messages, will be the subject of this chapter.

THREE ISSUES IN PERSUASIVE CINEMA

Any discussion of propaganda must treat three aspects of the deliberately persuasive movie. All such films may be seen in terms of three aspects: (1) effectiveness (or pragmatics), (2) honesty (or ethics) and (3) art (or esthetics). In considering a persuasive film's pragmatic side, we consider how effective the piece is at persuasion. Does it influence its audience? In considering the ethical side, we ask: Is the work honest? Does it argue its case fairly and reasonably? In treating the esthetic side, we ask in effect: Can we separate the film as a work of art from its moral, political, or ideological message? If so, by what standards do we judge it?

Effectiveness

One of the standard complaints about persuasive films is that they "preach to the converted." The reason for this is obvious: people do not like to be told they are wrong. It is fundamentally reinforcing for an audience to see its feelings confirmed in a film; it is threatening to see one's attitudes challenged by a different point of view. Viewers are suspicious of undue manipulation of their feelings, especially when they are unsure of their agreement with the film's point of view. Social psychologists have found that audiences build up a certain natural resistance to persuasive messages. People seek out and attend to messages they agree with; they avoid or ignore messages they disagree with.[2]

Is it so useless to "preach to the converted"? For people to maintain their commitment to a cause, their hatred for an enemy, or their interest in an issue, reinforcement through the media may often be necessary. In wartime, for example, the reaffirmation of the reasons for fighting may be very important to maintain morale and avoid discouragement. Audiences for films that do this may learn nothing new. Such films instead provide symbolic opportunities for reinvestment of audience energies toward a desired goal.

Social psychological research suggests that persuasion through the media is a long-term, gradual process. A single film in and of itself may not change minds but must act with other cultural influences to affect its audience. We can only judge the effectiveness of a propaganda film after the fact, when it has influenced or failed to influence its audience; even then it may be hard to determine whether the film itself was a cause of changed attitudes and behavior or whether it simply reflected attitudes that had already become accepted by the public.

Honesty

Because audiences are resistant to persuasive messages, one of the frequent approaches of the propaganda film is to try to efface its persuasive nature. To be seen as trying to persuade may subvert the persuasive process.

There are two essential points of view toward the ethics of cinematic persuasion. Some observers would argue that a film should present a total political or moral situation, including all of its ambiguities and contradictions. It should present all sides of an issue and leave the final judgment to the audience. We might call this an *investigative* approach, and it is one that often stands at the border between realist and persuasive cinema.

Others would say that to present a problem without offering solutions is an evasion of moral responsibility and that filmmakers should exercise their capacity for leadership. This we might call *activist* filmmaking. The latter risks demagoguery, but the former may lead to confusion and inactivity and to an ultimate support of the status quo.

Art

When a work is deliberately persuasive, we must finally decide whether it is to be judged in terms of its persuasive impact or if we have some other standards to use. Critics often find weighty political messages in films obtrusive, but the reverse side of this is suggested in a statement by the leftist German playwright Bertolt Brecht to the effect that people who want their political messages in a work of art to be subtle do not really want political messages in their works of art. The controversy becomes one of form over content. Do we ignore the film's subject matter in judging it as a film (as some critics have done in analyzing Nazi propaganda films, such as Leni Riefenstahl's *Triumph of the Will*)? Or must the film critic also be a political and moral critic?

THREE KINDS OF PERSUASIVE CINEMA

Let us keep these pragmatic, ethical, and esthetic issues in mind when discussing three major kinds of persuasive cinema and some representative examples of each:

1 Commercial "problem" films. These are generally Hollywood-financed movies that attract audiences by dramatizing topical or controversial issues.

2 Official government propaganda. These are works commissioned and financed by a government to encourage citizen support of its actions and policies.

3 Subversive or revolutionary films. These are movies financed by the government or commercial sources that attack, directly or indirectly, the economic or political system under which they are made.

In each case we shall see how methods of financing and assumptions about a film's eventual audience may strongly affect both its content and its manner of presentation.

The Commercial Problem Film

The *problem film* dramatizes social issues and conflicts in storytelling form. Problem films take the structures of the standard genre film but make deliberately political the forces of good and evil that inform usual storytelling.

If the early Hollywood narratives emphasized stock characters with good or evil qualities, Hollywood could link this typing to whatever political attitudes were prevalent at the time (Fig. 11.1). Before America's entry into World War I, when isolationism was the popular sentiment, films like Thomas Ince's *Civilization* (1916) championed the virtues of peace and morality. As anti-German sentiment grew, however, the Kaiser began to be portrayed as a brutal, bloodthirsty villain in *My Four Years in Germany* (1918) or *Beware* (1920).[3]

With the Depression, however, the problem film came into its own in Hollywood as a vehicle for the discussion of social issues. The Warner Brothers studio

11.1 Griffith as a propagandist. Persuasion and propaganda in the Hollywood film were employed as early as D. W. Griffith's *The Birth of a Nation* (1915). Griffith's description of the formation of the Ku Klux Klan proved inflammatory when first shown, and the film revealed the potential of the medium for molding public opinion.

in particular responded to the collapse of the economy with a series of socially conscious films that presented a bleak picture of conditions in America at the time.

The Warner Brothers gangster film, such as *The Public Enemy* (1931), was at least in part a response to very real social issues of organized crime in America. *I Am a Fugitive from a Chain Gang* (1932), the archetypal Warner problem film of the thirties, revealed faults in an unfair justice system, harsh prison conditions, and the hard realities of economic life that made it impossible for some to earn an honest living. Similar films followed, such as *Cabin in the Cotton* (1932), about sharecroppers in the South, and *Wild Boys of the Road* (1933), which treated adolescent boys trying to survive on their own without burdening their parents, in the harsh environment of joblessness and poverty.

Liberal in tone, these films were a kind of Hollywood muckraking, exposing and dramatizing problems of the time and sometimes offering tentative solutions. They were generally supportive of Roosevelt and the New Deal. Darryl F. Zanuck, production chief at Warners at this time, was largely responsible for this socially conscious approach, and he carried on this tradition when he became vice president in charge of production for Twentieth Century–Fox. In 1940, John Ford made *The Grapes of Wrath,* about migrant farm workers, under Zanuck's supervision. Many critics and historians consider it the film that most exemplifies a certain attitude of New Deal liberalism in America.[4]

Near the end of the thirties, Hollywood became less concerned with domestic problems and looked more toward international concerns. *Blockade* (1938) was the first major American production to take a partisan position toward the Spanish Civil War, and Warners' *Confessions of a Nazi Spy* (1939), in the style of the *March of Time* newsreels, took an inflammatory, anti-German stance. During World War II itself, the concerns of the war were evident both in movies about the fighting, such as *Wake Island* (1941) or *Bataan* (1943), and movies portraying Nazi atrocities in the occupied countries, such as *The North Star* (1943) and *Hangmen Also Die* (1943). The war's effects on domestic and family life were visible in a series of home-front movies, such as *Since You Went Away* (1944), glorifying the American way of life and showing how model American families coped with the disruptive effects of wartime.

Much of Hollywood's wartime output may be seen as a continuation of the social consciousness of the Depression period. The films continually demonstrated the need for action in confronting the international menace of Naziism, calling for popular concern and individual sacrifice. The success of America in its war effort gave birth to what is considered the golden age of the problem film in the late forties. In an effort to inform the public and produce reform, these films dramatized and analyzed postwar obstacles to building a better society—racism, anti-Semitism, juvenile delinquency, and the unfair treatment of veterans.

This trend began during the war with the production of several films (such as producer Val Lewton's *Youth Runs Wild*, 1944) about juvenile delinquency, which arose in direct conjunction with wartime prosperity. As the war drew to a close, a series of films dealing with problems of the returning veteran began, treating psychological difficulties (*I'll Be Seeing You*, 1945), blindness (*Pride of the Marines*, 1945), and paralysis (*The Men*, 1950). The most famous of these was William Wyler's *The Best Years of Our Lives* (1946). It dealt with the problems of a group of returning soldiers, which ranged from learning to live without hands to facing less than promising employment prospects. The problem film reached its height in the years immediately following and is best characterized by Elia Kazan's films from that period. These works treated anti-Semitism (*Gentlemen's Agreement*, 1947), racism (*Pinky*, 1949, Fig. 11.2), and questions of public health (*Panic in the Streets*, 1950). The first two, produced by Darryl Zanuck, were very much in the mode he had established in the thirties.

With the fifties, the major producer of the problem film became Stanley Kramer, who was responsible for such topical works as *The Men* and *Home of the Brave* (1949), which treated, respectively, the returning veteran and racial problems, and *The Wild One* (1953), a classic juvenile delinquency picture. On becoming a director, Kramer consciously attacked such issues as medical ethics (*Not as a Stranger*, 1955), racism (*The Defiant Ones*, 1958), nuclear war (*On the Beach*, 1959), Nazi guilt (*Judgment at Nuremberg*, 1961), interracial romance (*Guess Who's Coming to Dinner*,

1967), student unrest (*R.P.M.*, 1970), and ecology (*Bless the Beasts and Children*, 1971). Even as a director, Kramer produced his own films and was thus able to avoid official studio timidity about controversial subjects. Although some commentators have criticized Kramer's films for their technical awkwardness and lack of subtlety, no Hollywood director has more consciously followed a strong line of social concern and liberal humanism. Andrew Sarris has described Kramer as "the most extreme example of thesis or message cinema."[5]

Judgment at Nuremberg represents the apogee of Kramer's career, perhaps his greatest critical and commercial success. The film was a dramatization of the Nuremberg trials of 1948, in which four former German officials were found guilty of war crimes for enforcing laws in connection with the Nazi exterminations.

The sympathies of Kramer and his script writer, Abby Mann, were clearly with the prosecution, but to give the story dramatic interest for the film's three-hour running time, they had to keep the question of guilt ambiguous and open as long as possible. Although the movie does assume that the defendants are guilty, it leads the audience through the process of determining that guilt. In other words, it becomes what we have been calling an *activist film*, one that comes out forcefully in favor of a point of view after a pseudoinvestigative process in which it "objectively" examines the issues. Like the prosecution in the movie, it judgmentally presents a case, only more subtly.

Judgment at Nuremberg's casting is one of its most effective devices, and in most cases Kramer exploits the audience's association of actors with previous roles. The central character of the picture is the American judge presiding over the tribunal, played by Spencer Tracy. Given the actor Tracy's ethos of trustworthiness and solidity, the movie points up his determination not to make his decisions before he has carefully weighed the evidence. Tracy thus becomes an audience surrogate in the movie: we see things through his eyes. How can we, the audience, jump to conclusions when such an honest character refuses to? The device works in reverse as well. Do we dare disagree with him once he has made his decision?

The rest of the casting deliberately makes us ill at ease. Burt Lancaster, an actor whose roles are ordinarily heroic, plays Ernst Janning, the chief man on trial. Can Lancaster really be a Nazi villain? Marlene Dietrich, an actress known for her activities during the war in support of the Allies, portrays the wife of a Nazi officer whom she claims has been unjustly sentenced in a similar trial. Richard Widmark, who was noted for his many "bad guy" roles, makes the prosecution attorney somewhat petty, vindictive, and overenthusiastic. Montgomery Clift's performance

11.2 A post–World War II *problem* film. In *Pinky* (1949), directed by Elia Kazan, Jeanne Crain plays a black girl who passes for white. The film is one of the first major Hollywood productions to treat racial prejudice.

as a worker who has been ordered sterilized is particularly disturbing, since the defense's argument that this was because he was retarded seems all but justified by his odd behavior. We may see all these ambiguities as the film's way of postponing its eventual decision.

How is this eventual judgment—that the men are guilty and should be fully punished—reached, and how does the audience come to agree with it? Kramer and Mann use three tactics:

1. The defense attorney (Maximilian Schell) is particularly cruel in his treatment of the two most important witnesses. Clift is the first. Judy Garland, the second, plays a woman whom Schell accuses of having had, as an adolescent girl, illegal sexual relations with an older Jewish man (Fig. 11.3). Both Clift's and Garland's performances are keyed at such a high emotional level that Schell's grilling becomes particularly sadistic. We have no way of knowing if they are lying, but our sympathies are with them nonetheless. (Would a character played by Judy Garland, beloved in her youth as a Hollywood ingénue, really lie?) Kramer makes it dramatically necessary for Schell to meet defeat and thereby implies that there is no legitimate grounds for a defense.

2. The prosecution shows the tribunal (and us) documentary footage of concentration camp atrocities. The footage becomes realistic proof of Nazi cruelty, provokes our anger against the defendants, and makes all the more pressing our need to see retribution.

3. Janning admits his own guilt. In a scene that strikingly reverses roles, he accuses his defense attorney of distorting the facts. Our trust in Lancaster as a star is

11.3 Stanley Kramer's sense of casting. The casting of Judy Garland in *Judgment at Nuremberg* (1961) as a victim of Nazi brutality almost automatically produced audience sympathy for the character she played.

justified after all: he admits his former complicity and present responsibility. What is more, Lancaster is contrasted to the other defendants. One of them remains adamantly pro-Nazi (he is the least attractive physically); another claims he was only following orders (he looks physically slight and impotent); a third remains silent. The movie thereby acknowledges the full range of possible defenses open to them, one man representing each position.

Given American politics in 1961, *Judgment at Nuremberg* could hardly be thought particularly controversial for its condemnation of Nazism. The film appeared, however, at the time of the controversial Adolf Eichmann trial and was thus surely topical in the light of current interest in the question of German guilt. Israeli agents captured Eichmann, one of the engineers of the Nazi program to exterminate Jews, in May 1960; a court in Jerusalem found him guilty of crimes against humanity, but he was not put to death until May 1962. Thus the film may have effectively addressed its persuasion to those who objected to prosecuting war criminals on various grounds—that such prosecution was by nature selective and inconsistent, or that it was useless since the specific historical circumstances were unlikely to be repeated, or that such prosecution might be politically unwise.

Kramer and Mann meet these arguments throughout *Judgment at Nuremberg,* especially in portraying the political pressures that come to bear on Tracy by the U.S. government, anxious not to lose the support of the Germans in the cold war against Russia. Tracy's dismissal of such considerations in favor of a higher ideal of justice clearly articulates the filmmakers' point of view. In doing so, the movie attaches to a widely accepted position (that the crimes were indeed horrible and inexcusable) one that was not so widely accepted (that prosecution should be severe and forceful). The ending of the film, in which a title card states that not one of the convicted defendants of the Nuremberg trials was still serving his life sentence, is in effect a call for vigilance on the part of the audience.

Given the attractions of courtroom theatrics and a star-filled cast, it is easy to see why the film was a popular success. On the pragmatic level, it doubtless achieved its ends. Yet it raises certain ethical questions, since one can never be sure to what extent the filmmakers have "stacked the deck" in favor of the political position they will eventually take. And some critics have faulted it on esthetic grounds, finding it visually heavy-handed or uninteresting. It was shot in black and white and uses some artificial back projection for scenes in Nuremberg. Occasionally flamboyant camera movements and zooms, pointedly significant framings, and cutting to emphasize dialogue are all calculated to enliven a basically static, talky courtroom situation.

Judgment at Nuremberg uses a standard storytelling genre, the courtroom melodrama, to explore and editorialize on an important political problem. It typifies the emotional, humanistic approach to social questions so often employed by the Hollywood cinema.

The problem film is mainly an American phenomenon, yet one may see some parallel developments in the European cinema. The films of the Italian neorealists, for example, are also problem films in their depiction of conditions among the poor. André Cayatte, a former lawyer, is sometimes considered the Kramer of France, as he has made films highly critical of existing social structures. His works include attacks on the faults of the jury system (*Justice Is Done*, 1953), critiques of capital punishment (*We Are All Murderers*, 1957), or condemnations of bourgeois moral hypocrisy (*To Die of Love*, 1970).

Even more prominent has been the development of what is often called the *political thriller* as a standard form of international filmmaking. These are films that have exposed political oppression and the abuses of power within the framework of strong, Hollywood-style stories of mystery and adventure, often about heroes who uncover political corruption or conspiracy.

The most famous and imitated director of the political thriller is Constantin Costa-Gavras, usually known only by his last name. Costa-Gavras's *Z* (1969), an angry denunciation of totalitarianism in Greece, is the prototype of the genre. Among his other films are *The Confession* (1971), about Stalinist purges in Czechoslovakia; *State of Siege* (1973), about South American terrorism; and *Special Section* (1975), about the Nazi occupation of France. Critics have praised his films as able to reach mass audiences with political messages and damned them for their superficiality. In Italy, the films of Francesco Rosi (*The Mattei Affair*, 1972) and Elio Petri (*Investigation of a Citizen Above Suspicion*, 1970) have explored the ambiguities of Italian economics and the corruption of the country's politics within the framework of commercial moviemaking. In the United States, Alan Pakula (*The Parallax View*, 1974; *All the President's Men*, 1976) and Sydney Pollack (*Three Days of the Condor*, 1975) have made similar films exploring the potential for political conspiracy in the United States, real (as in Watergate) or imagined.

The late seventies saw the development of the Vietnam problem film in highly touted works dealing with both the morality of the conflict itself (*The Deer Hunter*, 1978) and problems of returning veterans (*Coming Home*, 1978). And questions of nuclear power received the political thriller treatment in *The China Syndrome* (1979), a film criticized by pronuclear forces as unethical and exploitative—until an incident similar to the one portrayed in the film occurred at Three Mile Island in

Pennsylvania within a week of the film's opening. Hollywood filmmakers continue to be ready to adapt the problem film to new situations and issues.

Yet while problem films are ideally suited to reaching a mass audience, they are often criticized for being inadvertently dysfunctional. The requirements of good storytelling are not always the same as those for responsible political analysis. The war film presents a particularly knotty example. In a survey taken among critics and filmmakers around 1960 about the production of antiwar films, the repeated worry of the respondents was that any portrayal of war on screen (whether in a heroic or pacifist context) is likely to glorify war.[6] The fascination of violence on film is perhaps unavoidable, for any war film is likely to make the audience more hostile to one side than the other. The antiwar film faces a constant contradiction: in opposing the prowar elements of society, a filmmaker may make violence exciting. In dramatic terms it makes sense to fight back; in moral terms it may not.

Similarly, a constant complaint leveled at films about concentration camps is that they trivialize their subject, often reducing to melodrama a subject of deeply tragic implications. Or consider Liliana Cavani's *The Night Porter* (1974), a superficially anti-Nazi film that has been criticized as a glorification of fascism. The movie deals with a former concentration camp officer, now a porter in a fancy hotel, who encounters a woman he had known when she was a prisoner years before in a concentration camp. Although Cavani demonstrates the cruelty of the Nazi oppressors, she also equates the relation between concentration camp prisoner and captor to that of a slave and master in a sadomasochistic love relation, which implies complicity on the part of the victim. Yet commentators have also praised Cavani for her political daring in raising this previously unthinkable point, on the grounds that it may indeed help us to understand the past better.[7] The problem is a complex one. If the purpose of a mythic narrative genre film is to explore (and thereby neutralize) bothersome contradictions within a culture, to what extent does building narratives around social issues turn them into myth and thus depoliticize them, neutralize their immediacy, and even produce complacency? On this level it is easy to see why so many political filmmakers naturally gravitate toward realist styles of moviemaking. The constant reminder of the film's concrete sources in the real world may serve to prevent the solidification of the political movie into myth.

Because they are made within existing systems of financing, problem films tend to preach reform rather than revolution. If they are in general constrained against taking stands that will be too unpopular, and thus uncommercial, they nonetheless represent that form of moviemaking in which strong narrative elements most customarily mix with didactic messages.

Official Government Propaganda

The potency of the film medium has not been lost on people directly seeking political power. Throughout the history of the medium, governments have deliberately used it to keep the people of their respective nations united under some particular political system or leader. This has been especially true in the Communist bloc countries, such as the Soviet Union in the twenties, Eastern Europe in the postwar era, and present-day Cuba. And the World War II era was a particularly rich one for government-sponsored propaganda, on the part of the Germans under Hitler and the Allies in England and the United States.

Filmmaking in Communist Countries In the Communist bloc countries, film production is state-organized and state-operated. And since Marxism, unlike ideologies organized around religious or humanistic precepts, is a philosophy of government that sees economic and political circumstances as the one primary driving force in human relations, there has been a tendency for these state-produced films to see the world in economic and political terms.

The history of film runs parallel to the establishment of the Communist bloc as a dominant, powerful force in the world today. Lenin, at the time of the Russian Revolution, saw that movies, then two decades old, were a primary means of reaching and rousing the masses. In our discussion of editing we treated the Soviet filmmakers of the Silent Period, who are well known for their innovative editing techniques. When we see their films today, we may have trouble putting them into their social contexts as persuasive messages aimed at the Soviet masses. We tend to be more interested in their technical mastery than their political messages.

What the great Russian makers of silent films most often did was take historical events, such as popular uprisings and revolutions, and dramatize them to serve as examples for the present. Eisenstein's *Potemkin* was about the unsuccessful revolution of 1905; *October* portrayed the October Revolution in 1917. In these works, Eisenstein strove to make the masses his hero, emphasizing not individual, personal drama but treating historical events as social movements arising out of the inevitable actions of a mass of individuals acting together. Even his treatment in *The General Line* (1929) of a contemporary topic, collectivized agriculture, emphasized the group nature of a community's struggle rather than individual people.

Vsevolod Pudovkin also preferred subjects from recent history. *Mother* was adapted from Gorki's novel of the 1905 revolt. *The End of St. Petersburg* (1927) treated the same subject as *October,* while *Storm over Asia* (1928) took place during an earlier popular uprising in Mongolia. Yet Pudovkin's films emphasize the awakening to political consciousness of individual, heroic characters with whom the audience can identify. In *Mother,* a woman's son inspires her to commitment; in *The End of St. Petersburg* a city Communist shows the way to a country peasant relative.

Let us consider at some length Eisenstein's first feature, *Strike* (1924). While some of the Russian director's later works are more polished (*Potemkin*) or more elaborate *(October),* *Strike* remains particularly accessible to audiences today.[8] Its directness and simplicity may occasionally slip into obviousness, but even this quality makes all the more clear Eisenstein's approach to the film medium as a tool for the development of political consciousness.

Strike was intended as a demonstration of the processes of social oppression and revolution. In this sense Eisenstein appeals to the audience's intellect as well as to its emotions, linking an investigation of economics with an activist celebration of the workers. Eisenstein divides the movie into six sections introduced by descriptive titles. Each section represents a step in the inevitable chain of events, from the mistreatment of the workers in a factory, through the strike itself, to the final massacre of the protestors by the army. Eisenstein indicates that the strike he presents is typical. At the end of the film a title card lists the Russian cities where similar conflicts took place before the revolution. The movie implies that the pattern of rebellion and suppression was the same for all of them.

As in his later silent films, Eisenstein refused to follow an individual hero through the course of the action but filled *Strike* with brief scenes (or even single shots) in which he edited the actions of individuals together to give a sense of collective unity among the workers. We see Eisenstein's approach most clearly in his staging of the walkout itself. As word of the strike spreads through the factory, he cuts from shot to shot of workers joining the strike as individuals. Through his editing, he emphasizes close-ups of their tools being thrown to the ground and of men fighting for control of the factory whistle. Only as the number of strikers increases does he cut to long shots of a crowd forming. This rhythmic progression, in which close-ups give way to long shots, is visually striking; it also drives home the idea that the crowd is a mass of individuals.

Reacting to the theatrical traditions he sees as bourgeois, Eisenstein rejects the usual notions of film characterization. He instead deliberately types characters according to their role in the struggle in keeping with the Marxist point of view that people are defined by their economic place in society. In the first section of *Strike,* when worker unrest is brewing, an obese factory manager calls his superior, who is dressed in white tie (Fig. 11.4). The man in evening clothes in turn calls an elaborately uniformed police officer. In three quick scenes, Eisenstein has established visually the links of power that unite the ruling class. Such typing invites the accusation that Eisenstein's works are excessively slanted propaganda, but there is more to this tactic than simply the creation of good guys and bad guys. He makes the capitalists fat and sloppy not just to make them ugly and despicable but to suggest that qualities of wastefulness and self-centeredness may be an inherent part of their social position. Eisenstein's use of types shows interest in the rule rather than the exception.

At times this portrayal of people approaches the fanciful. Each of the police antilabor spies has a nickname, such as The Fox, The Owl, or The Bulldog, that is based on features or mannerisms that make the comparison apt. For each spy, Eisenstein dissolves a shot of the man himself into one of his namesake from the animal world. Early in the film, this is mere caricature—the use of ridicule to denigrate the enemy. Subsequently these comparisons take on more significance, as the agents seek out the strike's organizers. Their hunt becomes predatory and animal-like. Their economic opportunism has reduced them to a dog-eat-dog level. Yet the device has a childlike simplicity, comprehensible to common people.

This creative use of metaphor is what Eisenstein is most famous for in *Strike.* In one scene the bosses, supposedly "considering the requests of the workers until late," engage in some heavy drinking amid plush furnishings and crystal decanters. A grotesque capitalist puts a lemon into a press and squeezes the juice from it. Eisenstein cuts to a simultaneous clash between police and workers (Fig. 11.5). In this way he suggests that juice will be squeezed from the latter too. Later, when the fire department uses hoses on the crowd, we see from the wild raging of the water the helplessness of the people against those who wield the power. In the movie's famed climax, Eisenstein intercuts shots of the massacre of the crowd with those of an

11.4 *Typage* in Eisenstein. In casting a factory boss in *Strike* (1924), Sergei Eisenstein typed the character as overweight and photographed him from a low angle to emphasize his fatness.

animal in a slaughterhouse. Like a well-worded speech, the film contains images that excite us by being both appropriate and unexpected.

Eisenstein followed *Strike* with his other silent film successes; but as time went on, he, Pudovkin, and Dziga Vertov all ran into increasing interference from the state, which accused them of excessive "formalism" in their approaches to filmmaking. With the coming of sound in the thirties and the change of regimes involving Stalin's rise to power, the official doctrine of *Socialist realism* supplanted the stylized editing and formal experimentation of these figures. The theory of Socialist realism asserted, in essence, that the most important aspect of a film was whether it contained a politically correct message. A correct film would combine strong elements of the realist function (presumably showing the world of economic relations as it really is) and the persuasive function (from a Marxist point of view). From Socialist realism came the notion of the *positive hero*—usually a figure moved by environment to fight against oppression for justice and the Communist state—to allow for audience identification and involvement. Extreme subjectivity, as we see in predominantly personal cinema, and formal experimentation (what we call *esthetic cinema*) were condemned as bourgeois and apolitical. Whereas the Soviet montage theorists had taken an esthetic approach to propaganda, Socialist realism advocated a "balanced" approach, and many of the works produced under its name were conventional story films, often similar in manner to the Hollywood problem film.

Yet even with the rise of Stalin and Socialist realism, a favorite tactic of the filmmakers was to inspire audiences with stories from the past. Sergei and Georgi Vassiliev's *Chapayev* (1934) and Alexander Dovzhenko's *Shors* (1939) treated national heroes who fought counterrevolutionary forces in the 1919 postrevolutionary period. Eisenstein's sound films went further back in history for their inspiration than his silent films had. *Alexander Nevski* (1938) and *Ivan the Terrible* (1944–1946) sought parallels to contemporary situations in historical figures. For example, Nevski would be shown leading the Russians to defend their country against invading

11.5 Idealizing the masses. Effective as propaganda, the film *Strike* arouses sympathy for the workers as they are repressed by violent military force.

Germans, or Ivan would be seen uniting feudal Russia for the benefit of the people. After World War II, films about the conflict and the resistance of the Russians and East European peoples became a standard genre of the period, a staple in these national film industries. Again, they would look to past heros for present uplift.

Yet in the fifties and sixties, a softening of the strict requisites of Socialist realism took place behind the Iron Curtain, particularly in countries like Hungary, Poland, and Czechoslovakia. Films from these countries began to take more subjective, experimental, and even politically critical points of view. Perhaps the major figure in this tendency was Poland's Andrzej Wajda, whose wartime trilogy—*A Generation* (1954), *Kanal* (1956), and *Ashes and Diamonds* (1957)—represents the earliest flowering of post-Stalinist cinema. Although these works continued the practice of drawing on the war years for material, they also deromanticized that era: a generation that filmmakers had presented as heroic was now viewed with skepticism or even cynicism. Wajda presented partisan heroics as often misguided or ineffective, criticized certain elements within the anti-Nazi camp, and even indulged in religious symbolism to avoid a simplistic "good guys versus bad guys" portrayal of the war. Wajda's bold, nonconformist cinema has investigated the ambiguities of political action, and the director has continued in this line for over twenty years. *Man of Marble* (1978), one of the most virulently critical attacks on the political repressiveness of Poland in the fifties, has surprised audiences both at home and abroad with its outspokenness.

The cinema of the Communist bloc countries raises certain unique questions about censorship. In the post–World War II period governments have periodically tightened and loosened their control over filmmakers, according to the mood of the current regime. Freedom of expression is always tentative, it would seem. In the sixties, for example, the Czech cinema flowered into one of the best national film industries in the world—until the Soviet invasion of 1968. A similar tightening of controls occurred at about the same time in Poland and Yugoslavia—controls that have only recently begun to be lifted. At the same time, filmmakers like Wajda in Poland, Miklós Janscó in Hungary, or Dusan Makavejev in Yugoslavia have all produced work that could perhaps never have emerged in a "free enterprise" film industry. The benefit of state control of filmmaking is that it can sometimes bring about works of great quality that would stand little chance of survival in a commercial marketplace. In effect the Communist filmmaker trades censorship by the box office for censorship by the state.

Propaganda and World War II　　When Hitler came to power, the German film industry began to produce Nazi propaganda justifying the regime, glorifying the German national heritage, and portraying Jews and Bolshevists as the primary threats to German peace and prosperity. In March 1933 Hitler appointed Joseph Goebbels minister of propaganda, ushering in a new era for the German film industry. Production companies were gradually nationalized and put under Goebbels's control. Goebbels believed the public wanted entertainment, and his program involved the injection of political comment into popular movie forms of the time, as well as the making of newsreels and documentary films.[9]

The most famous German filmmaker of this period preceding the war was Leni Riefenstahl. Her *Triumph of the Will* (1934–1935) documented the famed Nuremberg rallies and was a skillful glorification of National Socialism. *Olympia* (1936–1938) was less overtly political. Although it is ostensibly a record of the 1936 Berlin Olympic Games, some critics have seen in its portrayal of the athletic prowess of white Nordic athletes a celebration of the "Master Race"—despite the accomplishments of black athlete Jesse Owens.[10]

Riefenstahl worked in documentary formats, but critics consider her works classic examples of factual material manipulated for political purposes. They often cite *Triumph of the Will* as a challenge to the viewer to choose form over content, since even those commentators who completely reject its subject matter are impressed with its skillful technique (Fig. 11.6). *Triumph of the Will* is perhaps the supreme example of documentary film being used to create and support a living political myth. Hitler descends godlike from the skies in an airplane and arrives triumphantly at rallies—a savior to people chanting subserviently or marching in perfect formation under his leadership. The film strikes some viewers today as tedious and long-winded, but it is easy to see how Hitler's followers could become entranced by the sense of expectation and drama Riefenstahl puts into her imagery.[11]

During World War II, all mobilized governments sponsored films to solidify public support for their war efforts. We have already discussed some of these works,

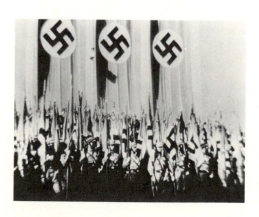

11.6 The seductive trappings of Fascism. Some critics have praised Leni Riefenstahl's *Triumph of the Will* (1934), even while resisting its message: the visual force of these swastikas is evident even if we find their specific political significance repulsive.

especially those produced in Britain, in connection with the documentary. In the United States, the government produced a series of films under the collective title *Why We Fight*. Made by such professional Hollywood directors as Frank Capra and Anatole Litvak, they were both training films for members of the service and morale boosters for the home front. These documentary works included *Prelude to War* (tracing the rise of the Nazis to power), *The Nazis Strike* (about German rearmament and the invasion of Poland), and *Divide and Conquer* (portraying developments in the early war years), all from 1943. Drawn almost exclusively from stock footage and newsreels—including segments of *Triumph of the Will* reedited to make Hitler seem menacing and vicious—the *Why We Fight* series took a lecture format. It wedded extensive narration and documentary footage with animated charts and diagrams, all explaining as simply as possible the political and military complexity of the struggle. The films are a classic example of a government using film to communicate to its people (Fig. 11.7).

In general, then, government propaganda calls not for change but for action to preserve or strengthen a regime already in power. It appeals to citizens' pride in what their government represents, points to its past and present accomplishments, and alerts the public to continuing threats to established order. If Communist countries are the chief examples of this mode of filmmaking institutionalized on the industrial level, the World War II era shows how almost any government may benefit from the medium.

Subversive Cinema

The late sixties were a period of great social unrest, particularly among those segments of society most likely to be frequent patrons of motion pictures—students, young people, minority groups. It was a period of great anti-Establishment feeling, in which rebellion against existing government systems was frequent in capitalist and

11.7 A *Why We Fight* film. *The Battle of Russia* (1943), directed by Anatole Litvak, is admired by some critics as the most powerful film of the *Why We Fight* series.

Communist countries alike. Films reflecting this spirit of revolt often found large audiences of young people, and movies advocating radical political change became a direct extension of the French New Wave and Young Cinema movements of the mid-sixties (which we will discuss shortly).

In some ways the 1969 Cannes Film Festival marks the change in sensibility as directly as the 1959 festival heralded the start of the French New Wave. A survey of the prize winners for that year shows that every title reflects a dominant spirit of political protest and cultural rebellion, despite the many international sources for the films:

- *If . . .,* Lindsay Anderson's parablelike study of rebellion in an English boarding school, which ends with students machine-gunning their elders from the rooftops (Grand Prize)

- *Adalen '31,* a film by Bo Widerberg presenting a strike in Sweden in the thirties in picturesque, romanticized terms (Special Jury Award)

- *Z,* Costa-Gavras's protest film about a Greek assassination (Jury Award and Best Actor for Jean-Louis Trintignant)

- *Antonio Das Mortes,* Brazilian director Glauber Rocha's work in which the title character is a kind of revolutionary Robin Hood (cowinner, Best Direction)

- *Moravian Chronicle,* one of the most politically outspoken films of the Czech New Wave, by Vojtech Jasny, condemning the government's insensitive disregard for the culture and way of life of Moravian peasants with the coming of collective farming after World War II (cowinner, Best Direction)

- *Isadora,* Karel Reisz's film biography of the American dancer Isadora Duncan, who advocated free love, Bolshevism, and commitment to art in a way that paralleled the radical sensibility of the sixties (Best Actress for Vanessa Redgrave)

- *Easy Rider,* a key film in the drug culture of the time, about two long-haired motorcyclists' alienation from the America they travel through (Prize for Dennis Hopper for a Director's First Film)[12]

Such an antiestablishment phenomenon was virtually unprecedented in world cinema. Even Hollywood studios began to finance works that attacked, or at least questioned, the very economic system of which Hollywood was a part. It was a contradictory situation: corporations could profit from films expressing anticorporate sentiments (Fig. 11.8). Yet comparable movements could also be found in the Eastern European countries. Movies such as Jan Nemec's *A Report on the Party and the Guests* (1968) and Jaromil Jires's *The Joke* (1969) from Czechoslovakia and Zelmir Zilnik's *Early Works* (1969) and Dusan Makavejev's *W.R.: Mysteries of the Organism* (1971) from Yugoslavia were bitter, satiric attacks on the enforced conformity and lack of personal freedom of a previous generation of Communist rule.

To a certain extent this new politicization grew out of the French New Wave, particularly the films of Jean-Luc Godard. As the sixties progressed, Godard became increasingly less interested in reworking Hollywood genres and more involved with loosely structured sociological inquests. By the time of *Masculine-Feminine* (1966), the rebellious Parisian youths of *Breathless* had become radicalized "children of Marx and Coca-Cola." In *Two or Three Things I Know About Her* (1966), Godard examined part-time prostitution among housewives in high-rise housing complexes. Godard was at the same time evolving, again with Raoul Coutard, a bright, decorative, pop-art style of shooting in which visual images consisted mainly of evenly lit planes of flat, clear color. It was a perfect visual style for film portrayals of a seductive French capitalist consumer-oriented environment of brightly colored plastics, ready-to-wear clothing, and clean, modern architectural lines—an environment Godard ironically saw as both a cause and an effect of economic injustice.

In 1967 Godard produced *La Chinoise*, a prophetic comedy about a group of Maoist students who form a collective cell for a summer. The film caught the mood of the time perfectly, for a year later the student-worker riots of May 1968 broke out and Godard became a major cinema spokesman for this new revolutionary sensibility. After *Weekend* (1967) Godard's work became increasingly theoretical and visually stylized. The so-called technical incompetence his detractors accused him of became a deliberate attempt to subvert the methods of the Hollywood, i.e., capitalist, repressive, exploitative cinema.

Godard's films from this period contain things not quite like anything the cinema had yet produced. They often seemed to be disconnected pastings together of

11.8 Anticapitalist Hollywood filmmaking. MGM's *The Strawberry Statement* (1970), winner of a major prize at the 1970 Cannes Film Festival, was a fictional portrayal of the student riots at Columbia University in 1968. In the United States, the film was not a success at the box office.

jottings, ideas, and sketches that could nonetheless be bizarrely funny and politically telling. In *Two or Three Things I Know About Her*, for example, a little girl tells about a dream she has had in which twins are walking along the edge of a cliff. As the road becomes narrower, there is no longer room for both of them, so the twins become one. The girl interprets the figures of her wonderful dream as North and South Vietnam. The episode, which has little to do directly with the story of the film, is both silly and provocative, coming in a work made when the political conflict over the Vietnam War was shaking both the United States and the countries of Western Europe.

Often Godard's films would emphasize exposition of ideas rather than stories. In *La Chinoise*, one of the Maoists writes the names of great writers in Western civilization on the blackboard. He then proceeds, without speaking further, to erase those that are expendable in light of revolutionary thought. Gradually every major literary figure in our culture is discarded and the order in which they go suggests a whole cultural esthetic summed up in a single gesture. When the Maoist finally comes to the name of Bertolt Brecht, the German playwright so important as a model to Godard and others of this period, he leaves the name. The sequence contains no dramatic development in any traditional sense and would be inaccessible to an uneducated audience, but it is nonetheless wittily economical to students of literature concerned, as Godard is, with the intersections of literary and political theory.

In *Weekend*, Godard stages one of his most technically brilliant scenes. In portraying a world of crass bourgeoisie who all leave Paris by car to go to the country for the weekend, Godard stages a traffic jam that he photographs in one of the longest traveling shots then executed in the history of cinema. The camera tracks past a seemingly infinite string of cars backed up, its inhabitants distraught, aggressive, or bored, as the director creates an apocalyptic vision of civilization and technology run amok. Viewers ask themselves, "When will the shot end?" and "When will the whole mad system end?" *Two or Three Things I Know About Her*, *La Chinoise*, and *Weekend* also contain scenes of somewhat less imagination or inspiration, but they are nonetheless vigorous works that challenged a whole generation of filmmakers and moviegoers.

While Godard was beginning his conversion to radical politics, other film-makers were already using the techniques of his cinema to address political issues. The most famous of these post–New Wave films was Vilgot Sjöman's *I Am Curious* (1967), a two-part work attacking the superficiality of Sweden's social advances. The film begins with a kind of homage to *Chronicle of a Summer* in which Sjöman's star,

Lena Nyman, asks people on the street in Stockholm whether they think Sweden has achieved a classless society. Throughout the film, Sjöman comments on the images and the process of shooting them through a voice-over soundtrack (a device used earlier by Godard in *Band of Outsiders* and *Two or Three Things I Know About Her*). As the movie traces the development of a sexual relation between Nyman and one of the actors in the film, we lose track of how much is real and how much is fiction, as well as the extent to which her alienation from Sjöman himself (she was supposedly his lover) is or is not invention. The argument the film develops attempts to link the violence of interpersonal relations, the dominant sexism of the society, and the personal frustration these factors produce to Sweden's inability to achieve any genuine social reform (Fig. 11.9). Sjöman followed the first part, *I Am Curious— Yellow*, with *I Am Curious—Blue*. Yellow and blue are the two colors of the Swedish flag. If the latter was less successful, it was probably because the former, much touted for explicit scenes of sexual intercourse and nudity, put emphasis on sex, whereas the latter went further into the structure of the Swedish welfare state. Yet Sjöman had incorporated Godard and even gone a bit beyond him, learning the main lesson that a fiction film can also be a sociological inquest, just as a sociological inquest can be a fiction film.

11.9 The post-Godard political essay. Swedish filmmaker Vilgot Sjöman explores some of the relationships between politics and sex in *I Am Curious—Yellow* (1967), a film that combines documentary reporting with fantasy and deliberate exaggeration.

The influence of this double-edged form of filmmaking extended not only to France and Sweden (not to mention the rest of Western Europe), but also Eastern Europe and the Third World (Fig. 11.10).[13] Zilnik's *Early Works* has been compared to *Band of Outsiders*, but where Godard's disaffected youths play self-destructively at being gangsters, Zilnik's play at being revolutionaries in a Socialist state they see as having betrayed the principles of Marx. Makavejev's *W.R.* goes even further by editing together, collage style, documentary, staged, and found footage to examine and in some ways celebrate the theories of Wilhelm Reich, the Marxist psychologist who saw sexual repression as the root of all totalitarianism (that of Hitler and Stalin included).

In Brazil a movement arose known as *cinema nôvo*. Although its quick shooting methods and improvised look were shared with works everywhere, *cinema nôvo* subjects were distinctly Brazilian and reflected South American political life and culture. The most famous director from the movement is Glauber Rocha, who achieved notoriety not only for *Antonio Das Mortes* but also for *Black God, White Devil* (1964) and *The Earth Entranced* (1967). Rocha's movies combine political allegory with peasant spectacle to the accompaniment of thumping rhythmic music, and the result is a seemingly contradictory mixture of revolutionary politics, primitive religion, and operatic spectacle.

Although the works of Glauber Rocha have achieved more fame in the United States, some critics consider Ruy Guerra's *The Gods and the Dead* (1970) to represent the finest work of the Brazilian *cinema nôvo* movement.[14] A mixture of Third World political concerns with contemporary *avant-garde* film esthetics, the film is a difficult one for an unprepared viewer, but it exemplifies perfectly how political cinema following the sixties has attempted to explore new modes of expression.

11.10 Africa and Third-World filmmaking. African directors have taken varied approaches in commenting on the political situations in their emerging countries. a. Sarah Maldoror's Angolan film *Sambizanga* (1972) uses a realistic style and heroic central characters to produce intense audience identification. b. Senegal's Ousmane Sembene takes a more satiric approach in *Xala* (1974), which pokes fun at the rising African bourgeoisie.

a

b

The film's most difficult challenge is its highly convoluted plot. Guerra's interest is not in giving us an easily followed, involving narrative, but in opposing to a conventional story a complicated one that requires the viewer's close and careful attention. One may easily gather that the story involves two rival plantation owners in the first part of the century, one headed by Santana da Terra, the other by Urbano D'Agua Limpa. It may take a second viewing to understand clearly how the plot portrays first the killing of D'Agua Limpa's two sons, Aurelio and Valeriano, then Urbano himself, before Seven, an opportunistic figure from the lower classes, marries into the Santana clan. Guerra gives his characters little or no introduction. One is left to figure out their roles and relationships in retrospect, putting pieces of information together after actions have taken place. Violent and grotesque to an extreme, the film has been compared with seventeenth-century Jacobean tragedy.[15]

One may find the political purpose of Guerra's story in the symbolic nature of all the characters. Each is made to represent a certain social class, a social force in the progress of history. Santana da Terra represents the old-fashioned colonial empire (one of his advisers is an internationalist banker). The D'Agua Limpas stand for "new money," linked to the corrupt politics of the new republican system (embodied in Urbano's ally, Dr. Venancio, a candidate for election). Urbano's two sons appear effete, impotent, spoiled by their privileged station, and easily overpowered. Santana has an epileptic daughter, Jura, and an ambitious mistress, Sol, both of whom suggest women who are perhaps more capable of continuing the Santana line.

The Gods and the Dead is thus a historical allegory of the struggle for power in Brazil. In the character of Seven, an ugly, scarred figure related in some ways to the archetypal gunman in the Italian Western, we see a demonstration of greed and cynicism (Fig. 11.11). Only Sereno, widow of one of Santana's employees, who kills Aurelio and later Santana himself, suggests a positive and fertile revolutionary force. As in *Judgment at Nuremberg,* individual characters represent various positions within a political system. But unlike Kramer, Guerra never pretends that his representative characters are also real people.

11.11 *The Gods and the Dead.* The character called Seven in Ruy Guerra's *The Gods and the Dead* (1970) is an ugly, scarred warrior who may represent the forces of opportunism latent in all revolutionary movements.

The style of *The Gods and the Dead* emphasizes this symbolic approach. Dialogue consists mainly of ritualistic litany (Seven says repeatedly, linking power to property, "I am the king, I am the queen, I am the prince, I am the sugercane, I am the mill, I am the husk") or poetic proclamation (Santana notes of his historical situation, "The conditions of an empire are to have its roots dipped in the blurs of time and blood.") Dramatic confrontations are inevitably verbal or physical duels. Guerra photographs these power struggles in long, uncut takes, circling hypnotically around his characters, creating a sense of tragic fate. In a long, intense battle between Seven and Valeriano, Seven opens the windows of the house in which they struggle, allowing Valeriano a chance to escape—only to have his victim close them again. Both see their confrontation as inevitable, as Guerra would argue that such power struggles are inevitable.

To the extent that Guerra's thinking is Marxist, this inevitability would be a reflection of laws of economics. In one scene, Guerra shows Urbano D'Agua Limpa assembling some troops in a square. He cuts to a businessman advising Dr. Venancio to align himself with the foreign economic interests, since they will triumph anyway; then he cuts back to the square, where we see that D'Agua Limpa's men have been slaughtered. The effect has been carefully planned: there was no need to show the battle, for its outcome was the inevitable result of *economic* power. It is a series of shots fully related to Eisenstein in its use of editing to create thematic meaning.

The Gods and the Dead is both a spectacle and a formalist experiment. As in most *cinema nôvo* films, exotic costuming, bright colors, and rhythmic music overshadow narrative considerations. Guerra's long, sinuous hand-held takes weave through rooms and corridors and circle about characters. Each scene shows great visual elegance even when its meaning may be ambiguous. Yet Guerra subverts any tendency the film may have simply to be beautiful, for the editing is deliberately choppy, putting lengthy, often single-take scenes abruptly next to one another. It is as if Guerra wants to jar us into intellectual awareness whenever we become too lulled by the allure of his images. In its disjointed plot structure and technique and its stylized dialogue, the film typifies the attempts by contemporary filmmakers to combine political observation and formal innovation. It defies the conventions of commercial moviemaking.

Guerra's film is not directly persuasive. But even if it advocates no particular practical solution, it does relate its study of Brazil's past to present-day life. In the beginning of the film, a man addressing peasants in the north of the country urges them to migrate south for jobs. We see a procession of them begin the journey, passing under a Shell Oil sign; they are followed by two men who divide up their catch of cheap labor, treating the people as commodities. The patterns of economic oppression and foreign domination continue. *The Gods and the Dead* is an act of anger against both and against the commercial narrative forms of filmmaking that it associates with these economic systems.

What almost all such subversive or revolutionary films have in common is a rejection of conventional forms of narrative and storytelling in favor of a style of filmmaking emphasizing direct political messages. Sometimes a lack of conventional plot and characterization serves to shock viewers accustomed to more standard formats and content. Interest on a popular level in subversive and revolutionary forms of filmmaking declined somewhat in the seventies, but the political questions raised by filmmakers like Godard, Sjöman, and Makavejev have become a central part of serious filmmaking today. In the seventies, questions of political filmmaking became increasingly theoretical, and it is perhaps best to treat them in that context.

PERSUASIVE CINEMA AND THE CRITICS

Throughout the history of cinema there have been critics whose primary interest has been the promotion of persuasive or didactic forms of filmmaking. That a film should have a concrete social purpose has been an ideal shared by many, although hardly all, film theorists. Political film theory tends to come from left of center in the political spectrum, since the position of the Left in politics has tended to be that of a challenger of the status quo, whereas the money required for film production has tended to make it a conservative medium, more available to those with power than without it. Political film theory has tended to come from Marxists, Socialists, and liberals, who put the persuasive value of the medium above all others. Frequently debates about issues of political film theory have been among factions of the Left rather than between Left and Right. Yet all factions are faced with a central problem: for whatever reason, the mass moviegoer seems to be more interested in entertainment than in politics. More often than not, the masses will flock to a popular, commercial film rather than one with a serious persuasive purpose.

We have already discussed several theorists and theories of political filmmaking, among them John Grierson, Dziga Vertov, and the school of Socialist realism. Grierson and Vertov's interests are, of course, also directly linked to questions of realism, since they are associated with two major approaches to the documentary. We may see already in these figures two primary drives in the development of theories of persuasive filmmaking. One sees political filmmaking as a question of subject matter, the other argues that one cannot separate political issues from esthetic or formal issues.

For Grierson and the Socialist realist, content is all-important. The persuasive film differs from the commercial storytelling film mainly in its directly political subject matter. The political film calls to the public eye the issues and problems of the day and suggests possible solutions for them. To reach the people, one must present issues to them in terms they understand. The political filmmaker seeks the widest possible audience.

Out of this attitude comes what some critics call the "sugar-coating" approach to political filmmaking.[16] If the public is uninterested in a certain issue, one must "sugar-coat" it—that is, present it by means of an exciting story, a heroic central figure, or deep human interest. In some cases it may be necessary to simplify issues to make them comprehensible to the masses. The sugar-coated approach emphasizes the pragmatic aspect of political filmmaking (Fig. 11.12). In general, this pragmatic approach was the dominant form in persuasive moviemaking in the world from the thirties to the sixties, the main period of both the problem film in Hollywood and Socialist realism in the Soviet Union.

It is only with the sixties that we have seen a revival of the Dziga Vertov tradition. Vertov and other Soviet montage theorists were highly influenced by a movement in Russian esthetics now known as *Russian formalism*. The Russian formalists postulated that the purpose of art is not to imitate reality (as centuries of Aristotelian theorists had proposed) but to make reality "strange." That is, art would be a set of devices used to aid in seeing the world in a fresh way, in surprising the viewer into a new awareness of his surroundings.

This theory was directly linked to a concept of political revolution. Any revolutionary art would have to shake the masses out of their complacency. By implication, the traditional forms of bourgeois art and conventional storytelling encouraged this antirevolutionary complacency. Thus Vertov's kaleidoscopic editing, for example, was intended to be a kind of sensory jolt to encourage in the people a

11.12 Political persuasion for the mass audience. *Wilson* (1944) is an example of the "sugar pill" approach to political filmmaking. In this film, producer Darryl Zanuck tried to persuade the American voter to learn from history and to re-elect Franklin D. Roosevelt.

new sense of the world around them. If the commercial cinema is one of mythmaking, Vertov's would be one of intentional demythicization. For the formalists, propaganda would be a matter of artistic form as well as content.

Influenced in part by Russian formalism, the theatrical theories of Bertolt Brecht, especially in such plays as *The Threepenny Opera, The Good Woman of Szechuan,* and *Mother Courage and Her Children,* began to be influential in the fifties, and by the late sixties his theories captured the sensibilities of a good number of filmmakers and theorists. Following Marx's notion that all culture is created by economic determinants, Brecht postulated that the conventional theater of his time—whether it was the tradition of Greek tragedy and classical theater or more contemporary realism—was essentially a product of capitalism. Brecht attacked such elements of traditional theater as audience identification with a main character, the resolution of stories by tragic fate, and the presentation of realistic settings; he even attacked Coleridge's notion of the "willing suspension of disbelief." He saw all of them as obstacles to the creation of a truly successful didactic theater, as devices that blunt the political awareness of the spectator (Fig. 11.13).

Instead, Brecht proposed an *epic theater,* in which actors would be seen as actors, not people, developing manifest political arguments on stage calculated to produce intellectual awareness on the part of the spectator. Brecht developed the notion of the *Verfremdungseffekt* ("alienation effect"—comparable to the notion of estrangement in the Russian formalists), whereby devices like stylized music, placards with written messages on them, or geometric groupings of actors would deliberately shatter theatrical illusion. The audience would have to question and evaluate, not simply be moved by, everything it saw.

Brecht had several bad experiences with the cinema, in which he felt that scripts he had written were mistreated by the filmmakers. In a text called "The Threepenny Lawsuit" he commented on his unsuccessful court action taken against the producers of the film version of *The Threepenny Opera* in 1934.[17] Today many film

11.13 Brecht on film. Exiled from Germany with the coming of Hitler, Bertolt Brecht worked in Hollywood on the script for *Hangmen Also Die* (1943), a film by Fritz Lang about the Nazi occupation of Czechoslovakia. Brecht later sued because he was denied screen credit on the finished film.

theorists consider it a landmark essay, for in it Brecht tries to show up the so-called art of film as a mask for the movies' real nature as merchandise, a simple commodity to be bought and sold. The capitalist system influences the forms and the content of the films produced under it. One cannot change the cinema simply by changing the content of films; one must also change their formal elements.

The debate on Brecht's theories has continued, mainly in French journals like *Cahiers du cinéma* and *Cinéthique,* with film critics and theorists attempting to apply them to the cinema.[18] If Brecht saw the techniques of theater as closely allied to capitalism, one could even make a greater case for film, the development of which has been directly allied, as we have seen in our earlier chapters, to capitalist innovation and industry. The narrative techniques of Griffith, the development of "correct" methods of shooting and editing in Hollywood, the growth of genres, the standards of realism developed by Bazin and others, and for some critics even the very technological nature of the camera—all these have been linked to the notion of film as a commodity designed indirectly to sell the ideological message of capitalism.

One immediate result of this interest in Brecht was the formation in 1970 by Jean-Luc Godard of the *Groupe Dziga Vertov,* whereby Godard announced a break with the bourgeois films of his past (which included even the political ones). The group's goal was to "make political films politically," calling for a revolution in both form and content in reaction against the methods of a commodity cinema. The Groupe tried to develop alternative forms of filmmaking that would treat political subjects without producing emotional identification through storytelling or relying on stylistic realism.[19] Thus *Wind from the East* (1970) borrows elements from the Western, but seeks through off-screen narration, the use of long static takes, the rejection of a story line to work toward the creation of a new kind of cinematic essay. Its technique of visibly penciling through yards of footage to show the collective's unhappiness with its own work serves as a radical reassessment of the politics of the filmmaking process. In *Tout va bien* (1971), a film modeled directly on some of Brecht's theoretical writings, the filmmakers describe how they had to hire two stars (Jane Fonda and Yves Montand) to get proper financing for the film; we see checks being cashed and papers changing hands—the film deliberately acknowledges its place in the commercial system. The rest of the film describes a strike in a French factory, but the film uses a huge, clearly studio-built set (inspired, reportedly, by a Jerry Lewis film) to suggest that the factory portrayed is not a real one (as location shooting would indicate) but rather the setting for a theoretical, archetypal strike, representative of a whole pattern in French industrial life.

All of Godard's recent films have been financial failures in their attempts to "deconstruct" the conventional commercial cinema, but their influence on critics and other filmmakers has been significant. Yet other leftist critics have reacted strongly against the films of the Groupe Dziga Vertov and those of other filmmakers working in this mode. The usual charge has been that such films partake of blatant elitism and have no contact with the very mass audience they must reach to be effective. One critic has rejoined that to reject the techniques of capitalist cinema and to refuse to apply them in a leftist context is like refusing to fight with guns that happen to be manufactured by the enemy. If a gun can be used to kill its maker, the techniques of commercial cinema can be used to kill the injustices of capitalism.[20]

Other leftist critics rejecting a tight, formalist line have looked to certain aspects of the recent Italian cinema for a model. A unique quality of a certain postwar Italian cinema has been, these critics argue, that directors of great political sincerity and concern have been able to create a popular cinema that repeatedly refers to and underscores Italian social issues—poverty, terrorism, the influence of the Catholic church, the role of trade unions in the economy, the legacy of fascism—all within the framework of the commercial cinema (Fig. 11.14). These

critics admire directors like Dino Risi, Luigi Commencini, and Ettore Scola, all of whom have been strongly influenced by neorealism, for being able to reach mass audiences with their messages.[21]

Debate about what constitutes an effective political cinema continues in such English and American periodicals as *Screen, Cinéaste,* and *Jump Cut,* and political and ideological criticism of individual films is a standard practice in serious film criticism today. Evaluation of films in terms of the portrayal of women and minorities, their implicit assumptions about the economic system, or the relation between form and political content are standard subjects for discussion and debate. If some approaches favor ethical and esthetic standards (such as the post-Brechtian line), others favor the pragmatic. Still others are trying to develop some middle ground between, let us say, the political tracts of the Groupe Dziga Vertov and the Hollywood world of *Judgment at Nuremberg.*

The issues are tantalizing. If indeed "all film is political," then every film presents a particular relationship between its subject matter, its method of financing and distribution, and its audience. But in choosing to be political, filmmakers have come to realize that what they do involves not the creation of a work of art in a vacuum, but rather a whole complex of economic and cultural aspects of film that occur before, during, and after the turning on of the camera.

SUMMARY

The persuasive function of film refers to the use of filmmaking to communicate political messages to an audience. Although we can see all films as having some persuasive function, certain kinds of film emphasize their influence on the audience more than others. In evaluating persuasive films we should consider their effectiveness, their honesty, and their artistic qualities.

There are three main kinds of political or persuasive film: (1) the commercial problem film, (2) official government propaganda, and (3) the subversive film.

The commercial problem film is a Hollywood-style narrative that links standard genre film storytelling to deliberately political messages. Some Warner Brothers films of the thirties (*I Am a Fugitive from a Chain Gang*), the films of Stanley Kramer (*Judgment at Nuremberg*), or those of Costa-Gavras (*Z*), are all commercial films examining social problems or issues.

11.14 The Italian social comedy. Some Italian filmmakers have received acclaim for their attempts to work political comment into familiar genre forms of comedy and melodrama. Ettore Scola's *Down and Dirty* (1975), for example, is an earthy, proletarian comedy that, nonetheless, shows the effects of poverty and urban blight on individual lives.

When governments finance their own motion pictures in a deliberate attempt to influence the governed, we have official government propaganda. The Soviet film of the twenties (as exemplified by Sergei Eisenstein's *Strike*) demonstrates how successful such works can be. World War II ushered in an era of full-scale use of government propaganda, as seen in Nazi Germany (*Triumph of the Will*) and the United States (the *Why We Fight* series).

Subversive cinema became particularly prominent in the late sixties, a period in which there could be such contradictions as anticapitalist films financed by big Hollywood studios or anarchistic movies produced by the Communist bloc countries. The films of Jean-Luc Godard led the way in the development of subversive film forms. Movements arose in Third World countries—most notably the *cinema nôvo* movement in Brazil—which produced films calling even more explicitly for revolution.

Theorists of political filmmaking have been divided between those favoring a "sugar-coating" method, whereby political filmmakers use the methods of popular, commercial cinema to reach the masses, and those advocating more "purist" approaches, who argue that a film cannot be truly subversive or revolutionary in content if it is traditional in form.

NOTES

1 Americans are not, of course, completely unaware of being manipulated by media, as one can tell from the constant satire on commercials that occurs on television and in other entertainment media. But that does not seem to make the manipulation less effective. Presumably the same would be true for workers in Russia or China and the type of propaganda they are exposed to.

2 This is referred to by some psychologists as *psychological reactance.* See Jack Brehm, *A Theory of Psychological Reactance* (New York: Academic Press, 1966).

3 Various film histories discuss the "problem films" produced by Hollywood in the 1910s and 1920s, but few of the works are remembered today. See Jack C. Ellis, *A History of Film* (Englewood Cliffs, N.Y.: Prentice-Hall, 1979), p. 154; John Davis, "Notes on Warner Brothers Foreign Policy, 1918–48," *The Velvet Light Trap,* No. 4 (Spring 1972), 23–33.

4 See also Russell Campbell, "Warners, the Depression and FDR—Wellman's *Heroes for Sale,*" *The Velvet Light Trap,* No. 4 (Spring 1972), 34–38.

5 Andrew Sarris, *The American Cinema: Directors and Directions, 1929–1968* (New York: Dutton, 1968), p. 260.

6 Robert Hughes, ed., *Film: Book II—Films of Peace and War* (New York: Grove, 1962).

7 The most articulate attack on *The Night Porter* is probably Bernard Sichère, "La bête et

le militant," *Cahiers du cinéma,* Nos. 251–252 (July–Aug. 1974), 18–28; a good defense is Teresa de Laurentis, "Cavani's *The Night Porter: A Woman's Film?" Film Quarterly,* 30 (Winter 1976–1977), 35–38.

8   See Norman Fruchter's comparison of *Strike* and *Potemkin* in "*Battleship Potemkin," Screen Education,* No. 30 (July–Aug. 1965), 37–52.

9   See David Stewart Hull, *Film in the Third Reich—A Study of the German Cinema, 1933–1945* (Berkeley: University of California, 1969); and Erwin Leiser, *Nazi Cinema,* trans. Gertrud Mander and David Wilson (London: Secker and Warburg, 1974).

10   To be fair, one should note that Riefenstahl reportedly did resist efforts to exclude from her film the victories of Jesse Owens and other black athletes, though she has also been criticized for not showing Hitler's insult to Owens when the German leader left the stadium just before the athlete's triumph. See Erik Barnouw, *Documentary: A History of the Non-Fiction Film* (New York: Oxford University Press, 1974), pp. 109–110; and Glenn B. Infield, *Leni Riefenstahl, The Fallen Film Goddess* (New York: Crowell, 1976), pp. 137–138.

11   See, in particular, Steve Neale, "*Triumph of the Will:* Notes on Documentary and Spectacle," *Screen,* 20 (Spring 1979), 63–86.

12   The phenomenon was not limited to Cannes. *Early Works* won the first prize at the Berlin festival that same year. *The Long Day's Dying,* a British antiwar film, took first prize at the San Sebastian Festival. And similar films of contestation were among the prize winners at Cannes in 1970.

13   One could mention, among others, Alexander Kluge's *Yesterday Girl* (1967) and *Artists Under the Circus Tent: Perplexed* (1968) from Germany; Nagisa Oshima's *Death by Hanging* (1968) and *Diary of a Shinjuku Thief* (1968) from Japan; and Robert Kramer's *Ice* (1970) from the United States as further examples of post-Godard filmmaking.

14   For a most thorough discussion of the film see Michel Ciment, "Cinéma épique, cinéma de la cruauté," *Positif,* No. 164 (Dec. 1974), 3–8.

15   Peter Cowie, "*Os deuses e os mortos,"* in *1972 International Film Guide* (New York: Barnes) p. 67. Cowie lists the running time of the film as 120 minutes. American prints are listed at 100 minutes, so it may be that some of the film's narrative difficulties are due to a shortened export version.

16   The idea of a "sugar-coated" cinema is not new, but it is nicely developed in James Monaco, "The Costa-Gavras Syndrome," *Cinéaste,* 7, No. 2 (1976), 18–21.

17   *Brecht on Theater: The Development of an Aesthetic,* ed. and trans. by John Willet (New York: Hill and Wang, 1964), pp. 47–51.

18   See in particular Jean-Louis Comolli and Jean Narboni, "Cinema/Ideology/Criticism," in *Movies and Methods: An Anthology,* ed. Bill Nichols (Berkeley: University of California, 1976), pp. 22–30.

19   "'La groupe Dziga Vertov,'" *Cahiers du cinéma,* No. 240 (July–Aug. 1972), 5–9.

20   Among these other examples would be films by Jean-Marie Straub and Marguerite Duras. See also Robert Benayoun, "Les enfants du paradigme," *Positif,* No. 122 (Dec. 1970), 7–26.

21   See in particular articles in *Ecran:* René Vautier, "Pour un cinéma plus populaire: 'Italianiser' le cinéma français," *Ecran 79,* No. 80 (May 1979), 21–22; Roland Duval, "En V.O.," *Ecran 76,* No. 43 (Jan. 1976), 8–9.

Chapter 12 / Personal Cinema

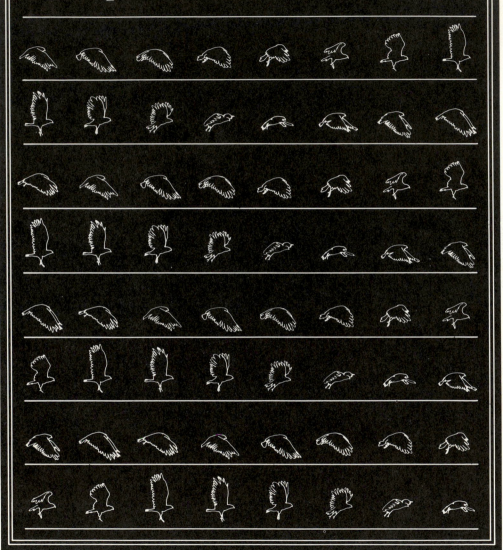

The persuasive function of communication deals with the message's effect on the *viewer*; the personal function refers to its full meaning for the *sender*. This meaning of a message for the sender may go beyond its simple literal sense and may be tied to a whole set of feelings about what is being communicated. With most communication, the sender conveys not only the message but an attitude toward that message. If the communication is effective, the receiver understands not only what was said but also something of the sender's feelings about it and reasons for articulating it.

Classic Hollywood movies can often be highly moving, and we have seen that much of our emotional involvement in such films comes from our identification with the privileged Hollywood actor—the star. The emphasis is on the doer, on action, on the dramatic. Yet we have also seen how certain Hollywood filmmakers, sometimes called *auteurs*, impose their personal imprint on the films they make. The movie no longer communicates anonymously but emphasizes an implied teller who communicates an attitude toward the story while telling it. These Hollywood films work on two emotive levels—one on which we identify with the feelings the actor is conveying, and another on which we identify with those of the filmmakers.

In dealing with personal cinema, we will concern ourselves with films that emphasize the teller—the filmmaker-narrator who can make his or her presence felt in a movie. In most cases the director will be the author of the film, but in other instances the writer may dominate. We will treat movies that are highly personal, emotional expressions on the part of an *auteur* whose personality infuses the whole film—whose subjective vision affects the viewer on many levels. The result is not the anonymous, collective myth making that is present in many Hollywood films, but a more individualist approach to the cinema.

We will examine three categories of personal cinema:

1 Autobiographical filmmaking, in which filmmakers emphasize themselves and their experiences as the primary subjects or referents of the film.

2 Hypersubjective cinema, in which filmmakers use the techniques of the medium to duplicate subjective experience.

3 Movies of aggressive individualism, in which filmmakers preach an ideology of self-reflection and self-involvement that may become political in nature.

These categories often overlap in personal cinema, but together form the range of possibilities open to filmmakers working in this mode.

395

AUTOBIOGRAPHICAL CINEMA

Home movies are perhaps the most familiar form of autobiographical cinema, and we all know a parent or other relative who methodically records every major family event or excursion with an 8-mm or super-8 movie camera. Home moviemakers record experiences they want to remember vividly, and their movies are about what the filmmakers have experienced and what they, their friends, and their loved ones have done together.

The closest analogy in literature to the home movie would be the diary, in which the diarist records daily experiences and observations. Like most diaries, most home movies are of little interest to the detached observer, but there are exceptions. Some experimental film exhibitors have invited their audiences to show home movies publicly, and occasionally there is revealed a naive, primitive poet of the genre who can give an unexpected expressiveness to a banal event like a back-yard get-together.

Some experimental filmmakers, working outside the conventional commercial system, have made films with essentially home-movie subject matter. Jonas Mekas, in *Diaries, Notes and Sketches* (1964–1969), merely strung together events he had casually photographed on various occasions. The films of Stan Brakhage also are like a private journal of his personal life. Brakhage has made intimate studies of the first months of his married life (*Wedlock House: An Intercourse*, 1959), the birth of his children (*Window Water Baby Moving*, 1959, and *Thigh Line Lyre Triangular*, 1961), and their growth (*Scenes from Under Childhood*, 1967–1970). Yet in these cases much of the interest in the film comes from the visual manipulation of the images, and we will be discussing Brakhage's work further in our chapter on esthetic cinema. A great cinematic diarist, like a great literary diarist, must offer more than simply an accurate recording of events.

Some filmmakers have wanted to produce work more akin to the memoir than the diary, work in which they describe or reflect on their past experiences rather than record present events. While some such autobiographers continue in the experimental tradition, others have moved into the realm of commercial filmmaking, creating a somewhat new kind of fiction film that has only truly developed in the past two decades or so. In the directly commercial, mass-audience film the predominance of conventionalized genre forms has traditionally precluded all but the most indirect forms of autobiographical expression. And even today, commercial autobiographical movies represent the exception rather than the rule.

The 400 Blows (1959), which we mentioned earlier in connection with the start of the French New Wave, marks a landmark in the autobiographical film and may yet be the most remarkable example of film autobiography ever made. The film dramatizes incidents from director François Truffaut's own childhood—his truancy from and problems in school, his relationship with parents whose feelings for him were highly ambivalent, his fascination with literature (particularly Balzac), the pranks that got him into trouble, and his ultimate aimlessness in running away from reform school. The film has a predominantly melancholy tone that captures effectively a sense of adolescent self-reflection that has appealed to a wide audience both in France and abroad.

The 400 Blows, like most New Wave films, has a deliberately semidocumentary look to it, and a scene in which Antoine Doinel (the boy who is Truffaut's stand-in in the film) is carried away in a paddy wagon is shot in a way that is a deliberate homage to a similar scene in De Sica's Shoeshine (1946), also about adolescent delinquents. Structually the film is very close to De Sica: it is built around seemingly banal, random, everyday events that are nonetheless carefully developed toward a moving, downbeat, and just slightly sentimental conclusion. The movie's most famous shot is its last one, in which the camera freeze-frames on the face of Antoine (an ending that is now a cliché, so that it may be difficult for young audiences to understand how jolting the original was in its time). It typifies the realist sense of film as a device to capture and freeze raw reality.

Yet although Truffaut sketches in aspects of working-class French life clearly and deftly, he understandably makes Antoine a special rather than a typical character, and there is almost no sense of social contestation to the film.[1] Truffaut in effect blames fate for Antoine's problems, not the economic system or social restraints; his problems are personal ones, not those of a society.

Antoine Doinel was acted by Jean-Pierre Léaud, whom Truffaut has used in a series of later films about the same character. He has followed Antoine through late adolescence (Antoine and Colette, a segment of the episode film, Love at Twenty, 1962), into adulthood (Stolen Kisses, 1968), through comic episodes of marriage, fatherhood, and adultery (Bed and Board, 1970), and finally to divorce and a career as a novelist (Love on the Run, 1978). Yet as one critic has commented, one can see in the Antoine Doinel films a gradual process whereby Antoine turns slowly from being Truffaut himself into a more artificially fictional character (Fig. 12.1).[2]

Yet Truffaut is clearly aware of the ambiguity of this process. In Love on the Run, Antoine meets a former girl friend; she has just read his first novel, in which she

a

b

figures as a central character. (Truffaut compares, through flashbacks from *Antoine and Colette*, how Antoine the novelist changes the "reality" from which he draws inspiration.) In talking to her about his writing career Antoine comments that he has an ambition to write a novel from a completely fictional idea, which he describes to her. In it, a man finds a torn-up picture of a woman; struck by her beauty, he tracks her down and falls in love with her. Only at the end of the film do we find that this is exactly how Antoine has met another girl with whom he is currently involved. Some artists, like Antoine, cannot help incorporating elements of their lives in their stories. *Love on the Run* is about this self-referential process of autobiographical creation. Like Renoir and Godard, Truffaut opposes fiction to reality, all the while acknowledging a difference between them.

The autobiographical film about childhood or adolescence has become almost a genre in the French cinema, and the decades since *The 400 Blows* have seen similar works. Some have been about childhood under the Nazi occupation (Claude Berri's *The Two of Us*, 1966; Michel Drach's *Les violins du bal*, 1974) or adolescence during the fifties or early sixties (Louis Malle's *Murmur of the Heart*, 1971; Diane Kurys's *Peppermint Soda*, 1978). The New Wave led to a movement known as Young Cinema, which established itself internationally, and many of the Young Cinema directors of the mid-sixties began their careers making semiautobiographical first or second features (Fig. 12.2). Polish director Jerzy Skolimowski started by making a series of short films at the Łódź film school that had enough continuity to be strung together as his first feature, *Identification Marks: None* (1964). In it, Skolimowski documents the day in the life of a young man, Andrzej, about to leave for military service. Andrzej, played by Skolimowski himself, goes on in the director's *Walkover* (1965) to become a boxer, a pursuit Skolimowski himself had briefly followed in his own youth. *David Holzman's Diary* (1968), by the American filmmaker (and former film student) Jim McBride, is about a film school student who obsessively records with his movie camera everything that happens to him. In some of the Young Cinema works we see the foreshadowing of the radical politicization of youth of the late sixties. The hero of Bernardo Bertolucci's *Before the Revolution* (1964) is a youth from a good family who flirts with communism while also having an affair with his aunt. Yet none of these works is quite imaginable without the precedent set by the New Wave.

These works exist on the periphery of the commercial cinema, and few Hollywood directors have attempted directly autobiographical films. One exception is Elia Kazan, who made *America, America* (1963), a film about his Greek ancestors

12.1 The maturing of Truffaut. In the character of Antoine Doinel, François Truffaut created an autobiographical stand-in for himself. a. Actor Jean-Pierre Léaud fell into mischief as the adolescent Antoine in *The 400 Blows* (1959) b. Léaud continued to play Antoine as an adult facing the problems of marriage and adultery in *Love on the Run* (1978).

and their emigration to the United States, and later *The Arrangement* (1967), an almost unsettlingly candid treatment of middle-aged sexual insecurity that would perhaps never have received financing if Kazan had not written the best-selling novel on which it was based. In other cases, however, directors have been remarkably adept at inserting elements of their own highly personal experiences into genre works or star vehicles. In *The Tenant* (1976), a horror film by Roman Polanski, Polanski himself plays an expatriate Russian who moves into a Paris apartment only to find himself abnormally preoccupied with the suicide of the apartment's former tenant (Fig. 12.3). The film can be seen simply as an occult chiller, but certain parallels to Polanski's own rather well-publicized life give the film an emotive significance that goes beyond simple identification with a character.

A similar instance of semiautobiography veiled in allegory, so to speak, may be found in Hollywood director Vincente Minnelli's *A Matter of Time* (1976). In it, Liza Minnelli, the director's daughter, plays an Italian hotel maid who is befriended by an aging countess (Ingrid Bergman) who helps the younger woman realize her talents and beauty and become a movie star. In this story of cross-generational love, Minnelli's casting subtly suggests his personal involvement in the subject. Bergman, an icon of the old Hollywood of which the elder Minnelli was a part, passes on a standard of beauty and elegance to the younger Minnelli, a sense underlined further by the presence of Bergman's own daughter, Isabella Rossellini, in a small role. The film is a testimony to the ideals, illusions, and ambitions that parents transfer to their children.

Not surprisingly, perhaps, none of the four American films just mentioned has been a box-office success, which may be some indication of why such personal filmmaking is the exception rather than the rule in commercial films. By this standard such films by Woody Allen as *Annie Hall* (1976) and *Manhattan* (1979) are remarkable achievements as semiautobiographical films aimed at—and reaching—a

Cinemabilia, NY/Audio Brandon/Directed and written by Melvin Van Peebles

12.2 The French tradition of personal filmmaking. The French film industry has offered opportunities for personal expression even to foreign filmmakers. In *The Story of a Three Day Pass* (1967), black American filmmaker Melvin Van Peebles was able to make his first feature, a possibly autobiographical portrayal of a black soldier's relationship with a French woman.

mass audience. In *Annie Hall,* Allen cast himself and his ex-wife Diane Keaton as a mismatched romantic couple, he an East Coast Jewish intellectual, she a Midwest Wasp, and it has been rumored that the relationship portrayed in the film very much paralleled their own. Although Allen's films carry in them strong elements of comedy, he repeatedly turns to a milieu familiar to him for his subjects, a New York of artists and writers, struggling with somewhat mixed-up love lives.

Of all the forms of predominantly personal cinema, autobiographical movies suggest a close alliance with the realist function we have previously discussed. In the autobiographical film the filmmaker suggests his own relation to reality; he uses the film medium to portray his own experiences. Autobiographical motion pictures may be highly subjective, but they emphasize the source in reality of their subject matter. Yet personal cinema also involves a crossover between these strong realist elements and personal ones that emphasize how filmmakers manipulate their media to underline the subjective nature of what they are doing. These esthetic aspects make up the techniques used in the creation of what we will call *hypersubjective cinema.*

HYPERSUBJECTIVE CINEMA

Movies like *The 400 Blows* and *The Tenant* use relatively conventional film technique to treat what may be highly personal subject matter. In other films, however, the demands of such self-expression require techniques that deliberately try to expand the use of the medium to replicate subjective experience. Hypersubjective film-making is deliberately selfconscious filmmaking that, overtly autobiographical or not, emphasizes the presence of an author trying to express himself or herself.

Filmmakers working in these hypersubjective modes tend to employ one of two approaches: they either use subjective forms of continuity to imitate mental processes and convey emotional feelings, or they rely on unusual *mise en scène* to create inner

12.3 The director as actor. Filmmakers sometimes cast themselves in their movies to indicate their personal involvement with the subject matter. In *The Tenant* (1976), expatriate Polish director Roman Polanski plays a Russian émigré living in Paris and tormented by what appear to be paranoid fantasies.

worlds of dream or fantasy. Sometimes they may combine these two approaches, but in both cases filmmakers calculatedly call attention to the personal significance of the images and to themselves as subjective mediators between the world they present and the audience.

Subjective Uses of Continuity

Filmmakers use subjective continuity in one or two ways. It may involve either a speeding up of the film's cutting rate to make the images more fragmentary and associative or slowing it down to make the work deliberate and meditative. Both approaches can be expressive, but let us consider the latter, simpler form first.

Slowing Down   Directors usually use slower editing rhythms in a film to make the viewer's experience more intense to produce a concentration on the purely physical sensations of a place or situation. Since the action of a standard storytelling film is often pared down to basic events to keep it moving quickly, such "decelerated" sequences are not necessarily slower than events might be in real time. The use of real time will often produce a sensation of slowness, especially to audience members accustomed to the speedier pace of the story film.

Perhaps the most common form of manipulating continuity for personal expression—one that occurs even in predominantly storytelling films as well—is the use of what the French call *temps mort* ("dead time"). Included in the film are scenes or moments whose sole purpose is to provide an artistic touch, emphasize a mood, underline a beautiful shot, or allow for a moment of reflection.

Some filmmakers have constructed stories with a minimum of plot, collecting and arranging incidents that are allowed to make the picture's rhythm deliberately slow. The entire film is dead time. The films of Michelangelo Antonioni work on this principle, and Antonioni's first big international success, *L'avventura* (1960), is still a landmark in the use of deliberate dedramatization in film.[3] In it a girl mysteriously disappears during a yachting trip, and the film deals with the half-hearted, desultory search for her on the part of her lover and a friend, who proceed to become sexually involved with each other after her absence. Antonioni is not really interested in unraveling the mystery, but in presenting a modern, industrial world in which human relationships have become stifled, in which affluence leads to boredom and complacency, in which sex becomes a substitute for love. *L'avventura*—like two of Antonioni's later films, *La notte* (1961) and *Eclipse* (1962), which together are often called his trilogy—uses studied compositions that emphasize setting as much as actors, and a slow pace in which the performers' deliberate, somnambulistic movements are weighted even further by the director's lingering on a landscape even after people have left it. Some critics would accuse Antonioni of trying to express the boredom of his characters by boring the audience, forcing them to experience things in the same aloof, uninvolved way. The slowness of rhythm in an Antonioni film does allow us more time to be aware of the techniques in making the film, so perhaps the best way to view his films is from the director's point of view, to watch and appreciate how line, form, and movement all express internal states of detachment and isolation.

Equally austere uses of unedited material are present in some of the Scandinavian films of Carl Dreyer or Ingmar Bergman. In Dreyer's last film, *Gertrud* (1964), the director takes for his subject a relatively unknown play from around the turn of the century that is composed of a series of conversations between a liberated woman of the time and her husband and various lovers. Because he does not resort to conventional dramatic cutting but photographs the *tête-à-têtes* in long, uninterrupted, beautifully composed single takes, the effect of the very subtly spoken, almost whispered dialogue is one of highly intense but repressed emotion. Because Dreyer's treatment of the material is so radical, and the material itself so paradoxically intense but undramatic, watching *Gertrud* suggests that Dreyer's personal attitude toward his subject took precedence over the commercial storytelling requisites of making it quick-paced and easily accessible.

Similarly, several of Swedish director Ingmar Bergman's films from the late sixties onward, such as *Persona* (1967) or *The Passion of Anna* (1969), contain lengthy monologues, taken in close-up and shot without cuts, in which a character talks directly into the camera, bearing his or her soul about personal anxieties and troubles. Both Dreyer and Bergman use a visual spareness to direct our attention away from merely watching the film passively and toward actively attending to words and the messages suggested in them.

The slower rhythms of many hypersubjective films are often the reason some segments of the public find them dull, boring, or intolerable. Even the defenders of this type of cinema admit that one must often be patient to reap the rewards. But the technique of fixing an image on the screen and concentrating on it, free from the distractions that usual editing produces, can also make for films that, when appreciatively viewed, are intense and powerful.

Speeding Up   As an alternative, the hypersubjective film may resort to a faster cutting rate, which fragments the film into small bits and pieces whose juxtaposition creates a new kind of message. This technique may be used for various purposes: to show the filmmaker's attitude toward the material, to reflect the subjective processes of memory, or to manipulate time and space the same way that dreams and free association do.

In Nicolas Roeg's *The Man Who Fell to Earth* (1976), nominally a science-fiction movie about a visitor from another planet, the director quickly intercuts a wild scene of a couple making love with a simultaneous scene of a staged, theatrical sword fight in a Japanese restaurant. The result is a commentary on the combative nature of eroticism. We may attribute this commentary directly to Roeg himself, since he has deliberately used more cutting than is purely functional to tell his story. Michel Drach's *Les violins du bal* alternates what are presumably Drach's own childhood memories of the Nazi occupation with scenes of the director himself in contemporary Paris, planning his film and comparing the past events to present experiences. The film thus becomes both a movie about the occupation and a commentary on that movie.

Les violins du bal reflects also what is perhaps the most common use of fragmentary editing in personalist filmmaking, namely, the use of editing to create the sensation of a subjective, mental reality that shows memory and dream with the same immediacy as the character's present experience. The classic example of this is Alain Resnais's New Wave film, *Hiroshima, mon amour* (1959), scripted by Marguerite Duras. In *Hiroshima,* the heroine's memories of her own tragic war-time experiences are intercut with scenes depicting her current relationship with a Japanese, who in turn has his own memories of the Hiroshima atrocity (Fig. 12.4). The subjective way in which past memory affects present experience is the theme of the film, and it creates a sense of flowing mental images of the past mingling with immediate perception. The last twenty minutes or so of the film is done in a contrasting editing style, in which the very quick editing of the early segments gives way to a slower, more extended form of continuity. Once it has portrayed the subjective experience of the stirring up of memories, the film settles down to record merely the slow passage of time as the couple spend their last hours together. In both cases Resnais matches the editing, whether elaborate or deliberate, to the subjective experience of the character.

Finally there is the use of fragmentary editing to condense, expand, or interchange space and time. This is a favorite technique of films that treat the world of fantasy and dream. In Germaine Dulac's *The Seashell and the Clergyman* (1928), a deliberately dreamlike work scripted by Antonin Artaud, there are shots of a priest running through streets, but Dulac edits the shots in such a way that their sequence of images is geographically impossible: she changes locations without allowing the clergyman time to get from one place to another. It is an effective way to suggest the dream experience of running and getting nowhere. Similarly, in Maya Deren's *Meshes of the Afternoon* (1943), which we will discuss at length, Deren includes a scene in which we see a woman's foot walk from sand to grass, to concrete, to living room carpet—all in a set of four physically impossible but continuous footsteps. Deren has used the illusion of continuity to create an illogical but arresting set of images.

By speeding up the cutting rate, filmmakers produce a different kind of intensity and force the viewer to make associations between images. Where the decelerated film calls attention to elements within the frame or on the soundtrack by isolating them, the fragmentary film achieves its emphasis by juxtaposition and comparison. Some audiences may be frustrated or confused by the seemingly arbitrary, associational cutting styles of the hypersubjective cinema. Others may find the same techniques stimulating and exciting. Whatever one's personal preference, the techniques involved in slowing down or speeding up the editing of the conventional story film have formed a major part of individualist filmmakers' range of technical options.

12.4 *Hiroshima, mon amour.* In Alain Resnais's *Hiroshima, mon amour* (1959), Emmanuelle Riva and Eiji Okada play lovers inhibited by their respective wartime experiences. Note the careful use of back lighting in this still.

Dreamlike *Mise en Scène*

If deliberately subjective continuity can help to achieve a sense of dislocation in space and time, certain types of *mise en scène* may confirm in a film an atmosphere of fantasy and dream. Dreamlike *mise en scène* is usually associated with two movements in art and literature prominent during the era of the silent film: expressionism and surrealism. Both movements influenced certain films of the Silent Period, and both involved the use of bizarre or unusual imagery to reflect internalized spiritual or emotional states. Expressionist or surrealist works refer not to the real, material world but to internal, symbolic worlds of imagination and fantasy.

Expressionism   From the earliest days, the films of northern Europe had shown a strong interest in the complexity of the psyche. The German cinema was the leading example. Before World War I, *The Student of Prague* (1913) and *The Other* (1913) told dark stories about men with diabolical alter egos and split personalities. In *The*

12.5 Two examples of German expressionism. a. In *Dr. Caligari* (1919), sets and costumes were designed to suggest a shadowy world of subjective anxiety—even though the lighting used was even. b. This still from *Der Golem* (1920) suggests the origins of the modern horror movie: the filmmakers used real shadows to create an expressionist mood.

a

Golem (1915, remade in 1920) and *Homunculus* (1916), forerunners of the Frankenstein films, men created monsters who came to sad ends through loneliness and a need for revenge. After the war, German films were briefly influenced by the art movement of expressionism, a movement in which artists asserted that they should not seek to reproduce reality in their work but instead destroy appearances to arrive at nonrational values—a sort of landscape of the mind. *The Cabinet of Dr. Caligari* (1919), was an archetypal example of cinematic expressionism, used to reflect the tormented world of a madman. Although expressionism in its purest form was short-lived in the German silent film, it left a tradition taken up by not only the commercial horror film but also by the personal, emotive kind of cinema we have been discussing.

A basic principle of expressionism is that the physical surroundings of the characters reflect their internal states. Thus, films we call expressionist usually emphasize highly contrasting light and shadow, the light-dark opposition suggesting a parallel conflict between intense good and evil (Fig. 12.5). Asymmetry and distortion imply a lack of balance and stability, a world of disorder and chaos. Huge, towering sets may suggest that characters are dominated by powers beyond their

1.

control, and exaggerated make-up may make us think we are looking through men's faces to their souls.

Perhaps the chief figure to carry on the tradition of German expressionism in what we have called hypersubjective cinema has been the Swedish director Ingmar Bergman. In *Cries and Whispers* (1972), Bergman tells the story of three sisters, one of whom is dying of cancer, and the effects of impending death on their lives. Yet Bergman sets his film not in anything like our real world, but in an isolated, enclosed universe of his own devising. The characters in the film wear period costumes, but the effect is not that of a specific year or epoch. Settings and costumes emphasize stylized reds and whites throughout, suggesting, according to Bergman, passion, blood, and feminity. In *The Serpent's Egg* (1977), a direct homage to German cinema of the twenties, Bergman went to great expense to create in the studio a post–World War I Berlin with decadent nightclubs, dirty streets, and a sinister mortuary. This effect was not intended primarily as historical re-creation; it was intended to be an environment suited to the tormented internal states of the main characters. Bergman may be the main practitioner of expressionism in the modern cinema, but shades of it still appear elsewhere in unexpected places. Antonioni, in *Red Desert* (1964), had objects in the set painted unexpected colors to reflect the mental states of his severely depressed heroine. Thus fruit might appear blue-gray, or the ceiling of a bedroom might suddenly switch from white to red.

Expressionism usually involves the creation of a somewhat unreal environment in front of the camera, through the use of stylized sets and costumes, dramatic lighting, and other effects—all used to convey subjective moods of anxiety or fear. It has had a limited but important influence on hypersubjective filmmaking.

Surrealism Far wider in range were the effects of the tradition of surrealism in film, which grew out of a movement in art in the twenties. In art and literature, the surrealists sought both political and cultural revolution by replacing bourgeois notions of art with works rooted in Freudian theories of the unconscious, in the world of dreams and fantasy.

Pure surrealist filmmakers were few, but the two most important works of the movement, *Un chien andalou* (1928) and *L'age d'or* (1930), had unique impact. Both were controversial in their time and strove for the disordered, irrational, but compelling atmosphere of dreaming. In the former, made by two Spaniards, Luis Buñuel and Salvador Dali, exotic dream imagery accompanies a strange succession of inexplicable, often erotically tinged incidents between a man and woman. A man slits a woman's eyeball with a razor (Fig. 12.6). A collar and tie suddenly dance around. A woman, hair cut short and dressed as a man, pokes with a cane at an amputated hand, which is later put into a box. Two grand pianos are filled with dead donkeys. *L'age d'or,* made by Buñuel alone, scandalized audiences with a bizarre society party portraying the rich as decadently dependent on erotic fetishes, with dreamlike episodes of American-style silent comedy and with anticlerical and scatological imagery. Both films reject the conventions of narrative for a kind of free association that conservative viewers saw as an attack on middle-class values. Both present impassioned love relations disturbed by the forces of society around them.

Other films made in France at the time on the fringes of the surrealist movement reflect similar preoccupations. *The Seashell and the Clergyman* also uses irreligious and erotic imagery: a priest's robes grow on the floor like Pinocchio's nose; a woman's bodice turns into a seashell-like plate over her breasts. Jean Cocteau's *The Blood of a Poet* (1930) combines both dream and personal symbolism to reflect on the nature of consciousness, memory, intuition, and poetry. Filled with eccentric visual ideas (an imaginary hotel inhabited by strange creatures viewed through keyholes, a remembered snowball fight from Cocteau's childhood), *Blood of a Poet* is a rough sketch for such semiautobiographical works as *Orpheus* (1950) and *The Testament of Orpheus* (1959, Fig. 12.7).

In the United States, surrealism was to influence a group of filmmakers who sought to work outside the Hollywood system to begin a movement that came to be known as the *underground film* or the *New American Cinema.* The first works of this movement are known now as *trance films.* These were individually financed and produced psychodramas in which the filmmaker would act out dreams or sexual fantasies of an intensely personal and narratively oblique nature.[4]

While critics consider Maya Deren's *Meshes of the Afternoon* (1943) a watershed film of the movement, the real outbreak of activity occurred around 1947, when three young California filmmakers—Kenneth Anger, Curtis Harrington, and Gregory Markopoulos—produced *Fireworks, Fragment of Seeking,* and *Psyche* respectively. The first of these films is doubtless the most extraordinary, if only for being an explicitly sadomasochist homosexual fantasy involving a youth and some sailors. Made when Anger was sixteen, it is noted for its extensive Freudian and sexual symbolism and contains direct references to Cocteau.

The usual technique of the trance film (and surrealist film in general) is to mix incongruous elements of *mise en scène* with experimental, hypersubjective forms of continuity such as we discussed earlier. This set of techniques is perhaps nowhere better seen than in Maya Deren's *Meshes of the Afternoon.* At the beginning of the film we see a woman (played by Deren herself) begin to chase a mysterious dark figure

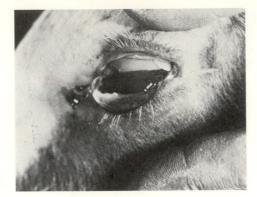

12.6 A surrealist image. The most famous shot from Luis Buñuel's and Salvador Dali's *Un chien andalou* (1928) depicts the supposed slitting of a woman's eyeball with a razor. Buñuel and Dali used the eyeball of a slaughtered animal for this shot.

12.7 Jean Cocteau. Although Jean Cocteau is not considered a true surrealist, his films use dreamlike *mise en scène*. Cocteau himself is seen here in *The Testament of Orpheus* (1959). Note how he emphasized his eyes—suggesting the subjectivity of his vision in the film.

who has left a flower in her path. Deren stops suddenly and abandons her pursuit to go up some stairs to a house. She knocks on the locked door. After dropping and retrieving a key, she enters a room scattered with newspapers. A knife inexplicably falls out of a loaf of bread on the table. The woman mounts a staircase, passing on her way a phone left off the hook. Upstairs, the woman enters a bedroom where there are curtains blowing in the wind, takes the arm up from a record turning on a phonograph, and sits down in a chair to sleep.

Deren repeats this basic structure of events three more times in the course of the fourteen-minute film, but each reprise includes variations that make it increasingly improbable, dreamlike, and disorienting. In the first variation, the woman pursued is shown as a cloaked figure with a mirror for a face; the knife and telephone appear upstairs near a bed; Deren produces the key from her mouth. As the cycle is repeated, the women seem to multiply so that at one point three identical women (who may simply be three sides of one woman) are seated at a table and watch the key turn into a knife, which one of them takes to attack her double asleep in the chair. In the final stages of the film, Deren follows a man up the stairs of the house, in much the same way she has previously followed the mirror-faced woman in an earlier variation. As he starts to make love to her on the bed, she throws the knife at him, but succeeds only in breaking a mirror image of him. In the final cycle he becomes the pursuer, entering the house and mounting the stairs, only to find the woman dead in her chair (Fig. 12.8).

Meshes of the Afternoon makes little sense as realistic storytelling. It operates rather like a dream, with the repetition of similar episodes creating a sense of fearful oppression—a sequence of events that must be repeated and cannot be stopped. The objects and visual elements in the film can all be seen as Freudian or sexual symbols. The phallic objects—the key, the knife—have a sinister, threatening quality. The mirrored face suggests a split sense of self (a theme found often in German expressionism). Yet the film is too complex to allow for a facile, easy interpretation. We cannot simply say that the woman is mentally ill, suicidal, or sexually deviant, although the film may be interpreted to indicate any of these things.

Although *Meshes of the Afternoon* shows the influence of Freud and surrealism, Deren does not merely give us a collection of symbols. Rather, part of the work's effectiveness is in the way it also uses the techniques of film to convey the subjective feelings of confusion and anxiety that such a dream or fantasy would elicit. When the woman drops the key from the top of the stairs, slow motion combines with editing in such a way that the space around the staircase is left ambiguous. The key seems to be self-propelled and falling to uncertain depths. Each time the woman or man enters the room, Deren uses the same subjective panning shot from left to right. With each subsequent use it creates an eerie sense of *déjà vu*, of repeating the same experience over again.

In another scene, the woman seems to be floating around the bedroom. Deren achieves this simply but effectively. She shows herself touching the walls and ceiling of the room (evidently standing on a chair or other support off camera), but rolls the camera dizzily about to suggest the character's lightheadedness and lack of control. Later the film puts her at various points on a staircase, moving her by pixillation rather than in real continuity. In an unreal world of a dream, the laws of gravity and physics may be distorted or ignored.

As a trance film, *Meshes of the Afternoon* suggests the dual nature of the genre. On the one hand it treats feelings and sexual anxiety of the most intensely personal sort. (The fact that Deren is the actress suggests that she is presenting her own fantasies and obsessions.) At the same time, the film expresses itself indirectly through symbolism, poetic imagery, and technical trickery. It is as if the film must say indirectly what the filmmaker may be too inhibited to say directly, just as a dream

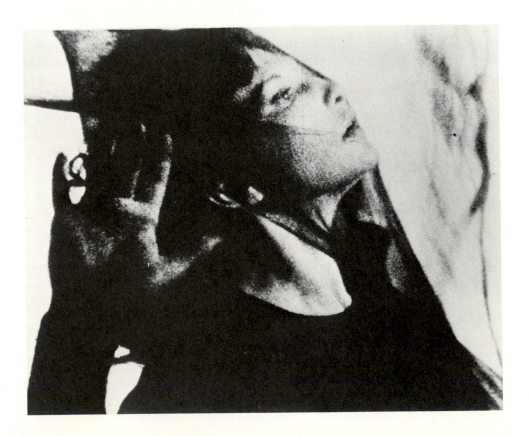

visualizes fears or concerns the conscious mind may be too inhibited to recognize. Thus, in its interest in dream, Deren's film is an outgrowth of surrealism, although it lacks the surrealist sense of striving for complete irrationality. At the same time it foreshadows the more coherent art film of the fifties and sixties in its elements of apparent autobiography.

The legacy of surrealism comes down to us today in the later work of Buñuel and a whole tradition of experimental film. But whether they use expressionist or surrealist means (the two are not always fully distinguishable), filmmakers exploring this mode of communication present an isolated, enclosed universe, the direct opposite of the world of the realist film. The environment of a personal film may be purely mental or even logically impossible apart from the world that the film sets up. One of the most famous finales in modern cinema is the ending of Federico Fellini's autobiographical *8 1/2* (1963), in which all the film's characters perform a joyous dance in a circle around the main character of Guido, the formerly depressed and indifferent film director. The characters come from different times and places in the story, and could never meet for the dance except in the character's imagination.

Such an environment is a *symbolic environment,* and the use of symbolism is a particular hallmark of certain kinds of personal cinema. We may recall here the distinction we made in Chapter 8 between the functional, transparent symbols of the standard Hollywood narrative and other, more self-conscious kinds of symbols. The hypersubjective film uses symbolism in a different way from the simple storytelling movie.

In the personal movie the use of symbols often requires interpretation by the audience if they are to appreciate the film: a person who does not interpret the symbol will miss the point. The viewer who fails to see that the dance at the end of *8 1/2* represents at least some kind of resolution or acceptance by Guido of the world around him will be unlikely to get much from the scene. Because the audience must view the symbolic meaning as intentional, this kind of symbolism emphasizes the presence of the filmmaker, the work's specific meaning for him or her.

The personal use of symbols calls for active viewing on the part of the spectator. Directors may call attention to multiple levels of interpretation they intend in their works. An explicit invitation to interpret a work sets up a kind of transaction between filmmaker and audience whereby the former addresses the latter all but directly, begging from it an awareness that the movie is not just an entertainment but a personal statement.

12.8 Maya Deren. As customary in a *trance film,* Maya Deren herself acts in *Meshes of the Afternoon* (1943).

The intentionally symbolic levels of meaning may thus often be the most important. The famous scene in Ingmar Bergman's *The Seventh Seal* (1956), in which Max von Sydow plays chess with the black-hooded figure of Death, might be confusing or irrelevant in a classic story film. When an entire film uses an extended form of symbolism, it may become an *allegory*, as is the case with *The Seventh Seal*. Hiroshi Teshigahara's *The Woman in the Dunes* (1964), about an entomologist who becomes trapped in a sand pit with a strange woman who teaches him her daily task of scooping out the sand that has fallen into the pit the night before, has little point if taken literally. But as a symbolic representation of the relative pointlessness of daily life, the story becomes personally meaningful.

Consider Fellini's use of symbolism in *Amarcord* (1974), an autobiographical work based on the director's remembrances of his childhood in Italy under Mussolini. Fellini constructs the environment of his movie around a single repeated symbolic motif: the use of imagery in which idealized objects of desire and fascination are physically elevated, with ordinary people remaining on the ground. The director includes images of a huge bonfire, a gramophone playing an anti-Fascist song in a church bell tower, a harem of Arab beauties in the top floor of a posh hotel, a huge insignia at a Fascist rally, a gigantic ocean liner that people row out in boats to see (Fig. 12.9). A madman climbs a tree and refuses to come down; falling snow looks magical from above, and the fallen snow is pushed aside into huge, monumental piles. Only at the end of the film, when Fascism is overthrown, are we presented with dominantly horizontal imagery of a table at a wedding reception. The episodes of *Amarcord* are disconnected; it is composed of incidents only tenuously related. What is important is Fellini's subjective perception of life in Fascist Italy, which is unified by its sense of towering height and imposing threat. He substitutes unity of imagery for unity of narrative line.

What we have been calling hypersubjective film may thus use one of two approaches, or combine them. It may manipulate continuity—by speeding up cutting, slowing it down, or dissolving the conventional barriers of time and

12.9 *Mise en scène* as metaphor. Federico Fellini's *Amarcord* (1974) is about childhood, when everything large looks even more imposing to the child, and also about Fascism and how it works to keep the people in a state of childlike submission.

space—or it may use different, symbolic forms of *mise en scène*, such as expressionism or surrealism, to suggest the world of dreams. In each case, however, filmmakers emphasize their work as portraying individual, subjective, personal responses to the world, highlighting through technique their emotional attitudes toward it.

A CINEMA OF INDIVIDUALISM

If autobiographical filmmaking represents personal communication in film with a strong realist emphasis, and hypersubjective filmmaking is personal filmmaking with a strong bias toward the esthetic, we may wish to ask in what ways personal movies may also lean toward the persuasive. Personal moviemaking is often criticized for its apolitical nature, in that its strong elements of subjectivity and emphasis on technique run counter to the usual political conception of man (evidenced, for example, in Socialist realism) as shaped primarily by economic forces. The kinds of subject matter typically treated in personal films—psychological maladjustment, sexuality, religious or spiritual experiences—are not the usual subjects of the political or persuasive motion picture.

On an ideological level, personal cinema preaches a value system strongly rooted in individualism, a system that values reflection and introspection as activities to be encouraged and cherished in people. Implicit in personal cinema is often the strong humanist message that an individual's feelings (often the filmmaker's) are as important as any political statement might be. The individualism in personal cinema is often in implicit protest against a society perceived as stifling human feeling and creativity.

Sometimes this ideology of individualism is conscious on the part of the filmmaker. The surrealists, for example, considered themselves a viable political movement, a branch of more traditional Socialist or Communist politics. They saw personal liberation—a freedom from sexual restraint, the self-knowledge of psychoanalysis, an appreciation for the poetic incongruities that are a part of the way the human mind works—as prerequisite of political revolution. (On this score, of course, they often alienated conventional representatives of Communist or Socialist movements.) In other cases, filmmakers have steadfastly avoided political engagement. François Truffaut, for example, has in some eighteen features consistently avoided any direct political issues, a position that has caused some commentators to fault his work as reactionary or right-wing.

This elevation of individualism to the level of a political stance can be seen in an early film scripted by Ingmar Bergman, Alf Sjöberg's *Torment* (1944). In it, a young student is persecuted by one of his teachers for falling in love with a girl whom the teacher is also involved with. While the film is not without underlying political significance (some commentators note that Sjöberg encouraged a resemblance between the actor who plays the teacher and Joseph Goebbels), its main emphasis is on the young man's personal problems. The film is in part autobiographical, a protest against what Bergman saw as an oppressive school system; but its techniques hark back to German expressionism, and its emphasis is on the particular individual rather than students in general. As Bergman's first successful work in film, *Torment* introduces what is to become the implicit ideology of all his work: that human beings are by nature fragile, sensitive, scared creatures, that the human condition is one of guilt and fear. The film was in its time prophetic of the themes and preoccupations that were to dominate much of the postwar art cinema.[5]

On this ideological level, one cannot fully discuss either Bergman or other examples of subjective or personal cinema without also considering existentialism as a dominant philosophical movement in the mid-twentieth century. The whole phenomenon of the postwar art film may have its roots in expressionism and surrealism, but its political and philosophical bias is heavily toward an existentialist view of the world. Existentialism was the fashionable philosophy in intellectual circles in the fifties and early sixties, to the point that much of the existentialist sensibility of the period was a vulgarization of the philosophy itself. Its ideas were popularized by journalists, commercialized by superficial, would-be philosophers, and absorbed into the beatnik movement of that time. Indeed, some of the films we will discuss might be considered examples of second-hand, predigested existentialism— more viable as art, perhaps, than systematic philosophy. Still, let us summarize some of the ways in which movies expressed themes of the movement, allowing that any such brief summary must partake of some of the vulgarization and imprecision by which existentialism was popularized.[6]

The philosophy of existentialism grew up in the nineteenth century out of a sense that the usual formulas and explanations for describing man's place in the world had become inadequate. Organized religion and traditional political thought came to seem antiquated in a new industrial society. A belief in God no longer appeared the correct starting place for considering the world, but neither did the new industrial order's trust in science, which can be a depersonalized, equally unsatisfying alternative. We may see existentialism as a partial attempt to adapt human values to a world made mechanical by technological advancement.

Some commentators would consider the formula "existence precedes essence" as the cornerstone of existential philosophy. That is, human beings can begin only with their own experience—not with God or with scientific law—in understanding the world. The themes approached in the writings of existentialist philosophers and in the work of existentialist artists cluster around three different areas. First, they emphasize the subjectivity of experience, and, by extension, the subjectivity of truth and meaning in the world. Second, they see alienation and anguish as characteristic and inescapable states in modern human beings. Third, they emphasize the recognition of free choice and responsibility as the basis of human morality and ethics, as the way of achieving meaning in life. Each of these themes is significant in much of world cinema, and particularly European cinema, after World War II. They are the themes that give these works, which by nature emphasize the personal function of communication, ideological unity or consistency.

The Subjectivity of Experience   We have already discussed certain techniques used in the creation of what we have termed hypersubjective cinema, and we have considered in particular modes of editing that seem to accelerate or decelerate time. These techinques reflect very precisely the existentialist view that makes a distinction between objective and subjective time. Time exists as something meaningful only as it is experienced; it may fly or stand still depending on the individual and the surroundings.

   Similarly, the existentialist feels that the past and future are not really separable from the present. The past continues to influence people in their present actions, forming a part of the subjective way in which people view the world—both in terms of their own past experience and the experiences of society in general.[7] Thus the flashbacks in *Hiroshima, mon amour* illustrate not only how the past is a part of the present for the heroine (who must overcome her memories in order to have a successful love relation in the present) but suggest the influence of historical events in forming the collective or communal subjectivity of nations and peoples. The woman may be seen as representing France, traumatized by the Occupation; the man is her Japanese counterpart, traumatized by Hiroshima. The subjectivity of the past and the expectations for the future are what make the present meaningful for all of us.

   This emphasis on subjectivity leads existentialist philosophers to place great emphasis on the meaningfulness (or meaninglessness) of everyday experience. We have, as it were, only the present in which to act: the past is finished, the future not yet here. The deceleration techniques used in, let us say, *L'avventura* emphasize the banality and boredom of everyday experience, even for the rich and privileged. In François Truffaut's *The Soft Skin* (1964), the director tells an ordinary, somewhat routine love story, but there is an emphasis throughout the film on the everyday objects that surround the adulterous lovers. One critic's review mentioned the work's endless procession of "door-handles, keys, gear-levers, airplane instrument panels, and doors, radio buttons, light switches, lift panels, starter buttons, petrol-tank caps, pens, pump-dials, telephone dials. . . ."[8] Yet the end result of this technique is to emphasize the subjective, moment-to-moment experience of the philandering hero (and the film is reportedly at least somewhat autobiographical). Truffaut may not be what one would call an overtly existential director, but the attitude that infuses *The Soft Skin* is one of concentrating on the concrete moment and finding meaning (or lack of it) simply in the material details of existence, as experienced by a character.[9]

Alienation and Anguish　To the existentialist, alienation (a sense of being disconnected from one's surroundings) and anguish (the sense of unmotivated fear of nothing in particular) are signs that modern men and women are unable to come to terms with the nature of the world. Loneliness, dread, and the inability to communicate are the rule rather than exceptions. Roberto Rossellini's abandonment of neorealism in the fifties signaled the shift toward such themes. With films like *Stromboli* (1949), *Europa 51* (1951), and *Voyage in Italy* (1953), Rossellini invariably cast Ingrid Bergman as a foreign woman in Italy at odds with unfamiliar surroundings that in one way or another reflect her internal state of detachment and spiritual isolation. Her wanderings through strange environments have metaphysical significance, turning neorealist landscapes into landmarks in a spiritual search for self (Fig. 12.10).

　　Rossellini's work from this period is perhaps better appreciated now than it was in its time, but it had great influence both on the French New Wave and on Antonioni.[10] In Antonioni's *Red Desert*, the wife of an Italian industrialist becomes withdrawn and passive, presumably due to some psychological maladjust-

12.10 From neorealism to alienation. (a) Roberto Rossellinni's *Voyage in Italy* and (b) Michelangelo Antonioni's *Camille Without Ca-* mellias, both made in 1953, show a tension between the troubled emotional states of their heroines and their impersonal surroundings.

a　　　　　b

ment. But Antonioni portrays her surroundings, the industrial city of Ravenna, as contributing to her sense of oppression and detachment with their coldness, their lack of vegetation, their pollution. Alienated by industrial life, she seeks refuge in a loveless affair.

In much of the modern personal cinema, sex becomes a substitute for human communication, as in *Red Desert* or Bernardo Bertolucci's *The Last Tango in Paris* (1972). In *Last Tango*, a couple decides to enter into a relationship based entirely on sex, deliberately keeping from each other all other aspects of their lives. The relation is of course unsatisfying, but when the man seeks to enlarge it, he creates a situation the younger woman cannot tolerate. The problem becomes a symptom of the depersonalization of modern society.

At the same time, the inadequacy of religion becomes a common theme in the work of a number of directors. In both Robert Bresson's *Diary of a Country Priest* (1950) and Ingmar Bergman's *Winter Light* (1963), clergymen in rural communities face personal crises in which they can no longer communicate with their parishioners, can no longer successfully lead them to Christ, can no longer confidently have faith themselves (Fig. 12.11). Yet the secular religions of science and psychology often fare no better. *Face to Face* (1976), Bergman's study of a psychologist facing an emotional break-down, suggests the same sense of quandary, of an inability to believe in anything.

In short, what one might call existentialist personal cinema dwells on the inadequacies of formerly successful social structures—the working world, marriage and the family, organized religion—to satisfy human needs. For people are by nature alienated, dissatisfied, unsure of themselves in the modern world.

Choice and Responsibility   Liberation from alienation and anguish comes from freeing oneself from the paralysis of excessive reflection. The passive, indecisive, overly reflective hero is a standby in the work of the directors we have been discussing.

MOMA/Audio Brandon

12.11 The failure of religion. In *The Diary of a Country Priest* (1950), Robert Bresson explores the seeming inability of religion to provide an alternative to modern despair. Bresson's films offer a view of the world that is both religious and existentialist in orientation.

L'avventura ends simply with one character patting the head of another, making a final attempt to communicate genuinely and to act with some decisive commitment toward another.

This notion of commitment and acceptance of responsibility is the key theme of one of Jean-Luc Godard's most personal early works, *My Life to Live* (1962), in which a young woman drifts into prostitution and is finally murdered by her pimp when she falls genuinely in love with someone (Fig. 12.12). But at one point in the film, the girl, Nana, gives a quiet speech in a café about responsibility in which she embraces the existentialist stance. "I lift my hand; I am responsible. I smoke a cigarette; I am responsible. I am unhappy; I am responsible." In another scene, Nana goes to the movies and sees Carl Dreyer's 1928 *The Passion of Joan of Arc*. Godard intercuts shots of Joan on screen with those of Nana in the theater. Joan achieves sainthood by decisively choosing to die, despite all of her uncertainty about the correctness of her choice. Nana is martyred in her own way, and the implication is that she is equally eligible for canonization because she takes full responsibility for her fate. She accepts her life as a streetwalker and the fact that she has chosen it.

By the late sixties this emphasis on commitment and responsibility in part grew into the political radicalism that produced, among other things, the events of May 1968 in Paris and the student and minority group demonstrations in the United

MOMA/Courtesy Corinth Films

States. In films, if not necessarily in philosophy, the apolitical, individualist existentialism of the early part of the decade grew into a more programmatic assertion of the rights of the individual over an alienating, corporate state. Filmmakers like Antonioni (in *Zabriskie Point,* 1970) and Godard (in *La Chinoise,* 1968) began examining political radicals and their actions as one form of confrontation with the existential dilemma. But we have considered this trend in part in our chapter on persuasive or political filmmaking.

In retrospect, then, the period around 1960 represents a full flowering of this personal, subjective, existentialist cinema. With *The 400 Blows,* subjective, apolitical autobiography achieved a first milestone; *Hiroshima, mon amour* and *L'avventura* developed their techniques of hypersubjectivity to a new level of sophistication; Jean-Luc Godard's *Breathless* pointed to a kind of nihilistic individualism. But the popular or mass market was conquered by Federico Fellini's *La dolce vita* (1959), a film combining autobiography and hypersubjectivity with all of the existentialist themes we have discussed. It assumes the subjectivity of experience, takes alienation and anguish to be characteristic of modern life, and sees choice and commitment as the only solution. It also proved at the box office to be one of the top-grossing non-Hollywood films of all time.

The roots of Fellini's cinema are in neorealism, and the director was formerly a coscripter of Rossellini's *Open City.* In Fellini's early films, such as *The White Sheik* (1952) and *I vittelloni* (1953), he emphasized not so much the social concern of De Sica or early Rossellini as he did the poetic side of Italian provincial life, remembered from his own childhood. The films are photographed with a neorealist look, but a Fellini film always has a strongly subjective cast: everything is seen through his eyes, eyes that emphasize small elements of the grotesque, the lonely, the desolate. As the 1950s progressed and Fellini made films starring his wife, Giulietta Masina, he was developing a repertoire of religious symbols and personal images that were to mark his films as distinctly his own. As one critic pointed out, every Fellini film has its abandoned, empty city squares or its drunken revelers working their way through the streets in the early hours of the morning.[11]

With the sixties, however, Fellini began to work in directly autobiographical forms. If such later works as *8 1/2* and *Amarcord* have moved into the realm of dreamlike imagery and ingenious shuffling of space and time, *La dolce vita* represents a perfect transition picture in which we can see a tradition of neorealism shifting decisively toward a far more personal kind of moviemaking.

12.12. "I lift my hand; I am responsible." In a discourse on existentialist themes, Jean-Luc Godard tells the story of a prostitute in *My Life to Live* (1962)—how she reacts to the world around her and how she takes responsibility for her actions.

La dolce vita is the story of Marcello (Marcello Mastroianni), a reporter for a Roman scandal sheet who specializes in covering jet setters. The film is three hours long, and, although filled with incident, contains very little developed plot. It emphasizes instead the daily life of its main character. In his professional life, Marcello covers the visit to Italy of an American movie star named Sylvia (Anita Ekberg) and the reported apparition of the Virgin Mary to two children. In Marcello's personal life, he is involved with Maddalena, a wealthy, bored, oversexed woman, and lives with Emma, who has become depressed and suicidal due to unfulfilled needs for security, marriage, and a family. He takes his father out for a night on the town when the older man visits Rome. An intellectual writer friend named Steiner kills himself and his children. Little else happens in the movie, except for the ever-present parties and nightclub acts that make up much of its background.

Marcello is clearly something of a stand-in for Fellini, and the director himself has described the work as his observations of Roman society of the time. Having himself been a caricaturist for a newspaper and a part of the Roman film scene for over a decade, he was clearly familiar with the milieu he was portraying. Yet Fellini makes no claims to objectivity. "The public demands exaggeration," Marcello says at one point of his profession as a reporter, adding that he could report events faithfully if he wanted to. This may well be Fellini excusing his work's obvious excesses, putting it in a context that goes beyond the supposedly objective school of Italian neorealism.

Marcello's detachment from and fundamental indifference to others unifies the episodes of the film thematically. When he comes home after a night with Maddalena, he finds Emma unconscious in a suicide attempt and rushes her to the hospital—only to try to telephone Maddalena shortly after. When his father comes to visit, only after the old man has become ill and must leave does his son urge him to stay an extra day and spend some time with him. When the police ask Marcello about Steiner's suicide, he says simply, "He was a friend, but I didn't see him often." At the end of *La dolce vita*, a young girl he has met earlier tries to talk to him across a shallow stretch of water at the beach, but the waves and noise frustrate communication and he walks away. Inability to achieve human contact is a problem shared by almost everyone in the movie. Fellini portrays it as a malaise of the times.

The outlining of this spiritual problem becomes more important to the film than telling a story. Fellini constructs whole sequences as demonstrations of the fleeting quality of the sensual pleasures that people use as a substitute for genuine love. His favorite tactic is to guide a long scene through a series of measured mood changes that invariably end in sadness, using music to underline the shifts of feeling. When Marcello takes his father to the nightclub and introduces him to a French dancer there, the music calculatedly changes from a wild Charleston to a sad trumpet solo and finally a romantic waltz as the old man dances with the younger woman.

The incidents of this same scene are linked not so much narratively as by their relation to the themes of disillusion, frustration, and loneliness. The father tells of having watched a beautiful woman strip in a Paris nightclub once—only to find out the stripper was a female impersonator. The Charleston recalls the younger days the father has mentioned, foreshadowing his coming attempt to recapture his youth. The trumpet soloist's act features the bursting of a balloon and the player's inability to reach a high note. As his father dances, Marcello comments that he has never really known his father, who was always traveling when he was growing up. The father's visit is unrelated to the rest of the film, but the sequence emphasizes the futility of pleasure seeking and the emptiness of even the closest of family relationships. Marcello's father and his friend Steiner suggest a past that now may seem more satisfying than the present.

La dolce vita was in its time a controversial film for its mingling of the themes of religion and sex, since it implied that the latter had replaced the former in contemporary life. The opening scene shows a statue of Christ being transported by helicopter to the Vatican. Later a love goddess appears from a plane in the form of Sylvia, an event as vulgarized and exploitative as the supposed appearance of the Virgin Mary that follows it. The film constantly presents a confusion between spiritual and secular values, as seen in Sylvia's wearing of an outfit imitating a priest's garb for her visit to Saint Peter's.

In Fellini's world, sex has become a public rather than a private event. We see this in Nadia's party celebrating the annulment of her marriage, at which she does a striptease for her friends. In one witty shot, Fellini shows her lying on the floor, undressing, with the feet of onlookers in the corner of the frame, tapping to the music (Fig. 12.13). At another orgylike party, some characters indulge in sexual adventures, while others seek their spiritual excitement in séances and hunting for ghosts. The intellectual world of Steiner, the world of books and art, offers no alternative: while Marcello envies Steiner for the seriousness of his writing, and Emma admires his family and children, the man turns out to be locked into an unexplained and probably inexplicable sense of futility and impotence.

Thus Fellini creates a picture of upper-class Rome in 1960 as mediated through his personal vision. The techniques of the movie emphasize the subjectivity of experience. Point-of-view shots frequently show us exactly what Marcello is seeing, as when Steiner's wife, answering the door, looks straight into the camera and says "I've been expecting you." The camera moves often during *La dolce vita*, but invariably *with* the action. When people dance, it follows with the same pace and rhythm. When Marcello mounts a staircase, as when he follows Sylvia to the top of Saint Peter's, again the camera is close behind, giving the audience a sense of breathless chase. As candle-carrying party-goers proceed through a castle in a mock hunt for ghosts, we get no idea of the total layout of the surrounding architecture. Rather, we experience a sense of moving through darkened, undefined corridors and rooms.

At the end of *La dolce vita*, Marcello announces that he has given up writing, both serious and journalistic, to do advertising. With this admission, Fellini may be expressing self-consciousness about making a film whose subject matter is on the surface so exploitative. Like Emma in the film, who prays to the virgin amidst hypocrisy, Fellini appears to be attempting a sincere statement on morality and commitment within a sensational context. In doing so, he shows both a showman's ability to get an audience as well as a potent and purposeful seriousness.

Audio Brandon/Ivy Film, NY/National Telefilm Associates, Inc.

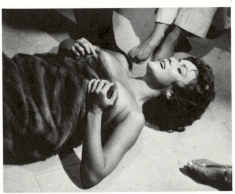

12.13 Women in *La dolce vita*. Although the main protagonist of Federico Fellini's *La dolce vita* (1960) is male, the two women characters shown here, Emma and Nadia, symbolize what Fellini sees as two alternatives offered by modern society—despair leading to suicide or self-abandonment to sensual pleasure.

Film as a personal, subjective medium has been a less prominent subject for film theorists than have issues of realism, political effectiveness, or formalist esthetics. Although many critics have admired the work of the filmmakers we have discussed, two movements in film criticism have shown particular interest in individualist or personal cinema: surrealism and auteurism. Both movements are French in origin, and while we have considered auteurism with regard to the Hollywood narrative film, its premises have influenced other schools of filmmaking, especially the French New Wave.

Surrealism

Although the surrealists themselves made only a few films, the writers and artists of the movement were often avid moviegoers. Their tastes ran to vulgar, commercial, mass-audience products, precisely in reaction against bourgeois notions of art and culture. The surrealists lauded the American silent comedy, for example, well before it became truly respectable to do so, and many of them have praised genres such as the horror film or the melodrama for their uneasy confrontations between reality and the fantastic.[12]

The surrealists, of course, saw the world of dream and the unconscious as the major realm of human creativity. Jacques Brunius, an actor, writer, and filmmaker connected with the movement, has suggested that the film medium itself is by nature surrealist, that it produces and exploits a dreamlike state in the viewer. He has written:

The darkness of the auditorium, tantamount to the closing of the eyelids on the retina, and for thought, to the darkness of the unconscious; the crowd that surrounds and isolates you, the deliciously stupid music, the stiffness of the neck necessary for the orientation of one's gaze, provide a state like being half asleep; . . . Neither chronological order nor relative values of duration are real. Contrary to the theater, film, like thought, like the dream, chooses some gestures, defers or enlarges them, eliminates others, travels many hours, centuries, kilometres in a few seconds, speeds up, slows down, stops, goes backwards. It is impossible to imagine a truer mirror of mental performance. Despite the wishes of the majority of filmmakers the cinema is the least realistic of the arts, even when photographic reproduction succeeds in creating an illusion of the concrete reality of each separate element.[13]

Brunius's position has been taken up recently even by nonsurrealist Freudian critics, who suggest that the medium is a kind of mental writing in which subconscious elements may emerge in images and juxtapositions.[14]

The result of this dreamlike nature of film is personal rather than rational. Surrealist filmmaker Luis Buñuel has observed, "Because it acts in a direct manner upon the spectator in presenting to him concrete people and objects, because it isolates him by virtue of the silence and darkness from what might be called his 'psychic habitat,' the cinema is capable of putting him into a state of ecstasy more effectively than any other mode of human expression."[15] To the surrealist, the personal function of cinema is its primary one; its capacity to communicate deep, often irrational or unbridled feelings—and particularly erotic excitement—is its primary glory (Fig. 12.14).

Of course most of the films the surrealists admired did not intentionally strive for this dreamlike quality. Rather, they represented a kind of "found" surrealism. Often the surrealists would admire the way certain shots, taken completely out of context, might be exciting, bizarre, or beautiful.[16] They derided, by contrast, the

12.14 Surrealism in film and painting. What Luis Buñuel offers in his film *The Exterminating Angel* (1964) is comparable to Salvador Dali's painting *Cardinal, Cardinal!* (1934). Both emphasize incongruous juxtapositions of objects as well as social decay in modern civilization.

impressionist movement in the French film of the twenties, which tried to develop a full range of camera techniques and cinematic devices to raise movies to the full level of a serious art form (see Chapter 13, Esthetic Cinema). Such an attempt to make film into art was, to the surrealists, too calculated, elitist, and ultimately reactionary. They preferred films in which the artist's subconscious could speak in unexpected, uncontrived ways, precisely because an artist may be unaware of what his or her work is really saying.

Surrealism has influenced a whole branch of serious film criticism, particularly in France.[17] Today, certain partisans of melodrama, science fiction, and horror films look to surrealism for a kind of intellectual respectability. They argue that these genres are the most successful use of the film medium precisely because they go to the depths of human fear and anxiety. The French film journal *Positif,* significantly influenced by surrealism, emerged in the seventies as the most serious publication in France to champion the commercial Hollywood film—even while exalting such figures as Buñuel and Fellini.[18]

Surrealism is, therefore, both a movement in filmmaking itself and a movement in film criticism. As the latter, it suggests that successful filmmaking emphasizes the personal function over the realist, the persuasive, or even the esthetic.

Auteurism

Auteurism is most commonly thought of as a method for seeing stylistic and thematic unity in the work of directors working under the commercial Hollywood genre system. It also has a theoretical basis that suggests a strong bias toward the individualism of much personal cinema.

In 1948 Alexandre Astruc wrote a famous essay in which he coined the term *caméra-stylo* ("camera-pen"). Astruc argued that the modern film had the technical ability "to become a means of writing just as flexible and subtle as written language." In part Astruc opposed adaptation, the use of standards and material from literature and the other arts as subject matter for movies or standards for judging them. Calling for a cinema in which "the scriptwriter ceases to exist," Astruc wrote: "Direction is no longer a means of illustrating or presenting a scene, but a true act of writing. The filmmaker-author writes with his camera as a writer writes with his pen." (Fig. 12.15) The notion of the *auteur* became for Astruc a way of advocating direct expression by filmmakers of their ideas and emotions. Although Astruc was partly talking about the film medium's ability to present abstract ideas, he was also clearly calling for an individualist freedom of expression.[19]

This same approach to auteurism is found in François Truffaut's own early writings as a film critic. His most famous essay, "A Certain Tendency in the French Cinema," is also an attack on a tradition of literary adaptation in French films of the

Hampton/*La Proie Pour L'Ombre* produced by Marceau Cocinor.

forties and fifties. Truffaut lashed out against Jean Aurenche and Pierre Bost, calling them formulaic, mechanical adapters of literary masterpieces. To Truffaut, these screenwriters lacked a sense of the true spirit of the original works, a genuine feeling for the capacities of the film medium, and all originality or creativity.[20] As a theoretical leader of the New Wave, Truffaut established the movement as one in which filmmakers tried to express themselves spontaneously and immediately, by writing and directing their own films and by rejecting the traditional division of labor in commercial filmmaking. Truffaut wrote:

It seems to me that tomorrow's film will be even more personal than a novel, more individual and autobiographical than a confession or a private diary. Young cinéastes will express themselves in the first person, and talk about things that have happened to them; perhaps an account of their first love or their most recent, the growth of their political awareness, or a travel tale, an illness, their military service, their marriage, their last holidays. . . . Tomorrow's film will not be made by employees going about their daily routine, but by artists for whom the shooting of a film constitutes an exciting and exalting adventure.[21]

Auteurism may thus be seen as referring not only to those Hollywood studio directors who succeeded in putting a personal stamp on their work, but also to writer-directors who could conceive their ideas directly for film. Many of the French filmmakers Truffaut admired—like Jean Cocteau, Roger Leenhardt, and Robert Bresson—wrote and directed their own works, using film to express their own personal involvements and feelings. Subsequent generations of filmmakers that have followed the New Wave have done so too.

Critics who cite directors like Bergman, Fellini, Antonioni, and Truffaut as the great filmmakers generally embrace, either implicitly or explicitly, this latter form of auteurism. In all of these men's works we may find elements of autobiography, extreme subjectivity, and existential thought. For such critics, emotion in film is meaningful when traced back to a single person who has felt it: an author and source of the message whose sensibility the audience can share. For these critics, great cinema is personal cinema, a cinema of the subjective individual.

SUMMARY

Personal cinema involves film that expresses the point of view of a single individual, for which one filmmaker is the dominant "voice."

There are three aspects to personal cinema: (1) autobiography, (2) hypersubjective technique, and (3) a philosophical bias toward subjectivity and individualism.

12.15 *Le caméra-stylo* in practice. Known as a critic, Alexandre Astruc is also a highly regarded filmmaker. In *Shadow of Adultery* (1961), Astruc achieved what commentator Joel Magny called "a cinema founded exclusively on the comprehension of space and time by the camera."

Autobiographical films are those in which filmmakers use the medium to relate past experiences from their lives. François Truffaut's *The 400 Blows* is probably the single most influential example of autobiographical filmmaking.

Hypersubjective cinema refers to the use of certain techniques to capture the qualities peculiar to individual, subjective experience. Through editing, filmmakers may slow down or speed up the experience of passing time. Through atypical styles of *mise en scène*, such as expressionism or surrealism, filmmakers can present their internal states of mind. Maya Deren's *Meshes of the Afternoon* is a key example of a film that communicates through such a symbolic, metaphorical environment.

Individualist cinema may be best understood in the context of existentialism as a dominant postwar philosophy. Personalist filmmakers consistently emphasize in their movies such typically existentialist themes as the subjectivity of experience, the oppressiveness of alienation and anguish in a postindustrial world, and the importance of choice and responsibility in modern life. Federico Fellini's *La dolce vita* is an archetypal example of film exploration of these preoccupations.

Two main schools of critical thinking have championed such personalist filmmaking. Surrealist theorists have argued that film is an inherently surrealist medium, one that duplicates the sensations of dreaming. Auteurist film critics, such as Alexandre Astruc and François Truffaut, have argued for films that are as subjective and individually expressive as any works of literature or painting.

NOTES

1 Not every commentator would agree. William Bayer writes: "How can one watch this film about the battering of a child and not read into it an indictment of everything in bourgeois culture, everything that is heavy, routine, stifling, without compassion?" But Bayer also notes, comparing Truffaut's film to *Bicycle Thief:* "De Sica's film is focused on the outside forces that crush the individual; Truffaut's film is about the inner life of a child who resists." See *The Great Movies* (New York: Grosset and Dunlap, 1973), pp. 217–218.

2 Vincent Canby, "Truffaut's *Love on the Run:* An 'Au Revoir' to Old Friends," *New York Times,* Apr. 22, 1979, Sec. 2, pp. 19, 21.

3 Marcel Martin develops this notion of de-dramatization, arguing that what Antonioni began with *L'avventura* became one of the key techniques of the cinema of the seventies. See "Notes sur le cinéma des années 70, " *Ecran 76,* No. 53 (Dec. 1976), 36.

4 P. Adams Sitney is the principle source of the term *trance film.* See *Visionary Film* (New York: Oxford, 1974), pp. 3–19.

5 See in particular the discussion of *Torment* in Benjamin Dunlap and Paula Franklin, *Cinemat-*

ic Eye, *Study Guide I* (Columbia: South Carolina Educational TV Network, 1978), 5–7.

6 For further themes of existentialism, see Kurt F. Reinhardt, *The Existentialist Revolt: The Main Themes and Phases of Existentialism* (New York: Ungar, 1960), pp. 228–243.

7 Ibid., pp. 237–239.

8 C. G. Crisp, *François Truffaut* (New York: Praeger, 1972), p. 78.

9 One may consider *The Soft Skin* as part of a "subjective experience of sexual indulgence" genre of film, comparable to such other works as *Red Desert*, Jorn Donner's *Black on White* (1968), or John Schlesinger's *Sunday, Bloody Sunday* (1971). See also Allen Thirer, "The Existential Play in Truffaut's Early Films," *Literature/Film Quarterly*, 5 (Summer 1977), 183–188.

10 "It might be noted also that Rossellennui preceded Antoniennui by several years." See Andrew Sarris, *The American Cinema: Directors and Directions, 1929–1968* (New York: Dutton, 1968), p. 152.

11 Gilbert Salachas, *Federico Fellini*, trans. Rosalie Siegel (New York: Crown, 1969), pp. 39–51.

12 See in particular J. H. Matthews, *Surrealism and Film* (Ann Arbor: University of Michigan Press, 1971); Paul Hammond, ed., *The Shadow and Its Shadow: Surrealist Writings on Cinema* (London: British Film Institute, 1978); Ado Kyrou, *Le surréalisme au cinéma*, 2nd ed. (Paris: Le Terrain Vague, 1963); Alain and Odette Virmaux, *Les surréalistes et le cinéma* (Paris: Seghers, 1976).

13 Jacques Brunius, "Crossing the Bridge," in *The Shadow and Its Shadow*, ed. Paul Hammond, p. 61.

14 See in particular Christian Metz, "Le film de fiction et son spectateur," *Communications*, No. 23 (1975), 108–135; John Michaels, "Film and Dream," *Journal of the University Film Association*, 32 (Winter–Spring 1980), 85–87.

15 Luis Buñuel, "Cinema, Instrument of Poetry," in *The Shadow and Its Shadow*, ed. Paul Hammond, p. 66.

16 See in particular Ado Kyrou, "The Marvellous Is Popular," in *The Shadow and Its Shadow*, ed. Paul Hammond, pp. 39–41; J. H. Matthews, *Surrealism and the American Feature Film* (Boston: Twayne, 1979).

17 In the United States, the chief surrealist critic is Parker Tyler. See, among other works, *The Hollywood Hallucination* (New York: Simon and Schuster, 1970); *Sex, Psyche, Etcetera in the Film* (New York: Horizon, 1969).

18 *Positif*'s history underlines the ambiguity of the surrealist position. During the fifties and early sixties *Positif* was both the leading postsurrealist and leftist French film journal. Its current championing of Hollywood film, although consistent with its past, puts the magazine in the eyes of many to the right of a number of other journals in France today.

19 Alexandre Astruc, "The Birth of a New Avant-Garde: La Caméra-stylo," in *The New Wave*, ed. Peter Graham (New York: Doubleday, 1968), pp. 17–23.

20 François Truffaut, "A Certain Tendency of the French Cinema," in *Movies and Methods*, ed. Bill Nichols (Berkeley: University of California Press, 1976), pp. 224–237; also in *The New Wave*, ed. Peter Graham.

21 François Truffaut, quoted in C. G. Crisp, *François Truffaut*, 15.

Chapter 13 / Esthetic Cinema

The esthetic function of communication sees the message not as something referring directly to the real world, or moving an audience to action, or expressing the sender's feelings, but rather as something to be enjoyed and experienced for its own formal and artistic qualities. The form of the message becomes exciting in itself. We appreciate the message as an artificially constructed device, and we take pleasure as much in seeing how it is constructed (and how it compares with other works of art) as we do in discovering any further meaning the work may have.

One may well imagine in film a continuum between the realistic and the esthetic. At one extreme would be the purely realistic, completely functional film. The movie would be important only for what it represents, not for what it is. For example, a videotape taken in a bank during a hold-up has little or no esthetic interest, yet it is highly realistic and can be used to prove the identity of the robber.[1] At the other extreme, a completely abstract animated cartoon might look like nothing in particular but still please the eye with color, line, and form. In most movies there is some interplay between how the movie refers to the real world and how the filmmaker's techniques make it different from the real world.

In this chapter we will discuss those films whose bias is heavily toward the esthetic side of the continuum. In the Hollywood cinema, genres such as the historical spectacle, the science fiction film, and the musical are all forms of expression somewhat more weighted toward taking pleasure in the medium for its own sake, an exploration of technical and special effects. With the experimental film, we find an esthetic approach to animation, abstract film, and schools of *minimal* or *structural* cinema. In both cases, however, the film becomes something to be admired for its own sake, as an artifact rather than as a portrayal of the real world.

Both of these traditions may be traced back to Georges Méliès, to whom film historians customarily oppose the Lumière brothers. If the Lumières took a documentary approach, recording aspects of reality faithfully and with minimal manipulation, Méliès emphasized two things in his work. He shot in a tightly controlled studio environment, making free and creative use of artificially constructed sets, and he used the continuity devices available in film to create magical effects.

Méliès's background was, of course, in magic lantern shows and stage magic, and film was to him an extension of these two popular theatrical traditions of the nineteenth century. Avoiding the practice of open-air location shooting that was also developing in his time, Méliès painted all his sets, building *trompe-l'oeil* perspective into them. He did this partly out of economic and technical necessity;

433

although the sets may look stylized and artificial today, according to some reports (which may be apocryphal) audiences of the time took some of them for real. They were frightened, for example, by the supposed eruption of a volcano in a Méliès film, in much the same manner that they were supposedly taken in by Lumière's train coming into the station.[2]

Méliès made films on various subjects and in various styles. Some were elaborate studio reconstructions of actual events, done often with extensive research; they might be on recent subjects (*The Coronation of Edward VII,* 1902) or historical subjects (*Joan of Arc,* 1900; *Benvenuto Cellini,* 1904). Only recently have film scholars discovered that such Méliès comedies as *The Mad Kitchen* (1904) and *The Infernal Cakewalk* (1903) were skillfully made and highly advanced for their time.[3] Méliès was a highly prolific filmmaker and made several hundred short films from 1896 to 1913.

But the pioneer filmmaker's primary reputation rests on his science fiction and fantasy films. Some were adapted from fairy tales or literature (*Cinderella,* 1899; *The Damnation of Faust,* 1903), and he is particularly famous for his adaptations of Jules Verne and similar stories of adventure and exploration. By far his most famous is *A Trip to the Moon* (1902), considered the first major science fiction movie. In it, Méliès used imaginative stage trickery, whimsical settings, and frequent touches of satire on the world of science. It was enormously popular, though Méliès was soon victimized by entrepreneurs who pirated his work and was outclassed by those who moved faster than he did in developing the medium even further.

The principle in Méliès's fantastic films is an appealing one that makes them effective even for audiences today. That is, his pictures assume that if one must use artificially dressed sets, it makes sense to use subjects that allow them to be as fanciful and elaborate as possible, subjects that could effectively be shot no other way. A whole tradition in Hollywood cinema came from Méliès's use of elaborate sets, for in genres like the historical spectacle or the science-fiction film audiences can take pleasure in cinematic environments of great imagination, whimsy, and decorative style that are hard to achieve through location shooting.

a

b

The fantastic films of Méliès made use not only of a whole repertoire of stage magic for the screen, but also established a tradition of movie special effects. Méliès experimented with almost all the devices of continuity we discussed earlier—fades, dissolves, stop motion, reverse action, over- and undercranking, as well as double exposure, masking, and animation techniques. These effects appealed to mass audiences as magic, but the surrealists also admired them as techniques to allow the cinema to go beyond simple realism. We see in a whole tradition of experimental film (in *Meshes of the Afternoon,* for example, discussed in the preceding chapter) a Méliès-like tradition of cinematic trickery used to somewhat different ends.

Let us consider both these lines of esthetic cinema—the spectacle film and the experimental film—as extensions of the Méliès approach to filmmaking (Fig. 13.1). Both forms provide the filmmaker with opportunities for great flights of imagination and cinematic fancy. The film's credibility (its acknowledged reference to the real world) becomes less important than its visual creativity. These films use the techniques of the medium to amaze us with their technical expertise or visual beauty.

THE SPECTACLE FILM

The spectacle film is Hollywood's form of purely esthetic cinema, the genre in which the most attention is given to purely visual effects and elaborate imagery. Hollywood spectacles, although they certainly partake of storytelling traditions, combine these with the use of the medium for its own sake. We may examine three subgenres of Hollywood spectacle—historical spectacle, the science-fiction film, and the musical.

Historical Spectacle[4]

Historical spectacle occupies a special place in the history of cinema, for its development is uniquely linked to that of the Hollywood genre film. The first big historical spectacles came from Italy, with its heritage of classical antiquity. The films of Enrico Guazzoni, such as *Quo Vadis?* (1912), were among the very first to use three-dimensional, artificially constructed scenery; those of Giovanni Pastrone, especially *Cabiria* (1913), gave D. W. Griffith some of the inspiration to work in grand, epic scale on films like *Judith of Bethulia* (1913), *The Birth of a Nation,* and *Intolerance.* With these Italian spectacles the feature film was born, for they demonstrated the viability of movies longer in length than was customary at the time (Fig. 13.2a). Yet they also established a precedent for a mode of filmmaking that emphasized visual sumptuousness as a selling point, done with a style that went

13.1 Two films by Georges Méliès. Although Georges Méliès is most famous for making some of the first attempts at science fiction and fantasy, such as (a) *The Impossible Voyage* (1904), he also made elaborate costume dramas and historical reconstructions, such as (b) *The Death of Anne Boleyn* (1905).

beyond stage spectacle to use some of the capacities of the medium. Similarly, the first great period of the German silent film is one of massive, elaborate costume movies, shot with detailed sets and crowds of extras. The foremost director of this cycle was Ernst Lubitsch, who, in works like *Madame du Barry* (1919) and *Anne Boleyn* (1920), sought to lighten the gravity of historical events with touches of comic and sexual titillation (Fig. 13.2b).

The origins of the feature-length storytelling film in spectacle suggest a dual relationship. On the one hand, spectacle gave a sensational quality to narrative films, assuring producers that audiences might sit through longer films if tantalized by scenery and splendor. On the other hand, stories gave filmmakers structures on which they constructed their experiments in *mise en scène* and special effects, so that they did not have to string them together arbitrarily. The first spectacles demonstrate an awareness on the part of early filmmakers of a potential for esthetic manipulation of the medium that would go beyond the simple recording of everyday events or the performing of magic tricks.

One of the fascinations for spectacle in the silent era lay in the involvement with the effects that could be achieved working in a studio. The movies of Fritz Lang from the twenties are a good case in point. His retelling of the Siegfried story, *Die Nibelungen* (1924), used myth and legend as subject matter in creating, through stylized, decorative sets, a storybook world of dragons, knights, and castles. While some of the great German films of the twenties may also be categorized as personal (*The Cabinet of Dr. Caligari*) or realist (the works of Pabst), almost all were also inspired by the visual world of painting and graphic design. What was said in such films was sometimes less important than their visual sophistication. Even in the Hollywood film, one may relate the studio spectacles of Cecil B. De Mille (such as *The Ten Commandments*, 1923, or *King of Kings*, 1927) or large-scale epics like *Ben-Hur* (1926) to the visual manner of the baroque or of nineteenth-century salon painting.[5]

a

b

Fascination with the use of the studio and the creation of stylized spectacle reached its high point in the thirties with the cinema of Josef von Sternberg. Even when he worked in sound, Sternberg's sensibility was often that of a silent director, for his films tend to be verbally slow and stilted, even while visually sophisticated or opulent. His motion pictures, especially those made with Marlene Dietrich (such as *Shanghai Express,* 1932, or *The Scarlet Empress,* 1934) have a kind of hothouse exoticism in which stories are merely excuses for extravagant lighting, fancifully elaborate decor and costumes, and mannered compositional effects achieved with intruding foreground objects. Critics often describe them as triumphs of form (because of their great craftsmanship) over content (the plots are often creaky, superficial, or trivial). They are a kind of ultimate hybrid between Hollywood glamour and the visually developed studio technique of the silent German cinema.

Although spectacles and historical films like those from the silent era were produced in Hollywood throughout the thirties and forties, this kind of spectacle acquired new significance in the Hollywood of the fifties and sixties, which had to compete with television. The most significant development was the introduction of wide-screen formats as standard filmmaking practice, but the perfection of improved color techniques also promised something that television of the time could not offer. Following the success of *The Robe* (1953), which introduced CinemaScope, wide-screen films on spectacular, usually historical and biblical subjects dominated the movies for a full decade, reaching a climax with the most expensive and publicized film up to that time, *Cleopatra* (1963).

The late fifties and early sixties were thus an era in which the potential success of a movie was often measured by the size of its sets, the number of extras, the expansiveness of locations, the quality of special effects, and, in some instances, its running time. Bigger was better. Superproductions were Hollywood's order of the day. Movies like Cecil B. De Mille's *The Ten Commandments* (1956) and William Wyler's *Ben-Hur* (1959), both remakes of silent era successes, became top box-office hits. The spectacle became Hollywood's primary genre for showing off its technical expertise, for introducing new wide-screen processes and special effects techniques. The films were in part excuses to explore the potential of new film technology.

Other commercial producers, particularly in Italy, imitated this genre, as in the Italian cycle of Hercules films starring Steve Reeves. There was born in the late fifties a cycle of Italian films featuring muscular heroes, mythical or ancient historical backgrounds, and wide-screen techniques. Religious or mythological settings often allowed for sensational special effects in these works, which played in the United

13.2 The silent film tradition of historical spectacle. (a) *The Last Days of Pompeii* (1913), an early Italian film, and (b) *Madame du Barry* (1919), a historical spectacle of Ernst Lubitsch, are among the first important European feature films. In the former, note the decorative use of pattern in the costumes; in the latter, note the towering sets and the use of crowds.

States for mass audiences in drive-ins and for double features. Let us consider Vittorio Cottafavi's *Goliath and the Dragon* (1960) as an example of this genre, a film which combines both Méliès-like magic and historical splendor in a single work.

Vittorio Cottafavi is the most famous director of the Italian spectacle. In the early sixties Michel Mourlet idolized Cottafavi as one of the great directors in the world; Mourlet, a French writer and spokesman for a group of critics known as the MacMahonists, argued that Cottafavi's visual skills far outweighed any deficiencies in his film stories or characterizations.[6] Elsewhere, *Goliath and the Dragon* has been praised by some, downgraded as inferior Cottafavi by others, or in some cases virtually ignored.[7] American prints of the film are hard to judge fairly, for the film's importer reportedly had some special effects animation footage shot and added to the film.

The plot involves a struggle by Goliath (Mark Forest) against the machinations of the bad king Eurytheus (Broderick Crawford) to conquer Goliath's native city of Thebes. (The original Italian title of the film is *Vendetta di Ercole* or *Hercules' Revenge;* the American distributor clearly did not hesitate to mix Greek mythology with the Bible.) Yet the story is conceived not so much for its own interest as for a framework on which to hang magical and stylistic effects.

In the opening minutes of the film, Goliath confronts a two-headed, fire-breathing dragon and a kind of flying ape with bat wings. Both are somewhat rubbery, unconvincing dummies, but what is surprising is the fascination that even such obviously fake monsters can have. The effect is partly achieved by skillful framing; a brief close-up shot in which a bat wing covers Goliath's face is startling, even frightening: it suddenly seems too close for comfort. We are also fascinated by these creatures precisely because they are at once harmless and manifestly synthetic while they are at the same time just effective enough to be unnerving. The effect is one of pleasure at being fooled, but pleasure also at seeing how we are fooled.

The film is filled with other fantastic sights. When Goliath returns a fabulous red "blood diamond" to his goddess's temple, the diamond floats from his hand into a hole in the statue's forehead. Editing and various effects allow Goliath to fell a huge tree single-handed, battle a bear, and topple the walls of his home in anger. In a later scene, Polymorphous, a centaur, appears and changes forms before our eyes. While all of these scenes are connected by a narrative, we are never so much concerned about the outcome as we are involved in the game the movie plays with our simultaneous belief and disbelief.

Other effects in the movie are not so much tricks as bravura exercises in *mise en scène*. A scene in which political prisoners are executed by being trampled by elephants contains both fluid camera movements following the elephant procession and subjective shots from the victim's point of view. When Goliath later enters the temple to defy the goddess, he walks toward the statue in such a way that the camera passes between his legs while doing an upward 180°-tilt that ends with the frame upside down. When the centaur dies, Cottafavi paints a circle of red around him in the grass—for no other reason than visual emphasis.

Such obvious technique would be bothersomely gratuitous in a conventional, relatively realistic movie; in a film with mythical subject matter, it is perfectly acceptable. Cottafavi, using a subject that causes us to expect and enjoy visual surprises and gaudy display, frees his camera to be as imaginative, excessive, and unpredictable as possible.

If a work of art must have philosophical or thematic substance, then Cottafavi surely fails. On a narrative level, *Goliath and the Dragon* is so formulaic and uncreative that it suggests a complete immersion in popular myth. And the work may be questioned on sociological grounds: does it reflect a totalitarian need for mythic heroes on the part of the masses? In terms purely of *mise en scène* and spectacle, however, *Goliath and the Dragon* reveals genuine film craftsmanship, particularly in its exploitation of wide-screen format in asymmetrical compositions and graceful, lateral camera movements coordinated with action. Cottafavi explores the pleasures of wide screen, color, movement, and light with little need for worry about the credibility, taste, or intellectual pretension of his story.

Science Fiction

The science-fiction film is similar to the historical spectacle in that both genres involve displacements in time. The latter explores the past (the more remote the past, the freer the filmmaker is to invent), the former the future.[8] Both genres create other-world environments by means of sets, costumes, and special effects—the same techniques of spectacle used by Méliès in his early experiments. We may include in the science-fiction film all manner of subgenres: the space exploration story, the extraterrestrial invasion movie, the end-of-the-world picture, the nuclear monster film, the *1984*-like parable about the future.[9] Almost all rely on visual and graphic effects to achieve their impact.

The most famous and lavishly mounted production of this sort in the late Silent Period was Fritz Lang's *Metropolis* (1926), about a city in the future ruled by a mechanistic and totalitarian regime. Like *Die Nibelungen*, *Metropolis* exploited the resources of the studio and revealed further Lang's splendid architectural sense in its emphasis on massive, monumental sets (or in some cases skillful models) in which the workers of the city, forced into lives of conformity, become robotlike and form geometric groupings. This emphasis on geometric order and symmetry came to represent restriction and enforced conformity and became a standard visual motif in later science-fiction films. If some critics discredit *Metropolis* for a certain banality of story line and theme, few find fault with its threatening visualization of future life as a rigid, depersonalizing machine in which humans are moving parts like any others.

Things to Come (1936), the most noteworthy science fiction film of the following decade, took a similar approach. Based on a tract by H. G. Wells, it was directed by a set designer, William Cameron Menzies, who conceived the parts of the film set in the future in terms of grandiose, white plaster sets that suggest human values dwarfed by a predominantly antihuman environment. Technically, *Things to Come* went further than *Metropolis* to combine *process shots* of models with live actors in the same frame, although the quality of such work may be somewhat lacking by today's standards.[10]

Things to Come was the last great science-fiction film before World War II, and it was not until after the war that the genre blossomed in the fifties to become a standard Hollywood product. The *auteurs* of the fifties were not so much the directors of the films as the special effects men, like George Pal and Ray Harryhausen, who both developed cult reputations even as the genre went into temporary decline in the sixties. Pal, whose earlier work involved puppet animation, did the effects for *War of the Worlds* in 1953, a key film in the Martian invasion cycle. He later went on to direct *The Time Machine* (1960), also from a story by H. G. Wells, considered by some to be his best work. Harryhausen achieved fame for his effects in *The Beast from 20,000 Fathoms* (also from 1953, a key year for science fiction), a film largely responsible for setting off a series of monster films, such as *Them!* (1954, featuring giant ants) or the Japanese-made *Godzilla* (1954). In many of these films, the arousing of the monster is in some way connected to modern nuclear science, reflecting popular anxiety about the atomic and hydrogen bombs.

Interest in the science fiction genre waned somewhat in the sixties, although some critics see the popularity of elaborate electronic gadgetry in the James Bond films as a combining of the science fiction film with the spy adventure movie. In 1968, however, Stanley Kubrick clearly broke new ground with *2001: A Space Odyssey*. The story of the film was simple, centering around a voyage to Jupiter in

13.3 Science fiction as esthetic filmmaking. In *2001: A Space Odyssey* (1968), Stanley Kubrick used the science-fiction film to explore some of the more complex formal possibilities of the film medium. As critic Max Kozloff points out, Kubrick plays with our perceptions of distance, space, relative sizes of objects, and speed of movement. Yet all is within the relatively familiar context of the space travel movie.

which a malfunctioning computer kills all but one of the space-ship crew members. The destination is the point to which a huge black monolith found buried on the moon has been sending signals, and the one remaining astronaut's "landing" on Jupiter is really a cross-dimensional move involving an evolution of man to a new physical state, implying a different relation between space and time.

What Kubrick did in *2001*—apart from using special effects of quality unseen up to that time—was to use the visual materials of science fiction for their fullest esthetic and formal potential. With a slender plot and little dialogue, but a 165-minute running time, Kubrick could deal simply with the arrangement of figures in space—in both senses of that word.[11] Freed from a world in which gravity is an organizing physical principle, the filmmaker could compose in the frame with greater freedom. Using outer space for visual milieu, Kubrick could suggest *infinite depth of field*. As one critic noted, perhaps no film has ever used changes in scale between two objects so extensively to suggest the passage of time, as one object moves forward or away from another (Fig. 13.3).[12] Kubrick's pace is lingering and decelerated, calling attention to compositions within the wide-screen Cinerama format, even while our usual senses of time, depth, proportion, and balance are all disoriented. In the final sequences, the suggestion that the spaceman transcends space and time comes through completely abstract imagery in which colored-light effects and moving forms give a sense of rushing forward at great speed. A radical example of a commercial film working within a traditional subject, *2001* explores the formal capacities of the medium.

The major science fiction films of the seventies—like *Star Wars* (1977), *Close Encounters of the Third Kind* (1978), and *Alien* (1979)—all owe a certain amount of their visual interest to *2001*, although in every case they are more tied to traditional dialogue and storytelling than Kubrick's work. They are, in effect, more "balanced" Hollywood products, with less exclusive interest in the esthetic function of film. Yet, like most science-fiction films, their bias is—at least in their most spectacular moments—against the realistic and toward the purely imaginative. That

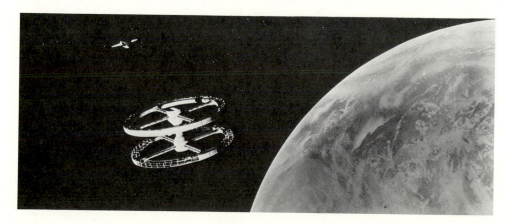

is, they present worlds very much apart from the mundane reality of the audience's experience, worlds that can be more fully manipulated for esthetic and visual effect.

Musicals

Of all the Hollywood genres, the musical is the one that most fully frees the cinema from any constraints of either realism or storytelling, to become purely esthetic. Singing and dancing are stylized forms of expression, and even though many musicals use songs and choreography for breaks in a story of show business and backstage romance, few fans of the musical would complain that a well-done production number slows down rather than emphasizes narrative action. Instead, production numbers become an opportunity for the appreciation of form, movement, camera work, and cutting, all for their own sakes.

The musical was, of course, originally a response to the sound technology that came in in the thirties, for music is one of the most aurally expressive forms of communication. The most famous and elaborate of the thirties musicals are those with production numbers by Busby Berkeley. Noted for their huge choruses of pretty girls, they emphasize geometric movements in unison rather than actual dancing. Berkeley would line up choruses of girls dancing with violins (*Gold Diggers of 1933*), seated at a seeming infinity of grand pianos (*Gold Diggers of 1935*), or in rocking chairs (*Gold Diggers of 1937*) and capture complex geometric patterns in overhead shots. He made his early movies, including the famous *Forty-Second Street* (1933) and *Dames* (1934) for Warner Brothers, but worked for MGM in the forties on such bright, attractive projects as *For Me and My Gal* (1942) and *The Gang's All Here* (1943), which is famous for its production number featuring Carmen Miranda surrounded by a chorus carrying giant bananas. Berkeley's *mise en scène* is one of quantitative fantasy.

Musicals in the 1940s lent themselves to color, especially at MGM, which turned out the best of them. With *Meet Me in St. Louis* (1944), *Yolanda and the Thief* (1945), and *The Pirate* (1948), Vincente Minnelli emerged as a major creator of stylized production numbers in which color was integrated into the visual whole, and which attempted somewhat more storytelling than their thirties counterparts. In the "Limehouse Blues" number of *Ziegfeld Follies* (1946), for example, Minnelli not only created an "atmospheric" London Chinatown but told an anecdotal story of the love of a poor Chinese worker (Fred Astaire) for a glamorous woman of the streets (Lucille Bremer). The number begins in sombre, nighttime tones accented only by whites and yellows, but a dream sequence in which Astaire dances with his desired woman switches strikingly to garish, unreal reds, while still carrying through a mystical

Oriental motif. Camera and performers move together in flowing unison in what has been called "the most exquisite review number ever filmed in the history of screen musicals."[13] (Fig. 13.4)

Famous musicals of the fifties, such as *The Band Wagon* (1953) also by Minnelli, and *Singin' in the Rain* (1952), by Stanley Donen and Gene Kelly, continued in the MGM tradition. Making use of backstage show-business stories, they created stylized, imaginative, colorful production numbers as the justification for slender, familiar plots. By the sixties, musicals suffered something of a decline. The few popular successes were invariably based on major Broadway productions like *My Fair Lady* (1964), *The Sound of Music* (1965), *Funny Girl* (1968), or *Cabaret* (1972). In such films stage elements were reworked for the screen, and few major advances were made in the musical genre. Only toward the late 1970s did Hollywood resume any widespread production of musicals conceived directly for the screen. Bob Fosse led the way with *All That Jazz* (1979), a highly subjective—sometimes even surrealist—autobiographical work. Productions like *Fame* (1980), *Can't Stop the Music* (1980), *The Blues Brothers* (1980), and *Xanadu* (1980) quickly followed, all in the hope that the public was again eager for the energy and razzle-dazzle unique to this form of spectacle.

At their best, musicals use their production numbers to explore an esthetic of style, grace, and physical movement. To examine how a scene from a musical might extend the Méliès tradition, we will discuss the "Shadow Waltz" number from Busby Berkeley's *Gold Diggers of 1933*, a largely conventional backstage comedy about

13.4 The Minnelli musical number. The "Limehouse Blues" number from *Ziegfeld Follies* (1946) is an example of Hollywood craft at its most skillful. To create an unsettling, dreamlike atmosphere, Vincente Minnelli uses a stylized red and black color scheme, Chinese motifs, graceful choreography, and camera movement—thereby revealing how the musical can be one of the most esthetic forms of commercial moviemaking. The dancers are Fred Astaire and Lucille Bremer.

chorus girls in search of rich husbands. Other numbers in the film contain elements of comedy ("Pettin' in the Park" is filled with sight gags) or even persuasive political comment ("Forgotten Man" is a critique of society's indifference to war veterans during the Depression). But the "Shadow Waltz" number experiments with elements of film comparatively unaffected by political or other interests, becoming an almost pure exploration of formal devices in both dance and film.

The entire sequence consists of six-and-a-half repetitions of a nine-line song, plus an introductory verse. Dick Powell first sings it to Ruby Keeler himself, then a background female chorus joins him and later dances to instrumental versions of the song. The sequence thus takes on a theme and variation structure, as such repetition elaborates on or modifies what has gone before.

Berkeley creates his own fantastic world. While Dick Powell is singing in front of a staircase, the chorus fades in behind it. When the chorus begins to dance, Berkeley pulls the camera back for an increasingly full shot of his multitude of dancers. The effectiveness of the number is not in the cleverness of its lyrics, nor in particularly expressive choreography, but in the sheer size and elaborateness of the presentation.

The most spectacular feature of the number is the neon violins the girls pretend to play in the dark while they are dancing. Viewed from above, the lights on the violins separately outline the curved shapes of the instruments and collectively form circular patterns as the girls dance. The dancing moves further toward abstraction. It need no longer be just women dancing, but shapes, lights, and shadows. The costumes and decor emphasize this abstract quality. The chorus members' skirts are conical, tiered hoops. They perform on sloping ramps above pools of water. Everything is decorative. Everything—choreography, costumes, decor, and camera placement—emphasizes an arrangement of curvilinear shapes that is not quite like anything in the real world.

While the effect is enchanting, Berkeley is careful to fascinate us with suggesting how it was achieved. He inserts, for example, a close shot of the girls marching forward, lighted only by the glow of the violins under their chins. In a startling bit of technical play, Berkeley starts with a high-angled, overhead close shot of a violinist, only to move quickly out as all the surrounding violins move into formation to outline a single giant neon violin shaped from all the small ones. Without cutting, Berkeley has shown us in one shot both the whole and one of its parts. It is technique for its own sake, and it delights audiences.

While one may read into the "Shadow Waltz" significant meanings about the thirties' fascination with technology (the electric violins), its pressures toward conformity (the dancers are anonymous and perform in perfect unison), or its mechanized eroticism, the sequence is explicitly nothing more than a celebration of love. Even *that* meaning is found in the lyrics of the song rather than the images themselves. At one point, Berkeley tilts the camera so that a shot in which the girls dance on a reflective surface is held vertically, and the symmetrically balanced skirts of the dancers move up and down the screen, splitting it evenly down the center. Physically and gravitationally impossible, this effect disorients us as to where or how the girls are actually dancing. In ornaments like these, the musical comes very close to the art of the abstract, experimental film. One enjoys the kinetic spectacle of moving objects for its own sake.

Berkeley's filmmaking thus approaches being a pure exercise in *mise en scène*. In the "Shadow Waltz" the camera becomes in effect one more musical instrument. It makes visual patterns that combine harmoniously with the notes on the soundtrack. We enjoy watching not because it gives us ideas, or because it allows us to identify with the feelings of an imagined character, but simply because, like most effective popular music, it makes us feel good in a direct, visceral, childlike way.

What finally separates spectacle films from regular Hollywood films is their emphasis on setting, costumes, physical movement, and special effects as much as—or even more than—characters and their feelings. In one sense, spectacle films depersonalize their actors, making them simply part of the scenery. The important elements are quantity (thousands of extras or dozens of dancers) and quality (towering sets, vast panoramas). Delight in excess makes the spectacle fascinating and attractive to the mass audience, so that spectacle, when combined with Hollywood storytelling expertise, can weight that storytelling tradition heavily in the direction of the esthetic.

THE EXPERIMENTAL FILM

Experimental cinema is perhaps best understood in contrast to the Hollywood genre film. In commercial genres, filmmakers tell stories that combine familiar plot and stylistic elements in a series of new variations whereby the genre—Western, gangster film, or "two-hanky weepy"—provides the audience predictable elements to follow. Genres are closely linked to the Hollywood economic system. The audience is buying entertainment, and it wants to know more or less in advance what it is getting.[14]

The notion of experimentation in film, on the other hand, suggests a different approach to the cinema. Almost any kind of film may, of course, have some experimental or unconventional elements, and we have seen them already as a major part of personal cinema with its techniques of acceleration and deceleration and its tendency toward nonrealist *mise en scène*. But the film whose main purpose is to be experimental usually shows a particular set of qualities:

1. It is produced and marketed outside the standard systems of production and distribution. To be genuinely experimental, to be radically different, is to work against the commercial dictum of giving the audience something reasonably familiar and comprehensible.

2. Its experimentation implies a trying out of techniques for their own sake, to see what will happen when they are used. Experimental films often break the rules of commercial filmmaking, and professional filmmakers often call such films amateurish because—by Hollywood standards at least—experimental filmmakers often expose and edit film "incorrectly." In other instances, experimental filmmakers work with technical devices, such as the optical printer, in a way that goes beyond the simple creation of special effects in the story film. Instead, the effects achieved *are* the primary content of the film.

3. The experimental film suggests a different attitude toward film content. If the story is the fundamental interest of the commercial film, the experimental movie is more interested in the formal properties of the medium itself. Qualities of line, shape, light, color, and movement may be emphasized over plot, characterization, and theme.

The experimental film is esthetic filmmaking par excellence. In the experimental film the emphasis is not so much on what the film *means* (in relation to the filmmaker, the real world, or the audience), but on what the film *is* as an object of esthetic interest.

In considering the experimental film, we shall treat three varieties of what one might call such "cinematic research":

1 The Dadaist film, which emphasizes randomness and anarchy in film organization.

2 The abstract film which emphasizes the formal qualities of film over all others, whether or not it has recognizable subject matter.

3 The minimalist or structural film, which pares down elements of film imagery to extremely simple, reductive forms.

These categories are not mutually exclusive, and some experimental works may combine aspects of all three, but let us examine each separately to see how various filmmakers have used them to explore the medium in which they work.

The Dadaist Film

The Dada movement in art and literature began in Europe following World War I as a reaction against the supposed rationalism and high ideals that had led to the war. The Dadaists sought to shock the middle class and to call into question all bourgeois forms of art. The movement's most famous statement on art is doubtless Marcel Duchamp's exhibition of a urinal (signed "R. Mutt") as a piece of sculpture.

The Dadaists produced only a few films, but these were to be of major importance to the experimental movements coming after them. Marcel Duchamp himself made *Anemic Cinema* (1926), which grew out of the painter's experiments with optics. *Anemic Cinema* uses concentric circles placed slightly off center, which, when Duchamp revolved them, looked like cones and spirals. Duchamp's work would be an ancestor of the op art movement in painting in the sixties, in which painters exploited the physiological phenomena and potential perceptual confusions involved in optical processes. Duchamp also included revolving slogans, written in spiral form, containing elaborate multilingual puns and anagrams. He playfully contrasts the purely visual to the verbal and conceptual.

With *Entr'acte* (1924) by René Clair and painter Francis Picabia, the Dada movement found its fullest expression in film. The work got its title because it was intended to go between the acts of a stage performance called *Relâche* (which means "No Show Today"). The film is filled with seemingly random imagery, edited together in a wild, chaotic manner, much of which wryly attacks the pomposity of high art. A ballerina's skirts are seen from below, and when we finally get to see her face, she turns out to be an eccentric, bearded gentleman (Fig. 13.5). A group of matchsticks form a grouping that resembles a set of pillars, and the image suddenly turns into the Parthenon. The ending of the film builds to a Sennett-like chase (itself an esthetic statement, since the Dadaists and surrealists—and many of the latter began as Dadaists—loved the American silent comedies, even while the middle class found them vulgar) in which the editing accelerates to breakneck speed. At one point Clair's camera is suddenly on a roller coaster: editing for movement takes precedence over spatial or narrative logic. Although it all makes little coherent sense, it entertains us with its unpredictability and abundance of reckless movement.

The qualities of *Entr'acte* that epitomize Dada are a sense of humor achieved through incongruous juxtaposition of images, an irreverence toward polite society and serious esthetics, and a rejection of careful technique in favor of raw energy and deliberate crudity. While the movement quickly blended into the surrealist movement, the spirit of Dada revived in the late fifties and early sixties as part of the American underground film. (This latter movement began, one may recall, with the trance film.) West Coast filmmaker Bruce Conner, for example, began to make collage films constructed from newsreel footage or "found" materials edited together in fragmentary, mosaic style. In *Report* (1965), Conner, with deliberate tastelessness, intercut footage from the Kennedy assassination with images of American technology (a garbage disposal, a switchboard operator, the installation of telephone wires) and violence (e.g., a toreador being gored by a bull). Its combination of illogical but poetically apt imagery makes us uncomfortable; it has the same satiric impoliteness and shock value as twenties Dada.[15] Similarly, Robert Nelson's *O Dem Watermelons* (1965) borrows the chase motif from *Entr'acte*, but in its raucous and anarchic imagery of white men chasing and destroying animated watermelons it also suggests a persuasive critique of racial stereotyping and intolerance.

13.5 Dada. This figure from René Clair and Francis Picabia's *Entr'acte* (1924) shows the typical Dadaist's disdain for middle-class art. The Dada movement saw such so-called culture as window dressing for a politically corrupt society.

13.6 Neo-Dada. Dada has left a powerful legacy to experimental cinema. Recent young independent filmmakers, such as Stuart Sherman in *Five Films* (1978), frequently revel in nonsensical, incongruous imagery.

Perhaps the most direct expression of a neo-Dada sensibility, however, may be found in the early films of Ken Jacobs and Jack Smith. In Jacobs's *Blonde Cobra* (1963), the filmmaker constructed a film in which the image track would go completely blank and the audience would have to listen to Jack Smith tell fantastic, erotic, and sometimes very funny stories (about a boy who burns another boy's penis or a convent of sexually active nuns). The film would thus be an assault on the audience's expectations—what little narrative structure the film has comes from its spoken sections rather than its visual ones—as well as on any standards of coherence or conventional mastery of the medium. That same year Smith produced *Flaming Creatures,* a black-and-white short feature that portrayed a transvestite orgy in which a Hollywood–Arabian Nights imagery merged with outrageous off-hand nudity. The film shocked in its time and was subject to police raids and legal action. In one famous shot, a man puts on lipstick while a limp penis dangles over his shoulder. Yet the film combines, in an unexpected way, elements of the Dadaist sensibility, for it is incongruously funny, pointedly offensive (by conventional standards), and technically primitive. The exposure of the film is carelessly gray and misty; the editing is slapdash; Smith suggests an earthquake simply by shaking the camera. Still, many critics admire the work for its surprising sensuousness and voluptuous imagery.[16]

What the Dadaist mentality suggests is that a work can be viewed as a put-on and an esthetic achievement at the same time. For the Dadaist, the purpose of the film is to jolt, to shock, and to surprise; Dadaist films are experimental in the sense that they deliberately do many of those things conventional movies avoid, both to subvert the assumptions of a complacent audience and to play with the medium in a spirit of fun and whimsy (Fig. 13.6).

The Abstract Film

The aims of the abstract film may be more complex. By abstract cinema, we mean films that present moving shapes and forms for their own esthetic effect rather than as referents to the real world, thus eliminating or minimizing the realist function of communication. Abstract films generally adopt the model of music, emphasizing a rhythmic flow of images and forms to be appreciated for their sensuousness and beauty.

Commentators on the subject often make a useful distinction between two forms of abstraction in cinema. One is the totally abstract film, which has no subject matter recognizable from the real world. Such films, often animated, use only geometry and movement to communicate. The other form uses images from the real world and may even have a slight story, but photographic pictures play down the content of the images in favor of form. These are two different kinds of abstraction. Let us treat them separately, as *pure abstraction* and *mixed abstraction* respectively (Fig. 13.7).

Pure Abstraction   Historian and critic of the *avant-garde* film, P. Adams Sitney sees four central works from the twenties as "pillars or directions upon which most of what has been called 'the pure' in cinema (or the abstract or the graphic) are built."[17] These are Hans Richter's *Rhythmus 21* (1921), Viking Eggeling's *Symphonie diagonale* (1924), Fernand Léger's *Ballet mécanique* (1924), and Marcel Duchamp's *Anemic Cinema*. We have discussed the Duchamp film as Dada, and *Ballet mécanique* falls into what we will call *mixed abstraction*. Let us now consider the seminal works by Richter and Eggeling.

The Swede Eggeling and the German Richter influenced each other. Evidence suggests that Eggeling was more the theorist, Richter more the spontaneous practitioner.[18] Eggeling, who died in 1925, tried continuously to work out a method for animating his drawings; *Symphonie diagonale* is the surviving example of his theories put into practice. In it, he presents a series of white geometric figures on a black field, organized always about a diagonal axis that changes in slope from left to right. Eggeling then adds pieces to make the figure more elaborate—or else subtracts lines or shapes, at times making the entire figure disappear. Sometimes a figure will

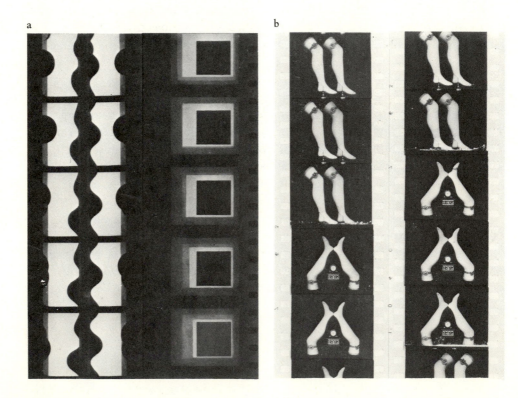

a   b

grow parts in one place and lose them in another. Each figure is on screen for only a few seconds, but since many of them resemble one another, the effect is one of a series of variations on a few given forms. The figures always seem to rest flat on the screen surface—with very little illusion of depth—and only rarely do they reach the edges of the frame.

By contrast, Richter found it easier to work by cutting out and animating paper shapes. *Rhythmus 21* consists mainly of squares and rectangles in white, gray, and black, which in becoming bigger or smaller seem to come forward or recede in depth. Richter plays with this illusion of depth as well as with a sense of the images continuing past the edges of the frame. He also experiments with changing a white ground to a black one and vice versa, by means of a wipelike effect. Unlike Eggeling's work, the emphasis is not so much on isolated changing forms as on movement and rhythm.

Together, Richter and Eggeling suggest two approaches to the animation of purely abstract shapes and forms. A number of other animators have followed in their footsteps, but we can trace just about all pure abstraction back to Richter and Eggeling.

Mixed Abstraction   With Fernand Léger's *Ballet mécanique* we come to the first major work that attempts to mix abstract shapes with recognizably photographed objects. The latter are often everyday objects photographed in extreme close-up, or photographed with lighting that disguises their nature as objects and renders them unrecognizable. Léger, fascinated by machinery, saw the camera as creating a beautifully mechanistic view of the world. In one of *Ballet mécanique*'s most famous shots, a woman comes up a staircase carrying a sack on her shoulder. Léger repeats the image over and over again, until it is no longer so much a representation of a human as simply a rhythmic movement. Elsewhere Léger edits into his film black leader, simply for rhythmic effect.[19] The rapid-fire editing used in the work suggests the Dadaist or neo-Dadaist experiments discussed earlier, but Léger's intent was not so much to scandalize as to reduce imagery simply to formal elements. Léger all but completely strips his imagery of narrative and thematic context.

Many of the movements we have discussed already in connection with the personal and esthetic functions of film—Dada, surrealism, the trance film, the abstract film of the twenties—eventually led to the movement variously known as the New American Cinema, the American underground film, or American

13.7 Two kinds of abstract film. We see in Hans Richter's *Rhythmus 21* (1921) and Fernand Léger's *Ballet mécanique* (1924) two classic examples of abstract filmmaking. a. Richter's work might be called pure abstraction since it animates simple geometric shapes. b. Léger treats recognizable objects as graphic forms—for their exclusively visual and esthetic qualities.

independent or *avant-garde* filmmaking. The movement's beginnings are in the trance film, but many of the filmmakers involved became less interested in self-absorbed psychodrama and more involved with the formal properties of the medium. Maya Deren, for example, followed *Meshes of the Afternoon* with a series of films using dance motifs, such as *Choreography for the Camera* (1945) and *Meditation on Violence* (1948). Whereas the underground movement has had a personal, romantic strain to it, much of it has also been preoccupied with esthetics and the finding of new, more abstract forms of film expression.[20]

Many of the movement's films look back to *Ballet mécanique* in their use of what we will call mixed abstraction, and we can see in the New American Cinema four consistent technical preoccupations that give it a quality somewhere between pure abstraction and traditional storytelling. These are (1) an interest in abstract photographic styles, (2) superimposition, (3) fragmentary editing, and (4) the use of extraphotographic forms of image making. Let us consider each of these devices and some of the filmmakers who have used them.

We may first consider what we will call abstract photographic styles. Most cinematography emphasizes subject matter: a good photograph or movie is usually thought to be the one in which style most appropriately suits what is being viewed. In *avant-garde* films, however, the emphasis is often more on the shapes, line, and movement of the image than on the subject matter, as we have already seen in *Ballet mécanique*.

One early experiment along these lines was *Geography of the Body* (1943) by Willard Maas and Marie Menken, made about the same time as *Meshes of the Afternoon*. In it, the filmmakers showed close-ups of different portions of the human anatomy, shot through a magnifying glass, framed so as to be ambiguously unidentifiable at first glance. Human flesh becomes abstract form. In the semisurrealist *The Lead Shoes* (1948), Sidney Peterson stretched and contracted his images with an anamorphic lens during shooting.

Perhaps the most important figure in the development of the semiabstract film esthetic has been Stan Brakhage. Brakhage's early films were out of the trance film genre, but he gradually developed a method of approaching filmmaking in which the camera was to become a kind of substitute for his own eye, his films more exercises in the processes of seeing rather than drama or documentary. In the course of Brakhage's work over almost thirty years he has used a whole repertoire of photographic techniques to distort or alter his images. He has employed deliberately

13.8 The influence of abstract expressionism. Movements in modern painting have influenced experimental filmmakers. Abstract expressionists in the 1950s employed bold, painterly brush strokes to convey subjective feelings. Note how the scratches on the eyes in Stan Brakhage's *Reflections on Black* (1955) are similar to those in Willem de Kooning's painting *Woman VI* (1954), in which traces of physical gestures—strokes, drips, scratches—are an essential part of the artist's visual vocabulary.

out-of-focus photography, outdated film, various lenses and filters (used "incorrect-ly") to emphasize the formal qualities of his images. He has put spittle on the lens to diffuse the image, and he once shot an hour-long film, *The Text of Light* (1974), entirely through a crystal ashtray to produce patterns of light and color. A favorite device has been to move the camera so quickly that the imagery becomes hardly recognizable, and in this regard some critics have seen *Sirius Remembered* (1959) as a key short film in Brakhage's development. Although it uses personal subject matter—Brakhage photographs the decaying corpse of a pet dog—the camera movements take on an importance in themselves, to be enjoyed and appreciated as hypnotic, abstract movement (Fig. 13.8).[21]

Other filmmakers, such as Scott Bartlett or Richard Myers, have experimented with the optical printer to give their images photographic interest. Filmmakers from Méliès onward have of course used optical printing to produce magic and special effects, but experimental filmmakers have discovered that by rephotographing their images, they can impose on them two levels of manipulation. After photographing their images one way in the camera, they can then speed them up, slow them down, reverse their movement, emphasize grain, or alter the black-and-white or color balance.

Thus in *Akran* (1971), a semiautobiographical feature about an alientated young man, Richard Myers rephotographs his footage to slow it down (using various rhythms), stopping the frame completely in spots before resuming, to create a sense of playing with the footage, stretching out the perception process, savoring the pictures. Part of the effect is the kind of subjective deceleration we talked about as

a
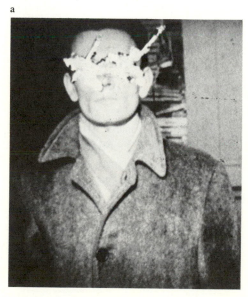

b

characteristic of emotive cinema, but part is also formal experimentation. Myers implicitly acknowledges the movie's nature as a succession of stills by contrasting the slowed-down image with the more completely illusory motion at full speed.

In all of these cases, whether the method is simple (photographing something in extreme close-up so that it is unrecognizable) or complex (optical printer manipulation) what is prized is not the clarity or directness of the photographic image (the ideal in commercial cinematography) but rather its expressive form as an image, often apart from subject matter.

A second major technique is superimposition. To the storytelling filmmaker, techniques of superimposition are of limited use, being confined to conventionalized indications of time transition (as in a dissolve), dream sequences, or special effects. To the filmmaker interested in esthetic issues, however, the technique has a particular richness: not only can the two images create formal and compositional effects when superimposed, but their poetic juxtaposition can suggest metaphoric or associative meanings between them.

One of the pioneers in the use of superimposition to esthetic ends was Ian Hugo, whose films about Times Square (*The Jazz of Lights*, 1954) and Venice (*The Gondola Eye*, 1964) create rhythmic and flowing effects for which the subject matter is merely something of a pretext. *Chumlum* (1964), a short by Ron Rice, who died in his twenties, takes the subject matter of *Flaming Creatures*, a group of lounging, zombielike transvestites, and photographs them in multiple superimposition and exotic color to create a languid, almost drugged effect. Rice's superimpositions were created by rewinding the film and reshooting; some of Hugo's involve the use of multiple projectors; other filmmakers have the work done in the laboratory. But in all, the effect is visually stimulating in a way that suggests an approach to film based on "reading through" layers of images rather than linking them in time to tell a story.[22]

Perhaps the most elaborate and systematic use of superimposition in film has been in Stan Brakhage's *Dog Star Man* (1961–1964) and a work derived from the same material, *The Art of Vision* (1965). The "plot" of *Dog Star Man* (and *The Art of Vision*) is simple: "A woodsman attempts to climb a mountain. He struggles with a dead white tree, throws it down and chops at it."[23] But in the film, Brakhage, who plays the woodsman himself, incorporates all manner of imagery to describe the woodsman's environment and subjective thoughts. *Dog Star Man*, which runs an hour and ten minutes, consists of a prelude and four parts, each successively denser in the number of layers of superimposition. The images range from landscapes of mountains and trees, shots of the sun and moon, portraits of one of Brakhage's children, intimations of sexual activity with his wife, and scientific footage of bodily organs such as the heart and blood vessels. In *The Art of Vision* each roll of film used to construct the superimposed images for the respective parts of *Dog Star Man* is presented in every possible permutation and combination with other rolls from the same part. Brakhage originally edited each roll with the idea of eventually superimposing them in the lab, so that the images are in some ways coordinated. Thus, part three of *Dog Star Man* is constructed from what Brakhage has labeled an A, B, and C roll that he put together in *Dog Star Man* for three-layer superimposition. In *The Art of Vision*, however, we get a progression of A alone, B alone, C alone, AB, AC, BC, and ABC. The audience can thereby follow the interrelation of images much more thoroughly in the four-and-a-half-hour *Art of Vision* than in the shorter *Dog Star Man*.

The other art that resembles such a method in its own way of working is music, in which compositions may take a theme-and-variation structure. But what Brakhage clearly wants us to do is use his films to associate images ourselves as active viewers, to get caught up in a meditative, almost mystical approach to viewing the world. The content of *Dog Star Man* may be Brakhage's own emotive obsessions and fantasies, but the form is so rigorous that what becomes important is Brakhage's esthetics—his interest in the act of seeing—rather than his feelings or ideas about any particular subject.

Third, abstract experimental filmmakers often use fragmentary editing. A primary stylistic trait of the *avant-garde* or underground film of the late fifties or early sixties was the use of extremely quick, fragmentary editing that went beyond the associational editing of personal cinema. The camera movements in *Sirius Remembered,* for example, are linked to a rapid, exaggerated cutting rate, a style that Brakhage also uses in *Anticipation of the Night* (1958) or the prelude section of *Dog Star Man*. Similarly, the neo-Dada films of Conner and Robert Nelson share this penchant for assaulting the eye with images that come at us almost too quickly for us to process them completely (Fig. 13.9).

13.9 A Robert Nelson film. The films of California filmmaker Robert Nelson often reveal a full range of experimental approaches, including neo-Dadaist imagery and fragmentary editing. In this still from *Suite California Stops and Passes* (1978), note how the background is in sharper focus than the foreground—in reverse of our usual expectations.

In some instances, experimental filmmakers have edited even single frames into their works, which theoretically may be missed by the viewer, since the eye needs more than 1/24 of a second to fully register an image. Gregory Markopoulos's *Twice a Man* (1963) was one of the first films to use such single-frame editing, and in parts of it rapid-fire images come in quick bursts, suggesting a flurry of overload of mental activity. The effect is of impressionistic cinema pushed to an extreme. Markopoulos extended this fragmentary mode of editing to his soundtrack as well, using clusters of words and sounds that had been chopped up and reassembled, collage-style.

This move toward fragmentation in editing has been taken to full extreme by Peter Kubelka, an Austrian. Two of Kubelka's early works, *Adebar* (1956–1957) and *Schwechater* (1957–1958), were edited "metrically," that is, in patterns of two, four, eight, and sixteen frames per shot. Neither film runs more than a minute and a half. Kubelka's most famous work, *Our Trip to Africa* (1961–1966), is a minutely edited work compressed into 12 1/2 minutes, based on footage shot during an African hunting expedition. Kubelka edits the footage not for chronology or for any kind of coherent action, or even to establish specific places and events, but for similarities and juxtapositions between shapes, actions, and sounds. The most precise analogy would again be to music, which is also involved with the rhythmic manipulation of durational units. Kubelka has said, "Cinema is a projection of stills—which means images that do not move—in a very quick rhythm."[24]

Thus, editing in the *avant-garde* film does not so much create an illusion of continuity as it usually does in the storytelling movie; rather, it becomes a device for comparing and contrasting images and movement. The fragmentary editing of a Brakhage, a Markopoulos, or a Kubelka suggests that editing may be used not so much to emphasize or clarify the meaning of images, but for its own sake, as an esthetic effect central to the nature of the medium.

A final approach to mixed abstraction is through the use of extraphotographic materials. The underground filmmaker will often find materials and means to put an image on film other than traditional photographic techniques or animation. Again Brakhage has been a leader in this area. In *Reflections on Black* (1955) Brakhage put scratches in the film over the blind protagonist's eyes, acknowledging his own creative level of intervention in the film illusion. (See Fig. 13.8a.) In *Dog Star Man* there are sections in which one level of superimposition involves painting directly on film to replicate what the filmmaker has called "closed eye vision"—the afterimages and geometric shapes one sees when one closes one's eyes. Perhaps Brakhage's most radical experiment in this regard has been *Mothlight* (1953), a film made by gluing objects—moth wings, seeds, flowers—directly to film that was then processed to retain the images (Fig. 13.10).

There have also been experiments in "expanded" cinema, using multiple projectors, live actors, or unique projection environments as part of the work. Such motion pictures question the very conventions of traditional film conception and exhibition. Stan Van Der Beek, for example, has designed and built what he has called a Movie-Drome, a planetariumlike structure in which a domed projection surface can be filled with images from motion-picture, slide, and overhead projectors. Van Der Beek calls such multiple projector works "movie murals."[25] With such activities we move directly back to the light and magic shows that were part of the medium's birth. We are in a realm that is partly a live performance, for the final presentation of the work is in the hands of a projectionist—whose role is now somewhat more complicated than simply getting the reels in the right order and the image in focus.

All of these formal devices—abstract photographic techniques, superimposition, fragmentary editing, and extraphotographic image making—suggest a point of view that treats the film more as an esthetic object to be appreciated in itself than as a second-hand or mediating representation of the world. All indicate a strong personal involvement by the filmmakers in what they present to an audience. All reject realism as a dominant purpose in the work. They emphasize the esthetic: the film is as much about filmmaking as it is about anything else.

Minimal Cinema

If by the mid-sixties filmmakers like Brakhage and Markopoulos were working in an increasingly formalist vein, the trend toward a less personal cinema was well defined by the end of the decade. There arose by 1970 a group of filmmakers working in a mode that might be described as *minimalist,* although some critics labeled such work *structuralist.* The films produced in this movement usually have explored single, very simple visual ideas for the duration of a film.

13.10 Extraphotographic materials. Exploration of extraphotographic materials is common in the work of Stan Brakhage. In *23rd Psalm Branch: Part 2: Nietzsche's Lamb* (1967), Brakhage produced controlled growth of mold directly on his film to get this unique effect.

A major influence in the development of minimal filmmaking was the work of Andy Warhol. In *Sleep, Haircut, Ear,* and *Kiss* (all from 1964), Warhol would simply set up the camera and record simple human events in single uncut takes. To a certain extent, one can see Warhol's work as neo-Dada, but one commentator wrote:

A strange thing occurs. The world becomes transposed, intensified, electrified. We see it sharper than before. Not in dramatic, rearranged contexts and meanings, not in the service of something else . . . but as pure as it is in itself: eating as eating, sleeping as sleeping, haircut as haircut.[26]

Other extremes in the minimal film were the *flicker film* and the *loop film*. In flicker films, there is no recognizable image, but simply alternations of black and white (or sometimes color). Peter Kubelka was responsible for one of the first flicker films, the 6 1/2 minute *Arnulf Rainer* (1958–1960), but the major film of the genre is Tony Conrad's forty-five minute *The Flicker* (1966). Loop films use film constructed in an endless loop, so that a strip of the same image is repeated over and over again. The most famous practitioner of the loop film is George Landow, although other filmmakers have used a similar practice of repeating almost identical images shot, edited, and projected the conventional way.[27]

Among the most famous minimalist or structural films is Ken Jacobs's feature *Tom Tom the Piper's Son* (1969) in which Jacobs took an early short silent film and dissected it by reshooting sections on a homemade optical printer, thereby enabling him to reedit and analyze it, collage-style, in numerous variations. Hollis Frampton's *Zorns Lemma* (1970) includes a forty-five-minute segment in which he substitutes pictures for letters of the alphabet flashing in succession.

The most touted of minimal filmmakers, however, has been Michael Snow. His ←——————→ (1969) consists of repeated back-and-forth camera movements in a classroom. *La region centrale* (1970) explores circular patterns made by putting the camera on a specially designed remote control machine. Yet Snow's most influential work is one of his earlier ones, *Wavelength* (1966–1967), a forty-five-minute film that consists, in effect, of a single zoom from the widest possible angle of an eighty-foot loft to an extreme close-up of a picture of some waves on the room's far wall. The camera seems to inch closer and closer to that wall, so that the movie represents a progressive narrowing of our field of vision within the frame.

As the film opens, we see some workmen carry a bookcase into the room. Two women enter, cross the floor, and later leave. Midway through the movie, there are some crashing sounds; a man then stumbles into the room and falls to the floor, presumably dead. Later, a woman enters, goes to the phone at the end of the room,

13.11 *Wavelength.* The effect of light through a window at various times of day is one of the subjects of Michael Snow's *Wavelength* (1966– 1967), considered by some to be a masterpiece of "contemplative" cinema.

and makes a call, apparently reporting the death. Nothing else happens in the film, and the number of minutes in which people are even in the frame are comparatively few.

By suggesting violence in an essentially nondramatic film, Snow invites us to compare his *avant-garde* work with more traditional storytelling forms. The suddenness and unexpectedness of the dying man's entry is shocking and unsettling. How are we to react to this? The film contrasts the arbitrariness of this single dramatic event with the complete predictability of the narrowing of the field of the lens. As the dead figure on the floor slowly slips out of view, Snow's priorities become even more apparent: the mechanical completion of the single zoom is far more important to him than any human interest the body may have.

The filmmaker does not attempt to make this zoom technically perfect, nor does he preserve any continuity of real time. He keeps in flashes of light that indicate the end of a roll of film. Snow shoots at different times of the day, under varying natural and artificial lighting conditions (Fig. 13.11). Not only does this lighting change, but he overexposes and underexposes at will, thus obtaining various photographic effects. Color tonalities, for example, will change from seemingly natural shades to exotic distortions that make everything brown and white or pink and white. The movie explores a range of effects not in editing but simply in exposing film.

Snow's real subject, if he may be said to have one, is a favorite of painters and photographers alike: the effects of light through a window. *Wavelength* becomes a series of variations on a theme. Sometimes the buildings outside the windows are visible, at other times not, depending on lighting and exposure conditions. Sometimes the interior is dark, the outside light—sometimes vice versa. As Snow manipulates these elements, he produces a series of views of the same subject that suggest the repetition and variation found in modern painting, such as Monet's series of paintings of haystacks or the Rouen cathedral.[28] The film becomes a comprehensive exploration of a certain lighting situation and the visual effects it can produce.

Wavelength also uses occasional superimposition. Images of the room are repeated over one another. As the camera reaches its goal of the picture on the far wall, the close-up of the waves appears somewhat earlier than expected, superimposed over a more distant shot. When a woman talks on the phone, there is a second image of her superimposed over the first. This is yet another visual variation—a frill the filmmaker allows himself within the rigid structure of the movie.

The sound of the picture also mixes the carefully structured with the arbitrary. The opening minutes of *Wavelength* contain natural street sounds, presumably from outside the important loft windows. For the larger part of the work, however, the soundtrack consists of a synthetically produced hum that begins at 50 cps (the lowest sound audible to humans) and goes to 12,000 cps (the highest sound humans hear). The soundtrack progression thus parallels the visual progression.

At the end of *Wavelength*, we see only the two-dimensional photograph of waves. (The visual pun, relating this to the sound-waves of the hum and the title *Wavelength*, is surely intentional.) Snow throws the image out of focus as though to acknowledge the ephemeral nature of photographic illusion. This is a two-dimensional motion picture image of a two-dimensional photograph. Snow has built his film around a pair of illusions—that a zoom lens can make us seem to move closer to an object being photographed and that a succession of projected still frames (which is what a motion picture is) will seem more three-dimensional than a still frame alone.

Snow has constructed a film around an interplay between stasis (the room) and movement (the zoom), between the arbitrary (the obtrusive narrative and photographic effects) and the planned and predictable (the formal structure of the work). *Wavelength* explores the medium of cinema in a way that is at once playful and carefully structured while minimizing or rendering arbitrary the usual narrative elements of the commercial film.

If the abstract film often involves the production of increasingly rapid, fragmented imagery, in the seventies the trend was toward a paring down, a simplification of film ideas. In both cases, we appreciate the film medium differently. Experimental films (like most modern painting, music, drama, poetry, or fiction) are as much about themselves, about the processes of filmmaking, as they are about the "real" world.

Spectacles and experimental films thus form a noteworthy contrast. Both take delight in seeing what the film medium can do, but where the former work within the conventions of storytelling to emphasize *mise en scène,* the latter look for alternatives to narrative either in anarchic disorganization (Dada), attention to formal elements (abstraction), or a paring down to simple, essential elements (minimalism).

ESTHETIC CINEMA AND THE CRITICS

Those types of filmmaking heavily inclined toward the esthetic have long produced great controversy and partisanship on the part of critics and theorists. On the one hand, the popular vision of historical spectacles, science fiction, and musicals has been that they are empty-headed genres that appeal to a mass audience's attraction to flash rather than substance. Defenders of these genres have had to react against this image. On the other hand, the experimental film has always had an elitist, overly intellectual image to its detractors, even while attracting theorists of a highly serious (some would say pompous) bent and highly vocal, intense, disputatious partisans.

Spectacle and the Critics

What one might call the middle-brow bias against those genres that gravitate toward spectacle can probably be traced to Aristotle and his influence on Western culture.[29] In Aristotle's six components of tragedy—plot, character, diction, thought, spectacle, and melody—spectacle is lowest. It is, according to him, "the least artistic and connected least with the art of poetry." Aristotle continues, "For the plot ought to be constructed so that, even without the aid of the eye, he who hears the tale will thrill with horror and melt to pity at what takes place."[30] The standards of Aristotle are in some ways directly opposed to a visually dominant cinema.

This bias against spectacle continues among more contemporary critics. Siegfried Kracauer, whom we discussed earlier as a primary advocate of realism, sees historical and fantastic films as anathema to the nature of the medium. In them, Kracauer argues, the filmmaker "seems no longer concerned with physical reality but bent on incorporating worlds which to all appearances lie outside the orbit of actuality."[31] In the dialectic that is traditionally established between Lumière and Méliès, Lumière still has vocal partisans. Very recently, one critic has even written: "With each insensitive praising of Méliès, it is Lumière whom they kill. Anything that counts in the cinema of today or yesterday . . . has absolutely nothing to do with Méliès."[32] For these critics, the Méliès-style cinema offers simple escapism or blindness to the real world, and by extension for some, an indifference to the political and social realities of life.

For other critics, however, the Méliès line is the major line of cinema—a line of magic and illusion. Partisans of this cinema have four primary arguments they make in its defense:

1. Magic and illusion are the basis of mass-audience popular cinema. This is what the public wants to see and pays for. "The cramped melancholy poverty of the so-called natural settings of *cinéma vérité* is now outmoded,"[33] one observer has written, citing the return to spectacular sets and special effects in movies like *The Exorcist* (1974) and *The Towering Inferno* (1974)—and the return of people to the box office.

2. The big superproduction is the surest gauge of genuine professionalism in filmmaking. Spectacles are "a genre where the scale of money required has never permitted even inspired amateurs to excel; where the technical difficulty of certain sequences requires that the filmmaker possess an in-depth knowledge of his art and craft; where the filmmaker finds that his primary function behind the camera, even before questions of style, of personal signature, or the art of editing, is to have a sense of organization."[34]

3. The alternative to spectacle, realism, is fundamentally limiting and unimaginative. Thus, in the extreme heroism of the semimythical, lavish, historical film, some critics have seen a glorification of humanity at its noblest—that is, the human as demigod freed from the limitations of the mundane world that the realists usually portray.[35] Others have found certain musicals to epitomize an ideal of erotic cinema, whereby a discreet expression of passion takes totally visual and symbolized terms.[36] And science fiction has always allowed for a blend of parable with conventional storytelling in a way that would be impossible in genres more tied to the earth as we know it.

4. The spectacle film offers the fullest potential for a cinema based on *mise en scène*. Historical spectacles, musicals, and science-fiction films allow for a cinema based largely on formal elegance.

What these last enthusiasts ultimately favor is a cinema that could best be described as baroque. The notion of the baroque in art is usually opposed to that of the classical. A key stylistic quality of the latter is a sense of balance and moderation; the former favors movement in place of balance, excess in place of moderation (Fig. 13.12). In terms of the visual style of filmmaking, the balanced, classical narrative we have discussed would have a certain visual moderation—a lack of technique for its own sake. Baroque commercial filmmaking would be a more estheticized form that prizes elaborate technique and often flourishes in the spectacle-oriented genres.[37]

The baroque idealization of movement comes directly into this mode of esthetic cinema, for what most so-called *mise en scène* critics favor is a cinema of long takes and camera movement rather than montage or editing. Many *mise en scène* critics have been influenced by the theories of André Bazin that we discussed earlier. But where they may differ from Bazin is that they do not so much see the uncut take as more realistic, but rather as a technique that emphasizes elegant movement. The musical, of course, is the *moving* picture par excellence, and those who find Vincente Minnelli a great director would usually cite his precise and graceful crane shots as an important stylistic trait. Similarly, when a critic like Andrew Sarris praises the films of Max Ophuls as the finest work ever produced in film, it is essentially out of reverence for a baroque sensibility. For not only did Ophuls characteristically work with elaborately decorated period sets (in films like *The Earrings of Madame De . . .*, 1953, and *Lola Montez*, 1955), but his stylistic trademark has always been the fluid tracking shot, which portrays a world in flux and

13.12 The baroque in painting. In *The Last Judgment* (1608), baroque painter Peter Paul Rubens creates dynamic movement and presents several actions occurring simultaneously. Baroque painting foreshadowed many effects that are possible in film.

movement (a baroque approach) rather than order and balance (a classical approach).[38] (See Fig. 4.5.) Critic Pierre Pitiot has even suggested that film by its very nature, because it is based on movement, should be considered a baroque medium.[39] Partisans of the baroque in film value the medium's esthetic side.

Experimental Film and the Critics

Theorists of the experimental film have very often been filmmakers themselves, and their writings on film have tended to emphasize two major arguments: (1) Experimentation in film exists in reaction to and is incompatible with the standard Hollywood apparatus for financing and producing motion pictures; (2) the film medium must establish its own modes of expression that are uniquely cinematic.

Let us consider each of these areas and some of the critics who have written about them.

The Reaction Against Hollywood   Experimental filmmaking has been, by and large, anti-Establishment filmmaking and most experimental filmmakers and theorists have reacted against the standards of commercial filmmaking we considered earlier in discussing the "balanced" Hollywood cinema. Thus Jonas Mekas, one of the primary spokesmen for the New American Cinema for many years (and particularly during the sixties), wrote in 1959 of a new generation of international filmmakers who "mistrust and loathe the official cinema and its thematic and formal stiffness" and "seek to free themselves from the over-professionalism and over-technicality that usually handicaps the inspiration and spontaneity of the official cinema, guiding themselves more by intuition and improvisation than by discipline."[40]

Even earlier, Maya Deren had argued that the Hollywood cinema, with its division of labor and its prizing of technical skill, propagandized its professionalism as a form of self-protection. The expense and time used in commercial moviemaking, she asserted, was Hollywood's way of maintaining cinema as an industry rather than as an art form in order to keep moguls and businessmen, rather than artists, in power. For her, ideas and imagination were more important than technical skill in filmmaking.[41]

Partisans of the Hollywood cinema have frequently criticized experimental films for their technical incompetence, but filmmakers and theorists within the movement, reacting defensively to the charges, have dismissed them as simply irrelevant. Gregory Markopoulos, who has contributed a signifcant body of theoretical writing on the experimental film, has written:

An over-exposure or an under-exposure is like a painter mixing his colors . . . A scratching of the film is like the scratches that may be found in paintings which are called masterpieces . . . Just as a poor surface or canvas may be used by a painter, just as a cheap note book may be used by a writer, just as ordinary clay may be used by a sculptor, so too any materials, that a film-maker may utilize for his own work. In the end it is not the materials that reveal the spirit of the artist but rather the soul of the artist that is revealed by the contents of the film.[42]

Similarly, Jonas Mekas has argued: "If we study the modern film poetry, we find that even the mistakes, the out-of-focus shots, the shaky shots, the unsure steps, the hesitant movements, the overexposed and underexposed bits, have become part of the new cinema vocabulary, being part of the psychological and visual reality of modern man."[43]

Experimental film is thus partly a protest against the filmmaking establishment, and words like *subversive* or *radical* are often used to describe it.[44] Shocking content (as in, let us say, *Flaming Creatures*) may be taken as a form of political revolt against bourgeois morality and a complacent society, an attitude similar to the militant existentialism we discussed with regard to the personal film. Primitive, or "unprofessional," form serves to carry the attack to the esthetic level as well. (One can only recall the reaction of a British censor to Germaine Dulac's *The Seashell and the Clergyman*. The film was found "so cryptic as to be almost meaningless. If there is a meaning, it is doubtless objectionable.") A cinema that is revolutionary in form, the argument would go, can be a first step toward the construction of a new political and social awareness.

Some recent theorists would attach this principle particularly to the minimal film. They see what they call the *structural-materialist* film as a "deconstruction" of the bourgeois Hollywood cinema, one that trains viewers not to be taken in by the mystifications of capitalist moviemaking. For these critics, the films of Peter Kubelka and Michael Snow are comparable to those of Godard's Groupe Dziga Vertov as alternative forms of filmmaking. In this respect the progression of the *avant-garde* film from the sixties through the seventies may well be that of a change from the amorality of, let us say, a Jack Smith and *Flaming Creatures*, to a new morality (even, perhaps, a new puritanism based on a rejection of fantasy and magic in favor of literal, "demystified" imagery) based on political, Marxist standards instead of religious ones.[45]

The Search for the Uniquely Cinematic To many theorists of experimental film, for film to become an art form it must go beyond realism and beyond the use of the camera merely as a recording device. Hans Richter has noted: "The main esthetic problem in the movies, which were invented for reproduction (of movement) is, paradoxically, the overcoming of reproduction." The film, Richter continues, "is overwhelmingly used for keeping records of achievements: of plays, actors, novels or just plain nature, and proportionately less for the creation of original filmic sensations."[46] The same argument occurs in the writings of Maya Deren, who rejects not only the conventional Hollywood cinema as film art, but also the documentary:

. . . All who have read fine poetry would not confuse even the finest reportorial account with a poem. Documentaries are the visual counterparts of reportorial dispatches, and bear the same relationship to cinema art as the dispatches do to poetry.[47]

What Richter and Deren sought, instead, was a film defined purely in terms of the medium and its unique abilities to manipulate time and space. This had been the goal of *avant-garde* theorists and filmmakers throughout the history of the medium. They have seen the traditional forms of narrative cinema as a hindrance to film's becoming a genuine art form and have often advocated a cinema modeled on painting or music rather than theater or literature. One of the earliest commentaries on film esthetics, by the French critic Elie Faure, calls for film as an art of "cinéplastics" in which story, if any exists, is simply a pretext for expression by means of "volumes, arabesques, gesture, attitudes, relations, associations, contrasts and passages of tones—the whole animated and insensibly modified form one fraction of a second to another."[48] Faure is associated with a movement in France during the twenties known as *impressionism,* in which critics (the most famous of whom was Louis Delluc) sought this kind of "pure" film expression of a cinema freed from stage or literary conventions. One impressionist theorist and filmmaker, Jean Epstein, wrote in 1923:

The film should positively avoid any connection with the historical, educational, romantic, moral, or immoral, geographic or documentary subjects. The film should become, step by step, finally exclusively photogenic elements.[49]

A later theorist of experimental film, Gene Youngblood, couched the argument in different terms. He argues that what contemporary experimental cinema has moved toward is a new kind of experience which he calls *synesthetic.* Whereas the traditional narrative film is limiting, linear, literary, and predictable by its very nature, experimental film can offer a more freely structured art in which what seem to be chaotic, random elements are really a perception of the world in terms of its totality rather than an attempt—as occurs in standard narrative—to understand it piece by piece. Youngblood sees the new cinema rendering old categories like fiction and documentary obsolete. What a synesthetic cinema achieves is a stimulation of the processes of perception and experience. He writes, "The natural phenomenon explained by synesthetic cinema is the filmmaker's consciousness."[50] A film need not "make sense" in terms of narrative design or structure. It need simply stimulate visually, as *Dog Star Man* and *Wavelength* do.

The usual negative criticism of this attitude is that it leads to an "anything goes" attitude in which formlessness and self-indulgence predominate. Even Amos Vogel, who for many years ran Cinema 16, a society in New York devoted to the screening of experimental films, was by the sixties raising objections:

Lack, failure and disregard of form is the overriding weakness of today's avant-garde. Current tendencies in all the arts toward improvisation, fluidity and chance are mistaken for a total absence of form, and the temptation is to disregard the fact that it is precisely the achieved works of this kind that reveal an inner structure and logic.[51]

The two sides of experimental film theory are ultimately related, because breaking Hollywood rules and distrusting convention may well indicate a distrust for the collective myths of a society and to prize the esthetic and the uniquely cinematic above all functions is to reject the way in which more balanced films take images with some realistic impact and turn them into collective myth. By subverting the realistic side of cinema and emphasizing the esthetic, one asks the audience not to take part in these myths but to examine the processes whereby filmmakers make film.

Whether this is really a purer form of cinema may be open to question, and the *avant-garde* film has always had to content itself with a small, partisan audience. If the spectacle film provides for an estheticized cinema in terms the masses can understand, the experimental cinema works with similar problems and issues—space, form, line, movement, color—in terms that may be too idiosyncratic or indirect for the average viewer but which may also excite and stimulate an audience alert to the challenges involved.

The implicit assumption of this chapter has been that the superficial opposition between these two kinds of esthetic cinema may hide certain basic similarities between them. Although spectacle films and experimental films come from different cultural contexts and aim at different audiences, the qualities that make, let us say, a musical production number engaging may often be the same ones that inspire us when we see an exciting piece of abstract animation.[52] We enjoy the pure sensuousness of the medium, the visual stimulation of figures in motion, the effects of pace, tempo, and physical grace that movies can offer.

SUMMARY

The esthetic function of film communication involves an appreciation of the medium for its own sake, a delight in the purely physical or formal properties of the medium. We see this approach to film—which, one may argue, goes back to Georges Méliès—in two kinds of cinema, the spectacle movie and the experimental film.

Spectacle films include such genres as the historical spectacle, the science-fiction film, and the musical. Spectacle films may often be considered short on ideas, but they can be appreciated for the sophistication with which their makers use the film medium. A film like *Goliath and the Dragon* or the "ShadowWaltz" sequence from *Gold Diggers of 1933* can reveal great skill in dealing with movement, line, form, color, and sound.

The experimental film deemphasizes narrative in favor of filmmaking that creates striking images and forms for their own sake. We can consider three kinds of experimental film: (1) the Dadaist film, (2) the abstract film, and (3) the minimalist or structural film.

Dadaist films, such as *Entr'acte* and later works influenced by the Dada movement, try to be deliberately incoherent or confusing, to shock or surprise audiences out of their complacent attitudes about what art should be.

Abstract films may be completely abstract, as in those that use animation of geometric forms, or they may use real photographic images that are distorted or manipulated through special kinds of photography, superimposition, fragmentary editing, or the introduction of extraphotographic materials. We may see all of these techniques in the work of Stan Brakhage and other experimental filmmakers.

Minimal or structuralist filmmaking has produced motion pictures built around an intentionally limited number of images and range of techniques for each film. Examples of minimalist or structural movies are the early films of Andy Warhol, which focus for hours on end on single subjects, photographed without editing, or those of Michael Snow, such as *Wavelength*. This film in effect shows a single, forty-five-minute zoom into a close-up of a photograph on the opposite wall of a room.

Esthetic forms of filmmaking have sharply divided theorists and critics. Critics oriented toward realism react negatively to spectacle films, whereas advocates of spectacle see it as the most genuine form of popular, professional, and imaginative filmmaking. Some of them would argue that the spectacle movie allows for the fullest expression possible of a baroque sensibility.

Experimental films are often criticized for being unprofessional and elitist, but advocates of experimental cinema argue that it is the only form of film that allows the filmmaker to be a genuine artist and to escape the limiting restrictions of Hollywood-style work.

NOTES

1 Calvin Pryluck discusses bank surveillance images, describing them as purely "indexical." That is, meaning in them comes not from the image itself, but from its connection to the object depicted. See *Sources of Meaning in Motion Pictures and Television* (New York: Arno, 1976), pp. 100–101.

2 Leon Barsacq, *Caligari's Cabinet and Other Grand Illusions: A History of Film Design*, ed. Elliot Stein, foreword by René Clair (Boston: New York Graphic Society, 1976), p. 6.

3 See Marcel Martin, "Méliès: Pionnier du burlesque," *Ecran*, No. 79 (April 1979), 2–3.

4 We have avoided the term *epic*, commonly used by critics and theorists, because it implies a certain kind of narrative structure, and a certain relation to the epic genre in literature, rather than the approach to the visual aspects of film that interests us here. For a treatment of the epic film as a genre, one may consult Louis Phillip Castelli, "Film Epic: A Generic Examination and an Application of Definitions to the Work of David Lean," unpublished doctoral dissertation, Northwestern University, 1977; or Foster Hirsch, *The Hollywood Epic* (New York: Barnes, 1978).

5 Critics have related De Mille in particular to this visual tradition. See Jacques Doniol-Valcroze, "Samson, Cecil et Dalila," *Cahiers du cinéma*, 1 (Sept. 1951), 19–31; and Foster Hirsch, *The Hollywood Epic*, p. 31.

6 Michel Mourlet, *Sur un art ignoré* (Paris: La Table Ronde, 1965). See also the special Cottafavi number of *Présence du cinéma*, No. 9 (Dec. 1961).

7 Gérard Legrand, "Le péplum et le cape," *Positif*, No. 45 (May 1962), 173–174; Charles Barr, "*Hercules Conquers Atlantis*," in *The Movie Reader*, ed. Ian Cameron, (New York: Praeger, 1971), p. 119.

8 Film director Martin Scorsese has written with regard to *The Silver Chalice*: "We don't know what ancient Rome was like, so why not take the attitude Fellini did with *Satyricon*: make it science fiction in reverse?" See "Martin Scorsese's Guilty Pleasures," *Film Comment*, 14, (Sept.–Oct. 1978), 63–66.

9 We have borrowed these categories from Philip Strick, *Science Fiction Movies* (London: Octopus, 1976).

10 Jeff Rovin, *A Pictorial History of Science Fiction Film* (Secaucus, N. J.: Citadel, 1975), p. 25.

11 The original running time of *2001* was 165 minutes; it was subsequently cut to 141 minutes, and 16-mm prints run 139 minutes.

12 Max Kozloff, "*2001*," *Film Culture*, Nos. 48–49 (Winter–Spring 1970), 53–56.

13 Albert Johnson, "The Films of Vincente Minnelli, Part I," *Film Quarterly*, 12 (Spring 1959), 30.

14 Some would argue that the experimental

film is indeed a genre unto itself—i.e., that experimental films share certain thematic and stylistic traits that make them comparable to one another in the way that Westerns, let us say, are comparable to one another. We will stick here, however, to the term *genre film* as it is commonly used, to refer to Hollywood genres.

15 See in particular Ken Kelman's "The Anti-Information Film: Conner's *Report,*" in *The Essential Cinema: Essays on Films in the Anthology Film Archives,* ed. P. Adams Sitney (New York: Anthology Film Archives and New York University Press, 1975), pp. 240–244.

16 See in particular Susan Sontag's "Jack Smith's *Flaming Creatures,*" in *The New American Cinema: A Critical Anthology,* ed. Gregory Battcock (New York: Dutton, 1967), pp. 204–210.

17 P. Adams Sitney, "The Idea of Abstraction," *Film Culture,* Nos. 63–64 (1976), 14–15.

18 Malcolm Le Grice, *Abstract Film and Beyond* (London: Studio Vista, n.d.), pp. 19–26.

19 Malcolm Le Grice argues that the blank leader and repeated imagery in Léger's film mark it as the first historic appearance of both the "structural" film and the "loop" film (*Abstract Film and Beyond,* pp. 38–40). See our section on minimal cinema.

20 In this section and the one on minimal cinema, our examples will be drawn primarily from the American cinema, since these are the films most available to viewers in this country. This should not be construed to minimize the importance of the British and Continental *avant-garde* film movements.

21 Malcolm Le Grice, *Abstract Film and Beyond,* p. 89.

22 For a full discussion of superimposition, see

Stephen Dwoskin, *Film Is . . . : The International Free Cinema* (London: Peter Owen, 1975), pp. 152–153.

23 Fred Camper, "*The Art of Vision,* a Film by Stan Brakhage," *Film Culture,* No. 46 (Autumn 1967), 41. Much of our discussion here is based on Camper's description.

24 Jonas Mekas, "Interview with Peter Kubelka," in *The Film Culture Reader,* ed. P. Adams Sitney (New York: Praeger, 1970), p. 291.

25 Sheldan Renan, *An Introduction to the American Underground Film* (New York: Dutton, 1967), pp. 184–190, 233.

26 "Sixth Independent Film Award," *Film Culture,* No. 33 (Summer 1964), 1.

27 Both Joyce Wieland's *Sailboat* (1967) and Peter Gidal's *Clouds* (1969) repeat almost identical images that are really shot separately. The esthetic is similar to that of the loop film, but the viewer may see subtle differences between the images. See Malcolm Le Grice, *Abstract Film and Beyond,* p. 113.

28 See John Coplans, *Serial Imagery* (Pasadena, Calif.: Pasadena Art Museum and the New York Graphic Society, 1968).

29 The authors thank William O. Huie for this insight, and for the observation that it is perfectly demonstrated in Vincente Minnelli's *The Band Wagon* (1953). In his musical, Minnelli opposes a pompous stage director concerned with Greek tragedy to popular entertainers more concerned with song and dance, as evidenced in the song "That's Entertainment."

30 Aristotle, *On the Art of Poetry* trans. S. H. Butcher, ed. Milton C. Nahm (Indianapolis: Bobbs-Merrill, 1956), pp. 11, 17–18.

31 Siegfried Kracauer, *Theory of Film: The Redemption of Physical Reality* (New York: Oxford, 1965), pp. 77.

32 Gérard Courant, "Méliès: La fin d'un mythe?" *Cinéma 79*, No. 245 (May 1979), 9. See in response, M. A. M. Quevrain, "L'idéologie de Méliès et son époque," *Cinéma 79*, No. 249 (Sept. 1979), 10–12.

33 Elliot Stein, in Léon Barsacq, *Caligari's Cabinet and Other Grand Illusions*, p. 193.

34 Roland Lacourbe, "L'invasion des amateurs," *Ecran 77*, No. 59 (June 1977), 44.

35 Michel Mourlet, *Sur un art ignoré*, pp. 50–56; Jacques Joly, "Esther et les autres," *Cahiers du cinéma*, 21 (Aug. 1961), 17–25.

36 Ado Kyrou, "Notes sur l'erotisme des films dansés," *Positif*, 2 (Nov.–Dec. 1954), 35.

37 For a graphic comparison of classic and baroque styles, see Germain Bazin, *The Baroque: Principles, Styles, Modes, Themes* (Greenwich, Conn.: New York Graphic Society, 1968), p. 53.

38 This particular kind of camera movement, as well as its implications for erotic subject matter, is discussed in Stephen Heath, "The Question Oshima," *Wide Angle*, 2 (1977), 48–57.

39 *Cinéma de Mort: Esquisse d'un baroque cinématographique* (Fribourg: Editions du Signe, 1972), 85.

40 Jonas Mekas, "A Call for a New Generation of Film Makers," *Film Culture*, No. 19 (1959), 2.

41 Maya Deren, "Cinema as an Art Form," in *Introduction to the Art of the Movies*, ed. Lewis Jacobs (New York: Farrar, Straus and Giroux, 1960), pp. 254–255.

42 Gregory Markopoulos, "Projection of Thoughts," *Film Culture*, No. 32 (Spring 1964), 5.

43 Jonas Mekas, "Notes on the New American Cinema," in *The Film Culture Reader*, ed. P. Adams Sitney, p. 105.

44 See in particular Annette Michelson's "Film and the Radical Aspiration," in *The Film Culture Reader*, ed. P. Adams Sitney, pp. 404–422; also in *The New American Cinema*, ed. Gregory Battcock, pp. 83–101.

45 See Stephen Heath, "Repetition Time: Notes Around 'Structural/Materialist Films,' " *Wide Angle*, No. 2, 3 (1978), 4–11.

46 Hans Richter, "The Film as an Original Art Form," in *Introduction to the Art of the Movies*, ed. Lewis Jacobs, pp. 282–283.

47 Maya Deren, "Cinema as an Art Form," p. 260.

48 Elie Faure, "The Art of Cineplastics," in *Film: An Anthology*, ed. Daniel Talbot (Berkeley: University of California, 1970), p. 7.

49 Jean Epstein, quoted in Hans Richter, "The Film as an Original Art Form," p. 286.

50 Gene Youngblood, *Expanded Cinema*, introd. by R. Buckminster Fuller (New York: Dutton, 1970), pp. 107-108. See also our discussion of Eisenstein's notion of synesthesia in Chapter 4.

51 Amos Vogel, "Thirteen Confusions," in *The New American Cinema*, ed. Gregory Battcock, pp. 130–131.

52 The connection between spectacle and experimental forms of filmmaking is evident in a recent interview with George Lucas, creator of *Star Wars*, accompanying the release of a *Star Wars* sequel, *The Empire Strikes Back* (1980). Lucas announced his desire "to go back to what I was exploring in film school," to make "a combination of visual tone poems and *cinéma vérité*. They'll have people, but no plots or characters. I like to play with pure film." Presumably the same sensibility that finds science fiction attractive also likes the notion of "pure film." See David Ansen, "More 'Stars' in His Eyes," *Newsweek*, May 19, 1980, p. 107.

Chapter 14 / Summary

Cinema and

Our Sense of Balance

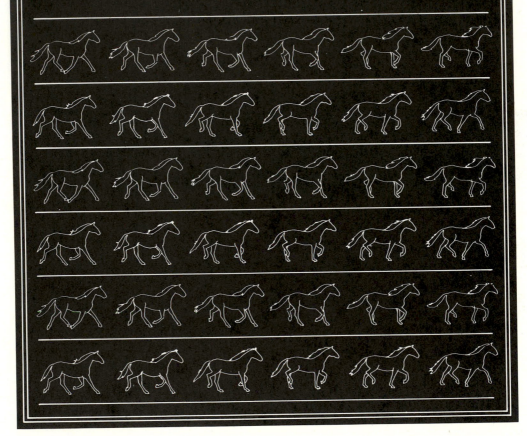

I n this book we have attempted to analyze the different types of cinematic experience in terms of the *medium*, by which we mean the various technical means available to filmmakers, and the *message*, considered in terms of four functions of communication. We have considered a movie as a system in which there are various tensions and balances among these techniques and these functions. And the complexity of these interrelated aspects is what makes movies fascinating.

Film was born out of a basic human desire to capture or imitate reality. It is, to use Aristotle's word, a *mimetic* medium. And it was invented and grew out of various cultural motivations: scientists wanted to explore areas of human perception, entrepreneurs wanted to make some money, magicians wanted to improve their craft. All worked together to produce one of the most potent cultural phenomena in human history. For the medium they created collectively plays on certain *perceptual fascinations* and the messages they were able to send have produced their own *conceptual fascinations*. The two are linked: the mimetic capacities of the medium make for a kind of communication very different from that of the printed page or the spoken word.

In considering the perceptual fascinations of the medium we have examined how early inventors created the illusion of movement and captured a sense of reality. Later filmmakers developed continuity techniques to create an illusion of time and space either recorded exactly or broken apart and analyzed, depending on the filmmaker's approach. We have followed a historical progression in the development of the medium from the time when anything that moved on film was exciting to an audience, to the development of editing practices that emphasized storytelling and heightened audience involvement, to the coming of sound and color, which provided for a greater sense of mimetic completeness.

We have studied what has been, for better or worse, the dominant form of filmmaking in the world—the *Hollywood cinema*, which we might also refer to as the *classic narrative cinema*. We have discussed this classic Hollywood film in both its social and artistic contexts, and we have noted that the Hollywood comedy is essentially a disruption of these standard storytelling forms. In examining the Hollywood movie as the dominant kind of film message, we have considered four functions of communication often cited by linguists and communication theorists:

■ A realist function, concerned with what the film communicates about the world. In the Hollywood film, there is a tension involving the way filmmakers create a superficial realism that may mask the truly mythic nature of characters and events.

473

■ A persuasive function, concerned with how the film influences the way its audience lives, works, and sees the world, both politically and socially. In the Hollywood film, the tension lies between implicit propaganda, in which the film takes certain values for granted, and explicit propaganda, in which its attempts at persuasion may be more conscious or deliberate.

■ A personal function, concerned with the way in which movies can express the feeling of the sender. In the Hollywood film, we can see this in the way certain directors, often called *auteurs,* impose a personal vision on what may be familiar genre material, while others may emphasize the star as the primary figure with whom the audience identifies.

■ An esthetic function, concerned with the ways in which Hollywood filmmakers have developed standard storytelling forms, called genres, and use familiar patterns of *mise en scène* and editing to tell these stories. In the Hollywood film, the tension is between the transparent (the technique that will go unnoticed) and the opaque (the technique that, effectively or not, may call attention to itself).

We have argued that the standard Hollywood film is a *balanced* form of filmmaking. No one function dominates the others. The result is a motion picture in which the manipulations of the filmmaker are often invisible, creating a kind of seamless narrative that lets the audience become unquestioningly involved in its story, which never stops to linger for very long on any one of these four aspects of the message.

We have also examined forms of filmmaking that, unlike the typical Hollywood film, dwell on one function or aspect of the cinematic message. These forms of what we call *weighted messages* are:

■ Realist cinema, including the documentary and various forms of realism in film, which emphasize the real world that the film is supposedly about.

■ Persuasive cinema, filmmaking concerned with affecting the audience, which emphasizes political or persuasive messages (such as films of propaganda or protest).

■ Personal cinema, by which we mean those kinds of moviemaking that emphasize the filmmakers themselves, either through autobiographical subject matter, subjective techniques of editing and *mise en scène* or a militantly individualistic point of view.

■ Esthetic cinema, which, when commercial, has extended a tradition (begun with Méliès) of elaborate spectacle, as in the musical or science-fiction film. In its noncommercial forms, esthetic cinema has involved experimental filmmaking. In both instances, filmmakers emphasize form over content, the techniques of filmmaking over any particular importance of subject matter.

All of these are what we consider self-conscious forms of film expression. Their single-minded emphasis on a single function of filmmaking often makes them less accessible to a mass audience, and of more interest to movie-going devotees and specialists seeking something other than simply entertainment.

Yet film is a pluralistic medium, and as with any attempt to classify human activity, there have been overlaps, inconsistencies, and anomalies in this system that we have sometimes overlooked and sometimes acknowledged, depending on their importance. We have tried to apply our categories in an evenhanded manner, and we have tried to include all the common—and some uncommon—forms of film experience.

Because movies can be diverse and so varied, we have tried not to advocate one use of the medium over any other. We prefer to leave to the reader any preference for balanced over weighted forms—or for one function of film over another. Most polemics about motion pictures argue for a single use of the medium over all others, and then argue that this single use is the most truthful, beautiful, or important kind of filmmaking. One writer will praise the old-fashioned mass-audience film as what movies are all about. Another will see realism as that form of expression for which the medium has the greatest affinity. A third will see forms of filmmaking that are not self-consciously artistic (or politically expressive) as unimportant or trivial. Such critics offer the reader an either-or choice. A film is either realist or not, popular or elitist, art or trash, political or pointless. In arguing for realism, art, or social commitment, many critics lump the alternatives into a single pile. By describing several functions of filmmaking, we have hoped to avoid this kind of over-simplification.

The difficulty with putting the whole history of film into categories is that all films perform more than one function simultaneously. They have multiple and sometimes even conflicting purposes. We have already discussed several particularly common combinations of functions. Political filmmakers often use a documentary approach, shaping their observations of the world to provoke audience commitment.

Filmmakers involved in personal expression often also explore the formal potential of the medium they work in. We have seen how narrative mixes with observation of the world in *The Bicycle Thief* and with exploration of the medium in *Wavelength*. We have discussed *The Gods and the Dead* as political spectacle. Almost any combination of functions is possible.

Certain films in the history of the medium have, however, had particularly high ambitions. They have tried, in a word, to do everything. Some have worked in deliberately commercial forms, yet have attempted at the same time to stretch their interests out over all of the functional areas we have described. Rather than being balanced in the sense that we have seen, like the traditional Hollywood narrative that effaces all particular emphasis on any one of these functions, these movies are what we may call *multiweighted*. That is, they show an emphatic interest in all of the functions, calling attention—in alternation, perhaps, and even with some degree of self-consciousness—to the way in which the film treats all of them. These works represent great *synthetic works* of the medium: they are achievements that exploit all the possibilities of film.

THE CLASSIC CINEMA

A glance at two highly regarded classics of the medium suggests the way in which all the functions can be so combined. Let us consider Jean Renoir's *The Rules of the Game* (1939) and Orson Welles's *Citizen Kane* (1941), to demonstrate how their richness, their status as classics, comes from their synthetic nature. They are works that do not limit themselves to a single preoccupation, but rather partake of many.

The Rules of the Game   Some critics consider *The Rules of the Game* to be Jean Renoir's finest motion picture. One can see in it, and in Renoir's work as a whole, a comprehensiveness of vision that allows for no simple classification.

The Rules of the Game is superficially a sex comedy about the various flirtations, pairings, and jealousies among a group of wealthy people and their servants. The mechanics of its plot are familiar. A wealthy couple entertain friends at a country chateau. The woman, Christine, rejects the advances of a young aviator until after she has seen her husband together with his mistress. She is unaware that they have just broken up and that their kiss is "for old time's sake". Her relationships are reflected in those of her maid, Lisette, who must conceal from her gruff husband, the

14.1 A comparison of social classes. In *The Rules of the Game* (1939), director Jean Renoir compares various levels of a class structure. He suggests that a wealthy woman and her maid are in many ways alike—even though fate has placed them in different positions in society.

gamekeeper, her interest in Marceau, a poacher whom the master of the house has capriciously made a servant (Fig. 14.1). Although we can enjoy most of the film as a simple amusement, Renoir thwarts our expectations by ending the film tragically—with an accidental murder through mistaken identity.

Such unexpected changes of mood are characteristic of Renoir's films. By breaking with the simple conventions of storytelling and comedy, Renoir creates a more personal kind of film. *The Rules of the Game*'s subjective nature may be seen in Renoir's casting of himself as Octave. The director claims to have been inspired to make the film by observing how the love affairs of friends would completely take over their lives.[1] Through most of the film Octave is merely an observer. Although he is instrumental in the beginning in getting the aviator and Christine together (and thereby sets the mechanism of the comedy in motion, in much the same way Renoir the director has set the film in motion), only near the end do he and Christine decide to run away together. The movie's tone is similar to that of Octave's in that he is interested and understanding, but also critical of himself and others.

Although other films by Renoir are somewhat more realist in tone, *The Rules of the Game* is still shot with typically Renoirian casualness. Renoir moves the camera

almost as if discovering things randomly, as a documentary filmmaker might. He generally avoids dramatic effects of light and shadow and is known for allowing actors to improvise, to be themselves. The exteriors of the film are clearly real locations, and the famed scene of the rabbit hunt has a particularly clinical objectivity to it. We can tell that real animals are being shot.

In discussing the question of realism in film, we pointed out the tendency of realism to deal with the lower classes, if only because the upper classes make a kind of theater of their lives, putting an emphasis on etiquette, show, and role playing. Renoir is very much aware of this tendency and reflects on it within the film. The culmination of the action is at a costume party involving impromptu stage performances, through which Renoir suggests that the characters' real lives are as false as anything they may be pretending. One of the most exciting effects in the film comes when we see in a distance a Méliès-like stage performance involving some rather convincing ghosts and skeletons (Fig. 14.2). Renoir then cuts to a shot from the stage, so that we can see something of the mechanics of the illusion. Like many of Renoir's films, *The Rules of the Game* becomes a reflection on both theater and life, realism and illusion. In his own way, Renoir explores the medium.

Finally, although one may debate the extent to which Renoir intended it as such, *The Rules of the Game* was a film with significant political repercussions. Seen today, it hardly seems the stuff of significant controversy, but audiences at the time saw it as a scathing critique of the upper classes. The work was banned as demoralizing by the French government some months after it opened and was later

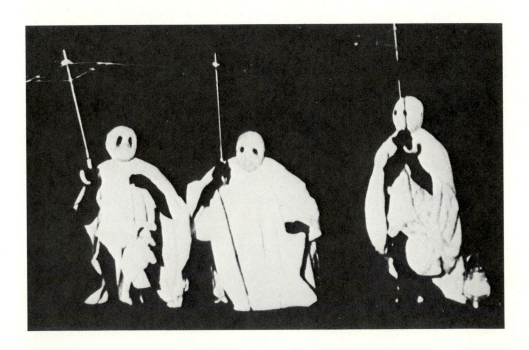

blacklisted by the Germans during the occupation. A modern audience may find *The Rules of the Game* stylized and not very realistic, but the reception it received suggests that Renoir came too close for comfort in his portrayal of bourgeois hypocrisy.

Citizen Kane A film of equal or greater prestige is Orson Welles's *Citizen Kane* (1941), which we have discussed as a landmark film in the development of deep-focus cinematography. Yet the film is noteworthy not simply for its technical innovation. In polls conducted by the magazine *Sight and Sound* in 1962 and 1972, critics named *Citizen Kane* more often than any other film as one of the ten best films of all time.[2]

Why so much critical enthusiasm? The answer again lies in the film's multifaceted nature. Welles chose for his film a politically hot subject. *Citizen Kane* was a thinly disguised biography of newspaper tycoon William Randolph Hearst, and although it was hardly a flaming piece of anti-Hearst propaganda, it presented the newspaperman in a negative enough light to cause some to try to block its release. In its portrayal of Kane's arrogant rise to power, his subsequent demagoguery and loss of ideals, *Citizen Kane* casts a critical glance at American industry and the ideology of rugged individualism.

Yet *Kane* also has a good story to tell. It begins with Charles Foster Kane on his deathbed and traces the attempts of newspapermen to find out the significance of Kane's dying word, "Rosebud." In hearing accounts from people who knew him, we come to see Kane's life from varying points of view. We follow his success in the newspaper business, his failure to make a career in politics, and his final attempt to turn into an opera star the woman who had wrecked his political career through scandal. As critics have pointed out, *Kane* exploits audience familiarity with several film genres, especially the detective story and the newspaper comedy. The narrative structure, although it consists of complicated and often overlapping flashbacks, is never difficult to follow, and even unsophisticated audiences find it exciting.

It is this skill at combining an involving narrative with technical innovation that is *Citizen Kane*'s chief claim to fame. Not only did the movie experiment with deep-focus photography, but its elaborate flashback structure allowed for inventive sound montages and fanciful editing. As a first feature made by an ambitious young man new to Hollywood, *Kane* is a technical bag of tricks. But as one critic has remarked, "what makes Welles' directorial style so satisfying in this movie is that we are constantly aware of the mechanics—that the pleasure *Kane* gives doesn't come

14.2 The ghost show in *The Rules of the Game*. The fine line between illusion and reality—and between theater and life—is a constant theme in Jean Renoir's films. The ghost show near the end of *The Rules of the Game* (1939) can be interpreted as a subtle comment on the nature of the film medium as shadow play or magic.

from illusion but comes from our enjoyment of the dexterity of the illusionists and the working of the machinery."[3] *Citizen Kane* is one of the few films in which such deliberately showy experimental continuity does not get in the way of a storytelling structure.

What gives Welles's work its greatest substance, however, is its awareness of film as a medium that can both look at the world with objectivity and duplicate subjective experience. At times *Citizen Kane* pretends to a realist, documentary quality: it even includes a parody of the *March of Time* newsreels to summarize Kane's life. It presents Kane (and Hearst) as a relatively evenhanded journalist might, observing without really passing judgment. At the same time, by presenting several points of view and by reflecting these subjective points of view in sets and lighting effects that owe more than a little to German expressionism, the film emphasizes the capacity of the medium to express subjective experience and feeling.

David Bordwell has pointed out how this duality in *Kane* is evident in its first few minutes. Welles portrays the death of Kane in ambiguous, poetic imagery reminiscent of the art films of the twenties, but follows it immediately with the film's pseudo-newsreel (Fig. 14.3). Bordwell even goes so far as to see in *Kane*'s subjectivity a prototype for the art cinema of Godard, Bergman, Fellini, and others.[4] While the movie does not hold to a single subjective viewpoint, certainly one may see this work as a substantial precedent for the kind of continuity we have noted in such personalist works as *Hiroshima, mon amour* and *Les violins du bal*. In all, past and present mix, linked more by emotional than narrative chronology, forming a single stream (Fig. 14.4).

14.3 *Citizen Kane* as an experimental film. During the course of *Citizen Kane* (1941), Orson Welles uses a full range of self-consciously artistic techniques. The distortion at the moment of Kane's death, shown here, is one example.

14.4 Symbolism in *Citizen Kane.* Orson Welles makes frequent use of symbols in *Citizen Kane* (1941), though an audience need not be aware of all the symbols to appreciate the film. The ice sculptures in this scene may represent anything from Kane's inner coldness to the imperma-nence of human success or happiness.

Works like *Citizen Kane* and *The Rules of the Game* cannot be neatly classified without some injustice to one or another aspect of them. Some movies achieve greatness through supreme single-mindedness, performing effectively only one function of the medium. Others, like the Renoir and the Welles, are rich precisely because they attempt a bit of everything. Film historians particularly admire these two works, but we might as easily have chosen other classic films to illustrate the same point. D. W. Griffith's *Intolerance*, Erich von Stroheim's *Greed*, Alexander Dovzhenko's *Earth* (1930), Charles Chaplin's *Modern Times*, Luis Buñuel's *Los Olvidados*, Yasujiro Ozu's *Tokyo Story* (1953), Elia Kazan's *On the Waterfront*, or Luchino Visconti's *Rocco and His Brothers* (1960) all present unique blendings of the functions we have identified (Fig. 14.5).

THE CONTEMPORARY CINEMA

It is difficult to tell exactly where the film medium is going. Researchers tell us about developments in film technology, but it is impossible to predict which ones will catch on with the public and which, like 3-D movies, will be passing novelties. The recent success of old-fashioned entertainment works like *Jaws* (1975) and *Star Wars* (1977) has demonstrated that traditional forms of genre film are remarkably durable, despite the fact that few people would have predicted the popularity of such films ten or fifteen years ago.

There is one trend in film, however, which seems unique to the last decade, particularly in the European cinema. We have witnessed the development of an

14.5 Multifunctional filmmaking. Many films generally considered classics are not easily categorized. a. Luis Buñuel's *Los Olvidados* (1950), for example, is a film that combines some of the documentary aspects of neorealism with the sense of dream associated with surrealism. b. Yasujiro Ozu's *Tokyo Story* (1953) is on some levels simply a familiar family melodrama, but it reveals calculated, formal patterns of camera placement and editing.

a.

b.

attitude toward filmmaking that consciously attempts to synthesize into single works most of the functions of film we have described above. In preceding chapters we discussed how the Young Cinema movement of the sixties became politicized by the end of the decade. The seventies saw the maturing of many of these directors into major forces both in their respective national cinemas and on an international level. What has resulted is a new type of film. Many of these now not-so-young directors have produced works that put personal feelings into political contexts or vice versa, works that are often simultaneously aware of problems of narrative, realism, and formal experimentation.

Let us consider two examples of this kind of filmmaking, *Padre Padrone*, a film by Paolo and Vittorio Taviani that won the grand prize at the 1977 Cannes Film Festival, and *Apocalypse Now*, cowinner of that same award some two years later. The latter was directed by Francis Coppola, one of the promising young film school graduates of the sixties who later became a major commercial figure when he made *The Godfather* (1972) and its sequel, *Godfather II* (1975). Although *Apocalypse Now* is far more commercial in nature than *Padre Padrone*, both suggest the kind of synthetic sensibility that was probably the single most important trend in film in the late seventies.

Padre Padrone   The Taviani brothers' film, which was financed by Italian television (doubtless without the expectation that it would receive the wide acclaim that it did), is personalist in conception. It is based on the autobiography of Gavino Ledda, a noted linguist who did not learn to read or write until he was an adult. It chronicles the childhood and adolescence of Ledda, the son of a poor Sardinian shepherd, who after less than a year of elementary school was sent by his parents to the mountains to tend their flocks. The Tavianis give cinematic form to Ledda's personal experiences, and at the beginning and end of the film the real Ledda introduces and concludes his true story.

The film is thus a realist work as well, rooted in fact. It documents the everyday life and culture of a poor class of people, and it is little wonder that the Taviani brothers have acknowledged the influence of Roberto Rossellini on their work. In structure, much of *Padre Padrone* is not so much a strong narrative or drama as it is a series of episodes portraying routine occurrences during Gavino's upbringing. We see, for example, how his father teaches him to carry heavy buckets of water or kill a snake, or how the man beats his son mercilessly as a regular part of his training for the life of a shepherd. The work is all but an ethnographic study, filtered through the eyes of a participant in the culture being scrutinized (Fig. 14.6).

The Tavianis and Ledda show us the Sardinian culture, but they also analyze it and evaluate it. We may consider *Padre Padrone* a political film, for it connects the sadism of Gavino's father with a sadistic political and economic system (Fig. 14.7). At the beginning of the film, when we see Gavino's father pull him out of the classroom, the Tavianis emphasize, through voice-overs on the soundtrack, the fears of his classmates that the same thing will happen to them. Gavino is only one of many; all of the children face a dismal, empty future. When Gavino and other young men attempt to emigrate in search of a better life, they show venomous contempt for their impoverished background. When Gavino's father starts to move out of his class by acquiring an olive grove, the film documents—in a single, intentionally dry, didactic scene of business bickering—the cutthroat nature of the olive oil market. *Padre Padrone* unites psychology, sociology, and economics into a single discourse.

As a political film we must class *Padre Padrone* as investigative rather than as advocating a specific program or solution. And, like much modern European cinema, the film links political comment to formal experimentation. In this case, much of the work's exploration of the medium is in the area of sound. When Gavino struggles with a heavy load, for example, we hear him vocalizing the strain, even though his lips are closed. When he hears an accordionist playing a Viennese waltz, we hear a fully orchestrated version on the soundtrack. The Tavianis suggest in this unrealistic use of sound the broader area of culture the accordion represents for the young man. The soundtrack provides *Padre Padrone* with some of its most beguiling comic effects. When the movie portrays the sexual practice of bestiality among the shepherds, isolated in the mountains away from wives or other women, we hear eager and impassioned panting on the soundtrack—a touch that renders the sequence comic rather than offensive. At another point, Gavino has an imagined dialogue with a goat who has been dropping turds into the bucket he uses to milk her. This use of sound undercuts the film's realism and suggests a style that experiments with form to convey ideas.

If there is one area of filmmaking *Padre Padrone* excludes or underplays (and some critics would argue this is its major failing), it is that of efficient narration or storytelling. As leftist filmmakers, the Tavianis may have tried to avoid the techniques of identification and narrative involvement that characterize the commercial cinema. They stage several key scenes with the actors' backs to the camera, subverting conventional dramatic effectiveness. Rather than have a smooth narrative flow, the story seems to lurch forward with abrupt starts and stops. Many of Gavino's triumphs near the end of the film—his successful building of a radio in an army electronics class, the dawning in his mind of concepts about symbolization and

14.6 The family in *Padre Padrone*. A film that uses unconventional methods of storytelling, the Taviani brothers' *Padre Padrone* (1977) attempts a comprehensive exploration of a rural culture. It shows personal relationships, such as between parents and children, as inseparable from the political structures of a society.

language, his learning of both basic Latin and the ability to feel friendship for a well-educated army buddy—all these emphasize mental processes rather than the physical conflicts and action stressed in the classic genre film. The film does build to a physical confrontation between father and son, but there is no real suspense, for the outcome has been suggested to us by the beginning of the film.

Apocalypse Now   Unlike *Padre Padrone*, *Apocalypse Now* has a commercial premise: it is a military adventure film set during the Vietnam war. Its plot tells of a Captain Willard (Martin Sheen), who is sent on a difficult secret mission to find a certain deserted general, Walter Kurtz (Marlon Brando), who has gone off into the jungle to continue fighting the war without consulting his superiors. During the movie Willard and his men face various forms of danger, from tigers to Vietcong, and much of the movie works as a modern-day war picture. Coppola even uses the standard war movie device of making Willard's squad a cross section of American ethnic and social types, from the soldier who had been a *saucier* in a fancy New Orleans restaurant to a surfer from California looking for a good wave in Southeast Asia.

But the film's intentions go beyond those of the standard genre film. For one thing, it has a significant antimilitary and anticolonialist tone. Coppola does not present Willard's or his men's actions as heroic, but simply as attempts to cope with an environment that has made sensible behavior impossible. It is possible to see *Apocalypse Now* as a parable about our entire military action in Vietnam: as Willard goes further and further up the river, his goals seem more and more impossible and unattainable, a product of the lunacy of the entire wartime enterprise. Like Willard's mission, the film suggests, Vietnam became a hopeless quest that the United States could neither get out of nor complete successfully. On this level, the film plays with a fundamental ambiguity. Shot in the Philippines, on locations that convincingly suggest the jungles of Vietnam and Cambodia, *Apocalypse Now* suggests that it is a realistic portrayal of what the war looked like, even while it pursues a line of allegory or metaphor.

Yet Coppola's film is also a spectacle of sorts. Almost every commentator on it has mentioned a dazzlingly choreographed air attack involving the napalming of a village and its surrounding forest, set to Wagner's *Ride of the Valkyries*. The spectacle of such scenes becomes revolting and fascinating at the same time, and Coppola seems intentionally to suggest by this duality an ambivalent attitude: we are struck by the beauty of the fiery, physically mobile images even while we may be shocked or

14.7 The father in *Padre Padrone*. The filmmakers see the father as both the victim of a social system into which he has been fully absorbed and as an oppressor who would inflict that system on his son.

sickened by their implications. This section of the movie emphasizes intricately worked out camera movements in which the camera slides past panicked natives, attacking soldiers, burning debris to create a sense of confusion, chaos, and nightmare.⁵ *Apocalypse Now*, a film that cost well over $30 million, clearly spent a good bit of its budget on striking, extravagant visual effects that could only be achieved in a large-scale production.

Finally, *Apocalypse Now* has many of the qualities of the emotive, introspective film we have also discussed. As Willard finally confronts Kurtz, he realizes that he himself has become what he had set out to destroy, that the supremely alienating environment of a jungle battlefield has all but completely dehumanized him. Kurtz has become a kind of imperial lord over the natives, a vision of colonialism taken to an extreme degree: he exploits the natives as slaves for want of any other means of survival. Marlon Brando's performance includes some fairly long, intense monologues about the moral ambiguities of the situation, staged with much of the actor's face plunged into semidarkness, an effect suggesting the familiar expressionist tactic of graphically portraying moral conflicts in terms of dark-light contrasts. These scenes use subjective, decelerated editing to intensify the sense of anguish and despair that links *Apocalypse Now* to the existentialist sensibility of the sixties art film. Vietnam comes to represent the human condition as a whole. Willard's confrontation with Kurtz at the end can as easily be seen as a discourse on the meaninglessness of life in general as much as it is about the meaninglessness of Vietnam.

And on this level one may question whether Coppola's achievements in *Apocalypse Now* quite live up to his ambitions. One could complain, for example, that the film's attempt to make a universal message blunts its effectiveness in making

a

b

a specific political message about the war. If Vietnam is simply a metaphor for what is wrong with humankind, the film cannot fully explore the particulars of a very real historical conflict. Similarly, does the work's exhilarative emphasis on the fire and gore of the battle scenes not glorify what it presumes, apparently, to condemn? *Apocalypse Now* clearly operates on metaphoric, realist, political, spectacular, and philosophical levels, but some critics have objected that it simply doesn't gel. As one commented, "to add Ingmar Bergman to Cecil B. De Mille can hardly give more than a feeble idea of the human condition."[6]

Still, *Apocalypse Now* is exciting in its ambition, its attempt to make a film of global, all-encompassing significance. That there are so many levels on which it may be analyzed make it as rich a film—though some would argue that it is not as successful a film—as *Citizen Kane* or *The Rules of the Game.*

Both *Padre Padrone* and *Apocalypse Now* typify much of contemporary filmmaking in their attempts to make a kind of total film, one that consciously manipulates all the communicative elements—realist, persuasive, personal, and esthetic—that we have discussed. We might have cited instead of these two any number of recent movies that take a pluralist approach within fairly traditional narrative formats. Rainer Werner Fassbinder's *Fox and His Friends* (1975), for example, grafts a parable of class exploitation onto a purposely melodramatic story of a homosexual who wins a lottery and is preyed upon by would-be friends and lovers. Bernardo Bertolucci's *1900* (1976) is an elaborate historical epic of modern Italy, conceived at once as spectacle, as propaganda for the Italian Communist party, and as a study of sexual obsession. André Téchiné's *French Provincial* (1975) covers much the same period as *1900* but mixes a broad parody of Hollywood formulas with an intelligent reworking of Eisensteinian montage in its survey of French history. These works and others seem particularly modern in their attempts to integrate disparate influences and combine several functions in a single film (Fig. 14.8).

CONCLUSION

We have attempted two things in this book. One has been to give an overview of the techniques and equipment used in filmmaking. The second has been to offer a set of contexts within which one can view a film. We offer our contextual categories not as pigeonholes in which one can conveniently classify a film and then forget it but rather as tools for understanding how filmmakers use their medium.

14.8 The movie as microcosm for a whole society. Two recent European films that tie overt political messages to popular entertainment are (a) André Téchiné's *French Provincial* (1975) and (b) Rainer Werner Fassbinder's *The* *Marriage of Maria Braun* (1979). Both analyze the operations of capitalism as embodied in central female characters who rise to phenomenal success in the male-dominated business world.

Only by studying the contexts by which human works (whether artistic or not) are produced, sold, bought, used, interpreted, and evaluated can one fully understand them. We hope our contextual, functional approach promotes fruitful analysis and understanding. If we have tried to leave judgments of what may be good or bad to the reader, let us end with one tentative value judgment. The film that invites us to look at it in a variety of frameworks, the film that tries to make itself meaningful on several levels at once, the film that is open to varying interpretations—such as *The Rules of the Game, Citizen Kane, Padre Padrone,* or *Apocalypse Now*—may be the richest film of all.

NOTES

1 Jean Renoir, *My Life and My Films,* trans. Norman Denny (New York: Atheneum, 1974), p. 169.

2 "Top Ten 72," *Sight and Sound,* 41 (Winter 1971–1972), 12–16. *The Rules of the Game* placed second in 1972, third in 1962.

3 Pauline Kael, "Raising Kane," in *The Citizen Kane Book* (Boston: Little, Brown, 1971), pp. 61–62.

4 David Bordwell, "*Citizen Kane,*" *Film Comment,* 7 (Summer 1971), 38.

5 Some critics claim to have detected in these sections the influence of the Hungarian filmmaker Miklós Jancsó (see Chapter 4).

6 Jean Pierre Le Pavec, "*Apocalypse Now,*" *Cinéma,* No. 250 (October 1979), 71.

Index

Credits

The following archive sources have been particularly helpful in providing most of the film stills used in this book. In the credits list, these sources are abbreviated as follows: **Academy** Margaret Herrick Library, Academy of Motion Picture Arts & Sciences, 8949 Wilshire Blvd., Beverly Hills, CA 90211 **Audio Brandon** Audio Brandon Films, Inc., 866 Third Avenue, New York, NY 10022 **Hampton** Hampton Books, P.O. Box 76, Newberry, SC 29108 **HRC, Gernsheim/HRC, Hoblitzelle** The Gernsheim Photography Collection, The Hoblitzelle Theatre Arts Library, Humanities Research Center, University of Texas at Austin, Austin, TX 78712 **MOMA** Museum of Modern Art, Film Stills Archive, 11 West 53rd Street, New York, NY 10019 **Ed Neal** Ed Neal, The Texas Movie Emporium, P.O. Box 12965, Austin, TX 78711.

In the following list, archive sources are listed first, followed by the copyright holder and/or the authorized grantor(s) of reproduction rights (unless that still is in the public domain).

CHAPTER ONE **1.2** Academy; **1.3** HRC, Gernsheim; **1.4** HRC, Gernsheim; **1.5** HRC, Gernsheim; **1.6** HRC, Gernsheim; **1.8** HRC, Gernsheim; **1.9** MOMA; **1.10** MOMA; **1.11** MOMA; **1.13** HRC, Gernsheim; **1.14** New York Historical Society; **1.16** International Museum of Photography, George Eastman House; **1.17** Academy; **1.19** Academy.

CHAPTER THREE **3.1a** MOMA/From *Don't Look Back* by D.A. Pennebaker; **3.1b** Ed Neal/From the MGM release *Anchors Aweigh* © 1945 Loew's Inc. Copyright renewed 1972 Metro-Goldwyn-Mayer Inc.; **3.2** George Wead; **3.3** George Wead; **3.4** Academy; **3.5** HRC, Hoblitzelle/From the MGM release *Roberta* © 1935 RKO Radio Pictures, Inc. Copyright renewed 1962 Metro-Goldwyn-Mayer Inc.; **3.6** HRC, Hoblitzelle/Copyright © by Universal Pictures, a Division of Universal City Studios, Inc. Courtesy of MCA Publishing, a Division of MCA, Inc.; **3.7** MOMA; **3.8** MOMA; **3.13** Academy/Courtesy of RKO General Pictures; **3.14a** Ed Neal/From the MGM release *The Split* © 1968 Metro-Goldwyn-Mayer Inc.; **3.15** HRC, Hoblitzelle/From the MGM release *The Great Ziegfeld* © 1936 Metro-Goldwyn-Mayer Corporation. Copyright renewed 1963 Metro-Goldwyn-Mayer Inc.; **3.16a** HRC, Hoblitzelle/From the MGM release *Gone With The Wind* © 1939 Selznick International Pictures, Inc. Copyright renewed 1967 Metro-Goldwyn-Mayer Inc.; **3.17a** HRC, Hoblitzelle; **3.17b** HRC, Hoblitzelle/*The Singing Fool* © 1928. Warner Bros. Pictures, Inc. Renewed by United Artists Television. All Rights Reserved; **3.17c** MOMA/Courtesy of RKO General Pictures; **3.20** George Wead; **3.21** George Wead; **3.22** George Wead; **3.23** Academy; **3.24** UCLA Theatre Arts Library/*The Jazz Singer* © 1927. Warner Bros. Pictures, Inc. Renewed 1955, United Artists Television. All Rights Reserved; **3.28** Academy/Courtesy of RKO General Pictures; **3.29** Academy; **3.31** MOMA/Courtesy of RKO General Pictures.

CHAPTER FOUR **4.2** Ed Neal/Copyright © by Universal Pictures, a Division of Universal City Studios, Inc. Courtesy of MCA Publishing, a Division of MCA, Inc.; **4.3** Ed Neal; **4.4** MOMA/Courtesy of the Samuel Goldwyn Company; **4.6** Academy; **4.7** Library of Congress; **4.8** George Wead; **4.10** Courtesy of Festival Films.

CHAPTER FIVE **5.1** HRC, Hoblitzelle; **5.12** Academy; **5.13** Academy; **5.15** From *The Film Sense* by Sergei Eisenstein, translated by Jay Leyda, copyright © 1942, 1947 by Harcourt Brace Jovanovich, Inc.; renewed 1970, 1975 by Jay Leyda. Reproduced by permission of the publisher.

CHAPTER SIX **6.8** Academy; **6.9** Redrawn from *Film and Its Techniques*, Raymond Spottiswoode, 1965, p. 212. Reprinted by permission of the University of California Press.

CHAPTER SEVEN **7.1** Ed Neal/Copyright © by Universal Pictures, a Division of Universal City Studios, Inc. Courtesy of MCA Publishing, a Division of MCA, Inc.; **7.2** Ed Neal/Copyright © by Universal Pictures, a Division of Universal City Studios, Inc. Courtesy of MCA Publishing, a Division of MCA, Inc.; **7.3** MOMA/TV-Cinema Sales Corporation; **7.4** HRC, Hoblitzelle/Copyright © by Universal Pictures, a Division of Universal City Studios, Inc. Courtesy of MCA Publishing, a Division of MCA, Inc.; **7.5** MOMA/Copyright © by Universal Pictures, a Division of Universal City Studios, Inc. Courtesy of MCA Publishing, a Division of MCA, Inc.; **7.6** MOMA/Copyright © by Universal Pictures, a Division of Universal City Studios, Inc. Courtesy of MCA Publishing, a Division of MCA, Inc.; **7.7** MOMA; **7.8** HRC, Hoblitzelle/Copyright © by Universal Pictures, a Division of Universal City Studios, Inc. Courtesy of MCA Publishing, a Division of MCA, Inc.; **7.9** MOMA/Copyright © by Universal Pictures, a Division of Universal City Studios, Inc. Courtesy of MCA Publishing, a Division of MCA, Inc.; **7.10a** Ed Neal/Courtesy of RKO General Pictures; **7.10b** Ed Neal/From the MGM release *A Patch of Blue* © 1965 Metro-Goldwyn-Mayer Inc. and Pandro S. Berman Productions, Inc.; **7.11** HRC, Hoblitzelle/Courtesy of RKO General Pictures; **7.12** MOMA/Copyright © by Universal Pictures, a Division of Universal City Studios, Inc. Courtesy of MCA Publishing, a Division of MCA, Inc.; **7.13** MOMA/From the MGM release *Ride The High Country* © 1962 Metro-Goldwyn-Mayer Inc.; **7.15** MOMA/Copyright © 1967, Embassy/Lawrence Turman, Inc.; **7.16** MOMA/Copyright © by Universal Pictures, a Division of Universal City Studios, Inc. Courtesy of MCA Publishing, a Division of MCA, Inc.; **7.17** Ed Neal/From the MGM release *Shaft* © 1971 Metro-Goldwyn-Mayer Inc.; **7.18** Ed Neal/Copyright © by Universal Pictures, a Division of Universal City Studios, Inc. Courtesy of MCA Publishing, a Division of MCA, Inc.

ABCDEFGHIJ-H-8210